PREACHING CHRIST FROM GENESIS

PREACHING CHRIST FROM GENESIS

Foundations for Expository Sermons

SIDNEY GREIDANUS

William B. Eerdmans Publishing Company
Grand Rapids, Michigan

Wm. B. Eerdmans Publishing Co.
4035 Park East Course SE, Grand Rapids, Michigan 49546
www.eerdmans.com

Published 2007
Printed in the United States of America

23 22 21 20 19 18 9 10 11 12

Library of Congress Cataloging-in-Publication Data

Greidanus, Sidney, 1935-
Preaching Christ from Genesis: foundations for expository sermons / Sidney Greidanus.
p. cm.
Includes bibliographical references and index.
ISBN 978-0-8028-2586-5 (pbk.: alk. paper)
1. Bible. O.T. Genesis — Sermons. 2. Preaching. I. Title.

BS1235.54.G74 2007
251 — dc22

2007014689

To Marie, my best friend and faithful wife for fifty years,

and our wonderful children:

Renee and John Vandermeer

Sheri and Frank Huizinga

Nathan and Heather Greidanus

Contents

Preface

I have written this book for preachers, seminary students, and Bible teachers. My primary aim is to encourage and help busy preachers and teachers to proclaim the Genesis narratives. This book will enable them to uncover rather quickly the important building-blocks for producing sermons and lessons on Genesis: to detect the story line of each narrative (the plot); to formulate the heart of the message for Israel (the theme); to discover the response sought from Israel and by analogy from the church today (the goal); to uncover various ways to link each narrative to Jesus Christ in the New Testament; and to obtain relevant biblical exposition of key verses.

This book, as a companion to my *Preaching Christ from the Old Testament,* is further intended to demonstrate and reinforce the redemptive-historical Christocentric method. While Christocentric preaching is always theocentric, it moves beyond the theocentric focus to the fullness of God's self-revelation in Jesus Christ. As the apostle John explains, "No one has ever seen God. It is God the only Son, who is close to the Father's heart, who has made him known" (John 1:18).

Readers will notice that I follow the same basic pattern for each narrative. This pattern is based on the ten steps from text to sermon I developed for first-year seminary students (see Appendix 1).[1] The resulting repetition in each chapter is intended to inculcate a basic hermeneutical-homiletical approach to the biblical text. First we search for the narrative unit and check its context. Next we note important literary features and especially the plot line, which is important not only for understanding the narrative but also for preaching the sermon in a narrative form. After theocentric interpretation, we seek to formu-

1. I have explained these ten steps and applied them to Genesis 22 in my *Preaching Christ from the Old Testament,* 279-318.

late the textual theme and goal. With the theme in mind, we can brainstorm for various roads that lead from this particular narrative to Jesus Christ in the New Testament. Having seen the Old Testament message in the context of the New Testament, we are ready to extend the textual theme and goal to the sermon theme and goal. I conclude each chapter with a section on "sermon exposition," which can be used not only for better understanding the narrative but also for gathering insights to incorporate into one's sermon. This section seeks to provide a model for the sermon by using oral style as much as possible, giving the verse reference *before* the quote so that the congregation can read along (comprehension is much better when the congregation not only hears but sees the words), and keeping the narrative moving (most quotations, complex arguments, and technical details are relegated to footnotes). I have indicated where in the exposition and how I might make the move(s) to Christ in the New Testament. These moves are intended only as suggestions, for while writing the actual sermon one may discover better ways and places to move to Christ. Finally, related to the goal, I make brief suggestions for application. In actual sermons, these "applications" will need to be fleshed out with illustrations and concrete suggestions appropriate to the situation of the congregation being addressed.

In the past, I have had several essays on Genesis passages published.[2] For this book I have revised these articles and expanded them considerably. In Appendix 2 I have reproduced the expository sermon model I developed for first-year students at Calvin Theological Seminary. This model aims for sermons that are biblical, relevant, and well organized. I have also included three of my own sermons on Genesis narratives to further demonstrate the practical outcome of following this model in sermon construction (see Appendixes 3 to 5).

Unless otherwise noted, the Bible version quoted is the NRSV. In these quotations I have occasionally emphasized words by italicizing them. Without notation, every reader will understand that these are *my* emphases since they are neither in the original Hebrew nor in the NRSV.

Hebrew transliterations throughout have been regularized using the pattern found in Willem A. VanGemeren, gen. ed., *New International Dictionary of Old Testament Theology and Exegesis,* V, xxi (see p. xvii below).

References in the footnotes have been kept to a minimum: full references

2. The publication started with Genesis 22:1-19 in my *Preaching Christ from the Old Testament,* 292-318. Next Roger Van Harn invited me to submit some essays for *The Lectionary Commentary* he was editing. I wrote on Genesis 6:9–8:22; 24:1-67; 28:10-22; 29:15-36; and 37:1-36 — respectively, pp. 11-16; 43-48; 52-56; 56-60; and 64-68 of Vol. 1. Then Dallas Theological Seminary invited me to give some special lectures on preaching Christ from the Old Testament. Here I tried out the format of expository essays which, with some changes, I am using in this book. These lectures on Genesis 1:1–2:3; 2:4–3:24; and 4:1-26 were subsequently published in *BSac* 161 (2004) — respectively, pp. 131-41; 259-73; and 387-97.

can be found in the Bibliography. When a book or article is not included in the Select Bibliography, complete information is found in the footnote. The Table of Contents has been designed to function as a Subject Index for the major subjects treated in Chapter 1 and as a Text Index for the major texts treated in Chapters 2 to 24. More detailed Subject and Scripture Indexes are found on pp. 510-18.

I send this book into the world with the hope and prayer that it may stimulate many preachers to preach the Genesis narratives as it spawns ideas, in text and footnotes, for developing sermons that will build up God's people with the biblical vision of paradise restored, the coming kingdom of God.

Grand Rapids, Michigan SIDNEY GREIDANUS

Acknowledgments

I started research for this book during a three-month sabbatical in 2001, and retired from full-time teaching in 2004 in order to complete this project as quickly as possible. I thank the Administration and Board of Calvin Theological Seminary for granting me the sabbatical and for encouraging research and writing also of its retired professors. My research started at the Free University in Amsterdam, and continued especially at my home base, Calvin Theological Seminary in Grand Rapids, Michigan. I thank the staff at these two libraries for their friendly, helpful service, as well as the staff of Eerdmans for their competent work in publishing this book.

My thanks go out to my student assistant, Tim De Jonge, who typed an early version of the Bibliography, and my M.Div. and Th.M. students at Calvin as well as my D.Min. students at Biblical Theological Seminary, Hatfield, PA, who struggled with me through some of these Genesis narratives. I wish to express my gratitude especially to my proofreaders, who alerted me to weaknesses in content and style: my former students, the Revs. Ryan Faber of Pella, IA, and Ken Vander Horst of Imlay City, MI; my hometown friend, the Rev. Cecil Van Niejenhuis of Edmonton, AB; and my brother-in-law, Dr. George Vandervelde of the Institute for Christian Studies, Toronto, ON, whose superb insights into theology and English style have benefitted all four of my books. (The Lord called George home on January 19, 2007.)

I am grateful to the Lord for health and strength to complete this work, for surprising discoveries and unexpected flashes of insight, and for daily joy in working on this project. Finally, I thank my wife, Marie, for her constant support, her quiet encouragement, and for creating a home and atmosphere which enabled me to concentrate on this project. I dedicate this book to her and our children.

Abbreviations

BAR	*Biblical Archaeology Review*
BBR	*Bulletin for Biblical Research*
BSac	*Bibliotheca Sacra*
CBQ	*Catholic Biblical Quarterly*
CovQ	*Covenant Quarterly*
CTJ	*Calvin Theological Journal*
EvQ	*Evangelical Quarterly*
JBL	*Journal of Biblical Literature*
JETS	*Journal of the Evangelical Theological Society*
JSOT	*Journal for the Study of the Old Testament*
NIB	*The New Interpreter's Bible*
NIBC	New International Bible Commentary
NICOT	New International Commentary on the Old Testament
NIDOTTE	*New International Dictionary of Old Testament Theology and Exegesis*
TDOT	*Theological Dictionary of the Old Testament*
TynBul	*Tyndale Bulletin*
VT	*Vetus Testamentum*
WW	*Word and World*

Transliterations

Hebrew

א = ʾ	ו = *w*	כ, ך = *k*	ע = ʿ	שׂ = *ś*
ב = *b*	ז = *z*	ל = *l*	פ, ף = *p*	שׁ = *š*
ג = *g*	ח = *ḥ*	מ, ם = *m*	צ = *ṣ*	ת = *t*
ד = *d*	ט = *ṭ*	נ, ן = *n*	ק = *q*	
ה = *h*	י = *y*	ס = *s*	ר = *r*	

No distinction is made between the *bgdkpt* with or without the dagesh lene.
Compare: תּוֹרָה = *tôrâ* הַתּוֹרָה = *hattôrâ* תּוֹרָתוֹ = *tôrātô*

Vowels

◌ָה = *â*	◌ֶ = *e*	וֹ = *ô*
◌ָ = *ā*	◌ְ = *ĕ* (if vocal)	◌ֹ = *ō*
◌ַ = *a*	◌ֱ = *ĕ*	◌ָ = *o*
◌ֲ = *ă*	◌ִ = *i*	◌ֳ = *ŏ*
◌ֵ = *ē*	◌ִי = *î*	וּ = *û*
◌ֵי = *ê*		◌ֻ = *u*

CHAPTER 1

Issues in Preaching Christ from Genesis

Before preaching the Genesis narratives, preachers should take note of some of the problems they will encounter and how they may be able to resolve them. This introductory chapter will first review issues involved in preaching Christ, next, reasons for selecting Genesis narratives as preaching-texts, third, issues in interpreting Genesis, and finally, issues in preaching these narratives.

Issues in Preaching Christ

This book is about preaching Christ from the Genesis narratives. Unfortunately, there is much confusion about what preaching Christ means precisely.[1] On the basis of New Testament testimony, I have previously defined preaching Christ as "preaching sermons which authentically integrate the message of the text with the climax of God's revelation in the person, work, and/or teaching of Jesus Christ as revealed in the New Testament."[2]

Two Hermeneutical Moves

The above definition of preaching Christ assumes two moves in interpretation. First, it assumes that the interpreter understands the message of the text in its own historical context, that is, the interpreter seeks to discern the message the writer wanted Israel to hear.[3] Second, it assumes that the interpreter under-

1. See my *Preaching Christ from the Old Testament*, 2-3.

2. Ibid., 10.

3. Ibid., 228-30.

stands the message of the text in the contexts of the whole canon (including the New Testament) and all of redemptive history.[4]

There are two major reasons for this move to the New Testament. First, a crucial hermeneutical rule is that a text must always be understood in its context. The context of the Genesis narratives in the Christian Bible, of course, is not just the Old Testament but also the New Testament. For example, when the narrative about God's covenant with Abraham (Gen 17) contains God's commandment: "Every male among you shall be circumcised" (17:10), preachers instinctively sense that they cannot apply this commandment directly to the congregation today. Rather, they understand this text in the context of the New Testament, where the Holy Spirit guided the church to replace circumcision as a sign of God's covenant (Acts 15:28-29) with the New Testament sign of baptism (Col 2:11-14). Similarly, when a narrative contains a promise of the coming Messiah, such as Genesis 3:15 about the seed of the woman, preachers cannot stop at the promise but must go on to its fulfillment in Jesus Christ. Or, when a narrative contains a type of Christ, such as Genesis 22:13 about the ram offered "instead of Isaac," preachers cannot stop at the type but must go on the Antitype, Jesus Christ, who was offered "instead of" God's people.

A second reason for this move to the New Testament is the New Testament requirement that Christian preachers preach Jesus Christ. Christian preaching is different from Jewish preaching precisely because Christian preachers understand Old Testament passages in the context of God's further revelation in the New Testament. As Graeme Goldsworthy aptly puts it: "The story is never complete in itself and belongs as part of the one big story of salvation culminating in Jesus Christ. Simply telling a story based on a piece of Old Testament historical narrative, however complete in itself, is not Christian preaching."[5]

Seven Ways of Preaching Christ

Throughout the church's history, preachers have preached Christ from the Old Testament in various ways. Sometimes they used ways that we today would consider illegitimate, such as allegorizing and typologizing.[6] In *Preaching Christ from the Old Testament* I identified seven ways in which preachers can move legitimately from the periphery to the center, from the Old Testament passage to Jesus Christ in the New Testament.[7] These seven

4. Ibid., 230-32.
5. Goldsworthy, *Preaching the Whole Bible as Christian Scripture,* 150.
6. See my *Preaching Christ from the Old Testament,* 70-109.
7. See ibid., 234-77.

ways are: redemptive-historical progression, promise-fulfillment, typology, analogy, longitudinal themes, New Testament references, and contrast. We shall briefly review each of these roads to Christ in the New Testament.

Redemptive-Historical Progression

The broadest and foundational path from an Old Testament text to Jesus Christ is the way of redemptive-historical progression. It traces God's history with the world from his good creation (Gen 1), to the human fall into sin and God's plan of redemption through the seed of the woman (Gen 3:15), to a long history of God continuing the line of the seed of the woman (Gen 3–Malachi), to Christ (the Gospels), the church (Acts and New Testament Letters), and finally to the new creation (Rev 22). In other words, in the Bible we can trace a continuous redemptive history which centers in the life, death, and resurrection of Jesus Christ, who then ascends to rule his church from heaven until he comes again. In broad strokes, we can picture redemptive history as follows:[8]

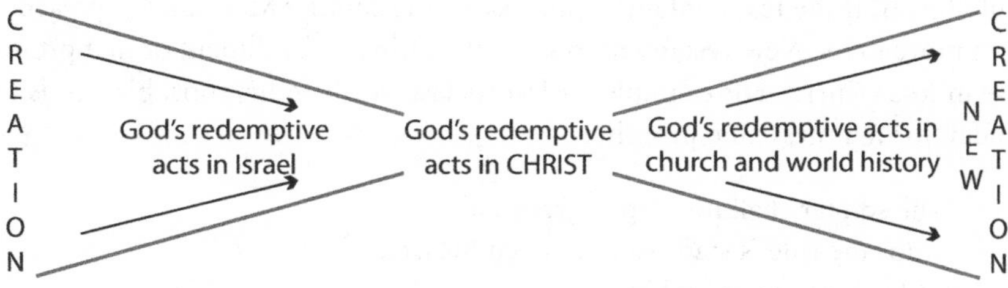

When a text witnesses to God's saving activity in history, we find ourselves on a road that progresses steadily through the Old Testament, leads to God's ultimate saving act in the sending of his Son, Jesus Christ, and culminates in Jesus' victorious Second Coming. For example, when one is preaching on the narrative of Cain murdering Abel (Gen 4), the fact that God provides Seth "instead of Abel" (4:25) to continue the line of the seed of the woman constitutes a link in the chain of redemptive-historical progression that leads to the birth of Jesus Christ, *the* Seed of the woman (Gal 3:16), and ultimately to his victorious Second Coming.

In the following chapters we will trace the plot lines of each individual narrative. It may be helpful here to visualize the Bible's meta-narrative as a single plot:

8. See Oscar Cullmann, *Christ and Time: The Primitive Christian Conception of Time and History* (trans. Floyd V. Filson; rev. ed.; Philadelphia: Westminster, 1962), 178.

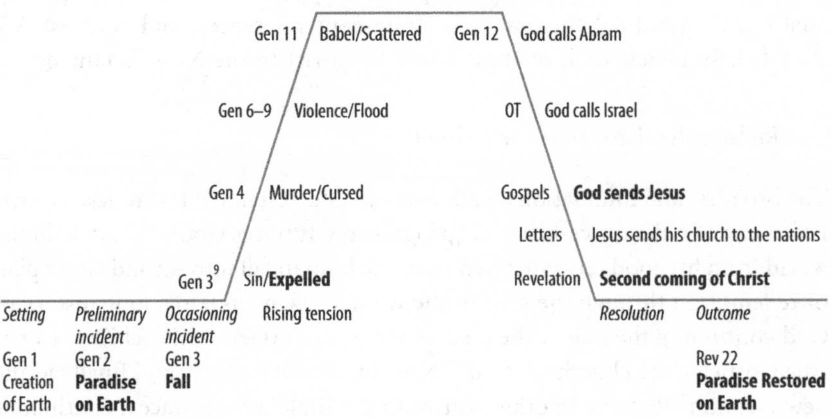

Promise-Fulfillment

A more direct road to Christ from an Old Testament text is the way of promise-fulfillment. If the text contains a promise of the coming Messiah, the preacher can move to the New Testament to show the ultimate fulfillment of that promise in Jesus Christ. For example, in Jacob's last words to his sons, his words to Judah form a messianic promise:

> "The scepter shall not depart from Judah,
> nor the ruler's staff from between his feet,
> until tribute comes to him;
> and the obedience of the peoples is his."
>
> (Gen 49:10)

In preaching this narrative, one can easily move from this Old Testament promise to its New Testament fulfillment in Jesus Christ, the King of kings born of the tribe of Judah and the house of David (Matt 1:1-17).

Typology

A third road from an Old Testament text to Christ is typology. Old Testament redemptive events, persons, or institutions can function as types which foreshadow the great Antitype, the person and/or work of Jesus Christ. For example, if one preaches on the Fall of Adam and Eve (Gen 3), one notes that the first Adam as representative of the human race prefigures the second Adam, Jesus.

9. God declaring enmity between the serpent and the woman in Gen 3:15 is a turning point, but the fallout from the Fall into sin keeps spreading and going from bad to worse.

In fact, Paul calls Adam "a type *(typos)* of the one who was to come" (Rom 5:14).[10] Adam is an antithetic (death vs. life) type (representing humanity) of the Antitype, Jesus Christ.

Analogy

A fourth and more general road from an Old Testament text to Christ is the way of analogy. Analogy exposes parallels between what God taught Israel and what Christ teaches the church; what God promised Israel and what Christ promises the church; what God demanded of Israel (the law) and what Christ demands of his church. For example, if the message of Genesis 12:1-9 is that Israel must claim Canaan for the worship of the LORD, one can use analogy to move to the New Testament and show that Jesus mandates his church to claim all nations for God (Matt 28:18-20).

Longitudinal Themes

A fifth road from an Old Testament text to Christ is the way of longitudinal themes. While this way will often overlap with redemptive-historical progression,[11] it is distinct in focusing on the development of theological ideas rather than development in redemptive history. "Longitudinal themes" is a technical term in the discipline of Biblical Theology. It refers to themes that can be traced through the Scriptures from the Old Testament to the New — themes such as God's coming kingdom, God's covenant, God's redemption, God's presence, God's love, God's faithfulness, God's grace, God's judgment, God's providence. We can utilize this concept of longitudinal themes for preaching Christ because every major Old Testament theme leads to Christ. For example, the theme of God's law can be traced from the creation account (Gen 2:16-17), through the patriarchs, to Sinai, to the prophets, and to Christ, who not only lived God's law perfectly and thus fulfilled the law for us, but who also showed us the depth-dimension of God's law and expects us to live by it (Matt 5–7; 22:37-40).

10. For a quick overview of the use of typology by New Testament authors, see O. Palmer Robertson, *The Israel of God,* 4-6. For a more elaborate presentation focusing on Matthew, see David Holwerda, *Jesus and Israel,* 31-58.

11. Compare the overlap between the disciplines of the history of redemption and the history of revelation. Progression in redemptive history generally involves progression in God's revelation.

New Testament References

A sixth road from an Old Testament text to Christ is that of New Testament references. Sometimes the New Testament alludes to or quotes the selected preaching-text and links it to Christ. In this case, the New Testament citation may possibly serve as a bridge to Christ. For example, if one preaches on the creation account of Genesis 1, the message for Israel is that the King of the universe by his Word created the earth as his good kingdom. After explaining the significance of God creating by his *word* (ten times "God said"), one can move to the New Testament, where John picks up on this "word" *(logos)* and identifies it as Jesus. In fact he quotes Genesis 1:1 when he writes, "*In the beginning* was the Word. . . . All things came into being through him . . ." (John 1:1, 3). This New Testament reference by itself is sufficient to function in the sermon as a bridge to Christ. Most often, however, New Testament references can best be used to support one of the other roads to Christ.[12]

Contrast

A final road from the Old Testament to Christ is the way of contrast. Because of the coming of Christ the text's message for the contemporary church may be quite different from the original message for Israel. For example, God commanded Abraham/Israel to circumcise every male among them as a sign of covenant membership (Gen 17:11). For two thousand years circumcision functioned as God's sign of covenant membership for Israel. But for Gentile converts the first council of the Christian church repealed this ancient ordinance with its shedding of blood (Acts 15:28-29). Instead of circumcision, baptism gradually became the sign of covenant membership (Col 2:11-14). The contrast between circumcision and baptism exists because of Jesus Christ, who shed his blood once for all, thereby ending the bloody rites and sacrifices of the old covenant.

Reasons for Selecting Genesis

To demonstrate the Christocentric method of interpretation and preaching I have selected the book of Genesis. There are several reasons for this choice. The most weighty reason is the importance of Genesis for the church; a second reason is the current lack of preaching from Genesis; and third, the challenge of preaching Christ from Genesis.

12. See the New Testament references used above to support the ways of redemptive-historical progression, promise-fulfillment, typology, analogy, and longitudinal themes.

The Importance of Genesis for Christian Understanding

The primary reason for selecting the book of Genesis to demonstrate the Christocentric method is the crucial importance of this book for the Christian church. For Genesis provides Christians with a worldview that is assumed but not necessarily taught by later Scriptures. If we fail to preach Genesis, we deprive our congregations in a large measure of this foundational worldview. A worldview is "a consistent conception of all existence" (Webster), or, better, "the comprehensive framework of one's basic beliefs about things."[13] It is a foundational view of all of reality that enables us to see individual elements and events in the light of the whole. Basically, a worldview consists of the knowledge of three entities and their interrelationship: God, the cosmos, and human beings.

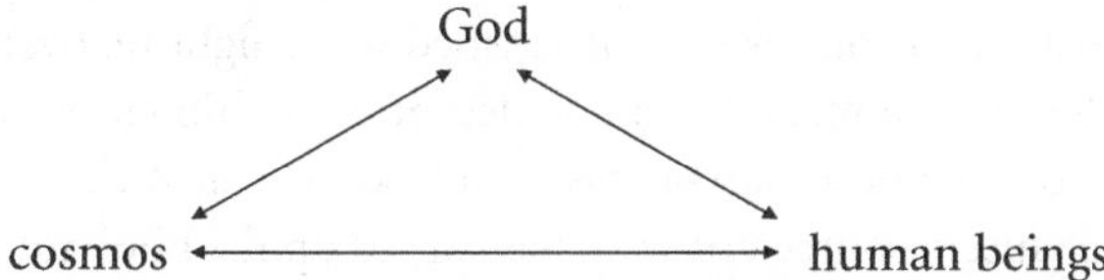

Genesis teaches that God is sovereign (vs. atheism) and wholly other than this universe (vs. pantheism), the only true God (vs. polytheism), the Creator of this universe (vs. secularism and naturalistic evolutionism), who has made a covenant with his creation and upholds it (vs. deism), and made human beings in his image to manage the world on his behalf (vs. hedonism). Genesis further teaches that God is not the source of evil but created everything good so that his creatures can enjoy the physical world (vs. gnosticism). The source of the evil and brokenness we see in the world today is human disobedience to God's command, which resulted in God's curse on creation. But God immediately promised to restore his creation to the beautiful kingdom he intended it to be. And so Genesis sketches the beginnings of redemptive history: God seeking to restore his creation and creatures, finally making a special covenant with Abram, who was to be a blessing to "all the families of the earth" (Gen 12:3).

As Genesis sketches the beginnings of redemptive history, it teaches about God's coming kingdom, God's love for his creation and his creatures, God's judgment of sin, God's grace for sinners, God's covenant faithfulness, God's sovereign providence, and God's presence with his people. As Ken Mathews puts it: "If we possessed a Bible without Genesis, we would have a 'house of cards' without foundation or mortar. We cannot insure the continuing fruit of

13. Albert M. Wolters, *Creation Regained: Biblical Basics for a Reformational Worldview* (Grand Rapids: Eerdmans, 1985), 2.

our spiritual heritage if we do not give place to its roots."[14] The church today needs to get in touch with its roots. After TV, videos, DVDs, pop music, and magazines have bombarded God's people for a whole week with a worldview that excludes God, God's people need "a reality check"[15] on Sunday, that is, sermons that expound the biblical worldview. God's people need to hear more sermons from the book of Genesis.

The Lack of Preaching from Genesis

In selecting preaching-texts for their congregations, preachers have many reasons to avoid the book of Genesis.[16] One author characterizes the Genesis narratives as follows: "They seem to be a conglomeration of very secular legends that have little if anything to do with faith. Their content (rape, murder, strife and jealousy between brothers, two unsatisfied wives fighting over the sexual attentions of their husband, and cunning deception within families) seems more appropriate to afternoon soap operas than God's revealed word."[17] Moreover, ever since Wellhausen, source criticism has carved up the book into debatable J, E, P, D, and more segments. This fragmentation makes the preaching-text uncertain and loses sight of the final author's message for Israel. Furthermore, in preaching Genesis, preachers are currently confronted with such troublesome questions as: Is the earth young or old? Were the days in Genesis 1 twenty-four-hour days or long periods of time? Was the flood universal or local? Were Abraham, Isaac, and Jacob historical figures or fictional characters? Because of this combination of hermeneutical, homiletical, and pastoral problems, modern preachers may think it the better part of wisdom to avoid preaching the Genesis narratives.

The Challenge of Preaching Christ from Genesis

A third reason for selecting Genesis is the challenge of preaching Christ from Genesis. Genesis is said to contain only seven "messianic texts," where one can employ the promise-fulfillment scheme. The traditional messianic texts listed for Genesis are:

14. Mathews, *Genesis 1–11:26*, 22.

15. A favorite saying of Jack Roeda, my colleague in teaching first-year preaching at Calvin Theological Seminary. For the significance of the biblical worldview for Christian living in every area, see Nancy R. Pearcey, *Total Truth: Liberating Christianity from Its Cultural Captivity* (Wheaton, IL: Crossway, 2004).

16. For reasons for the lack of preaching from the Old Testament in general, see my *Preaching Christ from the Old Testament*, pp. 16-25.

17. Throntveit, "Preaching from the Book of Genesis," *WW* 14/2 (1994) 212.

Genesis 3:15, the seed of the woman;
Genesis 4:25, the line of Seth;
Genesis 9:26, the blessing of Shem;
Genesis 12:3, the blessing of Abraham for "all the families of the earth";
Genesis 26:3, the blessing of Isaac's seed;
Genesis 46:3, the promise to Jacob; and
Genesis 49:10, the promise of kingly rule to Judah.

To preach Christ from these passages may seem fairly straightforward. But how does one preach Christ from the many other narratives in Genesis?

Preachers have tried to solve this problem in various ways. Some simply identified "Jehovah" with Christ, that is, whenever the text mentions Yahweh, we can substitute Christ.[18] Others, taking their cue from John 1 ("In the beginning was the Word"), look for the eternal Logos at work in the Old Testament. In Genesis, they claim, the Angel of Yahweh is the eternal Logos, the second person of the Trinity.[19] But this is not very helpful, for the Angel of Yahweh appears in only a few passages. Moreover, identifying Christ with the Angel of Yahweh is not preaching Christ as the fullness of God's revelation in Jesus of Nazareth. Still others seek to preach Jesus by using allegorical interpretation: they simply import the New Testament story of Jesus into the Old Testament without doing justice to the Old Testament message (a form of eisegesis). Still others seek to preach Jesus by understanding mere narrative *details* as types of Christ (the error of typologizing in distinction from proper typology).

A few examples of flawed efforts may help disclose the difficulties preachers face in preaching Christ from the Genesis narratives. A popular radio preacher presented the following allegorical interpretation of Genesis 2:18-25:

> While Adam slept, God created from his wounded side a wife, who was part of himself, and he paid for her by the shedding of his blood. . . . Now all is clear. Adam is a picture of the Lord Jesus, who left His Father's house to gain His bride at the price of His own life. Jesus, the last Adam, like the first, must be put to sleep to purchase His Bride, the Church, and Jesus died on the cross and slept in the tomb for three days and three nights. His side too

18. See, e.g., William Robinson, "Jesus Christ Is Jehovah," *EvQ* 5 (1933) 145; T. W. Calloway, *Christ in the Old Testament* (New York: Loizeaux, 1950); and Howard A. Hanke, *Christ and the Church in the Old Testament* (Grand Rapids: Zondervan, 1957).

19. See James D. G. Dunn, *Christology in the Making: A New Testament Inquiry into the Origins of the Doctrine of the Incarnation* (London: SCM, 1980), 149-62.

> was opened after He had fallen asleep, and from that wounded side redemption flowed.[20]

Others moved from the mark of protection God put on the murderer Cain (Gen 4:15) to the cross of Christ, speculating that Cain's mark was "in the form of a cross."[21] Similarly, "In Melchisedek's bringing of bread and wine [Gen 14] we have a clear allusion to the sacrament of the New Covenant which Jesus instituted for the completion and dissolution of the old."[22] Many have preached Isaac carrying the wood up the mountain (Gen 22:6) as a type of Christ carrying his cross.[23] One modern dictionary of types moves allegorically to Christ from the narrative of Abraham sending his servant to find a wife for Isaac (Gen 24):

> Abraham is a type of the Father who sent His servant (the Spirit) to obtain a bride (Rebecca) for his son Isaac. The servant represents the Holy Spirit, and Isaac represents the Lord Jesus Christ. . . . Rebecca represents the Church.[24]

Still others have preached the details of Joseph's life as the life of Christ:

> I need not say to you, beloved, who are conversant with Scripture, that there is scarcely any personal type in the Old Testament which is more clearly and fully a portrait of our Lord Jesus Christ than is the type of Joseph. You may run the parallel between Joseph and Jesus in very many directions. . . . In making himself known to his brethren, he was a type of our Lord revealing himself to us. . . . I. Notice, first, that the Lord Jesus Christ, like Joseph, reveals himself in private for the most part. . . . II. The second remark I have to make is this, — when the Lord Jesus Christ reveals himself to any man for the first time, it is usually in the midst of terror, and that first revelation often creates much sadness. . . . III. Now, thirdly, though the first appearance of Jesus, like that of Joseph, may cause sadness, the further revelation of the Lord Jesus Christ to his brethren, brings them the greatest possible joy.[25]

These flawed efforts illustrate the sincere desire as well as the difficulty of authentically preaching Christ from the Genesis narratives. However, if the fol-

20. Martin R. DeHaan, *Portraits of Christ in Genesis* (Grand Rapids: Zondervan, 1966), 32-33.

21. E.g., Vischer, *The Witness of the Old Testament to Christ,* 75.

22. Ibid., 132.

23. From the church fathers to preachers today.

24. W. L. Wilson, *Wilson's Dictionary of Bible Types* (Grand Rapids: Eerdmans, 1957), 15.

25. Charles Spurgeon, *Christ in the Old Testament: Sermons on the Foreshadowing of Our Lord in Old Testament History* (London: Passmore & Alabaster, 1899), XLVII, 93-97.

lowing essays can demonstrate that one or more of the seven ways of preaching Christ enables us legitimately to preach Christ from the Genesis narratives, we should be able to preach Christ from almost any Old Testament book.[26]

Issues in Interpreting Genesis

Before proceeding to the expository essays, we need to explore some crucial issues in interpreting the book of Genesis. We shall first discuss issues in literary interpretation and then move on to issues in historical interpretation.

Issues in Literary Interpretation

Source Criticism

Source criticism was first called "literary criticism." Most modern commentaries on Genesis will acquaint students with the Graf-Wellhausen Documentary Hypothesis of J, E, P, and D sources, which critical scholarship "widely accepted from about 1878 to 1970, [though] there have been significant dissenters at various points."[27] It was held that J (Yahwist) dated from Israel's monarchy around 950 B.C., E (Elohist) from the time of the divided kingdom around 850 B.C., D (Deuteronomist) from shortly before the exile around 620 B.C., and P (Priestly Code) from after the exile around 500 B.C. The result of this Documentary Hypothesis was the rejection of the traditional Jewish and Christian position that Moses was the primary author of the Pentateuch since Moses would predate these sources by at least 300 years. Moreover, with most of its efforts going into source criticism, Old Testament scholarship largely abandoned the church and its preachers, for preachers do not preach hypothetical sources behind the text but the final text the church received in its canon as the inspired Scriptures (2 Tim 3:16–4:2).

Happily, after a century of exploring blind alleys, "the hypothetical character of the results of modern criticism" was finally acknowledged[28] and the

26. I say "almost" because wisdom literature will still be a major challenge. Because of its unique nature, with wisdom literature one normally cannot use redemptive-historical progression, promise-fulfillment, or typology. Hence one is limited to four ways to Christ: analogy with the teaching of Christ, longitudinal themes, New Testament references, and contrast.

27. Wenham, *Genesis 1–15,* xxvi. For an enlightening history of source criticism, see Wenham, *Exploring the Old Testament,* 159-85.

28. Ibid., xxxv. For some of the disagreements among source critics, see, e.g., Wenham,

new literary criticism of the last few decades returned scholarly concentration to the final text. In fact, the new literary criticism has undermined the Documentary Hypothesis. Gary Rendsburg has shown that "the same or similar vocabulary appears in matching units which are usually assigned to different sources." He concludes, "All of this material demonstrates how attention to redactional structuring greatly weakens the Documentary Hypothesis, indeed according to the present writer, renders it untenable."[29] With the collapse of the Documentary Hypothesis, its dating of the sources of Genesis also collapses.[30] Gordon Wenham comments, "Without denying the presence of sources within the narrative, the new literary critic wants to understand how the final editor viewed his material and why he arranged it in the way he did."[31] This new literary criticism, as well as its precursors such as redaction criticism and rhetorical criticism, can help preachers discern the message of the preaching-text.[32]

The Tôlĕdôt *Structure of Genesis*

Genesis is frequently divided into two distinct parts:

1. Primeval History (Gen 1:1–11:26), and
2. Patriarchal History (Gen 11:27–50:26).

Although God's call of Abram clearly begins a new section in Genesis, for purposes of proper interpretation and preaching it is crucial also to see the overall literary structure of this book. Awareness of the unity of Genesis will enable us to interpret each narrative in the light of the whole book.

The most obvious literary feature unifying the Genesis narratives is the author's carefully crafted *tôlĕdôt* structure. *'Ēlleh tôlĕdôt* is variously translated in our English versions as: "These are the generations of . . ."; or, "These are the descendants of . . ."; or, "This is the history of. . . ." *Tôlĕdôt* "stands for that

Genesis 16–50, 18-19, 79, 203-4, 219-21. Cf. R. K. Harrison, "The Historical and Literary Criticism of the Old Testament," in *Biblical Criticism*, ed. Harrison et al., 27-29, and Waltke, *Genesis*, 24-29.

29. Rendsburg, *Redaction of Genesis*, 104. Cf. p. 105, "The standard division of Genesis into J, E, and P strands should be discarded."

30. Though Rendsburg holds to a fairly late date for the *redaction* of Genesis (the united monarchy of the tenth century B.C.), he acknowledges that "Genesis is replete with evidence indicating the antiquity of the book." Ibid., 114. For example, "various customs reflected in Genesis . . . contradict later Pentateuchal law," such as Abram marrying his half-sister and Jacob marrying his sister-in-law. Ibid., 115. See pp. 107-20.

31. Wenham, *Genesis 1–15*, xxxiv.

32. See my *Modern Preacher and Ancient Text*, 51-67, and my article, "The Value of a Literary Approach for Preaching," 509-19.

which was produced, for the result."[33] By way of *ten*[34] sets of generations, the author traces Israel's roots back from enslavement in Egypt to Adam and Eve in Paradise.

Ten Sets of *Tôlĕdôt* Genesis begins with God creating his good kingdom on earth in *seven*[35] days, and the first *tôlĕdôt* (of heaven and earth, Gen 2:4–4:26) shows what happened to that good kingdom: human rebellion against God, banishment from Paradise, Cain murdering his brother Abel, and the depth of depravity in the *seventh* generation when Lamech boasts of killing a young man for striking him (4:23). But God gives Adam and Eve another child "instead of Abel" (4:25), Seth, and the line of the seed of the woman can continue.

The second *tôlĕdôt* is the *tôlĕdôt* of Adam (Gen 5:1–6:8). In *ten* generations it runs from Adam through Seth to Noah. This is the line of the seed of the woman. The *seventh* generation in this line is the polar opposite of Lamech, the seventh generation in the first *tôlĕdôt:* "Enoch walked with God; then he was no more, because God took him" (5:24). And the tenth generation is Noah, of whom his father said, "Out of the ground that the Lord has cursed this one shall bring us relief from our work and from the toil of our hands" (5:29). Yet in the time of Noah such evil prevails that God decides to "blot out from the earth the human beings I have created" (6:7). "But Noah found favor in the sight of the Lord" (6:8). Again the line of the seed of the woman can continue.

The third *tôlĕdôt* is that of Noah (6:9–9:29). "Noah walked with God. And Noah had three sons, Shem, Ham, and Japheth" (6:9-10). But "the earth was corrupt in God's sight, and the earth was filled with violence" (6:11). God instructs Noah to build an ark so that a remnant can survive the great flood that is about to scour and cleanse the earth. After the flood subsides, God makes a covenant with the earth and with Noah and his sons. "God blessed Noah and his sons, and said to them, 'Be fruitful and multiply, and fill the earth'" (9:1). Noah is another Adam starting out on a clean earth. But evil still lurks in people's hearts. Noah becomes drunk and lies naked in his tent. His son Ham dishonors him. When Noah discovers this, he curses Ham's son Canaan (9:21-25). Canaan is another Cain — seed of the serpent. But Noah may also bless Shem and Japheth (9:26-27), and the line of the seed of the woman can continue.

The fourth *tôlĕdôt* is the *tôlĕdôt* of Noah's sons, Shem, Ham, and Japheth (10:1–11:19). Reversing the chronological order, it first lists seventy (10 × 7) nations that "spread abroad on the earth after the flood" (10:32) and then relates

33. Martin Woudstra, "The *Toledoth* of the Book of Genesis and Their Redemptive-Historical Significance," *CTJ* 5/2 (1970) 187.

34. "Ten" is the number of fullness; "seven" the number of completion or perfection.

35. See the note above.

the story of God confusing the language at Babel so that people will be scattered "abroad over the face of all the earth" (11:9). The author may well have changed the chronological order so that this fourth *tôlĕdôt* parallels the first three by ending once again in human disobedience: (1) Cain cursed and Lamech's detestable boast, (2) extreme violence, (3) Canaan cursed, and (4) Babel rebellion. With this repeated sequence the author calls attention to constant human rebellion and to God's grace in making new starts to continue the line of the seed of the woman.

The fifth *tôlĕdôt* is that of Shem (11:10-26). It moves quickly through the generations until it reaches another number "ten," Abram and his brothers (cf. the second *tôlĕdôt,* Adam to number "ten," Noah).

The sixth *tôlĕdôt* is the *tôlĕdôt* of Terah (11:27–25:11). It relates God's call of Abram, the blessings promised, and God's covenant with Abram. God makes a new start with Abram, who, like Noah, is another Adam. The line of the seed of the woman can continue. But Sarai is barren and, as was customary in that culture, gives her maid Hagar to Abram to raise up children. Ishmael is born (16:1-16). Later Sarah conceives and Isaac is born. Now Abraham has two sons, Ishmael and Isaac, but the LORD tells him that "it is through Isaac that offspring [seed] shall be named for you" (21:12). This *tôlĕdôt* concludes with the death of Sarah (ch. 23), the marriage of Isaac and Rebekah (ch. 24), and the death of Abram (ch. 25).

The seventh *tôlĕdôt* is that of Ishmael (25:12-18). With only seven verses, it is the shortest list. Since Ishmael is a son of Abraham, the author includes this *tôlĕdôt,* but he can hardly wait to get back to the line of the seed of the woman.

The eighth *tôlĕdôt* is the *tôlĕdôt* of Isaac (25:19–35:29). It deals briefly with Isaac but soon moves to the twins Esau and Jacob and concentrates especially on Jacob: his bargaining for the birthright from his older brother, deceiving his aged father for the blessing, his escape to uncle Laban, his marriage to two sisters, Leah and Rachel, and their maids, Bilhah and Zilpah, Jacob's flight back to Canaan, his meeting with God at Peniel, and his reconciliation with brother Esau. This *tôlĕdôt* ends with the death of Rachel, a listing of Jacob's twelve sons, and the death of Isaac.

The ninth *tôlĕdôt* is that of Esau (36:1–37:1).[36] It is similar to the *tôlĕdôt* of Ishmael. It seeks to give a brief account of the descendants of Esau, who is, after all, Isaac and Rebekah's son. But the interest of the author lies with the chosen son Jacob and his descendants.

The tenth *tôlĕdôt* is the *tôlĕdôt* of Jacob (37:2–50:26). As clearly as any-

36. I take the repetition of *tôlĕdôt* in 36:9 to be just that, a repetition of 36:1 expanding on the same *tôlĕdôt.*

where, we see here that a *tôlĕdôt* deals not primarily with the person named but the one begotten by that person: "This is the story of the family (*tôlĕdôt*) of Jacob. Joseph, being seventeen years old, was shepherding the flock with his brothers . . ." (37:2). This final *tôlĕdôt* tells the story of Joseph being sold by his brothers, his imprisonment in Egypt, his rise to power, his testing of his brothers, and his arranging for Jacob and his family to settle in Goshen. The *tôlĕdôt* ends with the last days of Jacob, his blessing of Joseph's sons, prophesying to his own sons, Jacob's death in Egypt and burial in Canaan, and Joseph's death. Genesis ends with the words, "He [Joseph] was embalmed and placed in a coffin in Egypt" (50:26). The story that began with life in Paradise appears to end with death in Egypt. But this is not the end of the story. God has called a new generation of Israelites into being. Joseph's last words are, "When God comes to you [to bring you to the land that he swore to Abraham, to Isaac, and to Jacob], you shall carry up my bones from here" (50:24-25). The diagram on page 16 will help visualize the author's overall literary structure of Genesis and some of its intricacies.

Functions of the *Tôlĕdôt* Structure The *tôlĕdôt* structure fulfills several functions in Genesis. First, from Israel's later perspective as a nation, the "genealogies display the existing relationship between kinship groups by tracing their lineage back to a common ancestor."[37]

Second, the linear genealogies of Genesis 5:1-31 and 11:10-26 (each ten generations) serve to link one narrative to another. They "establish continuity over stretches of time without narrative."[38]

Third, the genealogies, some individually and as a whole, mark the process of the narrowing of God's channel of redemption. The first *tôlĕdôt,* of heaven and earth, begins universally and ends with Seth, with whom God will continue the seed of the woman. The second *tôlĕdôt,* of Adam, narrows the field from many people who are destroyed in the flood, to Seth's descendant Noah, whom God selects to survive the devastation. The third *tôlĕdôt* begins with Noah and his three sons, Shem, Ham, and Japheth, but ends with the blessing of Shem. Although the fourth *tôlĕdôt* is of Shem, Ham, and Japheth, the fifth narrows the line of the seed of the woman down to Shem. The sixth *tôlĕdôt* begins with Terah and his three sons, Abram, Nahor, and Haran, but focuses on Abram as the recipient of God's covenant promises. Abraham has two sons, Ishmael and Isaac, but Isaac is God's chosen instrument. The seventh *tôlĕdôt* about Ishmael's

37. Waltke, *Genesis,* 106.

38. Ibid. This obvious literary structure of a full number of ten generations from Adam to Noah and ten generations from Shem to Abram should caution interpreters not to use the *tôlĕdôt* structure to calculate the date of Adam.

Tôlĕdôt *Structure of Genesis*

- A *tôlĕdôt* discloses primarily what comes *after* the character(s) for whom the *tôlĕdôt* is named.
- The *tôlĕdôt* structure of Genesis begins universally with all creation, narrows down to all humanity, and narrows still further to one family and nation: Abram, Isaac, Jacob, and Israel.
- In its *tôlĕdôt* structure Genesis highlights the numbers "ten," the number of fullness, and "seven," the number of perfection or completion.

"These are the generations of":

I. **Heaven and Earth** (Gen 2:4–4:26):
Adam (rebellion) → Cain (murder) → Lamech *(7)* → Seth

II. **Adam** (Gen 5:1–6:8):
Adam → Seth → Enoch *(7)* Noah *(10)* → Violence → Noah favor

III. **Noah** (Gen 6:9–9:29):
Noah → Violence → Flood → Shem blessed → Canaan cursed

IV. **Noah's sons** (Gen 10:1–11:9):
descendants → nations *(70)* → Babel

V. **Shem** (Gen 11:10-26):
Shem → Abram *(10)*

VI. **Terah** (Gen 11:27–25:11):
Terah → Abraham

VII. **Ishmael** (Gen 25:12-18):
twelve sons

VIII. **Isaac** (Gen 25:19–35:29):
Isaac → Jacob

IX. **Esau** (Gen 36:1–37:1):
descendants

X. **Jacob** (Gen 37:2–50:26):
Jacob → Joseph → (*70* Israelites in Egypt; 46:27)

descendants is brief in order to put the full weight on Isaac's descendants in the eighth *tôlĕdôt.* Isaac also has two sons, Esau and Jacob, and again, the author spends little time on Esau's descendants in the ninth *tôlĕdôt,* in order to concentrate on Jacob's descendant, Joseph, in the final *tôlĕdôt.*

Finally, and most importantly, the genealogies reveal the sovereignty and the grace of God as he provides for the continuation of the line of the seed of the woman with a view to re-establishing his good kingdom on earth.[39]

Unifying Biblical-Theological Themes

There are also many biblical-theological themes that weave Genesis into a unified composition. We shall briefly note six intertwined strands: the kingdom of God, God's blessing and curse, God's covenant, covenant promises, the promise of seed, and the beginnings of redemptive history.

The Kingdom of God Genesis sketches the beginnings of the kingdom of God. Bruce Waltke observes, "Although the expression 'kingdom of God' never occurs in the Old Testament and its equivalents are relatively rare and late, the concept informs the whole. The Primary History, which traces Israel's history from the creation of the world (Gen 1) to the fall of Israel (2 Kings 25), is all about what the New Testament calls 'the kingdom of God.'"[40] Genesis 1 relates that God created this earth as his kingdom and that he created human beings in his image to manage this world on his behalf. Human beings were to obey the great King without question (Gen 2:15-17). Genesis 3 relates the tragic rebellion against God and God's subsequent punishment, but also God's resolve to restore his kingdom on earth (Gen 3:15). When Cain killed Abel, God continued the line of the seed of the woman with the birth of Seth. When terrible violence later made life impossible, God cleansed the earth with a flood and made a new start with Noah. When people subsequently disobeyed God at Babel, God confused their language and made a new start with Abram with a view to spreading his kingdom across the entire earth: "In you all the families of the earth shall be blessed" (Gen 12:3) — a promise subsequently repeated to Isaac (26:4) and Jacob (28:14).

God's Blessing and Curse God promotes the cause of his kingdom by giving his blessing. The word "blessing/bless" *(bĕrakâ/bārak)* is used eighty-eight

39. The genealogies highlight "the existence of a unique line of 'seed' which will eventually become a royal dynasty. Members of this lineage enjoy a special relationship with God who actively provides and sustains each new generation." Alexander, "Genealogies, Seed and the Compositional Unity of Genesis," "Covenant and Creation," *TynBul* 44/2 (1993) 269-70.

40. Waltke, *Genesis,* 44.

times in Genesis, "more than in any other biblical book."[41] The note of God's blessing is first struck in Paradise. God blessed the animals (Gen 1:22) as well as humankind: "God blessed them, and God said to them, 'Be fruitful and multiply, and fill the earth and subdue it; and have dominion . . .'" (1:28). Allen Ross succinctly explains the word "to bless": "A study of its uses in Genesis shows that the giving of a blessing bestowed prosperity with respect to fertility of land and fertility of life. The gift of blessing included the empowerment to achieve what was promised."[42]

With the Fall into sin, God's curse entered the picture. God cursed the serpent as well as the ground (Gen 3:14, 17). "The curse in Genesis involved separation or alienation from the place of blessing, or even from those who were blessed."[43] God expelled Adam and Eve from his presence in the garden(3:24). Cain was "cursed from the ground" for murdering his brother (4:11). At the climax of the cycle of violence, God cursed the ground (see 8:21) with a great flood. And even though God blessed Noah and his sons and said to them as to Adam, "Be fruitful and multiply, and fill the earth" (9:1), Noah cursed his grandson Canaan and blessed his son Shem (9:25-26). Blessing and curse — which one will win out in the end?

God's call of Abram leaves little doubt: "I will bless you, and make your name great, so that you will be a blessing. I will bless those who bless you, and the one who curses you I will curse; and in you all the families of the earth shall be blessed" (Gen 12:2-3). Many times God repeated these promised blessings to Abraham, to Isaac, and to Jacob.[44] In the book of Genesis we see a partial fulfillment of this universal promise of blessing especially in the life of Joseph, for the author records that "*all the world* came to Joseph in Egypt to buy grain, because the famine became severe throughout the world" (41:57). Under God's blessing, the goodness of God's original kingdom will eventually spread to "all the families of the earth."

God's Covenant God administers his kingdom on earth by way of the covenant he makes with his creation and with his special people. Although the word "covenant" *(bĕrît)* is not used in the early chapters of Genesis, we can detect in them some of the usual elements of covenant treaties.[45] For example, in the

41. Mathews, "Genesis," 141.

42. Ross, *Creation and Blessing,* 66.

43. Ibid.

44. For Abram, see also Genesis 13:14-18; 15:4-5, 13-21; 17:4-8; 18:17-19; 22:15-18. For Isaac, see 26:4, 24; and for Jacob, see 28:13-15; 35:11-12; and 46:3.

45. In the second millennium B.C., the usual elements in international (Hittite) covenant treaties were: a preamble identifying the king, a historical prologue relating the king's deeds, covenant stipulations that spelled out the obligations of the vassal to the king, where the treaty

narrative about Paradise, a preamble identifies the great King as "the LORD God" (Gen 2:4); a historical prologue recalls what the LORD has done (2:7-15); covenant stipulations follow: "The LORD God commanded the man, 'You may freely eat of every tree of the garden; but of the tree of the knowledge of good and evil you shall not eat, for in the day that you eat of it you shall die'" (2:16-17); and finally there is God's curse: "Cursed are you [the serpent]. . . . Cursed is the ground" (3:14, 17).

The word *bĕrît* is first used when God announces that he will continue[46] his covenant with Noah, "But I will establish my covenant with you" (Gen 6:18). This is a covenant not only with Noah and his descendants but with "every living creature of all flesh" (9:9-17). In this covenant God promises "that never again shall all flesh be cut off by the waters of a flood" (9:11). The sign of God's covenant with his creation is the rainbow (9:13).

Later God makes a special covenant with Abram, promising to give his descendants the land from the river Nile to the Euphrates (Gen 15:18). Still later God promises Abram: "I will make nations of you, and kings shall come from you. I will establish my covenant between me and you, and your offspring after you throughout their generations, for an everlasting covenant, to be God to you and to your offspring after you. And I will give to you, and to your offspring after you, the land where you are now an alien, all the land of Canaan, for a perpetual holding; and I will be their God" (17:6-8). The sign of this covenant is circumcision (17:10-14). This covenant of grace is extended to Isaac (17:19), to Jacob (35:11-12) and to all of Israel (Exod 6:2-8).

God's Covenant Promises The covenant, we have seen, is marked by God's special promises. The repetition of these promises runs like a golden thread through Genesis. Frequently three major covenant promises are highlighted: a special relationship with God, numerous seed, and the land of Canaan. The fulfillment of all three promises will be required for establishing a theocratic kingdom in Canaan. These promises are repeated at various times in Genesis:

---

was to be kept and when read in public, witnesses, blessings if obedient and curses if disobedient. The book of Deuteronomy is structured on these very elements. See also the structures of Exodus 20 and Joshua 24. See G. E. Mendenhall, "Covenant," in *The Interpreter's Dictionary of the Bible* (Nashville: Abingdon, 1962), 719-20; Meredith G. Kline, *Treaty of the Great King: The Covenant Structure of Deuteronomy* (Grand Rapids: Eerdmans, 1963), 28-44, and Kitchen, *On the Reliability of the Old Testament,* 283-94.

46. William Dumbrell, *Covenant and Creation,* 26, argues that the use of *hăqim bĕrît* instead of *kārat bĕrît* in Genesis 6:18 "makes it more than likely that . . . the institution of a covenant is not being referred to but rather its perpetuation." For a contrary position, see John H. Stek, "'Covenant' Overload in Reformed Theology," *CTJ* 29 (1994) 12-41, esp. 22-24. See also the rejoinder by Craig G. Bartholomew, "Covenant and Creation," *CTJ* 30 (1995) 11-33.

1. The promise of a special relationship with God: 10 times.
2. The promise of numerous seed: 19 times.
3. The promise of land: 13 times.
4. Allusions to God's threefold promise: 17 times.[47]

Not to be overlooked, however, is God's promise to Abram, "In you all the families of the earth shall be blessed" (Gen 12:3). This promise is all the more important because it comes at a crucial juncture: right at the end of God's dealings with "all the families of the earth" (Gen 1–11) and at the beginning of God's redemptive activity being channeled through one family (Abraham's) and one nation (Israel). God tells Israel that he is not giving up on the nations; he will channel his grace through one family with a view to blessing "all the families of the earth." This promise is repeated seven times in Genesis.[48]

God's Promise of Seed The promise of seed is especially prominent in Genesis. The Old Testament uses the word "seed" *(zeraʿ)* 229 times, and 59 of these are in Genesis.[49] In Genesis 1 the word is first used for the seed of plants and fruit trees, but in Genesis 3:15 the word "seed" takes on a deeper, spiritual dimension as well. God says to the serpent: "I will put enmity between you and the woman, and between your offspring [seed] and hers." Like plants and trees, human beings will also produce seed, but this seed will be of two kinds: the seed of the serpent and the seed of the woman; those who rebel against the great King and those who seek to follow God in obedience. Genesis will follow the development of these two kinds of seed, tracing especially the line of the seed of the woman, whose continued existence often appears in doubt: Abel is killed (4:8); Sarai is barren (11:30); Rebekah is barren (25:21); Rachel is barren (29:31); Jacob and his family are about to starve in Canaan (42:2). But in his grace, God continually intervenes so that the seed of the woman can advance from Adam and Eve to Seth, to Noah, to Abram, to Isaac, to Jacob, and, by the end of Genesis, to the beginning of numerous seed — the full number of 70 (10×7) people (Gen 46:27; Exod 1:5).

The Beginnings of Redemptive History Our final biblical-theological theme in discerning the unified structure of Genesis doubles back to the first, the beginnings of the kingdom of God. Genesis 1 tells of God creating this earth as his

47. For the specific references, see Clines, *Theme of the Pentateuch,* 32-40. See further VanGemeren, *Progress of Redemption,* 104-8.

48. It is first given in Genesis 12:3, repeated to Abraham in 22:18, to Isaac in 26:4, and to Jacob in 28:14. It is implied in Genesis 17:4-6, 16, and remembered in 18:18.

49. Alexander, "Genealogies, Seed and the Compositional Unity of Genesis," *TynBul* 44/2 (1993) 259-60.

beautiful kingdom, but Genesis 3 relates the tragic rebellion against God, the King, and God's punishment of humanity. However, God resolves to restore his kingdom on earth; he breaks up the unholy alliance between Adam/Eve and the serpent. God says to the serpent, "I will put enmity between you and the woman, and between your offspring [seed] and hers; he will strike your head, and you will strike his heel" (Gen 3:15). This declaration of enmity against Satan signals the start of redemptive history. The book of Genesis relates the beginnings of this redemptive history. In focusing on this single history, Genesis exhibits a unified structure.

The Literary Structure of Individual Narratives

To understand a biblical narrative and to preach it in a narrative form, it is crucial to detect the plot line in the narrative. To discover the plot line, one should ask, What is the conflict in this story and how is it resolved? All narratives will have some of the following components: a setting for the story, some preliminary incidents, an incident that generates the conflict, buildup in the tension till it reaches a climax, the turn in the narrative to the beginning of a resolution, the full resolution, an outcome, and perhaps a conclusion. Tremper Longman has provided a helpful diagram of the typical elements in a single plot.[50]

The Structure of Biblical Narrative

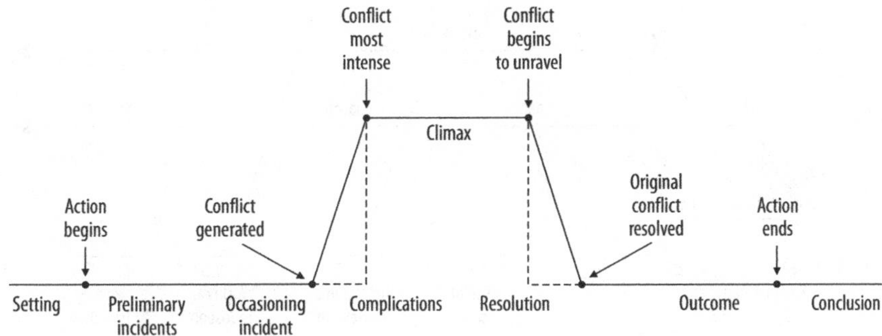

Hebrew narratives have various plot lines: a single plot which relates a single narrative conflict and resolution (e.g., Babel, Gen 11:1-9), a single plot with subplots or complications (e.g., the call of Abram, 11:27–12:9), a complex plot which relates conflict and resolution only to usher in a new conflict leading to another resolution (e.g., the Fall into sin, 2:4–3:24), an overarching plot in

50. Tremper Longman III, *Literary Approaches to Biblical Interpretation* (Grand Rapids: Zondervan, 1987), 92.

which the initial conflict (e.g., God's promise to make of Abram a great nation when his wife is barren, 11:30; 12:2) is not resolved until the birth of Isaac (21:1-7) and then only partially, and the Bible's meta-narrative plot from Genesis 1 to Revelation 22 (see the plot line on p. 4 above).

Moreover, these various plot lines do not neatly follow one after the other but are intricately interwoven. A single plot may have embedded in it settings for overarching narratives. For example, the single plot of God calling Abram (11:27–12:9) has embedded in it God's promise to Abram of "a great nation" (12:2). The conflict of this overarching narrative begins to be resolved only with the birth of Isaac (21:1-7), then Jacob, Jacob's sons, and the full number of seventy Israelites going down to Egypt (46:27). The single plot of God calling Abram also contains God's promise of land (12:7). The conflict of this overarching narrative begins to be resolved only when Abram is able to buy a burial plot for Sarah (23:1-20) but by the end of Genesis is still waiting for full resolution. God also promises Abram, "in you all the families of the earth shall be blessed" (12:3).[51] This overarching narrative conflict receives an initial resolution only when "all the world came to Joseph in Egypt to buy grain" (41:57) but is still waiting for full resolution. The following diagram shows the interweaving of single and overarching narratives that begin to be resolved in Genesis but reach beyond it for full resolution:

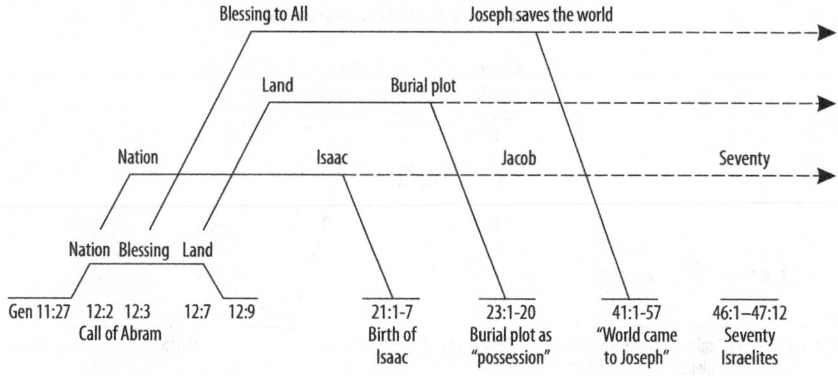

The Genre of the Genesis Narratives

Another important issue one faces in literary interpretation is the question of the *kind* of literature one is interpreting. Although this question is a literary question, for the Genesis narratives it is often informed by a judgment of their

51. Walter Kaiser argues that God's "promise-plan" "embraces both testaments in one unified, single plan." *Preaching and Teaching from the Old Testament,* 38. Cf. his *Toward an Old Testament Theology.*

historicity. Granted that these narratives are not the genre of modern historical narrative, what are they? A multitude of answers have been offered to this question, the three most prominent being legend, myth, and saga.

Legend Some have suggested that the Genesis narratives are legends. For example, George Coats states that the legend "employs a relatively static narration. The structure of the legend features recurring emphasis on some particular characteristic of the narrative's hero. . . . The structure does not develop an arc of tension that moves from point of complication to point of resolution. . . . The goal of the legend is edification of its audience. Thus, the hero may serve as a model whose virtue can be duplicated by subsequent generations."[52] Coats identifies specifically Genesis 22 (Abraham) and 39–41 (Joseph) as legends. However, as we shall see, these narratives do exhibit the buildup of tension from conflict to resolution. It also seems far-fetched to suggest that Israel, with its penchant for historical foundations, would seek to base its history with God and its claim to the land of Canaan on mere legends.

Myth Others have suggested that the Genesis narratives are "myths." But "myth" is a slippery term, witness the fact that scholars use at least nine different definitions of "myth."[53] According to McCartney and Clayton, "the common meaning of the term myth in popular parlance is 'a fabulous and untrue story.'" This denotation, they say, makes the term "myth" totally inadequate for Genesis, for "biblical history is not myth, but a true story, told with theological purpose and vantage point. It may use the images and linguistic forms of its environment, but slipping in the term myth by redefinition really results in a reduction of the uniqueness of the biblical history."[54] Moreover, the Genesis narratives *de*mythologize pagan mythologies.[55] Surely, the label of "myth" is inappropriate for narratives that demythologize pagan mythologies.

Saga Hermann Gunkel first introduced the name "saga" for the Genesis narratives. "Saga," a Norse term, has been defined as "a long, prose, traditional narrative having an episodic structure developed around stereotyped themes or objects."[56] The major unresolved issue with saga is whether and how much of the narrative is historical.[57] Although Donald Gowan bemoans the fact that it is

52. Coats, *Genesis*, 8-9.

53. Hamilton, *Genesis 1–17*, 57.

54. McCartney and Clayton, *Let the Reader Understand*, 212-13.

55. See Ross, *Creation and Blessing*, 52-54.

56. Coats, *Genesis*, 319.

57. See, e.g., von Rad's struggle to ground Israel's "sagas" "in the 'real' history." *Old Testament Theology*, I, 108. Cf. his *Genesis* (rev. ed., 1972), 31-43.

a "vague" label, he asserts that "nevertheless the term saga can be used in a helpful way to denote a type of literature which is different in form, content, and intention from history-writing, so different that it ought to be preached in a distinctive way."[58] By contrast, Dillard and Longman judge that labels such as saga, legend, fable, and myth "are obviously prejudicial to the historical intentionality of the book. They are . . . motivated more by modern interpreters' unwillingness and inability to accept the reality of the world of Genesis than by a clear insight into the intention of the text."[59] Asking about the "intention of the text" may lead to a more solid footing than the vague and slippery labels above.

Redemptive-Historical Narrative In discussing the *tôlĕdôt* structure of Genesis, we noted that the author has gone to great lengths to unify his composition by structuring the whole as ten sets of *tôlĕdôt.* The author's intention clearly is to link the nation of Israel via the patriarchs to the very beginning of history. "The frequent *tôlĕdôt* formulae that structure the book . . . indicate a historical impulse to the book."[60] Bruce Waltke argues effectively that Genesis is some form of history writing: "The author of Genesis presents himself as a historian. . . . He gives an essentially coherent chronological succession of events, using the Hebrew narrative verb form. He validates his material as much as possible by locating his story in time and space (e.g., 2:10-14), tracing genealogies (e.g., 5:1-32), giving evidence of various sorts that validate his history (e.g., 11:9), and citing sources (5:1 ['the written account']). . . . The narrator's evidence will not satisfy the demands of modern historiography, but it shows that he intended to write real history, not myth or saga or legend."[61]

If it is clear that Genesis contains a form of history writing, it is also clear that it is a special form. This is no national history, not even tribal or family history. The author focuses on *God's* history with the world and the patriarchs. Therefore we can call the genre of Genesis narratives redemptive-historical narrative.[62] We can define redemptive-historical narrative as narrative which recounts the history God makes in the world to restore his kingdom on earth and

58. Gowan, *Reclaiming the Old Testament,* 35.

59. Dillard and Longman, *Introduction to the Old Testament,* 49.

60. Ibid.

61. *Genesis,* 29. Cf. Dillard and Longman, *Introduction to the Old Testament,* 49, "If we are speaking of the original intention of the biblical writer(s), the style of the book leaves little space to argue over the obvious conclusion that the author intended it to be read as a work of history that recounts what has taken place in the far-distant past." Cf. Provan et al., *A Biblical History of Israel,* 111, "One cannot conceive of the original audience as thinking of Abraham as other than a real person, or of his movements from Ur to Haran to Palestine as other than a real journey."

62. Some prefer "salvation history" to "redemptive history," but "redemptive history" is more precise in signaling *how* God saves, namely by redeeming, rescuing and delivering, his creation and creatures from enslavement to Satan (Gen 3:15) and sin (Gen 8:21).

redeem his people. In contrast to legend, myth, and saga, the genre of redemptive-historical narrative not only acknowledges that this is a form of history writing but also connects these Genesis narratives to other biblical narratives which together, like frames in a film, constitute the meta-narrative from fallen creation (Gen 3) to new creation (Rev 22).

Redemptive history is not above ordinary history; redemptive history unfolds in ordinary history.[63] Yet the common historical-critical method is incompetent to evaluate redemptive history because it assumes that it can apply to biblical narratives the principles of analogy and correlation in a universe closed to God.[64] Because of this starting point, this method is inherently incapable of competently assessing redemptive history. For example, the historical-critical method may some day be able to confirm the probability that Jacob's son Joseph rose to high power in Egypt, but it cannot confirm the biblical message that "God intended it for good, in order to preserve a numerous people" (Gen 50:20). To do justice to the genre of redemptive-historical narrative, one needs to utilize a holistic historical-critical method, that is, a method that presupposes an open universe where God can act in history either mediately or immediately.[65]

Issues in Historical Interpretation

With the discussion of the genre of the Genesis narratives we have already entered the field of historical interpretation. Here we will discuss three major is-

63. This redemptive-historical approach is not to be identified with the *Heilsgeschichte* school of von Rad and others who separate *geschichte* from *historie* (facts).

64. In 1898, Troeltsch taught that "the means by which criticism becomes possible is the employment of analogy. The analogy of what takes place before our eyes . . . is the key to criticism. . . . Correspondence with normal, customary, or at least repeatedly attested ways of occurrence . . . , as we know them, is the mark of probability for occurrences which criticism can acknowledge as really having happened" (*Gesammelte Schriften* [Tübingen: Mohr, 1913], II, 732, my translation). The principle of analogy with *our* experience of reality places a large question mark behind the historicity of the Genesis narratives where God walks and talks with people. In addition to the principle of analogy, Troeltsch employed the principle of correlation, that is, all events must be understood in terms of their causes and effects (ibid., 732-37). This principle applied in a *closed* universe allows only for immanent causes and eliminates God as a possible agent in human history. Cf. von Rad, *Old Testament Theology*, II, 418, "The modern view of history . . . finds it very hard to assume that there is divine action in history. God has no place in its *schema*. The realization that the men who give us the history of ancient Israel were not only men of faith, but that . . . their conceptions of history centred completely on God, brings out the tremendous difference between their view of history and the modern scientific one." For a more detailed analysis of the historical-critical method, see my *Modern Preacher*, 25-36.

65. See my proposal in *Modern Preacher*, 36-47. See also Grant R. Osborne, "Historical Narrative and Truth in the Bible," *JETS* 48/4 (Dec. 2005) 684.

sues: first, the historicity of the Genesis narratives; second, their indispensable historical foundations; and third, their original readers.

The Historicity of the Genesis Narratives

The Genesis narratives are obviously not modern historiography. For one, they are not eyewitness accounts. If, as tradition has it, Moses was the original author, he lived at least six centuries after Abraham. Having led Israel out of Egypt, he wrote about Israel's ancestors, pushing its origins back ever further: to its patriarchs, to the first nations, to the first humans, to the beginning of the world. We can describe the history-writing of Genesis as ancient, kerygmatic historiography.

Ancient Historiography The ancient author is clearly not confined by nineteenth-century standards of exactitude. He is unashamedly selective. "Only that which contributes to the story of God, i.e., to the theological intention of the text, is worthy of comment. Thus, whole centuries can be bypassed . . . or long chapters can be devoted to a relatively brief period of time."[66] For example, the author devotes thirteen long chapters to the life of Joseph while he simply skips over more than three centuries between Jacob's death (Gen 50) and Moses' birth (Exod 2). The author of Genesis selects some facts here and ignores others there; he details particulars here and summarizes others there; he arranges certain events in chronological order and then switches to a topical order (e.g., the reversal in Gen 10 and 11:1-9); he uses anachronism by pushing the distinction between clean and unclean animals back to Noah; he employs hyperbole to make his point when he reports that "*all the world* came to Joseph in Egypt to buy grain" (Gen 41:57); he uses the seven-day week known to Israel as a literary framework to proclaim that Israel's God created all things; he places Enoch who "walked with God" seventh in the line of the seed of the woman to contrast him with the murderous Lamech, seventh in the line of the seed of the serpent; he uses round, symbolic numbers: ten sets of *tôlĕdôt* from the creation of heaven and earth to Israel in Egypt, ten generations from Adam to Noah and ten generations from Shem to Abram, forty days and forty nights of rain causing the flood, seventy nations descended from Noah (Gen 10), seventy persons descended from Jacob (Gen 46:27). Even the ages listed for the patriarchs may be intended as symbolic numbers when one considers that Abraham's age of 175 (25:7), Isaac's of 180 (35:28), Jacob's of 147 (47:28), and Joseph's of 110 (50:26) form a refined symmetry which begins and ends with the perfect number seven:[67]

66. Merrill, "Old Testament History," 72.

67. Duane L. Christensen, "Josephus and the Twenty-Two Book Canon of Sacred Scripture," *JETS* 29 (1986) 45-46. Cf. Hamilton, *Genesis 18–50*, 709.

$175 = 7 \times 5^2$
$180 = 5 \times 6^2$
$147 = 3 \times 7^2$
$110 = 1 \times 5^2 + 6^2 + 7^2.$

Evidently the author of Genesis did not intend to give Israel exact information about the distant past, and the narratives should not be understood as such.[68]

Kerygmatic Historiography It is better to understand Genesis as kerygmatic historiography. The author sketches in broad strokes the beginnings of God's redemptive history in order to acquaint Israel with the God of their ancestors and his acts to preserve a people and to restore his kingdom on earth. For preachers and teachers this kerygmatic character is advantageous, for "the bare facts of history are usually capable of several different interpretations, and the inner meaning of the events, Yhwh's purpose behind the occurrences, is not clear unless it is disclosed in words which Yhwh speaks to his chosen messengers."[69] The Genesis narratives may be described as sermons addressed to ancient Israel; they seek to impart God's relevant message to Israel.[70] As such they can be used for relevant proclamation to the new Israel, the church, today.

Christian preachers should honor the intention of the author of Genesis, of course: they should not put questions to the text which the author did not intend to answer. For example, they should not ask Genesis about the age of the earth or the sequence in which things came to be. Instead of raising these modern questions, they should use Genesis to listen in on the relevant message that came to ancient Israel and apply that message to the church today.

The Sources of Genesis Since Genesis was written long after the recorded events, the author must have used ancient sources to compose his work.[71] Eugene Merrill observes, "The tradition is silent as to how Moses (or any author)

68. For more details on biblical history writing, see my *Modern Preacher,* 82-94 and 191-97. For historical incongruities in Genesis, see LaSor et al., *Old Testament Survey,* 108-9.

69. Bertil Albrektson, *History and the Gods* (Lund: Gleerup, 1967), 119.

70. "It must be admitted that Genesis . . . is not attempting to be as close as possible to a dispassionate reporting of events. Rather, we have proclamation — with the result that the history is shaped to differing degrees. The point is that the Biblical narrators are concerned not only to tell us the facts but also to guide our perspective of and responses to those events." Longman, "The Literary Approach to the Study of the Old Testament: Promises and Pitfalls," *JETS* 28/4 (1985) 395.

71. Just as Luke (see Luke 1:1-4) used sources to write his Gospel. See Numbers 21:14 about "the Book of the Wars of the LORD."

gained access to the events of that pre-Mosaic era, though perhaps terms such as *tôlĕdôt* might suggest written texts."[72]

As far as primeval history is concerned, Ken Mathews suggests that "Genesis appears to be following an ancient pattern for the way origins were told among the peoples of the Near East. The closest parallels are the Akkadian *Atrahasis* (1600 B.C.) and the Sumerian *Eridu Genesis* (1600 B.C.) which give an account of the period from creation to the great Flood. Other parallels to Genesis may be drawn from such myths as the Akkadian *Enumah Elish* and *Epic of Gilgamesh*." Mathews judges, "There is no evidence that outright borrowing occurred between the Hebrews and others; rather, there was general knowledge of early traditions shared by all antiquity."[73]

These sources, their dates, and how they were used is a never-ending debate — a debate preachers may be inclined to sidestep. In seeking to understand the message of the text, however, awareness of underlying sources or parallel developments may be helpful.[74] For the way the biblical author uses, changes, or counters his sources may sharpen the particular message he wishes to bring to Israel. For example, all the ancient myths speak of a multitude of gods. In sharp contrast, Genesis begins: "In the beginning God created the heavens and the earth." In the creation account *Atrahasis,* the gods persuade the goddess Mami to "create a human being that he bear the yoke," that is, the "forced labor" of the lesser gods.[75] By contrast, Genesis 1 proclaims that God created human beings not as slaves but as the crown of his creation, made in his image, his representatives, to take care of the earth. Again, "*Atrahasis* and the *Eridu Genesis* attribute the Flood to the last desperate attempts of the gods to rid themselves of the overpopulated, bothersome humans. The survival of their 'Noah' was unintended and only accepted by the gods after a compromise. The Bible, on the other hand, presents the population of the earth as good in the eyes of God; procreation is a blessing and will bring to pass God's reign on earth through Adam's lineage. More importantly, the Flood is God's judgment against the encroaching world-wide practice of human sin."[76]

As far as patriarchal history is concerned, though the author may not be as far removed from his subject matter as from primeval history, he is still at least six cen-

72. Merrill, "Old Testament History," 77.

73. Mathews, "Preaching in the Pentateuch," 268. Cf. Ross, *Creation and Blessing,* 62, "We conclude, with others, that the two traditions must be parallel traditions, perhaps going back to one source." Cf. Kitchen, *On the Reliability of the Old Testament,* 422-27, 447.

74. A convenient place to find these myths in English translation is Hallo, ed., *The Context of Scripture:* Vol. I, *Enuma Elish,* 390-402; *Atrahasis,* 450-53; *Gilgamesh,* 458-60; *Eridu Genesis,* 513-15.

75. *Atrahasis,* lines 190-97.

76. Mathews, "Preaching in the Pentateuch," 269.

turies removed from Abraham. Where did he get his information? Allen Ross suggests that "besides the primeval traditions and genealogies brought from the East, the family traditions of the patriarchs would have been handed down from generation to generation. Joseph, and later Moses, would have had every facility for recording and preserving the traditions that the ancestors brought with them."[77]

The Reliability of Genesis Archeologists have discovered interesting parallels to places and customs described in Genesis. Victor Hamilton sums up some of the evidence: Tablets from Mari (19th century B.C.) "revealed place names and personal names (a) equivalents of which are found in the early chapters of Genesis . . . , and (b) most of these names were restricted to the Bronze Age." Further, texts from Nuzi (15th century B.C.) showed the following parallels:

1. A marriage to a niece (11:29)
2. A husband obtains the status of a brother by adopting his wife (12:1-20; 21:1-34; 26:1-35)
3. A childless couple might adopt someone, even a servant, to take care of them; in the end this person would inherit their property. Any naturally born son, however, replaces the adoptee (15:2-3)
4. A barren wife must provide her husband with a surrogate, normally the wife's slave girl (16:1-2; 30:1-13)
5. The status of the slave girl and her offspring is protected against the jealousy or whims of either wife or husband (21:9-14)
6. A brother may adopt his sister in order to give her in marriage to someone else, providing she agrees (24:1-67)
7. A birthright might be sold to another (25:29-34)
8. A patriarchal blessing carries the weight of law and is not to be subjected to revision (27:35-37; 48:8-22)
9. A couple might adopt a son-in-law as their own son (30:1-2)
10. Possession of the household gods was seen as legal title to an inheritance (31:34)[78]

John Sailhamer judges, "However Moses may have obtained his information, one thing is certain: the Pentateuch depicts accurately the age and historical period of the patriarchs. . . . Many of the historical details and customs in the lives of the patriarchs are now known to us from contemporary documents."[79]

77. Ross, *Creation and Blessing,* 62. Cf. Kitchen, *On the Reliability of the Old Testament,* 368-71.

78. Hamilton, *Genesis 1–17,* 62. Cf. Kitchen, *On the Reliability of the Old Testament,* 324-28, 352-60.

79. Sailhamer, *Pentateuch as Narrative,* 23-24. Cf. Wenham, *Genesis 16–50,* xx-xxx. Cf.

Still, it is well to remember that the authority of the preacher's message is not dependent on nineteenth-century concepts of historical accuracy. As Clyde Francisco observes, "The truths of Genesis 1–11 are not to be found so much in the exactness with which the original event has been preserved as in the witness to that event. Witnesses in court give clues to the judge concerning the actual event; they cannot reproduce it. . . . Even so, the biblical accounts, regardless of their condition in transmission, give authentic witness to the redemptive acts of God which are both before and beyond their words."[80]

Indispensable Historical Foundations

Although fiction can surely proclaim truth (e.g., Jesus' parables), preachers cannot proclaim redemptive-historical truth on the basis of fiction. When preachers proclaim with Genesis that God acted in world and human history, their message has integrity only when they themselves assume that God acted in history.

Creating a Narrative World In the section on literary interpretation above, we saw how the author/compiler of Genesis was able to present a compelling narrative linking the history of Israel as a nation to the patriarchs and ultimately to the creation of this world. With the recent paradigm shift in biblical scholarship from historical criticism to the new literary criticism and especially narrative criticism, biblical scholars have opened up wonderful vistas for preachers of biblical narrative. Narratives are now carefully analyzed according to their setting, characters, dialogue, plot, point of view, narrator and narratee, implied author and implied reader, and real author and real reader.[81]

Unfortunately, in the quest for literary meaning and in reaction to the onslaught of secular historical-criticism, biblical scholars now frequently ignore the historical referent.[82] They simply wish to "bracket out" the question of historicity. For example, Mark Ellingsen writes, "The strength of the biblical narrative approach for preaching on the strange biblical accounts is precisely that formal

---

Kitchen, *On the Reliability of the Old Testament*, 365, "In terms of content, these narratives give a picture of real human life as lived by West Semitic pastoralists, derived mainly from conditions observable in the early second millennium, with a very moderate amount of minor retouches in at least three later periods." See also the evidence gathered by Kitchen, "The Patriarchal Age: Myth or History?" *BAR*, Mar./Apr. 1995, 48-57.

80. Francisco, "Preaching from the Primeval Narratives of Genesis," 20.

81. See my *Modern Preacher*, 197-213; Waltke, *Genesis*, 31-43; Osborne, *Hermeneutical Spiral*, 154-64; Mathewson, *The Art of Preaching Old Testament Narrative*, 44-66.

82. "Many literary critics radically deny any historical element in reading a text." Osborne, *Hermeneutical Spiral*, 164. See also my "The Value of a Literary Approach for Preaching," 513-14.

historical claims are not made on their behalf." "The preacher's job is simply to report the biblical accounts, not to insist that the strange stories happened."[83] Grant Osborne, by contrast, insists, "If cut off from historical and referential meaning, they become arbitrary and subjective. Therefore, any proper methodology must blend the two (literary and historical) in such a way that they modify one another, magnifying the strengths and avoiding the weaknesses of each."[84]

The Genesis Narrative World Depicts the Real World John Goldingay observes that "large tracts of the Old Testament such as Genesis are put in the form of narrative about the factual past. Israel was capable of producing fictional parable and present testimony, but in the patriarchal stories she did not: she makes a point of telling a story about the factual past, and refers to it (in a passage such as Isaiah 51) in such a way as to make it rather clear that she understands the story to be fundamentally factual."[85] In other words, the narrative world of Genesis depicts the real world. In opposition to Frei and others who suggest that biblical narratives are only "history-like," Sailhamer maintains, "It is not enough to say that the biblical narratives are only 'history-like' and to relegate them to the level of 'realistic narrative [Frei].' . . . The authors of the biblical narratives give every indication of intending their works to be taken as history rather than fiction. . . . There is reasonable evidence that the history recorded in these narratives corresponds to the events themselves."[86] Sailhamer's diagram will help clarify the relationships between the reader, redemptive-historical narrative, the narrative world, and the real world:[87]

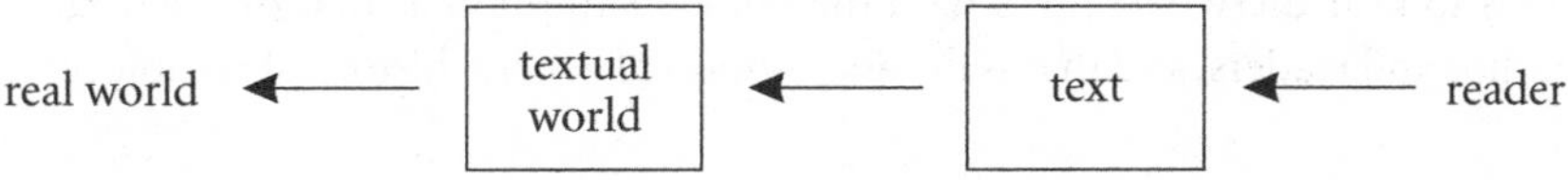

The Necessity of Historical Foundations Redemptive-historical narrative requires historical foundations for its message to stand.[88] Not all narratives, of

83. Ellingsen, *The Integrity of Biblical Narrative* (Minneapolis: Fortress, 1990), 68 and 92.

84. Osborne, *Hermeneutical Spiral*, 168. See also his "Historical Narrative and Truth in the Bible," *JETS* 48/4 (Dec. 2005) 673-88. Cf. Philips Long, "Reading the Old Testament as Literature," 110-11, "To leave aside historical concerns entirely and interminably is misguided in dealing with texts that appear to make historical truth claims — as misguided as focusing on the artistry of a portrait to the exclusion of any interest in the *historical* subject of which the portrait is a representation."

85. Goldingay, "Patriarchs in Scripture and History," 39-40.

86. Sailhamer, *Pentateuch as Narrative*, 16.

87. Ibid., 14.

88. See my *Modern Preacher*, 194-97. Cf. Goldingay, "Patriarchs in Scripture and History," 36: "While the historicity of the events is not sufficient evidence of the truth of the narrative's

course, require historical foundations. Parables and allegories carry their messages without historical foundations. But for redemptive-historical narratives, the lack of historical foundations is fatal, for the factuality that God acted in history is part and parcel of their message. For example, if the message of Genesis 1 is that God created this world good, then preachers cannot preach this text with integrity if they adhere to the theory of naturalistic evolutionism. Questions of *how* God created and *when* he created and the *order* in which he created are secondary. But doubts about God being the Creator of this universe or about God creating this world good (as in the hypothesis of gnosticism) undermine and negate the message of Genesis 1. Or, to take another example, the message that God judged human violence with a great flood (Gen 6–9) requires an actual, historical flood. The question whether it was a universal flood or a local flood is secondary. We may never find indisputable proof of these historical events at the dawn of human history, but "absence of evidence is *not* evidence of absence."[89]

Or, to give a few more examples, if the author's message of Genesis 12 is that God calls Abram from Haran to the land of Canaan and Abram is a fictional character, the message is groundless. If the message of Genesis 28 is that God promises the land of Canaan to Jacob and his descendants, and Jacob is a fictional character, the message evaporates. If the message of Genesis 39 is that God was with Joseph in his suffering, and Joseph is not a historical figure, the message melts away. One should not use the pulpit, of course, to try to "prove" the historical nature of Genesis. It is sufficient for modern preachers and congregations to hear these narratives with the same assumption as that of the original author and readers, and that is the assumption of general historical reliability.[90]

The Original Readers of Genesis

A frequently overlooked dimension of historical interpretation is the historical situation of the original readers of Genesis. Knowing the situation of the first

---

interpretation, it is necessary evidence of its truth. The narrative builds its interpretation on the factuality of the patriarchal events, so that without this factuality, faith in Yahweh as the giver of blessing, the one who keeps his promises, the God of grace, and so on, may be true but is nevertheless groundless."

89. Kitchen, "The Patriarchal Age: Myth or History?" *BAR*, Mar./Apr. 1995, 50. See Wenham, *Exploring the Old Testament*, 30, for the most recent evidence of a cataclysmic flood at the Black Sea basin. See ibid., 38-39, on the historicity of the patriarchal stories, and 53 on the historicity of the Joseph story.

90. By "general historical reliability" I mean that there is a real historical core to these narratives, but, given the literary shaping we have noted above, it would be contrary to the author's intention to press for historical accuracy in the details.

recipients of Genesis is of crucial importance for catching the relevance of the Genesis narratives. At this level one raises questions such as: Who wrote this book? To whom? When? Where? And why?

Let's look at a simple example to illustrate the importance of historical interpretation at this level. Suppose the selected preaching-text is from 1 Corinthians. The preacher asks: Who wrote this text? To whom? When? Where? And why? Biblical scholars respond with clear answers: Paul wrote this letter to a struggling church in the sinful harbor city of Corinth, around A.D. 55, because Paul received word of immorality and other problems in this church. These answers of the date and of the intended readers/hearers and their needs allows preachers to hone in on the goals Paul had in mind in writing this letter. For example, some of Paul's goals were to encourage the Corinthian Christians to live a distinctively Christian life in the midst of their sinful culture, to warn them against divisions in the church, to motivate them to walk in love, and to convince them of the reality of Jesus' resurrection. Inasmuch as these Corinthian problems still exist in the church today, preachers can readily and relevantly transfer to their congregations Paul's various messages to the church in Corinth.

But who was the author of Genesis? The answer to this question is difficult because Genesis is an anonymous work and gives evidence of later "updates." There is no doubt, however, that "early Jewish and Christian tradition . . . is virtually unanimous in ascribing Genesis through Deuteronomy to him [Moses]."[91] Modern source criticism, because of its late dating of the Genesis sources, abandoned this traditional view. Still, there are good reasons to continue to assume that Moses was the author/compiler of at least the original core of the Pentateuch — what Waltke calls "Ur-Genesis."[92] Exodus 2 relates that Moses was adopted by Pharaoh's daughter — a position that would have given him access to a superior education.[93] Moreover, the Pentateuch recounts that the LORD at various times instructed Moses to write certain events in a book for posterity: "Write this as a reminder in a book" (Exod 17:14), and Moses did so. Again, "Moses wrote down their starting points, stage by stage, by command of the LORD" (Num 33:2). The LORD also instructed Moses to write down the LORD's words.[94] By the time of Joshua, as Israel was about to cross the Jordan, the LORD warned Israel to be "careful to act in accordance with all

91. Dillard and Longman, *Introduction to the Old Testament,* 39.

92. Waltke, *Genesis,* 22-28.

93. Cf. Stephen's speech to the Council, "So Moses was instructed in all the wisdom of the Egyptians . . ." (Acts 7:22).

94. "Write these words; in accordance with these words I have made a covenant with you and with Israel. . . . And he wrote on the tablets the words of the covenant, the ten commandments" (Exod 34:27-28; cf. 24:4 and Deut 4:13; 5:22; 31:9, 22, 24).

the law that my servant *Moses* commanded you. . . . *This book of the law* shall not depart out of your mouth . . . (Josh 1:7-8).[95] Later, "the exilic and postexilic writers refer to the Pentateuch as the Law, the Law of Moses, the Book of Moses, and the Book of the Law of Moses."[96] In the New Testament, Jesus and his disciples, as well as his opponents, ascribe the first books of the Bible to Moses.[97] Bruce Waltke concludes, "The founder of Israel [Moses] is the most probable person to transpose its national repository of ancient traditions into a coherent history in order to define the nation and its mission."[98] But John Sailhamer cautions, "We should not lose sight of the fact that the Pentateuch itself comes to us as an anonymous work and was apparently intended to be read as such."[99]

For preaching purposes, however, the important question to answer is not so much, Who wrote the text? but to whom? when? where? and especially, why? These are the questions that get at the questions *behind* the text, the problems Israel encountered to which the text may be a response. Where was Israel when they received this word, and what were their needs? Was the author addressing his message to a terrorized Israel enslaved in Egypt, or to a fearful Israel about to enter Canaan, or to a confident and proud Israel during the heady times of David and Solomon, or to a crushed and confounded Israel (Judah) in exile? Unfortunately, biblical scholars have no clear answers to these questions, and that makes interpreting and preaching Genesis much more complicated than preaching 1 Corinthians.[100] Scholars have suggested several different backgrounds for Genesis.

Israel about to Enter the Promised Land Some have suggested that Moses wrote Genesis while Israel was enslaved in Egypt,[101] but that is not a likely setting. Rather, evidence suggests that Genesis was written *after* Israel received God's laws at Sinai, for specific Sinaitic laws have made their way into Genesis. For example, Israel's week of six days of work and one day of rest are reflected

95. Cf. Josh 8:31; see also 1 Kings 2:3; 2 Kings 14:6; 21:8.

96. Waltke, *Genesis*, 22, with references to 2 Chron 25:4; 35:12; Ezra 3:2; 7:6; and Neh 8:1 See also Ezra 6:18 and Neh 13:1. See ibid., 22-24, for more arguments for Mosaic authorship of "Ur-Genesis."

97. A concordance will give a multitude of New Testament references to verses that identify Moses and "the law," the first books of the Bible. See, e.g., Luke 24:27, 44 and John 5:46.

98. Ibid., 23. Cf. Kitchen, *On the Reliability of the Old Testament*, 295-99, 306.

99. Sailhamer, *Genesis*, 5.

100. As we search for answers to these foundational questions, we should remember that the message of the preaching-text does not change with different historical circumstances but that the goal and consequently the application of that message may change.

101. For example, Norman L. Geisler, *A Popular Survey of the Old Testament* (Grand Rapids: Baker, 1977), 38-40.

in the creation account. Further, God's "ten words" (Exod 34:28) of the law are reflected in his ten words in creating the world (10 × "God said," Gen 1:3-29).[102] "Noah distinguishes between clean and unclean animals, works on a seven-day cycle and presumably keeps the Sabbath."[103] Later the LORD says to Isaac that "Abraham obeyed my voice and kept my charge, my commandments, my statutes, and my laws" (Gen 26:5). These are indications that Genesis was written to Israel *after* God gave his law at Sinai.

Moreover, as John Sailhamer observes, "It becomes clear as one reads through the second half of the Pentateuch that it was not written primarily to the generation that came out of Egypt. Its readership was specifically the generation of Israelites that was about to go into the Promised Land. All the events of the Exodus and the wilderness journey as well as the giving of the Law at Mount Sinai were cast as something that happened in the past. . . . The focus of the writer was on the future, the next generation."[104] Joseph's final words in Genesis underscore this focus on the future: "God will surely come to you, and bring you up out of this land to the land that he swore to Abraham, to Isaac, and to Jacob" (Gen 50:24).

Accordingly, we should probably see the original addressees of the original book of Genesis as Israel in Moab, soon to enter the land of Canaan.[105] Israel had tried to enter the land earlier but failed miserably because of their great fear: "Our kindred [the spies] have made our hearts melt by reporting, 'The people are stronger and taller than we; the cities are large and fortified up to the heaven!'" (Deut 1:28).[106] God punished their lack of faith with a forty-year desert journey marked with graves: everyone in that generation died in the desert, except Moses, Caleb, and Joshua. Now Israel still fears to enter the land, as we see in Joshua 1 with its repeated command, "Be strong and courageous" (vv 6 and 7), which is repeated for good measure in verse 9 with antithetic parallelism, "Be strong and courageous; do not be frightened or dismayed." Moses could well be focusing the Genesis narratives on Israel's fresh memories of that disastrous desert journey and their present fear of entering the Promised Land. As they are caught between a rock and a hard place, he reminds them that their LORD is the great Provider for his people, that nothing is impossible for him, that he promised this land repeatedly to their fathers Abraham, Isaac, and Jacob, that he is faithful in fulfilling his promises, and that his presence with them

102. Sailhamer finds the ten words also repeated in God recreating the world (Gen 6:7–9:17). See his *Genesis*, 94.

103. Wenham, "The Face at the Bottom of the Well," 206.

104. Sailhamer, *The Pentateuch as Narrative*, 6. See also Merrill, "Old Testament History," 72-75.

105. Moab is also the setting claimed for the book of Deuteronomy (see Deut 1:5).

106. Cf. Num 13:28-33.

(as with Jacob and Joseph) means protection and life. Therefore, "Do not be frightened or dismayed!"[107]

Moreover, before entering Canaan, Israel had to understand "who they were, how they originated, and what purpose they were to serve as the covenant people of Yahweh. This required a sketch of their history to that point, first as a people delivered from Egyptian bondage to become at Sinai a covenant nation, and second as descendants of a common father who found themselves in Egypt in the first place. What was required next was a narrative linkage between themselves and those ancestors of ancient times."[108] These are some of the reasons why Moses would have written the original book of Genesis to Israel in Moab.

But just as there are later additions to "The proverbs of Solomon son of David, king of Israel" (Prov 1:1; see Prov 30:1 and 31:1) as well as later additions to the book of Isaiah of Jerusalem (Isa 1:1; see Isa 40–66), so there may well be later additions to Moses' account and revisions to bring into focus its relevance for later Israel. Israel in Moab, therefore, is not the only historical background of Genesis we need to consider.

Israel in the Promised Land Some post-Mosaic additions (glosses) in Genesis suggest that a later editor clarified these narratives for Israel in Canaan, probably in the time of David and Solomon. The phrase, "At that time the Canaanites were in the land" (Gen 12:6b; 13:7b), seems to point to an editor living in Israel when there were no Canaanites in the land. Genesis 14 contains at least five later geographical updates (see vv 2, 3, 7, 8, and 17). Moreover, v 14 states that "Abram pursued Lot's captors as far as Dan, yet the place did not receive this name until the Danites captured it following the Conquest (Josh. 19:47; Judg. 18:29)."[109] The story of Jacob's wrestling at Peniel now ends with the later comment, "Therefore to this day the Israelites do not eat the thigh muscle that is on the hip socket, because he struck Jacob on the hip socket at the thigh muscle" (Gen 32:32). "Genesis 36:31, at the beginning of a list of Edomite kings, states that they all ruled 'before any king reigned over the Israelites.' Obviously the writer's viewpoint can only be sometime after Saul."[110] These post-Mosaic additions do not necessarily change the original relevance of these messages; they seek only

107. Cf. Richard Pratt, *He Gave Us Stories*, 282, "Israel could be confident in conquest because: 1) God's actions in the primeval history reveal his plan to give them possession of Canaan; 2) God promised, led, and protected the patriarchs, and he will do the same for the nation as they move toward Canaan; 3) God ordered the twelve tribes in the days of Joseph in order to bring them to the land."

108. Merrill, "Old Testament History," 74.

109. LaSor et al., *Old Testament Survey*, 60.

110. Ibid.

to clarify these messages for later Israel under David and Solomon when God's promises to the patriarchs come to major fulfillments.[111]

Israel in Exile In time, Genesis became part of a single narrative that runs from Genesis through 2 Kings — from creation to exile. This unified collection of books probably received its final form around the time of Israel's (Judah's) exile. John Goldingay asserts, "Since they ultimately came to belong to a work that culminates in the exile, it is appropriate to interpret them against this historical context."[112] This lengthy narrative doubles back on itself. "The narrative that begins in Genesis by creating order from formlessness and then by taking Abram out of Ur of the Chaldeans [a first-millennium term used in Genesis 11:28 and 31] into the Promised Land ends in 2 Kings with chaos triumphant and Israel back in the power of the Chaldeans [2 Kings 25]."[113]

Since Genesis through 2 Kings is a single narrative in the final canonical form, Israel's exile from the Promised Land is another major historical horizon in which we can hear the relevance of the Genesis narratives. Israel (Judah) is in exile, driven out of the Promised Land, banished from God's presence, the covenant seemingly in tatters. The nation has been overrun by the mighty Babylonian armies supported by their powerful gods. How would Israel in exile hear the Genesis narratives? How would they hear the creation story of their God, just by speaking, bringing order out of chaos? How would they hear the story of their God creating the pagan gods Sun, Moon, and Stars only on the fourth day? How would they hear the flood story of a God who punished sin with death, yet in his grace saved a remnant? How would they hear the story of their father Abraham migrating from Ur of the *Chaldeans* (Gen 11:31), responding to God's call to go to a land and being promised that land "forever" (13:15)? How would they hear the story of God's promise to father Jacob before leaving the Promised Land for Haran: "Know that I am with you and will keep you wherever you go, and will bring you back to this land" (28:15)? Read against the background of the exile, the Genesis narratives begin to throb again with relevance. They can speak with renewed relevance because the needs of Israel in exile are very similar to the needs of Israel in Moab.

Today, of course, the Genesis narratives are part of an even larger literary unit that encompasses the whole Old Testament as well as the New Testament

111. See Goldingay, "The Patriarchs in Scripture and History," 30-33. According to P. Wayne Townsend, "Genesis assumes the exodus from Egypt and conquest of Canaan and how it uses the Sinai code." See his "Eve's Answer to the Serpent," *CTJ* 33 (1998) 402.

112. Ibid., 26.

113. Ibid., 33. See p. 41, n. 19, "'Chaldeans' is a term that strictly belongs only to the first millennium (cf. its prominence in Isaiah, Jeremiah, etc.), and in Genesis 11 it may deliberately make the point that Israel has returned to the land that Abram was called from."

and runs from creation (Gen 1) to the new creation (Rev 22). This metanarrative gives Christian preachers a final window for discerning the relevance of these narratives for the church today. The challenge for preachers, therefore, is to hear the message of each Genesis narrative first as Israel would have heard it against the backdrop of the needs in these various historical situations and to sense the inherent relevance of these narratives for Israel. The second challenge for preachers is to hear the theme and goal of each narrative in the light of the good news of Jesus Christ in the New Testament and to prepare their sermons against the backdrop of contemporary needs similar to those that Israel faced.

Issues in Preaching the Genesis Narratives

Before launching into our expository essays, we need to touch on a few more practical issues: preaching a sermon series on Genesis; how to handle lengthy narratives; the reasons for formulating the theme and goal of narratives; the application of narratives; the narrative sermon form; and oral style.

A Sermon Series on Genesis

Like links in a chain, the Genesis narratives are connected to the foregoing and the following narratives. As such they are ideally suited for a sermon series. But preachers must be cautious not to extend the series so long that people start losing interest. Variety holds interest. I suggest, therefore, that one plan a series of five or six sermons on Genesis, then switch to different topics for a few months before returning to another series of sermons on Genesis. The book of Genesis breaks up into natural divisions for a number of such short series: five or six sermons on Israel's prehistory (Gen 1:1–11:26), five or six on the Abraham cycle (11:27–25:11), five or six on the Jacob cycle (25:19–35:29), and five or six sermons on the Joseph narratives (37:2–50:26).

Lengthy Narratives

Preachers are frequently tempted to preach on a catchy phrase in a narrative or on an intriguing character. But this procedure fails to do justice to the inspired writer, for he does not proclaim his message in a single phrase or verse or character but in literary units. The smallest literary unit in the narrative genre is a scene, but usually single scenes don't tell the whole story. It is normally best, therefore, to select as one's preaching-text a single narrative. The practical problem is that some of these narratives in Genesis are quite long. For example, the flood narrative runs from Genesis 6:9 to 9:17 — more than three chapters. Do we have time in the worship service to read such a lengthy narrative before the sermon? Even if we do, how do we keep people listening? The first requirement is good interpretive reading. Preachers can do this themselves or they can ask excellent readers from the congregation. They can also assign three or more readers: a narrator, and two readers for the dialogue of the characters (usually two per scene). If the narrative is too long to read because of much repetition in Hebrew style, one can perhaps skip over some of the repetition, as long as the main story line is read. Or one can consider incorporating some of the reading into various parts of the sermon.

The Theme and Goal of Narratives

Some homileticians have objected to turning a dynamic biblical plot into a static theme for preaching purposes.[114] But a dynamic plot and a static theme are not polar opposites. The relationship between plot and theme has been described as "two sides of the same formal principle with plot being theme in movement and theme being plot at a standstill."[115] True, the theme is an abstraction of the dynamic narrative. But the preacher needs that theme to focus the sermon so that the congregation gets the author's point of telling the narrative. The issue of discovering the theme of the narrative is ultimately the issue of seeking to do justice to the message intended by the inspired author. The sermon itself should turn that static theme back into a dynamic narrative.

The goal, or aim, of the narrative raises the question why the author told Israel this particular story: what needs did he address? what response(s) did he seek? what was the relevance of this narrative for Israel? The goal must be determined on the basis of the message (theme)[116] and the questions behind the text. When preachers observe a similar need in their congregations, they can retell the narrative with a goal similar to that of the biblical writer. The issue of discovering the goal of the narrative is ultimately the issue of the relevance of the sermon.

114. See my *Modern Preacher,* 132-33.

115. Dan Via, *The Parables: Their Literary and Existential Dimension* (Philadelphia: Fortress, 1967), 96-97.

116. The theme of a literary unit is the only objective point of control when the precise historical reason for writing is uncertain. Therefore the theme is primary in determining what the author's objectives may have been in writing this message.

The Application of Narratives

The goal of the sermon sets the stage for the application of the sermon. With inductive sermon development, the point (theme) of the narrative for Israel will not be disclosed until the narrative has been retold. This means that narrative sermons will usually have end application rather than continuous application. End application has much to commend it. First, the sermon can better keep the tension of the narrative and keep people *in* the story. Second, in saving the application for the end of the sermon, the application can be more concentrated and powerful than continuous application. And third, people will remember the application better because it is the final part of the sermon. To establish relevance, preachers should not feel obliged to sprinkle the sermon with practical asides (moralisms), for such comments, though practical, detract from the real relevance of the sermon. Current applications should be extensions of the original relevance of the narrative for Israel.[117]

In the following expository essays, I will try to show the direction for current application, but, not knowing the situation in the local church, I cannot go into detail. Preachers using this book for preparing sermons should expand the applications with personal observations and powerful illustrations to meet the needs of their local church.

The Narrative Sermon Form

Narrative texts are best preached in the narrative sermon form.[118] This form not only allows preachers to follow in their sermon the form of the text (the plot line) but it also allows their hearers to be holistically engaged in the story (emotions as well as intellect). In preaching Old Testament narratives, however, preachers cannot simply retell the Old Testament story. For modern hearers, preachers will have to suspend the story from time to time to explain the historical background and cultural customs that were obvious to ancient Israel. Moreover, they will have to retell the narrative in such a way that its message for

117. See my "Application in Preaching Old Testament Texts," 233-44. Cf. Walter Russell, "Literary Forms," 281-98; and Richard Pratt, *He Gave Us Stories*, 307-402.

118. See my *Modern Preacher*, 224-26; Eugene Lowry, *The Homiletical Plot* (Atlanta: John Knox, 1980), 88-95; Eugene Lowry, *How to Preach a Parable: Designs for Narrative Sermons* (Nashville: Abingdon, 1989), 38-41; Calvin Miller, "Narrative Preaching," in *Handbook of Contemporary Preaching* (ed. Michael Duduit; Nashville: Broadman, 1992), 103-16; David C. Deuel, "Expository Preaching from Old Testament Narrative," in *Rediscovering Expository Preaching* (ed. John MacArthur; Dallas: Word, 1992), 273-87; and Mathewson, *The Art of Preaching Old Testament Narrative*.

Israel becomes evident to contemporary hearers. Furthermore, the message to Israel needs to be channeled via the New Testament and Christ to the church today. Therefore contemporary preachers cannot use a pure narrative form but will have to use a hybrid form.

Moving from the Old Testament to the New to the church today does not mean that all sermon forms will have the predictable movement:

1. Message for Israel;
2. Message in the context of the New Testament;
3. Application to the church today.

These are the standard hermeneutical moves in one's study, but to repeat these moves from the pulpit Sunday after Sunday might prove boring for the congregation. For variety, as well as for other reasons, one can start with a need in the church today, then flash back to the Old Testament, the New, and back to the church. Or one may be able to start in the New Testament, then flash back to the Old, then to the church today.

The Narrative Sermon's Oral Style

Many narrative sermons fail because they are delivered in written style. The narrative sermon, more than any other sermon form, ought to be written and delivered in a style that hearers can immediately absorb. That requirement calls for an oral style. Some of the characteristics of oral style are:[119]

1. Short sentences — mostly principal clauses, few relative clauses.
2. Short, familiar words.
3. Vivid, picture words — language that helps us to see the action.
4. Strong nouns and verbs — words that enable us to see the action without complicating adjectives and adverbs.
5. Specific, concrete language instead of general or abstract.
6. The active voice instead of the passive.
7. Narration in the present tense instead of the past tense.[120]

119. For further elucidation on many of these characteristics, see Mark Galli and Graig Brian Larson, *Preaching that Connects: Using the Techniques of Journalists to Add Impact to Your Sermons* (Grand Rapids: Zondervan, 1994).

120. Narration in the present tense is more vivid and immediate than the past tense. Unfortunately, when preachers seek to tell biblical stories in the present tense, they are hampered in quoting the text itself since translators usually translate the Hebrew "perfect tense" as an English past tense.

8. Verse reference *before* quoting a verse so the hearers can read along.
9. Direct quotation of the dialogue of characters instead of indirect.
10. Use of the indicative mood instead of imperative.
11. Use of questions to involve people.
12. Use of gender-inclusive language without calling attention to it.
13. Use of the first person plural "we" rather than the second person "you."
14. Verbal punctuation with words like "and," "well," "now," "by the way."
15. Important words at the end or beginning of clauses and sentences.
16. Use of repetition and parallelism.

In the following expository essays I seek to model the oral style as much as is possible in essays, highlight the theme and goal of each narrative, suggest ways of preaching Christ, and offer sermon expositions for each narrative. My intent is not that preachers incorporate all this material in their sermons, which would merely lead to information overload on the part of the hearers. Rather, my intent is that preachers would prudently select from the expositions as well as the ways of preaching Christ in order to produce sermons that are focused on the theme, biblical, relevant, and that communicate well in this postmodern age.

CHAPTER 2

God Creates the Universe

Genesis 1:1–2:3

In preaching the creation narrative, preachers face several difficulties. The first difficulty is how to preach Christ from this account. Genesis 1 tells of a perfectly good creation in which there was no need for a Messiah Savior. Genesis 1 gives no promise of the coming Christ and it has no type of Christ. How then can one preach Christ from this narrative?

A second difficulty is to formulate a single theme that does justice to the central thrust of this narrative. For this passage has several sections that can serve as preaching-texts in their own right: for example, Genesis 1:26-31, God created human beings in his own image to have dominion; and Genesis 2:2-3, God hallowed the seventh day.

A third, more troubling, difficulty is that one can easily be drawn into the controversies of what has been called "the conflict between Genesis 1 and science." What is the age of the earth? Is the earth six thousand years young or some four billion years old? And related to this question, Are the days of Genesis 1 twenty-four-hour days or long periods of time? On the one hand, if we come down on the side of long periods of time, we face some serious problems. For the text clearly says: "And there was evening, and there was morning — the first day," and so on. Evening and morning indicates a Hebrew twenty-four-hour day, which began at sunset. Moreover, if plants and trees were created in the third eon of time, how could they have survived without the sun, which was not created until the fourth eon? On the other hand, if we come down on the side of twenty-four-hour days, we face several other problems. For example, scientists claim that dinosaurs roamed the earth two hundred million years ago and that humans appeared two hundred thousand years ago, but Genesis 1 states that land animals as well as humans were created on the sixth day, that is, within a twenty-four-hour period. We also face some textual problems. For example, how could there be days, "evening and morning," on the first three days before the creation of the sun on the fourth day?

Unfortunately, because of these difficulties many preachers in our generation avoid preaching on Genesis 1. But this is a tragic omission, for Genesis 1 lays the foundation of our Christian faith. The very first article of the Apostles' Creed states, "I believe in God the Father Almighty, *maker of heaven and earth.*" If we fail to preach the message of Genesis 1 because of contemporary problems, we undermine the faith of the church. So how do we preach Genesis 1 today?

A sound rule of interpretation is that one must first hear an Old Testament text as the author intended Israel to hear it. Now it seems obvious that Israel was not concerned about the age of the earth or precisely how God created the world. These are modern issues which may or may not be answered by the text. If we wish to do justice to the inspired author of Genesis, we must begin by carefully *listening* to the text. Instead of imposing our modern questions on the text, we must hear this creation narrative as ancient Israel would originally have heard it. After establishing the textual unit, therefore, we must seek to determine the author's message for Israel (the theme) and why he wrote this message to Israel (the goal).

Text and Context

The textual unit runs from Genesis 1:1 to 2:3, as most versions have it, and not to the *tôlĕdôt* formula of 2:4a, as the NRSV has it. The *tôlĕdôt* formulas in Genesis, "these are the generations of," always introduce a new sequence and never function as a conclusion.[1] The obvious conclusion of this narrative is the seventh day recounted in 2:1-3. This section also forms an artistic inclusio with 1:1, "2:1-3 echoes 1:1 by introducing the same phrases but in reverse order: 'he created,' 'God,' 'heavens and earth' reappear as 'heavens and earth' (2:1), 'God' (2:2), 'created.' This chiastic pattern brings the section to a neat close which is reinforced by the inclusion 'God created' linking 1:1 and 2:3."[2] Moreover, verse 4a, "These are the generations of the heavens and the earth when they were created," forms a fitting introduction to the next narrative, which shows what happened to God's good creation.

Literary Features

The narrative reveals an omnipresent narrator who was "present" before any humans were created. He is also omniscient, knowing the thoughts of God,

1. See Hamilton, *Genesis 1–17*, 151, for the argument that "the *tôlĕdôt* formula is always followed by the genitive of the progenitor, never of progeny."

2. Wenham, *Genesis 1–15*, 5.

"God saw that it was good," and knowing the deliberations of God, "Let us make humankind in our image" (v 26).

The narrator has carefully structured this narrative using the perfect number "seven" and its multiples: seven days, seven times "And it was so," seven times "God saw that it was good/very good," twenty-one times (3 × 7) heavens *(šāmayim)* and twenty-one times earth *('ereṣ),* thirty-five times (5 × 7) God *('Ĕlōhîm).*[3] He also utilized the number "ten," the number of fullness: ten times "And God said." In addition, he has composed the first six days as two sets of three days, with the second set of three days running parallel to the first three days — an ABC A′B′C′ structure.

The Plot Line

Though not as obvious as in other Hebrew narratives, we can still detect a plot line in Genesis 1:1–2:3. There is a preliminary incident ("In the beginning God created the heavens and the earth" [TNIV]),[4] an occasioning incident with rising conflict ("Now the earth was *formless* and *empty, darkness* was over the surface of the *deep*"), a gradual resolution to the tension ("the Spirit of God was hovering over the waters," followed by ten words of God forcing back the chaos and gaining order, cosmos), and outcome ("God rested and blessed the seventh day"). We can sketch this single plot as shown on page 46.

Theocentric Interpretation

In order to do justice to the Old Testament as God's story with his world and creatures, it is well to highlight theocentric interpretation prior to formulating the text's theme. One should raise the questions, Where is God in this narrative? What is God doing? What is the author here teaching about God? In the creation account the theocentric focus is so obvious it cannot be missed. It begins with God, "In the beginning *God* created the heavens and the earth," that is, the

3. See Cassuto, *Commentary on Genesis,* I, 13-15.

4. Although the NRSV's translation, "In the beginning *when* God created the heavens and the earth . . ." is grammatically possible, the traditional translation is to be preferred for various reasons. See von Rad, *Genesis,* 46-47 and Anderson, *Contours,* 88-89. Cassuto, *Commentary on Genesis,* I, 20, argues that "*v.* 2 begins a new subject. It follows, therefore, that the first verse is an independent sentence that constitutes a formal introduction to the entire section, and expresses at the outset, with majestic brevity, the main thought of the section." From a narrational point of view, one would also expect the major preliminary incident (God created) to be highlighted and not to be subordinated to the resultant conflict.

God Creates the Universe

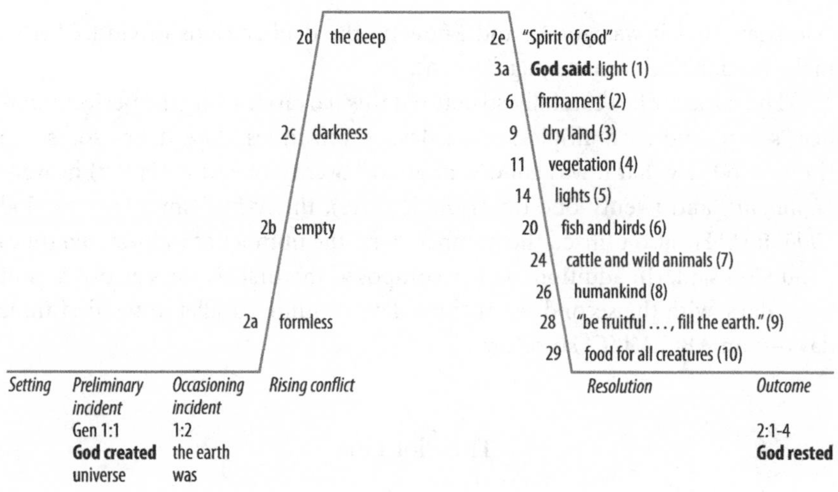

entire universe. Verse 2 notes that "the Spirit of God swept over the face of the waters." Next we read ten times, "God said. . . . And it was so," and seven times that "God saw that it was good/very good." Meanwhile the author notes that "God called the light Day, and the darkness he called Night. . . . God called the dome Sky. . . . God called the dry land Earth, and the waters . . . Seas" (vv 5, 8, 10). God also blessed the animals, next the humans, and then the seventh day (1:22, 28; 2:3). And, finally, "God rested from all the work that he had done in creation" (2:3). Derek Kidner observes, "It is no accident that *God* is the subject of the first sentence of the Bible, for this word dominates the whole chapter and catches the eye at every point of the page: it is used some thirty-five times in as many verses of the story."[5]

Textual Theme and Goal

Listening carefully to the text as Israel was intended to hear it, we seek to discern the theme ("the big idea") of the text and the author's goal for Israel. We could perhaps understand verse 1 as a thematic statement and formulate the theme as, "In the beginning God created the heavens and the earth" (TNIV). However, this theme would not cover major points the rest of the narrative makes, especially the tenfold repetition of "God said" and the sevenfold repetition of "it was good." For the whole narrative, a more appropriate theme would be: "With his word, God created the earth as his good kingdom."[6] But we can

5. Kidner, *Genesis*, 43.

6. Waltke's statement regarding "kingdom of God" bears repeating: "Although the expres-

refine this theme still further. God is portrayed as the supreme King: he speaks and it is done; he brings order out of chaos; and he names Day, Night, Sky, Earth, and Seas. A more graphic theme would therefore be, *With his powerful word, the King of the universe created the earth as his good kingdom.*

As to the goal for Israel, the author may have had several objectives in mind. His most obvious goal was to teach Israel that its God is the sovereign King who, in the beginning, created the earth as his good kingdom.[7] Of course, the goal of every biblical text is to teach something. We can often get to a deeper, even more relevant goal if we raise the question, *Why* did the author wish to teach Israel this message? We should first check the text for any clues. One clue in Genesis 1 is that the author relegates the creation of the sun, moon, and stars to the fourth day; another clue is that he does not give the names of the sun and the moon but merely calls them "the greater light to rule the day and the lesser light to rule the night" (v 16). Why does he not name the sun and the moon? Because these were the names of the pagan gods of Israel's neighbors. Clearly, the author is carrying on a polemic against the pagan worldview with its gods of Sun and Moon and Stars. Israel's God created these so-called gods only on the fourth day, after the vegetation of the third day. They are only "lights." Therefore a more specific goal than simply to teach is to oppose the influence of pagan mythologies and to shape or correct Israel's worldview.[8] One can certainly develop a sermon on the creation account with this primary goal in mind, biblically to correct people's worldview in contrast to the contemporary secular worldview.

But we can dig still deeper. We can look for clues to the author's goal not only in the text itself but also in the historical circumstances in which Israel found itself. Suppose Israel heard this creation account when they were in exile in Babylonia. The powerful Babylonian armies had overrun their little country, killed many of them, and taken others away into exile. It seemed that the Babylonians had defeated Israel's God, Yahweh. They had burned his temple, destroyed his city Jerusalem, and enslaved his people. Israel's God appeared to be

---

sion 'kingdom of God' never occurs in the Old Testament and its equivalents are relatively rare and late, the concept informs the whole. The Primary History, which traces Israel's history from the creation of the world (Gen. 1) to the fall of Israel (2 Kings 25), is all about what the New Testament calls 'the kingdom of God.'" *Genesis,* 44. See also S. G. De Graaf, *Promise and Deliverance,* I, 29-35.

7. Cf. Cassuto, *Commentary on Genesis,* I, 7, "The purpose of the Torah in this section is to teach us that the whole world and all that it contains were created by the word of the one God."

8. "Genesis 1 again affirms the unity of God over against the polytheism current everywhere else in the ancient Near East. In particular it insists that the sun, moon, stars, and sea monsters — powerful deities according to pagan mythology — are merely creatures." Wenham, *Genesis 1–15,* xlix. On the conceptual affinities with and the polemic against ancient Near Eastern cosmologies, see John Stek, "What Says the Scripture?" 226-32.

no match for the powerful Babylonian gods. According to the ancient Babylonian creation epic *Enuma Elish,* their head god Marduk (known in the Hebrew as Merodach)[9] was the creator of heaven and earth. It all began when Marduk battled the ocean goddess Tiamat:

> The Lord spread out his net, encircled her,
> The ill wind he had held behind him he released in her face.
> Tiamat opened her mouth to swallow,
> He thrust in the ill wind so she could not close her lips.
> The raging winds bloated her belly,
> Her insides were stopped up, she gaped her mouth wide.
> He shot off the arrow, it broke open her belly,
> It cut to her innards, it pierced the heart.
> He subdued her and snuffed out her life,
> He flung down her carcass, he took his stand upon it. . . .
> He split her in two, like a fish for drying,
> Half of her he set up and made as a cover, heaven.
> He stretched out the hide and assigned watchmen,
> And ordered them not to let her waters escape.
> He crossed heaven and inspected (its) firmament. . . .[10]

Marduk next "made position(s) for the great gods, he established (in) constellations the *stars*. . . . He made the *moon* appear." Returning to the other half of the slain Tiamat, he spread half of "her as a cover, he established the netherworld."[11] Then Marduk said, "I shall create humankind, They shall bear the gods' burden that those may rest." And he made humankind from the blood of the executed traitor god Qingu.[12] After this "the great gods convened, They made Marduk's destiny highest. . . . They established him forever for lordship of heaven and earth. . . . His word shall be supreme above and below. . . . He shall appoint the black-headed folk to serve him."[13]

These great gods, people thought, had enabled the Babylonian armies to destroy the temple of the LORD (Yahweh) in Jerusalem and to carry his people off into exile. It was only natural that Israel would be afraid of these mighty gods. Jeremiah (10:5) seeks to comfort Israel by writing pointedly,

9. See Jer 50:2, "Babylon is taken, Bel is put to shame, Merodach is dismayed. Her images are put to shame, her idols are dismayed."

10. *Enuma Elish,* tablet IV, lines 95-104, 137-41, as translated in Hallo, *The Context of Scripture,* I, 390-402.

11. Ibid., tablet V, lines 1-2, 12, 63.

12. Ibid., tablet VI, lines 7-8, 34.

13. Ibid., tablet VI, lines 95-96, 100, 104, 113.

Their idols are like scarecrows in a cucumber field,
  and they cannot speak;
they have to be carried,
  for they cannot walk.
Do not be afraid of them,
  for they cannot do evil,
  nor is it in them to do good.

The creation narrative, similarly, would not only correct Israel's worldview but also give them good hope that they were not at the mercy of fickle pagan gods but were under the protection of their sovereign God, the Creator of heaven and earth. In this context a deeper, more relevant, goal of this message for Israel would be, *to comfort God's fearful people with the knowledge that their God is the sovereign Creator God who controls the world's destiny and theirs.*

Ways to Preach Christ

Preaching Christ from this creation story is a challenge because it speaks of a perfect world which has no need of a Savior. One will not find in this text, therefore, a *promise* of Christ or a *type* of Christ that would allow one to move to the New Testament fulfillment in Jesus Christ. But even though the text speaks of a pre-Fall world, we should remember that it was addressed to Israel in a post-Fall world. Given the theme, *With his powerful word, the King of the universe created the earth as his good kingdom,* what are legitimate bridges to Jesus Christ in the New Testament? Let us check the seven possible ways to Christ.

Redemptive-Historical Progression

Redemptive-historical progression is a possible bridge to Christ in the New Testament since the message is about God creating the earth as his good kingdom. Human rebellion against the King ruined this kingdom, but God decided to restore his kingdom on earth. In the New Testament era, Jesus brought this kingdom near with his First Coming when he proclaimed, "The time is fulfilled, and the kingdom of God has come near" (Mark 1:15). Jesus' miracles were signs of the presence of God's kingdom. Jesus said, "If it is by the finger of God that I cast out the demons, then the kingdom of God has come to you" (Luke 11:20). Jesus now rules as King, having received "all authority in heaven and on earth" (Matt 28:18), being seated at the right hand of God the Father (Eph 1:20-23). When he comes again on the last day, Jesus will bring this kingdom in perfection — as John testified, "Then I saw a new heaven and a new earth" (Rev 21:1).

Promise-Fulfillment

There is no promise of Christ in the creation narrative.

Typology

There is no type of Christ in this passage.

Analogy

The bridge of analogy can often be detected by considering the goal of the passage. We formulated the goal as, "to comfort God's fearful people with the knowledge that their God is the sovereign Creator God who controls the world's destiny and theirs." Does Jesus also teach this comforting message in the New Testament? Do the New Testament letters teach this with a reference to Jesus? In the Sermon on the Mount Jesus does indeed teach that his Father in heaven is sovereign (Matt 6:9-11) and that we need not worry. He encourages us, "Look at the birds of the air; they neither sow nor reap nor gather into barns, and yet your heavenly Father feeds them. Are you not of more value than they?" (Matt 6:26). With respect to New Testament letters, Hebrews 1:2-3 comes to mind, "In these last days God has spoken to us by a Son, whom he appointed heir of all things, through whom he also created the worlds. . . . He *sustains* all things by his *powerful word*."

Longitudinal Themes

Longitudinal themes offer another way of preaching Christ from the creation account. For example, one can trace the longitudinal theme of the powerful creative word of God which not only created the world (ten times "God said") but subsequently sought to redeem the world by calling Abram ("the Lord said") from his pagan surroundings (see Josh 24:2) to Canaan and promising to make of him a great nation. At Sinai God spoke ten words to shape the nation of Israel according to kingdom standards. When Israel failed to manifest the kingdom of God, the word of God spoke of judgment through the prophets but also of rebuilding after the exile (Isa 40:12-31; 42:5-9; Jer 31:35-40). In the fullness of time the Word of God became incarnate in Jesus. He was the Word of God, and he spoke the word of God in order to establish God's kingdom on earth.

One can also trace the longitudinal theme of the goodness of God's creation. Though this goodness was spoiled by the Fall, enough remains for the Old Testament to praise God for his marvelous creation (e.g., Pss 8, 19, 136). In the New Testament, Jesus begins to restore the goodness of God's creation with his miracles, and on the final day he will set the creation itself "free from its bondage to decay" (Rom 8:21).

Other important subthemes in this creation narrative can be traced to Jesus Christ in the New Testament. Think of the sovereignty of God displayed in this narrative and throughout the Old Testament and claimed by Jesus in the New Testament: "All authority in heaven and on earth has been given to me" (Matt 28:18). Or the theme of humans being created in the image of God, which comes to a climax in Jesus Christ, "*the* image of the invisible God" (Col 1:15; 2 Cor 4:4). Or the theme of Sabbath-rest which God commanded Israel to follow (Exod 20:8-11; 31:13-17), which Jesus set in proper perspective (Mark 2:27), and which points forward to the final "Sabbath-rest" Jesus gained for "the people of God" (Heb 4:1-12; Rev 14:13). In using the way of longitudinal themes, however, preachers must be careful to select themes that support the textual theme lest the sermon loses its unity; moreover, they should not include too much detail lest the hearers tune out because of information overload.

New Testament References

New Testament references offer another option. The appendix to the Greek New Testament[14] lists twenty-three New Testament passages that quote or allude to this narrative. For example,

For Genesis 1:1 it lists Hebrews 11:3, "the worlds were prepared by the word of God," and John 1:1, "In the beginning was the Word."

For Genesis 1:3, 6, and 9, "God said," it lists 2 Peter 3:5, "By the word of God heaven existed long ago."

For Genesis 1:31, "very good," it lists 1 Timothy 4:4, "Everything created by God is good, and nothing is to be rejected, provided it is received with thanksgiving."

Since these passages refer to the verses of the narrative rather than its theme, many will not be helpful in carrying the theme of the narrative forward to Christ. But when a verse in the narrative comes close to expressing the theme, some of the listed New Testament passages may be useful not only in supporting the theme but in carrying it over into New Testament times. For example, Genesis 1:1, "In the beginning God created the heavens and the earth,"

14. Nestle and Aland, *Novum Testamentum Graece* (27th ed.; Stuttgart: Deutsche Bibelgesellschaft, 1993), 770-801.

comes close to expressing the theme of the narrative. The New Testament passages listed for this verse are Hebrews 11:3 and John 1:1. Hebrews 11:3 does not establish a direct link with Jesus Christ, but John 1 does: "the Word became flesh." John 1 not only calls Jesus "the Word," but he deliberately quotes Genesis 1:1, "In the beginning," and states that "all things came into being through him." Moreover, John 1 adds several allusions to other concepts in Genesis 1, such as light and darkness and life. Some other New Testament references that can possible be used in the sermon as a bridge to Christ are: 1 Corinthians 8:6, Colossians 1:15-17, Ephesians 1:10, Hebrews 1:2, and John 3:16.

Contrast

There is no contrast between the message of the creation narrative and the New Testament.

Sermon Theme and Goal

Since the context of canon and redemptive history does not change this particular message of God for Israel, we can re-proclaim the same message to the church today. Accordingly, the textual theme can be the sermon theme: *With his powerful word, the King of the universe created the earth as his good kingdom.* Although this theme (as all sermon themes) reduces the dynamic narrative to a static proposition, preachers require a thematic statement for at least two reasons: to do justice to the unique blend of textual elements in each narrative, and to keep the sermon on track. The sermon itself should turn the static theme back into an engaging, dynamic form.

The goal of the sermon should be in harmony with the author's goal for Israel. We formulated the author's goal as, "to comfort God's fearful people with the knowledge that their God is the sovereign Creator God who controls the world's destiny and theirs." With slight revisions we can make this textual goal the sermon goal: *to comfort God's fearful people with the knowledge that our God is the sovereign Creator God who controls the world's destiny and ours.* This goal provides a clue to the need addressed by this sermon: like Israel of old, God's people today are fearful of unknown, unpredictable powers: terrorists, weapons of mass destruction, disasters, disease, death.

The Sermon Form

In preaching a narrative text, it is usually best to use a narrative form that follows the story line. But in the case of Genesis 1, I am concerned that the sermon may get bogged down in the details of the seven days or the ten times "God said." Therefore, I would opt instead for a three-point sermon, each point highlighting an aspect of the passage that supports the theme. The theme can also be communicated more clearly if the sermon is developed deductively, that is, if the theme is stated in the introduction. These considerations lead to the following outline:

Introduction: our fears today; transition to Israel's fears in the past.

Statement of the theme: With his powerful word, the King of the universe created the earth as his good kingdom.

I. The King of the universe created the earth with his powerful *word.*

II. The King of the universe completed his work in *seven* days.

III. The King of the universe created his kingdom *good.*

Conclusion: the comfort of knowing that our sovereign God controls the world's destiny and ours.

Sermon Exposition

The sermon introduction is usually best when it opens up the congregational need that will be addressed in the sermon. This need can usually be derived from the sermon goal. In this case, it is our fear of unknown, unpredictable powers. I would begin, therefore, by illustrating our fear of these powers, whether asteroids on a collision course with the earth, or category five hurricanes, or weapons of mass destruction in the hands of terrorists. Then transition to Israel and its fears of powerful but fickle foreign gods. This sets the stage for the congregation to hear this comforting message as Israel heard it. "With his powerful word, the King of the universe created the earth as his good kingdom."

First, the King of the universe created the earth with his powerful *word.* Genesis 1 begins, "In the beginning God created[15] the heavens and the earth." "The heavens and the earth" means the entire universe. The Bible begins with this powerful message: Not any of the pagan gods but *'Ĕlohîm* in the beginning created everything. In the next chapter, this God will be identified as Israel's God, *Yahweh,* "the Lord God" (2:4).

The conflict in the narrative is generated in verse 2, which shifts the focus to this earth: "The earth was formless and empty, darkness was over the surface of the deep" (TNIV). The conflict escalates from "formless and empty" *(tōhû wābōhû)* — a formless desert where nothing can live — to "darkness was over the face of the deep." It is pitch black; no light at all. All that exists is a formless, empty, dark, deep ocean. Nothing can grow or develop on this earth. It is utter chaos.[16]

15. On the meaning of *bārā',* see John Stek, "What Says the Scripture?" 207-13.

16. I understand v. 2 to describe God's incomplete creation (chaos) which requires order-

But there is a ray of hope. Verse 2 continues, "the Spirit [*rûaḥ*] of God was hovering over the waters" (TNIV). The Spirit of God is not part of the chaos; it hovers above the chaos like a mighty eagle "*hovers* over its young," seeking to stir them into flight (Deut 32:11). And this Spirit of God, or breath of God, is about to bring order out of chaos. God begins to speak, and his first word takes on the lethal darkness. Verse 3, "Then God *said,* 'Let there be light,' and there was light." God forces back this deadly darkness with radiant light — light that will make life on earth possible. Verse 4, "And God saw that the light was good; and God separated the light from the darkness. God called the light Day, and the darkness he called Night." God separates the light from the darkness; he sets limits to the darkness by relegating it to the night. The first three days are days of separation, of God forcing back the powers of chaos (darkness and water) in order to form a liveable cosmos.

After limiting the darkness, the word of God takes on the destructive waters. Verse 6, "And God *said,* 'Let there be a dome in the midst of the waters, and let it separate the waters from the waters.' So God made the dome and separated the waters that were under the dome from the waters that were above the dome. And it was so." Now the earth starts to take on form: water below and water above and air to breath. But still life as God intended is not possible.

So again God speaks: Verse 9, "And God *said,* 'Let the waters under the sky be gathered together into one place, and let the dry land appear.' And it was so." God separates the land from the waters. The waters recede and land appears. Now the earth has a definite form: there is not only the sky, but there are oceans and land. When God further commands the land to bring forth vegetation (v. 11), the earth is able to sustain life. In contrast to the earlier chaos which was formless *(tōhû)* and empty *(bōhû),* a dark, dark ocean, now there is form: day and night, the sky above and water below, and seas and dry land with vegetation. Now the earth is ready to be inhabited, that is, filled with living creatures in contrast to being empty *(bōhû).*[17]

The picture that stands out on the first three days is that God forces back the destructive powers of chaos with his powerful word (cf. Job 38:8-11; 2 Pet

---

ing for six days before it becomes a very good cosmos. As God's pronouncements of "good" show, incompleteness (such as on the first day) is not evil. If Ross, *Creation and Blessing,* p. 107, is right that v. 2 describes "not the results of divine creation but a chaos at the earliest stage of this world," the conflict in the narrative would be even more pronounced but at the cost of the polemic of *creatio ex nihilo* against pagan myths of preexistent matter. Cf. von Rad, *Genesis,* 51, "The theological thought of ch. 1 moves not so much between the poles of nothingness and creation as between the poles of chaos and cosmos. It would be false to say, however, that the idea of the *creatio ex nihilo* was not present at all (v. 1 stands with good reason before v. 2!)."

17. Cf. Kidner, *Genesis,* 46, on "form" for the first three days and "fullness" for the last three. Others, e.g., Hughes, *Genesis,* 25, speak of "form" and "filling."

3:5-7). But this does not mean that the powers of chaos can no longer affect the earth. True, God separated the waters above from the waters below, but God could withdraw his powerful word as he did later in the great flood: "All the fountains of the great deep burst forth, and the windows of the heavens were opened. . . . And all flesh died that moved on the earth" (Gen 7:11, 21). True, God relegated darkness to the night, but he could withhold the light and allow the darkness to rule again. He did so with the ninth plague in Egypt (blocking out their sun god Re): "There was dense darkness in all the land of Egypt for three days. People could not see one another, and for three days they could not move from where they were" (Exod 10:22-23). The prophets describe the coming Day of the LORD as "a day of darkness and gloom, a day of clouds and thick darkness" (Joel 2:2; cf. Amos 5:18, 20). Every cloudy night is a reminder to Israel of the inky blackness that shuts out meaningful life. But in his covenant faithfulness (Gen 8:22), God protects his creatures and every morning drives out the darkness with radiant light.

Ten times Genesis 1 repeats the phrase: "God said; God said; God said." Ten is the number of fullness. How would the Israelites have heard the message that God spoke *ten* words in creating this world? They would undoubtedly have been reminded of the ten words of God's covenant at Mount Sinai, the decalogue. In ten words, Exodus 20 sets forth God's law for Israel. In ten words, Genesis 1 sets forth God's law for his creation.[18]

Psalm 33 has caught the significance of God's ten words for his creation:

By the *word* of the LORD were the heavens made,
  their starry host by the *breath* of his mouth. . . .
For he *spoke*, and it came to be;
  he *commanded*, and it stood firm.

(33:6, 9; cf. Ps 148:5-6)

How would the Israelites have heard the message that God created all things with his powerful word? "The imagery is of a powerful sovereign who utters a decree from the throne, issues a fiat, and in the very utterance the thing is done."[19] In ancient times kings were the law of the land. The king spoke and it was done. Genesis 1 portrays God as the King of the universe. This means, first, that God is the owner of the universe (see Pss 24:1-2; 89:11; 95:5). Second, that God is the law of the universe. His word is powerful. He speaks and it is done; he commands and it happens; he wills and it comes to pass. Our God is the sovereign King of the universe. Nothing on earth happens without his will. There is no such thing as chance happenings. Our King is sovereign and in control of

18. See Wenham, *Genesis 1–15*, 38.

19. Brueggemann, *Theology of the Old Testament*, 146.

the universe. With his powerful word he brought order out of chaos. With his powerful word he controls the universe.

When the apostle John writes his Gospel, he intentionally echoes the majestic words of Genesis 1:

> *In the beginning* was the *Word,* and the Word was with *God,* and the Word was God. He was in the beginning with God. *All things* came into being through him, and without him not one thing came into being. In him was *life,* and the life was the light of all people. The *light* shines in the *darkness.* . . . The Word became flesh and lived among us. (John 1:1-5, 14)

John identifies Jesus Christ as the Word of God through whom all things were made. Christ was there in the beginning. He is one with the sovereign Creator God.

Paul expresses similar ideas this way:

> He [Jesus] is the *image* of the invisible *God,* the firstborn of all creation; for in him *all things* in *heaven* and on *earth* were created, things visible and invisible, whether thrones or dominions or rulers or powers — all things have been created through him and for him. He himself is before all things, and in him all things hold together. (Col 1:15-17)

Our Lord Jesus is one with the King of the universe. By him all things were created, and "in him all things hold together." Seeing the exalted nature of Jesus makes us more aware of his tremendous sacrifice in becoming a human being. John proclaims that this eternal Word "became flesh" (John 1:14), and Paul says that he "emptied himself, taking on the form of a slave" (Phil 2:7). The King of the universe became a slave. When the world was headed for destruction, God spoke his word again through Jesus. "God so loved the world (*ton kosmon*) that he gave his only Son, so that everyone who believes in him may not perish but may have eternal life" (John 3:16). The Word of God, Jesus, created this world, and the Word of God, Jesus, will redeem this world.

In addition to this message that God created this earth *with his word,* the narrator also emphasizes that the King of the universe completed his work in *seven days.* The author of Genesis highlights the number "seven" and its multiples. In the Hebrew, verse 1 has exactly seven words: "In the beginning God created the heavens and the earth." Verse 2 has exactly fourteen words, 2 × 7. In this narrative the name of God *('Ĕlōhîm)* is mentioned thirty-five times, 5 × 7, while heavens *(šāmayim)* and earth *('ereṣ)* are each mentioned twenty-one times (3 × 7).[20] "Seven" is the number of completeness, perfection.[21] Israel

20. See Cassuto, *Commentary on Genesis,* I, 13-15, and Mathews, *Genesis 1–11:26,* 120-21.

21. "Throughout the ancient Near East the number seven had long served as the primary

knew the number "seven" especially from its weekly cycle. When Israel traveled through the desert, the LORD taught them to gather manna six days a week and to trust God that the manna gathered on the sixth day would not spoil for the seventh (Exod 16). Later at Sinai this pattern was codified in the decalogue: "Six days you shall labor. . . . But the seventh day is a sabbath to the LORD your God" (Exod 20:9-10).

The author of Genesis 1 uses Israel's week of six days of work followed by rest on the seventh as a pattern to proclaim to Israel that God himself completed his work of creating in six days and rested the seventh day. The author faced a problem, however, because a week has only six workdays and he wished to report eight creative acts. He solved this problem by placing two acts of creation on the third day and two on the sixth day. This solution highlights the beautiful parallelism between the days.

Origen and Augustine already observed that the author constructed days 4, 5, and 6 to parallel days 1, 2, and 3, resulting in an ABC A′B′C′ pattern.[22]

Day 1	light	Day 4	the light bearers: sun, moon, and stars
Day 2	firmament	Day 5	the inhabitants of the sea and sky: fish and birds
Day 3	two creative acts: the land and vegetation	Day 6	two creative acts: land animals and human beings

Day 7 God rested

Obviously, the author was not interested in giving us a chronological report of what happened exactly. He was not there at the creation to give a chronological account, nor was any other human being. Instead of an objective chronological report, he has prepared a carefully crafted sermon to comfort Israel and us today.

Remember how Israel feared the powerful pagan gods? Notice where the author places the creation of sun, moon, and stars: he places them on the fourth day, right between the creation of vegetation (day 3) and the creation of fish and birds (day 5). He is saying to Israel that these powerful pagan gods, the sun, moon, and stars, are as much God's creatures as are vegetation and fish and

---

numerical symbol of fullness/completeness/perfection, and the seven-day cycle was an old and well-established convention." Stek, "What Says the Scripture?" 239.

22. N. H. Ridderbos, *Is There a Conflict between Genesis 1 and Natural Science?* trans. John Vriend (Grand Rapids: Eerdmans, 1957), first brought to my attention the "literary framework theory," and claims (p. 11) that "this view was already current in the early church (Philo of Alexandria, Origen, Augustine)."

birds.[23] Why do we fear them? Notice that in verse 16 the author deliberately avoids the names of sun *(šhemeš)* and moon *(yārēaḥ)*, the names of the pagan gods; he writes, "God made the two great lights — the greater light to rule the day and the lesser light to rule the night — and the stars."[24] These powerful gods of the pagans are only lights made by Israel's God.

Do we hear what fearful Israel heard? Our God created absolutely everything in the universe. The pagan gods, the Sun, Moon, and Stars, are God's creatures.[25] Our destiny is not held by the stars. We need not fear chance or anything in this universe. Our sovereign God made everything and controls everything. He will take care of his people.

The author of Genesis 1 emphasizes a third point: The King of the universe created his kingdom *good.* Six times we read, "and God saw that it was good." The light was good; the dry land was good; the vegetation was good; the light of sun, moon, and stars was good; the fish and birds were good; the land animals were good. Six times. Finally God created human beings, and the seventh time we read in verse 31, "God saw everything that he had made, and indeed, it was very good."

God created his kingdom on earth very good. We can see this especially on days six and seven. On day six God created the land animals and then seemed to pause. The narrator slows the pace — this is important! God either deliberates with himself or announces his intention to his royal court.[26] Verse 26, "Then God said, 'Let us make humankind in our image, according to our likeness. . . .'" In the ancient world, a king would place images of himself, statues, in far-off provinces. The images of the king told everyone that these provinces were part of the king's domain.[27]

God made human beings in his image and placed us on this earth. In other words, the world we live in is God's domain; it is his kingdom. In sharp contrast

23. Cf. Westermann, *Genesis,* 9, "The narrator . . . consciously places the creation of the heavenly bodies between that of plants and animals. He claims that the heavenly bodies, which in the ancient Near East were gods of supreme importance, are creatures like plants and animals."

24. The stars are relegated to an afterthought partly as a put-down of those who worship the stars as gods (see Isa 47:13) but also because, from verse 2 on, the author concentrates on this earth, and the sun and moon are more directly lights that "give light upon the earth."

25. On "the great sea monsters" (v 21), see Cassuto, *Commentary on Genesis,* I, 49-51. Cf. Ross, *Creation and Blessing,* 102, "Those gods were identified with the sun, moon, stars, animals, rivers, and a host of other things. In short, everything that the pagans worshiped God had made. Consequently, their gods should pose no real threat to Israel, for the creation must be subject to the Creator."

26. Stek, "What says the Scripture?" 233: "Both in itself and in the language employed, this announcement recalls the scene in a royal council chamber in which a king announces his impending action to the members of his court." Hamilton, *Genesis 1–17,* 208-9, argues against this position and takes "us" as "a reference to God." Cf. Cassuto, *Commentary on Genesis,* I, 55-56.

27. Von Rad, *Genesis,* 60.

with the Babylonian creation epic *Enuma Elish,* which portrays humans as slaves of the gods,[28] Genesis 1 proclaims that we were created in God's image, that is, we are God's representatives in this world.[29] As images of God we may manage this kingdom on God's behalf. That is God's good plan for his kingdom and for human beings. God carefully deliberates:

> "Let us make humankind in our image, according to our likeness; and let them have dominion over the fish of the sea, and over the birds of the air, and over the cattle, and over the wild animals of the earth, and over every creeping thing that creeps upon the earth."
>
> So God created humankind in his image,
> in the image of God he created them;
> male and female he created them. (Gen 1:26-27)

As God earlier blessed the fish and birds so that they could be fruitful and multiply, so now God blesses male and female both with an eye to reproduction and to having dominion.[30] Verse 28, "God blessed them, and God said to them, 'Be fruitful and multiply, and fill the earth and subdue it; and have dominion. . . .'" Both male and female receive the high honor and authority of being rulers on this earth on behalf of the King of the universe.

God next makes provision for food for his creatures. In contrast to the ancient *Atrahasis* epic where the gods made humans to provide food for the gods,[31] here God provides food for human beings. Again we sense the goodness of God's creation. Then follows verse 31: "God saw everything that he had made, and indeed, it was very good." The King of the universe judges that he created everything very good. The conflict of chaos obstructing the formation of life has been completely resolved. The original chaos has become a well-ordered cosmos, and "it was very good." It was superb! It was splendid! God's creation is his marvelous gift for us to enjoy and to develop responsibly.

28. See at nn. 12 and 13 above.

29. Over the centuries theologians have sought to identify precisely what is the image of God in human beings. Some have suggested it was the soul, others thought it was human reason, self-consciousness, recognition of right and wrong, communion with God, etc. Genesis 1 with its proximity of "image" and having "dominion" suggests that the image of God makes us representatives of God on this earth. Walton, *Genesis,* 131, defines image as "a physical manifestation of divine (or royal) essence that bears the function of that which it represents; this gives the image-bearer the capacity to reflect the attributes [such as love, faithfulness, justice, and wisdom] of the one represented and act on his behalf."

30. Stek, "What Says the Scripture?" 251: "This word addressed to humankind is not a directive or commission, as long and still widely supposed. It is a benediction. . . . By his blessing they will fill the earth, and by his blessing they will rule over the creatures about them."

31. *Atrahasis,* lines 190-97.

The outcome of the narrative underscores the goodness of God's creation. For we read in chapter 2:1-3 that God rested on the seventh day and hallowed it:

> Thus the heavens and the earth were finished,
> and all their multitude.
> And on the *seventh* day God finished the work that he had done,
> and he rested on the *seventh* day from all the work that he had done.
> So God blessed the *seventh* day and hallowed it,
> because on it God rested from all the work that he had done
> in creation.[32]

God's creation is complete; his kingdom on earth is well established. God blesses the seventh day and makes it holy. What God created on the other days God declared good, even very good. But this seventh day God makes *holy,* that is, God sets it apart from the six days of work as his very special day. This special day accents and symbolizes God's communion with his creation.[33]

Like God, God's images on earth may rest from their labors and enjoy the fruit of their work. This special day is good for us. Jesus says, "The sabbath was made for humankind, not humankind for the sabbath" (Mark 2:27). The Sabbath is good for us. We need that day of rest. If our life were only work, work, work, we would all burn out. But God provides so richly for us so that we can rest one day in seven. We can rest from our work; we can gather with God's people to worship God and reflect on the meaning and direction of our life; we can take delight in God's good creation as well as in the work of our hands; we can enjoy family and friends. God created everything good. That is the gospel message, the joyful tiding, of Genesis 1.

Genesis 1 sketches God as the King of the universe who created this earth as his good kingdom. Scientists today are discovering just how great the universe is. Especially the Hubble telescope has given us amazing pictures of the stars and the galaxies. Scientists now think that there may be a billion galaxies, each with a billion stars. And in the midst of this ever-expanding universe floats a little planet called earth. For those who do not believe in the Creator God, this can be a frightening picture. We seem to be all alone in a dark, terrifying universe. The earth is but a frail little ship floating among mighty neighbors. Who knows when the earth will be struck again by a devastating asteroid? We seem to be at the mercy of powers that are far beyond our control.

But God's Word assures us that God is in control. "In the beginning God created the heavens and the earth." With his powerful word he created order out

32. "The threefold mention of the seventh day, each time in a sentence of seven Hebrew words, draws attention to the special character of the Sabbath." Wenham, *Genesis 1–15*, 7.

33. De Graaf, *Promise and Deliverance*, 30.

of chaos. This God is greater than any asteroid, greater than any star, greater than any galaxy, greater than the whole universe. And this God created everything good. This almighty God will take care of his people. No matter what dangers threaten us, we can find security and rest in him.[34]

Great are you, O Lord,
  and wondrous are your works,
  and no word will suffice to sing your wonders.
For you by your will
  have out of nothingness brought all things into being,
and by your power sustain all creation,
  and by your providence direct the world.[35]

"You are worthy, our Lord and God,
  to receive glory and honor and power,
for you created all things,
  and by your will they existed and were created."

(Rev 4:11)

34. My sermon based on some of this research is found in Appendix 3.
35. Excerpt from the Orthodox Great Blessing of Water.

CHAPTER 3

Paradise Lost

Genesis 2:4–3:24

This rather lengthy narrative about the Fall into sin introduces several topics that can be treated in sermons: the formation of human beings as dust and breath (2:7), human work (2:15), marriage (2:18-25), the Fall into sin (3:1-7), and God's punishment (3:14-19). One of the challenges for preachers will be to formulate a single theme that encompasses the entire narrative. Another challenge will be to keep the sermon itself on track (theme) and not be sidetracked into other interesting topics.

Text and Context

Genesis 2:4 to 3:24 is clearly a narrative unit. Genesis 2:4 introduces the first *tôlĕdôt* of the ten in Genesis: "These are the generations of the heavens and the earth when they were created." In other words, this is what happened to the universe *after*[1] God created everything "very good" (1:31). This narrative continues the theme of "very good" of chapter 1 by showing how the LORD God placed humankind in a beautiful garden, Paradise,[2] but it ends with the man being expelled from the garden (3:24).

This literary unit is confirmed by a chiastic structure of seven scenes with the climax coming at D., the Fall into sin (3:6-8).[3]

1. See p. 44 above for arguments supporting the narrative break between 2:3 and 4 and not, as the NRSV has it, between 2:4a and 4b. *Tôlĕdôt* "stands for that which was produced, for the result." Martin Woudstra, "The *Toledoth* of the Book of Genesis and Their Redemptive-Historical Significance," *CTJ* 5 (1970) 187. See further Hamilton, *Genesis 1–17*, 151, and Mathews, *Genesis 1–11:26*, 189.

2. The LXX translated *garden* as *paradise* — "a Persian loan word, originally meaning a royal park." Wenham, *Genesis 1–15*, 61.

3. Adapted from Radday, "Chiasmus in Hebrew Biblical Narrative," 98-99. See also

A Narrative: God, man (2:4b-17)
From *'ădāmâ* (ground) to garden
  B Narrative: God, man, woman, animals (2:18-25)
  Relationship among creatures
  God's goodness in making a partner for man
    C Dialogue: Serpent, woman (3:1-5)
    About eating from the tree
    Three statements
      D Narrative: Woman, man (3:6-7)
      They eat from the tree[4]
      Rebellion in God's kingdom
    C′ Dialogue: God, man, woman (3:8-13)
    About eating from the tree
    Three questions and answers
  B′ Monologue: God, man, woman, serpent (3:14-19)
  Relationships among the creatures
  God's judgment and grace
A′ Narrative: God, man (3:20-24)
From garden to *'ădāmâ* (ground)

As to the context, Genesis 1 and Genesis 2–3 display some striking differences. Genesis 1 begins, "In the beginning God created the heavens and the earth," that is, the entire universe. Then verse 2 narrows the focus to the earth: "The earth was formless and empty." Genesis 2 narrows the focus even more: it zeroes in on a garden and the first man and woman. Whereas Genesis 1 refers to God as *'Ĕlōhîm,* the almighty King of the universe, Genesis 2–3 uses the name *Yahweh 'Ĕlōhîm,*[5] "the

---

Jerome T. Walsh, "Genesis 2:4b–3:24: A Synchronic Approach," *JBL* 96/2 (1977) 161-77; Wenham, *Genesis 1–15,* 50; Stordalen, *Echoes of Eden,* 218-20, 476-77; and Mathews, *Genesis 1–11:26,* 184.

4. "Within this central scene, the same device [chiasm] is used; the midpoint 'and he ate' employs the key verb of this tale — 'eat.' On either side we have the woman's hopes of eating, 'good to eat,' 'delight to the eyes,' 'giving insight,' balanced by its effects, 'eyes opened,' 'knowing they were nude,' 'hiding in the trees.'" Wenham, *Genesis 1–15,* 75. If scene four consists of verses 6-7, the final element might better be identified as "making loincloths" (v 7).

5. In fact, the narrator uses the name "*Yahweh 'Ĕlōhîm*" more often (20 times) in this one narrative than it is used in the rest of the Old Testament (16 times). Wenham suggests that the narrator "deliberately used this form to express his conviction that Yahweh is both Israel's covenant partner and the God (*'Ĕlōhîm*) of all creation." Wenham, *Genesis 1–15,* 57. Cf. Mathews, *Genesis 1–11:26,* 192-93, "*'Ĕlōhîm* is appropriate for the majestic portrayal of God as Creator of the universe since it properly indicates omnipotent deity, whereas Yahweh is the name commonly associated with the covenant relationship between deity and his people, Israel (cf. 15:7; Exod 3:14-15). Its combination with Elohim achieves an overlapping of these theological emphases: Yahweh, the Lord of his people, is in fact the all-wise and powerful *'Ĕlōhîm*-Creator."

Lord God," the personal God who led his people Israel out of Egypt, who fed them in the desert, who made a covenant with them at Mount Sinai and called them to obey his commandments. And whereas in Genesis 1 God *speaks* as the almighty King and it comes to be, here the Lord is sketched in more intimate terms as a potter who stoops down and fashions a delicate object (2:7), as a horticulturist who plants a garden (2:8), as a sculptor who fashions a woman from a rib of the man (2:21-22), as a person who walks in the garden (3:8), and as a judge who conducts a hearing and renders judgment (3:9-19).

Literary Features

The narrator reveals that he is writing from a later perspective when he comments, "Therefore a man leaves his father and his mother and clings to his wife, and they become one flesh" (2:24). But he is also omniscient. He knows about a time when there were no plants on the earth (2:5), gets inside the woman's mind when she contemplates the tree (3:6), and knows the thoughts of God as God considers what to do about these rebellious creatures who still have access to the tree of life (3:22).

The narrator does not intend to give us a precise chronological account of what happened in the beginning. This is most evident from the order in which he sketches the creation of various creatures. In Genesis 1 we saw the ascending order of complexity: vegetation, animals, and, as a climax, human beings. Here the order seems to be: the man Adam, trees, animals, and finally the woman. The arrangement is not chronological but topical. This is not a modern historical report but, as we can see in the chiastically structured scenes, this is literary art.

The Plot Line

Although the narrative has several subplots (complications),[6] it has one overall plot: it begins with God forming a man and placing him in a garden, and it ends with the man being expelled from the garden. With several subplots, the challenge will be to keep the focus on the overall plot.[7] We can sketch a simplified version of this complex plot as shown on the following page:

6. For example, Genesis 2:18, the conflict begins with the man being alone; vv 19-20, rising tension because no animal is equal to being his partner; vv 21-22, resolution, God made the woman; v 23, outcome; vv 24-25, conclusion. Cf. Stordalen, *Echoes of Eden,* 221-33 and 447, who calls these subplots "plot segments" (p. 221). I will simply call them "subplots" or "complications."

7. Hartley, *Genesis,* 58 and 64 suggests considering Genesis 2:4-25 as Act 1 and Genesis 3:1-24 as Act 2. "In act 1 the narrator introduces the characters and defines the crucial props in a topical, not a chronological, order. . . . Act 2 of the drama begins with the introduction of a new actor, the serpent. . . ."

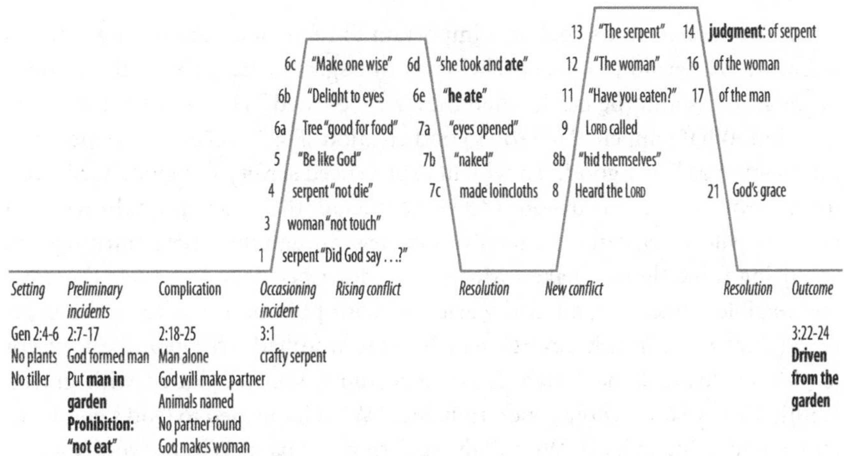

Theocentric Interpretation

Although there are several characters in this narrative, the LORD God, the man, the woman, and the serpent, it is the LORD God who clearly is the central character. The LORD God formed the man, planted a garden, made the trees grow, put the man in the garden, commanded him not to eat of the tree of the knowledge of good and evil, formed animals and birds, caused a deep sleep to fall on the man and fashioned a woman from one of his ribs, walked in the garden, called for the man, interrogated the man and the woman, pronounced judgment on the serpent, the woman, and the man, made garments for the man and his wife, expelled them from the garden, and placed the cherubim to guard the way to the tree of life.

Textual Theme and Goal

A major theme in this narrative is God's judgment tempered by God's grace. We see God's grace after the Fall when he calls the man, puts enmity between the serpent (Satan) and the woman, promises her children, though born in pain, promises food, though gained with toil, and makes garments for Adam and Eve. Thus we can formulate the textual theme as: "The LORD responds to human rebellion with judgment and grace." But this theme is rather general and does not capture the plot of this narrative: put in the garden, disobedience, expelled from the garden. So it would be better to formulate the theme as follows: *In banishing his rebellious creatures from his presence in Paradise, the LORD still extends his grace.*

As to the narrator's goal, it is important to remember that this narrative is intended as a sermon to Israel. The narrator begins in 2:4, "This is the account of the heavens and the earth when they were created." He seeks to answer the question: What happened to God's good creation? For Israel did not experience the creation as "very good." Israel had experienced slavery in Egypt: hard labor from dawn to dusk, no freedom to worship God, their baby boys drowned in the river Nile. Then came the terrible journey through the desert: burning sun, agonizing thirst, lethal snakes. Moses later described this desert as "the great and terrible wilderness, an arid wasteland with poisonous snakes and scorpions" (Deut 8:15). In this desert every Israelite who had left Egypt died, except for Moses, Joshua, and Caleb. It was a tortuous journey dotted with graves. Within forty years a whole generation dead! What happened to God's good creation? Why is life so hard? Why all the suffering and pain? Why do we all die?

Therefore the narrator's goal is probably more than to teach Israel about the origin of the brokenness of life. Given Israel's painful circumstances after the desert journey and again later during the exile, the narrator probably had a deeper goal in mind than simply to teach. We can get at this deeper goal by asking the question: *Why* did the narrator wish to teach suffering Israel that the LORD, in banishing his rebellious creatures from his presence in Paradise, still extends his grace? This question suggests a few deeper goals such as: to give suffering Israel hope that evil will eventually be overcome through the seed of the woman; or, more closely matched with the theme, *To give suffering Israel hope that the LORD's judgment of sin is tempered by his grace.*

Ways to Preach Christ

The strongest bridge to Christ in the New Testament usually follows the textual theme to the New Testament (the main exception is typology, when a *person* is a type of Christ). As we brainstorm and look for legitimate roads to Christ, we should, therefore, keep in mind the theme, "In banishing his rebellious creatures from his presence in Paradise, the LORD still extends his grace." We ask if and how each way would lead to Christ in the New Testament. Although we will not use all these ways in the sermon (information overload), we'll still check each in turn so that later we can select two or three of the most prominent ways for the sermon.

Redemptive-Historical Progression

One can preach Christ from this narrative by tracing through redemptive history the instances of God's grace in judgment. This narrative contains in a nutshell the first three of the four basic components of redemptive history: Creation, Fall, Redemption, New Creation. The narrative begins with God creating a perfect world, then relates the human Fall into sin. Redemptive history starts right after the Fall with God cursing the serpent, declaring enmity between the seed of the serpent and the seed of the woman, and holding out defeat for the serpent (cursed, eating dust) and by implication the victory for the seed of the woman. With its *tôlĕdôt* structure, Genesis traces the seed of the woman from Abel to Seth to Noah to Abraham, Isaac, Jacob, and Judah (49:10). Other writers pick up the trail and trace it to King David and his "seed" (2 Sam 7:12-13; Ps 89:4). In the New Testament Matthew retraces the trail starting with Abraham, moving to King David, and ending with Jesus Messiah (Matt 1:1-17). Luke traces Jesus' lineage all the way back to "Seth, son of Adam" (Luke 3:38). And Paul identifies Christ as the "seed" of Abraham who received God's promises regarding the inheritance (Gal 3:16). Jesus is the Seed of the woman who will ultimately gain the victory over the Satan.

One can also follow the trail of Paradise. This narrative ends with Paradise lost but also shows God's grace. The prophets single out this note of grace and hold out hope that Paradise will be restored. Isaiah (11:1, 4-9) prophesies:

> A shoot shall come out from the stump of Jesse. . . .
> With righteousness he shall judge the poor. . . .
> Righteousness shall be the belt around his waist,
> and faithfulness the belt around his loins.
> The wolf shall live with the lamb,
> the leopard shall lie down with the kid,
> the calf and the lion and the fatling together,
> and a little child shall lead them.
> The cow and the bear shall graze,
> their young shall lie down together;
> and the lion shall eat straw like the ox.
> The nursing child shall play over the hole of the asp,
> and the weaned child shall put its hand on the adder's den
> [the serpent has been rendered harmless].
> They will not hurt or destroy on all my holy mountain;
> for the earth will be full of the knowledge of the LORD
> as the waters cover the sea.

But Israel kept disobeying God and was eventually driven out of the land, which was "like the garden of the LORD" (Gen 13:10), as Adam and Eve had been "driven out" of the garden. Still, during the Babylonian exile Isaiah (65:17, 24-25) could comfort them with the LORD's word:

> I am about to create new heavens and a new earth;
> the former things shall not be remembered or come to mind. . . .
> Before they call I will answer,
> while they are yet speaking I will hear.
> The wolf and the lamb shall feed together,
> the lion shall eat straw like the ox;
> but the *serpent* — its food shall be dust!
> They shall not hurt or destroy on all my holy mountain,
> says the LORD.

One day peace and harmony will be restored on this earth. For the serpent has "licked the dust."

In the book of Revelation (22:1-5), John comforts persecuted Christians with a vision of Paradise restored. The river flowing out of Eden is back, as is the tree of life, easily accessible from "either side of the river," with plenty of fruit; the curse has vanished, and instead there is God's royal presence and that of the Lamb:

> Then the angel showed me the river of the water of life, bright as crystal, flowing from the throne of God and of the Lamb through the middle of the street of the city. On either side of the river is the tree of life with its twelve kinds of fruit, producing its fruit every month; and the leaves of the tree are for the healing of the nations. Nothing accursed will be found there any more. But the throne of God and of the Lamb will be in it, and his servants will worship him; they will see his face, and his name will be on their foreheads.

Paradise is not lost after all. Through the Lamb, Jesus Christ, it will come again. "Blessed are those who wash their robes, so that they will have the right to the tree of life and may enter the city by the gates" (Rev 22:14).

Promise-Fulfillment

Redemptive-historical progression dovetails with the way of promise-fulfillment. The church has always interpreted God's curse of the serpent in Genesis 3:15 as a promise of the ultimate victory of the seed of the woman.[8] In

8. The Septuagint (third century B.C.) and Jewish targums understand this verse "as referring to a victory over Satan in the days of King Messiah." Alexander, "Messianic Ideology," 27; cf. 37-41. See further my *Preaching Christ from the Old Testament,* 245-48, and Hamilton, *Handbook on the Pentateuch,* 49-51.

fact, the Church Fathers called this verse the *protevangelium*, the first gospel. Jesus' resurrection from death is proof positive that he is the Seed of the woman who gained the victory over Satan. As Hebrews 2:14 puts it, Christ shared our flesh and blood, "so that through death he might destroy the one who has the power of death, that is, the devil" (cf. Rev 12). And Paul adds, "The God of peace will shortly crush Satan under your feet" (Rom 16:20).

Typology

From this narrative one can also preach Christ by way of typology, for, as the New Testament demonstrates time and again, Adam is a type of Jesus Christ. As Adam was tempted by Satan, so Jesus would be tempted by Satan.[9] But whereas Adam disobeyed God and followed Satan, Jesus obeyed God and sent Satan away (Matt 4:1-11). Because of this contrast (as well as others) between Adam and Christ, one can label this "antithetic typology."

In Romans 5 Paul calls Adam "a type *(typos)* of the one who was to come" (Rom 5:14) and draws many analogies between Adam and Christ, shows escalation, and highlights antitheses:

> Therefore, just as sin came into the world through one man, and death came through sin, and so death spread to all because all have sinned. . . . Yet death exercised dominion from Adam to Moses, even over those whose sins were not like the transgression of Adam, who was a *type* of the one who was to come. But the free gift is not [*antithesis*] like the trespass. For if the many died through one man's trespass, much more surely [*escalation*] have the grace of God and the free gift in the grace of the one man, Jesus Christ, abounded for the many [*analogy*]. And the free gift is not [*antithesis*] like the effect of the one man's sin. For the judgment following one trespass brought condemnation, but the free gift following many trespasses brings justification [*antithesis*]. If, because of one man's trespass, death exercised dominion through that one, much more surely [*escalation*] will those who receive the abundance of grace and the free gift of righteousness exercise dominion in life through the one man, Jesus Christ [*analogy*]. Therefore just as one man's trespass led to condemnation for all men, so [*analogy*] one man's act of righteousness leads to justification and life for all [*antithesis*]. For just as by one man's disobedience the many were made sinners, so [*analogy*] by one man's obedience the many will be made righteous [*antithesis*]. (Rom 5:12-19)[10]

9. Luke (3:23-38) highlights the analogy between Adam and Jesus by inserting Jesus' genealogy just before Jesus' temptations and tracing Jesus' lineage back to "Adam, son of God."

10. Cf. 1 Cor 15:21, 45, 47-49: "For since death came through a human being, the resurrec-

James Dunn comments on the antithesis between Adam and Christ: "By freely following out the consequences of Adam's disobedience (i.e. death), Jesus burst through the cul-de-sac of death into life. He went all the way with the first Adam to the end of Adam in death. But beyond death he re-emerged as a new Adam whose hallmark is life from the dead."[11]

Analogy

Since we have discovered such major highways for preaching Christ as redemptive-historical progression, promise-fulfillment, and typology, it is not likely that we will use analogy. But it is still well to indicate how analogy can be used to preach Christ from this narrative. Analogy can often be discovered by reflecting on the narrator's goal. We determined earlier that the narrator's likely goal was to give hope to suffering Israel. Did Jesus ever try to give hope to suffering people in an analogous way? Did the New Testament writers ever try to give hope in an analogous way by proclaiming the good news of Jesus?

These reflections lead to several possible analogies: as God gave Israel hope that through his grace Paradise would one day be restored on earth, so Jesus gives his church hope for the restoration of Paradise on earth with his Second Coming. This analogy would have to be supported by New Testament references. One can use such passages as John's vision of Paradise restored through the Lamb of God (Rev 22:1-3), or even Jesus' word to the criminal on the cross, "Today you will be with me in Paradise" (Luke 23:43).

Another analogy would be, as God gave Israel hope that evil would eventually be overcome through the victory of the seed of the woman, so Jesus gives his church hope that evil is being overcome by his victory over Satan. A New Testament reference that supports this analogy is when the seventy say to Jesus, "Lord, in your name even the *demons* submit to us." And Jesus responds, "I watched Satan fall from heaven like a flash of lightning. See, I have given you authority to tread on *snakes* and scorpions, and over all the power of the enemy" (Luke 10:18-19).

---

tion of the dead [*antithesis*] has also come through a human being [*analogy*]; for as all die in Adam, so [*analogy*] also will all be made alive in Christ [*antithesis*]. . . . Thus it is written, 'The first man, Adam, became a living being' [Gen 2:7]; the last Adam became a life-giving spirit [*antithesis*]. . . . The first man was from the earth, a man of dust; the second man is from heaven [*antithesis*]. As was the man of dust, so [*analogy*] are those who are of the dust; and as is the man of heaven, so [*analogy*] are those who are of heaven. Just as we have borne the image of the man of dust, we will also bear the image of the man of heaven [*antithesis*]."

11. Dunn, *Christology in the Making,* 111.

Longitudinal Themes

In preaching Christ from this narrative, one can also trace longitudinal themes that move from the heart of this narrative through the Old Testament to Jesus Christ in the New Testament. For example, one can trace the theme of *God's presence with his people* from the garden where the LORD walked with his people, to Adam and Eve driven out of the garden and kept from returning by cherubim, to the tabernacle and temple, where God dwelt in the midst of his people as represented by the cloud and yet could not be approached by sinners — the way being blocked by curtains embroidered with images of cherubim (see Exod 26:1, 31 and 2 Chron 3:14). This theme of God's presence can be traced further to the New Testament to Jesus who is called Immanuel, that is, "God is with us" (Matt 1:23), who calls his body "the temple" (John 2:19), at whose death the temple curtain with the cherubim tears "from top to bottom" (Matt 27:51), thus reopening the way into the holy of holies (the presence of God), to Jesus' promise, "I am with you always" (Matt 28:20), to Pentecost when Jesus pours out God's Spirit to dwell in his people, to the new earth where "the home of God is among mortals. He will dwell with them" (Rev 21:3).

Or one can trace the theme of *God's grace in his judgment* through the Old Testament to Christ in the New Testament. In Jesus Christ God's judgment and grace merge. On the cross Jesus carries God's judgment so that God's grace may save many.

New Testament References

In addition to the passages mentioned above, a few other possibilities are:

1 Corinthians 15:25, "He [Christ] must reign until he has put all his enemies under his feet."

2 Corinthians 5:17, "If anyone is in Christ, there is a new creation; . . . see, everything has become new."

1 John 3:8, "The Son of God was revealed for this purpose, to destroy the works of the devil."

Revelation 2:7, where the risen Jesus says, "To everyone who conquers, I will give permission to eat from the tree of life that is in the Paradise of God."

Contrast

There are many contrasts between Adam and Christ listed under typology (above), but there is no contrast between this message of the Old Testament and that of the New.

Sermon Theme and Goal

The context of the New Testament clarifies the message of this narrative by showing that Satan was the tempter who was and will be defeated by Jesus Christ. Further, the New Testament proclaims that Jesus with his Second Coming will restore Paradise on earth, that is, he will make all things new.[12] We formulated the textual theme as follows, "In banishing his rebellious creatures from his presence in Paradise, the LORD still extends his grace." For the sermon theme we can add the New Testament hope by making it, "In banishing his rebellious creatures from his presence in Paradise, God still extends his grace in order eventually to restore Paradise on earth." A shorter, more memorable theme for use in the sermon would be, *God banishes sinners from Paradise with a view to restoring his perfect Paradise on earth.*

Our goal in preaching this sermon should be in harmony with the narrator's goal in relating this narrative to Israel. We saw that the narrator probably aimed to teach Israel the origin of the brokenness it experienced. He sought to answer the questions: What happened to God's good creation? Why is it that in our present life we experience pain, toil, tensions in marriage, enmity with the animal world, and finally death? Since we have the same questions today, we can also make it our goal to teach our hearers the origin of the brokenness we experience daily.

But we can aim at more than simply to teach. We should ask, *Why* do I wish to teach my hearers about the origin of the brokenness we experience? The narrator, we saw, probably aimed for the deeper goal, "To give suffering Israel hope that the LORD's judgment of sin is tempered by his grace." In line with the narrator's goal, we can therefore make our goal for preaching this sermon, *To give suffering people today hope that God in his grace will restore Paradise to earth.*[13]

12. Cf. Childs, *Old Testament Theology in a Canonical Context,* 226, Humanity "was not created in alienation from God, his fellows, or himself. The theological significance of a period of innocence is to testify to a harmony in God's creation at the beginning which overcame the threat of non-being in the presence of God. It also bears witness to the eschatological restoration of God's new creation in which all threats will have been removed."

13. This goal is similar to that of Isaiah (51:3), who prophesied to Israel in exile:

> For the LORD will comfort Zion;
> he will comfort all her waste places,

The Sermon Form

Since the text is a narrative, the sermon is best presented in a narrative form, that is, the preacher follows the plot line but suspends the story now and then for explanation, application, and moves to Christ in the New Testament. The narrative form keeps its suspense best if the theme is saved for the end of the narrative, that is, inductive development. Since this narrative has a complex plot with several subplots, care must be taken not to get bogged down in the subplots and lose the main thrust of this narrative. In the sermon, the subplots can be treated as complications that are rather quickly resolved in order to keep the focus on the main plot.

Sermon Exposition

I suggest beginning the introduction with an illustration of how contemporary suffering can lead to a loss of hope. Then transition to Israel's loss of hope when they suffered. While enslaved in Egypt, they had given up hope of ever reaching the Promised Land; when they failed to capture Canaan the first time, they lost all hope and wished to return to Egypt; when God later drove them out of Canaan into exile, they lost all hope of ever returning to the land. The writer of this narrative wishes to give God's people hope.

He begins in chapter 2:4, "These are the generations of the heavens and the earth when they were created." This is what happened to the kingdom of God on earth which he declared to be "very good." "In the day that the Lord God made the earth and the heavens" the earth was barren: no plants, no herbs, no rain, "no one to till the ground" (2:5).

The action begins in Genesis 2:7, "The Lord God formed man from the dust of the ground, and breathed into his nostrils the breath of life; and the man became a living being." The point of this verse is not precisely *how* God made the man but that he is made from the "dust of the ground" (see 3:19). Human beings are not gods, as some ancient people believed their kings to be. The man, *hā'ādām,* is made from *hā'ădāmâ,* the ground. The earthling is made from earth. Humans are mere earthlings, frail, made from the dust of the ground.

Still, they are God's special creatures. For God himself carefully, lovingly

---

and will make her wilderness like Eden,
    her desert like the garden of the Lord;
joy and gladness will be found in her,
    thanksgiving and the voice of song.

formed the first man and shaped him into an elegant vessel. And, in another personal touch, he "breathed into his nostrils the breath of life."[14] It is the breath of God that gives us life; it is the breath or Spirit of God that keeps us breathing and living.[15]

In verses 7 and 8 the narrator informs us that the LORD planted a lush garden on earth. "And the LORD God planted a garden in Eden, in the east; and there he put the man whom he had formed. Out of the ground the LORD God made to grow every tree that is pleasant to the sight and good for food, the tree of life also in the midst of the garden, and the tree of the knowledge of good and evil." The garden is a true Paradise. When we try to picture the garden, we should probably think of a lush, secure, Eastern garden. It had a wall all around it except for a gate on the east side (see 3:24). Elsewhere in the Old Testament the garden is referred to as "the garden of the LORD" (Gen 13:10; Isa 51:3) and "the garden of God" (Ezek 28:13; 31:9). Just like the later tabernacle and temple, this garden is the special dwelling place of God on earth.[16]

The garden, however, is more than a symbol. The narrator spends a large amount of narrative time (2:10-14) pinpointing the location of the garden with respect to four rivers and three countries. Paradise was on this earth. Two of the rivers are not known today,[17] but mention of the Tigris and the Euphrates in verse 14 would indicate that the location of the garden was in Mesopotamia, perhaps present-day Turkey or Iraq.

In any event, the garden is pictured as a beautiful, peaceful place where the man can commune with God and enjoy God's good gifts: "every tree that is pleasant to the sight and good for food" (2:9). And in the middle of the garden "the tree of *life*" — apparently a tree whose fruit could keep him alive forever. In addition to these gifts, the LORD provides the man with meaningful work. Verse 15, "The LORD God took the man and put him in the Garden of

14. "*Breathed* is warmly personal, with the face-to-face intimacy of a kiss and the significance that this was an act of giving as well as making; and self-giving at that. Cf. . . . John 20:22." Kidner, *Genesis*, 60.

15. "Man is more that a God-shaped piece of earth. He has within him the gift of life that was given by God himself." Wenham, *Genesis 1–15*, 60.

16. In some respects the narrator sketches the garden as an early tabernacle/temple. "(1) The LORD God walks in Eden as he later does in the tabernacle (3:8; cf. Lev 26:12). (2) Eden and the later sanctuaries are entered from the east [Ezek 41:1] and guarded by cherubim (3:24; Exod 25:18-22; 26:31; 1 Kings 6:23-29). . . . (4) The pair of Hebrew verbs in God's command to the man 'to work it (the garden) and take care of it' (2:15) are only used in combination elsewhere in the Pentateuch of the duties of the Levites in the sanctuary (cf. Num 3:7-8; 8:26; 18:5-6)." Alexander, *From Paradise to the Promised Land*, 20, with credit to Wenham, "Sanctuary Symbolism in the Garden of Eden Story," 19-25. Cf. Sailhamer, *Pentateuch as Narrative*, 98; and Mathews, *Genesis 1–11:26*, 52.

17. But see Kitchen, *On the Reliability of the Old Testament*, 428-30.

Eden to till it and keep it." Work, even in Paradise, gives meaning and purpose to human life.

The narrative develops somewhat along the lines of the ancient Hittite covenant treaties.[18] The great King is identified as *Yahweh 'Ĕlōhîm,* which is followed by an enumeration of all the good things the King has done for the man. Now follow the covenant stipulations. At Sinai Israel heard ten commandments: "You shall have no other gods before me," etc. Here there is only one commandment. Verse 16, "And the LORD God *commanded* the man, 'You may freely eat of every tree of the garden; but of the tree of the knowledge of good and evil you shall not eat, for in the day that you eat of it you shall die.'" We see how good God is also in giving this commandment: they are free to eat from *every* tree in the garden. That includes the tree of life. There is only one prohibition, "of the tree of the knowledge of good and evil you shall not eat," and this is also good because God treats the man, in contrast to the animals, as a moral agent who can decide to obey God willingly.

Even though this commandment is good, in the narrative it is this prohibition that raises the conflict and sets the tension. God places the man before a clear choice: continue in communion with God by trusting and obeying him, or break communion with God by disobeying his commandment. But disobedience will result in the penalty of death: "you *shall* die." The choice is an obedient life with God in Paradise or disobedience and death. The stakes are high. What will happen?

The narrator, however, keeps us in suspense. Amazingly, God discovers something that is not good in Paradise. Verse 18, "The LORD God said, 'It is not good that the man should be alone; I will make him a helper as his partner.'" So God let all the animals pass by Adam, but, we read in verse 20, "for the man there was not found a helper as his partner." Animals can be good companions for human beings, but they are inferior. Only human beings were made in the image of God, and only human beings received dominion (Gen 1:26, 28). Adam had just exercised his dominion by naming the animals, but not one of them could function as his partner. So God goes to work again, this time fashioning a woman from one of Adam's ribs.[19] When Adam sees the woman he is ecstatic. He says, verse 23,

18. One does not necessarily need the word "covenant," *bĕrît,* to discern a covenant; one can recognize a covenant by the presence of its elements. The usual elements in these covenant treaties were: a preamble identifying the great King, the historical prologue recounting what the King had done for his people, covenant stipulations, the place where the treaty must be kept, witnesses, and curses and blessings. See p. 18, n. 45.

19. "By using a part of the man to create the woman, there can be no doubt that the woman is on the same level as Adam. To deny her is to deny himself. Commitment to each other and dependence on each other must be total." Baylis, *From Creation,* 42.

"This at last is bone of my bones
  and flesh of my flesh;
this one shall be called Woman (*'iššâ*),
  for out of Man (*'îš*) this one was taken."

The parallelism in the poetry shows how closely men and women are related: the same flesh, the same bones, but the opposite sex. *'Îš* and *'iššâ* will complement each other perfectly.

Verse 25 tells us, "The man and his wife were both naked, and were not ashamed." This statement must have been astonishing for Israel, for they had a strong sense of shame, covering most of their bodies with long robes and scarves. But here are Adam and Eve, "both naked, and not ashamed."[20] They are innocent like little children at play. It is a perfect marriage in a perfect home: Paradise, the garden of the LORD.

The narrator emphasizes how good God made everything in the beginning for human beings: God himself fashioned the man, giving him life with his divine breath, placing him in a safe garden where he had plenty of food and meaningful work, and to top it off, God formed a perfect partner for him. At the end of chapter 2, God could have looked back as he did in chapter 1 and said: "Behold, it is very good." But that is about to change. A new character enters this idyllic setting.

Genesis 3:1, "Now the serpent was more crafty than any other wild animal that the LORD God had made." The serpent sounds like a sinister character. In the ancient world, however, the serpent was often worshiped as a god of healing.[21] Even today medical doctors identify themselves as healers with the figure of a coiled serpent. But the biblical author makes sure that we do not think of this serpent as a god. The serpent, he says, like all the other animals, had been made by the LORD God. Therefore it was originally good.

Hebrew narrators seldom use character description, but when they do, it is often a key for understanding the narrative. Here the serpent is described as "more crafty than any other wild animal that the LORD God had made." That sounds ominous.[22] Remember also that Israel considered serpents their archenemies. In the desert, the plague of fiery serpents had killed many Israelites (Num 21). People always had to be careful where they walked. A serpent could

20. "Nakedness among the Hebrews was shameful because it was often associated with guilt." Mathews, *Genesis 1–11:26*, 225.

21. "This reptile figures prominently in all the world's mythologies and cults. In the Near East the serpent was a symbol of deity and fertility, and the images of serpent-goddesses have been found in the ruins of many Canaanite towns and temples." Sarna, *Understanding Genesis*, 26.

22. Although *'ārûm* (crafty) can be a positive trait, the context here clearly shows it to be negative. Cf. Exod 21:14; Job 5:12; 15:5; Ps 83:3.

be lying behind a rock and with its deadly fangs strike a passerby in the heel. Serpents were deadly enemies.[23]

But there is something special about this serpent. Not only is it "more crafty than any other wild animal." This serpent speaks! Israel had never heard a serpent speak. Serpents do not speak, not even in Paradise. We can only conclude that the narrator wants us to understand that some other being has taken possession of the serpent and speaks through it. And this is an evil being because it questions God's command and even calls God a liar. In the New Testament Jesus describes the devil as "a liar and the father of lies" (John 8:44). And in the book of Revelation (12:9) John writes about "that ancient serpent who is called the Devil and Satan, the deceiver of the whole world." It is the devil or Satan who speaks through the serpent.

The serpent, alias Satan, says to the woman, verse 1, "Did God say, 'You shall not eat from *any* tree in the garden'?" Notice how craftily Satan twists God's words. God had said, "You may freely eat of every tree of the garden" except for that one tree. Satan ignores God's good gifts of plenty of food and makes God's commandment sound unreasonable. All these trees here that are "pleasant to the sight and good for food," and God said, "You shall not eat from *any* tree?"

The woman is quickly drawn into the conversation. She responds, verse 2, "We may eat of the fruit of the trees in the garden, but God said, 'You shall not eat of the fruit of the tree that is in the middle of the garden, nor shall you touch it, or you shall die.'" She has it almost right. But the suggestion that God's command is unreasonable has entered her mind. God had said, "Of the tree of the knowledge of good and evil you shall not eat." The woman quotes God as saying, "You shall not eat of the fruit of the tree that is in the middle of the garden, *nor shall you touch it,* or you shall die." That does sound rather unreasonable, doesn't it?[24] Touch that tree and die?

Satan sees his opening. He calls God a liar. In verse 4 he says to the woman, "You will not surely die,[25] for God knows that when you eat of it your eyes will be opened, and you will be like God, knowing good and evil." Satan suggests

23. See Gen 49:17; Eccl 10:8; Amos 5:19. "According to the classification of animals found in Lev 11 and Deut 14, the snake must count as an archetypal unclean animal. Its swarming, writhing locomotion puts it at the farthest point from those pure animals that can be offered in sacrifice. Within the world of OT animal symbolism a snake is an obvious candidate for an anti-God symbol, notwithstanding its creation by God." Wenham, *Genesis 1–15*, 73.

24. But see Townsend, "Eve's Answer to the Serpent," *CTJ* 33 (1998) 406-7, who argues that "the original readers of Eve's words would have understood the story in the context of God's commands concerning unclean food, and would have understood that the fruit of the Tree of the Knowledge of Good and Evil was unclean food." As such, it should not be touched (see Lev 11:8 for similar vocabulary and sentence structure as Gen 3:3).

25. "It is the serpent's word against God's, and the first doctrine to be denied is judgment." Kidner, *Genesis*, 68.

that God has not been generous with them, creating them only in his image. They can do much better: they can be "like God." It's as if God created them blind. But eat of that tree and "your eyes will be opened, and you will be like God, knowing good and evil." Imagine, they can decide for themselves what is good and what is evil.[26] They can be like God![27]

With that temptation Satan leaves. We are left with Adam and Eve and how they will deal with the temptation to be like God. This central scene (scene 4) is the climax of the story. The narrator retards the pace in verse 6 by sketching every detail as the woman contemplates eating from the forbidden tree: "So when the woman saw that the tree was good for food [like all the other trees] and that it was a delight to the eyes [again like all the other trees], and that the tree was to be desired to make one wise [they could be wise like God], she took of its fruit and ate; she also gave some to her husband, who was with her, and he ate."

Her husband, who had received the commandment directly from God, should have stopped her: "Don't do this! God told us not to eat of this tree! God honored us by creating us after his likeness, but as his creatures we should not try to be *like* God." However, Adam keeps silent. He allows his wife to transgress God's commandment, and then he transgresses it himself. "She took . . . and ate. . . .[28] She gave . . . and he ate." The creature desires to be *like* God.[29] God's creature no longer trusts God's goodness. Sin enters God's perfect Paradise.[30] Rebellion in God's kingdom!

The results of the fall into sin show up immediately. Verse 7, "Then the eyes of both were opened, and they knew that they were naked;[31] and they sewed fig

26. "The serpent holds out . . . the independence that enables a man to decide for himself what will help him or hinder him." Von Rad, *Genesis,* 89.

27. "From usage in the rest of the passage (2:16f; 3:3-7, 22), the tree must symbolize the right of complete freedom of choice over good and evil. The first human pair, by eating of the tree, aim at being 'as God' (3:5, 22) by determining for themselves what is good and bad, establishing moral autonomy over good and evil, thus usurping the divine prerogative." LaSor et al., *Old Testament Survey,* 80-81. Cf. W. M. Clark, "A Legal Background to the Yahwist's Use of 'Good and Evil' in Genesis 2–3," *JBL* 88 (1969) 266-78.

28. "So simple the act, so hard its undoing. God will taste poverty and death before 'take and eat' become verbs of salvation." Kidner, *Genesis,* 68.

29. "A counterpart of Adam's action is clearly the attitude of Jesus referred to in Philippians 2:6." Dumbrell, *Covenant and Creation,* 38.

30. "Man has stepped outside the state of dependence, he has refused obedience and willed to make himself independent. The guiding principle of his life is no longer obedience but his autonomous knowing and willing, and thus he has really ceased to understand himself as creature." Von Rad, *Genesis,* 97.

31. "The effect of the Fall was not simply that the man and the woman came to know that they were *'ārôm* ('naked' [in the sense of 2:25]). Specifically, they came to know that they were *'êrôm* ('naked') in the sense of being 'under God's judgment,' as in Deuteronomy 28:48 (cf. Eze 16:39; 23:29)." Sailhamer, *Pentateuch as Narrative,* 103.

leaves together and made loincloths for themselves." The first result of sin is the loss of childlike innocence. They are ashamed of their own bodies and make coverings for themselves to hide themselves from each other. Their perfect marriage has broken down.

A second result of sin is fear of God. Verse 8, "They heard the sound of the LORD God walking in the garden at the time of the evening breeze, and the man and his wife hid themselves from the presence of the LORD God among the trees of the garden." Fear of God! Innocence has been replaced by guilt and fear. Communion with the LORD of life has been broken. Adam and Eve are spiritually dead.

But the covenant God does not give up on his distrustful and disobedient creatures. In scene 5 the LORD seeks the lost. Verse 9, "The LORD God called to the man,[32] and said to him, 'Where are you?' He said, 'I heard the sound of you in the garden, and I was afraid, because I was naked; and I hid myself.' He said, 'Who told you that you were naked? Have you eaten from the tree of which I commanded you not to eat?'" Adam tries to defend himself, "The woman whom you gave to be with me, she gave me fruit from the tree, and I ate" (v 12). Talk about marriage breakdown. Now Adam blames his wife for his transgression. And he even dares to blame the Judge himself: "The woman whom *you* gave."[33]

Verse 13, "Then the LORD God said to the woman, 'What is this that you have done?' The woman said, 'The serpent tricked me, and I ate.'" Both Adam and Eve pass the blame to others. They fail to take responsibility for their own sin.

The heavenly Judge does not need much time to render a verdict. In the sixth scene the LORD passes judgment in reverse order: the LORD begins with the serpent, next the woman, and finally the man. Notice that the verdict in verse 14 to 15 is written in a poetic form to emphasize the word of God:[34]

> The LORD God said to the serpent,
> "Because you have done this,
>   *cursed* are you among all animals
>   and among all wild creatures;
> upon your belly you shall go,

32. "Perhaps God speaks to the man alone because it was the man alone who heard the initial prohibition. The narrative, as usual, does not provide any explanation. Perhaps none would have been needed in ancient Israelite culture if men were assumed to speak on behalf of their families." Stratton, *Out of Eden,* 51.

33. "As an index of the extent of humanity's fall, the author shows that the man saw God's good gift as the source of his trouble." Sailhamer, *Pentateuch as Narrative,* 106.

34. "Since poetry is our best human model of intricately rich communication, not only solemn, weighty, and forceful but also densely woven with complex internal connections, meanings, and implications, it makes sense that divine speech should be represented by poetry." Robert Alter, *The Art of Biblical Poetry* (New York: Basic Books, 1985), 141.

and dust you shall eat all the days of your life.
I will put enmity between you and the woman,
and between your offspring [Heb. seed] and hers;
he will strike your head,
and you will strike his heel."

(vv 14-15)

"Cursed are you." This is the first time we read in the Bible about God's curse. God's curse is the opposite of God's blessing: God's curse removes creatures from his blessing.[35] In Genesis 1 we read three times that God blessed: God blessed the animals, God blessed human beings, and God blessed the seventh day. After the Fall we read three times that God cursed, that is, turned his blessing into its opposite.[36] God cursed the serpent, God cursed the ground, and in the next narrative God will curse the murderer Cain. Here God's curse falls the serpent.

Next God turns to the woman, but note that he does not curse her. He punishes her in her role as mother and wife. Verse 16,

"I will greatly increase your pangs[37] in childbearing;
in pain you shall bring forth children,
yet your desire shall be for your husband,
and he shall rule over you."

Whereas she should have been fulfilled as a mother, she will experience great pain in becoming a mother. And whereas she should have been fulfilled in ruling in partnership with her husband, now she will desire to rule over her husband[38] and experience that "he shall rule over you." Pain in becoming a mother; anguish in the struggle for dominance in marriage.

Finally, God turns to Adam and punishes him in his role as provider and as head of the human race. Verses 17-19,

35. "The curse in Genesis involved separation or alienation from the place of blessing, or even from those who were blessed." Ross, *Creation and Blessing,* 66.

36. "'To curse' is the antonym of 'to bless' (cf. Gen 12:3). In the Bible, to curse means to invoke God's judgment on someone, usually for some particular offence." Wenham, *Genesis 1–15,* 78.

37. "The NRSV unfortunately obscures this relationship [of the man's 'toil' in 3:17 echoing the woman's 'toil' in 3:16] by translating 'pangs' in 3:16 and 'toil' in 3:17. NIV does a better job since it uses 'pains' in 3:16, reflecting the plural, and 'painful toil' in 3:17." Stratton, *Out of Eden,* 61, n. 2.

38. For the same Hebrew construction, see Gen 4:7b:

"Its [sin's] desire is for you
but you must master it."

See Bruce Waltke, "The Relationship of the Sexes in the Bible," *Crux* 19/3 (Sept. 1983), 16, with credit to Susan Foh, *Women and the Word of God* (Grand Rapids: Baker, 1981), 67-69, for pointing out the parallel between Gen 3:16 and 4:7b.

"Because you have listened to the voice of your wife, and have eaten of the tree about which I commanded you, 'You must not eat of it,'

> cursed is the ground because of you;
>   in toil you shall eat of it all the days of your life;
> thorns and thistles it will bring forth for you;
>   and you shall eat the plants of the field.
> By the sweat of your face you shall eat bread
> until you return to the ground,
>   for out of it you were taken;
> you are dust,
>   and to dust you shall return."

This is the most painful judgment of all. Instead of living in a blessed Paradise with plenty of food, people will live on an earth that God has cursed. It will produce thorns and thistles. Meaningful work becomes toil: "By the sweat of your face you shall eat bread." And then comes the ultimate punishment: "until you return to the ground, for out of it you were taken; you are dust, and to dust you shall return." Every human being is made from the ground and will return to the ground. The ultimate punishment for sin is death.

Yet there is hope, for the narrative focuses on God's curse of the serpent. Scenes 5 and 6 together form a chiasm:

A God interrogates the man; he blames the woman. (3:9-12)
   B God interrogates the woman; she blames the serpent. (3:13)
      C God curses the serpent. (3:14-15)
   B′ God punishes the woman. (3:16)
A′ God punishes the man. (3:17-19)

At the heart of this chiasm God curses the serpent and sets enmity between the serpent and its seed and the woman and her seed. It will be a drawn-out, deadly battle. It looks like a draw: "He will strike your head, and you will strike his heel."[39] But there is hope that the woman's seed will win out in the end. For God has cursed the serpent, and its crawling in the dust is a sign of its ultimate defeat.[40] It will bite the dust![41]

39. "It will *šûp* your head, and you will *šûp* its heel." Since the same verb is used for what each will do, it seems better not to follow the TNIV with, "He will *crush* your head, and you will strike his heel," but to use "strike" in both instances, as in the TNIV note and most other versions.

40. The serpent "is cursed in his mode of locomotion — simply to move from one place to another will require grovelling." Walsh, "Genesis 2:4b–3:24," *JBL* 96/2 (1977) 168.

41. The serpent crawling on its belly and seemingly eating dust is a sign of humiliation and

But meanwhile the punishment for sin must be borne. We read in verse 22, "The LORD God said, 'See the man has now become like one of us, knowing good and evil'" — that is, human beings have become independent, autonomous, determining for themselves what is good and what is evil. The LORD said, "and now, he might reach out his hand and take also from the tree of life, and eat, and live forever." Can you imagine what a disaster it would be if sinful human beings, like the ancient murderer Lamech or the modern murderer Hitler, would live forever? No matter how great the reign of terror of evil people, we know that they will all die and their evil reign will come to an end.

Verse 23 concludes: "Therefore the LORD God *sent him forth* from the garden of Eden, to till the ground from which he was taken. He *drove out* the man. . . ." Banished from the garden. Banished from Paradise. Banished from the presence of God. That is the worst punishment of all. "The expulsion of Adam and Eve from the garden was in the narrator's view the real fulfillment of the divine sentence. He regarded their alienation from the divine presence as death."[42] "He drove out" "is a stronger term than 'send out.' . . . It is often used in the Pentateuch of the expulsion of the inhabitants of Canaan (e.g., Exod 23:28-31)."[43] With this escalation of terms, the narrator would have Israel feel the awful disaster that has taken place: Adam and Eve driven out of the garden just like the Canaanites must be driven out of the Promised Land, and just like disobedient Israel will be driven out of the Promised Land into exile. Adam and Eve forfeited their place in the garden of God. "Sin separates from God. Intimacy with God is replaced with alienation from God."[44]

And there is no way back into Paradise. For we read in verse 24, "He drove out the man; and at the east of the Garden of Eden he placed the cherubim, and a sword flaming and turning to guard the way to the tree of life." The cherubim as guardians are a reminder to Israel of the two cherubim guarding the sacred ark in the tabernacle (Exod 25:22) and later in the temple. Images of cherubim were also embroidered on the curtains of the tabernacle/temple (Exod 26:1, 31; 2 Chron 3:14), warning people that sinners are not allowed in the presence of God. The story that began with God placing human beings in his beautiful Paradise ends with their expulsion from Paradise.[45] And there is

---

defeat. See Wenham, *Genesis 1–15*, 79, with references to Ps 72:9, Isa 49:23, and Mic 7:17. See also Isa 65:25.

42. Wenham, "Sanctuary Symbolism," 404.

43. Wenham, *Genesis 1–15*, 85.

44. Hamilton, *Genesis*, 210. Cf. Sailhamer, *Pentateuch as Narrative*, 40, "According to the regulations in Leviticus, if one were found to be unclean. . . . 'He must live alone; he must live *outside the camp*' (Lev 13:46)."

45. "Paradise is irreparably lost; what is left for man is a life of trouble in the shadow of a crushing riddle, a life entangled in an unbounded and completely hopeless struggle with the

no way back into the garden (presence) of God unless God removes the guarding cherubim.

God's judgment of human rebellion is a reversal of the blessings of Paradise. God's judgment of sin means banishment from the full presence of the holy God. It introduces pain in childbearing, strife for dominance in marriages, thorns and thistles in our fields and gardens, work that becomes painful toil to eke out a living, and then death. "You are dust, and to dust you shall return." It's a tragic story. It's the story of Paradise lost. And it seems that we cannot get back to the peace and harmony of Paradise. Mighty cherubim guard the way back.

And yet, we see hints of hope in this sad narrative. Could it be that in banishing his rebellious creatures from Paradise, God still extends his grace in order eventually to restore Paradise on earth? In verse 20 we read that "the man named his wife Eve, because she was the mother of all living." In spite of pain in childbirth, God's blessing of procreation would remain. The birth pangs themselves are not only a reminder of God's punishment but also a sign of God's grace. In spite of the penalty of death, the generations of human beings will continue. Eve will become "the mother of all living."

In verse 21 we see God's grace in that He "made garments of skins for the man and for his wife, and clothed them." God equips them to face the hostile environment outside the garden.[46]

But we see God's grace especially in verses 14 and 15. In cursing the serpent, God says, "Upon your belly you shall go, and dust you shall eat." The way the serpent moves on its belly is a sign that Satan will bite the dust — he will be defeated. God says further,

> "I will put enmity between you and the woman,
> and between your offspring [Heb. seed] and hers;
> he will strike your head,
> and you will strike his heel."

In this judgment of the serpent, God breaks up the unholy alliance between Satan and the woman. Instead of Satan and humanity being pitted

---

power of evil and in the end unavoidably subject to the majesty of death." Von Rad, *Genesis,* 102.

46. Gordon Hugenberger observes that God covering their nakedness shows God's grace, for it shows that he will deal with the problem of sin ("to forgive" in Hebrew = "to cover [Ps 32:1]"). Special lecture at Calvin Theological Seminary. See his *Marriage as a Covenant: A Study of Biblical Law and Ethics Governing Marriage, Developed from the Perspective of Malachi* (Leiden: Brill, 1994). Cf. Wenham, *Genesis 1–15,* 84. "Clothing, besides its obvious protective function, is one of the most pervasive of human symbols through which a person's position and role in society is signalled."

against God, God says he will draw the battle lines differently: He will put enmity between Satan and the woman and between Satan's seed and her seed. Human history will consist of a long struggle between evil and good. But in the end, God says, someone from the seed of the woman will strike the serpent's head, and the serpent will strike his heel.

This prediction the church has called the *protevangelium,* the first gospel. This is the good news that evil will not rule forever but that the seed of the woman will fatally strike the serpent's head. Genesis traces this seed of the woman from Adam to Seth to Noah to Abraham, Isaac, Jacob, and Judah. And then the rest of the Bible will follow this trail to David and to Jesus Christ.

Jesus is *the* Seed of the woman, another Adam. He too was tempted by Satan. But Jesus was much more vulnerable. Unlike Adam in Paradise, Jesus was in the wilderness, and, Matthew tells us, "He fasted forty days and forty nights, and afterwards he was famished." When Jesus was starving, Satan came to him and said, "If you are the Son of God, command these stones to become loaves of bread." But Jesus resisted the temptation. Satan tempted Jesus a second time, and then the third time he offered Jesus "all the kingdoms of the world." Jesus could become King of the universe — like God. But Jesus said, "Away with you, Satan! For it is written: 'Worship the Lord your God, and serve only him'" (Matt 4:2-10).

Unlike Adam, Jesus withstood Satan's temptations. But Satan still had that poisonous bite that could strike the heel of the seed of the woman. At Satan's instigation the people killed Jesus. It looked like a defeat for the seed of the woman; the seed of the woman died.

But an amazing thing happened. Matthew (27:51) reports that when Jesus breathed his last, "at that moment the curtain of the temple was torn in two, from top to bottom." This curtain barred people from the presence of God. This curtain was embroidered with cherubim as a reminder that sinful people cannot come into the presence of a holy God. But when Jesus died, this curtain was torn in two and the cherubim no longer blocked the way to God's presence.

Satan's victory turned into his defeat. On the third day Jesus rose from the dead and ascended to the right hand of God the Father; "from there he shall come to judge the living and the dead." The book of Revelation tells us that the first one to be judged will be Satan: "The devil who had deceived them was thrown into the lake of fire and sulfur" (Rev 20:10).

And then notice what John sees:

> Then the angel showed me *the river* of the water of life, bright as crystal, flowing from the throne of God and of the Lamb through the middle of the street of the city. On either side of the river is *the tree of life* with its twelve kinds of fruit, producing its fruit each month; and the leaves of the tree are for the

> healing of the nations. *Nothing accursed* will be found there any more. But the throne of God and of the Lamb will be in it, and his servants will worship him. . . . *Blessed* are those who wash their robes, so that they will have the right to *the tree of life* and may enter the city by the gates. (Rev 22:1-3, 14)

Paradise is not lost after all. Through Jesus Christ Paradise will be restored on earth. That is the hope and comfort for all those who suffer in this in-between time. Paradise will one day be restored on earth, and we will once again enjoy full communion with God.

> Joy to the world! the Lord is come;
> let earth receive her King.
> Let every heart prepare him room,
> and heaven and nature sing.
>
> No more let sin and sorrow grow,
> nor thorns infest the ground;
> *he comes to make his blessings flow*
> *far as the curse is found.*[47]

47. Isaac Watts, 1719, based on Ps 98.

CHAPTER 4

Cain and Abel

Genesis 4:1-26

With Genesis 4, the narrator completes the first *tôlĕdôt* (account), relating what happened to God's good creation. He has sketched the rebellion in God's kingdom. The first human pair fell for the temptation to be like God, knowing good and evil. That is, they wished to decide for themselves what is good and what is evil; they wished to be autonomous — a law unto themselves. Genesis 4 sketches what became of this rebellion in the next seven generations. It is a sad story of increasing violence. Some of the challenges for preachers will be to detect God's grace in this narrative as well as how to preach Christ.

Text and Context

The narrative unit is clear because Genesis 4:1 begins this new narrative and 5:1 begins a new *tôlĕdôt*. The literary unit is also signaled by the double inclusio,

A "Now the man knew his wife Eve" (4:1)
  B Cain and Abel bring offerings to the LORD (4:3-4)
A′ "Adam knew his wife again" (4:25)
  B′ People "began to invoke the name of the LORD." (4:26)

As to context, the Cain-Abel narrative has many similarities to the narrative of the Fall. Like Adam and Eve, Cain is tempted to sin (4:7), is warned to master it (4:7), but succumbs to the temptation (4:8), whereupon the LORD seeks him out, "Where is your brother?" (4:9) and curses him (4:11) as earlier he cursed the serpent and the ground, pronounces the penalty, "When you till the ground, it will no longer yield to you its strength" (4:12); Cain will be "hidden" from the LORD's "face" (4:14), and settles "east of Eden" (4:16).[1]

Literary Features

The narrative consists of a double plot: Cain murders Abel (4:1-16) and Cain's descendants (4:17-24). The narrator's careful literary crafting is highlighted by his use of the number "seven" or its multiples. In Genesis 4:1-17, the name "Abel" occurs seven times and the name "Cain" fourteen times. Moreover, the narrator underscores that Abel is Cain's brother by using the word "brother" seven times. The last verse of this *tôlĕdôt* (4:26) states that people "began to invoke the name of the LORD." The narrator underscores the significance of this event by making this the seventieth time he uses one of the divine names. He has used the name *'Ĕlōhîm* thirty-five times (5 × 7) in Genesis 1:1–2:3, and in this first *tôlĕdôt* (Gen 2:4–4:26) he uses several names for God a total of thirty-five times.[2] The evil Lamech is the seventh generation from Adam. In the next *tôlĕdôt,* in Genesis 5, Lamech will be contrasted with the seventh generation in the line of Seth, that is, Enoch who "walked with God."

In the first plot (Gen 4:1-17) we note a possible chiastic structure:[3]

A Cain produced "with the help of the LORD" (4:1)
 B Cain and Abel bring offerings to the LORD (4:3-4)
  C The LORD judges between Abel and Cain (4:4b-5)
   D The LORD warns Cain: "sin is lurking at the door" (4:6-7)
   D′ Cain kills his brother Abel (4:8)
  C′ The LORD judges Cain (4:9-12)
 B′ Cain pleads with the LORD and finds mercy (4:13-15)
A′ "Cain went away from the presence of the LORD" (4:16)

1. For more details, see Fishbane, *Text and Texture,* 24-27, and Alan J. Hauser, "Linguistic and Thematic Links between Genesis 4:1-16 and Genesis 2–3," *JETS* 23/4 (Dec. 1980) 297-305.

2. See Cassuto, *Commentary on Genesis,* I, 191-92, and Wenham, *Genesis 1–15,* 96.

3. Adapted from Lion-Cachet, "Die prediking oor die historiese stof van die Ou Testament," *In die Skriflig* 23/1 (1989) 31. Cf. Wenham, *Genesis 1–15,* 99:

(1) 2b-5	Narrative	Cain, Abel main actors; Yahweh passive.
(2) 6-7	Dialogue	Yahweh questioning Cain.
(3) 8	(Dialogue) narrative	Cain and Abel alone.
(4) 9-14	Dialogue	Yahweh and Cain.
(5) 15-16	Narrative	Yahweh active, Cain passive.

The Plot Line

The setting of this narrative is Adam "knowing" his wife and the birth of Cain and Abel (4:1-2). The preliminary incidents consist of Cain and Abel bringing offerings to the LORD (vv 3-4a). The occasioning incident is that the LORD has "regard for Abel and his offering" but not for Cain and his offering (vv 4a-5a). This results in Cain's anger and rising tension as to what he will do. The LORD warns Cain about sin, but Cain invites Abel "out to the field" and murders him (vv 5b-8). The tension begins to resolve when the LORD confronts Cain and curses him and seems to be fully resolved when Cain, after receiving a mark of protection, moves away from the presence of the LORD, "east of Eden" (vv 9-16). But a question remains: What will happen to the promised seed of the woman? The new narrative conflict begins when Cain "knows" his wife and receives a son (v 17). The narrator traces Cain's line through seven generations and reaches the climax with Lamech's defiant boast of killing a man for wounding him and taking vengeance seventy-sevenfold (vv 18-24). There is no hope in Cain's line for the seed of the woman. The tension is resolved when the narrator reports, "Adam knew his wife again, and she bore a son and named him Seth, for she said, 'God has appointed for me another child instead of Abel'" (v 25). The outcome of this narrative is that Seth also receives a son and "at that time people began to invoke the name of the LORD" (v 26).

We can sketch this narrative as a complex plot:

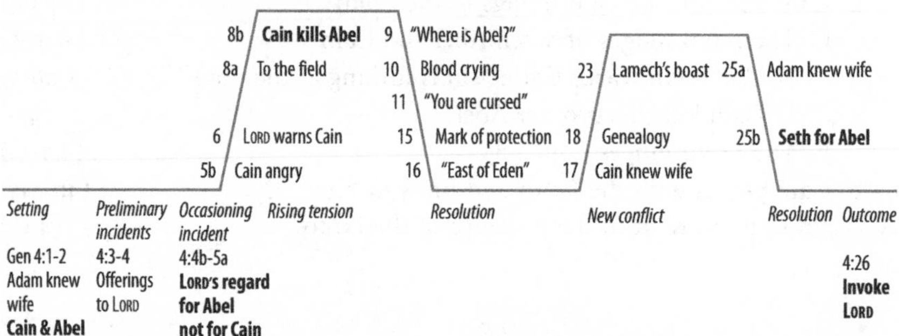

Theocentric Interpretation

Preachers frequently focus on human characters such as Cain, Abel, and Lamech, and how we should emulate or shun their behavior. Theocentric interpretation functions as a good corrective of such an anthropocentric approach and calls us back to listening to the story as God's story with humanity. What does the narrator reveal about God in this narrative?

At the beginning Eve confesses that she "produced a man with the help of the LORD." Then Cain and Abel bring an offering to the LORD. The LORD has "regard for Abel and his offering," but not for Cain and his offering. The LORD interrogates the murderer Cain and passes sentence on him. The LORD puts a mark of protection on Cain. Cain goes away from the presence of the LORD. Significantly, in the sequel about the descendants of Cain (Gen 4:17-24) we do not hear about the LORD anymore. But the narrative ends with Eve's confession that "God has appointed for me another child instead of Abel," and the final note, "At that time people began to invoke the name of the LORD."

Textual Theme and Goal

The narrative sketches the beginnings of the battle between the seed of the serpent and the seed of the woman (3:15). After relating Cain's murder of Abel and briefly tracing Cain's descendants through the seventh generation, the narrative returns to Adam and Eve and their new son Seth. Although the narrative appears to be about murder and violence, the concluding verses call attention to God's faithfulness in continuing the line of the seed of the woman. Eve's confession at the birth of Seth says as much: "God has appointed for me another child *instead of Abel,* because Cain killed him" (4:25). We can therefore formulate the textual theme as follows: *In the battle between the seed of the serpent and the seed of the woman, God provides for the continued existence of the seed of the woman.* The likely goal of the narrator is: *To assure Israel that God is faithful in maintaining in human history his covenant people.* Knowing the theme and goal for Israel, we can now look for ways to extend this theme to Jesus Christ in the New Testament.

Ways to Preach Christ

Redemptive-Historical Progression

The author of Genesis himself sketches the redemptive-historical progression of the line of the seed of the woman from Seth, the "seed" that replaced the martyred Abel (4:25), to Noah, to Abraham, Isaac, Jacob, and Judah. Beyond Genesis the trail continues to the nation of Israel (the collective seed of the woman), to its king, David, and finally to Jesus Christ, "the son of Seth, the son of Adam" (Luke 3:38), *the* Seed of the woman.

One can trace through redemptive history how God provides for the continued existence of the seed of the woman, providing Seth for the murdered

Abel, providing Abram and the barren Sarai with a son, providing Isaac and the barren Rebekah with a son, calling Israel out of Egypt, returning a remnant from the Babylonian exile, sending his own Son, pouring out the Spirit at Pentecost and growing his church on earth until Jesus returns.

Promise-Fulfillment

This narrative contains no promise of the coming Christ.

Typology

One can preach Christ from this passage with Abel-Christ typology. Abel, the seed of the woman who was killed by the seed of the serpent, is a type of Jesus Christ, *the* Seed of the woman who would be killed by Satan. Note the analogy and escalation. This typology can be supported by quoting Hebrews 12:24, which makes the same point: You have come "to Jesus, the mediator of a new covenant, and to the sprinkled blood that speaks a better word than the blood of Abel." Why a "better word than the blood of Abel"? 1 John 1:7 provides the answer: "The blood of Jesus . . . cleanses us from all sin."

Analogy

One can also preach Christ with the following analogy: As God assured Israel that he would maintain his covenant people in human history, so Christ assures his church that "the gates of Hades will not prevail against it" (Matt 16:18).

Longitudinal Themes

Longitudinal themes provides another option. One can trace through Scripture the theme of the antithesis, that is, the battle between the seed of the serpent and the seed of the woman. The battle, which God predicted in Genesis 3:15, begins here with the conflict between Cain against Abel. Later the battle broadens with Egypt against Israel (Pharaoh drowning Israel's baby boys), Canaan against Israel, and even Israel's kings against God's prophets (Matt 23:35). The New Testament shows the continuation of the battle with Herod against Jesus, Satan against Jesus, the world against the church, until the final defeat of Satan (Rev 20:10) and the victory of Christ.

New Testament References

Under typology (above) we have already noted Hebrews 12:24. In Matthew 23:35 Jesus speaks of "the blood of the righteous Abel" (par. Luke 11:51). Other New Testament passages refer to Abel but do not link him directly to Christ. For example, Hebrews 11:4 uses this narrative to illustrate that "faith is the assurance of things hoped for": "By faith Abel offered to God a more acceptable sacrifice than Cain's. . . . He died, but through his faith he still speaks." Jude 11 refers to false teachers who "go the way of Cain." And 1 John 3:12-13 admonishes, "We must not be like Cain who was from the evil one and murdered his brother. And why did he murder him? Because his own deeds were evil and his brother's righteous. Do not be astonished, brothers and sisters, that the world hates you." We can use these New Testament references to preach Christ only if we can link them to Christ.

Contrast

There is no contrast between the theme of this passage and the message of the New Testament. But preachers can possibly use the way of contrast to preach Christ from this narrative by contrasting the seed of the serpent (Cain and Lamech) with the seed of the woman (Jesus). Cain did not master the devil "lurking at the door" (4:7); Jesus mastered the devil when tempted (Matt 4:1-11). Cain took the life of his brother; Jesus gave his life for his brothers and sisters. Lamech boasted that he would be avenged "seventy-sevenfold"; Jesus taught his disciples that they should forgive "seventy-sevenfold" (Matt 18:22).

Sermon Theme and Goal

We formulated the textual theme as, "In the battle between the seed of the serpent and the seed of the woman, God provides for the continued existence of the seed of the woman." Since the New Testament confirms the message of this Old Testament narrative, the sermon theme can be practically identical to the textual theme, perhaps adding the New Testament note of Christ gaining the final victory. The sermon theme then reads, "In the battle between the seed of the serpent and the seed of the woman, God provides for the continued existence of the seed of the woman until Christ gains the final victory." We can simplify this theme somewhat by making it, *God is faithful in continuing the line of the seed of the woman till Christ gains the final victory.*

We formulated the narrator's goal as, "to assure Israel that God is faithful in maintaining in human history his covenant people." The goal in preaching this sermon can be very similar, *to assure the church that God is faithful in maintaining his people in human history till Christ gains the final victory.*

This goal points at the need addressed by this sermon, the target: God's people today fear for the continued existence of the church under the onslaught of secularism and persecution. Europe has suffered through "a hurricane of secularism," while other nations of the world have seen more Christian martyrs than ever in world history. God's people fear that the church is dying. In response to this fear, a sermon on this narrative can assure God's people that even though the battle is fierce and bloody, God is faithful and will preserve his people till Christ claims final victory over Satan.

Sermon Exposition

Genesis 4 begins: "Now the man knew his wife Eve, and she conceived and bore Cain, saying, 'I have produced a man with the help of the LORD.'" The name Cain *(qayin)* is a play on the verb "I have produced" *(qānîtî)*. More important, Eve says, "I have produced a man *('îš)* with the help of the LORD." Not just a baby, not just a boy, but a *man.* Cain, for Eve, is another Adam. A man produced with the help of the LORD. Is this the promised seed of the woman who will conquer the evil serpent?

Cain certainly has much going for him. His mother testifies that he is born "with the help of the LORD." He starts his life with the LORD. As the firstborn, according to the understanding of the Israelites, he would also have the rights of inheritance. And indeed, like his father, he is "a tiller of the ground" (4:2). Cain is the seed of the woman — so Eve must have thought.

Eve also gives birth to another son, Abel. Abel may have been a twin brother,[4] but Cain has the rights of the firstborn. Abel's name *(hebel)* means "breath," vanity, as in Ecclesiastes, "Vanity of vanities! All is vanity." And in this narrative Abel lives up to his name of being a mere breath. He is vulnerable; he is passive; he does not speak in this narrative; he does not defend himself. Abel reminds us of Isaiah's description of the Suffering Servant: "Like a lamb that is led to the slaughter, and like a sheep that before its shearers is silent, so he did not open his mouth" (Isa 53:7b).

The narrator brings out the contrast between the brothers with inverted parallelism:

4. Since the narrator here mentions only once, "the man knew his wife" (4:1).

A Eve "bore Cain" (4:1).
B "Next she bore his brother Abel" (4:2a).
B′ "Abel was a keeper of sheep" (4:2b).
A′ "Cain a tiller of the ground" (4:2c).

The narrative conflict begins with verse 3, "In the course of time Cain brought to the LORD an offering of the fruit of the ground, and Abel for his part brought of the firstlings of his flock, their fat portions. And the LORD had regard for Abel and his offering, but for Cain and his offering he had no regard." Here the narrator continues to use inverted parallelism to highlight the contrast between the two brothers:

A. Cain brought "an offering of the fruit of the ground" (4:3).
B Abel brought "of the firstlings of his flock, their fat portions" (4:4a).
B′ "The LORD had regard for Abel and his offering" (4:4b).
A′ "But for Cain and his offering he had no regard" (4:5).

The narrator highlights the contrast even further with inverted antithetic parallelism in verses 4b and 5:

A "The LORD *had regard*
B for Abel and his offering.
B′ But for Cain and his offering
A′ he had *no regard*."

The question has often been raised, Why did the LORD have regard for Abel and his offering and not for Cain and his offering? The Israelites would have known the answer instinctively. We read, "Abel for his part brought of the *firstlings* of his flock, their *fat portions*." Abel obeyed God's law which called for an offering of the very best: the firstborn, a perfect specimen, including especially the fat portions for burning on the altar.[5] Abel obeyed God's law; he showed total dedication to the LORD; he gave the very best.

Notice also that the LORD looks on the *person* before he looks at the gift. "The LORD had regard for *Abel* and his offering." The LORD looks first at the heart of a person, at the motivation, before he looks at the offering. Hebrews 11:4 says, "By *faith* Abel offered God a better sacrifice than Cain did."

Cain, by contrast, just brought some of "the fruit of the ground." The word "firstfruits" is noticeably absent.[6] His offering seems rather superficial. It is

5. See, e.g., Exod 13:2, 12; Lev 3:16; 22:17-25; 27:26; Deut. 12:6.

6. For this requirement, see, e.g., Exod 23:19, 34:26; Lev 2:14; 23:9-14.

something he has to do, but his heart isn't in it.[7] Therefore, "for *Cain* and his offering he had no regard." God bypasses Cain, the firstborn, and accepts the younger Abel — a theme that will be repeated in Genesis with the younger Isaac being chosen over Ishmael, the younger Jacob over Esau, the younger Joseph over his brothers, the younger Ephraim over Manasseh.

As a result of God's rejection, "Cain was very angry, and his countenance fell" (4:5). Cain was very angry with God for not accepting his offering. And he was jealous of his younger brother Abel. His anger even showed in his face: "His countenance fell."

But like a loving parent going after an angry child, the LORD pursued Cain. Verse 6: "The LORD said to Cain, 'Why are you angry, and why has your countenance fallen? If you do well, will you not be accepted?'" Even after the Fall into sin, the LORD suggests that Cain can still do well, that is, "do what is right" (TNIV), obey God's law. He is not a helpless victim of Satan or of Adam's original sin. He can fight sin, do well, and be accepted.

But this is followed by the warning in verse 7, "And if you do not do well, sin is lurking at the door." This is the first time the Bible uses the word *sin.* And sin is personified as a violent animal. "If you do not do well, sin is *lurking* ["crouching," TNIV] at the door," like an animal crouching to pounce on its victim. If you do not do well, you leave yourself wide open to attack by this ferocious animal.[8] Like a lion crouching for the kill. That is the picture Peter brings to mind in his first letter (5:8): "Like a roaring lion your enemy the devil prowls around, looking for someone to devour. Resist him, steadfast in your faith. . . ."

One can think of a lion. But in the context of Genesis another animal comes to mind, namely the serpent — the archenemy of Israel; the serpent that tempted Adam and Eve.[9] The serpent is ready to strike again in the second generation. This time he tempts Cain, the firstborn.

God warns Cain, "Do well." But Cain refuses to listen to God; instead he nurses his anger at God and his jealousy of his brother Abel. The story reaches a climax in verse 8, "Cain said to his brother Abel, 'Let us go out to the field.'" For Israelites, this reference to "the field" had a foreboding sound. What is Cain doing, taking his brother *out to the field?* Any crime committed in the field was considered premeditated.[10] Killing someone far away in the field muffles the

7. "Cain's sin is tokenism. He looks religious, but in his heart he is not totally dependent on God, childlike, or grateful." Waltke, *Genesis,* 97.

8. Cf. Jesus' teaching in John 8:34, "Everyone who commits sin is a slave to sin."

9. "The participle 'crouching' or 'lies' *(rōbēṣ)* is cognate to an Akkadian term used of a type of demon. The first edition of the Jewish Publication Society's *Torah* offered the translation: 'Sin is the demon at the door.'" Ross, *Creation and Blessing,* 158.

10. "In the law the circumstance that a crime is committed 'in the field,' i.e., out of range of help, is proof of premeditation; cf. Deut 22:25-27." Wenham, *Genesis 1–15,* 106.

victim's screams for help and leaves no witnesses. Surely Cain is not planning to kill his brother? But he is: "When they were in the field, Cain rose up against his brother Abel, and killed him." This is no accident; the Hebrew word *hārag* indicates that he murders his brother intentionally.[11]

"His *brother* Abel." Seven times this narrative tells us that Abel is Cain's brother. He does not kill an enemy, not even a stranger. He kills his very own brother! Unbelievable! This is what Adam and Eve's sin leads to in only the second generation: fratricide — the murder of a brother.

And no witnesses — except one. God has seen Cain's awful deed, and the tension in the narrative begins to be resolved. As with the sin of Adam and Eve, God immediately sets up court and begins to interrogate Cain.[12] Verse 9, "Then the Lord said to Cain, 'Where is your brother Abel?' He said, 'I do not know; am I my brother's keeper?'"

It's a bold-faced lie. Jesus said that the devil is "the father of lies" (John 8:44). Cain's murder and now his lie show that he has moved into the camp of the devil. When he was born, Eve thought he was the seed of the woman who would conquer the serpent. But Cain, nursing his anger against God and his jealousy of his brother, gives an opening to the devil. He intentionally kills his brother and lies to God. It is clear that Cain is not the seed of the woman. He is the seed of the serpent out to destroy the seed of the woman.

The heavenly Judge confronts Cain with his crime: "What have you done? Listen: your brother's blood is crying out to me from the ground!" (v 10). Cain has allowed himself to be mastered by Satan; he has become a traitor to the kingdom of God; he has murdered his brother Abel. Abel turns out to be the seed of the woman, and Abel's blood is crying out to the Lord from the ground.

In verse 11 the heavenly Judge pronounces sentence: "Now you are cursed from the ground, which has opened its mouth to receive your brother's blood from your hand."[13] In Genesis 3 God had cursed the serpent and cursed the ground, but God never cursed Adam and Eve: they represented the seed of the woman. Now God curses their son Cain, confirming that Cain is indeed the seed of the serpent. The enmity between the seed of the serpent and the seed of

11. Hamilton, *Genesis 1–17*, 230: "Cain kills *(hārag)* Abel. This is the common verb meaning 'to murder intentionally' and is to be distinguished from the one mentioned in the sixth commandment (*rāṣaḥ*, Exod 20:13), which also encompasses manslaughter."

12. "The remainder of the narrative (vv. 9-16) is a lawsuit. Yahweh tries Cain for his life. The narrative has close parallels to the lawsuit of Gen. 3:9ff. as the drama moves through investigation (vv. 9-10), sentence (vv. 11-12) and, finally, to banishment (v. 16)." Brueggemann, *Genesis*, 60.

13. Shed blood pollutes the land. God told Israel, "You shall not pollute the land in which you live; for blood pollutes the land . . ." (Num 35:33).

the woman will split the human race into two camps: some will be on the side of Satan, and some will be on the side of God (see 1 John 3:8-10).

God continues sentencing Cain: "When you till the ground, it will no longer yield to you its strength; you will be a fugitive and a wanderer on the earth" (v 12). The farmer Cain will be exiled from civilization.[14] What is worse, he will be exiled from the presence of God.

Cain appeals to the LORD: "My punishment is greater than I can bear! Today you have driven me away from the soil, and I shall be hidden from your face; I shall be a fugitive and a wanderer on the earth, and anyone who meets me may kill me" (vv 13-14).

The Israelites reading this story would have understood Cain's fear. A murderer could be killed at any time by "the avenger of blood." In Israel when a person had been killed, a relative of the dead person would become "the avenger of blood."[15] In American terms, Cain has a bounty on his head. "Then the LORD said to him, 'Not so; whoever kills Cain will suffer a sevenfold vengeance' [that is, complete vengeance; perfect justice]. And the LORD put a mark on Cain, so that no one who came upon him would kill him" (v 15).

We don't know what kind of mark the LORD put on Cain. The text does not tell us. That is not very important either. What matters is what the mark stood for, and that is simply amazing. Cain had switched sides in the battle between the seed of the woman and the seed of the serpent. Cain had joined forces with the devil. He had become a traitor in God's kingdom. He had murdered the seed of the woman. God rightly cursed him. Now we would expect God to condemn him.

But what happens? God puts a mark on him to protect his life. It is a mark of God's goodness and mercy. God bestows his good gifts even on traitors to his cause. As Jesus says in the Sermon on the Mount, "Your Father in heaven . . . makes his sun to rise on the evil and on the good, and sends rain on the righteous and on the unrighteous" (Matt 5:45). That's God's goodness and mercy. Even the traitor Cain receives God's mercy.

The first plot ends with verse 16, "Cain went away from the presence of the LORD, and settled in the land of Nod, east of Eden." Cain, who was produced "with the help of the LORD" (v 1), "went away from the presence of the LORD and dwelled in the land of Nod." The name of the land of Nod is a play on the verb "wandering."[16] Wherever the land of Nod is, it is "east of Eden." When

14. "In some ways it is a fate worse than death. It is to lose all sense of belonging and identification with a community. It is to become rootless and detached. . . . Cain, once a farmer, is now ousted from civilization and is to become a vagabond." Hamilton, *Genesis 1–17*, 232.

15. See, e.g., Num 35:12; Deut 19:1-13; Josh 20:1-9.

16. "He who had been sentenced to *nād* settles in the land of *nôd*. The wanderer ends up in the land of wandering." Hamilton, *Genesis 1–17*, 235.

Adam and Eve fell into sin, they were driven out of the garden, away from the presence of God, "east of Eden." Now Cain is forced to move even further away from God's holy presence, "east of Eden."[17]

But God's mercy goes with him. God's curse on Cain does not entirely remove God's original blessing, "Be fruitful and multiply." We read in verse 17, "Cain knew his wife, and she conceived and bore Enoch; and he built a city, and named it Enoch after his son Enoch." Cain is seeking security in a human fortress. In Genesis, Cain's city anticipates the later city of Babel (Gen 11), built in defiance of God's command to "fill the earth." Augustine rightly observed that "Cain was the first-born, and he belonged to the city of men; after him was born Abel, who belonged to the city of God."[18] In quick succession the narrator speeds down Cain's genealogy to the seventh generation, and then stops at Lamech, whose family reveals both the height of the development of culture and the depth of sin in the human race: "To Enoch was born Irad; and Irad was the father of Mehujael, and Mehujael the father of Methushael, and Methushael the father of Lamech" (4:18). Lamech represents the seventh generation from Adam in the line of Cain. Lamech is special.

The narrator highlights the tremendous cultural developments in this line of the seed of the serpent.[19] Verse 19, "Lamech took two wives; the name of the one was Adah, and the name of the other Zillah. Adah bore Jabal; he was the ancestor of those who live in tents and have livestock. His brother's name was Jubal; he was the ancestor of all those who play the lyre and pipe. Zillah bore Tubal-cain, who made all kinds of bronze and iron tools." Again we see God's goodness and mercy in the cultural developments that enable people to cope and experience some joy in a harsh environment under God's curse.

But all is not well. Lamech, in the seventh generation, breaks God's creation order of marriage between one man and one woman. He marries *two* women. And then he begins to brag to these two wives (v 23):

17. "The author's mention of the direction 'eastward' is not a mere geographical detail. Throughout Genesis, the author carefully apprises the reader of the direction of the characters' movement. In doing so, he plants a narrative clue to the meaning of the events he is recounting. At this point in the narrative, 'eastward' has only the significance of 'outside the garden.' Later in the book, however, the author will carry this significance further by showing 'eastward' to be the direction of the 'city of Babylon' (11:2) and the 'cities of Sodom and Gomorrah' (13:11). Moreover, he will show that to return from the east is to return to the Promised Land and to return to the 'city of Salem'" (14:17-20). Sailhamer, *Pentateuch as Narrative,* 110-11.

18. Augustine, *The City of God,* trans. Marcus Dods (New York: Random House, 1950), XV.1 (pp. 478-79).

19. "It should not escape our attention that from the very beginning, the greatest development is to be found not among those who fear the Lord but among unbelievers. Apparently the unbelievers' drive for independence from the Lord is stronger than the believer's drive to serve the Lord." De Graaf, *Promise and Deliverance,* I, 54.

Lamech said to his wives:
"Adah and Zillah, hear my voice;
you wives of Lamech, listen to what I say:
I have killed a man for wounding me,
a young man for striking me.
If Cain is avenged sevenfold,
truly Lamech seventy-sevenfold."

Lamech is a brutal killer. God's law for Israel demanded that punishment must fit the crime: "life for life, eye for eye, tooth for tooth, . . . [and, the very words of Lamech] wound for wound, stripe for stripe" (Exod 21:23-25). But Lamech moves far beyond this principle of justice: He *kills* a man for wounding him, a young man for striking him. And then he brags,

"If Cain is avenged sevenfold,
truly Lamech seventy-sevenfold."

He takes God's words to Cain of complete vengeance and goes them seventy times better. He vows unending vengeance. No one, but no one, will touch the violent Lamech. He does not need God's protection. He can fend for himself.

The story is almost finished. The narrator has sketched the awful development of sin in human history. Only seven generations from Adam, a complete number of generations, and sin has come to full fruition: human beings boast about their power to defend themselves; they don't need God; they don't need his law; they themselves will decide what is good and what is evil (3:4); they can be gods for themselves. This is the sin of Adam and Eve, only far more defiant. With their cultural developments, they can fend for themselves. Only seven generations, and humanity has disintegrated from a world where God was worshiped and adored to a world where humans think they can live without God.

But instead of ending the narrative on this awful note, the narrator flashes back to Adam and Eve again. Verse 25, "Adam knew his wife again, and she bore a son and named him Seth, for she said, 'God has appointed for me another child instead of Abel, because Cain killed him.'" Eve now knows that Cain was not the promised seed of the woman. The younger Abel was. And Cain killed him. But in his faithfulness, "God has appointed me another child (*zeraʿ*, seed) instead of Abel, because Cain killed him." "Eve's use of the word *zeraʿ* in 4:25 associates the birth of Seth with the earlier divine pronouncement of judgement upon the serpent [3:15]."[20]

20. Alexander, "From Adam to Judah," *EvQ* 61 (1989) 15. "In such narratives as these, the author clearly betrays his interest in the 'seed' (*zeraʿ*, 3:15) of the woman. Chapter 5 shows just how seriously the author takes the promise in 3:15. The focus is on the 'seed' and the one who

The point of this narrative now becomes clear: In the battle between the seed of the serpent and the seed of the woman, God is faithful in continuing the line of the seed of the woman.

The narrator concludes with the significant observation, "To Seth also a son was born, and he named him Enosh [that is, 'weakness']. At that time people began to invoke the name of the LORD" (v 26) — as Abram would later invoke or "call on" the name of the LORD" (12:8; 13:4). In the line of Cain we see rich cultural developments but increasingly people declaring that they don't need God. In this line of the seed of the woman we see people who are weak, a mere breath (Abel), but people who "call on the name of the LORD." They recognize their dependence on the LORD, their King, and make the LORD central in their lives: they pray to God and worship him. As Ken Mathews puts it, "Cain's firstborn and successors pioneer cities and civilized arts, but Seth's firstborn and successors pioneer worship."[21]

The narrator accentuates this positive development by making this the seventieth time he uses the divine name. In the creation narrative he uses *'Ĕlōhîm* thirty-five times and in the following *tôlĕdôt* (Gen 2:4–4:26) he uses several divine names a total of thirty-five times. This seventieth time he uses God's name is very special. In contrast to the seed of the serpent sketched in the line of Cain, in this line of Seth people "began to invoke the name of the LORD." This is the line of the seed of the woman (cf. 1 John 3:8-10).

God is faithful in continuing the line of the seed of the woman. If God would not have been faithful, this line would have ended with the death of Abel. But God raised up Seth and his descendants to continue his people on earth. This also means, of course, that the bitter battle with the seed of the serpent continues.

Abel was the first of many martyrs. The Egyptians drowned the Israelite boys in the river Nile. Jezebel killed so many prophets of the LORD that Elijah thought he was the only one left. But God kept the seed of the woman alive until the Messiah could be born. Finally Satan managed to kill *the* Seed of the woman, Jesus Christ. And the persecution did not stop there. Jesus had warned his disciples: "I am sending you out like sheep into the midst of wolves. . . . You will be hated by all because of my name. . . . A disciple is not above the teacher . . ." (Matt 10:16, 22, 24). Soon these words came true.

A mob stoned the deacon Stephen; Herod Agrippa killed James; the Romans killed the apostles Peter and Paul. The early church suffered great persecution which resulted in many Christian martyrs. But the church fathers saw

---

will crush the head of the snake. A pattern is established in chapter 4 that will remain the thematic center of the book." Sailhamer, *Pentateuch as Narrative,* 69.

21. Mathews, *Genesis 1–11:26,* 291-92.

rightly that the blood of the martyrs was the seed of the church. In the battle between the seed of the serpent and the seed of the woman, God has provided for the continued existence of the seed of the woman to this very day.

We may think that we are not involved in this battle. The church in North America lives in relative peace today. But we *are* involved in this battle. We belong to the one church of Jesus Christ. And our brothers and sisters are being martyred all around us. The twentieth century has seen more Christian martyrs than fell in all the preceding nineteen centuries. A recent book puts the number of Christian martyrs in the twentieth century at a staggering 45 million people. The author estimates that since 1990 every year an average of 160,000 Christians have been killed in countries all around us.[22] How will we respond if the battle comes to our country? How will we react when martyrs fall in the United States, in our state, in our town?

John's first letter is instructive. He writes this letter to a persecuted church: "We must not be like Cain who was from the evil one and murdered his brother. And why did he murder him? Because his own deeds were evil and his brother's righteous. Do not be astonished, brothers and sisters, that the world hates you" (1 John 3:12-13). John continues by telling his readers about "the spirit of the antichrist, of which you have heard that it is coming, and now is already in the world." And then he writes, "Little children, you are from God, and have conquered them; for the one who is in you is greater than the one who is in the world" (1 John 4:3-4). The seed of the woman will conquer even under the pressure of persecution today "because the one who is in you is greater than the one who is in the world." We will be victorious in the battle against Satan because Jesus poured his Spirit into our hearts. No matter how hard the battle, God is faithful in preserving his church till Christ comes again to establish his kingdom in perfection.[23]

22. David Barrett and Todd M. Johnson, *World Christian Encyclopedia* (2d ed.; New York: Oxford University Press, 2001), I, 11.

23. My sermon based on this research is found in Appendix 4.

CHAPTER 5

Noah and the Flood

Genesis 6:9–9:17

One of the challenges preachers face in preparing a sermon on the narrative of the flood is its length. With a text covering more than three chapters, how does one stay within the expected time-limits for Scripture reading and sermon? Depending on the circumstances, one can perhaps read the entire narrative before the sermon, but it may be better to read only selected narrative portions such as Genesis 6:9-22; 7:11–8:3a; 8:13-22; and 9:8-17. Or one can read only a few key verses, such as Genesis 6:11-14, 18-19; 7:11-12; 8:1; and 9:8-10. Or one can consider doing what I did: Before preaching this lengthy narrative, I read only its beginning (Genesis 6:9-22) and then invited the congregation to keep their Bibles open so that we could read together other selected sections as the narrative unfolded.

Text and Context

From Cain's murder and Lamech's proud boasting about murder, Genesis 6 continues to develop the theme of the spread of sin and violence: "The LORD saw that the wickedness of humankind was great in the earth, and that every inclination of the thoughts of their hearts was only evil continually. . . . Now the earth was corrupt in God's sight, and the earth was filled with violence" (6:5, 11). The narrative of the flood discloses the final outcome of human sin and violence: God's judgment and death.

Though some begin the narrative of the flood with Genesis 6:5, the narrative proper begins with Genesis 6:9 which opens a new *tôlědôt,* "These are the descendants of Noah." The narrative takes us through the rising flood and the receding flood, and ends with God establishing his covenant with "all flesh that is on earth" (9:17). This conclusion of the narrative unit is confirmed because

Genesis 9:18 begins a new narrative. Some scholars end the narrative earlier, at 8:22, God's resolve not to destroy humankind.[1] Although this is a more manageable text for one sermon and chapter 9:1-17 provides more than enough material for another sermon, the narrative proper does not end till chapter 9:17.

This narrative unit is confirmed by a chiastic structure:[2]

Transitional introduction (6:9-10)
  A Violence in God's creation (6:11-12)
    B First divine address: resolution to destroy (6:13-22)
      C Second divine address: command to enter the ark (7:1-10)
        D Beginning of the flood (7:11-16)
          E The rising flood waters (7:17-24)
            GOD'S REMEMBRANCE OF NOAH
          E′ The receding flood waters (8:1-5)
        D′ The drying of the earth (8:6-14)
      C′ Third divine address: command to leave the ark (8:15-19)
    B′ God's resolution to preserve order (8:20-22)
  A′ Fourth divine address: covenant blessing and peace (9:1-17)
Transitional conclusion (9:18-19)

The value of this chiastic structure is not only that it confirms the narrative unit, but it also shows that this narrative is carefully crafted,[3] it gives us an overall view showing parallels between various parts, and it clearly exposes the central point of the narrative: "God remembered Noah."

Understanding this narrative in its literary context reveals many similarities between the flood narrative and the creation narrative of Genesis 1. In both we have the *tĕhôm,* "the deep" (7:11; 8:2; cf. 1:2), the earth covered by water (7:24;

1. See the chiasm suggested by Ross, *Creation and Blessing,* 191.

2. First proposed by Anderson, "From Analysis to Synthesis," *JBL* 97 (1978) 38, and since supported by many scholars: see, e.g., Wenham, *Genesis 1–15,* 156, and Turner, *Genesis,* 43. I have changed Anderson's numbers 1 through 10 to the current convention of capital letters. For a more detailed chiastic structure (A through P, also centering on "God remembers Noah"), see Wenham, "The Coherence of the Flood Narrative," *VT* 28 (1978) 338.

3. Wenham, *Genesis 1–15,* 157, also alerts us to the parallel number of days inverted after 8:1:

7 days of waiting for flood (7:4)
  7 days of waiting for flood (7:10)
    40 days of flood (7:17a)
      150 days of water triumphing (7:24)
      150 days of water waning (8:3)
    40 days' wait (8:6)
  7 days' wait (8:10)
7 days' wait (8:12)

cf. 1:2), the *rûaḥ* (Spirit or wind) of God over the waters (8:1; cf. 1:2), the waters recede (8:1-5; cf. 1:9), dry land appears (8:5; cf. 1:9), the classification of animals (6:20; 7:14, 21, 23; cf. 1:21, 24-25), God blessed them (9:1; cf. 1:28), "be fruitful and multiply" (8:17, 9:1, 7; cf. 1:28), and human beings in God's image (9:6; cf. 1:27).[4] In other words, the narrator wishes us to understand that the flood is the undoing of creation and the world after the flood is a new creation, or at least God's new beginning with his creation.

Further, just as Adam had three sons, of which Cain was cursed and Seth would carry on the line of the seed of the woman, so Noah has three sons, of whom Canaan (son of Ham and father of the Canaanites) is cursed (9:25) and Shem is blessed (9:26) to carry on the line of the seed of the woman.

Literary Features

As the narrator of this account sought to link Israel's history via the patriarchs back to the beginning of time, he apparently made use of contemporary accounts of a great flood. Gordon Wenham has helpfully diagramed the similarities[5] as well as the differences. For preaching purposes the differences are more important, for they enable us to spot the specific emphases of the biblical author. Whereas Mesopotamian accounts speak of many gods who were angry at human noise and overpopulation, the biblical author speaks of a single God who is "grieved to his heart" (Gen 6:6) at human "wickedness" (6:5), which is destroying his good creation with "corruption" and "violence" (6:11-13). Whereas the pagan accounts tell of the gods being terrified and helpless once the flood has started ("The gods became frightened of the deluge, They shrank back and went up to Anu's highest heaven"[6]), the biblical author sees God as sovereign, in full control of the rising flood ("forty days" of rain, 7:12, 17) and its recession ("God made a wind blow over the earth, and the waters subsided," 8:1). And whereas the Mesopotamian gods after the flood wished to limit hu-

4. Sailhamer, *Genesis,* 94, seeks to make a case for the repetition of the ten words of creation, "God said," in the flood account, but he counts as the first "God said" Gen 6:7a, which is before the narrative proper as delineated by the new *tôlĕdôt* at 6:9. For a detailed listing of "parallel thoughts and theme-words," see Rendsburg, *Redaction of Genesis,* 9-12. Cf. Mathews, *Genesis 1–11:26,* 383.

5. These accounts include a "divine decision to destroy mankind, warning to flood hero, command to build ark, hero's obedience, command to enter, entry, closing door, description of flood, destruction of life, end of rain, etc., ark grounding on mountain, hero opens window, birds' reconnaissance, exit, sacrifice, divine smelling of sacrifice, and blessing of flood hero." Wenham, *Genesis 1–15,* 163-64.

6. *Gilgamesh,* Tablet XI, lines 113-14.

man population growth, the biblical author notes that God encouraged population growth as he did at the creation: "Be fruitful and multiply" (9:1, 7).[7]

The narrator again is omniscient: he sees what God sees (6:12) and knows what God says "in his heart" (8:21). He begins the story by sharing God's point of view. John Sailhamer explains, "We, the readers, are allowed to look down from heaven over all the earth and see what the Lord himself sees; we are allowed to listen in on his conversations and follow his judgments (6:5–7:5). With the onset of the Flood, however, we lose our privileged position. We no longer see what God sees. . . . Our perspective is horizontal. . . . With Noah, we must wait for the waters to recede and rely only on the return of the raven and the dove sent out through the little window of the ark (8:5-14). Once the dry land has appeared (8:14), the reader's perspective returns to that of the Lord in heaven, and we hear and see his point of view as at the beginning of the story."[8]

The Plot Line

Although one can seek to divide this narrative into various scenes,[9] for preaching the plot line is much more important, for this not only shows the tension in and the point of the narrative but it also aids in retelling the story in a narrative sermon form.

The setting for this narrative is the narrator's statement that Noah is a righteous man, walking with God (6:9-10). The preliminary incident consists of God seeing that the earth is corrupt and filled with violence (6:11-12). The occasioning incident is God's decision to destroy all flesh (6:13). What will happen to the seed of the woman? The tension rises as God commands Noah to make an ark (6:14), enter it (7:1), take with him his family and selected animals (7:2), "for in seven days I will send rain . . . for forty days" (7:4). Noah, his family, and the animals enter the ark (7:7-9); then "the fountains of the great deep burst forth, and the windows of the heavens were opened" (7:11). It rains for forty days (7:12). The water bears up the ark (7:17); the waters swell and cover the mountains (7:19), and all flesh on earth dies (7:22), except for those in the ark (7:23). "The waters swelled on the earth for one hundred fifty days" (7:24).

The narrative turns toward resolution with the key statement, "But God remembered Noah" (8:1a). God makes a wind blow (8:1b), and closes the fountains and windows (8:2). The waters begins to recede (8:3), subsiding for forty

7. Wenham, *Genesis 1–15*, xlix and 164-66. See also Hamilton, *Handbook on the Pentateuch*, 66-72.

8. Sailhamer, *Genesis*, 79-80.

9. Wenham's result of ten scenes is debatable (6:22 a scene?) and not very helpful. See his *Genesis 1–15*, 157-58.

days (8:6). Then Noah sends out a raven (8:7), and three times a dove (8:8-12). Finally the earth is dry (8:13), and God commands him, "Go out of the ark" (8:16). Noah and his family go out and the tension is resolved.

The outcome is that Noah builds "an altar to the LORD" (8:20), and the LORD promises, "I will never again curse the ground" (8:21) but maintain the regularity of the seasons (8:22). The LORD blesses Noah and his family (9:1a), gives regulations for life on this cleansed earth (9:1b-7), establishes his covenant with them and every living creature (9:8-10), promising never again to send such a flood (9:11) and appointing the rainbow as sign of his covenant (9:13-17).

We can sketch the plot line of this lengthy narrative as a single plot:

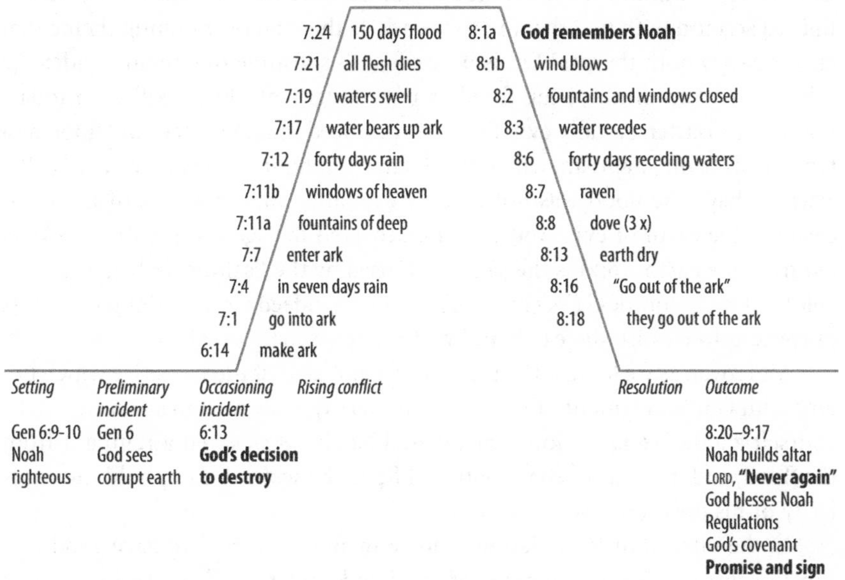

Theocentric Interpretation

The theocentric emphasis, as in the creation narrative, is obvious. God is the main actor: "God saw that the earth was corrupt" (6:12); he "determined to make an end of all flesh" (6:13); he commanded Noah to make an ark (6:14); he commanded Noah, "Go into the ark" (7:1); he promised to send rain in seven days (7:4); he closed the hatch (7:16); he "remembered Noah" and "made a wind blow over the earth" (8:1); he told Noah, "Go out of the ark" (8:15); he said in his heart, "Never again," and promised to maintain the regular order of nature (8:21-22); he blessed Noah and gave him detailed instructions (9:1-7); and he made a covenant with Noah and all living creatures, promising never again to send such a disastrous flood and appointing the rainbow as its sign (9:8-17).

Besides God, the other main character in this narrative is Noah. Noah does not have a single line in this drama, but his actions speak louder than words: he "walked with God" (6:9); "he did all that God commanded him" (6:22; 7:5, 9, 16); he "built an altar to the LORD" and offered burnt offerings to the LORD (8:20). Noah's life is totally God-directed.

Textual Theme and Goal

This narrative seems to have a dual theme: God judges all flesh with a flood *and* God saves a remnant from the flood. But homiletically we cannot develop a unified sermon with two themes, so we ask, Is there an overarching theme that encompasses both themes? Or, is it possible to subsume one theme under the other? I used to think of the flood as pure judgment: floods kill even today; floods are disasters, totally evil. But then I noticed that Peter sees the flood as a type of baptism: "Baptism, which this [water] prefigured, now saves you" (1 Pet 3:21). Perhaps the flood was not entirely evil; after all, the waters of the flood cleansed the earth of evil. And then I discovered that God's intention to "*blot out* from the earth" (6:7) is the same verb used by the Psalmist in begging God, "blot out my iniquities" (Ps 51:1, 9). The flood is indeed God's judgment, but its purpose is to cleanse the earth and make a new start.

Moreover, as we look at the plot line, we notice that the narrative which begins with God's judgment of the flood tilts very quickly to God's mercy: "Make yourself an ark" (6:14), "God remembered Noah" (8:1), saved a remnant from the flood, and made a covenant with "all flesh," henceforth to uphold the regularity of his creation.

In the interest of formulating a single theme, we therefore have good reason to subsume God's judgment of the flood under God's grace in saving a remnant. Accordingly, we can formulate the single theme somewhat as follows: *Even as God judges the world for human sin and violence, in his grace he continues his kingdom on earth by making a new start with Noah, his family, and selected animals.*

Given this theme, what could have been the narrator's goal with this message for Israel? It could have been simply to teach them about God's justice: punishment for the wicked and salvation for the "righteous" (6:9). Or, at a more existential level, the narrator's goal could have been to warn them against violence and to motivate them to live righteously. But these goals seem rather superficial and moralistic (Don't be wicked like the world; be righteous like Noah). Hearing this message in Israel's historical context will lead to a deeper, more relevant goal.

Suppose Israel first heard this message in Moab after their forty-year desert journey. This generation had witnessed God's judgment on their parents and grandparents who died in the desert for their wickedness. How would they hear the message, "Even as God judges the world for human sin and violence, in his grace he continues his kingdom on earth by making a new start with Noah, his family, and selected animals"? Would they not see themselves as another remnant with which God was about to make a new start in the Promised Land? The narrator's goal would then be, to encourage Israel with the message that, though God judges wickedness, in his grace he will save a remnant to continue his good kingdom on earth.

The goal would have been similar for Israel in exile. The exile for them was like the flood, "the collapse of the known world."[10] But while Israel was undergoing God's judgment, God encouraged the exiles through the prophet (Isa 54:9-10):

> This is like the days of Noah to me:
> Just as I swore that the waters of Noah
> would never again go over the earth,
> so I have sworn that I will not be angry with you
> and will not rebuke you.
> For the mountains may depart
> and the hills be removed,
> but my steadfast love shall not depart from you,
> and my covenant of peace shall not be removed,
> says the Lord, who has compassion on you.

Thus in the setting of the exile, the goal of the flood narrative would also have been, *to encourage Israel with the message that, though God judges wickedness, in his grace he will save a remnant to continue his good kingdom on earth.*

Ways to Preach Christ

As we explore ways to preach Christ from this narrative, we should keep in mind the theme, "Even as God judges the world for human sin and violence, in his grace he continues his kingdom on earth by making a new start with Noah, his family, and selected animals.

Redemptive-Historical Progression

In making a new start with Noah, clearly another Adam and the seed of the

10. Brueggemann, *Genesis,* 87.

woman (walking with God), God ultimately prepares the way for *the* seed of the woman, Jesus Christ. One can follow the same trail that we noted in Genesis 4 with the birth of Seth. The author of Genesis himself sketches the redemptive-historical progression of the line of the seed of the woman from Seth, the "seed" that replaced the martyred Abel (4:25), to Noah and the "blessed" Shem (9:26), to Abraham, Isaac, Jacob, and Judah. Beyond Genesis the trail continues to the nation of Israel (the collective seed of the woman), to its king, David, and finally to Jesus Christ, "the son of Noah" (Luke 3:36), *the* Seed of the woman.

Another way to use redemptive-historical progression is to focus on the flood as God's judgment of human sin. After the flood we meet God's judgment of sin at crucial junctures in redemptive history. We see God's judgment of human sin at the tower of Babel where God again "sees" and judges by confusing "the language of all the earth" (Gen 11:5, 9). We see God's judgment again when God completely destroys Sodom and Gomorrah (Gen 19). We see God's judgment of Israel when a whole generation is not allowed to enter the Promised Land but dies in the desert (Num 14:20-23). We see God's judgment again in the deportation of Israel to Assyria (722 B.C.) and of Judah to Babylon (587 B.C.). Finally we see God's judgment of human sin at Calvary, where Jesus' "blood of the covenant . . . is poured out for many for the forgiveness of sins" (Matt 26:28). All these judgments of God are precursors of God's final judgment at Jesus' Second Coming (Matt 24:39) when "the heavens will be set ablaze and dissolved, and the elements will melt with fire" (2 Pet 3:12) and all will be judged by the heavenly Judge on the "great white throne" (Rev 20:11-15). Note that in his grace, as in the flood narrative, God rescues a remnant from each of these judgments.

Promise-Fulfillment

This narrative contains no direct messianic promise. God does promise to save a remnant and establish his covenant with them (6:17-20). Although this promise was fulfilled right after the flood (8:20–9:17), it becomes a pattern in subsequent redemptive history, a promise that keeps filling up till the final fulfillment of eternal salvation through the blood of the new covenant of Jesus Christ (Matt 26:28).

God also promises never again to send such a flood and guarantees the regularity of the seasons. Although these promises do not directly involve Jesus Christ as fulfillment (but see Col 1:17), given God's acknowledgment that "the inclination of the human heart is evil from youth" (8:21), God can keep these promises only because in the fullness of time Jesus will take away "the sin of the world" (John 1:29; 1 John 2:2).

Typology

Noah is clearly a type of Jesus Christ. Noah is the seed of the woman, a new Adam representing the human race (cf. Rom 5:14), "a righteous man, blameless in his generation . . . , [who] walked with God" (Gen 6:9), a person who obeyed God without question (Gen 6:22; 7:5, 9, 16; 8:18), a person through whom God made a new start with his world. But Christ is greater than Noah. Through Christ God makes a completely new start with his people: he gives them clean hearts and the hope of a new creation that is "free from its bondage to decay" (Rom 8:21), "new heavens and a new earth, where righteousness is at home" (2 Pet 3:13).

The flood, too, is a type of God's judgment of human sin — a judgment that forms a pattern in redemptive history and culminates in God's final judgment, "the day of God" when "the heavens will be set ablaze and dissolved, and the elements will melt with fire" (2 Pet 3:12). The connection between God's final judgment and Jesus is that Jesus on the cross endured God's judgment for human sin and Jesus will be the Judge who will save some and condemn others. As Jesus says, "When the Son of Man comes in his glory . . . , he will sit on the throne of his glory. All the nations will be gathered before him, and he will separate people one from another as a shepherd separates the sheep from the goats . . ." (Matt 25:31-46; cf. Acts 17:31).

Peter also uses a form of typology to link the salvation from the waters of the flood with the waters of baptism and Jesus Christ. He writes, "Eight persons were saved through water. And baptism, which this prefigured *(antitypon)*, now saves you — not as a removal of dirt from the body, but as an appeal to God for a good conscience, through the resurrection of Jesus Christ" (1 Pet 3:20-21).[11]

11. Some commentators understand Noah's burnt offerings from the perspective of Leviticus 1: Noah does what God's law prescribes; he brings burnt offerings of clean animals and birds, turning "the whole into smoke on the altar as a burnt offering, an offering by fire of pleasing odor to the LORD" (Lev 1:9, 13, 17). The burnt offerings are understood as offerings that appease God; they atone for sin. This position leads to the conclusion that God makes his covenant with the creation only because Noah's offerings atone for sin. Thus these burnt offerings are seen as a type of Jesus' offering at Calvary that atoned for the sin of the world. Only through Jesus' atoning death does God uphold his creation order so that we can live in an orderly world. However, there are good reasons to see these particular burnt offerings not as atonement offerings but as thank and dedication offerings. First, the narrative describes a pre-Israelite setting. Second, Noah is described as "righteous." Third, it is precisely because God acknowledges the presence of human evil that he says "never again" (8:21). And fourth, the covenant God makes here is an unconditional, "Royal Grant" type of covenant (see *The NIV Study Bible* at Gen 9).

Analogy

Analogy can also be used as a bridge to preaching Christ. For example, as God encouraged Israel with the message that, though God judges wickedness, in his grace he will save a remnant to continue his good kingdom on earth, so Jesus teaches that on "the day of the Son of Man" he will judge many but save a remnant. This claim can be supported by New Testament references such as Jesus' analogy, "For as the days of Noah were, so will be the coming of the Son of Man" — unexpected; moreover, "one will be taken and one will be left" (Matt 24:37-41; cf. 25:31-46).

Longitudinal Themes

One can also use longitudinal themes to move from this narrative to Christ in the New Testament. One can use the theme of God making new beginnings, saving a remnant to continue his kingdom on earth: from the remnant saved from the flood, to Abram and Sarai called to the Promised Land after the dispersion at Babel, to the remnant of Israel saved to enter the Promised Land after forty years of death in the desert, to the remnant of Israel saved from Babylonian exile to return to the Promised Land, to the new beginning God makes by sending his only Son, to the continuation of this new beginning through Jesus' disciples and the church, to the remnant saved from the final judgment to inherit the new creation.

One may also be able to use the longitudinal theme of God's covenant with all creation leading to "the eternal covenant" made by the blood of Christ (Heb 13:20), whose powerful word "sustains all things" (Heb 1:3; cf. Col 1:17), culminating in God's perfect kingdom when Jesus comes again (Rev 21–22).

New Testament References

In addition to the New Testament references mentioned above, one can also consider the following passages.

2 Corinthians 5:17, "If anyone is in Christ, there is a new creation. . . ."

Hebrews 11:7, "By faith Noah, warned by God about events as yet unseen, respected the warning and built an ark. . . ."

2 Peter 2:5, "And if he [God] did not spare the ancient world, even though he saved Noah. . . ."

2 Peter 3:6-7, "Through which the world of that time was deluged with wa-

ter and perished. But by the same word the present heavens and earth have been reserved for fire. . . ."

Revelation 21:1, "Then I saw a new heaven and a new earth; . . . and *the sea* was no more."

Of course, one can use these New Testament passages as a bridge to Christ only when one can clearly link them in the sermon to Jesus Christ.

Contrast

There is no contrast between this message of the Old Testament about God's grace in his judgment and that of the New Testament.

Sermon Theme and Goal

We formulated the textual theme as, "Even as God judges the world for human sin and violence, in his grace he continues his kingdom on earth by making a new start with Noah, his family, and selected animals." Since the New Testament confirms this basic theme but shows a final new beginning with Christ and those in him, we can formulate the sermon theme as, "Even as God judges the world for human sin and violence, in his grace he continues his kingdom on earth by making a new start with the seed of the woman (Noah and later Christ)." Although this is a good working theme, it is probably too long and involved to be used in the sermon. A shorter, more memorable sermon theme would be, *God makes new beginnings to continue his good kingdom on earth.*

The sermon goal should be in harmony with the narrator's goal for Israel. We noted that the narrator's goal was "to encourage Israel with the message that though God judges wickedness, in his grace he will save a remnant to continue his good kingdom on earth." The sermon goal can follow suit: *to encourage God's people today with the message that though God judges wickedness, he will save a remnant to continue his good kingdom on earth.* This goal indicates that the target for this sermon is the discouragement of people today who fail to see the reality of God's coming kingdom in the here and now.

Sermon Exposition

Genesis 6:9 begins a new *tôlĕdôt* ("account," "family history"): "These are the descendants of Noah." This is the third of ten such "accounts" in Genesis (cf.

2:4; 5:1). The narrator immediately provides some rare (for Hebrew narrative) but significant character description: "Noah was a righteous man, blameless in his generation; Noah walked with God." The words characterize Noah in ascending order: he was "righteous" *(ṣaddîq),* living in the right relationship with God, his neighbors, and all God's creatures; he was "blameless" (*tāmîm;* cf. 17:1), walking "with integrity of heart";[12] and "he walked with God," as only Enoch did before him (5:22, 24). This character description of Noah stands in sharp contrast to the violence, lawlessness, and godlessness of his contemporaries. Note the threefold repetition: "The earth was corrupt *(šāḥat)* in God's sight, and the earth was filled with violence. And God saw that the earth was corrupt *(šāḥat);* for all flesh had corrupted *(šāḥat)* its ways upon the earth" (6:11-12).[13]

"God *saw* that the earth was corrupt." In the beginning, when God created his kingdom on earth, "God saw everything that he had made, and, indeed, it was very good" (1:31). But now "God saw that the earth was corrupt"[14] — ruined like a spoiled potter's vessel (Jer 18:4). "And the earth was filled with violence" — such violence as to make the ordered development of society impossible (cf. Lamech's boast, 4:23-24). The earth no longer honored its Creator King; it was no longer a manifestation of the good kingdom of God. It grieved God to see this corruption of his beautiful creation; "it grieved him to his heart" (6:6).[15] What will God do to his ruined handiwork? Will he smash it as a potter smashes a spoiled clay pot?

The narrative conflict is generated when God says to Noah, "I have determined to make an end of all flesh, for the earth is filled with violence because of them; now I am going to destroy them along with the earth" (6:13). The heavenly Judge has seen the evidence of diabolical evil and pronounces sentence. But God's judgment is infused with redeeming grace. God intends to save a remnant: Noah, his family, and a selection of animals, for God instructs Noah to build an ark: a huge wooden vessel 450 feet long (140 m), 75 feet wide (23 m), and 45 feet high (13.5 m). And Noah obeys God's commands without question (6:22; cf. 7:5, 9, 16; 8:18). The narrator's repeated, Noah "did all that

12. See the synonymous parallelism in Ps 101:2. Fretheim, "Genesis," 390, comments, "This term [*tāmîm*], typical in ritual contexts for an unblemished animal, does not mean that Noah is sinless; rather he is a person of high integrity (see Ps 15:2-5)."

13. "Corruption *(šāḥat)* involves ruin, decadence, or decay, the effect of violence; it stands over against the 'good' God saw in chap. 1." Fretheim, "Genesis," 390. Cf. Turner, *Genesis,* 46, "The same root is employed to show that God's punishment will fit the crime, 'I am going to destroy *(šḥt)* them' (6.13)."

14. "The parallelism in the Hebrew text of these two passages is evident and obviously intentional." Rendtorff, "Covenant," *JBL* 108/3 (1989) 386.

15. Note the contrast between God's "grief" and the anger of the Mesopotamian gods about human noise.

God commanded him," calls attention to the fact that Noah indeed "walked with God."

God repeats, "For my part, I am going to bring a flood of waters on the earth, to destroy from under heaven all flesh in which is the breath of life; everything that is on the earth shall die" (6:17). The flood is no accident. It is a deliberate act of God to destroy that which has turned intrinsically evil. But again, God's judgment is infused with redeeming grace. God says to Noah, "But I will establish my covenant with you . . ." (6:18). This is the first of some 290 times the Old Testament uses the significant word *bĕrît,* "covenant." Eugene Merrill observes that "'my covenant' can refer only to something antecedent and the only possible antecedent is that covenant implied by Genesis 1:26-28 [see also p. 75 above on Genesis 2–3]. The old Adamic Covenant would be established with Noah, and all that the Lord had entrusted to and required of Adam would devolve on Noah and his descendants."[16] God will establish a special covenant relationship with Noah and promises at this point "to keep alive" (6:20) Noah, his family, and all creatures that enter the ark. God gives a detailed listing of all the creatures that are to enter the ark (the pace retardation underscores the importance): ". . . you shall come into the ark, you, your sons, your wife, and your sons' wives with you. And of every living thing, of all flesh, you shall bring two of every kind into the ark, to keep them alive with you. . . . Of the birds according to their kinds, and of the animals according to their kinds, of every creeping thing of the ground according to its kind, two of every kind shall come into you, to keep them alive" (6:18-20). The ark is to function as a rescue capsule that will keep alive human beings as well as representatives of all the kinds of birds and land animals God created in the beginning (see 1:21-25). If the ark survives, it will mark a new beginning for God's kingdom on earth. But if it doesn't survive?

In the next scene, the conflict intensifies when God orders Noah and his family and all the animals into the ark and states, "In seven days I will send rain on the earth for forty days and forty nights" (7:4). Forty days and forty nights indicates a full but critical period of time in redemptive history.[17] For a full period of time the corrupted earth will be subjected to God's judgment. God's judgment will be severe and complete.

The narrator uses pace retardation again by listing once more all the creatures that enter the ark to escape God's judgment, "to escape the waters of the flood" (7:7-9, 13-16).[18] And then it happens, verse 11: "In the six hundredth year

16. Merrill, "A Theology of the Pentateuch," 23.

17. Cf. Gen 7:12; 8:6; Exod 24:18; 34:28; 1 Kings 19:8; Jonah 3:4; Matt 4:2; Acts 1:3.

18. "What is most apparent in the description of the onset of the Flood is the focus of the author on the occupants of the ark. . . . No bit of information is too insignificant if it can contribute to the author's purpose of holding this picture before the reader as long as literarily pos-

of Noah's life, in the second month, on the seventeenth day of the month, on that day all the fountains of the great deep burst forth, and the windows of the heavens were opened." In the beginning God had separated the waters below from the waters above by a dome and set boundaries for the waters so that dry land could appear (1:6-10). Now God withdraws his upholding hand; he reverses his acts of creation, and chaos returns to the earth as in the beginning (1:2; cf. 2 Pet 3:5-7). But there is a glimmer of hope that this is not the end of God's kingdom on earth: there is the ark with all these creatures inside. Will it survive the flood? There are hopeful signs: in contrast to the Babylonian flood story *Gilgamesh,* where the hero was told to "batten the door" and where "the gods became frightened of the deluge,"[19] in the Genesis account it is the LORD who shuts the door of the ark (7:16), and the LORD is sovereign over the waters — he will let it rain forty days and forty nights (7:4), no more (7:17)!

The tension reaches a climax in chapter 7:17-24. The narrator again slows the pace, relating first that "the waters increased and bore up the ark" (7:17). Though bobbing in the dangerous flood like a cork in the ocean, the ark rises above God's judgment. Still, the waters keep swelling (repeated in 7:18, 19, 20, 24), reaching higher and higher until the highest mountains are covered. "And all flesh died that moved on the earth . . . ; everything on dry land in whose nostrils was the breath of life died" (7:21-22). The One who gave his creatures "the breath of life" (1:30; 2:7) has seen fit to take it away. God's judgment is complete. Verse 23, "He blotted out every living thing that was on the face of the ground."

God hates sin and judges it. In Genesis we next see God's judgment of human sin at the tower of Babel (Gen 11:9) and when God completely destroys Sodom and Gomorrah (Gen 19). We see God's judgment of Israel when a whole generation dies in the desert and does not enter the Promised Land (Num 14:20-23). Again we see God's judgment in the deportation of Israel to Assyria (722 B.C.) and of Judah to Babylon (587 B.C.). Finally we see God's judgment of human sin at Calvary, where Jesus dies for "the sins of the whole world" (1 John 2:2). All these judgments of God point to God's sudden, final judgment when people, like people in Noah's day, will be "eating and drinking, marrying and giving in marriage," and unexpectedly Jesus, the Son of Man, comes again (Matt 24:36-39) to judge the living and the dead (Matt 25:31-46).

God "blotted out every living thing that was on the face of the ground. . . . Only Noah was left, and those that were with him in the ark. And the waters swelled on the earth for one hundred and fifty days" (7:23-24). Will the inhabitants of the ark survive this awesome judgment?

---

sible. It is first and foremost this picture of Noah's salvation that the author wants his readers to take a long look at." Sailhamer, *Genesis,* 88.

19. *Gilgamesh,* XI, lines 114 and 93. Cf. Wenham, *Genesis 1–15,* 159-66.

The narrator quickly moves to the resolution: chapter 8:1, "But God remembered Noah." That's the turn in the narrative: "God remembered Noah." Not that God had forgotten Noah; when God "remembers" someone, he remembers in order to save (cf. 19:29; 30:22). God remembered Noah because he had made covenant with him (6:18). And God remembered not only Noah, but "all the wild animals and all the domestic animals that were with him in the ark. And God made a wind (*rûaḥ;* see 1:2) blow over the earth, and the waters subsided . . ." (8:1).[20]

By drawing parallels to the creation story of Genesis 1, the narrator seeks to show that God is making a new beginning with Noah and the creatures with him in the ark. As in Genesis 1, God reins in the destructive waters by closing "the fountains of the deep and the windows of the heavens" (8:2; cf. 7:11 and 1:6-9). Gradually the waters subside as they did in Genesis 1, and a cleansed creation rises from the chaos.[21]

Next the narrator highlights the new beginning by using a number of "firsts." Chapter 8:13, "In the six hundred first year, in the first month, the first day of the month, the waters were dried up from the earth."[22] Three times the narrator repeats this important fact that the earth was dry again (8:13-14). Then God said to Noah, "Go out of the ark, you and your wife, and your sons and your sons' wives with you. Bring out with you every living thing that is with you of all flesh — birds and animals and every creeping thing that creeps on the earth — so that they may abound on the earth, and be fruitful and multiply on the earth" (8:16-17; cf. 1:28). Noah is the new Adam in a renewed creation. God is making a new beginning with the seed of the woman.

The outcome of the flood narrative sees Noah building an altar to the LORD and offering "burnt offerings" on the altar. Noah follows the pattern of the line of Seth by calling on the name of the LORD (4:26). By bringing offerings to the LORD, Noah as new head of the human race dedicates himself and his family and the whole cleansed earth to the LORD. The earth is the place where the LORD will be worshiped; the cleansed earth is the kingdom of the LORD.

The LORD is indeed pleased[23] with this offering. "The LORD said in his heart, 'I will never again curse the ground because of humankind, for the incli-

20. "The description of God's rescue of Noah [remembering those in the ark and sending a wind] foreshadows God's deliverance of Israel in the Exodus." Sailhamer, *Genesis,* 89.

21. See Mathews, *Genesis 1–11:26,* 383.

22. "The date formula signals mankind's new beginning after the flood." *NIV Study Bible,* note on Gen 8:13.

23. "The LORD smelled the pleasing odor" (8:21). Compare Lev 1:9, 13, 17: "The priest shall turn the whole into smoke on the altar as a burnt offering, an offering by fire of pleasing odor to the LORD."

nation of the human heart is evil from youth; nor will I ever again destroy every living creature as I have done.

> As long as the earth endures,
> seedtime and harvest,
> cold and heat,
> summer and winter,
> day and night,
> shall not cease."
>
> (8:21-22)

God recognizes that "the inclination of the human heart is evil from youth." Human beings are still inclined to evil, as the next two narratives (Noah drunk and the tower of Babel) so clearly show. Yet God promises never again to send such a disastrous flood that turns his good creation into chaos. Why is that? Since the human heart has not changed, how can God now promise, "Never again"?[24] This is where we see God shifting from strict justice to pure grace (see the Royal Grant covenant below). God will try a different way of establishing his kingdom on earth — ultimately by sending his own Son. For, instead of destroying all sinful human beings, God promises to uphold the order of his creation "as long as the earth endures."

This divine promise is further elaborated in a two-part sequel each marked by inclusio. The first inclusio has to do with God's blessing, "God blessed Noah and his sons, and said to them, 'Be fruitful and multiply, and fill the earth. . . . And you, be fruitful and multiply, abound on the earth and multiply in it'" (9:1, 7).[25] These words are a clear reminder of God's words to Adam in Genesis 1:28. Even though the human heart is inclined to evil, God graciously sends his people out into the world again under his blessing. But things have changed. The peaceful harmony between creatures is broken. God now makes provision for his creatures in a broken world: "The fear and dread of you shall rest on every

24. "The same condition which in the prologue (viz., 6:50) is the basis of God's judgment in the epilogue reveals God's grace and providence. The contrast between God's punishing anger and his supporting grace . . . is here presented . . . as an adjustment by God towards man's sinfulness." Von Rad, *Genesis,* 123. Cf. Brueggemann, *Genesis,* 81, "The flood has effected no change in humankind. But it has effected an irreversible change in God, who now will approach his creation with an unlimited patience and forbearance."

25. "The single command to Adam to be fruitful is repeated to Noah no less than four times, perhaps to counteract the idea that God was opposed to the human race *per se*. . . ." This could also be a polemic against the *Atrahasis* epic, where "the flood was sent to stop the population explosion. . . . And after the flood's failure to deal with the problem completely, the gods decreed that infertility, miscarriage, and childhood ills would curtail population growth." Wenham, *Story as Torah,* 83.

animal of the earth . . . ; into your hand they are delivered" (9:2). And instead of a vegetarian diet (1:29), "Every moving thing that lives shall be food for you; and just as I gave you the green plants, I give you everything" (9:3). The earth displays no longer the perfect harmony of Paradise. People eat animals. But human beings must continue to show respect for animal life: "You shall not eat flesh with its life, that is, its blood" (9:4). For "the life of the flesh is in the blood" (Lev 17:11), and only God can give and take life. And most of all, people must respect human life: "For your own lifeblood I will surely require a reckoning: from every animal I will require it and from human beings, each one for the blood of another [brother],[26] I will require a reckoning for human life.

> Whoever sheds the blood of a human,
> by a human shall that person's blood be shed;
> for in his own image God made humankind."
>
> (9:5-6)

The second inclusio focuses on God's covenant. In spite of the evil inclination of the human heart, God affirms his relationship with the creatures made in his image, his representatives on earth. "Then God said to Noah and to his sons with him, 'As for me, I am establishing my covenant with you and your descendants after you. . . .' God said to Noah, 'This is the sign of the covenant that I have established between me and all flesh that is on the earth'" (Gen 9:8-9, 17). In this monologue, God repeats the word *bĕrît,* "covenant," seven times. This is a perfect, all-encompassing covenant in which God establishes his covenant not only with Noah but "with every living creature that is with you . . . as many as came out of the ark" (Gen 9:10). In this covenant, God promises again, "that never again shall all flesh be cut off by the waters of a flood, and never again shall there be a flood to destroy the earth" (Gen 9:11).

God establishes this covenant totally on his own initiative. God states explicitly that "the inclination of the human heart is evil from youth" (8:21). He places no conditions of obedience for maintaining this covenant; it is an unconditional covenant.[27] This is as much a covenant of grace as the covenant with Abram which scholars usually call a covenant of grace.

And, strangely but appropriately, the sign of this covenant is the bow, nor-

26. "This is the first time *'aḥ,* 'brother,' has been used since Gen 4 (cf. 4:8-11), where the term is harped on to highlight the incongruity of Cain's action, so it seems likely that here this story is being alluded to." Wenham, *Genesis 1–15,* 193.

27. In the context of ancient Near Eastern covenants, scholars have identified this Noahic covenant as a Royal Grant covenant where the divine promise is unconditional. For a clear distinction between the Royal Grant, the Parity, and the Suzerain-vassal treaties, see *The NIV Study Bible,* at Genesis 9.

mally understood in Israel as a weapon of war.[28] God hangs his bow of war in the heavens as a sign of peace linking heaven and earth. "I have set my bow in the clouds, and it shall be a sign of the covenant between me and the earth" (Gen 9:13). This is an appropriate sign for an unconditional covenant, for unlike the later covenant signs of passover and circumcision (Lord's Supper and baptism), human beings cannot control this sign.[29]

The fact that this is an unconditional covenant is underscored when God says twice that when he sees the bow in the clouds, not human beings but *he* will remember the covenant: "*I* will remember the everlasting covenant between God and every living creature of all flesh that is on the earth" (Gen 9:16; cf. 9:15). As God, at the climax of this narrative, "*remembered* Noah" (8:1) and saved him from the flood, so at the end of this narrative God promises (twice) to *remember* his covenant that he will never again send "a flood to destroy all flesh" (9:15). Like the creation narrative, the flood narrative ends with God declaring peace.[30] Life on earth can develop in full assurance of God's covenant faithfulness. "In spite of human sin and violence, God has committed himself to his world; the unconditional covenant of the rainbow, by which he binds only himself, is a sign of that. The story of the Flood is therefore an affirmation of the story of creation, and speaks ultimately not of divine punishment but of God's faithfulness to the works of his hands."[31]

God is a God who makes new beginnings (cf. Gen 9:1 with 1:28). Even as he judges the earth for its corruption, in his grace he continues his kingdom on earth by making a new start with Noah, his family, and the animals with him. God makes a new beginning with Noah.

Noah is clearly a type of Jesus Christ. Noah is a new Adam representing the human race; the seed of the woman; "a righteous man, blameless in his generation . . . , [who] walked with God" (Gen 6:9); a person who obeyed God without question (Gen 6:22; 7:5, 9; 8:18); a person through whom God made a new start with his world. But Jesus is greater than Noah. Jesus is God's *only* Son and, through Jesus, God makes a completely new start with his people and his creation. Jesus offers his life to atone for human sin once for all. Paul states, "For our sake he [God] made him to be sin who knew no sin, so that in him we might become the righteousness of God" (2 Cor 5:21). With his resurrection, Je-

28. See, e.g., Hab 3:9, "You brandished your naked bow, sated were the arrows at your command." Cf. Lam 2:4; 3:12.

29. Gowan, *From Eden to Babel,* 105.

30. "The bow at rest thus forms a parallel to the sabbath in 2:1-4a at the resolve of creation. The first creation (1:1–2:4a) ends with the serene rest of God. The recreation (8:20–9:17) ends with God resting his weapon. God's creation is for all time protected from God's impatience." Brueggemann, *Genesis,* 84-85.

31. Clines, "The Theology of the Flood Narrative," 140.

sus brings in God's kingdom with new life for all his followers and the hope of a new creation that is "free from its bondage to decay" (Rom 8:21).

This good news is not only hope for the future; it is also encouragement for the present. Peter uses the flood narrative to offer his persecuted readers encouragement: "If he [God] did not spare the ancient world, even though he saved Noah, a herald of righteousness, with seven others, when he brought a flood on a world of the ungodly . . . , then the Lord knows how to rescue the godly from trial, and to keep the unrighteous under punishment until the day of judgment . . ." (2 Pet 2:5, 9). "The Lord knows how to rescue the godly from trial." He is the God of new beginnings. He made a new beginning with Noah and all creatures with him in the ark. He made a new beginning with Israel when he brought a remnant back from exile. He made a new beginning with Jesus Christ. And we as the church, the body of Christ, are part of this new beginning. Even during persecution and trials, God's new beginnings give us hope and courage. For, as Peter puts it, "In accordance with his promise, we wait for new heavens and a new earth, where righteousness is at home" (2 Pet 3:13). So we can live in good hope. In Christ, we also can count on God's new beginnings both now and when Jesus comes again to restore his perfect kingdom on earth.

God is the prism
by whom the spectrum
is formed.

the seven colors of
his love
fall across my hands.

finding myself
on Mount Ararat
I see
in the sky the sign.

before me
passes the archeological
expedition
in search of Noah's ark.

but the sign —
they do not see the sign.[32]

32. A Frisian poem of the 1950s by Durk van der Ploeg, probably translated by Remkes Kooistra. Reprinted in *Christian Courier,* June 13, 2005, p. 6.

CHAPTER 6

The Tower of Babel

Genesis 11:1-9

In contrast to the flood narrative, the Babel narrative is extremely compact, only nine verses. The major challenge in preaching this narrative is how to preach Christ, for God's grace is hard to detect. The foregoing narratives all showed God's grace in his judgments: in the narrative of the Fall, Eve could still be called "the mother of all living" and God clothed Adam and Eve (3:20-21); the narrative of Cain and Abel concludes with God providing Seth as a replacement for the murdered Abel (4:25); in the narrative of the flood, God saved a remnant and promised "never again" (8:21; 9:15). But where is God's grace in his judgment at Babel? The narrative contains neither a promise of Christ nor a type of Christ. Nor does it contain an inkling that God will continue the line of the seed of the woman. The narrator very clearly indicates this continuation in the next *tôlĕdôt,* which takes us in ten generations from Shem to Abram (11:10-26), and in the next narrative God calls Abram to the Promised Land (11:27–12:9). But the Babel narrative itself contains no such inkling of the seed of the woman. In fact, the narrator seems to have purposefully eliminated this option of good news by reversing the chronological order of God's judgment at Babel (Gen 11) and the resulting seventy nations (Gen 10). It's as if the narrator with this final narrative on the theme of the spread of sin on earth wishes to highlight the incorrigibility of the human race and therefore concludes Israel's prehistory with a narrative of judgment without an obvious note of grace.[1] So how does one preach Christ from a narrative that seems to be totally concerned with God's judgment?

1. Clines, *The Theme of the Pentateuch,* 68-69, suggests, "If the material in ch. 10 had followed the Babel story, the whole Table of Nations would have to be read under the sign of judgement; where it stands it functions as the fulfillment of the divine command of 9:1."

Text and Context

Genesis 11:1-9 is clearly a textual unit. Verse 1 begins a new narrative, "Now the earth had one language," and it concludes at verse 9, "Therefore it was called Babel, because there the LORD confused the language of all the earth" — an inclusio. This completion of the narrative is confirmed by verse 10, which begins a new *tôlĕdôt.* The textual unit is also confirmed by a chiastic structure of key words:[2]

A "The whole earth had one language" (v 1)
 B "there" (v 2)
  C "each other" (v 3)
   D "Come let us make bricks" (v 3)
    E "let us build for ourselves" (v 4)
     F "a city and a tower"
      G "the LORD came down to see" (v 5)
     F′ "the city and the tower"
    E′ "which mankind had built"
   D′ "come . . . let us mix up" (v 7)
  C′ "each other's language"
 B′ "from there" (v 8)
A′ "the language of the whole earth" (v 9)

For preaching purposes, it may be helpful to see this narrative as two acts, the first describing human action (vv 1-4) and the second God's response (vv 5-9). Anderson[3] subdivides further:

Introduction: the original situation (v 1)
 Human action:
  a. Narrative report (v 2): wanderers settle in the plain
  b. Discourse with twofold invitational exclamations (vv 3, 4)
 Divine action:

2. Wenham, *Genesis 1–15*, 235. Wenham, 234, points out that D and D′ are phonetic allusions that "make the contrast between man's *nilbĕnâ* 'let us make (bricks),' v 3, and God's *nēbĕlâ* 'let us mix up,' v 7, the more dramatic." See also Fokkelman, *Narrative Art in Genesis*, 20-23, and Radday, "Chiasmus in Hebrew Biblical Narrative," 100. Van Wolde, *Words Become Worlds*, 84-91, compares, contrasts, and critiques various proposals and suggests that "the stylistic patterns in the text give grounds for regarding the story of the Tower of Babel as an iconic representation of a *ziggurat* or temple tower in Babylonia" — the chiasm turned on its side.

3. Anderson, *From Creation to New Creation*, 169-70.

a. Narrative report (v 5): investigation of the building
b. Divine discourse with twofold invitational exclamations (vv 6, 7)
c. Narrative report of divine action (v 9): dispersion
Conclusion: return to the beginning but on a new level of meaning (v 9)

To rightly understand this narrative, we need to see it in its broader context. In the creation narrative, God not only created human beings in his image, but "God blessed them, and God said to them, 'Be fruitful and multiply, and *fill the earth* and subdue it" (1:28). After the flood, we read again, "God blessed Noah and his sons and said to them, 'Be fruitful and multiply, and *fill the earth*'" (9:1). There is a reminder again that human beings are created in the image of God (9:6), followed by the repetition, "And you, be fruitful and multiply, abound on the earth and multiply in it" (9:7). At Babel people refuse to "fill the earth." Rather, like Cain before them, they seek to cope east of Eden (11:2 TNIV; cf. 3:24; 4:16) by building a city with "a tower with its top in the heavens." Their motive? "Otherwise we shall be scattered abroad upon the face of the whole earth" (11:4).

As the Lord was concerned after the Fall, "See, the man has become like one of us, knowing good and evil . . . — therefore the Lord God sent him forth from the garden of Eden" (3:22-23), so here the Lord is concerned, "Look, they are one people, and they have all one language . . . ; nothing that they propose to do will now be impossible for them" (11:6).[4] But since the Lord after the flood promised never again to destroy all flesh with a flood, he scattered the people at Babel by confusing their language.

It should also be noted that the Babel narrative is part of "the *tôlĕdôt* of Noah's sons, Shem, Ham, and Japheth; children were born to them after the flood" (10:1). The new beginning after the flood was soon spoiled by human power grabbing: Nimrod, a descendant of Ham, "was the first on earth to become a mighty warrior. . . . The beginning of his kingdom was Babel, Erech, and Accad, all of them in the land of Shinar" (10:8, 10).[5] By reversing the chronological order from the confusion of language at Babel (Gen 11) followed by various nations with different languages (10:5, 20, 31), the narrator concludes this *tôlĕdôt* with the major power grab at Babel and God's judgment.[6] For some

4. Wenham points out that "the structure . . . and sentiments closely resemble 3:22, 'Since man has become like one of us, knowing good and evil, now lest they reach out . . . and live forever." *Genesis 1–15*, 240.

5. "The following biographical notation [10:8-12] foreshadows the Tower of Babel and explains the racial, political, and spiritual origin of Babylonia and Assyria, the two great Mesopotamian powers that conquered Israel and held them as exiles." Nimrod means "we shall rebel." Waltke, *Genesis*, 168-69.

6. "The point of contact between the two chapters appears to be the birth of Peleg (and

reason he wished to end Israel's prehistory on a note of judgment.[7] Left to themselves, there is no hope for humanity.

Literary Features

The name "Babel" in verse 9, earlier mentioned in 10:10, is the Hebrew name translated elsewhere in the Old Testament as "Babylon." Although no similar stories about Babel/Babylon have been found in the ancient Near East,[8] the narrative may well recall ancient Babylon with its ziggurat temple tower to the god Marduk. Von Rad notes, "Babylon in ancient times, especially in the second millennium B.C., was the heart of the ancient world and its center of power (Hammurabi, 1728-1686), and the rays of its culture went out far into neighbouring lands. Thus even in Palestine there was legendary knowledge of its gigantic cultural achievements, especially of the mighty stepped towers in which the united civilized will of this strong nation had created an enduring monument."[9]

Like the narratives of creation and flood, this narrative is partly a polemic against Babylonian pagan notions. Wenham states, "The tower of Babel story is a satire on the claims of Babylon to be the center of civilization and its temple tower the gate of heaven . . . : Babel does not mean gate of god, but 'confusion' and 'folly.' Far from its temple's top reaching up to heaven, it is so low that God has to descend from heaven just to see it!"[10] Moreover, it was not built by the gods but by *běnê hā'ādām,* "sons of the earth" (v 5), mere earthlings, mortals. "The work was terrestrial, not celestial."[11]

The narrator again is omniscient. He knows the people migrating to Shinar: he records their plans and fears. He also sees the LORD coming down from heaven and is privy to his concerns and his deliberations for a counter plan.

---

thus his naming) in Genesis 10. ['The name of the one was Peleg, for in his days the earth was divided' (10:25).] At that point the incident of chapter 11 may have happened, causing the people to spread out into the earth until they settled in their tribes as described in chapter 10." Ross, *Creation and Blessing,* 243. Cf. Sailhamer, *Genesis,* 103-4.

7. "The story of the Tower of Babel concludes with God's judgment on mankind; there is no word of grace. The whole primeval history, therefore, seems to break off in shrill dissonance." Von Rad, *Genesis,* 153.

8. But for some interesting parallels, see Mathews, *Genesis 1–11:26,* 469-73.

9. Von Rad, *Genesis,* 150. For details, see John H. Walton, "The Mesopotamian Background of the Tower of Babel Account and Its Implications," *BBR* 5 (1995) 155-75.

10. Wenham, *Genesis 1–15,* xlviii-xlix; see pp. 236-37. Cf. Sarna, *Understanding Genesis,* 76. "The Bible has deliberately selected the mighty city of Babylon with its famed temple of Marduk as the scene for a satire on paganism, its notions, mythology and religious forms."

11. Ross, *Creation and Blessing,* 246.

The narrative is tightly structured and filled with repetition, wordplays, and irony. We have already noted the chiastic structure above. The words "whole earth" and "language" each occur five times. "Scattered" occurs three times. The human, "Come, let us make bricks," and, "Come, let us build," are balanced by the divine, "Come, let us go down, and confuse their language there." "The irony of mankind's attempt to 'make a name,' to overreach itself and immortalize its achievements, is reinforced by the tightly coiled acoustical sound track of the text, which plays back the initial achievements as failures. Mankind goes eastward to build 'there' *(shām)* a tower to the heavens *(shāmayim),* and so to make a 'name' *(shēm)* for itself. It was 'there' *(shām)* that human language was confounded, and it was 'from there' *(mi-shām)* that mankind was scattered over the broad earth."[12]

The Plot Line

The narrator gives the setting in verse 1, "Now the whole earth had one language and the same words." The preliminary incident consists of the migrants settling on a plain in Shinar. The occasioning incident is their plan to make bricks and kiln-burn them — a new invention. Combining these bricks with bitumen, they wish to build a city. The tension rises as they seek not only to build a city but also "a tower with its top in the heavens." They wish to "make a name for ourselves; otherwise we shall be scattered abroad upon the face of the whole earth" (11:4). The narrative turns to a resolution in verse 5 when the LORD comes down from his heavenly throne "to see the city and the tower." The LORD is deeply concerned about their plan: "Look, they are one people, and they have all one language; and this is only the beginning of what they will do; nothing that they propose to do will now be impossible for them" (v 6). The LORD decides to "confuse their language, so that they will not understand one another's speech" (v 7). The outcome is that they are scattered abroad "over the face of all the earth," and leave off building the city (v 8). The writer adds the conclusion, "Therefore it was called Babel, because there the LORD confused the language of all the earth; and from there the LORD scattered them abroad over the face of all the earth" (v 9).

We can sketch the plot line of this narrative as a single plot, as shown on page 125:

12. Fishbane, *Text and Texture,* 38. For more details, see Fokkelman, *Narrative Art in Genesis,* 11-45.

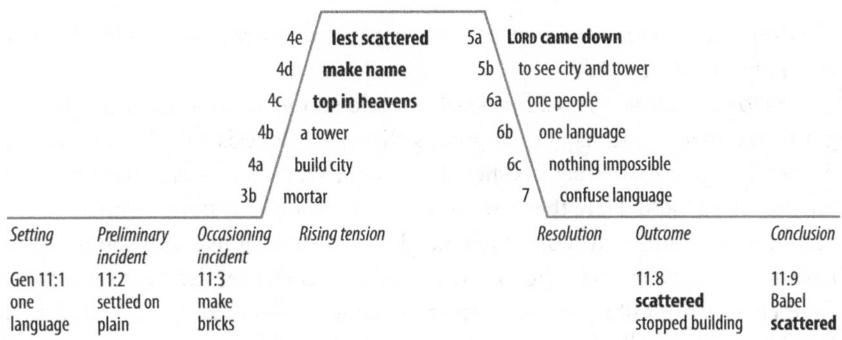

Theocentric Interpretation

In the first act of this narrative (11:1-4) God seems to be absent: it is all human planning and activity (cf. the story of Cain and Lamech's descendants in 4:17-24). But in the second act it is all God's activity. From highest heaven "the LORD came down to see the city and the tower" (11:5). The LORD deliberates about the disastrous consequences of this human building project (v 6) and says, "Come, let us go down, and confuse their language" (v 7). The narrator shows the outcome, "So the LORD scattered them abroad from there over the face of all the earth" (v 8). He repeats in the conclusion, "The LORD confused the language of all the earth; and from there the LORD scattered them abroad over the face of all the earth" (v 9).

Textual Theme and Goal

At Babel the LORD counters human efforts not to be scattered by scattering them "over the face of all the earth," thus accomplishing his original plan that human beings should "fill the earth." God's grace in this narrative is found in the very judgment of scattering, for God predicts, "This is only the beginning of what they will do; nothing that they propose to do will now be impossible for them" (v 6). At Babel God halts the unbridled human efforts to build a united, secular city, which would leave no room for the kingdom of God.

We might formulate the theme of this narrative somewhat as follows: "At Babel, the LORD scatters humankind which in disobedience seeks to build its own, secular kingdom." Although this is an accurate summation of the narrative, it fails to express the foregoing context of the LORD's intention that they fill the earth and God's grace in his judgment. Therefore a better thematic statement would be something like this, *The LORD scatters humankind, which in dis-*

obedience seeks to build its own, secular kingdom, in order to accomplish his plan that they "fill the earth."

As to the narrator's goal for Israel, it could simply be to teach Israel the origin of the many nations and languages (listed in Genesis 10). But we can dig deeper. Imagine that Israel first heard this story when they were about to enter the Promised Land. Here they would confront several city-states (similar to Babel) and be tempted to copy their neighbors and establish city-states.[13] The narrator's goal then might be to warn Israel not to rely on their own ingenuity for their security but to rely on their transcendent, sovereign LORD.[14] But since Israel feared the well-fortified city-states in Canaan, the narrator's goal with the tower of Babel story may also be somewhat different. The first set of spies had returned with discouraging reports: "The people are stronger and taller than we; the cities are large and fortified up to heaven *(wbṣwrt bšmym)*" (Deut 1:28). Now Israel hears the story of the LORD scattering the people who sought to build a tower "with its top in the heavens *(wr'šw bšmym)*" (Gen 11:4). The narrator's goal, then, is to give Israel hope that the LORD will indeed scatter the Canaanites living in their "great cities, fortified to the heavens *(wbṣwrt bšmym)*" (Deut 9:1) and give Israel the Promised Land.[15]

And how would Israel have heard this story when they were in exile in Babylon? Here the polemic against Babel/Babylon would really hit home. Babylon, which seemed so powerful, was lifted up of *bricks*, mere clay compared to solid *stones* used in Israel. Moreover, Israel's LORD had to "come down" to see their loftiest accomplishments. In the tragedy of exile, the narrator's goal would probably not be to warn but *to give hope to Israel that their sovereign LORD is able to break down the secular city (Babel/Babylon) in order to restore them to the Promised Land.*

Ways to Preach Christ

How can we move from the theme, "The LORD scatters humankind . . . in order to accomplish his plan that they 'fill the earth,'" to Jesus Christ in the New Testament? We shall check out the seven ways.

13. "Canaan's cities no doubt were attractive to the Israelite sons of Egypt's slaves." Mathews, *Genesis 1–11:26*, 486.

14. "That it was Babylon, the beginning of kingdoms under Nimrod from Cush [see 10:6-10], adds a rather ominous warning: Great nations cannot defy God and long survive. The new nation of Israel need only survey the many nations around her to realize that God disperses and curses the rebellious, bringing utter confusion and antagonism among them." Ross, *Creation and Blessing*, 248.

15. See Richard Pratt, *He Gave Us Stories*, 271.

Redemptive-Historical Progression

One can possibly use the way of redemptive-historical progression. At Babel God's judgment falls on human beings who seek security in building their own secular kingdom. This judgment is followed by God's judgment of the wicked cities of Sodom and Gomorrah (Gen 19). Again God "must go down" (18:21) to see the gravity of their sin, and he destroys these cities in Canaan.[16] Next God's judgment falls on a whole generation of Israelites who die in the desert because of their lack of trust and obedience (Num 14:20-23). Next God's judgment falls on the ten northern tribes of Israel, which are deported to Assyria (722 B.C.), and later on Judah, which is deported to Babylon (587 B.C.). Isaiah (13:19) prophesies that God will judge Babylon:

> And Babylon, the glory of kingdoms,
> the splendor and pride of the Chaldeans,
> will be like Sodom and Gomorrah
> when God overthrew them.

Ultimately, Babylon stands for secular human kingdoms, which Jesus will judge and overthrow when he establishes his perfect kingdom on earth (see Rev 18).

Promise-Fulfillment

There is no messianic promise in this narrative.

Typology

There is no type of Christ in this narrative. Babel becomes a type of human wickedness in the Bible and as the "city of man" functions as an antithetic type to Jerusalem, the "city of God." We shall explore these ideas further under Contrast below.

Analogy

One can use analogy to preach Christ from this narrative. For example, as God gave hope to Israel that their sovereign LORD was able to break down secular

16. Wenham, *Genesis 1–15,* 245-46, points out that Genesis 10:9-19 also links Babel and Sodom through Noah's son Ham by way of Nimrod and Canaan respectively.

cities in order to establish his kingdom on earth, so Jesus gives hope to his followers since all authority has been given to him (Matt 28:18) and his church cannot fail. This analogy can be supported by New Testament references such as Jesus' words in Matthew 16:18, "On this rock I will build my church, and the gates of Hades will not prevail against it."

Longitudinal Themes

One can also trace to Jesus in the New Testament the theme of God's judgment on Babel. Babel becomes a symbol of human rebellion against God's designs. In the Old Testament the prophets move from God's judgment on Babel to God's judgment on Babylon. The New Testament continues with the message of God's judgment on Babylon, "Fallen, fallen is Babylon the great!" (Rev 14:8; cf. 16:19). And again,

> "Fallen, fallen is Babylon the great!
> It has become a dwelling place of demons,
> a haunt of every foul spirit. . . .
> For all the nations have drunk of the wine of the wrath of her fornication,
> and the kings of the earth have committed fornication with her,
> and the merchants of the earth have grown rich from the power of her luxury. . . .
> With such violence Babylon the great city will be thrown down,
> and will be found no more . . . ;
> and an artisan of any trade will be found in you no more;
> and the sound of the millstone will be heard in you no more."
> (Rev 18:2-3, 21-22)

All this will take place because "the Lion of the tribe of Judah, the Root of David, has conquered, so that he can open the scroll and its seven seals" (Rev 5:5; cf. v 9).[17]

One can also follow the trail of the confusion of languages which divides people into different nations. Already in the Old Testament, Zephaniah (3:9) looks forward to the time when the nations will be restored to "pure speech" and serve the LORD:

17. The fall of Babylon is followed by rejoicing in heaven:

> "Hallelujah!
> For the Lord our God the Almighty reigns.
> Let us rejoice and exult and give him the glory,
> for the marriage of the Lamb has come,
> and his bride has made herself ready. . . ." (Rev 19:6-7)

> At that time I will change the speech of the peoples to a pure speech, that all of them may call on the name of the LORD and serve him with one accord.

This prophecy finds its initial fulfillment when Jesus pours out the Holy Spirit at Pentecost and people from different nations hear the mighty acts of God "in their own language" (Acts 2:11; see Contrast below). The final reversal of Babel will take place on the last day: "There was a great multitude that no one could count, from every nation, from all tribes and peoples and languages, standing before the throne and before the Lamb, robed in white, with palm branches in their hands. They cried out in a loud voice, saying, 'Salvation belongs to our God who is seated on the throne, and to the Lamb!'" (Rev 7:9-10).

New Testament References

In addition to the New Testament references mentioned above, one might consider making a link to Christ in the New Testament by using:

> John 11:51-52, "Jesus was about to die for the nation, and not for the nation only, but to gather into one the dispersed children of God."
>
> Hebrews 11:10, "For he [Abraham] looked forward to the city that has foundations, whose architect and builder is God."
>
> Hebrews 11:16, All these heroes of faith "desire a better country, that is, a heavenly one. Therefore God is not ashamed to be called their God; indeed, he has prepared a city for them."

Contrast

In contrast to the people of Babel who wished to "make a name" for *themselves* (11:4), the LORD promised Abram, "*I* will make your name great" (12:2). According to the New Testament, God gave Jesus "the name that is above every name, so that at the name of Jesus every knee should bend, . . . and every tongue should confess that Jesus Christ is Lord, to the glory of God the Father" (Phil 2:9-11). And Jesus promises to write on his people "the name of my God, and the name of the city of my God, the new Jerusalem that comes down from my God out of heaven, and my own new name" (Rev 3:12).

Further, in contrast to Babel, "the city of man," the Bible presents Jerusalem as "the city of God." In contrast to Babel, which represents the kingdoms of the world, Jerusalem represents the kingdom of God. In contrast to Babel, which represents human autonomy and might, Jerusalem represents the city where people rely on God for security and seek to obey his will (Isa 2:2-4). At Babel God confused human language resulting in division; at Jerusalem on the day of Pentecost God enabled people to "hear" each other again resulting in amazing unity (Acts 2:4-11, 41-47). The link to Jesus is that he poured out his Spirit at Pentecost to reverse the judgment of Babel for his church.

Sermon Theme and Goal

Earlier we identified the textual theme as, "The LORD scatters humankind, which in disobedience seeks to build its own, secular kingdom, in order to accomplish his plan that they 'fill the earth.'" The next chapter (Genesis 12) already indicates that the scattering created room for God to call an individual family to be his special people and eventually Israel to be a holy nation. When the Messiah is born, he calls on his followers to make disciples of all nations. The biblical context, therefore, shows God's ultimate purpose in scattering the people at Babel: it was to fulfill his plan to restore his kingdom on earth. Adding this dimension to the textual theme, we can make the sermon theme: "The LORD scatters rebellious humankind by confusing their language in order to accomplish his plan to restore his kingdom on earth." This theme is a good working theme for developing the sermon, but it is rather long and complicated for the hearers to remember and take home. How can we reduce this theme to a more striking one for use in the sermon itself? Perhaps, *God scatters the inhabitants of Babel in order to restore his kingdom on earth.* This theme might well be matched by the sermon title, "God Shatters the Monolith Babel."

Our goal in preaching this message should be guided by the narrator's goal for Israel. The likely goal of the narrator is, "to give hope to Israel that their sovereign LORD is able to break down the secular city (Babel/Babylon) in order to restore them to the Promised Land." Matching the sermon theme, we can make our sermon goal, therefore, *to give hope to God's people today that our sovereign LORD is able to break down secular kingdoms in order to restore his kingdom on earth.*

This sermon goal links up to the need of people today being discouraged about the prospects of the kingdom of God. Instead of relying on God, many still seek their security in their own ingenuity. They look for security in "towers" such as that of the United Nations, trade-center towers (money and stocks), global communication satellites, the internet, spy satellites, weapons of mass destruction, and missile shields.

Sermon Exposition

The narrator provides the setting of the Babel narrative in 11:1: "Now the whole earth had one language and the same words." The single language is significant in this narrative because it allows for perfect communication and cooperative work projects. A single language fits well after the flood since Noah and his family and their descendants would naturally have spoken one language.

The narrator describes in verse 2 a migration eastward to Shinar, that is, Sumer, between the Euphrates and Tigris rivers in southern Mesopotamia (later called Babylonia and presently Iraq): "And as they migrated from the east, they came upon a plain in the land of Shinar and settled there." The NRSV adds the footnote, "*migrated eastward*," which the TNIV uses in its text. The word *miqqedem* can be translated either as "from the east," or "eastward."[18] Since the narrator assumes that the ark landed on Ararat and that the people migrated toward Mesopotamia in the southeast, "eastward" is more in keeping with the context of this narrative. Moreover, "eastward" has symbolic overtones in Genesis: it is a movement away from Eden (3:24; 4:16).[19] Hence the term "eastward" raises concern in the careful reader: What is humanity up to now?

The conflict in the narrative arises because of a new human invention and the resulting plan. The invention is baking bricks in a kiln. They say to each other, verse 2, "Come, let us make bricks, and burn them thoroughly." The narrator explains this new invention for the Israelites who were used to building with stones and mortar, "And they had brick for stone, and bitumen [a tarlike substance] for mortar."

Verse 3 relates their plan: They say, "Come, let us build ourselves a city, and a tower with its top in the heavens, and let us make a name for ourselves; otherwise we shall be scattered abroad upon the face of the earth." Each element in this plan drives the narrative closer to the climax. First, in desiring to build a city, they seek to follow the lead of Cain, the seed of the serpent, who had sought to cope with the difficulties east of Eden by building a city (4:17). Sec-

18. Wenham comments, "The parallel with 13:11 [Lot journeying eastward to Sodom and Gomorrah] suggests that 'eastward' would be an apt translation here. This would be a possible rendering, if we suppose that mankind is seen as emigrating from Ararat to Mesopotamia." Wenham, *Genesis 1–15*, 238.

19. "Lot departs Abraham and journeys eastward (13:10-12), where he ultimately meets with disaster in the cities of Sodom and Gomorrah. Also Abraham's sons by Keturah are dispersed "to the land of the east" to detach them from the elect Isaac (25:6), and deceitful Jacob flees his homeland to live among the 'eastern peoples' of Aram (29:1)." Mathews, *Genesis 1–11:26*, 478. Cf. Sailhamer, *Genesis*, 104, "In the Genesis narratives, when a man goes 'east,' he leaves the land of blessing (Eden and the Promised Land) and goes to a land where the greatest of his hopes will turn to ruin (Babylon and Sodom)."

ond, this city has to have a tower. It should be a high tower that would be visible at a great distance so that people who wandered off on the plain would not be scattered but be able to find their way back to the city. Third, the plan calls for more than a high tower; this is to be a celestial tower, "with its top in the heavens."[20] It should be a tower that links heaven and earth. Most interpreters understand the tower to be a ziggurat, such as archeologists have discovered in Mesopotamia. A ziggurat is a stepped pyramid with a stairway on its side so as to encourage the god to descend to the temple next to the tower.[21]

The narrator raises the tension as he records the motivation of the builders. They wish to build this city and its huge tower, in order "to make a name" for themselves. The narrator subtly shows us that these people are seeking to defy God himself. He gave us a few hints earlier: the people moving "eastward," away from Eden — like Adam and Eve after the Fall (3:24), and Cain after murdering his brother (4:16); their plan to build a city, like Cain (4:17); and a tower "with its top in the heavens" — perhaps like Adam and Eve wishing to "be like God" (3:5). But now there is no doubt that they desire to defy God in heaven: "Let us make a name for ourselves." They lust for fame, for power, for world renown, for independence. Laurence Turner observes, "Previously, names have been given by superiors to inferiors (1:5, 8, 10; 2:20, 23; 3:20; 4:17, 25-26; 5:1, 3, 29). Read against this background, the human desire to make a name for themselves suggests not only a desire for a reputation, but also for autonomy. That, of course, was the original human offence (see 3:1-7, 20-24)."[22] From another angle, Gordon Wenham comes to a similar conclusion, "It is God alone who makes a name for himself (e.g., Isa 63:12, 14; Jer 32:20; Neh 9:10). Mankind is again attempting to usurp divine prerogatives."[23]

But in his grace God can make a name also for his people. In the very next chapter, God promises Abram, "*I* will make your name great" (12:2). Later God makes this promise to David, "I will make for you a great name" (2 Sam 7:9). According to Paul, God gives Jesus "the name that is above every name, so that at the name of Jesus every knee should bend, . . . and every tongue should con-

20. "Here the addition 'to the heavens' shows they are vying with God himself. The Lord, not humankind, dwells in the heavens (Gen 19:24; 21:17; 22:11, 15; Deut 26:15; Ps 115:16)." Waltke, *Genesis*, 179.

21. "The main architectural feature was the stairway or ramp that led to the top. In a small room at the top a bed was made and a table set for the deity. . . . In summary, the Tower of Babel project is a temple complex featuring a ziggurat, which was designed to make it convenient for the god to come down to his temple, receive worship from the people, and bless them." Walton, *Genesis*, 373-74.

22. Turner, *Genesis*, 60. Cf. later king Nebuchadnezzar bragging about "the magnificent Babylon, which I have built as a royal capital by my mighty power and for my glorious majesty" (Dan 4:30). God was not pleased!

23. Wenham, *Genesis 1–15*, 240.

fess that Jesus Christ is Lord, to the glory of God the Father" (Phil 2:9-11). And Jesus promises to write on his people "the name of my God, and the name of the city of my God, the new Jerusalem that comes down from my God out of heaven, and my own new name" (Rev 3:12). It is God's prerogative to make a name for his people. But at Babel, people desire to make a name for *themselves.* They wish to be like God.

Their second motive for building the city and the tower even more clearly shows their defiance of God. They say they wish to undertake this huge building project, for "otherwise we shall be scattered abroad upon the face of the whole earth" (11:4d). But human beings spreading across the earth was precisely God's intent. According to the creation narrative, God created human beings in his image, "blessed them, and God said to them, 'Be fruitful and multiply, and fill the earth and subdue it'" (1:28). God desired his image bearers to represent him in the whole world. They were to spread God's kingdom far and wide. After the flood, we read again, "God blessed Noah and his sons, and said to them, 'Be fruitful and multiply, and fill the earth'" (9:1). Clearly at Babel, people seek to disobey God's creation design to "fill the earth." Instead, for their own security, they wish to establish their own city-state. They seek salvation in their unity ("lest we be scattered"). Being one people with one language, their defiance threatens God's plan to restore his kingdom on earth.[24]

The LORD is quick to respond to this human rebellion. According to verse 5, "The LORD came down *to see* the city and the tower, which mortals had built." This response is similar to God's response to the threat to his kingdom before the flood when "God *saw* that the earth was corrupt; for all flesh had corrupted its ways upon the earth" (6:12).[25] But here the LORD has to *come down* from his heavenly throne to see this city and the tower whose top was supposed to be "in the heavens." The mocking of human pretension to greatness is biting. It reminds one of Isaiah's message to Israel in exile:

Have you not known?
  Have you not heard?
  Has it not been told you from the beginning?

24. "At Babel . . . rebellious man undertook a united and godless effort to establish for himself, by titanic human enterprise, a world renown by which he would dominate God's creation." *NIV Study Bible,* Genesis 11:4, n. Cf. von Rad, *Genesis,* 151, "The saga views such a development of power as something against God, rebellion against the Most High, as Babylon in many passages of the Bible is mentioned as the embodiment of sinful arrogance (Isa 12:14; 14:13; Jer 51:6ff.)."

25. This is "the decisive divine intervention that reverses the tide of human history. It is comparable to 'And God remembered Noah' in 8:1. Like 8:1, v 5 occurs at the midpoint of a story and heralds the undoing of what has gone before: there the flood waters start to fall; here the building stops." Wenham, *Genesis 1–15,* 236.

Have you not understood from the foundations of the earth?
It is he who sits above the circle of the earth,
and its inhabitants are like grasshoppers; . . .
who brings princes to naught,
and makes the rulers of the earth as nothing.

(Isa 40:21-23)

Israel's transcendent[26] LORD has to come down from his throne "to see the city and the tower, which mortals had built." "Which mortals had built" is another cutting remark. The Babylonians thought that their gods had built Babylon,[27] but the narrator states pointedly in the Hebrew, "which the sons of the earth had built" — mere earthlings. Will this human technology offer security to and save humankind? Far from it; it will have the opposite effect. It will push them over the brink of self-destruction. Because of his faithfulness and grace, God will intervene and foil their foolish plans for attaining their own salvation.

But how? In verse 6 the LORD says, "Look, they are one people, and they have all one language; and this is only the beginning of what they will do; nothing that they propose to do will now be impossible for them." The LORD expresses two concerns. His first concern is that the people are "one people and they all have one language." They are one, all in agreement, united in their defiance against God, a monolith, undivided. There is not a single righteous Noah among them. This leads to the LORD's second concern, "This is only the beginning of what they will do; nothing that they propose to do will now be impossible for them." If the people are successful in defying God now, who knows what they will propose next? "If the whole human race remained united in the proud attempt to take its destiny into its own hands and, by its man-centered efforts, to seize the reins of history, there would be no limit to its unrestrained rebellion against God. The kingdom of man would displace and exclude the kingdom of God."[28] For the sake of his kingdom, the LORD must intervene.

Twice the people had said, "Come, let us make bricks. . . . Come, let us build ourselves a city and a tower" (vv 3, 4). Now God responds with his own "Come, let us" in verse 7, "Come, let us go down, and confuse their language

26. "According to all accepted notions, this ziqqurat was to be a physical link between the divine and human realms. The Bible, by stressing that God 'came down,' sweeps away such a fancy. Before God's infinite superiority, elevation is meaningless and even the sky-capped tower becomes a puny creation. God's transcendence is absolute and his independence of materiality complete." Sarna, *Understanding Genesis,* 76.

27. "The temple of Marduk in Babylon was supposed to have been built by the Annunaki gods with specially prepared bricks. Its name, 'house with the uplifted head,' reflects its claim to have reached the heavens." Wenham, *Genesis 1–15,* 244.

28. *NIV Study Bible,* Genesis 11:6, n.

there, so that they will not understand one another's speech." Again the narrator emphasizes that the transcendent LORD has to come down to oppose these haughty people. The LORD counters this threat to his kingdom by confusing their language so that they can no longer understand each other. The single language had made their unity and defiant cooperation possible. By confusing their language the LORD shatters their unity and cooperation. God shatters the monolith Babel. This judgment reveals God's faithfulness to his plan of salvation.[29] For the LORD here breaks up Babel, a monolithic antigod kingdom, in order to begin his kingdom on earth anew with Abram and Israel and through Christ with his church. The evil empire will not control the whole earth, but nations will oppose each other, thus allowing room for God's kingdom, like yeast (Matt 13:33), to penetrate the world. The conflict of humankind seeking to make the world their united, secular empire is resolved.

In verse 8 the narrator relates the outcome of this narrative, "So the LORD scattered them abroad from there over the face of all the earth, and they left off building the city." The reason for building the city and its tower was, "otherwise we shall be scattered abroad upon the face of the whole earth" (v 4). The result of the LORD's action was precisely what they had feared, "the LORD scattered them abroad from there over the face of all the earth." They had tried to disobey God's will that they "fill the earth." In spite of their disobedience, the LORD accomplished his will.

Verse 9 concludes the narrative: "Therefore it was called Babel, because there the LORD confused *(bālal)* the language of all the earth; and from there the LORD scattered them abroad over the face of all the earth." God scatters defiant humanity across the whole earth. God scatters the self-reliant. "With exquisite irony those who wanted to make a name for themselves do indeed receive a name — Babel. . . . They had wanted to make a name by settling down in their city, but the name they receive through the Babel/*bālal* ('confuse') wordplay (11:9) actually describes their scattering."[30] Although the proud inhabitants of Babel thought they lived in Babel, "gate of the god," the narrator sarcastically claims that the name "Babel" derives from *bālal,* confusion;[31] Babel is mere babble.

God scatters the self-reliant. God scatters the inhabitants of Babel in order to restore his kingdom on earth. What a message of hope this was for Israel in

29. "God resolves upon a punitive, but at the same time preventive, act, so that he will not have to punish man more severely as his degeneration surely progresses." Von Rad, *Genesis,* 149.

30. Turner, *Genesis,* 60.

31. "The name 'Babel/Babylon' does not mean 'gate of the god,' as the Babylonians held, but 'confusion,' and it evokes the similar sounding words 'folly,' and 'flood.' Far from being the last word in human culture, it is the ultimate symbol of man's failure when he attempts to go it alone in defiance of his creator." Wenham, *Genesis,* 245.

Moab, who, like their fathers before them, must have stood in dread of the Canaanite cities, "large and fortified up to heaven!" (Deut 1:28). Yet they were about to be God's army entering Canaan to annihilate these secular city-states. "Babel exemplified the threat that the indigenous Canaanite cities presented for Israel. These cities were perceived as overwhelming fortresses (Num 13:28; Deut 1:28; 3:5; 9:1); nevertheless they would fall before the judgment of God."[32]

This Babel narrative certainly gave hope to Israel when they suffered in exile in Babylon. Israel's God had to come down from his throne in heaven to see this "great" city humans had built; and how puny it was compared to Israel's God, the Creator of heaven and earth. He scattered the defiant inhabitants of Babel in order to make room for his kingdom on earth. This God could also shatter the Babylon that had enslaved Israel and restore his people to the Promised Land. The Babel narrative offered Israel hope similar to that of Jeremiah's message (51:53),

> Though Babylon should mount up to heaven,
> and though she should fortify her strong height,
> from me destroyers would come upon her,
> says the LORD.[33]

The Babel narrative also gives hope to the Christian church. In New Testament terms, at Babel God shattered the consolidated power of the antichrist. "Babel/Babylon becomes in the Bible a symbol of a self-reliant, imperialistic secularism: control without accountability to the Creator. . . . John the apostle symbolically speaks of the Roman Empire and all kingdoms to follow as Babylon the Great. Babylon, the seducer of nations, kings, and merchants will fall (Rev 18)!"[34]

God scatters the inhabitants of Babel in order to restore his kingdom on earth. After shattering the monolith Babel, God can call Abram from among the idol worshipers (Josh 24:2) to continue the line of the seed of the woman. For the time being God's grace will be channeled through one family, Abram's,

32. Mathews, *Genesis 1–11:26*, 486.

33. Cf. Isaiah (47:10-11), who addressed Babylon:

> You felt secure in your wickedness. . . .
> You said in your heart,
> "I am, and there is no one besides me."
> But evil shall come upon you,
> which you cannot charm away;
> disaster shall fall upon you,
> which you will not be able to ward off.

34. VanGemeren, *Progress of Redemption*, 90.

and one nation, Israel. But God's concern is still to bring the nations into his kingdom. God promised Abram, "I will make of you a great nation, and I will bless you, and *make your name great,* so that you will be a blessing. . . . In you *all the families of the earth* shall be blessed" (Gen 12:2-3). God's promise to Abram was fulfilled in Abram's great descendant, Jesus Christ. When Jesus died at Calvary, he took away "the sin of the world" (John 1:29). When Jesus rose again, he commanded his disciples, "Go . . . and make disciples of *all nations.*"

God's promise of blessing to the nations received an initial fulfillment at Pentecost when the ascended Lord poured out the Holy Spirit. Luke reports that Jesus' followers "were filled with the Holy Spirit and began to speak in other languages, as the Spirit gave them ability. Now there were devout Jews from *every nation under heaven* living in Jerusalem. And at this sound the crowd gathered and was bewildered, because each one heard them speaking in the native language of each . . . about God's deeds and power" (Acts 2:4-6, 11). God enabled people to "hear" each other again, which resulted in amazing unity among people from different nations (see Acts 2:41-47). For the church of Jesus Christ, Pentecost reversed the judgment of Babel.[35] In contrast to Babel, which represents a human, secular kingdom, Jerusalem represents the kingdom of God. In contrast to Babel, which represents human autonomy and might, Jerusalem represents the city where people rely on God for security and seek to obey his will. But Jerusalem at Pentecost was only an initial fulfillment of God's promise to bless the nations. Exiled to the island of Patmos, John received a vision of the final fulfillment in the new Jerusalem: "And in the Spirit he carried me away to a great, high mountain [cf. Isa 2:2-4] and showed me *the holy city Jerusalem* coming down out of heaven from God. . . . The city has no need of sun or moon to shine on it, for the glory of God is its light, and its lamp is the Lamb. *The nations* will walk by its light, and the kings of the earth will bring their glory into it. . . . People will bring into it the glory and the honor of *the nations*" (Rev 21:10, 23-24, 26).

The church today lives in the time between the initial fulfillment of God's promise of blessings for the nations and the final fulfillment. Today the church finds itself in the age of fear. People are afraid of rogue states, terrorists, and the spread of nuclear weapons and other weapons of mass destruction. And nations seek to deal with this fear by arming themselves to the teeth: developing smart bombs, weapons of mass destruction, spy satellites, and missile shields. Christians, too, may be tempted to seek security not in God but in a nation bristling with armor and defensive shields. The story of Babel tells us that our

35. "The Spirit does not remove diverse languages but allows the regenerate people to hear and understand one another. The Spirit alters the effects of their languages from deconstructing the community to reconstructing the new community of the church." Waltke, *Genesis,* 184.

human ingenuity and mightiest accomplishments mean little in the eyes of God if they counter his purposes. Our ultimate security lies not in human "towers," whether United Nations towers or trade-center towers, intelligence, communication satellites,[36] or missile shields. Our security lies in the transcendent, sovereign God alone. He alone is able to break down kingdoms that oppose his redemptive purposes for his world and people. He alone is able to bring his peaceable kingdom on earth. And he will do it. John was privileged to see the new Jerusalem and pass this hopeful vision on to the persecuted church:

I saw a new heaven and a new earth. . . .
And I saw the holy city, the new Jerusalem,
  coming down out of heaven from God,
  prepared as a bride adorned for her husband.
And I heard a loud voice from the throne saying,
"See, the home of God is among mortals.
He will dwell with them;
  they will be his peoples,
and God himself will be with them;
  he will wipe every tear from their eyes.
Death will be no more;
  mourning and crying and pain will be no more,
for the first things have passed away."

(Rev 21:1-4)

36. One of the designers of the Early Bird, the first communications satellite planted 22,300 miles above the Atlantic Ocean, was quoted as saying, "What we are trying to do is to save the world."

CHAPTER 7

The Call of Abram

Genesis 11:27–12:9

This narrative relates God's call to Abram, "Go from your country and your kindred and your father's house to the land that I will show you," and Abram's obedient response. One of the challenges preachers face with this narrative is to formulate and focus the sermon on a single theme. Where will the emphasis fall: on God's call and rich promises, including the gift of the land, or on Abram's actions when he arrives in the land? Another challenge is to avoid superficial "character-imitation" preaching.[1] In their justified concern to preach a relevant message, preachers can easily turn this biblical narrative into a moral tale: God's call to Abram becomes God's call to everyone, and they, like Abram, must respond with unquestioning obedience. In such sermons preachers tend to apply God's unique call of Abram directly to everyone in the congregation, thus committing the error of generalizing/universalizing.[2] But since they realize that people cannot literally imitate Abram by actually leaving their country and moving to Canaan, they spiritualize the text: people must leave their "country," that is, their old way of life, and go to the new life God will show them. This message is not unbiblical, but it is not the message of this particular text. It fails to ask first what was the message the narrator intended to convey to Israel.

Text and Context

Having recorded the story of Babel, the final major rebellion of humanity in Israel's prehistory, the narrator quickly moves by way of the *tôlĕdôt* of Noah's son

1. See my *Modern Preacher,* 161-66.

2. See Ernest Best, *From Text to Sermon: Responsible Use of the New Testament in Preaching* (Atlanta: John Knox, 1978), 86-89.

Shem (11:10) in ten generations to Abram (11:26). Because God had scattered humanity at Babel, he can now call an individual (Abram) to carry the banner for God's kingdom. In contrast to Babel, where people sought to make a name for themselves (11:4), the LORD here promises Abram, "I will make your name great" (12:2).

The narrative begins at Genesis 11:27, which opens a new *tôlĕdôt,* "Now these are the descendants of Terah," and it ends at Genesis 12:9 with Abram reaching the Negeb, the southern border of the Promised Land. Genesis 12:10 begins a new narrative with Abram going down to Egypt.

As to the broader context, the narrator has carefully shaped the Abraham cycle of narratives in a chiastic pattern. This enables the reader to see not only progression in the narratives but also the parallels between narratives.

A Genealogy of Terah (11:27-32)
 B Start of Abram's spiritual odyssey (12:1-9)
  C Sarai in foreign palace; ordeal ends in peace and success; Abram and Lot part (12:10–13:18)
   D Abram comes to the rescue of Sodom and Lot (14:1-24)
    E Covenant with Abram; Annunciation of Ishmael (15:1–16:16)
    E′ Covenant with Abraham; Annunciation of Isaac (17:1–18:15)
   D′ Abraham comes to the rescue of Sodom and Lot (18:16–19:38)
  C′ Sarah in foreign palace; ordeal ends in peace and success; Abraham and Ishmael part (20:1–21:34)
 B′ Climax of Abraham's spiritual odyssey (22:1-19)
A′ Genealogy of Nahor (22:20-24)[3]

Literary Features

The narrator again is omniscient: he knows the situation in "Ur of the Chaldeans" (11:28), that is, Babylonia, where Abram is born and marries Sarai; he knows that Sarai is barren (11:30); he travels with Terah's family to Haran (11:31), overhears the LORD calling Abram (12:1-3), travels with Abram through the Promised Land, and explains to Israel, "At that time the Canaanites were in the land" (12:6).

The narrative proper has two scenes.

Scene 1: The LORD calls Abram to go and Abram goes (vv 1-5b).
Scene 2: Abram passes through Canaan building altars to the LORD (vv 5c-9).

3. Rendsburg, *The Redaction of Genesis,* 28-29. See pp. 29-52 for details.

Hebrew narrative usually has two characters in each scene, and here the LORD and Abram appear in each scene. Hebrew narrative seldom employs character description, but when it does, it is important. Here the narrator relates that "Sarai was barren"; repeated in parallel form for emphasis, "she had no child" (11:30). He also notes that "Abram was seventy-five years old" (12:4). These descriptions are important especially to set the tension for the macronarrative that will not be resolved until Genesis 21, the birth of Isaac.

Characters are usually fleshed out with dialogue. Like Abel and Noah before him, Abram does not get a line in this narrative, but his actions speak louder than words. The LORD commands Abram to go and promises rich blessings (Gen 12:1-3), and Abram responds obediently (vv 4-6). Further, the LORD promises to give the land of the Canaanites to Abram's seed (v 7), and Abram responds by building altars to the LORD (vv 7b-8).

Frequently the narrator will highlight the point of his narrative by repeating keywords. In this narrative he uses the keyword "go" in two strategic spots (vv 1, 4). He repeats the word "bless," "blessing" five times (vv 2-3). The narrator also uses the word "land" referring to Canaan seven times (11:31; 12:1, 5b, 5c, 6a, 6b, 7). And finally he reports twice in this narrative that Abram "built an altar to the LORD" (vv 7b, 8b, and again in 13:18).

The Plot Line

In the setting of this narrative (and of the whole Abraham cycle) the narrator introduces Terah's family and relates that Sarai was barren (11:27-30). The preliminary incidents consist of Terah migrating with his family to Haran and his death there (11:31-32). The narrative conflict begins with the LORD's call to Abram, "Go from *your country*," and rises with each segment, "and *your kindred* and *your father's house* to the land *I will show you*" (12:1). The LORD encourages Abram by promising rich blessings for Abram himself ("I will make of you a great nation, and I will bless you, and make your name great"), for his contemporaries ("so that you will be a blessing. I will bless those who bless you"), and for all families ("in you all the families of the earth shall be blessed") (vv 2-3). God's call of Abram obviously has a universal end in view — "all the families of the earth." These promises to Abram are so rich, one might well base a sermon on this subunit of verses 1-3 alone. But the story continues to the resolution of the conflict. The tension begins to resolve in verses 4-5, "So Abram went . . . ," but it flares up again when Abram finds the land occupied by Canaanites (v 6), descendants of Canaan whom Noah had cursed. This complication is quickly resolved when the LORD promises this land to Abram's seed (v 7). The outcome of the narrative relates that Abram builds altars to the LORD at Shechem and

Bethel and continues traveling toward the Negeb (vv 7-9). We can sketch the plot line as a single plot.

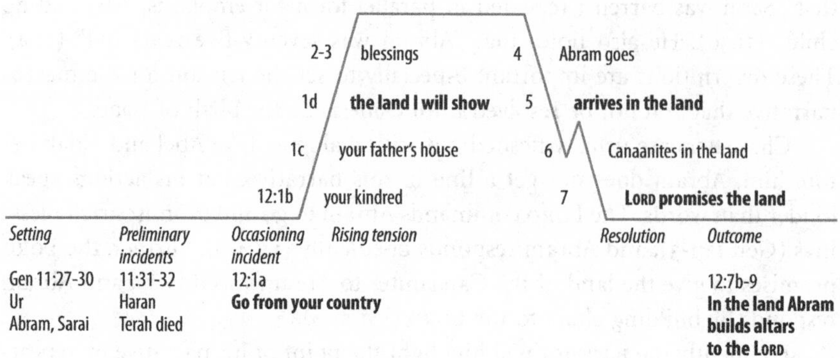

Theocentric Interpretation

It is clear that the narrative starting at 12:1 is theocentric throughout. The LORD is the subject of the very first verb;[4] he orders Abram, "Go" (v 1); he promises, "I will," "I will" — four times (vv 1-3); he appears to Abram in Canaan and adds another "I will" (v 7). Even Abram's actions are God-centered: in obedience to God's command he goes to the land and, arriving there, builds altars to the LORD.

Textual Theme and Goal

We have to choose between two themes in this passage. The first theme is found in verses 2 and 3: "The LORD promises to bless Abram so richly that in him all the families of the earth shall be blessed." These promises introduce a major theme in the book of Genesis as they are repeated many times to Abram, Isaac, and Jacob.[5] In fact, they are the theme of a macro-plot in Genesis that covers at least Genesis 12–36.[6] If one wishes to preach this theme, it would be better to se-

4. "Yahweh is the subject of the first verb at the beginning of the first statement and thus the subject of the entire subsequent sacred history." Von Rad, *Genesis,* 159.

5. For Abram, see also Genesis 13:14-18; 15:4-5, 13-21; 17:4-8; 18:17-19; 22:15-18. For Isaac, see 26:4, 24; and for Jacob 28:13-15; 35:11-12; and 46:3.

6. "There is a consensus among biblical scholars (e.g., von Rad, Westermann, Clines, Kaiser, VanGemeren) that the theological theme that unites at least Gen 12–36 is that of divine promise to the individuals Abraham, Isaac, and Jacob." Hamilton, "Genesis: Theology of," 666.

lect as a preaching-text the subunit of Genesis 12:1-3. We will cover these promises in three of the following chapters as the "settings" for later narratives which show their initial fulfillments: the initial fulfillment of the promise of seed in the birth of Isaac (21:1-7); the initial fulfillment of the promise of land in the burial plot for Sarah (23:1-20); and the initial fulfillment of a blessing to all the families of the earth in Joseph saving "all the world" (41:57).

Since we have selected as our text the whole narrative of God's call of Abram and his response, the theme that now becomes dominant has to do with the land (7×) that God said he would show Abram (v 1), the land of Canaan where they arrive (v 5), the land which the LORD promises to give to Abram's seed (v 7), the land on which Abram builds altars to the LORD (vv 7, 8). It seems clear that the narrator's theme of this whole narrative focuses on God's gift of the land and Abram's response of building altars to the LORD. The question that now becomes crucial is, What is the significance of Abram building altars to the LORD? He builds the first altar to the LORD in the center of the land at Shechem, where he hears God's promise, "To your seed I will give this land" (12:7). He builds this altar within view of the oak of Moreh, a Canaanite shrine. Then he moves south and stops at Bethel to build another altar to the LORD. And finally he moves on toward the Negeb, the southern border of the land (where he will build another altar "by the oaks of Mamre," 13:18). Why is Abram building altars to the LORD next to Canaanite shrines at strategic locations in the land? And why is he building altars only in the Promised Land and nowhere else? Many commentaries overlook this key question, but John Calvin has caught its import. He writes that Abram "endeavoured, as much as in him lay, to dedicate to God, every part of the land to which he had access, and perfumed it with the odour of his faith."[7]

Abram is doing the same thing as Noah did before him: by building an altar, Noah dedicated the cleansed earth to the LORD (8:20); now Abram dedicates this land of the Canaanites (the seed of the serpent) to the LORD. A good textual theme, therefore, would run something like this: "The LORD gives Abram/Israel the land of the Canaanites in order to reclaim it for the worship of the LORD." However, the meaning of "for the worship of the LORD" is not entirely clear. We can clarify this point by formulating the textual theme as follows: *The LORD gives Abram/Israel the land of the Canaanites in order to reclaim it for the kingdom of God.*[8]

7. Calvin, *Genesis,* I, 357. Cf. Kidner, *Genesis,* 115, "It was a foretaste of things to come that at this stronghold of other gods the Lord revealed His presence, allocated the land to His servant and received formal homage."

8. "Abraham sets out for this land (12:1-3), and when he arrives he sets up altars at Shechem and Ai, thereby claiming it for God (12:4-9)." "Abraham does not use a Canaanite altar. His altar is an expression of gratitude (see 8:20) and consecration of the Promised Land to God (see also 12:8; 13:18; 22:9; 26:25; 35:7; Ex 20:24; Josh 22:19)." Waltke, *Genesis,* 202 and 208.

As to the narrator's goal, we must remember that these narratives about Israel's patriarchs are more than stories about God and Abram, Isaac, and Jacob; these stories are also about God and Israel. The patriarchs are more than individuals; they also represent their "seed," Israel. Jacob, of course, was also called Israel. But Abram/Abraham, too, represents later Israel. "Thus the Abraham stories often need to be read on different levels, both for what they say about Abraham in his own right, and for what they show about Abraham as a type of Israel."[9] John Sailhamer observes, "It is as if the Pentateuch was telling its readers that just as God had given the land to Abraham, so also he would give the land to the 'seed' of Abraham as they were about to go in to take the land under the leadership of Joshua."[10] Therefore, if the narrator penned this narrative for Israel while they were in Moab, about to enter the Promised Land, his goal would have been, *to motivate Israel to reclaim the land of the Canaanites for the kingdom of God.*

Later, when Israel was in exile in Babylon, they would have been equally encouraged by this narrative. Here they found themselves captives in Abram's home country, for he was born "in Ur of the *Chaldeans*"[11] (11:28). But God had spoken to him, "I am the LORD who brought you from Ur of the Chaldeans, to give you this land to possess" (15:7). And Abram had responded to God's gift by building altars to the LORD, reclaiming the land for the kingdom of God. At this later stage in Israel's history, therefore, this narrative would also have motivated the returning remnant to reclaim the Promised Land for the kingdom of God. For, as Isaiah (51:3) prophesied to the exiles:

> The LORD will comfort Zion;
> he will comfort all her waste places,
> and will make her wilderness like Eden,
> her desert like the garden of the LORD;
> joy and gladness will be found in her,
> thanksgiving and the voice of song.

9. Moberly, "Genesis 12–50," 109. Cf. Mathews, *Genesis 1–11:26*, 52, "Patriarchal episodes prefigured events in the life of Israel, thus connecting the experiences of Moses' community with those of its fathers. We find this, for example, in the route of Abraham in Canaan by way of Shechem, Ai/Bethel, and the Negev (Gen 12:1-9), which is repeated by Jacob upon his return from Haran (Gen 33:18-20; 35:14-15, 27); both patriarchs build altars of worship at Shechem and Bethel. The pattern of traversing these three regions is repeated in the conquest narratives of Joshua: Ai/Bethel (Josh 7:2; 8:9), Shechem, where an altar is built (Josh 8:30), and south of Ai/Bethel toward the Negev (Josh 10) and then north of Shechem (Josh 11)."

10. Sailhamer, *Pentateuch as Narrative*, 4. Cf. Wenham, *Genesis 1–15*, 283, Abram's "actions, however briefly related, are an acted prophecy. They foreshadow the day when Israel will take possession of the whole land and worship the LORD there."

11. "'Chaldeans' is a term that strictly belongs only to the first millennium (cf. its prominence in Isaiah, Jeremiah, etc.)." Goldingay, "The Patriarchs in Scripture and History," 41, n. 19.

Ways to Preach Christ

Keeping in mind the theme, "The LORD gives Abram/Israel the land of the Canaanites in order to reclaim it for the kingdom of God," we now explore the seven ways of moving to Christ in the New Testament.

Redemptive-Historical Progression

One can preach Christ from this narrative by using the way of redemptive-historical progression. In the beginning God created the earth as his kingdom where he would be worshiped and served as the great King. God placed the first human pair in a beautiful garden, Paradise, "the garden of God," where they could live in the presence of God. But the human Fall into sin led to disastrous consequences: God drove them out of the garden; the close communion with God was broken. Human sin resulted in such violence that proper development of human life and culture became impossible. God sent a great flood to cleanse the earth and to make a new start with Noah, who built "an altar to the LORD" (8:20) to rededicate the cleansed earth to God. But humankind again defied God at Babel, resulting in God confusing their language and scattering them across the earth. Then God called Abram to leave his father's house and its gods. God would make a new start with him in the land of Canaan, which was watered "like the garden of the LORD" (13:10).[12] Canaan was to become another Paradise — a beachhead on earth for the kingdom of God.

As with Adam and Noah, the LORD promises to bless Abram. In fact, the LORD promises, "In you all the families of the earth shall be blessed" (Gen 12:3). In calling Abram/Israel to reclaim Canaan for his kingdom, God has the whole earth in view. Abram was the first to build altars to the LORD in this land. Later, Israel was to continue worshiping the LORD in this land, praising his name, obeying his commands (theocracy). Israel was to reveal in its national life the peace and justice of the kingdom of God. It was to manifest the kingdom of God in Canaan — not for Israel's benefit alone, but for the sake of the whole world (e.g., Ps 72:17; Isa 49:6). When Israel failed to manifest the kingdom of God, God banished the nation from the Promised Land.[13]

In the fullness of time God made a new start by sending his Son, Jesus. Jesus

12. "The land represented prosperity under God's watchful eye, fruitful fields and herds, an abundance of grain, wine, and oil, and numerous descendants. Such was the land promised by the Lord. But above all other blessings, the land symbolized safety, peace, and rest." David Holwerda, *Jesus and Israel,* 90.

13. "Just as faith and the obedience that flows from faith were necessary to enter the land, so faith and obedience are necessary to maintain possession of the land." Ibid., 90.

came preaching, "The time is fulfilled, and the kingdom of God has come near" (Mark 1:15). Jesus showed the reality of the kingdom in his miracles of feeding the hungry, healing the sick, casting out demons, and raising the dead. When some accused Jesus of casting out demons by Beelzebul, the ruler of the demons, Jesus said, "If it is by the finger of God that I cast out the demons, then the kingdom of God has come to you" (Luke 11:20). After his death and resurrection, Jesus mandated his disciples, "Go . . . and make disciples of all nations . . ." (Matt 28:19), and the kingdom of God started to spread throughout the world. When Jesus comes again, he will establish his kingdom on earth in perfection. The ascended Lord promises: "To everyone who conquers, I will give permission to eat from the tree of life that is in the paradise of God" (Rev 2:7). God "will dwell [tabernacle] with them; they will be his peoples, and God himself will be with them" (Rev 21:3). Paradise will be restored on earth (Rev 22:1-5).

One can also follow the trail of the seed of the woman. After Adam and Noah, Abram is the next important link in the line of the seed of the woman God promised in Genesis 3:15. Abram comes from the line of Shem (Gen 11:10) and is another number "ten" (11:26), like Noah. "He, like Noah before him, is a second Adam figure. Adam was given the garden of Eden: Abraham is promised the land of Canaan. God told Adam to be fruitful and multiply: Abraham is promised descendants as numerous as the stars of heaven. God walked with Adam in Eden: Abram was told to walk before God. In this way the advent of Abraham is seen as the answer to the problems set out in Genesis 1–11: through him all the families of the earth will be blessed."[14] God now promises to give the land of Canaan to Abram's "seed" (Gen 12:7), Israel, which is to be a witness of God's good kingdom to the nations of the world (e.g., Ps 105:1; Jonah). Even though Israel fails and God punishes her with exile from the land, God uses Israel to give birth to *the* Seed of the woman, Jesus Christ. Through his own Son, God again makes a new start at establishing his kingdom on earth. At his First Coming Jesus inaugurated the kingdom of God on earth; at his Second Coming he will bring it in perfection.

Promise-Fulfillment

The LORD makes several promises in this narrative. The LORD promises, "To your offspring I will give this land" (12:7). This promise gradually fills up beginning

14. Wenham, *Story as Torah,* 37. Cf. Sailhamer, *Genesis,* 91, "Both Noah and Abraham represent new beginnings in the course of events recorded in Genesis. Both are marked by God's promise of blessing and his gift of the covenant." See there also for the "striking thematic parallel between the picture of God's calling Noah out of the ark (8:15-20) and the call of Abraham (12:1-7)."

with Abraham's purchase of a burial plot for Sarah (Gen 23:18, 20); next, under Joshua, with the capture of the land around 1240 B.C. (Josh 21:43-45); and finally with the inheritance of the new earth:[15] "In accordance with his promise, we wait for new heavens and a new earth, where righteousness is at home" (2 Pet 3:13).

The LORD also promised, "I will make of you a great nation" (12:2). This promise gradually fills up: first with the birth of Isaac, then Jacob, the twelve sons and *seventy* Israelites going down to Egypt (Exod 1:5); next Israel in Canaan under Joshua, the nation reaching a high point under David and Solomon around 1000 B.C. (1 Kings 4:20-25). The New Testament writers see further fulfillment of this promise when Jesus mandates his followers to make disciples of all nations. Paul declares, "In Christ Jesus you are all children [sons = heirs] of God through faith. . . . There is no longer Jew or Greek . . . ; for all of you are one in Christ Jesus. And if you belong to Christ, then you are Abraham's offspring [seed], heirs according to the promise" (Gal 3:26-29). And John writes about the new Jerusalem: "The nations will walk by its light, and the kings of the earth will bring their glory into it. . . . People will bring into it the glory and the honor of the nations" (Rev 21:24-26).

The LORD also promised Abram, "In you all the families of the earth shall be blessed" (12:3). This promise, too, gradually fills up: first when Joseph is a blessing to the families of the earth, "all the world" (41:57) coming to Joseph for food; next when God uses Israel as a witness to the world (e.g., Jonah); and then when Jesus sends his followers to "make disciples of all nations" (Matt 28:19). This promise of being a blessing to all families of the earth also awaits its final fulfillment. Although this is not a direct messianic promise (but see Ps 72:17), the New Testament shows that this promise was and is being fulfilled in Jesus Christ. Paul writes, "And the scripture, foreseeing that God would justify the Gentiles by faith, declared the gospel beforehand to Abraham, saying, 'All the Gentiles shall be blessed in you' . . . in order that in Christ Jesus the blessing of Abraham might come to the Gentiles" (Gal 3:8, 14).[16]

If we had selected as a preaching-text Genesis 12:1-3, promise-fulfillment would certainly be an appropriate way of preaching Christ. But since we have selected the whole narrative as our text, our theme indicates that promise-fulfillment is not the best way of preaching Christ in this particular sermon.

15. "The New Testament has neither forgotten nor rejected the promise of the land. Earthly Jerusalem has been transcended, but the present location of the city in heaven is viewed within the continuing history of redemption, which will culminate on the renewed earth. The heavenly Jerusalem will descend as the new Jerusalem, but not until its citizens have been gathered from among the nations of the world." Holwerda, *Christ and Israel,* 111-12; see especially 101-12.

16. See also Gal 3:16 and Acts 3:25-26. Calvin, *Genesis,* I, 348-49, writes, "Therefore God (in my judgment) pronounces that all nations should be blessed in his servant Abram, because Christ was included in his loins."

Typology

Abram is a type of Christ: he not only represents the seed of the woman who is given the land (as Adam was given the garden) but in building altars to the LORD in Canaan, he reclaims this land for the LORD. "His actions . . . foreshadow the day when Israel will take possession of the whole land and worship the LORD there."[17] But Abram's actions foreshadow more than Israel worshiping the LORD in Canaan. As seed of the woman reclaiming the land for the LORD, Abram foreshadows Jesus Christ, *the* Seed of the woman, who restores true worship of God and who sends out his disciples to make disciples of all nations, thus reclaiming the whole world for the LORD. Moreover, as God made Abram's name great (12:2), so God "highly exalted" Jesus "and gave him the name that is above every name" (Phil 2:9).

Analogy

One can also use analogy to preach Christ from this narrative. Directly related to the goal, one can draw the analogy this way: As the LORD called Abram/Israel to reclaim Canaan for his kingdom, so Christ calls his disciples (past and present) to reclaim the ends of the earth for the kingdom of God. This analogy can be supported by quoting Jesus in the New Testament: either, "Go therefore and make disciples of all nations" (Matt 28:19), or, "You will be my witnesses in Jerusalem, in all Judea and Samaria, and to the ends of the earth" (Acts 1:8).

Longitudinal Themes

One can also trace in Scripture the theme of land where God is worshiped: from the garden of Eden (Gen 2), to expulsion from the garden (Gen 3), to Abram reclaiming the land of Canaan for the worship of the LORD (Gen 12), to Israel worshiping the Lord in the land (tabernacle, temple), to Israel being expelled from the land (exile), to Jesus teaching the Samaritan woman, "Woman, believe me, the hour is coming when you will worship the Father neither on this mountain [Mount Gerizim near Shechem] nor in Jerusalem. . . . The hour is coming, and is now here, when the true worshipers will worship the Father in spirit and truth" (John 4:21-23), to Jesus' teaching, "Blessed are the meek, for they shall inherit *the earth*" (Matt 5:5), to Jesus' mandate to make disciples of all nations (Matt 28:19), to Jesus' Second Com-

17. Wenham, *Genesis 1–15*, 283.

ing when "people will bring into it [the new Jerusalem] the glory and the honor of the nations" (Rev 21:26).

New Testament References

In addition to the New Testament references cited above, one can perhaps make use of the following texts:

Matthew 1:1, "An account of the genealogy of Jesus the Messiah, the son of David, the son of Abraham."

Matthew 24:14, Jesus words: "This good news of the kingdom will be proclaimed throughout the world, as a testimony to all the nations; and then the end will come."

Romans 4:13, where Paul sees God's promise of land to Abram in the light of Jesus' death and resurrection and speaks of it as "the promise that he [Abraham] would inherit the *world*."

Contrast

The way of contrast, finally, can be used as a bridge to Jesus in the New Testament because it was Jesus himself who mandated his disciples not to concentrate only on the land of Canaan as Abram and Israel had, but to bring the gospel of the kingdom "in Jerusalem, in all Judea and Samaria, and to the ends of the earth" (Acts 1:7; cf. Matt 28:19).

Sermon Theme and Goal

The sermon theme should be the same as that of the text unless there is good reason to change it in the light of the New Testament. Even then the theme of the sermon ought to be rooted in the theme of the text. In the light of Jesus' statement that "the meek . . . will inherit the *earth*" (Matt 5:5), and his broadening of the missionary mandate to *all nations* (Matt 28:19), the textual theme will have to be broadened so that it can function as the sermon theme for the church today. Therefore, instead of, "The LORD gives Abram/Israel the land of the Canaanites in order to reclaim it for the kingdom of God," we can make the sermon theme: *The LORD gives his people the earth in order to reclaim it for the kingdom of God.*

Our goal in preaching the sermon should match the sermon theme and be in line with the narrator's goal. Since the narrator's goal was "to motivate Israel to reclaim the land of the Canaanites for the kingdom of God," the goal of this sermon can be *to motivate God's people to reclaim the earth (all nations) for God's kingdom.*

Reflecting on the need addressed in this sermon, the question is, Why do we have to motivate God's people today to reclaim the earth for God's kingdom? What is it today that saps our missionary zeal? I suggest that today our missionary zeal is being undermined by the contemporary traps of materialism and consumerism.

Sermon Exposition

In the introduction to the sermon, one can illustrate the need addressed, namely that contemporary materialism and consumerism sap our missionary zeal. But God has a calling for his people. That call and calling came first to Abram.

As we read in Genesis 11:28, Abram was born "in Ur of the Chaldeans," that is, Babylonia, present-day Iraq. Babylonia is associated with Babel, where people rebelled against God's mandate to "fill the earth." Instead people tried to stick together by building a large city with a huge tower. They did not want to spread the kingdom of God around the world as God desired (Gen 1:28; 9:1). God quashed their rebellion by confusing their language and scattering the people to different lands (Gen 11 and 10). But people still did not serve the true God. Abram and his relatives worshiped pagan gods. Joshua later told the tribes of Israel as they gathered at Shechem, "Long ago your ancestors — Terah and his sons Abraham and Nahor — lived beyond the Euphrates and served other gods" (Josh 24:2).[18]

With God's judgment of the rebellion at Babel, the question is if God is giving up on his plan of establishing his kingdom on earth. The answer is a firm, No. After reporting on Babel, the narrator gives the family history of Shem, the son Noah blessed (9:26), the seed of the woman. And in ten generations he arrives at Abram (11:26). Abram is another Noah (who was the tenth generation from Adam) with whom God will make a new beginning.

This new beginning, however, requires a major test of Abram's obedience. Genesis 12:1, "Now the Lord said to Abram, 'Go from your country and your kindred and your father's house to the land[19] I will show you.'" The word of the

18. One of these gods was the moon-god Sin, which was worshiped both in Ur and in Haran. "In fact, the Abrahamic family names Terah, Sarah, Milcah and Laban, all reflect traces of a connection with moon worship." Sarna, *Understanding Genesis*, 98.

19. "As Adam and Eve had known God's blessing in Eden, so God would bless his people in

LORD that called the cosmos into being (10 × "God said") now calls Abram to reestablish God's kingdom on earth. But Abram has to make a complete break with his past. God calls for him to go and leave behind everything that is dear to him. In our highly mobile society we can hardly imagine the conflict the LORD's command raises for Abram: "Go from your country?" Very difficult. "And your kindred," your more distant relatives? Almost impossible. "And your father's house?" How could the LORD possibly ask Abram to leave his father's house, his immediate family? That is his very identity. He is Abram *bēn* Terah, son of Terah. His father's house is his house; his father's goods are his goods; his father's gods are his gods. "To leave home and to break ancestral bonds was to expect of ancient men almost the impossible."[20] Yet the LORD commands him, "Go from your country and your kindred and your father's house to the land I will show you." "To the land I will show you" raises the tension even further. Nothing is certain here. This is no emigration to the riches of the United States or Canada. Abram is asked to trust blindly that the LORD will lead him to a favorable land.[21]

The LORD encourages Abram by giving him seven great promises.[22] Verses 2-3, "[1] I will make of you a great nation, and [2] I will bless you, and [3] make your name great, [4] so that you will be a blessing. [5] I will bless those who bless you, and [6] the one who curses you I will curse; and [7] in you all the families of the earth shall be blessed." Seven promises. "Seven" is the number of perfection, of completeness. God's promises to Abram are complete. And five times these promises contain the word "bless(ing)." This fivefold blessing continues the fivefold use of blessing in Genesis 1–11.[23] God's fivefold blessing to Abram is "the gracious counterbalance to the five 'curses' against fallen creation and humanity (3:14, 17b; 4:11; 8:21; 9:25)."[24] Ultimately, this blessing will nullify

---

a new land. This idea of restoration to paradise provides the proper biblical context for understanding God's promise to give land to Abraham (Gen 12:1)." Robertson, *The Israel of God*, 7.

20. Von Rad, *Genesis*, 161. Cf. Dumbrell, *Covenant and Creation*, 57, "The call was to abandon all natural connections, to surrender all social customs and traditions, to leave land, clan and family. These were the very areas of strong attachment which in the ancient world would have been thought to provide ultimate personal security."

21. Calvin comments, "This is another test to prove the faith of Abram. For why does not God immediately point out the land, except for the purpose of keeping his servant in suspense, that he may the better try the truth of his attachment to the word of God? As if he would say, 'I command thee to go forth with closed eyes, and forbid thee to inquire whither I am about to lead thee, until, having renounced thy country, thou shalt have given thyself wholly to me.'" *Genesis*, I, 344.

22. "Doubtless it is also deliberate that the promises to Abram fall into seven clauses in vv 2-3, just as do the promises to Isaac and Jacob in 26:3-4; 27:28-29." Wenham, *Genesis 1–15*, 270.

23. See Genesis 1:22, 28; 2:3; 5:2; 9:1.

24. Mathews, "Genesis," 143.

God's curse. In fact, "the promise of land, nationhood, the presence of God, and blessing to the nations restores what has been lost by man through his misbehavior recorded in Gen 3–11."[25] For God's promises to Abram expand from promises for him personally (great nation, bless you, great name, will be a blessing), to his contemporaries, to the climax, "in you all the families of the earth shall be blessed."[26] This final promise can be fulfilled only in Abram's great son, Jesus Christ (Matt 1:1), who will send out his followers to "make disciples of all nations" (28:19).

Wonderful promises, but could they possibly come true? Take that first promise: "I will make of you a great nation." But "Sarai was barren; she had no child" (11:30). Moreover, Abram was "seventy-five years old" (12:4). How could God fulfill the promise of a great nation to an old man with a barren wife? Or take the last promise, "In you all the families of the earth shall be blessed." How could this ever come about? Lots of questions. Even accepting these promises required a great deal of faith. But we don't hear Abram questioning God. We don't even hear him talk over this dangerous undertaking with his wife Sarai. We don't see Abram tossing and turning in bed, wondering what to make of the voice he had heard.

After rapidly building up the tension in this narrative, the narrator resolves it even faster: verse 4, "So Abraham went, as the LORD had told him." God said, "Go" and Abram "went." Simple obedience. Just like Noah before him, simple obedience to the word of the LORD.

In verse 5 the narrator informs us of the people who went with Abram: "his wife Sarai and his brother's son Lot, and all the possessions that they had gathered, and the persons whom they had acquired in Haran; and they set forth to go to the land of Canaan. When they had come to the land of Canaan. . . ." The narrator hurries through the four-hundred-mile journey. One can hardly imagine how long that journey would have taken with sheep and goats, and how dangerous it may have been. But the narrator's interest lies elsewhere. In but one sentence he covers four hundred miles and then takes all of four verses to cover the next seventy-five: Abram's actions in the land. Obviously the narrator wishes to emphasize what Abram does in Canaan. Abram passes through the land from north to south. It is a good land. Moses will later tell Israel, "The

25. Wenham, *Genesis 1–15*, li. Cf. p. 275, "Blessing not only connects the patriarchal narratives with each other (cf. 24:1; 26:3; 35:9; 39:5), it also links them with the primeval history (cf. 1:28; 5:2; 9:1). The promises of blessing to the patriarchs are thus a reassertion of God's original intentions for man."

26. "It is agreed that the principal statement of these three verses is contained in the final clause of v. 3. The Hebrew syntax indicates this and the clause is most probably to be taken as a result clause. . . . That is to say, the personal promises given to Abram have final world blessing as their aim." Dumbrell, *Covenant and Creation*, 65.

LORD your God is bringing you into a good land, a land with flowing streams . . . , a land of wheat and barley, of vines and fig trees and pomegranates, a land of olive trees and honey" (Deut 8:7-8). It is like another Paradise,[27] "like the garden of the LORD" (Gen 13:10). But Abram's delight is short-lived.

Verse 6, "Abram passed through the land to the place at Shechem, to the oak of Moreh." The oak of Moreh was a shrine where the Canaanites worshiped their pagan gods.[28] The narrator adds ominously, "At that time the Canaanites were in the land." The Canaanites were the descendants of Canaan whom Noah had cursed (Gen 9:25). The land to which the LORD has led Abram is occupied territory and that by an accursed people, the seed of the serpent.

But this complication is quickly resolved, for here, in the midst of the land of the Canaanites, the LORD appears to Abram and promises: verse 7, "To your offspring [seed] I will give this land." God is going to *give*[29] this occupied land to Abram's seed. It will be their "inheritance."[30]

Abram's response to this gracious promise is profound: "He built an altar there to the LORD [Yahweh], who had appeared to him" (v 7). In the center of the land of Canaan, in view of the Canaanite shrine, Abram erects the first altar to the LORD.[31]

Then Abram moves further south to Bethel. And again (v 8), "he built an altar to the LORD [Yahweh] and invoked the name of the LORD." Abram then journeys on "by stages toward the Negeb" (v 9) — all the way to the southern

27. "The original idea of land as paradise significantly shaped the expectations associated with redemption. As the place of blessedness arising from unbroken fellowship and communion with God, the land of paradise became the goal toward which redeemed humanity was returning." Robertson, *Israel of God,* 4.

28. "The 'terebinth of Moreh' as a sacred tree was the focus of a Canaanite cultic center and still important in Israelite times (Gen 35:4; Deut 11:30; Josh 24:26; Judg 9:37)." Von Rad, *Genesis,* 162. Later Jacob, returning from Haran, would collect the foreign gods his household had brought along and bury them "under the oak that was near Shechem" (Gen 35:4; cf. 31:19, 34).

29. "The trophies that the people of Babel attempted to take for themselves — fame, security, and a heritage for the future — are God's *free* gift to Abraham." Bartholomew and Goheen, *The Drama of Scripture,* 54. Cf. Holwerda, *Jesus and Israel,* 93, "The nature of the land as a gift is reflected further in the fact that the land is divided by lot (Numbers 26:55), that its firstfruits must be given to the Lord, that the land must observe a sabbath, and that land sold for debt must be returned to the original family in the year of Jubilee. . . . Israel is chosen to possess the land as an inheritance from the Lord, but its title remains in the Lord's hands."

30. See, e.g., Ps 37:9, 11, 22, 27, 29, 34.

31. "Subsequently, after the gift of the Promised Land to Israel under the leadership of Joshua, Shechem became the first site of the central sanctuary of the twelve-tribe federation in the time of the judges. It was destroyed by the armies of Assyria in 722 B.C., but was then rebuilt about 350 B.C. and became the religious center of the Samaritans, who erected their temple there on Mount Gerizim (cf. John 4:21)." Elizabeth Achtemeier, "Genesis 12:1-9," in Van Harn, ed., *The Lectionary Commentary,* I, 26.

border of Canaan. In the next chapter, 13:18, we read that "Abram settled by the oaks of Mamre [again a Canaanite shrine] which are at Hebron; and there he built an altar to the LORD."

Why does the narrator emphasize that Abram, journeying through the Promised Land by stages, builds altars to the LORD right next to the Canaanite shrines? Clearly Abram is reclaiming this land for the LORD. Just as Noah before him had dedicated the cleansed earth to the LORD by building an altar to the LORD (8:20), so Abram now dedicates the Promised Land to the LORD. In this land, the LORD will be worshiped and obeyed (cf. Lev 20:22-24). As Calvin put it, Abram "endeavoured, as much as in him lay, to dedicate to God, every part of the land to which he had access, and perfumed it with the odour of his faith."[32] In this land, not the Canaanite gods but the LORD will be King. This is the LORD's country! We can liken Abram's actions to that of the American soldiers in the Second World War raising the American flag on the island of Iwo Jima in the Pacific Ocean. Abram is planting the LORD's flag at strategic locations in the Promised Land, thereby proclaiming that this is a land where the LORD will be worshiped. Abram is reclaiming the land for the kingdom of God.

How would Israel have understood this narrative? Imagine Israel in Moab, about to enter the Promised Land under Joshua. In this narrative they would hear that the LORD promised to give this land of the Canaanites to Abram's seed and that Abram responded to God's promise by building altars to the LORD, thus reclaiming the land for the kingdom of God. And now Abram's seed, Israel, is called to reclaim the Promised Land for the kingdom of God. But not just the Promised Land. Remember the climax of God's promises to Abram: "In you all the families of the earth shall be blessed" (12:3)? The LORD's plan of redemption goes far beyond the land of Canaan. The LORD is still interested in blessing "all the families of the earth." The LORD's design is to spread his kingdom to all nations. Canaan is but a first step.[33] Like the allied invasion of Normandy in 1944 was but a first step in liberating all of Europe (D-day to V-day), so Israel's theocracy in Canaan was but a first step in liberating the entire world by reclaiming all nations for the kingdom of God.

The Israelites were well aware of God's universal design. They prayed with Psalm 72:8, 17-19:

> May he [the king] have dominion from sea to sea,
> and from the River to the ends of the earth. . . .

32. Calvin, *Genesis,* I, 357.

33. "The land which once was the specific place of God's redemptive work served well in the realm of old covenant forms as a picture of paradise lost and promised. But in the realm of new covenant fulfillments, the land has expanded to encompass the whole world." Robertson, *Israel of God,* 31.

May his name endure forever,
his fame continue as long as the sun,
May all nations be blessed in him;
may they pronounce him happy.
Blessed be the LORD, the God of Israel. . . .
May his glory fill *the whole earth.*[34]

This prayer will be fulfilled through Jesus Christ. For in reclaiming Canaan for the kingdom of God, Abram prefigured his Seed, Jesus (Matt 1:1). But one greater than Abram was here. Jesus came to reclaim the whole world for the kingdom of God. "God so loved the world [*kosmos*] that he gave his only Son" (John 3:16). Jesus died to atone for "the sins of the whole world" (1 John 2:2). And he rose again to spread the kingdom of God "from sea to sea." After his resurrection Jesus mandated his disciples to reclaim all nations for the kingdom of God. He commanded them, "Go therefore and make disciples of all nations" (Matt 28:19). That call still comes to us today. As God called Abram and later Israel to reclaim Canaan for his kingdom, so Christ calls his church to reclaim all nations for the kingdom of God. Imagine being partners with Christ in reclaiming the whole earth for the kingdom of God. What a grand, glorious mission!

But it is also a difficult mission. As it was difficult for Abram to leave his country, his kindred, and especially his father's house (his immediate relatives), so Jesus declares that ours is a difficult mission. He says, "Whoever loves father or mother more than me is not worthy of me; and whoever loves son or daughter more than me is not worthy of me; and whoever does not take up the cross and follow me is not worthy of me. Those who find their life will lose it, and those who lose their life for my sake will find it" (Matt 10:37-39). We may lose our life on this mission, but in losing it we will find it.

Jesus begins his Sermon on the Mount with a ninefold blessing for his people — just as God sent Abram on his mission with a complete set of blessings. Jesus proclaims:

"Blessed are the poor in spirit, for theirs is *the kingdom of heaven. . . .*
Blessed are the meek, for they will inherit *the earth. . . .*[35]

34. Israel well knew that "the earth is the LORD's" (Exod 9:29; cf. 19:5; Deut 10:14-15); he had created it.

35. "Although the Greek term found in the Beatitudes for 'earth' is the same as that which is used in the Septuagint for 'land' [see Ps 37:9], the context of Jesus' statement requires a larger frame of reference than the land of Palestine. Jesus teaches not that the Jewish race will inherit the Promised Land, but that in the new covenant the 'meek,' regardless of their ethnic background, will inherit the 'earth,' wherever in this world they might live." Robertson, *Israel of God*, 26-27. The parallelism of receiving the "kingdom of heaven" and inheriting "the earth" also in-

> Blessed are those who are persecuted for righteousness' sake,
> for theirs is *the kingdom of heaven*."
>
> (Matt 5:3, 5, 10)

The poor in spirit will find life in the kingdom of heaven; the meek will find life on the new earth; the persecuted will find life in the kingdom of heaven.

Did you notice, Jesus says that the meek "will *inherit* the earth." The new earth will be the inheritance of God's people. As Canaan was Israel's inheritance,[36] so the new earth will be God's people's inheritance. The new earth will be God's gift to his people. John saw "the new Jerusalem, coming down out of heaven from God, prepared as a bride adorned for her husband." And he heard a voice from the throne saying,

> "See, the home of God is among mortals.
> He will dwell with them;
> they will be his peoples,
> and God himself will be with them."
>
> (Rev 21:3)

And then John sees Paradise on earth. He writes, "Then the angel showed me the river of the water of life, bright as crystal, flowing from the throne of God and of the Lamb. . . . On either side of the river is the tree of life. . . . Nothing accursed will be found there any more. But the throne of God and of the Lamb will be in it, and his servants will worship him; they will see his face" (Rev 22:1-4).

One day this earth will again be like Paradise, "the garden of God," a wonderful place with plenty of food and drink, meaningful work caring for God's creation, and above all, close fellowship with God. The restored earth[37] will be God's gift to his people.

But the gift-character of the new earth does not diminish our calling today

---

dicates that Jesus is thinking of God's kingdom encompassing the entire world. Cf. Rev 11:15, "The kingdom of the world has become the kingdom of our Lord and of his Messiah, and he will reign forever and ever."

36. Although God gives the land to his tenants to use, it remains his land. Cf. Lev 25:23, "The land shall not be sold in perpetuity, for the land is mine; with me you are but aliens and tenants." See also above, p. 153, n. 29 and p. 155, n. 34.

37. "John's vision in Revelation, indeed, the whole New Testament, does not depict salvation as an *escape* from earth into a spiritualized heaven where human souls dwell forever. Instead, John is shown (and shows us in turn) that salvation is the *restoration* of God's creation on a new earth. In this restored world, the redeemed of God will live in resurrected bodies within a renewed creation, from which sin and its effects have been expunged. This is the kingdom that Christ's followers have already begun to enjoy in foretaste." Bartholomew and Goheen, *The Drama of Scripture*, 211. See further 212-13.

to reclaim the world for God's kingdom. Jesus' command still holds: "Go . . . and make disciples of all nations. . . . And remember, I am with you always, to the end of the age" (Matt 28:19-20). God gives his people the earth in order to reclaim it for the kingdom of God.[38]

38. My sermon based on my early research is found in Appendix 5. Note that upon further research, reflection, and a comment by one of my proofreaders, I have adjusted the focus of the theme for this essay by placing more weight on the land as God's gift.

CHAPTER 8

God's Covenant with Abraham

Genesis 17:1-27

The narrative of God establishing his covenant with Abraham and his seed is "a water shed"[1] in the Abraham cycle. Not only is it central in the chiastic structure of the Abraham cycle (see at Genesis 12 on p. 140 above), the narrator may also signal its central position by time designations. Beginning with Terah's age in Genesis 11:32 the narrator has inserted eleven time designations in the *tôlĕdôt* of Terah and the central one, number 6, which contains "*two* indications of age,"[2] is found in Genesis 17:17, "Then Abraham . . . said to himself, 'Can a child be born to a man who is a hundred years old? Can Sarah, who is ninety years old, bear a child?'"

In this pivotal narrative God gives Abram and Sarai new names, establishes an "everlasting" covenant with them (17:7, 13, 19), clarifies his covenant promises ("I will make nations of you, and kings shall come from you" [v 6]), makes clear that these promises will be fulfilled through Sarah (v 16), and designates as the sign of this covenant, circumcision (vv 9-14), which Abraham obediently applies to all males in his household (vv 23-27).

Since no Christian preacher would preach that God today requires circumcision as a sign of his covenant, one advantage in preaching this narrative is that it forces preachers (and hearers) to consider this requirement in the light of the New Testament and redemptive-historical progression. One of the challenges in preaching this narrative is to formulate the precise theme of a passage that

1. Wenham, *Genesis 16–50*, 16. See also ibid., 17, "The significance of the occasion is marked too with literary devices: five long and elaborate divine speeches set this episode apart within Genesis."

2. Fokkelman, *Reading Biblical Narrative*, 41-42, counts Gen 11:32; 12:4; 16:3, 16; 17:1, 17, 24, 25; 21:5; 23:1; 25:7 and 17. Fokkelman argues for seventh of a string of thirteen. But he has listed only twelve and 25:17 is in the *tôlĕdôt* of Ishmael. But his suggestion that this is a "pivotal and meaningful center" is still valid because 17:17 is the sixth designation in a string of eleven in the Abraham cycle.

contains so many important topics: God establishes his everlasting covenant with Abraham; God promises Abraham and Sarah wonderful blessings; God promises to richly bless Ishmael; God promises a son to Sarah within the year; God requires circumcision as a sign of his covenant; and Abraham responds with immediate obedience. What is the specific theme of this narrative?

Text and Context

Genesis 17:1-27 is clearly a literary unit. The beginning of the narrative is unmistakable: Genesis 16:16 ends, "Abram was eighty-six years old," and Genesis 17:1 begins, "When Abram was ninety-nine years old" — a new narrative. The end of the narrative is equally clear since chapter 18:1 begins a new narrative.

As to the context, God's promise to Abraham in Genesis 17:6, "I will make you exceedingly fruitful" (cf. v 2), harks back to the creation story, "Be fruitful and multiply" (Gen 1:28), as well as God's covenant with Noah, "Be fruitful and multiply" (Gen 9:1, 7). Abram is another Adam, another Noah, with whom God makes a new beginning to establish his kingdom on earth. But "whereas Adam and Noah were simply commanded, 'be fruitful' (qal imperative) [under God's blessing], God makes Abraham a promise, 'I shall make you fruitful' (hiphil)."[3]

In the more immediate context, God's covenant with Abram in Genesis 17 harks back to God's covenant with him in Genesis 15. "The similarities with chapter 15 are obvious: God introduces himself (17:1, cf. 15:7); expands on the covenant (17:2-7, cf. 15:9-18); promises numerous descendants (17:8, cf. 15:5), land (17:8, cf. 15:18), and a son (17:19, 21, cf. 15:4); and Abram questions Yahweh (17:17, cf. 15:3, 8). These similarities actually highlight the significant development that takes place here. In chapter 15, believing the promises is righteousness (15:6); in chapter 17 being righteous is the condition for the fulfillment of the promises (17:1-2; see 22:1-19)."[4] In other words, whereas in Genesis 15 God declared his covenant with Abram/Israel as an *unconditional* promise, a "royal grant treaty," in Genesis 17 God emphasizes the *condition,* "Walk before me, and be blameless" (v 1), a "suzerain-vassal treaty."[5] Moreover, in Genesis 15 God's covenant promises focus primarily on the land and the nation of Israel, whereas in Genesis 17 God's promises focus primarily on numerous descendants and a multitude of nations. In addition, Genesis 17 includes God's covenant stipulation: circumcision.[6]

3. Wenham, *Genesis 16–50,* 22.

4. Turner, *Genesis,* 80.

5. See the helpful chart in *The NIV Study Bible* at Genesis 9.

6. For an elaborate comparison between the covenant of Genesis 15 and that of Genesis 17, see Williamson, *Abraham, Israel and the Nations,* 188-267.

Literary Features

The narrator again is omniscient: he knows what the LORD said to Abram in private and he knows what Abram "said to himself" (17:17). The narrative has two characters, the LORD and Abram. The narrator sketches the two characters partly by character description: significantly, he introduces the LORD as *'Ēl Šadday*, God Almighty (v 1), and *'Ĕlōhîm*, the transcendent Creator God, and Abram as being "ninety-nine years old" (v 1) and receiving the name Abraham, "father of a multitude of nations" (v 5). He also notes Sarai's new name, Sarah, princess, and that she is ninety years old and still without child (vv 15, 17).

But the narrator depicts the two acting characters primarily through dialogue: five lengthy speeches of God to Abraham promising rich blessings and giving him a stipulation, and two short speeches by Abraham, once to himself (v 17) and once to God pleading for Ishmael (v 18), as well as Abraham's obedient response to the stipulation (vv 23-27).

The narrator signals keywords with repetition: *bĕrît*, "covenant," thirteen times, "circumcise" ten times, "everlasting" covenant three times, Abraham "father of nations" three times, and "to be God to you" two times.

Sean McEvenue was the first to call attention to a chiastic structure which has since been adopted by other commentators:[7]

A Abraham 99 years of age (1a)
  B Yahweh appears to Abraham (1b)
    C God speaks (1b)
      D First speech (1b-2)
        E Abraham falls on his face (3a)
          F Second speech (name change, nations, kings) (4-8)
            G THIRD SPEECH [requirement of circumcision] (9-14)
          F′ Fourth speech (name change, nations, kings) (15-16)
        E′ Abraham falls on his face (17)
      D′ Fifth speech (19-21)
    C′ God ceases speaking (22a)
  B′ God goes up from him (22b)
A′ Abraham 99 years of age (and Ishmael 13) (24-25)

7. McEvenue, *The Narrative Style of the Priestly Writer*, 158. Cf. Radday, "Chiasmus in Hebrew Biblical Narrative," 105; Wenham, *Genesis 16–50*, 17. McEvenue called this pattern a "palistrophe." Note that the outcome of the narrative, vv 26-27, is not covered by this chiastic structure. For a critique of "McEvenue's stylistic analyses of Genesis 17," see Williamson, *Abraham*, 147-48.

In addition to this chiastic structure, McEvenue also suggested "a parallel development of the story in two panels":[8]

A Yahweh's intention to make an oath [covenant] about progeny (1-2)
B Abraham falls on his face (3a)
C Abraham father of nations (4b-6)
D God will carry out his oath [covenant] forever (7)
E The sign of the oath [covenant] (9-14)
A′ God's intention to bless Sarah with a progeny (16)
B′ Abraham falls on his face (17-18)
C′ Sarah mother of a son, Isaac (19)
D′ God will carry out his oath [covenant] forever (18b, 21a)
E′ The sign of the oath [covenant] (23-27)

Note that both panels, as well as the chiasm, climax in the sign of the covenant, circumcision.

Although Genesis 17 is not a covenant treaty but a narrative about God establishing his covenant, we can detect the elements of international (Hittite) covenant treaties.[9] Genesis 17:1 provides the preamble identifying the great King, "I am God Almighty." Covenant stipulations spell out the vassal's obligations to the King: "Every male among you shall be circumcised" (v 10). Blessings if obedient are spelled out in God's wonderful promises (vv 2, 4-8, 15-16), and curses if disobedient: "Any uncircumcised male . . . shall be cut off from his people" (v 14).

The Plot Line

This narrative features a single plot. The setting is given in verse 1a, Abram is ninety-nine years old. Preliminary incidents are God's appearance to Abram (v 1b), God's condition, "walk before me, and be blameless" (v 1c), his expressed intent to make a covenant with Abram (v 2a), followed by his promises (vv 2b-8). The narrative conflict is generated in verses 9 and 10 with the covenant stipulation, "Every male among you shall be circumcised." The tension rises with each further specification through verse 14. Verses 15 to 22 about Sarah bearing a child set the tension for the larger narrative (Gen 11:27–21:7) that will not be resolved until chapter 21:2, the birth of Isaac. But these verses also raise the ten-

8. McEvenue, *Narrative Style of the Priestly Writer,* 159.

9. For the usual elements, see above, p. 18, n. 45. On these elements in Genesis 17, see Meredith Kline, *By Oath Consigned,* 39-41.

sion in this narrative whether Abraham will obey God and circumcise all males. For God's declaration that the old, barren Sarah will bear a child is so far-fetched that Abram doubles up with laughter (v 17). In fact, he suggests to God that his son Ishmael is enough (v 18). But God insists that Sarah will bear a child within the year. Will Abraham believe this inconceivable news? Will he obey a God who promises the impossible?

As Abram's instant obedience immediately resolved the tension in Genesis 12, so here the tension is quickly resolved: "Then Abraham took . . . every male . . . of Abraham's house, and he circumcised the flesh of their foreskins that very day, as God had said to him" (v 23). The narrator lists the ages of Abraham and Ishmael when they were circumcised (vv 24-25) and states the outcome of the narrative in verses 26 to 27. We can sketch this single plot as follows:

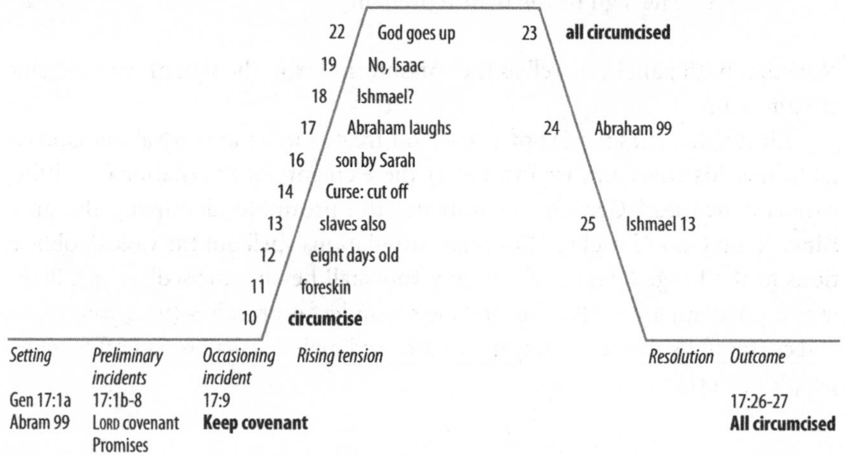

Theocentric Interpretation

Although Abraham is one of the two characters in this narrative, God is clearly the main character, the protagonist. The theocentric nature of this narrative is obvious from God's five lengthy speeches compared to Abraham's two short speeches. The LORD appears to Abram, reveals himself as God Almighty, commands "Walk before me, and be perfect," initiates his covenant with Abram, changes his name to Abraham, gives wonderful promises, stipulates circumcision as the sign of his covenant, changes Sarai's name to Sarah, gives similar promises to Sarah, promises to bless Ishmael but extends his covenant to the future Isaac. And Abraham follows God's order "as God had said to him" (v 23).

Textual Theme and Goal

This narrative is about God establishing his covenant (13 × "covenant") with Abraham and his seed, God's promises and his stipulation of circumcision, and Abraham's obedient response by circumcising all males in his house. The challenge is to preach these several topics under a single theme. One may consider, "God Almighty establishes with Abram and his seed an everlasting covenant with rich promises and obligations." But this theme is too general: it fails to cover the elaborated textual concern with the requirement of circumcision (17:9-14) and Abraham's obedient response to this specific requirement (vv 23-27). In order to incorporate these major elements into the theme, one may formulate the theme something like this, "God Almighty establishes with Abraham and his seed an everlasting covenant which includes rich promises as well as the requirement to keep the covenant by applying circumcision as the sign of the covenant, which Abraham fulfills by circumcising all the males in his house." But this theme is not only too long to give focus to preaching this narrative, it is merely a summary of the narrative.

The theme should be formulated as the main *message* Israel heard. Now we have to make some difficult choices as to where the primary emphasis lies in this narrative. Note that the plot line focuses on the covenant stipulation of circumcision: this requirement sets the tension in the narrative, Abraham's obedient response resolves this tension, and the outcome of the narrative states that all were circumcised. That circumcision is the main concern of this narrative is further supported by the chiastic structure which centers in God's third speech regarding circumcision and by the two parallel panels which reach a climax in God's requirement of circumcision (vv 9-14) and Abraham's obedient response (vv 23-27). With this evidence in mind, we can formulate the textual theme as follows: *God Almighty establishes with Abraham and his seed an everlasting covenant with the stipulation that all males be circumcised as a sign of membership in God's covenant family.*

As to the narrator's goal with this message for Israel, if Israel first heard this message in Moab it would clearly be to *persuade* Israel (with the LORD's wonderful promises, the threat of being cut off from the covenant community, and their Patriarch's example) to keep God's covenant by circumcising all males (in contrast to Moses' neglect of circumcision, Exod 4:24-26). If Israel heard this narrative while in Babylonian exile, its relevance would be even more pronounced. Gerhard von Rad suggests, "Because of the abolition of the great cultic regulations [in exile], the feasts, sacrifice, etc., which were binding on the national community, the individual and the family were suddenly summoned to decision. Each family with all its members, each of them personally, was bound to Yahweh's offer, and since the Babylonians (like all eastern Semites) did not practice circumcision, the observance of this custom was a *status confessionis* for the exiles; i.e., it became a question of their witness of Yahweh and his guidance of history."[10] In short, the narrator's goal of this message for Israel in exile was *to persuade Israel (with the LORD's wonderful promises, the threatened curse of being cut off, and the example of their Patriarch) to keep God's covenant by circumcising all males.*

Ways to Preach Christ

Keeping in mind the theme, "God Almighty establishes with Abraham and his seed an everlasting covenant with the stipulation that all males be circumcised as a sign of membership in God's covenant family," let us check the various legitimate ways to Jesus Christ in the New Testament.

Redemptive-Historical Progression

One can preach Christ from this narrative by following the road of redemptive-historical progression from God establishing his covenant with Abraham/Israel to be "their God" (17:7) to Jeremiah's prophecy of God making "a new covenant with the house of Israel" to be "their God" (Jer 31:31, 33), to its fulfillment in Jesus, who established the new covenant the night before he died, "This cup that is poured out for you is the new covenant in my blood" (Luke 22:20; cf. Matt 26:27-28). The author of Hebrews confirms this message when he writes, "For this reason he [Christ] is the mediator of a new covenant, so that those who are called may receive the promised eternal inheritance, because a death has occurred that redeems them from the transgressions under the first covenant" (Heb 9:15; cf. Eph 3:6).

Alongside this development in the covenant, one can follow the trail of redemptive-historical progression of God requiring circumcision as a sign of his covenant from Abraham to Israel throughout the Old Testament, to the first Church Council in Jerusalem, which, guided by the Holy Spirit, freed Gentiles from the requirement of circumcision (Acts 15:1-29), to its replacement by baptism as the sign of entrance into God's covenant. Jesus sent his disciples out not to circumcise but to baptize: "Make disciples of all nations, baptizing them in the name of the Father and of the Son and of the Holy Spirit" (Matt 28:19). Paul

10. Von Rad, *Genesis*, 201. Cf. Foster McCurley, *Genesis*, 42, "Circumcision, then, for Israel — at least in the time of exile — was a confessional act by which an individual appropriated to himself the gift of the eternal relationship between God and Israel."

wrote the Galatian church, "As many of you as were baptized into Christ have clothed yourselves with Christ. There is no longer Jew or Greek, there is no longer slave or free, there is no longer male and female; for you are all one in Christ Jesus. And if you belong to Christ, then you are Abraham's offspring, heirs according to the promise" (Gal 3:27-29; cf. Col 2:11-14). Moreover, whereas the sign of circumcision was applied only to males, the covenant sign of baptism is now applied to females as well as males.

Promise-Fulfillment

This narrative contains many covenant promises which are ultimately fulfilled in Jesus Christ. "You shall be the father of a multitude of nations" (17:4) was fulfilled in Christ when he sent his disciples to "make disciples of all nations" (Matt 28:19; cf. Rom 4:16-17; 15:8-12). "Kings shall come from you" (17:6; cf. 49:8-12) was ultimately fulfilled with the arrival of Abraham's son Jesus, the King of kings. "I will give you . . . all the land of Canaan" (17:8) will be fulfilled in Jesus on a far grander scale when God's people will inherit the new earth. "I will be their God," was fulfilled in Jesus, who with his sacrifice reconciled God and his people. If our text was confined to God's promises, these would certainly be legitimate roads to Christ in the New Testament. But since our text is the whole narrative and its theme focuses not so much on God's promises as on God's requirement of circumcision, we should select bridges to Christ in the New Testament in line with the theme.

Typology

Abraham, the seed of the woman obediently receiving circumcision, has a parallel with Jesus. Jesus, the Seed of the woman, also received the covenant sign of circumcision (Luke 2:21). But this analogy is insufficient to establish Abraham in this narrative as a type of Christ.

Analogy

There are several ways to use analogy to preach Christ. One can draw the analogy with the narrator's goal: As God through this narrative persuaded Israel to apply the sign of the covenant (circumcision) to God's people, so Christ persuades his church to apply the new sign of the covenant (baptism) to God's people. This analogy can be supported by Jesus' command, "Make disciples of all nations, baptizing them in the name of the Father and of the Son and of the Holy Spirit" (Matt 28:19).

One can also draw the analogy at the level of the covenant: As God made a covenant with Abraham to be his God, so God in Christ makes a new covenant with us to be our God. This analogy can be supported, for example, by Hebrews 9:15, "For this reason he [Christ] is the mediator of a new covenant, so that those who are called may receive the promised eternal inheritance" (see also Matthew 26:28).

Longitudinal Themes

One can also use longitudinal themes to preach Christ from this narrative. For example, one can trace the theme of circumcision as it develops theologically in the Old Testament from a literal cutting off of flesh ("You shall circumcise the flesh of your foreskins," 17:11), to the additional connotation of circumcising the heart in a spiritual sense ("Circumcise then the foreskin of your heart," Deut 10:16; cf. 30:6; Jer 4:4), to Paul's argument in the New Testament, "A person is not a Jew who is one outwardly, nor is true circumcision something external and physical. Rather, a person is a Jew who is one inwardly, and real circumcision is a matter of the heart — it is spiritual and not literal" (Rom 2:28-29). Paul can make this argument because Jesus inaugurated a new age: "Now, apart from law, the righteousness of God has been disclosed . . . , the righteousness of God through faith in Jesus Christ for all who believe" (Rom 3:21-22). Baptism, as the new sign of covenant membership, now implies this spiritual circumcision. Baptism now symbolizes that believers "in him [Christ] . . . were circumcised with a spiritual circumcision, by putting off the body of the flesh in the circumcision of Christ; when you were buried with him in baptism, you were also raised with him through faith in the power of God, who raised him from the dead" (Col 2:11-12).

New Testament References

In addition to the New Testament references supporting the other ways above, one may also be able to use one or more the following passages:

Luke 1:68-73, the song of Zechariah:

> "Blessed be the Lord God of Israel,
> for he has looked favorably on his people and redeemed them.

He has raised up a mighty *savior* for us
in the house of his servant David. . . .
Thus he has shown the mercy promised to our ancestors,
and has remembered his holy *covenant,*
the oath that he swore to our ancestor *Abraham*."

Romans 4:9-25, which speaks of Abraham, "about a hundred years old," believing before he was circumcised that he would become "the father of many nations."

1 Corinthians 7:14, "For the unbelieving husband is made holy through his wife. . . . Otherwise your children would be unclean, but as it is, they are holy."

1 Corinthians 7:19, "Circumcision is nothing, and uncircumcision is nothing; but obeying the commandments of God is everything."

Galatians 5:6, "For in Christ Jesus neither circumcision nor uncircumcision counts for anything; the only thing that counts is faith working through love."

Galatians 6:15, "For neither circumcision nor uncircumcision is anything; but a new creation is everything!"

Philippians 3:3, "For it is we who are the circumcision, who worship in the Spirit of God and boast in Christ Jesus and have no confidence in the flesh."

Contrast

There is a clear contrast between the old covenant and the new covenant and between circumcision as sign of the old covenant for Israel and baptism as the sign of the new covenant for the church. When the question is raised, Why does the church not practice circumcision as a religious rite, the answer is that Jesus has come and shed his blood once for all, thereby ending all the bloody rites of the old covenant. One can confirm this contrast with the decision of the first Church Council in Jerusalem, Acts 15:28-29, or by quoting Hebrews 8:6, 8, 13, "But Jesus . . . is the mediator of a better covenant. . . . 'The days are surely coming, says the Lord, when I will establish a new covenant with the house of Israel. . . .' In speaking of a 'new covenant,' he has made the first one obsolete."

Sermon Theme and Goal

We formulated the textual theme as follows: "God Almighty establishes with Abraham and his seed an everlasting covenant with the stipulation that all males be circumcised as a sign of membership in God's covenant family." In preaching this narrative to the Christian church, we will have to adjust this theme so that it covers both the Old Testament narrative and the New Testament context. Whereas the Old Testament sign of God's covenant with his people was circumcision, because of Christ's sacrifice on the cross this bloody sign is no longer required (Acts 15:28-29) and baptism replaces it (Matt 28:19; Col 2:11-14). Moreover, whereas circumcision was applied only to males, baptism is applied to females as well as males. Taking these changes into account, we can make the sermon theme more general to cover both circumcision and baptism and formulate it like this: *God Almighty establishes with Abraham and his seed an everlasting covenant with the stipulation that they receive the sign of membership in God's covenant family.*

The sermon goal should be in harmony with the narrator's goal, which was, "to persuade Israel (with the LORD's wonderful promises, the threat of being cut off, and their Patriarch's example) to keep God's covenant by circumcising all males." In line with the sermon theme, our goal in preaching this sermon can be, *to persuade the church to keep God's covenant by applying the sign of covenant membership to all its members.* This goal suggests that the need for preaching this sermon is a lack of obedience among God's people with respect to applying the sign of covenant membership to all its members, or at least insufficient knowledge about God's covenant and its required sign.[11]

Sermon Exposition

To set the stage for the relevance of this sermon, one can begin with some contemporary misuses of baptism. Sometimes people receive baptism because of custom or superstition. Sometimes people totally neglect baptism, or people who have been baptized never think about its implications again. One can then transition to Israel, which at various times neglected to apply God's sign of the covenant. Moses himself neglected to circumcise his son (Exod 4:25), and the entire generation of Israelites raised in the desert was uncircumcised (Josh 5:7). Later when Israel was in exile in Babylonia, the temptation was great to disregard circumcision, for this was not the practice among the Babylonians. At various times, therefore, it was necessary for the LORD to educate Israel with respect to the origin of his covenant with Abram and its sign and to persuade them to apply the sign of the covenant.

Verse 1, "When Abram was ninety-nine years old, the LORD appeared to Abram, and said to him, 'I am God Almighty; walk before me, and be blame-

11. See Henry De Moor, "Erosion at the Font," *CTJ* 29 (1994) 168-79.

less.'" The LORD introduces himself as the great King, *'Ēl Šadday,* "God Almighty." The etymology of *'Ēl Šadday* is "obscure, but wherever it is used in Genesis, it is associated with divine omnipotence, his ability to fulfill his promises and especially to make the barren fertile (28:3; 35:11; 48:3)."[12] The great King desires to make a covenant, a sacred treaty, with Abram. But before God Almighty specifies the covenant promises, he succinctly states the conditions Abram must meet: "Walk before me, and be blameless." Abram is to be like Noah, of whom we read, "Noah was a righteous man, *blameless* in his generation; Noah walked with God" (Gen 6:9).[13] With Noah God had also made a covenant. The sign of that covenant was the rainbow. Now God is ready to make with Abram a special covenant with the sign of circumcision. Like Noah, Abram has to walk with God — literally, he has to walk "*before* God" (v 1). "This phrase ['before God'] usually expresses the service or devotion of a faithful servant to his king."[14] It means to live in such a way "that every single step is made with reference to God and every day experiences him close at hand."[15] And like Noah, Abram is to be blameless. The Hebrew word translated "blameless" does not mean "sinless" but "whole": "It signifies complete, unqualified surrender."[16] Abram is to be wholly devoted to God, his King.

God continues speaking to Abram, verse 2, "And I will make my covenant between me and you, and will make you exceedingly numerous." Nine times in this narrative, God speaks of *my* covenant. It is God's covenant; he initiates this sacred treaty.[17] And God promises to make Abram "exceedingly numerous."

In response to God's words, Abram falls "on his face," that is, he prostrates himself before God the way servants bow down before their king. He acknowledges the "master-servant footing of the covenant."[18]

Then, while Abram is lying face down like a servant before his King, God says to him, verse 4, "As for me, this is my covenant with you: You shall be the ancestor [father] of a multitude of nations. No longer shall your name be Abram, but your name shall be Abraham; for I have made you the ancestor [father] of a multitude of nations." The great King gives his servant a new name —

12. Wenham, *Genesis 16–50,* 28.

13. "In light of the sparsity of these terms in Genesis, it seems likely that the author expected an association to be made between these two great men based on the close recurrence of both terms. 'Blameless' *(tāmîm)* occurs in Genesis only in these two texts." Sailhamer, *Genesis,* 141.

14. Hamilton, *Genesis 1–17,* 461.

15. Westermann, *Genesis 12–36,* 311.

16. Von Rad, *Genesis,* 198.

17. Cf. Genesis 15:17, where not God and Abram but God alone passed between the (halves of) the slaughtered animals.

18. Kidner, *Genesis,* 129.

a name that gives expression to God's covenant promise to make Abraham "the father of a multitude of nations."

"Throughout the Near East the inauguration of a new era or a new state policy would frequently be marked by the assumption of a new name expressive of the change on the part of the king."[19] Here God Almighty begins a new phase with his servant Abraham. God explains the meaning of the name Abraham: "father of a multitude of nations." Twenty-four years earlier, God had promised Abram, "I will make of you a great nation" (Gen 12:2). But now God promises that Abraham will be the "father of a *multitude* of nations." This is an important turning point for Abraham. The new name is "a divinely guaranteed statement about Abraham's identity and future destiny. His very name guarantees that he will father many nations."[20] It confirms God's initial promise to Abram: "in you all the families of the earth shall be blessed" (Gen 12:3).

God Almighty continues to stress this new phase in Abraham's life in verses 6 and 7, "I will make you exceedingly fruitful; and I will make nations of you, and kings shall come from you. I will establish my covenant between me and you, and your offspring after you throughout their generations, for an everlasting covenant, to be God to you and to your offspring after you." Two new items stand out. First, this is not a temporary covenant but an "everlasting covenant," similar to the "everlasting covenant" God made with Noah and every living creature (9:16). This covenant is made with Abraham and his seed after him "throughout their generations." Second, the promise "to be God to you" is the essence, the core, of this covenant. "The essential heart of the covenant is defined: 'I shall be their God.' I, El Shaddai the omnipotent creator of the world and redeemer of mankind, will be Israel's God. This nation descended from Abraham is to be unique, because unlike the other nations, Israel enjoys a unique relationship with the only true God."[21] In verse 8 God repeats the essence of his covenant, "And I will give to you, and to your offspring after you, the land where you are now an alien, all the land of Canaan, for a perpetual holding; and *I will be their God*." This is what God will do for Abraham and his seed.

In verses 9 to 14 God tells Abraham and Israel what is expected of them. This is the third of five speeches of God in this narrative. As the central speech this is also the longest. It begins with an emphatic "as for you." God says to

19. Sarna, *Understanding Genesis*, 130.

20. Wenham, *Genesis 16–50*, 21. Cf. Sarna, *Understanding Genesis*, 130, "The very fact of a new name distinguishes and even effectuates, to an extent, the transformation of destiny."

21. Wenham, *Genesis 16–50*, 29; cf. ibid., 22, "The covenant formula 'to be your God' . . . used twice here and not again till 28:21, expresses the heart of the covenant, that God has chosen Abraham and his descendants, so that they are in a unique relationship: he is their God, and they are his people (cf. Exod 4:16; 6:7; Lev 11:45; 26:12, 45)."

Abraham, "As for you, you shall keep my covenant, you and your offspring after you throughout their generations. This is my covenant, which you shall keep, between me and you and your offspring after you: Every male among you shall be circumcised."[22]

Two items call for special attention. First, in contrast to God's covenant with Noah and all creatures, a covenant marked by the sign of the rainbow, the sign of circumcision "has to be performed by the human beings who thereby acknowledge themselves to be God's partners in his covenant."[23] Second, in contrast to God's covenant at Sinai, which had ten covenant stipulations (the decalogue), here there is only one covenant stipulation: "Every male among you shall be circumcised." Why just one stipulation? Derek Kidner explains: "To be *committed* was all. Circumcision was God's brand; the moral implications could be left unwritten (until Sinai), for one was pledged to a Master, only secondarily to a way of life."[24] But in the very next chapter that way of life is already summarized: "to keep the way of the LORD by doing righteousness and justice" (Gen 18:19).

This single covenant stipulation sets the tension in this narrative. For we cannot take for granted that Abraham would simply obey God. Even though circumcision was practiced in Egypt and by some tribes in Palestine, it was foreign to Babylonia, Abraham's homeland. Moreover, circumcision was a painful, bloody rite (cf. Gen 34:25). It required that the foreskin be cut off with a flint stone (Exod 4:25; Josh 5:2). Would Abraham obey God? Verse 11 graphically portrays God's requirement, "You shall circumcise the flesh of your foreskins, and it shall be a sign of the covenant between me and you."

God continues in verse 12, "Throughout your generations every male among you shall be circumcised when he is eight days old,[25] including the slave

22. Twice these verses speak of circumcision as "my covenant" whereas verse 11 calls it "a sign of the covenant." "The designation of circumcision itself as a covenant is a synecdoche for covenant obligation: 'this is [the aspect of] my covenant you must keep.'" Hamilton, *Genesis 1–17*, 470.

23. Rendtorff, "'Covenant' as a Structuring Concept," *JBL* 108/3 (1989) 392.

24. Kidner, *Genesis*, 129.

25. Following Sarna, Waltke, *Genesis*, 261, remarks, "By the eighth day the baby has completed the cycle of time corresponding to the course of creation (cf. Exod 22:30; Lev 22:27)." Walton, *Genesis*, 451, suggests, "Waiting until the eighth day to perform this ritual may reflect the high infant mortality rate and the desire to determine if the child was viable." My student Nick Blystra suggested the best reason yet for waiting until the eighth day: he recalled his mother, a nurse, saying that infants, who today are circumcised when a few days old, need to be given a special clotting agent called vitamin K. Checking *The American Medical Association Home Medical Encyclopedia* (ed. Charles B. Clayman; New York: Random House, 1989) under "Vitamin K," I learned that vitamin K "is essential for the formation in the liver of substances that promote blood clotting. . . . Newborn infants lack the intestinal bacteria that produce vita-

born in your house." In ancient Near Eastern cultures males were usually circumcised to mark puberty.[26] But God demands that *infants* also be circumcised, for circumcision is not a rite of puberty but a sign of covenant membership.[27] Joyce Baldwin observes, "It was the extension of this rite to infants that characterized as different the role of circumcision in Israel. If infants are to be circumcised, the essence of circumcision must be what the Lord is saying to them, for they can say nothing to him."[28] The children of God's covenant people are included in God's covenant. Note that circumcision does not establish the covenant; *God* establishes the covenant, and circumcision is a sign of membership in the covenant family.

In addition to eight-day-old infants, God requires that Abraham circumcise "the slave born in your house and the one bought with your money from any foreigner who is not of your offspring" (v 12b). With these instructions, membership in God's covenant moves beyond biological lines of descent to include in God's covenant family even Gentiles who are part of Abraham's household.[29]

At the end of verse 13 God declares, "So shall my covenant be in your flesh an *everlasting* covenant." As circumcision is a permanent sign in the flesh of God's covenant, so God's covenant is permanent. As circumcision is irreversible, so God's covenant is irreversible. Bernhard Anderson clarifies, "Individuals may fail to 'keep the covenant' by not submitting to this rite of admission, but God's covenant with the community represented by the family of Abraham and Sarah stands forever."[30] But what happens when the whole nation becomes unfaithful? Does this abrogate God's everlasting covenant? Wenham responds,

---

min K and are therefore given supplements to prevent deficiency." Presumably waiting till the eighth day to circumcise a baby was not "to determine if the child was viable," but to make sure that he would remain viable after life-threatening surgery.

26. A "well-nigh universal practice." Sarna, *Understanding Genesis*, 132.

27. "Although the Israelites are not the only people in the ancient Near East to circumcise their sons, what is unique in their practice is that the ritual is used as a theological rite of passage into the covenantal community rather than a passage into adulthood or a new family group through marriage." Walton, *Genesis*, 451.

28. Baldwin, *The Message of Genesis 12–50*, 66-67. Cf. p. 68, "God's grace, not human merit, undergirded the covenant, and that grace enfolded the children of those who believed."

29. Abram, of course, "was originally nothing more than another pagan 'Gentile' before being called by God. He was simply one of many idol worshipers on the other side of the Euphrates River (Josh 24:2). . . . No racial barrier existed to keep Gentiles from becoming full participants in the covenant promises. As a Jewish commentator on the book of Genesis has noted, 'Indeed, differences of race have never been an obstacle to joining Israel which did not know the concept of purity of blood. . . . Circumcision turned a man of foreign origin into an Israelite.'" Robertson, *Israel of God*, 34-35, quoting Benno Jacob, *The First Book of the Bible: Genesis* (New York: KTAV, 1974), 233.

30. Anderson, *Contours of Old Testament Theology*, 98-99.

"Even when Israel rebels and disregards the covenant, bringing upon herself the curse of exile, the covenant is not thereby invalidated: national repentance will lead to national restoration, as Lev 26:40-45 and Deut 30:1-10 affirm."[31]

God underscores the seriousness of his covenant stipulation by concluding this lengthy speech with the covenant curse. Verse 14, "Any uncircumcised male who is not circumcised in the flesh of his foreskin shall be cut off from his people; he has broken my covenant." The warning that he "shall be cut off from his people" involves "a word play on *cut.* He that is not himself cut (i.e., circumcised) will be cut off (i.e., ostracized). Here is the choice: be cut or be cut off."[32] The one who will not submit to this painful rite of covenant membership has disobeyed the covenant stipulation and thereby broken God's covenant. Therefore he has forfeited his privilege of being part of God's covenant community, and God requires his excommunication from the community.[33]

In a fourth speech, God extends his rich covenant promises also to Sarai. Wives were included in God's covenant by virtue of their husbands' membership and daughters by virtue of their fathers' membership. Verse 15, "God said to Abraham, 'As for Sarai your wife, you shall not call her Sarai, but Sarah shall be her name. I will bless her, and moreover I will give you a son by her. I will bless her, and she shall give rise to nations; kings of peoples shall come from her." As God had changed Abram's name to Abraham, so God now changes Sarai's name to Sarah.[34] As Abraham entered a new phase in his life, so Sarah enters a new phase in her life. As God had promised Abraham, "I will make nations of you, and kings shall come from you" (17:6), so God promises that Sarah "shall give rise to nations; kings of peoples shall come from her." As Abraham's name expressed his destiny as "father of a multitude of nations," so Sarah's destiny is to be the mother of nations and kings. Waltke observes, "Both Sarai and Sarah are probably dialectical variants meaning 'princess.' The promise that she will bear kings supports this interpretation. Sarai, her birth-name, probably looks back on her noble descent, whereas Sarah, her covenantal name, looks ahead to her noble descendants."[35]

Abraham can hardly believe that God's promises of numerous offspring will be fulfilled through Sarah. Sarah has been barren all her life and is now

31. Wenham, *Genesis 16–50,* 31.

32. Hamilton, *Genesis 1–17,* 473.

33. See, e.g., von Rad, *Genesis,* 201, "'Cut off from his people' . . . scarcely means the death penalty [as some claim], which is expressed by P in a different way, but rather exclusion from the sacred community, a kind of excommunication."

34. "Sarah's importance to salvation history is borne out by the fact that she is the only woman in the Bible whose name is changed and whose age at death is detailed (23:1)." Waltke, *Genesis,* 262.

35. Ibid.

ninety years old. In fact, many years ago she gave up the idea of ever giving birth to her own child and, according to custom, had given her maid Hagar to Abraham. That union resulted in the birth of Ishmael. Ishmael is now thirteen years old. "For the last thirteen years Abraham has lived in the belief that Ishmael, the son of his old age, is the promised son and that God's covenant will be carried out through him. All of his love, all of his hopes, and all of his dreams have been poured into this boy."[36] Would God after all this time give a child to ancient, barren Sarah?

When God first spoke to Abram, he "fell on his face" and was silent. This time, we read in verse 17, "Abraham fell on his face and laughed." Some claim that this was joyful laughter about God's wonderful promises.[37] But as Abraham's questions imply, this is unlikely. This was incredulous laughter — very similar to the disbelieving laughter we hear from Sarah in the next chapter: "Sarah laughed to herself, saying, 'After I have grown old, and my husband is old, shall I have pleasure?'" (18:12). Similarly Abraham, too, laughed "and said to himself, 'Can a child be born to a man who is a hundred years old? Can Sarah, who is ninety years old, bear a child?'" Disbelief! "And Abraham said to God, 'O that Ishmael might live in your sight!'" Please let Ishmael be the heir.

God responds to Abraham's request with his final speech. God says in verse 19, "No, but your wife Sarah shall bear you a son, and you shall name him Isaac.[38] I will establish my covenant with him as an everlasting covenant for his offspring after him. As for Ishmael, I have heard you; I will bless him and make him fruitful and exceedingly numerous; he shall be the father of twelve princes, and I will make him a great nation.[39] But my covenant I will establish with Isaac, whom Sarah shall bear to you at this season next year." Then God goes up from Abraham.

What will Abraham do now? There can be no mistake. God stated twice that Sarah would bear a son and that God would establish his covenant with her son Isaac. But it was impossible for Sarah to bear a son: barren all her life and now ninety years old. How could that happen? True, God had revealed himself as *'Ēl Šadday*, God Almighty. If anyone could give Sarah a son it was God Almighty. But would God do this after twenty-five years of waiting? It seemed im-

36. Walton, *Genesis*, 451. Concerning Abraham's love for Ishmael, see Genesis 21:11.

37. For example, Vischer, *The Witness of the Old Testament to Christ*, I, 137, "The message which the patriarch heard in that hour is so prodigiously mighty that he sinks in adoration to the ground, and so prodigiously paradoxical, so joyous and so impossible, that — he cannot do otherwise — he laughs."

38. Isaac, *yiṣḥāq*, means "he laughs."

39. "God pastorally reassures Abraham that Ishmael will not be excluded from a blessing. Indeed he too will father a great nation, with twelve tribes corresponding to the twelve tribes of Israel (cf. 25:12-16)." Waltke, *Genesis*, 262.

possible! And then there was God's covenant stipulation, "Every male among you shall be circumcised" (17:10). A strange command. Why would God select such a painful procedure as the sign of his covenant? Why not something painless like the rainbow? Will Abraham obey a God who demands pain of his servants and promises the impossible?

The tension in the narrative is quickly resolved. Verse 23, "Then Abraham took his son Ishmael and all the slaves born in his house or bought with his money, every male among the men of Abraham's house, and he circumcised the flesh of their foreskins *that very day*, as God had said to him." "That very day"! "Whatever his doubts about the possibility of Sarah conceiving, they did not prevent Abraham from obeying God's commands. And his obedience as well as the content of the revelation itself make this day one of the greatest days in redemptive history."[40]

The narrator carefully lists the males that were circumcised — "Ishmael and all the slaves born in his house or bought with his money" — echoing verse 12 to show that Abraham not only fulfilled his covenant obligations promptly but also exactly "as God had said to him."[41] Verses 24 and 25 record the ages of the major participants: "Abraham was ninety-nine years old when he was circumcised in the flesh of his foreskin. And his son Ishmael was thirteen years old when he was circumcised in the flesh of his foreskin."[42]

The narrator reports the outcome of the narrative in verses 26 and 27, "*That very day* Abraham and his son Ishmael were circumcised; and all the men of his house, slaves born in the house and those bought with money from a foreigner, were circumcised with him." "That very day" is repeated. By repeating this phrase, "the narrator stresses that the day Abraham circumcised his family was one of the turning points in world history, comparable to Noah's entry into the ark or the exodus from Egypt (cf. 7:13; Exod 12:17, 41, 51)."[43] It was a momentous day in redemptive history: "this was the birthday of the church of the Old Testament."[44]

As Israel heard this story of God's command to Abraham, the father of their nation, they clearly heard God's command to them: Circumcise your sons and all the men in your household as a sign of God's covenant! All can be members of

40. Wenham, *Genesis 16–50*, 30. Cf. Waltke, *Genesis*, 263, "This expression marks a significant moment (see also 7:13): the scene's climax when Abram shows himself a faithful covenant partner by immediately fulfilling his obligations."

41. Wenham, *Genesis 16–50*, 27.

42. Arabs, who claim to be descendants of Ishmael, still practice circumcision at age thirteen.

43. Wenham, *Genesis 16–50*, 27.

44. Kidner, *Genesis*, 131, "In the sense that Pentecost was the birthday of the church, this was the birthday of the church of the Old Testament."

God's covenant family, including infants as well as domestic and foreign slaves. The women are included with their husbands and fathers. This broad range of covenant membership comes close to Paul's description of the new covenant: "there is no longer Jew or Greek, there is no longer slave or free, there is no longer male and female" (Gal 3:28; cf. Exod 12:48-49). God will be their God, and they will be his people. But the males have to carry the sign of God's covenant. If they fail to be circumcised, they have broken the covenant and are no longer part of God's covenant family. This penalty (curse) underscores the importance God attached to this sign. The sign of circumcision reminds God of his covenant promises and reminds God's people "to live in loyalty to the covenant."[45] God Almighty established with Abraham and his seed an everlasting covenant with the stipulation that they receive the sign of membership in God's covenant family.

Unfortunately, Israel soon broke God's covenant by failing to circumcise their sons. Strangely, Moses failed to circumcise his son (Exod 4:25), and, even stranger, the whole generation that grew up in the desert was uncircumcised (Josh 5:7). Worse, they failed to follow the way of the covenant, "the way of the LORD by doing righteousness and justice" (Gen 18:19). Finally God "cut off" the whole nation from the Promised Land and sent them into exile in Babylonia, back to the place where Abram lived before God called him. In exile, applying circumcision became even more a deliberate confession of belonging to God's covenant people "since the Babylonians . . . did not practice circumcision."[46] Those who were circumcised and thereby confessed to belonging to God's covenant people lived in hope, for God had promised that this was an "everlasting covenant" (17:7, 13, 18) and that the land of Canaan was "a perpetual holding" (17:8). "So . . . the prophets spoke encouragingly about the permanence of the covenant relationship (Isa 24:5). In particular they looked forward to a new and eternal covenant: new in that this time Israel, not just the LORD, would observe it loyally (Jer 31:31-37; 32:40; Ezek 16:60; 37:26)."[47] New because God's law would no longer be external but internal, written on people's hearts (Jer 31:33).

Jesus established this new covenant the night before he died. At the Last Supper he told his disciples, "This cup that is poured out for you is the *new* covenant in my blood" (Luke 22:20). The author of Hebrews confirms that Jesus established this new covenant: "For this reason he [Christ] is the mediator of a new covenant, so that those who are called may receive the promised eternal inheritance, because a death has occurred that redeems them from the transgressions under the first covenant" (Heb 9:15; cf. Eph 3:6).

45. Ross, *Creation and Blessing,* 333.

46. Von Rad, *Genesis,* 201.

47. "Indeed, through this new and eternal covenant, all nations would be blessed (Isa 55:3; 61:8)." Wenham, *Genesis 16–50,* 31.

But what happened to God's covenant stipulation that, as a sign of covenant membership, all males be circumcised? Jesus was circumcised (Luke 2:21), but after his resurrection he sent his disciples out not to circumcise but to baptize: "Make disciples of all nations, *baptizing* them in the name of the Father and of the Son and of the Holy Spirit" (Matt 28:19). The first Church Council in Jerusalem considered the all-important question whether Gentile believers should still be circumcised in this new age Jesus had inaugurated. This Council decided, "It has seemed good to the Holy Spirit and to us to impose on you no further burden than these essentials: that you abstain from what has been sacrificed to idols and from blood and from what is strangled and from fornication" (Acts 15:28).[48] The painful rite of circumcision is no longer required for covenant membership. Jesus shed his precious blood once for all, thus ending the bloody rites and sacrifices of the old covenant. Paul insists to the Galatians (6:15) that "neither circumcision nor uncircumcision is anything; but a new creation is everything!"[49] Baptism now becomes the sign of covenant membership. "As many of you as were *baptized* into Christ have clothed yourselves with Christ. There is no longer Jew or Greek; there is no longer slave or free; there is no longer male and female; for you are all one in Christ Jesus. And if you belong to Christ, then you are *Abraham's offspring,* heirs according to the promise" (Gal 3:27-29; cf. Col 2:11-14). In this new covenant, not only males but also females receive the sign of baptism.

The question is being raised today, Are infants also included in this covenant and should they receive the sign of membership? The New Testament nowhere declares that little children are now *ex*cluded. If eight-day-old infants were included in the old covenant, one would expect that infants are also included in the new covenant. Certainly God's grace is not less in the new covenant than it was in the old. In fact, Jesus was indignant when his disciples tried to block people with little children. He said, "Let the little children come to me; do not stop them; for it is to such as these that the kingdom of God belongs" (Mark 10:14). If the kingdom of God belongs to such little children, should they

48. Presumably going back to God's regulations for Noah and all peoples (Gen 9:4-5). "The rabbis understood the Noachian precepts, which they took to preclude idolatry, murder and adultery and the eating of flesh with the blood, to be binding upon Gentiles. . . . It may be that allusion is made to this in the Apostolic Decree found in Acts 15:29." R. Nixon, "The Universality of the Concept of Law," in B. Kaye and G. Wenham (eds.), *Law, Morality and the Bible* (Downers Grove, IL: InterVarsity Press, 1978), 115.

49. "The radicalness of the apostle's statement needs to be appreciated. Circumcision now means absolutely nothing in terms of the identity of the people of God. Lack of circumcision likewise means absolutely nothing in terms of the identity of the people of God. . . . The only thing that can establish a person as one of God's people is for him to experience a new creation by God's grace." Robertson, *Israel of God,* 39.

not receive the sign of membership in God's royal family? On the day of Pentecost (the birthday of the New Testament church), Peter encouraged the people, "Repent, and be baptized every one of you in the name of Jesus Christ so that your sins may be forgiven." And then, echoing God's original covenant promise "to be a God to you and to your offspring after you" (Gen 17:7), he declares, "For the promise is for you, and for your children" (Acts 2:38-39). Accordingly, when Paul was in Philippi and speaking to women, among them Lydia ("a worshiper of God"), "the Lord opened her heart to listen eagerly to what was said by Paul. . . . she and her household were baptized" (Acts 16:14-15). Later, when Paul "spoke the word of the Lord" to the Philippian jailer and those in his house, the jailer "and his entire family were baptized without delay" (Acts 16:32-33). Lydia, a woman, and her household were baptized; the Philippian jailer, a Gentile, "and his entire family were baptized." If there were any children in those households, they were also baptized,[50] for baptism can hardly be less inclusive than circumcision.

Both of these households were baptized "without delay" — a statement that reminds us of Abraham's action "on that very day." When people come to faith in Jesus Christ, they should also receive the sign of membership in God's covenant without undue delay. And when God gives children to his people, these children, too, should be baptized without undue delay. For baptism is a deeply meaningful, joyful occasion: it's a sign and seal of sins being washed away and being in a covenant relationship with the triune God. On the one hand, baptism reminds God of his covenant promise to be our God and the God of our children. On the other hand, it reminds those baptized of the wonderful privilege of being part of God's covenant family and of their obligation "to keep the way of the LORD by doing righteousness and justice" (Gen 18:19). Or, as Jesus summarized this way of the LORD: "You shall love the Lord your God with all your heart, and with all your soul, and with all your mind," and "You shall love your neighbor as yourself" (Matt 22:37, 39).

50. Cf. 1 Cor 7:14, where Paul calls children of a believing husband or wife "holy," i.e., set apart for God.

CHAPTER 9

The Birth of Isaac

Genesis 21:1-7

Genesis 21:1-7 in itself is not a complete narrative but provides the resolution to a larger narrative that began at Genesis 11:30 where the narrator emphatically informs us that Abram's wife "Sarai was barren; she had no child." Yet the LORD promised Abram, "I will make of you a great nation" (12:2). Abram at that time was seventy-five years old (12:4). How could God possibly fulfill this promise? That's the conflict in this larger narrative. Finally, after twenty-five years, many adventures, and ten chapters of Genesis, we hear the resolution to this conflict: "The LORD dealt with Sarah as he had said, and the LORD did for Sarah as he had promised" (21:1). One of the challenges in preaching this narrative will be to hold together this extended narrative by selecting appropriate Scripture readings and preaching it as a single, coherent narrative.

Text and Context

The text of Genesis 21:1-7 is clearly a literary unit. The narrative before it, about Sarah ending up in the harem of King Abimelech, concludes at the end of chapter 20, and a new narrative, about Abraham sending away Hagar and Ishmael, begins at Genesis 21:8. So Genesis 21:1-7, between these two narratives, is a literary unit. But it is not a complete *narrative* unit; as noted above, it is the resolution to an overarching narrative plot which began in Genesis 11:30 with the statement that "Sarai was barren" and that the LORD promised to make of Abram "a great nation" (12:2). The LORD repeated this promise of offspring at various times: "I will make your offspring as the dust of the earth" (13:16); "Look toward heaven and count the stars, if you are able to count them. . . . So shall your descendants be" (15:5); "I will make you exceedingly numerous" (17:2); "Your name shall be Abraham; for I have made you the ancestor of a multitude of nations. I will make you exceedingly fruitful" (17:5-6). At that point in time, God made unmistakably clear that his promise would be fulfilled through Sarah: "I will bless her, and she shall give rise to nations" (17:16). Finally, after twenty-five years of waiting, "The LORD dealt with Sarah as he had said, and the LORD did for Sarah as he had promised. Sarah conceived and bore Abraham a son in his old age, at the time of which God had spoken to him" (21:1-2).

Literary Features

In this scene (21:1-7) the narrator relates the initial fulfillment of God's promise to Abraham of numerous descendants. The LORD hovers in the background (21:1) while the narrator sketches the two main characters in this scene, Abraham and Sarah, with character description as well as action and speech. The narrator describes Abraham twice as being of "old age" (vv 2, 7) and as "a hundred years old" (v 5), emphasizing the impossibility of his fatherhood. He stresses Abraham's obedience to God in naming his son, Isaac (v 3), and circumcising him on the eighth day, "as God had commanded him" (v 4). He describes the barren Sarah as conceiving and bearing a son (v 2), and concludes the narrative with Sarah's substantial speech praising God (vv 6-7).

The LORD's prior word or promise is repeated three times: "as he [the LORD] had said," "as he had promised," "the time of which God had spoken to him" (vv 1-2). As noted above, Abraham is described three times as being old. The name Isaac ("he laughs") is repeated three times (vv 3, 4, 5) and its root "to laugh" two times (v 6). The passage has to do with the LORD miraculously fulfilling his promise to Abraham and Sarah and the laughter that results.

Repetition in sentence structure also alerts us to synonymous parallelism in verse 1:

A The LORD dealt with Sarah
  B as he had said,
A′ and the LORD did for Sarah
  B′ as he had promised.[1]

1. "In the original language, the number of stresses is exactly what it would be in poetry: 3 + 2, 3 + 2 (in v 1), 3 + 3+ 4 (in v 2) . . . 3 + 3+ 3 [in v 7]." Fokkelman, *Reading Biblical Narrative,* 176.

The Plot Line

The setting of this narrative is found in Genesis 11:30, where the narrator informs us that Abram's wife, Sarai, "was barren; she had no child" (11:30). The occasioning incident takes place in Genesis 12:2, where the LORD promised Abram, "I will make of you a great nation." The tension rises when the narrator reports that "Abram was seventy-five years old" (12:4). Years pass, and Abram and Sarai receive no child.

After waiting ten years, Sarai, following the customs of that culture, suggests to Abram, "You see that the LORD has prevented me from bearing children; go in to my slave-girl; it may be that I shall obtain children by her" (16:2). Abram agrees and takes Hagar as his wife. As a result of this union, Abram receives a son, Ishmael. The narrator emphasizes with repetition that this son was born not of Sarai but of Hagar: "*Hagar* bore Abram a son; and Abram named his son, whom *Hagar* bore, Ishmael. Abram was eighty-six years old when *Hagar* bore him Ishmael" (16:15-16). Abram must have thought that God's promise to make of him "a great nation" would be fulfilled through Ishmael. At least Abraham seemed content with Ishmael (see 17:18). The tension appears to be resolved — at least for the next thirteen years.

But the narrative conflict starts up again in Genesis 17 when the LORD appears to Abram, changes his name to Abraham, and promises him a son by Sarai/Sarah (17:16), who is now ninety years old. In response, "Abraham fell on his face and *laughed,* and said to himself, 'Can a child be born to a man who is a hundred years old? Can Sarah, who is ninety years old, bear a child?' And Abraham says to God, 'O that Ishmael might live in your sight!'" (17:17-18). But the LORD insists, "No, but your wife Sarah shall bear you a son, and you shall name him Isaac" (17:19), that is, "*he laughs.*"

A short while later the LORD again appears to Abraham and promises, "I will surely return to you in due season, and your wife Sarah shall have a son" (18:10). Sarah, overhearing this promise, "*laughed* to herself, saying, 'After I have grown old, and my husband is old, shall I have pleasure?'" (18:12).

The larger narrative about Abraham and Sarah is at this point interrupted by narratives about God sharing with Abraham his intent to destroy Sodom and Gomorrah (18:16-33), the depravity of Sodom (19:1-11), the saving of Lot and his daughters from the destruction of Sodom (19:12-29), and Lot's daughters conceiving through incest and giving birth to the ancestors of the Moabites and the Ammonites (19:30-38). The tension in the narrative of Abraham and Sarah receiving the promised child is picked up again and reaches a climax in Gerar when Abraham passes off Sarah as his sister. So "King Abimelech of Gerar sent and took Sarah" (20:2). Abraham is risking the mother of the promised child in the harem of Abimelech.

Finally, after all these harrowing experiences, the conflict is resolved: "The LORD dealt with Sarah as he had said, and the LORD did for Sarah as he had promised. Sarah conceived and bore Abraham a son in his old age" (21:1-2). The narrator informs us of Abraham's obedient response: he names his son Isaac and circumcises him on the eighth day (21:3-4). The narrator reminds us again that "Abraham was a hundred years old" (21:5). Sarah's joyful speech praising God for bringing "laughter" for her is the happy outcome of this lengthy narrative.

We can sketch the plot line of this extended narrative as a complex plot.

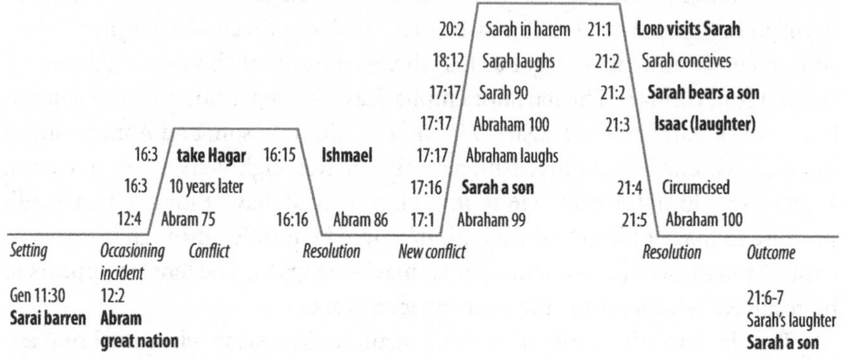

Theocentric Interpretation

The LORD is clearly the protagonist in this lengthy narrative covering twenty-five years. The LORD sets the tension by promising Abram, "I will make of you a great nation" (12:2) even while Sarai is barren. The LORD repeats this promise many times, even making it "a multitude of nations" (17:5). Finally, after twenty-five years, when all human scheming and planning to fulfill God's promise are utterly exhausted (Abraham is now one hundred and the barren Sarah is ninety), "The LORD visited Sarah as he had said, and the LORD did for Sarah what he had promised" (21:1). Sarah knows that only the LORD could have worked this miracle of a son to a barren woman at age ninety. She exclaims, "God has brought laughter for me" (21:6).

Textual Theme and Goal

It is tempting to formulate the theme of this narrative as, "The faithful LORD gives 'laughter' by fulfilling his promise of a child to Abraham and Sarah in their old age." Although this is a good summary of the narrative, it does not quite capture the message for Israel. How did Israel hear this narrative? What was the point for them? Israel, of course, would have identified with Isaac: had the LORD not been faithful in fulfilling his promise to Abraham and Sarah, there would have been no Israel. Moreover, the lengthy narrative focuses on the laughter of disbelief which the faithful LORD in the end turns into the joyful laughter of Sarah at the birth of Isaac ("laughter"). So we can formulate the theme (message) for Israel somewhat as follows: *Rejoice in the LORD's faithfulness in fulfilling his promise by miraculously calling Isaac/Israel into existence.*

The narrator's goal for Israel is evident in the formulation of the theme. Whether Israel was in Moab, discouraged after the deadly journey through the desert, or discouraged in exile in Babylonia for being banished from the Promised Land, this narrative would have encouraged Israel to rejoice ("laughter") in the LORD's faithfulness and miracle-working power. So the goal of this message for Israel can be formulated as, *to encourage Israel to rejoice in the LORD's faithfulness which miraculously called them into existence as the LORD's special people.*

Ways to Preach Christ

Redemptive-Historical Progression

One way to preach Christ from this narrative is to follow the road of redemptive-historical progression. With Sarah's miraculous conception and the birth of Isaac, the LORD provides another seed of the woman who provides genuine laughter for Abraham and Sarah. Later the LORD will provide another miracle child for Isaac and the barren Rebekah, Jacob/Israel. Eventually Jacob's sons give birth to the nation of Israel out of which, in God's time, the Messiah would be born (see Jesus' genealogy in Matthew 1 and Luke 3). When God works this even greater miracle of Jesus' conception and birth, there is great rejoicing by the angels, the shepherds, Simeon, Anna, and the wise men. Jesus' preaching of the good news and his healing miracles bring joy to many. When Jesus is about to die, he acknowledges to his disciples, "You have pain now; but I will see you again, and your hearts will rejoice, and no one will take your joy from you" (John 16:22).

Promise-Fulfillment

Since the message has to do with the faithful LORD fulfilling his promise of a child for Abraham and Sarah, the road of promise-fulfillment will probably be the most natural way of preaching Christ from this narrative. However, the passage does not have a direct messianic promise, for God's promise is fulfilled when Isaac is born. Yet the promise is open to further filling, for God had promised to make Abraham the "father of a multitude of *nations*." So the birth of Isaac is an initial fulfillment. God's promise to Abraham reaches for its fulfillment far beyond Isaac to Abraham's son Jesus Christ, who commands his disciples to "make disciples of all *nations*." But still the promise is not filled full. The church today is engaged in fulfilling this promise as it preaches the gospel of Jesus Christ to the nations. God's promise to Abraham will finally be fulfilled when Jesus comes again and a great multitude "from every nation, from all tribes and peoples and languages" will stand "before the throne and before the Lamb, robed in white, with palm branches in their hands" praising God and the Lamb (Rev 7:9-10).

This way of preaching Christ can be supported further by quoting Galatians 3:13-14, "Christ redeemed us from the curse of the law . . . in order that in Christ Jesus the blessing of Abraham might come to the Gentiles." Or by quoting Romans 4:16-20, Abraham

> is the father of all of us, as it is written, "I have made you the father of many nations" — in the presence of the God in whom he believed, who gives life to the dead and calls into existence the things that do not exist. Hoping against hope, he believed that he would become "the father of many nations," according to what was said, "So numerous shall your descendants be." He did not weaken in faith when he considered his own body, which was already as good as dead (for he was about a hundred years old), or when he considered the barrenness of Sarah's womb. No distrust made him waver concerning the promise of God, but he grew strong in his faith as he gave glory to God, being fully convinced that God was able to do what he had promised.

Typology

One can also preach Christ by using typology. Isaac is here a type of Jesus Christ. Note the analogies and escalations: Isaac was the continuation of the line of the seed of the woman — Christ is *the* Seed of the woman; Isaac's conception was a miracle — Christ's conception is an even greater miracle (born of a virgin); Isaac's birth brought laughter to a few old people — Christ's birth brings laughter to many people.

Analogy

Analogy offers another possibility. As the miraculous birth of Isaac encouraged Israel to rejoice in the LORD's faithfulness which called them into existence, so the miraculous birth of Christ and his outpouring of the Holy Spirit encourages the church to rejoice in God's faithfulness which called his church into existence.

This analogy can be supported by moving from Sarah's song of praise at Isaac's birth (21:6-7) to Mary's song of praise at the announcement of Jesus' birth:

> "My soul magnifies the Lord,
>   and my spirit *rejoices* in God my Savior,
> for he has looked with favor on the lowliness of his servant.
>   Surely, from now on all generations will call me blessed;
> for *the Mighty One has done great things for me. . . .*
> He has helped his servant Israel,
>   in remembrance of his mercy,
> *according to the promise he made to our ancestors,*
>   *to Abraham* and to his descendants forever."
>
> (Luke 1:46-55)

Longitudinal Themes

One can trace in Scripture the theme of the LORD's miracle-working power: creating the universe with his word, giving Abraham and barren Sarah a child in their old age, later answering the prayer of Isaac for barren Rebekah (25:21) by giving them twins, working miracles in Egypt to set Israel free, working miracles in the desert to sustain his people, knocking down the walls of Jericho so his people can enter the Promised Land, much later giving a special child to a virgin, raising Jesus from the dead, empowering Jesus to ascend to heaven to rule at his right hand until he comes again on the last day.

New Testament References

In addition to the New Testament references cited above, one may consider also the following passages:

Luke 1:68-73, the Song of Zechariah about the birth of Jesus,

> "Blessed be the Lord God of Israel,
>   for he has looked favorably on his people and redeemed them.

> He has raised up a *mighty savior* for us
> in the house of his servant David, . . .
> Thus he has shown the mercy promised to our ancestors,
> and *has remembered his holy covenant,*
> *the oath that he swore to our ancestor Abraham.*"

Luke 6:21, "Blessed are you who weep now, for you will *laugh.*"

John 8:56, "Your ancestor Abraham *rejoiced* that he would see my day; he saw it and was *glad.*"

Hebrews 11:11-12, "By faith he [Abraham] received power of procreation, even though he was too old — and Sarah herself was barren — because he considered him faithful who had promised. Therefore from one person, and this one as good as dead, descendants were born, 'as many as the stars of heaven and as the innumerable grains of sand by the seashore.'"

Revelation 19:6-7,

> "Hallelujah!
> For the Lord our God the Almighty reigns.
> Let us *rejoice* and exult and give him the glory,
> for the marriage of the Lamb has come,
> and his bride has made herself ready."

Contrast

There is no contrast between the message of this narrative and the New Testament.

Sermon Theme and Goal

We formulated the textual theme as, "Rejoice in the LORD's faithfulness in fulfilling his promise by miraculously calling Isaac/Israel into existence." The context of the Old and New Testaments shows that the promise of a child and ultimately "a multitude of nations" (17:5, 16) finds further fulfillment in the birth of Jacob, in the birth of the nation of Israel, finally in Israel's Messiah, Jesus Christ, who sends his disciples out to "make disciples of all nations" (Matt 28:19) and, ultimately, in Jesus' second coming when "the nations will walk" by God's light (Rev 21:23-24). In order to encompass this context as well as the original message, we can formulate the sermon theme as, *Rejoice in the LORD's faithfulness in fulfilling his promise by miraculously calling his people (Isaac/Israel/the church) into existence.*

The narrator's goal we formulated as, "to encourage Israel to rejoice in the LORD's faithfulness which miraculously called them into existence as the LORD's special people." Similarly, our goal in preaching this narrative can be, *to encourage the church to rejoice in the LORD's faithfulness which miraculously called them into existence as the LORD's special people.* This particular goal implies that the need addressed in this sermon is our lack of reflection on and joy in the miracle of the church and our membership in it.

Scripture Readings

Since this narrative from promise to initial fulfillment covers ten chapters, one of the challenges is to select an appropriate number of passages for Scripture reading. I suggest that one read passages about God's promises to Abraham and Sarah *before* the sermon but save the passage on the fulfillment, Genesis 21:1-7, for the sermon itself. This will enhance the possibility of capturing in the sermon some of the tension of this lengthy narrative. For example, before preaching the sermon one can read Genesis 11:27-30; 12:1-4a; and 15:1-6, and ask the people to keep their Bibles open at Genesis. In the sermon itself briefly explain these passages of God's promise of a child, even many descendants, and then continue quoting and explaining Genesis 16:1-4a; 17:15-19; 18:9-15; and perhaps 20:2, building up the tension until the resolution in Genesis 21:1-7.

Sermon Exposition

Given the sermon goal and need, the introduction can illustrate that many people take membership in the church of Jesus Christ for granted or even consider it a burden. Israel, too, frequently failed to appreciate the miracle of belonging to God's covenant people. And yet the existence of Israel was a miracle of God. Abram was seventy-five years old when God promised to bless him and make of him a great nation (12:2). But the narrator has just informed us that Abram's wife Sarai "was barren; she had no child" (11:30). How can God make a great nation of Abram when his wife is infertile?

After many years of waiting, Abram complained to God. We read in Genesis 15:2-5, "Abram said, 'O Lord GOD, what will you give me, for I continue childless, and the heir of my house is Eliezer of Damascus?' And Abram said, 'You have given me no offspring [seed], and so a slave born in my house is to be my heir.' But the word of the LORD came to him, 'This man shall not be your heir; no one but your very own issue shall be your heir.' He brought him outside and said, 'Look toward heaven and count the stars, if you are able to count them.' Then he said to him, 'So shall your descendants be.'" Three times now the LORD has repeated his promise to Abram on ever grander scale: in Genesis 12:2, "I will make of you a great nation"; in Genesis 13:16, "I will make your offspring [seed] like the dust of the earth"; in Genesis 15:5, Your descendants will be like the stars in the sky.

Still Abram and Sarai received no children. And it is becoming more and more unlikely that they will get children. Abram is now eighty-five years old and Sarai seventy-five. So Sarai comes up with an alternative plan. The LORD had promised Abram many descendants, but he had never said explicitly that this would be with his wife Sarai. In that culture, if a wife was unable to have children, the custom was for the husband to produce children with his wife's slave-girl.[2] In chapter 16:2 we read that Sarai says to Abram, "You see that the LORD has prevented me from bearing children; go into my slave-girl; it may be that I shall obtain children by her." This must have been an incredibly difficult step for Sarai, but it seemed that this was the only way for her to get children. And Abram agreed. So Sarai gave Hagar, her slave-girl, to Abram "as a wife" (16:3). The plan worked: Hagar became pregnant, and, as we read in verse 15, "Hagar bore Abram a son; and Abram named his son, whom Hagar bore, Ishmael." The narrator adds, "Abram was eighty-six years old when Hagar bore him Ishmael." Just in the nick of time did they resort to this plan. Abram had a son in his old age. The tension in the narrative is resolved. The LORD had fulfilled his promise.

For thirteen years Abram and Sarai seem to have accepted the idea that Ishmael was the promised son. Abram, at least, seems to have been content with that thought (see 17:18). But then the suspense starts all over again. We read in chapter 17:1, "When Abram was ninety-nine years old, the LORD appeared to him." On this occasion the LORD for the first time specifically includes Sarai in his promise of children. God changes Sarai's name to Sarah and says to Abraham, verse 16, "I will bless her, and moreover I will give you a son *by her.*" Abraham cannot believe his ears. A son by Sarah who now is ninety years old? And he almost a hundred! We read in verse 17, "Then Abraham fell on his face and *laughed,* and said to himself, 'Can a child be born to a man who is a hundred years old? Can Sarah, who is ninety years old, bear a child?'" It is the laughter of disbelief! It is now impossible for Abraham and Sarah to have children of their

2. According to "legal customs that were apparently widespread at that time, the wife could bring to the marriage her own personal maid. . . . If she gave her personal maid to her husband, in the event of her own childlessness, then the child born of the maid was considered the wife's child: The slave was . . . [to give birth] 'on the knees' of the wife, so that the child then came symbolically from the womb of the wife herself (cf. ch. 30:3, 9)! From the legal and moral standpoint, therefore, Sarah's proposal was completely according to custom." Von Rad, *Genesis,* 191. Cf. Sarna, *Understanding Genesis,* 128.

own. Abraham pleads with God (v 18), "O that Ishmael might live in your sight!" But God replies, "No, but your wife Sarah shall bear you a son, and you shall name him Isaac." The name Isaac means "he laughs." The very name of the promised son will remind Abraham and later Israel that Abraham laughed in disbelief of God's promise. It is simply impossible for a hundred-year-old man and his barren, ninety-year-old wife to conceive and have a child.

In chapter 18 the LORD appears to Abraham again and repeats the promise. Verse 10, "I will surely return to you in due season, and your wife Sarah shall have a son." Sarah is in the tent and overhears this comment. It seems that this is the first time she hears about receiving her own son, for we read in verse 12, "So Sarah *laughed* to herself, saying, 'After I have grown old, and my husband is old, shall I have pleasure?'" Sarah's language is quite crude: she describes herself literally as being "worn out" (TNIV), like clothing ready to be discarded (cf. Josh 9:13), and as incapable of sensual pleasure. The LORD asks Abraham in verse 13, "Why did Sarah laugh, and say, 'Shall I indeed bear a child, now that I am old?' Is anything too wonderful for the LORD? At the set time I will return to you, in due season, and Sarah shall have a son." But Sarah denies her disbelief. She says, "'I did not laugh'; for she was afraid." The LORD responds, "Oh yes, you did laugh."

First Abraham laughed in disbelief, and now Sarah laughs in disbelief. Sarah laughs at the sheer impossibility of her having a child. The LORD responds to this laughter of disbelief with the question, "Is anything too wonderful for the LORD?"[3] An important question that we will need to reflect on later. But here the narrator emphasizes Sarah's laughter by repeating the word four times. First he tells us in verse 12 that "Sarah laughed." Next the LORD asks (v 13), "Why did Sarah laugh?" Then Sarah denies it, saying (v 15), "I did not laugh"; to which the LORD responds, "Oh yes, you did laugh." The point is that God causes this laughter of disbelief because his promise of a child to a couple "as good as dead" (Rom 4:19) is really incredible!

The narrator leaves us hanging there with the laughter of disbelief ringing in our ears. He moves on to other stories: God's intent to destroy Sodom and Gomorrah (18:16-33), the depravity of Sodom (19:1-11), the angels saving Lot and his daughters from the destruction of Sodom (19:12-29), and Lot's incest with his daughters (19:30-38). The overarching narrative of Abraham and Sarah receiving the promised child is picked up again in chapter 20 and reaches a climax when Abraham in Gerar (near Gaza) again (see 12:13) passes off Sarah as his sister. So "King Abimelech of Gerar sent and took Sarah" (20:2).[4] Abraham

3. "The narrator works out the contrast very sharply: The unbelieving . . . laugh, and now this word which indignantly punishes the way of thinking that mistrusts Yahweh's omnipotence." Von Rad, *Genesis,* 207.

4. The question may be raised why Abimelech "took Sarah" who was now ninety years old (17:17) and who had just described herself as "worn out" (18:12). This is a question for us because

is risking the mother of the promised child in the harem of Abimelech.[5] Kidner comments, "On the brink of Isaac's birth-story here is the very Promise put in jeopardy, traded away for personal safety. If it is ever to be fulfilled, it will owe very little to man. Morally as well as physically, it will clearly have to be achieved by the grace of God."[6]

Finally, in chapter 21 we read of God fulfilling his promise to Abraham and Sarah. Verse 1,

> The LORD dealt with Sarah as he had said,
> and the LORD did for Sarah as he had promised.

The NRSV translates the Hebrew word *pāqad* as, "The LORD *dealt with* Sarah," while the TNIV translates, "Now the LORD *was gracious to* Sarah." The same word is also used in Genesis 50:24-25 to describe God *"coming to"* Israel to bring them up out of Egypt to the Promised Land. So the LORD here "comes to"[7] or "visits" Sarah to fulfill his promise: "as he had said, . . . as he had promised." The birth of a son for Sarah was "predicted twice (17:16-21; 18:10-15), and here the fulfillment of the promises is mentioned twice."[8] Calvin observes that there is "great emphasis in the repetition. . . . For he thus retains his readers, as by laying his hand upon them, that they may pause in the consideration of so great a miracle."[9]

Verse 2, "Sarah conceived and bore Abraham a son in his old age, at the time of which God had spoken to him." This is the third time the narrator reminds us of God's prior word: "as he [the LORD] had said," "as he had promised," "at the time of which God had spoken.'" Sailhamer comments, "The plan not only came about, but, more importantly, it happened as it was announced.

---

we tend to read this passage in the light of Genesis 12:11, "a woman beautiful in appearance," so that we assume that Abimelech "took Sarah" because she was still beautiful (indeed, many modern commentators treat Genesis 20:1-18 as a doublet of 12:10-20). But Abimelech could have had other reasons for taking Sarah, such as a political marriage in order to form an alliance with Abraham. Calvin may point in this direction when he suggests, "It might also be, that king Abimelech was less attracted to the elegance of her form, than by the rare virtues with which he saw her, as a matron, to be endued." *Genesis,* I, 522.

5. Hamilton, *Genesis 18–50,* 73, n. 7, as well as Calvin, *Genesis,* I, 521, suggests that Sarah may have been pregnant at this time, but 21:2 states rather clearly that she conceived after this episode. Hamilton seems to acknowledge this when he remarks, "In only two words *(wattahar* and *watteled)* the narrative covers nine months." Ibid., 73.

6. Kidner, *Genesis,* 137. Cf. Calvin, *Genesis,* I, 521, "In this history, the Holy Spirit presents to us a remarkable instance, both of the infirmity of man, and of the grace of God."

7. "Often this verb is used in contexts where the focus is on God's attentive care and concern." Sailhamer, *Genesis,* 164.

8. Wenham, *Genesis 16–50,* 79.

9. Calvin, *Genesis,* I, 538.

Thus the narrative calls attention to God's faithfulness to his word and to his careful attention to the details of his plan."[10]

In verse 3 we read that "Abraham gave the name Isaac to his son whom Sarah bore him. And Abraham circumcised his son Isaac when he was eight days old, as God had commanded him." Significantly, Abraham does not get a line thanking God for Isaac, but, as before (12:4), he obeys God to the letter. God had said, "You shall name him Isaac" (17:19), and Abraham names his son Isaac. God had said, "Every male among you shall be circumcised when he is eight days old" (17:12), and Abraham circumcises Isaac "when he was eight days old."

The Hebrew in verse 3 reads literally, "And Abraham called the name of his son *which was born to him,* whom Sarah had born to him, Isaac." Wenham observes, "Comparison with 16:15 shows that 'which was born to him' is unnecessary. But the repetition again serves to drive home the miraculous nature of the birth of a son to Sarah."[11] And to Abraham, we might add. For the additional phrase results in the repetition of "born to *him.*" For good measure the narrator adds in verse 5, "Abraham was a hundred years old when his son Isaac was born to him." Isaac is indeed a child who could only have been called into being by the miraculous power of the faithful LORD.

Interestingly, whereas Abram does not get a single line in this passage, it concludes with a substantial song of praise by Sarah. Verse 6, "Now Sarah said, God has brought laughter for me; everyone who hears will laugh with me." God has turned the laughter of disbelief into the laughter of joy. Every time she will call Isaac, she will be reminded of her laughter of disbelief. The LORD had asked, "Is anything too wonderful for the LORD?" (18:14). Well, that depends on how great your God is. Now Sarah knows: nothing is too wonderful for the LORD! He who created the universe with his word is able to fulfill his promise, no matter how impossible it seems. Jesus also had to remind his disciples, "For God all things are possible" (Matt 19:26).

With the miraculous fulfillment of his promise, the LORD has turned Sarah's laughter of disbelief into genuine laughter. Sarah says, "Everyone who hears will laugh with me." Certainly her household will laugh with her, but also later Israel. For in a real sense Israel was born that day. Had Isaac not been born, there would have been no Israel. Israel owed its existence to the LORD's faithfulness in miraculously calling Isaac into existence generations earlier. So when Israel heard this story, they were expected to laugh with Sarah, to rejoice in the LORD's faithfulness which miraculously called them into existence. And also to rejoice in the LORD's faithfulness which miraculously sustained them in their

10. Sailhamer, *Genesis,* 164.

11. Wenham, *Genesis 16–50,* 80.

trials, even bringing a remnant back from exile. Psalm 126:1-2 reflects this joy which echoes Sarah's laughter:

> When the LORD restored the fortunes of Zion,
> we were like those who dream.
> Then our mouth was filled with *laughter,*
> and our tongue with shouts of joy;
> then it was said among the nations,
> "The LORD has done great things for them."

Like Israel, we also are expected to laugh with Sarah, to rejoice in the LORD's faithfulness which miraculously, throughout the ages, calls his people into existence.

Sarah concludes her praise song with a rhetorical question in verse 7. She asks, "Who would ever have said to Abraham that Sarah would nurse children? Yet I have borne him a son in his old age." Who would ever have said it? Not Abraham. Certainly not Sarah. No one would have said it, for it is impossible for a ninety-year-old woman to nurse children. Yet the LORD made the impossible possible. He fulfilled his promise: Isaac was born. The son of the covenant was born, the first of a long line of descendants. God's covenant people began to multiply on earth. First it was one son, later a nation. And then Isaiah (9:6) would prophesy,

> For a child has been born for us,
> a son given to us;
> authority rests upon his shoulders;
> and he is named Wonderful Counselor, Mighty God,
> Everlasting Father, Prince of Peace.

Can God fulfill this promise of a divine son? "Is anything too wonderful for the LORD?"

Jesus' birth of the virgin Mary was even more miraculous than Isaac's birth of ninety-year-old Sarah. At Jesus' birth, too, there was much laughter. Mary sang her song of praise even before Jesus' birth (Luke 1:46-55).

> "My soul magnifies the Lord,
> and my spirit *rejoices* in God my Savior,
> for he has looked with favor on the lowliness of his servant.
> Surely, from now on all generations will call me blessed;
> for *the Mighty One has done great things for me. . . .*
> He has helped his servant Israel,
> in remembrance of his mercy,

according to the promise he made to our ancestors,
to Abraham and to his descendants forever."

At Jesus' birth the angels sang "Glory to God" and the shepherds rejoiced as well as Simeon, Anna, the wise men from the East, and many others. Yet this child was not named Isaac, laughter. God commanded Joseph, "You are to name him Jesus, for he will save his people from their sins" (Matt 1:21). The name "Jesus," Yahweh saves, is even more cause for rejoicing than the name "Isaac."

Jesus brought joy by preaching the good news of the kingdom of God, by healing people of their diseases, but especially by giving his life as a ransom for many. In a dispute with the Jews, Jesus said to them, "Your ancestor Abraham rejoiced that he would see my day; he saw it and was glad" (John 8:56). Jesus was referring to Isaac's birth and the laughter it brought about. How did Abraham see Jesus' day in Isaac's birth? Isaac's birth was in fulfillment of God's covenant promise to Abraham that he would have a child with Sarah. But God's promise was for much more than a child; God promised to make Abraham the "father of a multitude of *nations*." This promise was initially fulfilled in the birth of Isaac, but it reached for its fulfillment far beyond Isaac and the nation of Israel to Abraham's son Jesus Christ, who would command his disciples to "make disciples of *all nations*" and poured out his Spirit to enable them to do so (see Acts 2). In the birth of Isaac, Abraham saw Jesus' day, for he saw the initial fulfillment of God's promise to make him the "father of a multitude of nations."

When the New Testament church was born at Pentecost, some three thousand persons were baptized, joining the church of Jesus Christ, rejoicing and "*praising God*" (Acts 2:47). Later, when Paul and Barnabas preached in Antioch, they recalled their mission: "The Lord has commanded us, saying, 'I have set you to be a light for the Gentiles, so that you may bring salvation to the ends of the earth.'" Luke comments, "When the Gentiles heard this, *they were glad and praised the word of the Lord*" (Acts 13:47-48). What an awesome work God has done in grafting Gentiles into the stem of Abraham, in miraculously calling into existence the church of Jesus Christ as his special people.

How thankful we should be that God gave "laughter" to Abraham and Sarah and that he gave great joy to the virgin Mary. How we should rejoice that "God so loved the world that he gave his only Son, so that everyone who believes in him may not perish but may have eternal life" (John 3:16). Abraham saw Jesus' day and was glad; we have seen Jesus' day and should be *glad!* Paul exhorts the church in Colossae, "Let the word of Christ dwell in you richly . . . ; and with *gratitude* in your hearts sing psalms, hymns, and spiritual songs to God. And whatever you do, in word or deed, do everything in the name of the Lord Jesus, *giving thanks* to God the Father through him" (Col 3:16-17).

CHAPTER 10

The Call to Sacrifice Isaac

Genesis 22:1-19[1]

One of the challenges in preaching this well-known narrative is to make responsible choices between the divergent opinions of various commentators as to the meaning of this passage as well as its connection with Jesus Christ. Another challenge is to avoid the superficial applications suggested by many commentaries. In their legitimate concern for relevance, these commentaries frequently fail to ask first what message Israel received from this narrative; they blur the redemptive-historical distinction between Abraham and us; and they tend to attach their practical remarks to mere verses in the text. For example, one commentary suggests the following applications for this passage: verse 2, As Abraham was called upon to sacrifice his son, "so we, in like manner, may be called upon to make sacrifices"; verse 5, "He [Abraham] wanted not to be interrupted. . . . Great trials are best entered upon with but little company"; verse 11, "God delights to bring his people to the mount, to the very brow of the hill, till their feet slip, and then he delivers them."[2]

1. This chapter is a major revision of my exposition in *Preaching Christ from the Old Testament,* 292-318, which sought to demonstrate with this passage the ten steps from text to sermon.

2. T. H. Leale, *The Preacher's Complete Homiletical Commentary* (New York: Funk & Wagnalls, 1892), Genesis 22. Cf. James Hastings, *The Great Texts of the Bible* (Edinburgh: T&T Clark, 1911), 198, "God's true children must climb their mount of sacrifice. When our own hour shall have come, may we arise forthwith, cleave the wood for the burnt-offering, and go unflinching up the path by which our Heavenly Father shall lead us. So shall the mount of trial become the mount of blessing." Following the same method of application, a pastor in 1997 shared the following sermon outline on this passage with the cyberspace world: Sermon title, "The Journey of Faith." Sermon points: 1. Be in relationship with the Most High God; 2. Risk it all; 3. Be prepared and obedient; 4. Trust God to provide; 5. Receive God's blessing.

Text and Context

The narrative unit is easy to determine. Genesis 22:1 clearly begins a new narrative with the words, "After these things. . . ."[3] Along with the Common Lectionary, one might be tempted to end the textual unit at verse 14 when the conflict of offering Isaac is resolved, but the narrative continues with the LORD pronouncing again his covenant blessings (vv 15-18) and ends at verse 19 with Abraham and his companions returning to Beersheba, "and Abraham lived at Beersheba." Verse 20 begins a new unit with the now familiar, "Now after these things."

In the discussion of Genesis 12 we noted that the Abraham cycle is arranged as a chiastic structure:

A Genealogy of Terah (11:27-32)
  B Start of Abram's spiritual odyssey (12:1-9)
    C Sarai in foreign palace; ordeal ends in peace and success; Abram and Lot part (12:10–13:18)
      D Abram comes to the rescue of Sodom and Lot (14:1-24)
        E Covenant with Abram; Annunciation of Ishmael (15:1–16:16)
        E′ Covenant with Abraham; Annunciation of Isaac (17:1–18:15)
      D′ Abraham comes to the rescue of Sodom and Lot (18:16–19:38)
    C′ Sarah in foreign palace; ordeal ends in peace and success; Abraham and Ishmael part (20:1–21:34)
  B′ Climax of Abraham's spiritual odyssey (22:1-19)
A′ Genealogy of Nahor (22:20-24)[4]

For our present narrative, the important issue shown in this chiasm is the narrator's deliberate parallel development between Genesis 12:1-9 and Genesis 22:1-19 as well as further progression. In Genesis 12 the LORD commanded Abram to "go" [*lek-lekā*], offer up his past (country, kindred, father's house), and receive the promises of the LORD's rich blessings. In this narrative the LORD commands Abraham to "go" [*lek-lekā*],[5] but now to offer up his future, "your son, your only son Isaac, whom you love." The stakes are raised. Now Abraham has to rely on the LORD even when the LORD seems to go back on his covenant promises.

3. "The formula, 'after these things' is found only four times in the Pentateuch — all four in Genesis (15:1; 22:1; 22:20; 48:1)" — twice in chapter 22 providing clues to the limits to this narrative. JoAnn Davidson, "Eschatology and Genesis 22," *Journal of the Adventist Theological Society* 11/1-2 (2000) 233.

4. Rendsburg, *The Redaction of Genesis*, 28-29.

5. Used in the Bible only in these two passages and, in the feminine form, in Song 2:10, 13.

But when he obeys, the LORD speaks to him a final time — the promised blessings in even heightened form.[6]

Literary Features

The narrator shows his hand most clearly in verse 14b, "as it is said to this day, 'On the mount of the LORD it shall be provided.'" But the narrator's hand is evident throughout the narrative. He lets Israel know at the outset (v 1) that God did not really require child sacrifice as did the pagan gods but that God was testing Abraham.[7] Abraham, of course, did not know this; he only heard the command, "Take your son, your only son Isaac, whom you love, and . . . offer him. . . ." Here the character description of Isaac as "your son, your only son Isaac, whom you love," drives home the enormity of God's request. This character description of "your son, your only son" is repeated at the climax of the narrative (v 12) as well as at its conclusion (v 16).

The narrator slows the pace of the narrative at two crucial points, at Abraham's preparation for the journey (v 3) and at the climax of the conflict where he carefully reports every action: "Abraham built an altar there and laid the wood in order. He bound his son Isaac, and laid him on the altar, on top of the wood. Then Abraham reached out his hand and took the knife to kill his son" (vv 9-10).

The narrator uses repetition to emphasize key concepts. The word "son" *(bēn)* is repeated ten times, showing the severity of the test for Abraham, "burnt offering" six times, "wood" five times, "place" four times, and "provide" three times. The word "provide" is particularly significant. In response to Isaac's question, "Where is the lamb for a burnt offering?" Abraham answers, "God himself will provide *(yir'eh)* the lamb for a burnt offering, my son" (v 8). God does indeed provide the lamb for a burnt offering, the ram caught in a thicket by its horns (v 13). Is it any wonder that Abraham called that place, *Yahweh-yir'eh,* "The LORD will provide" (v 14)? For good measure the narrator adds for a third time that to his day people use the proverb, "On the mount of the LORD it shall be provided" *(yērā'eh)* (v 14).[8]

Repetition also alerts one to an underlying chiastic structure. Gordon

6. For many more parallels between these two narratives and shared theme-words, see Rendsburg, *Redaction of Genesis,* 30-35.

7. "This frees the reader to concentrate on the interaction between Abraham and God rather than wrestle with the entangling perplexity of how God could resort to human sacrifice." Kenneth Mathews, "Preaching Historical Narrative," 36.

8. Since this is the niphal of the verb, some scholars translate, "On the mount of the LORD he shall be seen" (NRSV note) or "appear."

Wenham suggests an intricate chiastic pattern based on both the scenes and subgenres.[9]

Introduction (1a)	Narration
A God's command, "Sacrifice your son" (1b-2)	Monologue
B Preparation for the journey (3)	Narration
C The third day at the foot of the mountain (4-6c)	Dialogue
C′ Journey up the mountain (6c-8)	Dialogue
B′ Preparation for sacrifice (9-10)	Narration
A′ Angel of the LORD's command, "Do not. . . ." (11-18)	Monologue
Epilogue: Return to Beersheba (19)	Narration

The narrator underscores the importance of God's covenant promises (vv 15-18) by noting that "the angel of the LORD called to Abraham *a second time* from heaven," the LORD swearing a formal oath, and this being the longest speech in the narrative. "The prominence of the denouement is indicated also by its location in the Abraham cycle; it is the last of 35 speeches [5 × 7] delivered by God (or the angel of the LORD)."[10]

The Plot Line

The setting of the text: "after these things" (v 1) refers especially to the foregoing chapter, where we read of the birth of Isaac and the expulsion of Ishmael. The conflict is generated by God's demand, "Take your son, your only son, whom you love, . . . and offer him . . . as a burnt offering . . ." (v 2). The tension rises with the three-day journey, the father and son's lonely climb up the mountain, Isaac's question, "Where is the lamb for a burnt offering?" and Abraham's ambiguous response, "God himself will provide the lamb for a burnt offering . . ." (vv 3-8). The conflict reaches a climax when Abraham builds an altar, puts the

9. Wenham, *Genesis 16–50,* 100. I have slightly changed the wording in his proposal. A possible weakness in this structure is that it covers vv 11-18 in one scene, ignoring the break indicated in verse 15 by "a second time." Stanley Walters, "Wood, Sand and Stars," *Toronto Journal of Theology* 3 (1987) 311-15, divides the narrative into a chiastic structure based on the repetition of groups of words (centering on "Where is the lamb?" and "God himself will provide the lamb") followed by a parallel pattern of seven units repeated in the same order. Brueggemann, *Genesis,* 186, suggests "three series of summons/response statement interchanges" which also highlight verse 8: "There can be little doubt of the cruciality of this statement on structural grounds."

10. Mathews, "Preaching Historical Narrative," 31. See p. 87 above for the use of the name *'Ĕlōhîm* thirty-five times in Genesis 1:1–2:3 and thirty-five times various names for God in the first *tôlĕdôt,* Genesis 2:4–4:26.

wood on it, binds Isaac, puts him on the altar, reaches for the knife, and is ready to kill his son (vv 9-10). At that excruciating pinnacle the angel of the LORD cries out, "Do not lay your hand on the boy!" and the tension breaks (vv 11-12). The conflict is completely resolved when Abraham spots a ram and offers it up "as a burnt offering instead of his son," and names the place, "The LORD will provide" (vv 13-14). The angel of the LORD calls a second time, and the LORD repeats his covenant blessings (vv 15-18). The narrative ends with Abraham back in Beersheba (v 19).

We can diagram the plot line as a single plot:

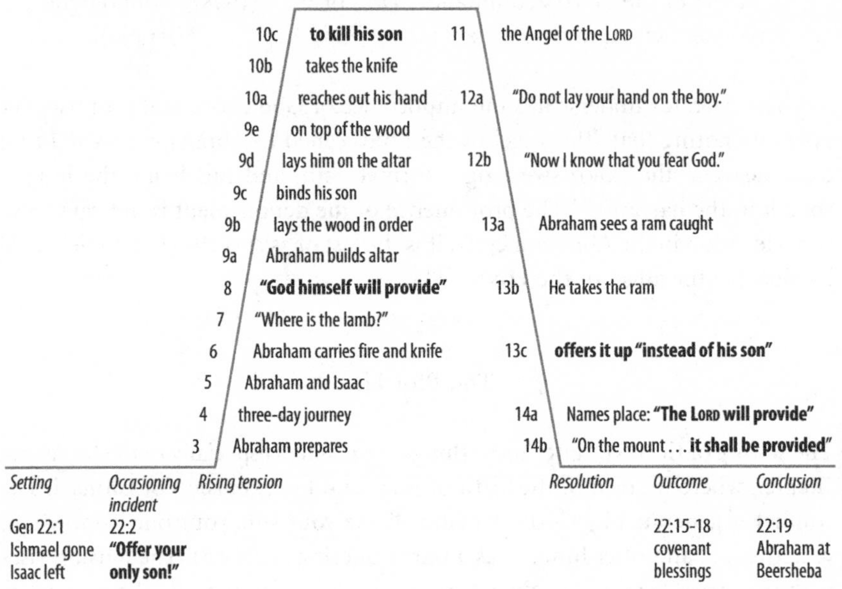

Theocentric Interpretation

Westermann observes, "The majority of interpreters . . . see the narrative holding Abraham up as an exemplar. . . . It seems to me, however, that when one refers the praise to Abraham (Kierkegaard), one has not understood the narrative. . . . The narrative looks not to the praise of a creature, but to the praise of God."[11] Although Abraham[12] and Isaac appear to be the main characters, in reality God is the protagonist. "God tested" (v 1); Abraham assures Isaac, "God will provide" (v 8); the LORD stops Abraham from offering Isaac (v 12); the

11. Westermann, *Genesis 12–36*, 364-65.

12. John Holbert, *Preaching Old Testament*, 86, holds that "This story is about *Abraham*, not Isaac, or even God." For Holbert's "pure narrative sermon" with explanations, see ibid., 79-92.

LORD provides the ram (v 13); Abraham names the place, "The LORD will provide" (v 14); the narrator adds, "as it is said to this day, 'On the mount of the LORD it shall be provided'" (v 14); and the LORD promises to bless Abraham, his offspring, and the nations (vv 15-18).

Textual Theme and Goal

In formulating the textual theme, we have to choose between two alternatives. The first and most frequently used entrance into the text takes its cue from verse 1, "God tested Abraham." Von Rad maintains that one of the main thoughts in this narrative is "the idea of a radical test of obedience. That God, who has revealed himself to Israel, is completely free to give and to take, and that no one may ask, 'What doest thou?' (Job 9:12; Dan 4:32), is without doubt basic to our narrative. . . . Yahweh tests faith and obedience."[13] Wenham also contends that "the central thrust of the story [is] Abraham's wholehearted obedience and the great blessings that have flowed from it."[14] These comments suggest that Israel heard in this narrative the message that God is sovereign and free to test his people's faith, and that he expects the unquestioning obedience and total trust that Abraham displayed. The ideas of God sovereignly testing Abraham's faith and Abraham modeling obedience for Israel can be merged into a single textual theme formulated like this: "Whenever the sovereign God tests the faith of his people, he demands unquestioning, trusting obedience." Although this theme is not unbiblical, I believe that it misses the specific theme of this particular narrative.

To hear the more specific theme of this narrative we first need to hear it as the narrator intended Israel to hear it. In this connection, a key question is, With whom would Israel have identified? This is often a difficult question to answer with any degree of certainty.[15] In this narrative the choices are limited to Abraham and Isaac. Initially the hearers would probably have identified with Abraham and the excruciating choice he had to make. But at a deeper level, there can be little doubt that Israel would have identified with Isaac:[16] Would

13. Von Rad, *Genesis*, 244.

14. Wenham, *Genesis 16–50*, 112.

15. See my *Modern Preacher*, 175-81.

16. This view is confirmed by von Rad, *Genesis*, 244-45: "When Israel read and related this story in later times it could only see itself represented by Isaac, i.e., laid on Yahweh's altar, given back to him, then given life again by him alone. That is to say, it could base its existence in history not on its own legal titles as other nations did, but only on the will of Him who in the freedom of his grace permitted Isaac to live." Cf. idem, *Biblical Interpretations*, 39, "In Isaac the community saw itself represented; in Isaac it saw itself offered up to God; in Isaac it confessedly had

Isaac die or live? If he had died on the altar, there never would have been a people called Israel; the ram died so that Isaac, that is, Israel, might live. Even in modern times, Jews identify with Isaac and read this narrative of what they call "The Binding of Isaac" on the Jewish New Year's day.

Moreover, it is clear that "God will provide" is a "turning point of the story," as Wenham and others admit.[17] But "God will provide" is not merely a turning point of the story, it is the heart of the message of this narrative for Israel. When Israel heard this narrative of Isaac on the altar, it heard the story of its very existence hanging in the balance. For Israel, Isaac's death or life is the heart of the plot. At the climax, Isaac is only a knife-thrust removed from death; then he receives his life back and a ram is offered "instead of" Isaac. This entry into the text not only does greater justice to the narrator's plot line in verses 2 to 14 but also to his explicit signals of meaning given in the repeated keywords, "God will provide." As we have seen, we hear these words first in Abraham's testimony to Isaac, "God will provide" (v 8), next implicitly in God's actual provision of a ram to be offered "instead of" Isaac (v 13), then in Abraham calling that place, "The Lord will provide" (v 14), and finally in the narrator's own testimony, "On the mount of the Lord it shall be provided" (v 14). This focus on Isaac is even supported by the concluding covenant blessings which, in contrast to the blessings in Genesis 12:2-3, now deal not so much with Abraham as with his seed: "I will surely bless you and make your descendants [seed] as numerous as . . . the sand on the sea shore. Your descendants [seed] will take possession of the cities of their enemies, and through your offspring [seed] all nations on earth will be blessed . . ." (vv 17-18, TNIV). Therefore, we can formulate the theme of this narrative for Israel as: *The Lord provides a lamb for a burnt offering so that Isaac/Israel may live.*

In seeking to determine the goal of this narrative for Israel, one might immediately think of the goal, to teach Israel that it lives only by the grace of the Lord who provides; or the deeper goal, to motivate Israel to gratitude for the Lord's grace in providing a substitute offering so that Israel can live. But we may be able to get better at the original relevance if we raise the question, Where was Israel when they first heard this narrative? Suppose Israel had just completed the desert journey and was about to enter Canaan. "They would possess a land of their own, in spite of their enemies. What a comfort this re-

---

received back from God's hand its entire existence and now knew itself to be living solely by his grace and entrusted to his will." Cf. Roland de Vaux, *Ancient Israel* (New York: McGraw-Hill, 1965), 443, "Any Israelite who heard this story would take it to mean that his race owed its existence to the mercy of God."

17. Wenham, *Genesis 16–50*, 109. Cf. Brueggemann, *Genesis*, 186, "There can be little doubt of the cruciality of this statement ['God himself will provide the lamb for a burnt offering'] on structural grounds."

peated promise must have been to the wilderness generation, standing on the verge of entering the Promised Land. . . . They too would learn what Abraham learned: that God would provide, one way or another, and that his promise would stand forever."[18] Most telling for Israel, God promised Abraham this time, "Your offspring shall possess the gate of their enemies" (22:17). The narrator's goal in relating this narrative to Israel would then be, "to assure Israel that their faithful covenant Lord can be trusted to provide their redemption."

Or suppose Israel heard this narrative when it was in exile. McCurley, noting various sixth-century formula parallels, states, "Thus, it is by no means unlikely that the story has expanded in the sixth century B.C. to address Israel, the son of God on the brink of tragedy. It came to exiles with the assurance that because of Abraham's faithfulness, the promise of blessing, descendants, and land will be fulfilled — and that the blessing for all nations of the earth will indeed be secured."[19] In this case, too, the narrator's goal for Israel is, *to assure Israel that their faithful covenant Lord can be trusted to provide their redemption.*

Ways to Preach Christ

Given the textual theme, "The Lord provides a lamb for a burnt offering so that Isaac/Israel may live," what are legitimate ways to Jesus Christ as revealed in the New Testament?

Redemptive-Historical Progression

This narrative relates that the Lord provides a ram as a substitute offering so that Isaac/Israel may live. Later, when Israel was enslaved in Egypt, the Lord saved their firstborn sons by means of the blood of a one-year-old ram: the passover lamb. Still later, when Israel was in the Promised Land, they offered burnt offerings, sin offerings, and guilt offerings at the tabernacle/temple in order to pay the penalty for sin (death) so they could live. In the fullness of time, the Lord provides his Son Jesus as a substitute offering so that his people may live. John the Baptizer introduces Jesus as "the Lamb of God who takes away the sin of the world" (John 1:29). Jesus himself proclaims that he came "to give his life as a ransom for many" (Mark 10:45).

18. Duguid, *Living in the Gap between Promise and Reality,* 136-37.

19. McCurley, *Genesis,* 46. McCurley mentions, e.g., that the oath formula occurs elsewhere only in prophetic preaching and that "as the sand on the seashore" has "exact parallels only in the sixth-century B.C. Deuteronomistic history (1 Sam 13:5; 1 Kings 4:29)."

Promise-Fulfillment

The covenant blessings (vv 17-18) contain promises for Abraham and his seed. Especially the promise, "through your offspring [seed] all nations on earth will be blessed" (v 18, TNIV) is fulfilled and is being fulfilled in Jesus Christ (cf. Matt 28:19). But since this way of promise-fulfillment is not directly related to the theme of the narrative, it is better not to make it a way to Christ in this sermon.

Typology

Although many see a type of Christ in this narrative, there is no agreement on whether it is Abraham,[20] Isaac, or the ram. In a sermon on Genesis 22, Chrysostom presents both the ram and Isaac as types: "All this . . . happened as a type of the Cross. Hence Christ too said to the Jews, 'Your father Abraham rejoiced in anticipation of seeing my day; he saw it and was delighted.' How did he see it if he lived so long before? In type, in shadow: just as in our text the sheep was offered in the place of Isaac, so here the rational lamb was offered for the world. . . . Notice . . . how everything was prefigured in shadow: an only-begotten son in that case, an only-begotten in this; dearly loved in that case, dearly loved in this. . . . The former was offered as a burnt offering by his father, and the latter his Father surrendered."[21]

20. E.g., von Rad, *Biblical Interpretations,* 39, sees "christological features in Abraham, who suffered being forsaken by God and who himself surrendered the promise." Cf. his *Genesis,* 244. Without using the word "type," Brueggemann, *Genesis,* 192-94, suggests a form of Abraham-Christ typology. He writes, "The life of Abraham, then, is set by this text in the midst of the contradiction between the *testing* of God and the *providing* of God. . . . The dialectic of testing and providing, of taking and giving, may be linked appropriately to the reality of Jesus of Nazareth. . . . The crucifixion of Jesus is the ultimate expression of the testing of God. Like Abraham, Jesus in Gethsemane (Mark 14:32-42) is in a situation where he must choose. . . . Jesus, like Abraham, trusts only the promise. . . . The resurrection is the miracle by which God provides new life in a situation where only death is anticipated. The dialectic of *testing/providing* in our narrative becomes the dialectic of *crucifixion/resurrection* in the faith of the church." I judge that the dialectic which places the same weight on God's testing as on God's providing is a foreign structure which does not fit the text. In v 1, the narrator simply informs Israel, which knew of God's prohibition against child sacrifice, that this was a test, whereas in the narrative he puts all the emphasis on "God provides."

21. Chrysostom, "Homily 47 [Genesis 22]" (*The Fathers of the Church,* vol. 87; Washington, DC: Catholic University of America Press, 1992), 21-22. Cf. *St. Augustine on the Psalms* (New York: Newman, 1961), II, 38, "Isaac is the one beloved son typifying the Son of God, bearing the wood for himself, just as Christ bore his cross. Lastly the ram itself was a type of Christ." Charles Spurgeon, *Metropolitan Tabernacle Pulpit* (London: Passmore & Alabaster, 1881), XXXVII, 500, similarly asks, "When did Abraham see Christ? . . . On the top of Moriah, when his own son was

Although not many today would follow Chrysostom and others in presenting two figures in one passage as types of Christ, the decision as to who is a type of Christ is by no means resolved today. Von Rad cuts through the knot by declaring, "Isaac is not simply a type of Christ. . . . Furthermore, it is best not to regard the ram caught in the thicket as a type of Christ."[22] Still, influential commentators teach that "Isaac is here a type (prefiguration) of Christ."[23] However, a major problem with this position is that Isaac did not die on the altar. In other words, the Isaac-Christ typology breaks down on the decisive parallel. On the other hand, the ram that was offered does contain this crucial parallel; it was killed. Even more, it was offered "instead of" Isaac — thus a substitute offering, a ransom. Therefore not Isaac, who represents Israel,[24] but the ram is a type of Christ. The ram in this narrative functioned in Israel as a symbol of a substitute offering (think of the passover lamb)[25] so that Isaac/Israel may live. In the context of the whole of Scripture, therefore, the ram can function as a type of Christ who, as a substitute, offers his life so that his people may live.[26]

Analogy

One can also use the way of analogy to preach Christ by, for example, focusing on the goal of this narrative for Israel: As God through this narrative assured Israel that their faithful covenant LORD can be trusted to provide for their redemption, so Jesus assures his followers that their faithful covenant LORD can be trusted to provide for their redemption. This analogy would have to be supported by New Testament references such as Jesus' teaching, "I give them [my

---

on the wood, and his own hand was lifted up, he must have seen the Son of God, and the uplifted hand of God offering the Great Sacrifice. When he took the ram from the thicket, and so saved the life of his son, how clearly he must have understood that blessed doctrine of substitution, which is the very centre of the gospel."

22. Von Rad, *Biblical Interpretations,* 39.

23. See the *NIV Study Bible,* Gen 22:9, n. Cf. Gordon Talbot, *Study of the Book of Genesis* (Harrisburg, PA: Christian Publications, 1981), 144, "Abraham and Isaac serve as types of God and His Son in this particular incident." See also the references in Van Groningen, *Messianic Revelation,* 144, to John R. Rice, George Rawlinson, and Leopold Sabourin.

24. See von Rad, *Genesis,* 244-45, quoted above in n. 16.

25. "In later Jewish tradition (e.g., the book of Jubilees, 100 B.C.) a connection is made between passover and the sacrifice of Isaac." Wenham, *Genesis 16–50,* 116.

26. We should stick to this major parallel and not drift into typologizing by looking for more parallels in details of the narrative. For example, both Tertullian and Augustine liken the ram caught by its horns in a brier-thicket to Christ receiving a "crown of thorns on his head." Jean Daniélou, *From Shadows to Reality: Studies in the Biblical Typology of the Fathers* (Westminster, MD: Newman, 1960), 125-27, with references to Tertullian's *Adversus Judaeos,* 13, and Augustine's *City of God,* 16.38.

sheep] eternal life, and they will never perish. No one will snatch them out of my hand" (John 10:28); or, "On this rock I will build my church, and the gates of Hades will not prevail against it" (Matt 16:18).

Longitudinal Themes

The message that the LORD provides a substitute offering for Isaac/Israel is related to the theme of substitutionary atonement. This theme can be traced from the ram offered "instead of" Isaac, to the passover lambs slain in Egypt instead of Israel's firstborn (Exod 12:12-13), to the lambs and other animals slain to redeem the firstborn in Israel (Exod 13:13-15; 34:20; Num 18:15), to the daily burnt offerings of lambs so that Israel might live (Exod 29:38-42), to the sin offerings slain for the sins committed by God's people (Lev 4–7). Continuing into the New Testament, Jesus proclaims that he came "to give his life as a ransom for many" (Mark 10:45). This idea is echoed in many New Testament letters: for example, 1 Peter 1:18-19, "You know that you were ransomed . . . with the precious blood of Christ, like that of a lamb without defect or blemish." Or, 1 John 4:9-10, "God sent his only Son into the world so that we might live through him. . . . He loved us and sent his Son to be the atoning sacrifice for our sins."

New Testament References

The New Testament has many references and allusions to this well-known narrative. The author of Hebrews (11:17-19) uses it to illustrate that "faith is the assurance of things hoped for, the conviction of things not seen" (11:1), and James 2:21-22 uses it to illustrate that faith without works is dead (2:17). These references, of course, do not form a direct link with Christ.

But several New Testament allusions to this narrative do connect directly with Christ:

Matthew 3:17 (par. Luke 3:22), God says of Jesus at his baptism, "This is my Son, the Beloved," possibly an allusion to Isaac being Abraham's beloved ("your son, your only son, whom you love"). See also Matthew 17:5, "This is my Son, the Beloved."

John 3:16, "For God so loved the world that he gave his *only* Son." This familiar verse proclaims that because of his love for the world, God himself made the supreme sacrifice which he prevented Abraham from making: he gave his only Son in order to save his world and his people.

Romans 8:32, "He [God] who *did not withhold* his own Son, but gave him up for all of us," may be an allusion to Genesis 22:16, "Because you have done this, and have *not withheld* your son."

Contrast

With so many positive ways of preaching Christ, it is not likely that we would use the way of contrast. But there is a major contrast, of course (which can also be covered under the escalation of typology). Abraham offered a ram "instead of his son." Today we no longer offer animals for our lives. The reason for this contrast is Christ: Jesus offered his life "once for all" (Heb 10:1-18).

Sermon Theme and Goal

The textual theme reads, "The LORD provides a lamb for a burnt offering so that Isaac/Israel may live." In the contexts of the whole of Scripture and redemptive history the message needs to be broadened considerably from Isaac/Israel to people from all nations. If we change "Isaac/Israel" to "his people," this covers both Isaac/Israel and God's people today. The words "a lamb for a burnt offering" need to be amended to cover also the death of Christ. If we substitute "a sacrificial lamb," this covers the ram for Isaac, the lambs for Israel, and the "Lamb of God" for all God's people. The resultant sermon theme is, *The LORD provides a sacrificial lamb so that his people may live.*

We formulated the textual goal as follows, "to assure Israel that their faithful covenant LORD can be trusted to provide their redemption." The sermon goal can be similar: *To assure God's people that their faithful covenant LORD can be trusted to provide their redemption.*

Sermon Exposition

Assuming that this powerful biblical narrative will be read to the congregation before the sermon, good interpretive reading will automatically draw people into the narrative. It is therefore advisable to continue with a sermon introduction that keeps the hearers *in* the narrative. One can do this, for example, by picking up on a question that undoubtedly lives in people's minds, How could God ask Abraham to offer his son? If we raise this question through the character of Abraham,[27] we can set the narrative suspense right at the beginning of

27. See my proposed sermon introduction in *Preaching Christ from the Old Testament*, 317.

the sermon and can leave the issue of the test (v 1) till after the climax.[28] But it is also possible, of course, to begin the exposition with the first verse.

Verse 1, "After these things God tested Abraham." "After these things" refers back to all the narrated events in Abraham's life, but especially to the events recorded in the foregoing chapter: the birth of Isaac and the sending away of Ishmael. Isaac is now Abraham's "only son." "After these things" also implies the passage of time, for, according to verse 5, Isaac has now grown into a "boy" strong enough to carry a load of wood.

"After these things God *tested* Abraham." This was not Satan tempting him as Satan tempted Job. The Hebrew emphasizes that it was *God*[29] who was testing Abraham. "'Testing' shows what someone is really like, and it generally involves difficulty and hardship."[30] God also tested Israel in the desert to see, God said, "whether they will follow my instruction or not" (Exod 16:4; cf. Deut 8:2). So God gave Abraham this final test to see if he would follow God's instruction. But how perplexing was this test for Abraham!

God requested, verse 2, "Take your son, your only son Isaac, whom you love, and go to the land of Moriah,[31] and offer him there as a burnt offering on one of the mountains that I shall show you." How could God ask Abraham to kill his son!? It was in Egypt that human life was cheap. Pharaoh had ordered all the baby boys of Israel to be drowned in the river Nile. But God was opposed to killing creatures made in his image. He had instructed Noah, "Whoever sheds the blood of a human, by a human shall that person's blood be shed" (Gen 9:6). He had commanded Israel at Sinai, "You shall not murder" (Exod 20:13). He

28. If we begin the exposition with verse 1, the test, it is easy to lose the suspense: it was "only a *test!*" "This word ['test'] puts our mind at ease. It tells us that God does not intend the death of Isaac; he is testing the faith of Abraham." Fredrick Holmgren, "Abraham and Isaac on Mount Moriah," *CovQ* 40/1 (Feb. 1982), 77.

29. "The explicit description of *God's* responsibility is underscored both by the reversal in the Hebrew of the usual verb-subject sequence, and also with the unusual use of the definite article with God's name." JoAnn Davidson, "Eschatology and Genesis 22," *Journal of the Adventist Theological Society* 11/1-2 (2000) 234.

30. Wenham, *Genesis 16–50*, 103.

31. The only other time the Old Testament speaks of Moriah is in 2 Chronicles 3:1, where the author informs us, "Solomon began to build the house of the Lord in Jerusalem on Mount Moriah, where the Lord appeared to his father David. . . ." Because of this identification of Mount Moriah with Mount Zion, some interpreters have been quick to identify the place of the offering of Isaac with the later temple mount. Preachers could draw interesting links from the ram Abraham offered on this rock to the many animals Israel's priests offered on the temple mount, to Christ who offered his life not far from there. But since "the land of Moriah" of Genesis 22 is not necessarily "Mount Moriah" of 2 Chronicles 3 (the author links it to David, not Abraham), Moriah is a weak link for preaching Christ. Note, however, that Moberly, "Christ as the Key," 157-58, and Wenham, *Genesis 16–50*, 104-6, both argue for a connection between "the land of Moriah" and "Mount Moriah."

had warned Israel in Canaan not to imitate the Canaanites in burning their children to their pagan gods (Deut 12:29-31; cf. Lev 18:21). How could God contradict his own law by asking Abraham to offer his son as a burnt offering?[32]

But for Abraham God's request was even more contradictory, for Isaac was the son of the *promise.* When God first called Abram to leave his country, his kindred, and his father's house, he had to leave behind his past and move forward with God's promise of making of him a great nation. After ten years of waiting for a child he received Ishmael by Hagar. Could this be the son of the promise? But God had other plans. After another fifteen years of waiting, Abraham and Sarah received Isaac. There was Laughter in Abraham's household. But Abraham had to send Ishmael away, for Isaac was the son of the promise. Isaac was the future. In him all the blessings God had promised were guaranteed. Through Isaac, Abraham would become "a great nation" (12:2) — without Isaac it could not come true. Through Isaac, Abraham would become a blessing to "all the families of the earth" (12:3) — without Isaac it could not come true. Isaac was the embodiment of all God's promises; Isaac was the focal point of all of Abraham's hopes. And now God asks Abraham to offer Isaac on an altar as a burnt offering; God asks Abraham to turn Laughter into smoke.[33] God asks Abraham to burn his bridges in front of him as he had burned his bridges behind him (Gen 12:1, 4) and to walk with God alone, to rely solely on God.

More was at stake here, however, than a father being asked to offer his son, unbearable though this was. Through this son, Abraham was to become a blessing to "all the families of the earth." At its deepest level the trial was, as Calvin put it, that "in the person of this son, the whole salvation of the world seemed to be extinguished and to perish."[34]

God was aware of the excruciating test he put before Abraham. Notice the buildup of phrases in verse 2, "Take your *son,* your *only son* Isaac, *whom you love. . . ,* and offer him. . . ." Ten times this narrative uses the word "son" to indicate the enormous sacrifice God was requiring of Abraham. Moreover, it is now Abraham's "only son." It is the one he loves. Isaac. "Offer him . . . as a burnt offer-

32. Both Westermann, *Genesis 12–36,* 357-58, and Wenham, *Genesis 16–50,* 105, remark that the answer to our question lies in another peculiar law for Israel. God commanded, "The firstborn of your sons you shall give to me" (Exod 22:29; cf. 13:2). Therefore God's demand that Abraham offer his "only son" to God was within the parameters of his law. But in his grace, God had also specified for Israel a required alternative to this offering: "All the firstborn of your sons you shall redeem" (Exod 34:20; cf. 13:13). Parents were to redeem these firstborn with a substitute: a lamb at passover (Exod 12), a lamb at the mother's purification rite, or, "if she cannot afford a sheep, she shall take two turtle doves or two pigeons" (Lev 12:8; cf. Luke 2:22-24 for the offering made for Jesus).

33. "You shall cut the ram into its parts . . . , and turn the whole ram into smoke on the altar; it is a burnt offering to the Lord" (Exod 29:17-18).

34. Calvin, *Genesis,* I, 560.

ing!" A burnt offering totally consumed the sacrifice. There would be nothing left. It would be as if Sarah had never given birth to Isaac. Abraham's lengthy journey with God would come to naught. His future would go up in smoke.

Can you imagine what must have gone through Abraham's mind that night? I think he must have tossed and turned, wondering if he had been dreaming. Was it really God who had spoken to him or was his mind playing tricks on him? If it was indeed God who spoke, how could God request that he offer the son of the promise? Abraham's whole future depended on Isaac.

Verse 3, "So Abraham rose early in the morning, saddled his donkey, and took two of his young men with him, and his son Isaac; he cut the wood for the burnt offering, and set out and went to the place in the distance that God had shown him." Strangely, Abraham does not say a word. Remember how he had argued with God when God informed him that he would judge Sodom and Gomorrah? "Suppose there are fifty righteous within the city . . . ?" Forty-five? Forty? Thirty? Twenty? Ten? (18:16-33). Here Abraham does not say a word. Presumably he never even informed Sarah of the awful request God had made. Abraham simply obeys.

Meticulously the narrator informs us of Abraham's every move: he "rose early in the morning, saddled his donkey, and took two of his young men with him, and his son Isaac; he cut the wood for the burnt offering, and set out and went to the place in the distance that God had shown him." For three days they traveled. Why did God select such a distant place? Calvin suggests that "God . . . compels him to revolve this execution in his mind during three whole days. . . . This tended to make him persevere, so that he should not obey God by a merely sudden impulse. . . . It hence appears, that his love to God was confirmed by such constancy, that it could not be affected by any change in circumstances."[35] We can imagine how difficult this three-day journey must have been for Abraham. He alone knew the purpose for this journey. There was no one with whom he could share his questions and pain.

But on the third day they see the place far away. Abraham says to his young men, verse 5, "Stay here with the donkey;[36] the boy and I will go over there; we will worship, and then we will come back to you." "*We* will come back to you." Is this a white lie to keep the servants and Isaac in the dark about the real purpose

35. Ibid., 565-66. By contrast, Westermann suggests a literary reason: "In Exodus 3:18; 5:3; 8:23, it is a journey of three days to the place where the Israelites want to offer sacrifice in the desert; there is a possible allusion to this. In any case, three days is the period of preparation for more important events in the Old Testament." *Genesis 12–36*, 358, with further references to Gen 31:22; 34:25; 40:20; 42:18.

36. "Abraham must now leave behind the two servants, who represent his household. Father and son alone together on their journey constitutes the setting of verses 6-8. It is emphasized by the statement: 'So the two went on together.'" Westermann, *Genesis*, 161.

of this trip? Or does Abraham really think that he will return with Isaac? Waltke suggests, "Although he does not know how God will work it out, his faith harmonizes God's promise that in Isaac his offspring will be reckoned (21:1-13) with God's command to sacrifice Isaac. According to Hebrews 11:17-19, he expresses a type of 'resurrection faith.'"[37]

Verse 6, "Abraham took the wood of the burnt offering and laid it on his son Isaac,[38] and he himself carried the fire and the knife." Notice that the young Isaac gets the heavier load but Abraham "carries the dangerous objects with which the boy could hurt himself, the torch and the knife."[39] So the two of them walk on together — father and son.

But it isn't long before Isaac notices that something is missing. In verse 7 he says to his father Abraham, "Father! . . . The fire and the wood are here, but where is the lamb for a burnt offering?" The question cuts through Abraham's heart like a knife. Where is the lamb? What shall he say in reponse? Shall he tell Isaac the awful truth that he is the lamb? Abraham responds, "God himself will provide the lamb for a burnt offering, my son." Again we can raise the question, Is this a white lie? Does Abraham seek to postpone the pain for Isaac as long as possible? Or is this a statement of Abraham's faith in God? Westermann comments, "Abraham refers Isaac to God as the one who will answer the question. He does not deceive him, but simply opens up to him as a possibility what for himself (since God gave his command) is a fact. He throws the ball back into God's court, so to speak: 'God will provide.'"[40] And so father and son continue their difficult journey together.

Soon they come to the place where the offering is to be made. The narrator slows down and very deliberately records every action of Abraham. Verse 9, "When they came to the place that God had shown him, Abraham built an altar there and laid the wood in order. He bound his son Isaac, and laid him on the altar, on top of the wood." Will Abraham really go through with it? Does he trust God so much that he will offer not just his son but his whole future? Relentlessly the narrative pushes on to the climax: verse 10, "Then Abraham reached out his hand and took the knife to kill his son."

37. Waltke, *Genesis,* 307.

38. The allegorical interpretation of the Church Fathers enabled them to understand Isaac carrying the wood as Christ carrying his cross. Some contemporary commentators continue to propose this as a valid way of preaching Christ: "Even as Christ was later to carry His own cross on the road to Calvary, so Isaac here was required to carry the wood for his own sacrifice." Talbot, *Study of the Book of Genesis,* 145 (see n. 23). But since this connection is laid between a detail in this narrative and a detail in the New Testament, it is a form of typologizing. Isaac, we have seen above, represents Israel.

39. Von Rad, *Genesis,* 240.

40. Westermann, *Genesis 12–36,* 359. Cf. Wenham, *Genesis 16–50,* 109, "The organization of the story, which makes 'God will provide' the turning point of the story, does favor a positive reading, i.e., as an expression of hope, a prophecy, or a prayer. . . ."

At that moment, the angel of the LORD[41] calls to him from heaven, verse 11, "Abraham, Abraham!" It is an urgent cry. Can the LORD stop Abraham in time? Abraham says, "Here I am." The angel says, "Do not lay your hand on the boy or do anything to him; for now I know that you fear God, since you have not withheld your son, your only son, from me." "Now I know[42] that you fear God." "Fearing God" does not mean that Abraham is afraid of God. "Fearing God" here is practically equivalent to obeying God's commands.[43] God had requested Abraham to offer his only son, and Abraham has demonstrated that he is ready to obey. "Now I know that you fear God, since you have not withheld your son, your only son, from me.'"

Verse 13, "And Abraham looked up and saw a ram, caught in a thicket by its horns. Abraham went and took the ram and offered it up as a burnt offering instead of his son." Abraham offers the ram "instead of his son." Because the ram dies Isaac can live, and because Isaac can live, Israel can eventually become a nation. The ram "instead of" Isaac. The ram "instead of" Israel.

Verse 14, "So Abraham called that place [as can be seen in the footnote, *Jehovah Jireh,* that is,] 'The LORD will provide.'" The narrator adds, "as it is said to this day, 'On the mount of the LORD it shall be provided.'" This is the third time he uses the word "to provide." The first time was when Isaac asked, "Where is the lamb for a burnt offering?'" And Abraham responded, "God himself will provide the lamb for a burnt offering, my son." And God had provided a lamb he could offer "instead of his son." No wonder Abraham called that place, "The LORD will provide." The narrator adds that even in his day Israel still uses the popular saying, "On the mount of the LORD it shall be provided." You see, the point of this story for Israel is that the LORD provides a lamb for a burnt offering so that Isaac, and with him Israel, may live.

As the Israelites heard this story, they would be reminded of their passover feast. The passover feast was first celebrated in Egypt. Moses prescribed that the Israelites were to take a "lamb without blemish, a year-old male. . . . [They]

41. "In the first half of the story where God is acting in a strange, remote, and inexplicable way, he is called *'Ĕlōhîm,* but when he is revealed as savior and renews the covenant promises, his personal name, 'the LORD,' is appropriate and is reintroduced." Wenham, *Genesis 16–50,* 103.

42. "The narrator does not wrestle with God's omniscience, which entails that he knew Abraham's faith commitment beforehand. Instead, he focuses upon the reality that God does not experience the quality of Abraham's faith until played out on the stage of history (cf. Deut 8:2)." Waltke, *Genesis,* 308.

43. See the synonymous parallelism in Deut 5:29, "If only they had such a mind as this, to fear me and to keep all my commandments always." H. F. Fuhs, *TDOT,* VI, 310, states, "With an artful play on words, he [E] transforms the original *'ĕlōhîm yir'eh* (vv 8, 14) into *yĕrē' 'ĕlōhîm* (v 12). E here defines fear of God as obedience to God, trust that makes it possible to take the ultimate risk." Cf. von Rad, *Genesis,* 241, "Fearing God" refers "not to a particular form of strong emotions but rather to their consequence, i.e., to obedience." Cf. Moberly, "Christ as the Key," 155.

shall slaughter it at twilight. They shall take some of the blood and put it on the two doorposts and the lintel of the houses" (Exod 12:5-7). That night "the LORD struck down all the firstborn in the land of Egypt," but he passed over the houses whose doorposts were covered with blood (12:29, 13). Saved by the blood of the lamb. A lamb died instead of the firstborn in Israel.

The offerings at the tabernacle and later at the temple carried a similar message. God instructed Israel to offer to him as a burnt offering "two male lambs a year old without blemish, daily, as a regular offering. One lamb you shall offer in the morning, and the other lamb you shall offer at twilight" (Num 28:3-4). A lamb died so that Israel could live.

In the New Testament we read in the familiar John 3:16, "For God so loved the world that he gave his only Son." "His *only* Son." Just like Isaac. But God made the supreme sacrifice which he prevented Abraham from making: he gave his only Son in order to save his world and his people. You see, in the New Testament, too, the LORD provides a sacrificial lamb so that his people may live. The Lamb is Jesus Christ. John the Baptizer introduced Jesus as "the Lamb of God who takes away the sin of the world" (John 1:29). Jesus himself proclaimed that he came "to give his life as a ransom for many" (Mark 10:45). Jesus is now the sacrificial Lamb who died for the sins of God's people.

Verse 15, "The angel of the LORD called to Abraham a second time from heaven, and said, 'By myself I have sworn, says the LORD: Because you have done this, and have not withheld your son, your only son, I will indeed bless you, and I will make your offspring as numerous as the stars of heaven and as the sand that is on the seashore. And your offspring shall possess the gate of their enemies, and by your offspring shall all the nations of the earth gain blessing for themselves, because you have obeyed my voice.'"

This is the thirty-fifth[44] and last time that the LORD speaks to Abraham. This is a momentous announcement. The LORD begins with the only divine oath in Genesis:[45] "By myself I have sworn, says the LORD." "Says the LORD" is a formula often used in the prophets to mark a prophetic oracle as the very word of God. The LORD's promises are framed by references to Abraham's obedience, "Because you have done this, and have not withheld your son, your only son, . . . because you have obeyed my voice." "All the promises first made to Abraham decades earlier are now augmented and guaranteed by the LORD unreservedly."[46]

44. Mathews, "Preaching Historical Narrative," 31.

45. "This is the first and only divine oath in the patriarchal stories, though it is frequently harked back to (24:7; 26:3; 50:24; Exod 13:5; often in Deuteronomy." Wenham, *Genesis 16–50*, 111.

46. Ibid., 116. Cf. Moberly, "Christ as the Key," 161, "Abraham by his obedience has not qualified to be the recipient of blessing, because the promise of blessing had been given to him already. Rather, the existing promise is reaffirmed but its terms of reference are altered. . . . Abraham's obedience has been incorporated into the divine promise."

The LORD had promised to make Abraham's seed "as numerous as the stars of heaven" (15:5). Now the LORD makes this promise even more emphatic by adding, "and as the sand that is on the seashore."[47] The LORD had promised to give the land of the Canaanites to Abraham's seed (12:7). Now the LORD adds, "And your offspring shall possess *the gate of their enemies.*" The LORD had promised, "In you all the families of the earth shall be blessed" (12:3). Now the LORD promises, "Through your *offspring* [*seed*] all the *nations* on earth will be blessed" (TNIV). That seed was first of all Isaac, Jacob, and then Joseph. Joseph was a blessing to the nations when he saved them from famine. We read later in Genesis, "all the world came to Joseph in Egypt to buy grain" (41:57). But ultimately the "seed" was Jesus Christ, "the son of Abraham" (Matt 1:1) through whom all nations would be blessed because he was "the Lamb of God who takes away the sin of the world" (John 1:29). After his death and resurrection, Jesus sent his followers out to "make disciples of all nations" (Matt 28:19). God had provided his own Son as a sacrificial lamb so that his people around the world might live.

But just like Israel, people today sometimes wonder, Can we really trust God to provide for our redemption? Shouldn't we be working for it ourselves? And if God did provide for our redemption, why do we see so little of it in our life and world? Paul responds to some of these questions in Romans 8. In fact, he probably alludes to verse 16 of our text where God says to Abraham, "because you . . . have not withheld your son." Paul writes, "If God is for us, who is against us? He who did not *withhold his own Son,* but gave him up for all of us, will he not with him also give us everything else? Who will bring any charge against God's elect? It is God who justifies. Who is to condemn? It is Christ Jesus, who died, yes, who was raised, who is at the right hand of God, who indeed intercedes for us. Who will separate us from the love of Christ? Will hardship, or distress, or persecution, or famine, or nakedness, or peril, or sword? . . . No, in all these things we are more than conquerors through him who loved us. For I am convinced that neither death, nor life . . . , nor anything else in all creation, will be able to separate us from the love of God in Christ Jesus our Lord" (Rom 8:31-39).

The God who forbade child sacrifice, the God who stopped Abraham from offering his only son, is the God who loved us so much that *he* offered up his one and only Son. And now nothing at all "will be able to separate us from the love of God in Christ Jesus our Lord." No matter how difficult our circumstances, we can fully trust God for our salvation. He provided the ram so that Isaac and Israel could live; he provided "his only Son, so that everyone who believes in him may not perish but may have eternal life" (John 3:16). God provides!

47. "This is the only place in Genesis where two similes are brought together in connection with the promise of numerical increase. This has the effect of making this element of the promise more emphatic on the occasion." Williamson, *Abraham, Israel and the Nations,* 248.

CHAPTER 11

The Burial of Sarah

Genesis 23:1-20

One of the challenges in preaching this narrative is the absence of any mention of God — except for the Hittites calling Abraham a "prince of *'Ĕlōhîm* [God]." Brueggemann writes, "Perhaps the narrative reflects no more than a specific commercial transaction. Nowhere is there any mention of God. The narrative gives no hint of any theological intention."[1] How does one preach a Christian sermon on a text that appears secular?

Text and Context

The narrative unit is easy to detect. It begins with Sarah's death (vv 1-2) and ends with her burial in the cave of Machpelah (v 19) and a concluding statement that the field and the cave in it are now Abaham's possession (v 20). In between these bookends is the story of Abraham, "a stranger and an alien," seeking to buy property for a burying place (vv 3-18).

Before this narrative God calls on Abraham to give up his only son (Gen 22); here he has to give up his wife of many years. Also, immediately before this narrative, Abraham is informed that his brother Nahor has twelve sons, one of them being Bethuel, the father of Rebekah (22:20-24). While Nahor is back in Haran, the present narrative stresses that Sarah died "in the land of Canaan" (23:2) and was buried "in the land of Canaan" (23:19). After this narrative, Abraham instructs his servant to go back to his kindred to find a wife for Isaac so that Sarah's tent may be inhabited once again (24:67).

But the broader context is more important for understanding this narrative. When God had called Abram "to go to the land I will show you," Abram

1. Brueggemann, *Genesis,* 195.

found that "the Canaanites were in the land" (12:6). Abram would be "a stranger and an alien," ineligible to own any property.[2] But God promised, "To your offspring I will give this land" (12:7). Later God appeared to Abram and said, "I am the LORD who brought you from Ur of the Chaldeans, to give you this land to *possess*" (15:7; cf. 13:17). The present narrative ends with the statement, "The field and the cave that is in it passed from the Hittites into Abraham's *possession* as a burying place" (23:20). "Clearly this purchase was regarded as extremely important by the editors of the Book of Genesis, as it is mentioned on three further occasions: in connection with the burial of Abraham (25:9-10), with Jacob's will (49:29-32), and with Jacob's burial (50:13), each time referring explicitly to the details of the purchase and property rights."[3] It was only a small part of the land, but God was beginning to fulfill his promise of land — as he had earlier begun to fulfill his promise of countless offspring with the birth of Isaac (Gen 21). In God's time, Abraham's offspring would possess all the land.

Literary Features

Calvin detected a major literary feature. He commented, "It is remarkable that Moses, who relates the death of Sarah in a single word, uses so many in describing her burial: but we shall soon see that the latter record is not superfluous."[4] Today we would say that the narrator reveals the point of this narrative by deliberately retarding the pace of the narration in Abraham's negotiations for the land. In fact, the question whether Abraham as "a stranger and an alien" will be able to *buy*[5] a piece of land is the conflict in this narrative. Sarah's death notice takes up only two verses (1-2), whereas Abraham's negotiations for the land and its description take up sixteen verses (3-18). This is followed by one verse (19) on the burial of Sarah. One might expect this to be the end of the narrative: mission accomplished. But the narrator adds another verse (20) to highlight the significance of this event for Israel: "The field and the cave that is in it passed from the Hittites into Abraham's *possession* as a burying place."

The narrator also supplies "tracks of meaning" by repeating keywords. He

2. "Abraham labors under two disabilities that derive from his status as an alien. He cannot avail himself of local burial facilities without municipal permission, and he cannot acquire land. Second, even if these restrictions were to be overcome, he would still face the problem of procuring an inheritable estate to be used by future generations, for an alien could not normally own land in perpetuity (cf. Lev 25:23)." Sarna, *Genesis,* 156.

3. Amit, *Reading Biblical Narratives,* 53.

4. Calvin, *Genesis,* I, 575.

5. See n. 2 above.

repeats twice that Hebron is "in the land of Canaan" (23:2, 19). "Twice the narrator adds that the negotiations take place at the 'gate of the city' (23:10, 18), the legal center of an ancient Near Eastern city. . . . The phrase 'his/my/your dead,' a metonymy for Sarah, occurs eight times (23:3, 4, 6 [2×], 8, 11, 13, 15). . . . The repetition keeps at the forefront the urgent reason for the negotiations. . . . Correlatively, the root *qbr* occurs thirteen times, eight times as a verb 'to bury' (23:4, 6 [2×], 8, 11, 13, 15, 19) and five times as a noun, either alone as 'tomb' (23:6 [2×]) or in the phrase '[property] for a burial site' (*'aḥuzzāt-qeber*, 23:4, 9, 20). . . . The operative verb *ntn* 'to give' occurs seven times; it is rendered 'to sell' and 'to pay' in the mouth of Abraham (23:4, 9, 13) and 'to give' in the mouth of Ephron (23:11 [3×]).[6] Moreover, "The repeated emphasis on the public nature of the negotiations is evident (cf. vv 10, 11, 13, 16, 18). This was clearly of great importance to make Abraham's claim to the land clear beyond dispute."[7]

The Plot Line

This specific narrative is about Abraham gaining possession of a plot of land in Canaan. In the context of the larger Abraham narrative, the setting is God's repeated promise of the land of Canaan for Abraham and his offspring (e.g., Gen 12:7; 13:17; 15:7). The occasioning incident is the death of Sarah. Where will Abraham bury the "princess"? In a soon-to-be-forgotten Canaanite grave? Abraham knows that as "a stranger and an alien" (v 4) he has no right to buy property from the owners of the land. Yet he decides to approach the Hittites and asks for "a burying place" (v 4). The Hittites offer him the use of any of their burial places (v 6). A generous offer, but the property would not belong to Abraham. So Abraham asks them to entreat Ephron to sell him the cave of Machpelah "for the full price . . . as a possession for a burying place" (v 9). Ephron responds, "I give you the field, and I give you the cave that is in it" (v 11). Again, a generous offer, but the property would not be officially deeded over to Abraham. So Abraham answers, "I will give you the price of the field" (v 13). Ephron responds, "a piece of land worth four hundred shekels of silver — what is that between you and me?" (v 15). He has named a price, probably highly inflated.[8] The narrative conflict has reached a climax. Will Abraham haggle about the price, as is customary?[9] The tension is quickly resolved when Abraham immediately agrees and weighs out four hundred shekels of silver (v 16). There fol-

6. Waltke, *Genesis*, 316.

7. Wenham, *Genesis 16–50*, 126.

8. "A laborer or artisan at ten shekels per year would not expect to make this much in a lifetime." Walton, *Genesis*, 528-29. See also Hamilton, *Genesis 18–50*, 135, quoted below on p. 224.

9. See, e.g., Aalders, *Genesis*, II, 59.

lows a listing of the field, its location, the cave, and all the trees in the field that have been deeded over to Abraham "as a possession" (17-18). Abraham can now bury Sarah in his own property "in the land of Canaan" (v 19). The outcome of the narrative once more highlights the significance of this purchase: "The field and the cave that is in it passed from the Hittites into Abraham's possession as a burying place" (v 20).

We can diagram this narrative as a single plot:

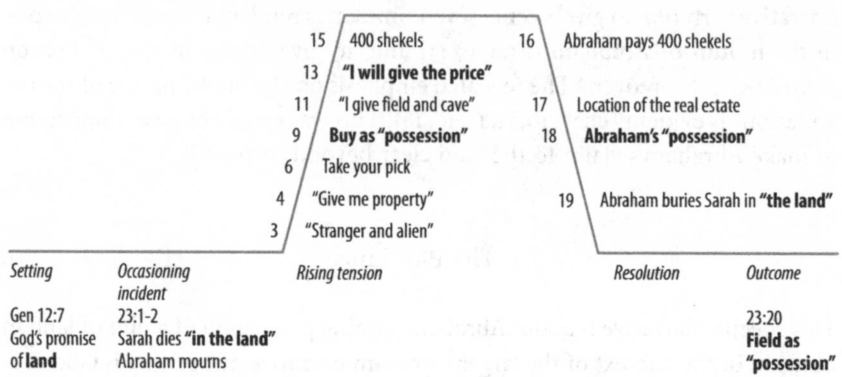

Theocentric Interpretation

As already indicated, there is no reference to God in this narrative except for the Hittites calling Abraham "a mighty prince," literally "a prince of *'Ĕlōhîm* [God]" (v 6). But the broader context provides the theocentric dimension. After calling Abram to "go . . . to the land I will show you" (12:1), the LORD promised, "To your offspring I will give this land" (12:7). The LORD frequently repeated this promise with respect to Abram's offspring (13:15; 15:18; 17:8; 22:17), but also made it specifically for Abram himself: "Rise up, walk through the length and the breadth of the land, for I will give it *to you*" (13:17; cf. 15:7). In this narrative, God does indeed give a small part of the land to Abraham as a permanent possession — a place in the Promised Land where he can bury his wife Sarah, where he can be buried later, as well as Isaac, Rebekah, Leah, and Jacob. God gave Abraham the stature and the mind to negotiate successfully for a piece of the Promised Land. God gave him the riches to weigh out four hundred shekels of silver for a field and a cave in "the land." God is here beginning to fulfill his covenant promises that his special people will inherit the land of Canaan.

Textual Theme and Goal

Noting the repetitions about death and burying his/my/your dead, Ross states, "It should be clear that Sarah's death is the central theme of the narrative, and the primary concern of the patriarch. The elaborate detail of the dialogue and the repetition of the theme obviously indicate that the narrator wanted to press the point home to the readers."[10] But this conclusion is not as obvious as Ross makes it out to be. If Sarah's death were the central theme, the narrator would not have spent sixteen verses on the negotiations of Abraham for a burial plot. Theocentric interpretation, the broader context, the plot line, and the narrator's pace retardation argue for a different theme. Sarah's death is the occasioning incident, but the point of the narrative is that Abraham receives a field and a burial plot as a permanent possession in the Promised Land. We can formulate the theme for Israel as: *The Lord begins to fulfill his promise of land by giving Abraham a field with a burial plot as his permanent possession in Canaan.*

As to the goal of the narrator for Israel, Brueggemann comments, "It is possible that securing the grave with a clear legal title is a symbolic but concrete guarantee of possession of the whole land. Since the text is assigned to the Priestly tradition and dated to the sixth-century exile, the memory of this transaction reassures exiles, those again made 'strangers and sojourners.' They do, in fact, have a secure place. This little piece of land signifies the whole land, certainly promised and undoubtedly to be possessed."[11] If Israel first heard this narrative when it was in exile, the goal of the narrator would be, "to assure Israel that the Lord can still be trusted to fulfill his promise of giving them the land of Canaan." If Israel first heard this narrative centuries earlier, as it was preparing in Moab to invade the Promised Land, the goal of the narrator would have been similar: *to assure Israel that the Lord can be trusted to fulfill his promise of giving them the land of Canaan.*

Ways to Preach Christ

Redemptive-Historical Progression

The way of redemptive-historical progression would trace the possession of land through the various epochs of redemptive history. In the beginning God mandated his people to "fill the earth" (Gen 1:28). After the flood God repeated this mandate to Noah (Gen 9:1). After people's refusal at Babel to fill the earth

10. Ross, *Creation and Blessing,* 410.

11. Brueggemann, *Genesis,* 196.

(Gen 11), God made a new start with Abram, calling him "to the land that I will show you" (12:1) and promising that land to his seed (12:7). Near the end of Abraham's life, God begins to fulfill his promise by giving Abraham a field and a burial plot as a permanent possession in the land. Four hundred years later, under Joshua, Israel will receive the whole land of Canaan. Under King Solomon the land expands from the river Euphrates to the border of Egypt (1 Kings 4:21). Under King Jesus the land expands to include the whole earth again (Matt 5:5; Rom 4:13). Jesus mandates his followers "to make disciples of all nations" (Matt 28:19). At his Second Coming God's people will receive a new earth. John saw "a new heaven and a new earth" (Rev 21:1).

Promise-Fulfillment

With the theme, "The LORD begins to fulfill his promise of land by giving Abraham a field with a burial plot as his permanent possession in Canaan," promise-fulfillment is the most obvious way to move to Christ in the New Testament. In this narrative the LORD *begins* to fulfill his promise of land. Israel experienced further fulfillment of God's promise when the LORD gave them the whole land of Canaan under Joshua (Josh 21:43-45). But when Israel proved unworthy of living in "God's country," God drove them out of the land into exile. After 587 B.C., a remnant of Israel returned to the land.

Jesus was born in the land of Canaan. But his view of the Promised Land was much larger than Canaan. He taught his followers, "Blessed are the meek, for they will inherit the earth" (Matt 5:5). This promise will not be fulfilled until Jesus comes again. Peter assures his persecuted readers, "We wait for new heavens and a new earth, where righteousness is at home" (2 Pet 3:13; cf. Rev 21:1). God's people today still wait for the final fulfillment of God's promise of land.

Typology

Some might look upon Abraham as a type of Christ because he was called "a prince of God" and purchased the Promised Land for Israel. This is a form of typologizing, for the Hittites calling Abraham "a prince of God" is an incidental detail, and Abraham purchased only a field and not the whole land. There is no type of Christ in this narrative.

Analogy

Analogy can be used to preach Christ from this narrative: As God through this narrative assured Israel that he can be trusted to fulfill his promise of giving them a homeland, so Jesus assures his church that he can be trusted to give his people a homeland. Jesus promised, "If I go and prepare a place for you, I will come again and will take you to myself, so that where I am, there you may be also" (John 14:3). That place, ultimately, is "a new heaven and a new earth" (Rev 21:1).

Longitudinal Themes

One can also move to Christ in the New Testament by tracing the longitudinal theme of the Land where God dwells with his people. This theme begins in Paradise where God walked and talked with Adam and Eve (Gen 2–3). Unfortunately, Adam and Eve disobeyed God and they were driven out of the "garden of God." "The original idea of land as paradise significantly shaped the expectations associated with redemption. As the place of blessedness arising from unbroken fellowship and communion with God, the land of paradise became the goal toward which redeemed humanity was returning."[12]

God made a new start with Abraham and his seed, promising them the land of Canaan, "like the garden of the LORD" (13:10), where he would be their God and they would be his people (17:7-8). Abraham received God's down payment on this land — a burial plot where his wife Sarah could rest in peace. Under Joshua Israel would receive the whole land and God was present among them in the tabernacle. Under Solomon the temple would be built where God dwelt in the midst of his people. But again God's people disobeyed, and the land "vomited" them out (Lev 18:28; 20:22).[13] But the LORD promised Israel in exile that they would return to the Land and that he would make "her wilderness like Eden, her desert like the garden of the LORD" (Isa 51:3).

In the fullness of time, Jesus was born in the Promised Land but expanded this idea to the entire earth (Matt 5:5).[14] Jesus taught, "The hour is coming

12. Robertson, *Israel of God,* 4.

13. "Entrance to the land was denied to those who lacked faith. . . . Just as faith and the obedience that flows from faith were necessary to enter the land, so faith and obedience are necessary to maintain possession of the land." Holwerda, *Jesus and Israel,* 90.

14. "The land which once was the specific place of God's redemptive work served well in the realm of old covenant forms as a picture of paradise lost and promised. But in the realm of new covenant fulfillments, the land has expanded to encompass the whole world." Robertson, *Israel of God,* 31.

when you will worship the Father neither on this mountain nor in Jerusalem. . . . The hour is coming, and is now here, when the true worshipers will worship the Father in spirit and truth" (John 4:21-23). Jesus sent his followers out to "make disciples of all nations" and promised, "I am with you always, to the end of the age" (Matt 28:19-20). When Jesus comes again to fully establish his kingdom on earth, God's "tabernacle" will be among his people: "He will dwell [tabernacle] with them; they will be his peoples, and God himself will be with them" (Rev 21:3). Paradise will be restored on earth (Rev 22:1-5).

New Testament References

Besides the New Testament references listed above, there is another passage that can possibly be used to support the move to Christ in the New Testament. The author of Hebrews uses this narrative to illustrate his theme that "faith is the assurance of things hoped for": "By faith he [Abraham] stayed for a time in the land he had been promised, as in a foreign land, living in tents, as did Isaac and Jacob, who were heirs with him of the same promise. For he looked forward to the city that has foundations, whose architect and builder is God. . . . All of these died in faith without having received the promises, but from a distance they saw and greeted them. They confessed that they were strangers and foreigners on the earth, for people who speak in this way make it clear that they are seeking a homeland" (Heb 11:9-14). Even now that homeland is being prepared for them and us by Jesus Christ (John 14:3).

Contrast

God's promise to Abraham was the land of Canaan. The New Testament authors expand this view to the whole earth. "For Paul [Rom 4:13], the promise to Abraham had a cosmic sweep, including not just the territory of Canaan but the entire inhabited world."[15] The reason for this expansion is Jesus Christ.

Sermon Theme and Goal

We formulated the theme of this narrative for Israel as, "The LORD begins to fulfill his promise of land by giving Abraham a field with a burial plot as his permanent possession in Canaan." The sermon theme would have to be broad-

15. Holwerda, *Jesus and Israel,* 103, with a reference to Sasse, *TDNT,* III, 888.

ened to take into account the further filling up of the promise of land when the LORD gave the entire land of Canaan to Israel and when the New Testament renews the promise in terms of the whole earth. A succinct sermon theme would be, *The LORD begins to fulfill his promise of a homeland for his people.*

The goal of the narrator for Israel was, "to assure Israel that the LORD can be trusted to fulfill his promise of giving them the land of Canaan." In line with this goal and matching the theme, the goal in preaching the sermon can be, *to assure the congregation that the LORD can be trusted to fulfill his promise of a homeland for his people.*

The goal of the sermon provides the target for this sermon and thus exposes the need it should address. This particular goal exposes the need that God's people today are giving up their hope for a new homeland, "a new earth, where righteousness is at home" (2 Pet 3:13).

Sermon Exposition

The introduction to the sermon can sketch the backdrop against which the relevance of this message will be highlighted. For example, one can begin with an illustration of a specific evil in our society: hunger, persecution, wars, weapons of mass destruction, terrorism, gangs — injustice seems to be at home on this earth. As a result, we tend to give up on God's promise of "a new earth, where righteousness is at home" (2 Pet 3:13).

The Israelites, similarly, were tempted to give up on God's promise of a homeland. In Moab, they feared the giants living in Canaan. In the exile, they were dragged from the Land while the temple was burned and Jerusalem destroyed. Will God ever give them a safe homeland? In that context they heard the story of Abraham and Sarah. God had promised the land of Canaan to Abraham and his offspring, but the whole time Abraham lived in the Promised Land he was "a stranger and an alien." And both Abraham and Sarah were getting on in age. For sixty-two long years they waited for God to fulfill his promise. Then Sarah died.

Verse 1, "Sarah lived one hundred twenty-seven years; this was the length of Sarah's life." The narrator begins with an inclusio, "Sarah lived . . . ; Sarah's life" (literally, "the life of Sarah . . . ; the life of Sarah"). The repetition focuses the reader's attention on Sarah — her age and her importance for Israel.[16] Sarah is the precious mother of Israel; the only woman whose life span is recorded in the Bible.

16. "The repetition underscores this unique biblical specification of a woman's age at death, testifying to Sarah's great importance as the first matriarch (cf. Isa 52:2)." Sarna, "Genesis Chapter 23," 18.

In verse 2 we read, "And Sarah died at Kiriath-arba (that is, Hebron) in the land of Canaan; and Abraham went in to mourn for Sarah and to weep for her." In contrast to Abraham's relatives who lived in Haran (22:20-24), the narrator emphasizes that Sarah lived out her life "in the land of Canaan." "This repetitive detail serves to link this story with God's earlier promise to give Abraham the land."[17]

"And Abraham went in to mourn for Sarah and to weep for her." Wenham notes that the use of both terms "to mourn" and "to weep" "suggests that Abraham did not just weep aloud but carried out other traditional mourning customs, such as rending his garments, disheveling his hair, cutting his beard, scattering dust on his head, and fasting."[18] But soon it was time to think about burying Sarah. They were in the land of Canaan, but they owned no property there. As "a stranger and an alien," Abraham had no right to buy land. Surely Abraham would not bury Sarah, the princess, in a Canaanite grave?! There she would soon be forgotten.

Verse 3, "Abraham rose up from beside his dead, and said to the Hittites,[19] 'I am a stranger and an alien residing among you; give me property among you for a burying place, so that I may bury my dead out of my sight.'" Abraham acknowledges that he is "a stranger and an alien among them" — a person who has no right to own property. Yet he asks for "property ['possession,' *'ăḥuzzâ*] for a burying place." "This key word to the transactions denotes a sepulchre in perpetuity (Lev 14:34; 25:25-28; Josh 21:12)."[20] In Genesis, the word *'ăḥuzzâ* harks back to God's covenant promise to Abraham, "I will give to you, and to your offspring after you, the land where you are now an alien, all the land of Canaan, for a perpetual *holding* [*'aḥuzzâ*]" (17:8; cf. 48:4). "So it seems that Abraham is asking for ownership of a piece of land for his permanent use as a burial ground."[21]

In verse 5 the Hittites answer Abraham, "Hear us, my lord; you are a mighty prince[22] among us. Bury your dead in the choicest of our burial places; none of us will withhold from you any burial ground for burying your dead."

17. Waltke, *Genesis,* 317.

18. Wenham, *Genesis 16–50,* 126.

19. "Hittites" here does not indicate citizens of the great Hittite empire in Asia Minor. "For the Israelites who came much later the name 'Hittite' was reduced to a designation for the Canaanite aborigines (Gen 15:20 and often)." Von Rad, *Genesis,* 247.

20. Waltke, *Genesis,* 318.

21. Wenham, *Genesis 16–50,* 127. Cf. Sarna, "Genesis Chapter 23," 19, *'ăḥuzzât-qeber* "denotes an inheritable sepulcher. This is the key to the transaction since the cave is to serve future generations."

22. Literally, "prince of God." "In the mouth of the Hebronites it is little more than urbane politeness; for Israel's ears, however, a lofty title of honor with which faith revered Abraham (cf. 'Yahweh's friend,' Isa 41:8)." Von Rad, *Genesis,* 248.

The Hittites are eager to do Abraham a favor, but they offer Abraham only the use of one of their *tombs,* not a *"perpetual holding"* (17:8) among them.[23] After Sarah's body has decomposed, the Hittites will be able to use the tomb again.[24]

But Abraham is not satisfied with the loan of a tomb. He has already selected a perfect spot and is willing to pay for it. In verse 7 we read that Abraham bows to the Hittites and says, "If you are willing that I should bury my dead out of my sight, hear me, and entreat for me Ephron son of Zohar, so that he may give me the cave of Machpelah, which he owns; it is at the end of his field. For the full price let him give it to me in your presence as a possession for a burying place." Abraham asks only for a little piece of Ephron's land: the cave at the end of his field. The cave apparently is easily accessible to Abraham, and Ephron can still use his field.[25]

Verse 10, "Now Ephron was sitting among the Hittites; and Ephron the Hittite answered Abraham in the hearing of the Hittites, of all who went in at the gate of his city, 'No, my lord, hear me; I give you the field, and I give you the cave that is in it; in the presence of my people I give it to you; bury your dead.'" Publicly Ephron responds to Abraham's request and raises the stakes: he offers Abraham the *field* as well as the cave. Three times he offers to *give* the field and the cave to Abraham, probably "a matter of oriental courtesy — offering to give when really he is proposing a sale."[26]

In response, verse 12, Abraham bows down before the people of the land and says to Ephron "in the hearing of the people of the land, 'If you only will listen to me! I will give the *price of the field;* accept it from me, so that I may bury my dead there.'" Publicly, "in the hearing of the people of the land," Abraham accepts Ephron's offer. He will take the field as well as the cave, but he insists on paying for it.

With a master stroke, Ephron next manages to mention a highly inflated price without asking it. He says, verse 14, "My lord, listen to me; a piece of land *('ereṣ)* worth four hundred shekels of silver — what is that between you and me? Bury your dead." Four hundred shekels of silver for a small field and a

23. "The change of terms from 'property for a burial site' to 'tomb' suggests that, while the Hittites are willing to grant this mighty prince the right to bury his dead on their land, they are reluctant to give him a permanent possession there." Waltke, *Genesis,* 318.

24. "A body was laid in a prepared shelf along with grave goods. . . . Later the skeletal remains were removed and placed in another chamber or an ossuary box or simply swept to the rear of the tomb to accommodate another burial." Walton, *Genesis,* 528.

25. "Presumably, the vault was conveniently approachable from the road without the necessity of traversing the field in which it was situated." Sarna, *Understanding Genesis,* 169.

26. Wenham, *Genesis 16–50,* 128. Wenham, ibid., keeps open the possibility that "he may simply be reiterating the former offer that Abraham can use his grave but implying that he does not intend to sell the land in perpetuity." But Ephron's offer to give "the field" in addition to the cave argues against this option.

cave? Four hundred shekels "would be more than a hundred pounds of silver. David paid only one-eighth that amount — 50 shekels of silver — for the purchase of the temple site from Araunah (2 Sam 24:24)."[27] Surely, Abraham knows that Ephron is taking advantage of his desperate need for a burial plot. Will he buy it at that exorbitant price? Will he follow custom and haggle down the price to a portion of the asking price? But that will give Ephron the opportunity to back out of the deal. Moreover, Ephron had mentioned the magic word "land," *'ereṣ*. To him it might have meant only a piece of land, but to Abraham and to later Israel *'ereṣ* means the Promised Land (see Gen 12:7). Furthermore, God had richly blessed Abraham.[28] Four hundred shekels of silver is not a big deal for him.

Verse 16, "Abraham agreed with Ephron; and Abraham weighed out for Ephron the silver that he had named in the hearing of the Hittites, four hundred shekels of silver, according to the weights current among the merchants." The narrative suspense is resolved. Abraham is now the legal owner of Ephron's field and cave. The narrator confirms this in verse 17, which reads like a real estate contract, "So the field of Ephron in Machpelah, which was to the east of Mamre, the field with the cave that was in it and all the trees[29] that were in the field, throughout its whole area, passed to Abraham as a possession in the presence of the Hittites, in the presence of all who went in at the gate of his city." Wenham comments, "In precise detail, the deal between Abraham and the Hittites is recorded. Note how the exact location of the land 'east of Mamre,' the property associated with it, 'the cave . . . and all the trees,' the names of the seller, 'Ephron,' and the purchaser, 'Abraham,' and the witnesses are all mentioned."[30] For the first time in his life, Abraham is legal owner of property in the Promised Land. Now he can bury his wife Sarah in hope — hope that one day all of this land will belong to Abraham and Sarah's offspring.

Verse 19, "After this, Abraham buried Sarah his wife in the cave of the field of Machpelah facing Mamre (that is, Hebron) in the land of Canaan." The narrator repeats for the second time, "in the land of Canaan," that is, the Promised Land. But Abraham did not have to bury her in a Canaanite grave where she would soon be forgotten. He could bury her in his own possession in the land

27. Hamilton, *Genesis 18–50*, 135. Other commentators equate "four hundred shekels of silver" with "about seven and a quarter pounds of silver." Walton and Matthews, *Bible Background Commentary*, 50.

28. "He . . . paid for it with money that the Lord had enabled him to acquire. Therefore he had to recognize that the field with its cave was a gift from the Lord, a divine guarantee that he and his seed would one day possess that land." De Graaf, *Promise and Deliverance*, I, 145.

29. "All the trees" is the ancient equivalent of selling property with "mineral rights."

30. Wenham, *Genesis 16–50*, 129. Cf. von Rad, *Genesis*, 249, "The affair is legally described in the terminology of the land register (Jac.)."

of Canaan.[31] Sarah, the mother of Israel, could be buried in her own inheritance. Sarah may rest in peace awaiting the fulfillment of God's promises.

The story is finished. The story that began with Sarah's death "in the land of Canaan" ends with Sarah's burial "in the land of Canaan." But the narrator adds an important summary about the significance of this narrative for Israel: verse 20, "The field and the cave that is in it passed from the Hittites into Abraham's *possession* as a burying place." It is now Abraham's "possession," his *'ăḥuzzâ* (cf. v 9). Finally, God has given Abraham a foothold in the Promised Land. God is beginning to fulfill his promise of giving Abraham and his offspring the whole land of Canaan as an *'ôlām 'ăḥuzzâ*, "a perpetual holding" (17:8). In fact, the same word *'ăḥuzzâ* is used when God invites Moses on Mount Nebo to "view the land of Canaan, which I am giving to the Israelites for a possession [*'ăḥuzzâ*]" (Deut 32:49; cf. Gen 48:4). The field with the cave of Machpelah represents the whole land of Canaan. God is giving Israel a down payment, a token of what is the come. Machpelah represents the "firstfruits," as it were; the whole harvest is sure to follow. Israel is acquainted, of course, with God's requirement that they give God the firstfruits (e.g., Deut 26:1-11). But when God gives Abraham a perpetual possession in Canaan, it is *God* who is giving the firstfruits. In God's time the whole land will be theirs.[32] The LORD is beginning to fulfill his promise of a homeland for his people.

Later, Abraham will be buried in his own possession in the Promised Land (25:9-10), and still later, Isaac, Rebekah, Leah, and Jacob (49:29-32). For centuries this grave site of their forefathers and mothers in Canaan was a silent witness to Israel that the LORD had begun to fulfill his promise of a homeland for his people. Even Joseph, whose wife was Egyptian, makes the Israelites in Egypt swear, "When God comes to you, you shall carry up my bones from here" (Gen 50:24). Joseph wishes to be buried in the Promised Land. Surely, the LORD can be trusted to fulfill his promise of a homeland for Israel.

Finally, under Joshua, the LORD fulfills his promise. "Not one of all the good promises that the LORD had made to the house of Israel had failed; all came to pass" (Josh 21:45). Israel receives the whole land of Canaan, from Dan

31. "In life the patriarchs were sojourners; in death they were heirs of the promise and occupied the land." Ross, *Creation and Blessing*, 412.

32. Calvin comments, Abraham "especially wished to have his own domestic tomb in that land, which had been promised him for an inheritance, for the purpose of bearing testimony to posterity, that the promise of God was not extinguished, either by his own death, or by that of his family . . . ; and that they who were deprived of the light of the sun, and of the vital air, yet always remained joint-partakers of the promised inheritance. For while they themselves were silent and speechless, the sepulchre cried aloud, that death formed no obstacle to their entering on the possession of it. A thought like this could have had no place, unless Abraham by faith had looked up to heaven." *Genesis*, I, 579.

to Beersheba. Sadly, they prove to be unworthy of living in "God's country," and God has to banish them from the land. God sends them into exile back to Babylonia — back to Abraham's homeland before God called him. Still, God gives Israel hope of one day returning to the land. On the eve of being taken into exile, Jeremiah buys a field at Anathoth for seventeen shekels of silver. He is as careful as Abraham was in following the correct legal procedures so that no one can ever dispute his claim to the land. He wants the deeds of purchase kept "in an earthenware jar, in order that they may last for a long time. For thus says the LORD of hosts, the God of Israel: Houses and fields and vineyards shall again be bought in this land" (Jer 32:14-15). After 587 B.C., a remnant of Israel does indeed return to the land. God fulfills his promise of returning Israel to the land, but it falls far short of the promised Paradise: to "make her wilderness like Eden, her desert like the garden of the LORD" (Isa 51:3).

Jesus, "the son of Abraham" (Matt 1:1) is born in the land of Canaan. But his vision of the Promised Land is much larger than Canaan. In the Old Testament God had promised his Anointed One, "Ask of me, and I will make the nations your heritage, and the ends of the earth your possession [*'ăḥuzzâ*]" (Ps 2:8). Accordingly, Jesus expands God's promise of land from the land of Canaan to the whole earth. Jesus declares, "Blessed are the meek, for they will inherit the *earth*" (Matt 5:5; cf. Rom 4:13).[33] But, like Abraham and Israel, God's people today still have to wait for the final fulfillment of this grand promise. The author of Hebrews states: "By faith he [Abraham] stayed for a time in the land he had been promised, as in a foreign land, living in tents, as did Isaac and Jacob, who were heirs with him of the same promise. For he looked forward to the city that has foundations, whose architect and builder is God. . . . All of these died in faith without having received the promises, but from a distance they saw and greeted them. They confessed that they were strangers and foreigners on the earth, for people who speak in this way make it clear that they are seeking a homeland" (Heb 11:9-14).

Christians today are still seeking a homeland. The world we live in is a foreign land, for it is filled with violence and injustice. Peter consoles Christians suffering injustice and persecution, "We wait for new heavens and a new earth, where righteousness is at home" (2 Pet 3:13). Even now that homeland is being prepared for us by Jesus Christ. Jesus promises his disciples and us, "If I go and prepare a place for you, I will come again and will take you to myself, so that where I am, there you may be also" (John 14:3). In a vision John receives a glimpse of this future, "a new heaven and a new earth" and "the holy city, the

33. "Promised land is grasped by faith, not by strength. It is the meek who will inherit the earth, those who possess confident faith in the God who always gives what he promises." Holwerda, *Jesus and Israel*, 89.

new Jerusalem, coming down out of heaven from God." And he hears a loud voice, "See, the home of God is among mortals. He will dwell with them; they will be his peoples, and God himself will be with them; he will wipe every tear from their eyes. Death will be no more; mourning and crying and pain will be no more" (Rev 21:1-4).

That is the future for which we wait eagerly.[34] For we still experience death and mourning and crying and pain. But as Abraham buried Sarah in Canaan in the hope of receiving the Promised Land, so, through Jesus, we today can bury our loved ones in the earth in the hope of receiving the new creation. How do we know that God can be trusted to fulfill his promise? God has also given the New Testament church a down payment, a token that he has begun to fulfill his promise. As God gave Israel the firstfruits of a grave site in the Promised Land, so God has given the New Testament church the firstfruits of an empty tomb. God's down payment of this promised new creation is Jesus' resurrection. Paul calls Jesus' resurrection, "the first fruits of those who have died. . . . For as all die in Adam, so all will be made alive in Christ. But each in his own order: Christ the first fruits, then at his coming those who belong to Christ" (1 Cor 15:20-23). And one day, Paul declares, "the trumpet will sound, and the dead will be raised imperishable. . . . When this perishable body puts on imperishability, and this mortal body puts on immortality, then the saying that is written will be fulfilled:

> 'Death has been swallowed up in victory.'
> 'Where, O death, is your victory?
> Where, O death is your sting?' . . .

Thanks be to God, who gives us the victory through our Lord Jesus Christ" (1 Cor 15:52-57). In his own time, God will provide us with a homeland, "new heavens and a new earth, where righteousness is at home" (2 Pet 3:13).

34. "The New Jerusalem has not yet come, and yet it is already here in the form of a sign as Jesus' disciples proclaim and live the righteousness that will fill the new earth. Enjoyment of the promise of the land has already begun, but only as a sign anticipating the future." Ibid., 112.

CHAPTER 12

A Bride for Isaac

Genesis 24:1-67

This is the longest narrative of all patriarchal narratives (Gen 12–36), and it contains the longest speech in all of Genesis (24:34-49).[1] This raises some questions for preachers: Should one read the whole narrative in church before preaching the sermon, or should one select only key sections for Scripture reading? And since much of the servant's lengthy speech repeats the narrator's story, how much time should the sermon spend on this speech?

A challenge in preaching this narrative is to avoid character-imitation preaching. Some commentators describe this narrative "as an example story, but now exemplifying the behavior of an ideal servant who faithfully carries out his master's instructions."[2] This may encourage preachers to look at the biblical characters as normative models for current behavior. For example, like the servant, we must be people of prayer and thanksgiving; or, like the servant, we must determine God's will by setting up tests and follow God's leading. And why stop with the servant when there are other interesting characters in his narrative? For example, like Abraham, believing parents today must see to it that their children do not marry unbelievers; or, like Rebekah, we must be friendly, help strangers, work hard, and respond positively to God's call to go; or, like Isaac, husbands must love their wives. These applications are not unbiblical, but they have nothing to do with the point of this narrative. In order to avoid these superficial asides, one should ask,

1. Brodie, *Genesis as Dialogue,* 277. Von Rad, *Genesis,* 253, states that it "ought to be called a *Novelle.*"

2. Wenham, *Genesis 16–50,* 140, mentions Wolfgang Roth, "The Wooing of Rebekah," *CBQ* 34 [1972] 177-87, and Coats, *Genesis,* 170. In countering Roth, Westermann, *Genesis 12–36,* 382, calls Genesis 24 a "guidance narrative,' that is, a narrative whose purpose is to attest the hand of God in the life of a small community. . . . Hence one cannot say that the main theme of Gen 24 is the wise, unselfish servant who is presented as an example."

How did the narrator intend Israel to hear this narrative? What was its relevance for Israel?

Text and Context

The narrative unit is easy to detect. Genesis 24:1 begins a new literary unit with the comment, "Now Abraham was old." Abraham sends his trusted servant on a mission to get a wife for Isaac from his "kindred." The servant returns with Rebekah. "Then Isaac brought her into his mother Sarah's tent. He took Rebekah, and she became his wife; and he loved her. So Isaac was comforted after his mother's death" (24:67). Mission accomplished.

As to the context, the chapter immediately preceding Genesis 24 relates the death and burial of Sarah (Gen 23). This sets up the need for the present narrative, for Sarah's tent is empty; there is no mother in Israel. Isaac, at age forty, is still single. But God had promised Abram, "I will make of you a great nation" (12:2). For this great nation to come about, Isaac, the only son of the promise, needs a wife. Just prior to the narrative about Sarah's death, the narrator relates that Abraham was told about his brother Nahor's twelve children, one of whom was Bethuel, "the father of Rebekah" (22:23). Now Abraham sends his servant on a mission to find a wife for Isaac among his kindred. The LORD leads him to Rebekah, who is more than kindred; she is Abraham's grandniece. Rebekah agrees to "go" and marry Isaac. The next chapter, Genesis 25, relates Abraham's death and Rebekah giving birth to Esau and Jacob.

Literary Features

The narrator shows his hand in this narrative especially in pace retardation. While he covers the servant's four-hundred-mile journey in one short sentence (v 10b), he slows the pace when the servant arrives at the well and prays (vv 12-14); he carefully informs his readers of Rebekah's lineage and notes her every action (vv 15-20); and he especially retards the pace with the servant's long speech which repeats much of what the narrator has already related (vv 34-49).[3]

The narrator uses character description when he informs his readers that

3. "The most striking feature of this version of the type-scene is its slow, stately progress, an effect achieved by the extensive use of dialogue, by a specification of detail clearly beyond the norm of biblical narrative, and, above all, by a very elaborate use of the device of verbatim repetition, which is a standard resource of the biblical writers." Alter, *Art of Biblical Narrative,* 53.

"Abraham was old, well advanced in years" (v 1), and that Rebekah was "very fair to look upon, a virgin, whom no man had known" (v 16). He provides character description of the servant through his monologues, especially the prayers but also the long speech, and he paints Rebekah's brother Laban as greedy: "As soon as he had seen the nose-ring, and the bracelets on his sister's arms . . . , he went to the man" (v 30).

The narrative consists of four scenes, with two main characters in each scene except for the fourth scene, which has three characters.

1. Canaan: Abraham and his servant (vv 1-9)
   2. Mesopotamia: the servant and Rebekah at the well (vv 10-28)
      3. Mesopotamia: the servant and Laban at the house (vv 29-61)
4. Canaan: Isaac, Rebekah, and the servant (vv 62-67)[4]

Repetition of several keywords and phrases again provide tracks of meaning. The narrator uses the word *bārak,* "blessed"/"had blessed" six times (24:1, 27, 31, 35, 48, 60; compare the name Rebekah[5]). Three times he uses the word *ḥesed,* "steadfast love," in the servant's prayers for the LORD "to show steadfast love to my master Abraham" (vv 12, 14, 27). He uses the word *yālak,* "go," eight times, which is particularly suggestive of his point in combination with "take": "Abraham's key command, 'Go and take (a wife for my son),' is eventually answered by Laban and Bethuel's response to the servant, '(Here is Rebekah) take her and go,' and fulfilled in v 61, 'The servant took her and went,' and in v 67, 'Isaac . . . took and married her.'"[6]

Even more suggestive of the theme are the sentences regarding the LORD making the servant's way "successful." When the servant comes to the well and watches Rebekah working hard to water his camels, he wonders "whether or not the LORD had made his journey successful" (v 21). This phrase is repeated twice in the servant's report to Laban: "The LORD . . . will send his angel with you and make your way successful" (v 40), and his reported prayer, "O LORD . . . if now you will only make successful the way I am going" (v 42). The servant uses this phrase a final time in trying to persuade Rebekah's family to let her go immediately: "Do not delay me, since the LORD has made my journey successful" (v 56). Von Rad remarks that this expression, "because it is used four times, must almost be considered the motif for the narrative."[7] This focus on the providence of God is further supported by the servant's words repeated

4. Adapted from Hamilton, *Genesis 18–50,* 138, and Wenham, *Genesis 16–50,* 138.

5. "Rebekah's name sounds even more like a play on the root 'to bless' . . . than does Abraham's." Wenham, *Genesis 16–50,* 151.

6. Ibid., 138.

7. Von Rad, *Genesis,* 257.

twice, "Let her be the one whom you have *appointed* for your servant Isaac" (vv 14, 44).

The Plot Line

This lengthy narrative has a complex plot. The distant setting is God's promise to make of Abram "a great nation" (Gen 12:2), but now Sarah is dead (Gen 23) and Abraham is old (Gen 24:1). The occasioning incident is Abraham's instruction to his trusted servant, "Go to my country and to my kindred and get a wife for my son Isaac" (v 4). This mission results in four distinct conflicts, each of which has to be resolved in turn: (1) Will the servant be able to find a suitable young woman? (2) If he does, will her family be willing to let her go to a far country to marry a stranger? (3) Will Rebekah be willing to go right away? And (4), Will Isaac be willing to marry this unseen bride?

We can sketch this complex plot as shown on pages 232-33.

Theocentric Interpretation

The LORD had promised Abraham, "I will make of you a great nation, and I will bless you" (12:2). This narrative begins, "the LORD had blessed Abraham in all things" (24:1). But what about the promise of making of him "a great nation"? Sure, Isaac had been born, but now Abraham is old, Sarah has died, and Isaac at age forty is still single. Abraham makes his servant swear an oath "by the LORD, the God of heaven and earth" (v 3), and sends him on an impossible mission with the assurance, "The LORD, the God of heaven, . . . will send his angel before you" (v 7). The servant is a man of prayer. He prays, "O LORD . . . please grant me success today" (v 12), and he sets up an almost impossible test for the young woman to pass (v 14). "Before he had finished speaking, there was Rebekah, who was born to Bethuel son of Milcah, the wife of Nahor, Abraham's brother" (v 15) — "Before he had finished speaking," the narrator assures his readers, the LORD answered his prayer. But the servant does not yet know Rebekah's identity and wonders "whether or not the LORD had made his journey successful" (v 21). When he finds out that she is "kindred," in fact, a grandniece of Abraham (v 24), he blesses the LORD and declares, "the LORD has led me on the way to the house of my master's kin" (v 27). In his long speech in Laban's house, the servant points again and again to the LORD (vv 35, 40, 42, 44, 48), and even Laban and Bethuel acknowledge, "the thing comes from the LORD" (50).[8] When

8. "Thus the reader has been given three witnesses that these events have been the work

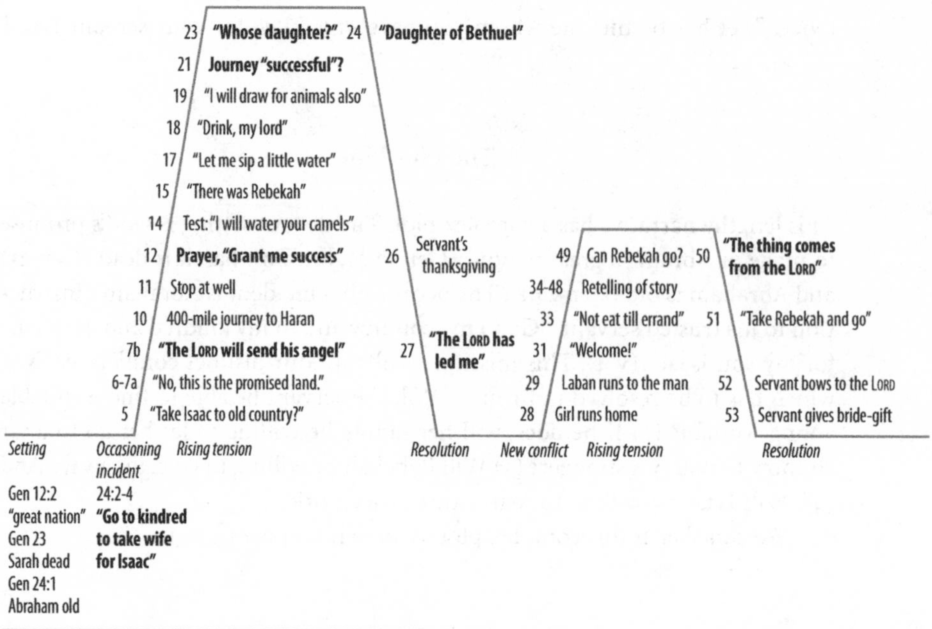

Rebekah's relatives do not want her to go right away, the servant plays his key card, "Do not delay me, since the LORD has made my journey successful" (v 56). This is the fourth time that the narrator has used the sentence that "the LORD made his [your/my] journey successful" (vv 21, 40, 42, 56). Clearly, the focus of this narrative lies in the LORD's providence guiding the servant in obtaining a wife for Isaac.

Textual Theme and Goal

The plot line of this narrative begins with Sarah's tent being empty, and it ends with Sarah's tent being occupied by Rebekah. Between these narrative bookends, the combination of Abraham's assurance, "The LORD, the God of heaven, . . . will send his angel before you" (v 7), the designation of the girl as the LORD's "appointed" (vv 14, 44), and the repetition of "the LORD made his journey successful," emphasize that it was the LORD who in his providence led the servant to the bride he appointed for Isaac. The servant's repeated appeal to the LORD "to show steadfast love *(ḥesed)* to my master Abraham" (vv 12, 14; v 27 has

of God: the narrator (vv 15-16), the servant (vv 26-27), and Laban (v 50)." Sailhamer, *Genesis,* 177.

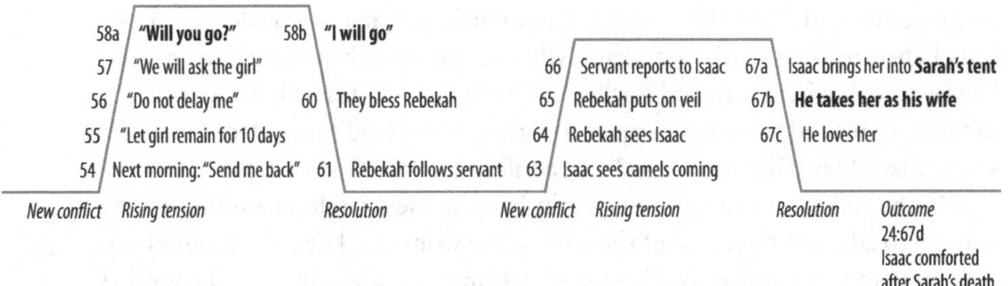

"steadfast love and faithfulness") indicate an appeal to the LORD's covenant faithfulness.[9] Therefore we can formulate the theme of this narrative as follows: "Because of his covenant faithfulness, the LORD continues to fulfill his promise of a great nation by providing Rebekah as his 'appointed' wife for Isaac."[10] In the light of the overall concern of Genesis with the seed of the woman (starting at Genesis 3:15), we can also formulate the theme something like this: *In his covenant faithfulness, the LORD provides Rebekah as his "appointed" wife for Isaac in order to continue the line of the seed of the woman.*

The goal the narrator sought to accomplish in addressing this narrative to Israel was at least twofold. The obvious goal was to teach Israel that it owes its existence solely to the LORD's providential care. But then we can raise the question, Why did the narrator seek to teach Israel this? This question leads to a second and deeper goal: *To encourage Israel to entrust itself for its existence to the LORD's providential care.* Whether Israel first heard this message in Moab prior to attacking Canaan, or in Canaan, or later in exile, its relevance for Israel is clear: Entrust your existence to the LORD's providential care!

9. On the close relation between "steadfast love" and "covenant faithfulness" see H. J. Zobel, *TDOT* (tr. David E. Green; Grand Rapids: Eerdmans, 1986), V, 60.

10. Cf. Ross, *Creation and Blessing,* 415, "This story . . . demonstrates how the Lord providentially ensured the continued development of the promise by guiding the faithful servant in the acquisition of a bride for Isaac."

Ways to Preach Christ

Redemptive-Historical Progression

The LORD continues the line of the seed of the woman by providing Rebekah as his "appointed" wife for Isaac. Had God not selected Rebekah as wife for Isaac, there would have been no Jacob, and no Israel. But God clearly is concerned about the continuation of the line of the seed of the woman. Here in his providence God selects Rebekah; later God's providence will encompass Laban's scheming as God blesses Jacob's wives, Leah and Rachel, and their concubines with twelve sons. By the time Jacob and his children move to Egypt, under God's providence there are seventy Israelites (Gen 46:27; Exod 1:4), a full number of God's people.

In the fullness of time, the LORD in his providence selects another young woman to advance the cause of the seed of the woman. "The angel Gabriel was sent by God to a town in Galilee called Nazareth, to a virgin. . . . The virgin's name was Mary" (Luke 1:26-27). And as Rebekah said, "I will go," so Mary replies to the angel, "Here am I, the servant of the Lord; let it be with me according to your word" (Luke 1:38). The son that was born to Mary was *the* Seed of the woman. "God so loved the world that he gave his only Son, so that everyone who believes in him may not perish but have eternal life" (John 3:16). Because God sent his Son, salvation is now offered not only to Israel but to "everyone who believes," in fulfillment of God's promises to Abraham that in him "all the families of the earth shall be blessed" (Gen 12:3).

Promise-Fulfillment

Although this narrative can be seen as God filling up his promise of making of Abraham "a great nation" (Gen 12:2), there is no promise of the coming Messiah in this narrative.

Typology

There is no type of Christ in this narrative.

Analogy

Analogy also offers a way leading to Jesus Christ in the New Testament. Taking one's cue from the narrator's goal, one can state the analogy as follows: As this story encouraged Israel to entrust itself for its existence to the LORD's providential care, so Jesus encourages the church to entrust itself for its existence to God's providential care. This analogy can be supported with a New Testament reference such as Jesus' teaching in Matthew 16:18, "On this rock I will build my church, and the gates of Hades will not prevail against it."

Longitudinal Themes

One can trace from the Old Testament to Christ in the New Testament the longitudinal theme of God's providence keeping alive the seed of the woman, here by providing a wife for Isaac, next by providing the barren Rebekah with the twins Esau and Jacob, then by placing Joseph in power in Egypt to save Israel from starvation, next by leading Israel out of Egypt and into the Promised Land, later enabling a remnant to return from exile in Babylon, to providing the virgin Mary to bear his own son Jesus, saving Jesus from Herod (Matt 2:13, 19-20), raising Jesus from death, pouring out the Holy Spirit, and protecting his church till Jesus returns.

New Testament References

The appendix of the Greek New Testament lists four references to this narrative: Genesis 24:3 — Mark 5:7; Genesis 24:7 — Galatians 3:16; Genesis 24:37 — Hebrews 11:13; and Genesis 24:65 — 1 Corinthians 11:10. None of these references can be used as a way to Christ.

Contrast

There is no contrast between the textual theme and the New Testament.

Sermon Theme and Goal

We formulated the textual theme as, "In his covenant faithfulness, the LORD provides Rebekah as his 'appointed' wife for Isaac in order to continue the line of the seed of the woman." We can try to broaden the sermon theme so that it will also encompass the LORD's continuing the line of the seed of the woman to Jesus. Unfortunately, this effort would lose the specificity of the textual theme. It seems best, therefore, to use the textual theme as the sermon theme: *In his covenant faithfulness, the* Lord *provides Rebekah as his "appointed" wife for Isaac in order to continue the line of the seed of the woman.*

We formulated the narrator's goal for Israel as, "To encourage Israel to entrust itself for its existence to the Lord's providential care." We can prepare the sermon with a similar goal in mind: *To encourage the church to entrust itself for its existence to the* Lord*'s providential care.* This goal shows that the need addressed in this sermon has to do with concern about the continued existence of the church.

Sermon Exposition

Since this is such a long narrative and the servant's rather repetitious speech tends to bore Western ears, one could skip reading the servant's speech and before the sermon read only the narrator's description of the servant's mission and its results (Genesis 24:1-33, 50-67). In the sermon, of course, one should certainly deal with the servant's long speech because his alterations sharpen the point (theme) of the narrative. If reading Genesis 24:1-33 and 50-67 still seems too long for Scripture reading, one could consider reading only the main challenge (conflict), Genesis 24:1-9, and read other sections of this narrative in the sermon itself.

The introduction could illustrate that the church today is under attack, both from within and without. We are concerned about the continued existence of the church. Will our children still be members of the church? Our grandchildren? Transition to Israel, which often feared for its existence as a nation. This narrative about God's providing Rebekah as his "appointed" wife for Isaac speaks directly to that need.

God had promised Abram the land of Canaan, many offspring, and that through him all the families of the earth would be blessed (Gen 12:1-7). Abraham and Sarah saw the initial fulfillment of these promises in their old age with the birth of the miracle child Isaac. But now God's promises seem to run into another dead-end. The narrator informs us in verse 1 that Abraham is old. For emphasis he adds, "well advanced in years." And Sarah, the matriarch, has died (Gen 23). There is no mother in Israel! Unless Abraham can find a wife for Isaac, who is now forty years old (Gen 25:20), there will not be any more offspring, and there will be no Israel, and ultimately no Messiah through whom "all the families of the earth shall be blessed" (12:3). It is high time, therefore, that Abraham, according to prevailing customs, arrange for the marriage of Isaac.

The easiest way for Abraham to arrange his son's marriage is to select one of the Canaanite girls. Abraham himself can then make the selection. Moreover, he may be able to arrange a marriage with a princess who owns property in Canaan. By combining the wealth of Isaac with the land holdings of a Canaanite princess, Abraham may be able to help God in fulfilling his promise of land. But Abraham adamantly refuses to go that route.

In verses 2-4 we overhear Abraham's last recorded words. Abraham says to his trusted servant, "Put your hand under my thigh and I will make you swear by the Lord, the God of heaven and earth, that you will not get a wife for my son from the daughters of the Canaanites, among whom I live, but will go to my country and to my kindred and get a wife for my son Isaac." Abraham insists that the servant not get a daughter from the Canaanites. Not marrying a Canaanite is important, for God had separated Abraham from the nations (Gen 12:1); for Isaac to marry a Canaanite would bring God's redemptive plan to naught.

Israel, of course, knows that God forbade his people from marrying Canaanites. God had warned them explicitly, "Do not intermarry with them, giving your daughters to their sons or taking their daughters for your sons, for that would turn away your children from following me, to serve other gods."[11] God is concerned that Israel will turn away from the only true God. That may have been part of Abraham's concern as well, but for Abraham the issue seems to be focused more on the land.[12] The descendants of Canaan live under God's curse while the descendants of Shem (and of Abraham) live under God's blessing (Gen 9:25-26). God had promised Abraham, "You shall go to your ancestors in peace; you shall be buried in a good old age. And they [your seed] shall come back here in the fourth generation; for the iniquity of the Amorites [read Canaanites] is not yet complete" (Gen 15:15-16). Hamilton perceptively observes, "If Isaac is to inherit the land, he must not marry among those destined to disinherit the land."[13]

That Isaac not marry a Canaanite is so important to Abraham that he makes his servant swear by "the Lord, the God of heaven and earth," that is, the covenant Lord who is God the creator (Gen 1). Abraham requires his servant to

11. Deut 7:3-4. The context for this law reads, "When the Lord your God brings you into the land that you are about to enter and occupy, and he clears away many nations before you — the Hittites, the Girgashites, the Amorites, the Canaanites, the Perizzites, the Hivites, and the Jebusites, seven nations mightier and more numerous than you — and when the Lord your God gives them over to you and you defeat them, then you must utterly destroy them. Make no covenant with them and show them no mercy. Do not intermarry with them, giving your daughters to their sons or taking their daughters for your sons, for that would turn away your children from following me, to serve other gods" (Deut 7:1-4; cf. Ezra 10; Neh 13:23-27).

12. "At this early stage, intermarriage with the people of the land would risk assimilation into those people and thus jeopardize the covenant promises of the land to Abraham's descendants. . . . This allows the Israel of Moses' audience to understand that the people that they are to drive out of the land are not related to them in any way." Walton, *Genesis,* 529.

13. Hamilton, *Genesis 18–50,* 140.

swear this oath while placing his hand under his thigh,[14] which is the ancient equivalent of our swearing an oath on the Bible.

But the servant immediately spots a problem in Abraham's request: verse 5, "Perhaps the woman may not be willing to follow me to this land; must I then take your son back to the land from which you came?" This is a good question. Which young woman would wish to leave her father and mother, her family and friends, and follow a stranger to a distant land to marry an unknown man? Why not have the groom move to the bride's country?

But Abraham is adamant that the servant not take Isaac back to Mesopotamia. Verse 6, "See to it that you do not take my son back there" (repeated in v 8). "See to it," or "take care" "often refutes a shocking or unworthy idea (cf. 31:24, 29; Exod 34:12; Deut 4:9)."[15] To take Isaac back to the land from which God called Abraham is to negate God's call of Abraham and his promise of the land. Abraham and Sarah's sixty-some years of living as "strangers and aliens" in the land would have been for nothing. Isaac is to stay in the land of his birth. His presence there will be a constant reminder of God's promise of the land.[16]

What an impossible assignment the servant faces: travel over four hundred miles to find a woman who is related to Abraham and who is willing to go back to Canaan with the servant in order to marry a stranger. But Abraham assures the servant, verse 7, "The LORD . . . will send his angel before you, and you shall take a wife for my son from there." "The LORD . . . will send his angel before you." The Israelites could relate to that message. As they left Egypt, "the LORD went in front of them in a pillar of cloud by day, to lead them along the way, and as a pillar of fire by night, to give them light" (Exod 13:21). Later, as they left Sinai for Canaan, the LORD promised, "I am going to send an angel in front of you, to guard you on the way and to bring you to the place that I have prepared" (Exod 23:20; cf. 32:34; 33:2). So Abraham here assures the servant of the LORD's providential leading.

With these words of Abraham ringing in his ears, the servant prepares a caravan of ten camels, loads them with provisions and gifts, and sets out for the distant country in the North. The narrator covers this month-long[17] journey in half a verse: verse 10b, "He set out and went to Aram-naharaim, to the city of Nahor." The journey itself is not important to the narrator; what is important is what happens when the servant reaches his destination (fifty-one verses for one

14. "Near the organ of procreation, probably because this oath was related to the continuation of Abraham's line through Isaac (see 47:29)." *NIV Study Bible*, Genesis 24:2, n.

15. Wenham, *Genesis 16–50*, 142.

16. As far as we know, Isaac spent his whole life in the Promised Land. When the land was plagued by a famine and Isaac thought of going to Egypt, "the LORD appeared to Isaac and said, 'Do not go down to Egypt'" (Gen 26:2).

17. Speiser, *Genesis*, 183.

evening and morning, vv 11-61). The servant stops by the well outside the city of Nahor. It is almost evening, and soon the women will come out in the cool evening air to draw water at the well. Perhaps one of these women will be a suitable wife for Isaac. But how will the servant know which is the right woman?

The servant is a man of prayer. He prays fervently: verse 12, "O LORD, God of my master Abraham, please grant me success today and show steadfast love to my master Abraham." The servant pleads with the LORD to show his steadfast love *(ḥesed)*, his covenant faithfulness, to Abraham by making his mission successful.

But how will the servant know which is the right woman? He puts out a fleece, as it were, asking the LORD to give him a clear sign of his guidance. He prays, verse 14, "Let the girl to whom I shall say, 'Please offer your jar that I may drink,' and who shall say, 'Drink, and I will water your camels' — let her be the one whom you have appointed for your servant Isaac." Von Rad comments that the servant "prays for a sign, not as generally for strengthening of his faith, but for knowledge of God's will. . . . He will recognize the maiden whom God has 'appointed' for him (*hōkîaḥ*, vv 14 and 44) by the readiness with which she complies with his request for water for men and beasts."[18] It is quite a test. Which young woman will offer to go down the steps to the spring and haul up enough water for ten thirsty camels? "A camel that has gone a few days without water can drink as much as twenty-five gallons. Ancient jars used for drawing water usually held no more than three gallons. In other words, this offer involves perhaps from eighty to a hundred drawings from the well."[19] This grueling test will not only indicate the right girl but also reveal something about her character: she will have to be kind, hospitable, and not afraid of hard work.

Verse 15, "Before he had finished speaking, there was Rebekah, who was born to Bethuel son of Milcah, the wife of Nahor, Abraham's brother." "Before he had finished speaking," God answers the servant's prayer. By telling us that Rebekah is Abraham's grandniece, the narrator raises our hopes that she may be the LORD's "appointed." He further provides unusual but important character description: verse 16, "The girl was very fair to look upon, a virgin, whom no man had known." She is beautiful, like Sarah before her. And she is a virgin. Surely Rebekah is the intended bride for Isaac.

But the servant is still in the dark. He doesn't have any of this information, except that he can see that the girl is beautiful. As the servant watches, Rebekah goes down the steps to the spring, fills her jar, and comes up again. As she is about to return home, the servant runs over and applies his test: verse 17, "Please let me sip a little water from your jar." She answers, "Drink, my lord," and lowers her jar to give him a drink. She is kind and hospitable, but she has

18. Von Rad, *Genesis*, 256.

19. Walton, *Genesis*, 530.

not passed the test by saying, "Drink, and I will water your camels" (v 14). "Is she the type that will oblige at request but offer nothing beyond? Does she overlook the camels thoughtlessly or deliberately? Is it one thing to 'lower' a pitcher for a single man and quite another to exhaust oneself on behalf of his thirsty beasts?"[20] The servant may already be giving up on her being God's "appointed." But then he hears the welcome words, verse 19, "I will draw for your camels also, until they have finished drinking." This girl may be the one!

Verse 20, "So she quickly emptied her jar into the trough and ran again to the well to draw, and she drew for all his camels." Sternberg observes, "The young woman's performance surpasses even the most optimistic expectations. Thus, the increased specificity largely derives from the references to haste that punctuate the narrative: 'she made haste and lowered her pitcher . . . she made haste and lowered her pitcher into the trough . . . she ran again to the well.' This spontaneous dispatch bears more than the obvious complimentary implications for character and judgment. It echoes nothing less than Abraham's model hospitality, 'He ran to meet them. . . . Abraham made haste into the tent. . . . Abraham ran to the tent . . . he made haste to prepare it' (18:2-7); and the elevating analogy stamps her as worthy of the patriarch himself."[21] The servant's hopes are raised. The girl is passing his test. But is she of Abraham's kindred? Verse 21, "The man gazed at her in silence to learn whether or not the Lord had made his journey successful." That is the key question in this narrative, "whether or not the Lord had made his journey successful." So after giving her a gold nose-ring and even costlier bracelets, he asks her straight out, verse 23, "Tell me whose daughter you are?" She answers, "I am the daughter of Bethuel son of Milcah, whom she bore to Nahor" (v 24).

When Abraham's servant hears that she is a grandniece of Abraham, he bows his head and worships the Lord. He says, verse 27, "Blessed be the Lord, the God of my master Abraham, who has not forsaken his steadfast love and his faithfulness toward my master. As for me, the Lord has led me on the way to my master's kin." The servant had asked the Lord to "show steadfast love to my master Abraham" (v 12), and now he confesses that the Lord has shown not only "steadfast love" to his master but specifically covenant "faithfulness." The Lord is faithful in fulfilling his covenant promises to Abraham that he would make of him a great nation and a blessing to "all the families of the earth" (12:2-3).

The servant also confesses that the Lord has led him to Rebekah: "The Lord has led me." God's providence! The narrator highlights the Lord's providence in this search for a wife for Isaac. Rebekah is literally a Godsend. Abra-

20. Sternberg, *Poetics of Biblical Narrative,* 139. The narrator has retarded "the plot with a view to heightened suspense." Ibid.

21. Ibid., 138.

ham testified that the LORD "will send his angel before you" (v 7). The servant himself prays at the well, "O LORD, God of my master Abraham, please grant me success today" (v 12). And now the servant testifies openly, "The LORD has led me on the way to the house of my master's kin" (v 27). In his providence, the LORD has brought the servant to the home of Rebekah, the young woman God "appointed" as wife for Isaac.

But there are still more hurdles to overcome. Will Rebekah's family be willing to let her go with a stranger to marry an unknown man? And will Rebekah herself be willing to go far from her family to marry a stranger?

Rebekah runs off to let her family know about the stranger she has just met by the well. Her brother Laban, as we learn later (31:7), is a greedy person. When he sees the gold nose-ring and bracelets (v 30), he can hardly wait for his sister to finish her story. He rushes out to the well and finds the servant, "standing by the camels" (v 30). Only the most wealthy had camels. Laban welcomes the stranger with open arms, takes him home, even unloads the camels for him (v 32), and offers a fine meal.

But before the servant will eat, he insists on telling Rebekah's family about his mission. He will have to convince them to let their beautiful daughter Rebekah go with him to a distant, foreign land to marry a total stranger. The servant repeats almost verbatim the narrator's words but makes a few strategic changes. Astutely, he begins by telling them about the riches of Abraham: verse 35, "The LORD has greatly blessed my master [cf. v 1], and he has become wealthy; he has given him flocks and herds, silver and gold, male and female slaves, camels and donkeys. And Sarah my master's wife bore a son to my master when she was old; and he has given him all that he has." There it is: by marrying Isaac, Rebekah will share in the riches of Isaac, and her family will receive a handsome bride-price.

The servant continues, verse 37, "My master made me swear, saying, 'You shall not take a wife for my son from the daughters of the Canaanites, in whose land I live; but you shall go to my father's house, to my kindred, and get a wife for my son.'" Well, not quite. Abraham had said, "Go to my country and to my kindred" (v 4) — rather general. The servant, now knowing Rebekah's lineage, makes it more specific and personal, "Go to my *father's house,* to my kindred."

The servant continues in verse 39, "I said to my master, 'Perhaps the woman will not follow me.' But he said to me, 'The LORD, before whom I walk, will send his angel with you and make your way *successful.* You shall get a wife for my son from my kindred, from my *father's house.*" The servant manages to repeat "my father's house" and combine Abraham's words about the LORD's angel leading him with his own concern about being "successful" (v 21). He stresses both Abraham's and his own reliance on God's providence in finding a wife for Isaac.[22]

22. "Understandably, the servant does not repeat Abraham's insistence that under no cir-

Next the servant recalls the events of the day: verse 42, "I came today to the spring, and said, 'O LORD, the God of my master Abraham, if now you will only make *successful* the way I am going! I am standing here by the spring of water; let the young woman who comes out to draw, to whom I shall say, "Please give me a little water from your jar to drink," and who will say to me, "Drink, and I will draw for your camels also" — let her be the woman whom the LORD has *appointed* for my master's son.' Before I had finished speaking in my heart, there was Rebekah coming out with her water jar on her shoulder; and she went down to the spring, and drew. I said to her, 'Please let me drink.' She quickly let down her jar from her shoulder, and said, 'Drink, and I will also water your camels.' So I drank, and she also watered the camels. Then I asked her, 'Whose daughter are you?' She said, 'The daughter of Bethuel, Nahor's son, whom Milcah bore to him. So I put the ring on her nose, and the bracelets on her arms.[23] Then I bowed my head and worshiped the LORD, and blessed the LORD, the God of my master Abraham, who had *led me* by the right way to obtain the daughter of my master's kinsman for his son." The servant stresses again the LORD's divine guidance: from his prayer at the well that the LORD will make his way "successful" (v 42), to the test he devised to discover which woman the LORD had "appointed" (v 44), to Rebekah's passing the test with flying colors (vv 45-47), to his final thanksgiving acknowledging that the LORD "had led" him (v 48).

The servant concludes his lengthy speech with the clincher, verse 49, "Now then, if you will deal loyally and truly with my master, tell me; and if not, tell me, so that I may turn either to the right hand or to the left." This is loaded language. "God has already shown 'kindness' *(ḥesed)* to Abraham (vv 12, 14, 27). Will Laban also extend *ḥesed* to Abraham (v 49)? Will Laban deal with Abraham as God has dealt with Abraham? Will divine kindness be complemented by human kindness?"[24] The family can hardly refuse. But if they should refuse to give Rebekah, the servant states, "tell me, so that I may turn either to the right hand or to the left." That is, "I will take my suit elsewhere, to relatives more mindful of God and humanity, kinship and wealth."[25]

In response, even Laban and Bethuel must testify, verse 50, "The thing comes from the LORD; we cannot speak to you anything bad or good," that is,

---

cumstances is the servant to take Isaac to Aram-Naharaim (vv 6, 8b). Diplomacy dictated this deletion." Hamilton, *Genesis 18–50*, 154. See ibid. for other subtle changes.

23. "Reversing the original order, he now puts the inquiry, 'Whose daughter art thou?' *before* the bestowal of the gifts, as though he would not commit himself as long as there remained the slightest doubt about the alignment of human wishes with divine disposition." Sternberg, *Poetics of Biblical Narrative*, 151.

24. Hamilton, *Genesis 18–50*, 155.

25. Sternberg, *Poetics of Biblical Narrative*, 151.

"we cannot contradict anything you say."[26] Since the LORD "has given his decision (Rebekah is the one for Isaac), . . . Laban is no longer free to exercise his own decision."[27] Rebekah's brother and father say, verse 51, "Look, Rebekah is before you, take her and go, and let her be the wife of your master's son, as the LORD has spoken."[28] Hearing this, the servant bows "to the ground before the LORD" (v 52) and then lavishes more costly gifts on Rebekah and presents a bride-price to her family. Business having been successfully concluded, it is time to feast.

The next morning the servant wishes to return to his master with Rebekah. But another problem crops up: Rebekah's brother and mother ask for a delay of at least ten days. But the servant insists on leaving right away, again appealing to the LORD's guidance: verse 56, "Do not delay me, since the LORD has made my journey successful. . . ." Rebekah is called in to decide the issue: either leave right away for a foreign land and an unknown husband or stay with her family at least another ten days. How will she respond? The relatives ask her, "Will you go with this man?" And just as Abram responded to God's call to go: he "went" (*yālak,* Gen 12:4), Rebekah says, "I will go" (*yālak,* v 58). Rebekah is indeed a suitable bride for Isaac.

Rebekah's relatives honor her decision and send her away with the blessing, verse 60, "May you, our sister, become thousands of myriads; may your offspring gain possession of the gates of their foes." This blessing is similar to the one the LORD gave Abraham after his willingness to offer up Isaac, "I will make your offspring as numerous as the stars of heaven. . . . And your offspring shall possess the gate of their enemies" (22:17). Isaac and Rebekah now share the same blessing.[29]

But in spite of this, there remains a final question: Will Isaac accept Rebekah as his bride? The scene switches back to Canaan where Isaac has "settled in the Negeb" (v 62). Verse 63, "Isaac went out in the evening to walk in the field; and looking up, he saw camels coming. And Rebekah looked up, and when she saw Isaac, she slipped quickly from the camel, and said to the servant, 'Who is the man over there, walking in the field to meet us?' The servant said, 'It is my master.' So she took her veil and covered herself." In that culture a bride would wear a veil when meeting the groom.[30] When Rebekah and the servant

26. Wenham, *Genesis 16–50,* 149.

27. Hamilton, *Genesis 18–50,* 155, n. 2.

28. "Their only reason for relinquishing her is the unmistakable hand of God throughout this whole episode. It is not the servant, Abraham, or Isaac, but rather their God, that Laban and Bethuel find persuasive." Hamilton, ibid., 157.

29. "The purpose is again to show just what careful attention to detail the Lord has shown in choosing this wife for Isaac. In God's plan the same blessing has been given to both Isaac and his bride." Sailhamer, *Genesis,* 178.

30. "The veil is not worn permanently, though the bride meets the bridegroom veiled." Westermann, *Genesis 12–36,* 390-91.

meet Isaac, the servant tells him all that has happened. Isaac also acknowledges that this is from the LORD, for, according to verse 67, he "brought her into his mother Sarah's tent. He took Rebekah, and she became his wife; and he loved her. So Isaac was comforted after his mother's death." Sarah's tent is occupied again. There is again a mother in Israel.

As Israel later read this story, it knew that again its very existence was in the balance. If Isaac had married a Canaanite princess, there would have been no Israel. If God had not guided the servant to Rebekah, there would have been no Israel. If Rebekah had refused to go, there would have been no Israel. But God gently worked through human deliberations and the servant's convincing arguments to bring about his special people Israel — a holy nation separated from the nations.

God is concerned about the continuation of the seed of the woman. Here God provides Rebekah; later God will incorporate in his providential plan the scheming of Laban and bless Jacob's wives, Leah and Rachel and their concubines, with twelve sons. By the time Jacob and his children move to Egypt there are seventy Israelites (Gen 46:27; Exod 1:4), a full number of God's people.

Centuries later, the LORD called on another young woman to advance the cause of the seed of the woman. "The angel Gabriel was sent by God to a town in Galilee called Nazareth, to a virgin. . . . The virgin's name was Mary. . . . The angel said to her . . . , 'You will conceive in your womb and bear a son, and you will name him Jesus. He will be great, and will be called the Son of the Most High, and the Lord God will give him the throne of his ancestor David. He will reign over the house of Jacob forever, and of his kingdom there will be no end." And as Rebekah said, "I will go," so Mary replies to the angel, "Here am I, the servant of the Lord; let it be with me according to your word" (Luke 1:26-33, 38). The son that was born to Mary was *the* Seed of the woman. Through Jesus, God would fulfill his promise to Abraham, "In you all the families of the earth shall be blessed" (12:3; cf. 22:18, "nations"). "God so loved the world that he gave his only Son, so that everyone who believes in him may not perish but have eternal life" (John 3:16). Because God sent his Son, the doorway to salvation has opened wide, not just to Israel but to all nations of the world.

As this story encouraged Israel to entrust itself for its existence to the LORD's providential care, so Jesus encourages the church to entrust itself for its existence to God's providential care. We may be very much concerned today about the inroads of materialism within the church and secularism battering the church from without. Will our children and grandchildren still be members of Jesus' church? Jesus said that he would build his church on the rock of Peter's confession, "You are the Messiah, the Son of the living God." And he promised, "The gates of Hades will not prevail against it" (Matt 16:16, 18). "The powers of death, i.e., all forces opposed to Christ and his kingdom"[31] will not prevail against the church. God is in control. Because of his covenant faithfulness, the LORD provides for the continuation of the seed of the woman from one generation to the next to the last day. Then, when Christ comes again to bring his kingdom in perfection, "The kingdom of the world . . . become[s] the kingdom of our Lord and of his Messiah, and he will reign forever and ever" (Rev 11:15). No matter how deep the distress of the church today, we can confidently entrust the continuing existence of Jesus' church to God's providential care.

31. *NIV Study Bible,* Matthew 16:18, n.

CHAPTER 13

Jacob and Esau

Genesis 25:19-34

One of the challenges in preaching this passage is to select a good textual unit, for commentators are quite divided on the conclusion of this unit. The beginning is clear since verse 19 starts a new *tôlĕdôt,* but where does the unit end? Some argue for verse 26, others for verse 28,[1] and the majority, according to Wenham,[2] opt for verse 34.

Text and Context

There is much to be said for selecting the literary unit of verses 19-26. The main conflict in this short narrative is the painful pregnancy of Rebekah. This conflict is resolved with the birth of the twins Esau and Jacob. Moreover, this unit is bracketed by an inclusio: "Isaac was forty years old" (v 20) and "Isaac was sixty years old" (v 26). It makes little sense to add verses 27 and 28 to this unit,[3] unless it be as the outcome of the first narrative highlighting more differences between Esau and Jacob as they grow older. But these verses are better seen as the setting for the narrative that follows: Esau selling his birthright. As I see it, therefore, the verses 19-34 consist of two short narratives (see plot line below), but because of their brevity and their linked themes, it is advisable to deal with both narratives in one sermon.[4]

1. Wenham mentions Gunkel and Westermann. *Genesis 16–50,* 172.

2. Ibid.

3. The NRSV's heading above verse 29, "Esau Sells His Birthright," may give this impression. Von Rad, *Genesis,* 265, opines, "The entire section vs 21-28 is not really a narrative . . . ; rather, it is apparently intended as an expository preface to the whole, i.e., in the form of a rather loose string of statements it acquaints the reader with those facts which are important for understanding the following stories."

4. Although one could also preach on verses 19-26 or 27-34, the danger of preaching on

As to the context, chapter 24 relates the search for a wife for Isaac and his marriage to Rebekah. Chapter 25 reports the death and burial of Abraham, a short *tôlĕdôt* of Abraham's other son, Ishmael (Gen 25:12-18), and then our text begins with the *tôlĕdôt* of Isaac, the younger son chosen to carry on the line of the seed of the woman.

A major feature in this first narrative is the LORD's oracle to Rebekah,

"Two nations are in your womb,
  and two peoples born of you shall be divided;
the one shall be stronger than the other,
  the elder shall serve the younger."

(25:23)

As the LORD's promises to Abraham in Genesis 12:2-3 set the stage for the following narratives about Abraham, so this oracle sets the stage for the following narratives about Jacob[5] striving with Esau in the womb and later acquiring his birthright.

After relating the story of Isaac and Abimelech, and of Esau marrying Hittite wives (Gen 26), the narrator returns to Jacob: deceiving his father Isaac for the blessing, fleeing from Esau, meeting God at Bethel, being deceived by his uncle Laban, striving with his uncle Laban, even striving with God, and finally making peace with Esau.

As in the Abraham cycle, scholars have detected an encompassing chiastic structure in the Jacob cycle (see p. 248).[6]

Literary Features

The narrator shows his hand most clearly when he explains to later Israel, "Therefore he [Esau, who asked for the "red, red" *('ādōm, 'ādōm)*] was called Edom [Red]" (v 30). But we also see the narrator's hand throughout the rest of

---

such a short narrative is that there is limited biblical exposition and preachers may be tempted to turn a sermon on verses 19-26 into a theological discourse on divine sovereignty and human freedom, and a sermon on verses 27-34 into a moralistic discourse on how we should not live for immediate gratification like Esau, nor be as calculating and unloving as Jacob.

5. It is also similar to Joseph's dreams at the beginning of the Joseph story. "This prediction, set at the beginning of the Jacob story, has a role somewhat similar to Joseph's dreams (37:5-11): at the beginning of a major section of Genesis it foretells how a younger son will achieve predominance." Brodie, *Genesis as Dialogue,* 299.

6. I have reproduced the one offered by Waltke, *Genesis,* 352. For slight variations, see also Fishbane, *Text and Texture,* 42; Rendsburg, *Redaction,* 53-69; Brueggemann, *Genesis,* 211-13; and Wenham, *Genesis 16–50,* 169.

A Births and genealogy: rivalry in the family, Jacob born	(25:19-34)
B Digression: Rebekah in foreign palace, pact with foreigners	(26:1-33)
C Jacob steals Esau's blessing	(26:34–28:9)
D Covenant blessings on Jacob and his exile	(28:10–32:32)
1 Encounter with the angel at Bethel	(28:10-22)
2 Arrival at Haran and conflict with Laban	(29:1-30)
3 Rachel and Leah: Birth of tribal fathers	(29:31–30:24)
2′ Jacob's prosperity and flight from Laban	(30:25–31:55)
1′ Encounter with angels at Mahanaim and Peniel	(32:1-32)
C′ Esau's reconciliation with homeward-bound Jacob	(33:1-17)
B′ Digression: Dinah in foreign palace, pact with foreigners	(33:18–34:31)
A′ Births and deaths	(35:1-29)

the narratives. He has included an unusual amount of character description in order to contrast Esau and Jacob: Esau was "red, all his body like a hairy mantle" (v 25); Jacob, "his brother came out, with his hand gripping Esau's heel" (v 26) and, we find out later, "smooth skin" (27:11). Esau was "a skillful hunter, a man of the field" (v 27a), while Jacob was "a quiet man, living in tents" (v 27b).

The narrator also gives character description through the characters' dialogue: "Esau speaks coarsely and acts on immediate demands without reflection. . . . Jacob, in contrast, acts with foresight. . . . He speaks with finesse and acts as one who reflects, who opts for future rewards over immediate sensual gratification."[7] Esau's narrated actions also reflect his character: "The quick succession of verbs, 'he ate and drank, and rose and went away' (25:34), completes the picture of an unsophisticated, unthinking (and vulnerable?) oaf."[8] Finally, the narrator gives his own evaluation of Esau (again, unusual in Hebrew narrative): "Thus Esau despised his birthright" (v 34). The narrator does not give a negative evaluation here of Jacob's calculated, unloving behavior. In fact, he characterizes Jacob as "a quiet man, living in tents" (v 27b). Amazingly, he characterizes Jacob as *tām,* which is more than "a quiet man" (NRSV), "content" (TNIV), or "peaceful" (NASB); it is a man "blameless" like Job (1:1, 8). "*All* the other biblical occurrences of the word — and it is frequently used, both in adjectival and nominative forms — refer to innocence or moral integrity."[9]

Noteworthy also is the narrator's pace acceleration and retardation. Like Sarah before her, Rebekah is barren. But instead of again spending a great deal

7. Waltke, *Genesis,* 361. Alter, *Art of Biblical Narrative,* 72, calls this "contrastive dialogue."

8. Turner, *Genesis,* 109.

9. Alter, *Art of Biblical Narrative,* 43 (his italics).

of narrative time on barrenness in the line of the seed of the woman (Gen 12–21), the narrator covers Rebekah's twenty years of bitter barrenness in one verse (v 21). Obviously, his interest here is not focused on barrenness but on the oracle that "the elder shall serve the younger" (v 23) and Jacob and Esau's birth (vv 24-26). Even the many years it took for the babies to grow into adulthood is covered in a single clause, "When the boys grew up" (v 27a). But the narrator retards the pace again when he describes the differences between Esau and Jacob and how Jacob obtained Esau's birthright (vv 27-34).

The most important repetition is found in the second narrative: four times the narrator uses the word *bĕkōrâ,* "birthright," the birthright of the firstborn — that's what the struggle between Jacob and Esau is all about. In Genesis 27 Jacob will try to clinch his birthright by going after the *bĕrakâ* (note the wordplay), the "blessing," of the one who has the *bĕkōrâ.*

We have already noted the inclusio enclosing the first narrative. Fokkelman cautiously suggests that in this narrative "we observe a tendency to a concentric structure":[10]

A Isaac was forty years old when he took as wife Rebekah	v 20
B Rebekah was barren; prayer for children answered	20-21
C his wife Rebekah conceived	21
the children struggle together	22
D Rebekah asks for an ORACLE	22
D′ Yahweh grants her an ORACLE	23
C′ her days to be delivered were fulfilled	24
and behold, there were twins in her womb	24
B′ birth and appearance of Jacob and Esau	25-26a
A′ Isaac was sixty years old when she bore them	26b

For the second narrative, Fokkelman is more certain of a chiastic structure:[11]

A Jacob was boiling pottage	v 29a
B Esau came in from the field; he was tired	29b
C *wayy'ōmer ʿĒśāw:* let me eat some of that red red pottage (. . .), I am so tired!	30
D *wayy'ōmer Yaʿăqōb:* first sell me your *bkrh*	31
X *wayy'omer ʿĒśāw:* I depart, I die; of what use is a *bkrh* to me?	32
D′ *wayy'ōmer Yaʿăqōb:* swear to me first. So he swore to him and sold his *bkrh* to Jacob.	33

10. Fokkelman, *Narrative Art in Genesis,* 93.

11. Ibid., 95.

C′ Jacob gave Esau bread and pottage of lentils; 34a
he ate and he drank
B′ He rose and went his way 34b
A′ Thus Esau despised his birthright *(bkrh)* 34b

These chiastic structures are helpful in confirming the focus of these narratives: the oracle and Esau's disdain for his birthright. For preaching purposes, however, the plot line is much more important not only for pinpointing the theme of the narrative(s) but also for retelling these narratives in the sermon while making the same point the narrator intended to make.

The Plot Line

The plot of these two interconnected narratives is the conflict between the twins Esau and Jacob. The pregnant Rebekah is at her wit's end because "the children struggled together within her" (25:22). In response to her inquiry of the LORD, the LORD said,

"Two nations are in your womb,
and two peoples born of you shall be divided;
the one shall be stronger than the other,
the elder shall serve the younger."

(25:23)

Who will have the rights of the firstborn *(bĕkōrâ)?* Esau is born first, but Jacob is close behind, in fact grabbing his heel. When they grow up, Jacob will overtake Esau by trading some common lentil stew for Esau's valuable birthright.

We can sketch the plot line of these two narratives as two connected single plots:

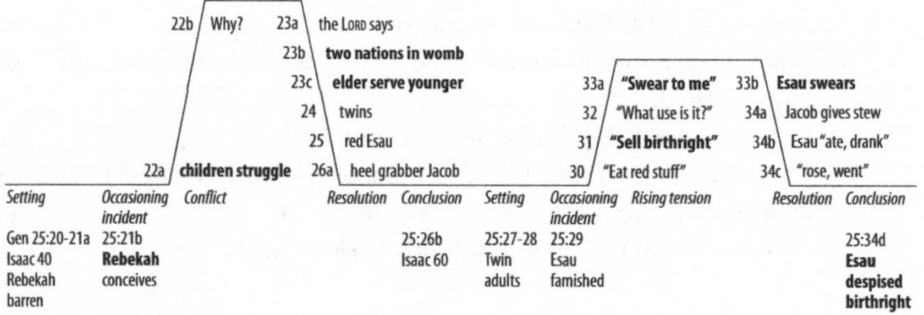

Theocentric Interpretation

The LORD appears only in the first of these two narratives. Isaac prayed to the LORD for his barren wife Rebekah, "the LORD granted his prayer," and Rebekah conceived (v 21). When the children struggled in her womb, Rebekah inquired of the LORD (v 22) and the LORD responded with an oracle (v 23). Although Jacob's bartering for Esau's birthright in the second narrative seems all too secular, this event takes place under the umbrella of the LORD's oracle, "The elder shall serve the younger."

Textual Theme and Goal

We have noticed the prominent place of the LORD's oracle. That makes the oracle a clue to where to look for the theme. Turner writes, "The details of the divine oracle in 25:23 need to be noted carefully. It functions as a thematic preface to the whole of the Jacob story, just as 1:28 did for the primaeval history, and 12:1-3 for the Abraham story."[12] The climax of the oracle is the LORD's prediction that "the elder shall serve the younger."

The context also provides insight into the theme. Just prior to our text the narrator has placed the *tôlĕdôt* of Ishmael (25:12-18) — only seven verses about the elder of Abraham's two sons who was sent away for the sake of the younger Isaac whom God chose to continue the line of the seed of the woman (17:19). Then comes the *tôlĕdôt* of Isaac, and again we hear of two sons; this time they are sons of the same mother as well as father. In fact, they are twins, Esau being just a few seconds older than Jacob. According to ancient Middle Eastern customs, this meant that Esau would have the rights and privileges of the firstborn. As readers of this story, the Israelites were acquainted with the firstborn birthright. God's law prescribed that the firstborn receive "a double portion of all that he [the father] has; since he is the first issue of his virility, the right of the firstborn is his" (Deut 21:17). But with Esau the LORD overturns human customs and even his own law. The LORD predicts, "the elder shall serve the younger." The first narrative describes the birth of the twins with Jacob grabbing the heel of Esau: Esau is first, but Jacob is literally hard on his heels. In the second narrative Jacob passes Esau by obtaining his firstborn birthright.

The narrator further emphasizes that this skirmish is not just between two individuals but between the two nations that will come from them: "Two na-

12. Turner, *Genesis*, 108. Cf. Fokkelman, *Narrative Art in Genesis*, 94, "By its centre of power, scene 1 [Gen 25:19-26] also obliges the reader to read all the events of Jacob's life in the light of the oracle."

tions are in your womb, and two peoples born of you shall be divided" (v 23); "Therefore he [Esau] was called Edom" (v 30; cf. 36:1, 8, 19). Jacob, of course, was later named Israel (32:28; 35:10) and was considered the father of the nation of Israel. We can capture these various ideas in a textual theme that runs something like this: *Contrary to human customs, in his grace God chooses the younger Jacob/Israel to rule the older Esau/Edom.*

As to the reason(s) why the narrator related this story to Israel, we need to remember the relationship between Israel and Edom. When Israel came out of Egypt, Moses requested the king of Edom for safe passage through his land, but Edom refused (Num 20:14-21). After this, the battles between Israel and Edom continued. Later Edom even allied herself with Babylonia and helped slaughter the Israelites and tear down the walls of Jerusalem.[13] One of the goals of the narrator in relating this story of Israel ruling Edom would be to teach Israel that in his sovereign grace God has chosen her to be his victorious people. Underlying this purpose is the more relevant goal: *To assure embattled Israel that in his sovereign grace God has chosen her to be his victorious people.*

Ways to Preach Christ

Redemptive-Historical Progression

God's choice of the younger brother over the older taps into a deep redemptive-historical vein. In Genesis 3:15 the LORD sets enmity between the seed of the woman and the seed of the serpent. Cain and Abel, probably twins,[14] were the first to experience this enmity. When they brought offerings to the LORD, "the LORD had regard for Abel and his offering, but for Cain and his offering he had no regard" (4:4-5). When Cain killed his younger brother Abel, God selected the younger Seth to carry on the line of the seed of the woman. Abraham also had two sons, Ishmael and Isaac, but God chose to establish his everlasting covenant with the younger Isaac (17:19). In our passage God chooses the younger Jacob over the older Esau. The struggle between Jacob and Esau extends beyond their own lifetimes into the lives of the nations of Israel and Edom. Edom refused her brother Israel safe passage through their country (Num 20:14-21). King David was finally able to subjugate Edom (2 Sam 8:13-14), but Edom regained its independence and later joined Babylonia in driving Judah into exile and tearing down Jerusalem (Ps 137:7).

The battle between Israel and Edom continued even into New Testament

13. See Ps 137:7; Ezek 25:12-14; Obad 10-19; and Mal 1:4.

14. See above, p. 92.

times. Matthew traces Jesus' lineage back to Isaac and his son Jacob (Matt 1:2). At that time King Herod ruled Israel harshly on Rome's behalf. He ruthlessly exterminated all who challenged his power. King Herod was an Idumean,[15] an Edomite. When Herod heard from the wise men that the "king of the Jews" had been born, he sought to kill Jesus (Matt 2:16). But an angel of the Lord warned Joseph, and Jesus escaped. Jesus was able to fulfill his mission and establish his church on earth. The battle between the seed of the woman and the seed of the serpent would continue between the church and the world, but Jesus promised that the church would gain the ultimate victory: "the gates of Hades will not prevail against it [the church]" (Matt 16:18).

Promise-Fulfillment

The Lord's oracle contains a promise that "the elder will serve the younger," which finds its initial fulfillment in the second narrative when Esau loses his birthright to Jacob. But there is no direct promise of Christ in this passage.

Typology

There is no type of Christ in this passage.

Analogy

As God assured Israel that in his grace he had chosen them to be his victorious people, so Christ assures the church that God in his grace has chosen the church to be his victorious people. This analogy can be supported by a New Testament reference such as Luke 10:18-19 where the seventy say to Jesus, "Lord, in your name even the *demons* submit to us." Jesus responds, "I watched Satan fall from heaven like a flash of lightning. See, I have given you authority to tread on snakes and scorpions, and over all the power of the enemy."

Longitudinal Themes

The theme of God choosing, contrary to human customs, the younger over the older can be traced from the Old Testament to Jesus in the New Testament. God

15. See *NIV Study Bible,* Matthew 2:1, n.

chose the younger Abel over Cain, the younger Isaac over Ishmael, here the younger Jacob over Esau, next the younger Joseph over his brothers, then the younger Ephraim over Manasseh, the younger David over his brothers, and the younger Solomon over Adonijah. Isaiah (53:3) prophesied about God's chosen Servant,

> He was despised and rejected by others;
> a man of suffering and acquainted with infirmity;
> and as one from whom others hide their faces
> he was despised, and we held him of no account.

But God allotted his Suffering Servant "a portion with the great" (53:12). Lowly Jesus, born in a stable, raised in Nazareth, poor and despised, was God's Suffering Servant. But God "highly exalted him and gave him the name that is above every name" (Phil 2:9).

New Testament References

There are only two clear references to this passage in the New Testament, neither of which link it directly to Christ. In Romans 9:10-13 Paul uses this passage to illustrate God's electing grace: "Something similar happened to Rebecca when she had conceived children by one husband, our ancestor Isaac. Even before they had been born or had done anything good or bad (so that God's purpose of election might continue, not by works but by his call) she was told, 'The elder shall serve the younger.' As it is written, 'I have loved Jacob, but I have hated Esau.'"

The author of Hebrews uses this passage to warn Christians who shortsightedly give up the Christian faith in order to escape persecution: "See to it that no one becomes like Esau, an immoral and godless person, who sold his birthright for a single meal. You know that later, when he wanted to inherit the blessing, he was rejected, for he found no chance to repent, even though he sought the blessing with tears" (12:16-17).[16]

Contrast

In contrast to this message for Israel which proclaims its victory over Edom, the New Testament views the continuing battle not between Israel and Edom but between the church and the world (e.g., Rev 12:9-17). The reason for this con-

16. Since the author of Hebrews is not preaching a sermon on a Genesis passage, his use of Esau for illustrative purposes in no way justifies preachers using Esau as a negative example when preaching on Gen 25:27-34.

trast is Jesus — Jesus who commanded his followers "to make disciples of all nations" (Matt 28:19; cf. already Ps 87:4).

Sermon Theme and Goal

We formulated the textual theme as: "Contrary to human customs, in his grace God chooses the younger Jacob/Israel to rule the older Esau/Edom." The ways of redemptive-historical progression as well as contrast show that we need to update this theme before it can serve as sermon theme, for Jacob/Israel shifts to the New Testament church and Esau/Edom shifts to the world. We can cover both Jacob/Israel and the church and Esau/Edom and the world in the following sermon theme: *In his grace God chooses the least to be his victorious people.*

We formulated the textual goal as: "To assure embattled Israel that in his sovereign grace God has chosen her to be his victorious people." The sermon goal can be similar: *To assure the embattled church that in his sovereign grace God has chosen her to be his victorious people.* This particular goal points to a specific need this sermon will target: because of widespread persecution, God's people lack confidence that the church will be victorious.

Sermon Exposition

The sermon could begin with an illustration of a local church that stands empty and forsaken. The church today hardly appears victorious. God's Old Testament people often experienced similar doubts, especially when, after forty years in the desert, Edom refused Israel safe passage through their country. This narrative about Jacob and Esau is addressed to people who feel defeated.

Our text begins a new chapter in God's dealings with the forefathers and mothers of Israel. Verse 19, "These are the descendants [*tôlĕdôt*] of Isaac, Abraham's son. Abraham was the father of Isaac." The normal *tôlĕdôt* formula would call for, "This is the *tôlĕdôt* of Isaac. Isaac was the father of Esau and Jacob." But here the narrator first reminds us that Isaac was "Abraham's son." And for emphasis again, "Abraham was the father of Isaac." The narrator wants Israel and us to recall the history of Abraham: how the LORD called him to go to the land of Canaan; how the LORD gave him rich promises of land, a great nation, and being a blessing to all the families of the earth; how the LORD above all promised to be his God and the God of his seed; and how the LORD began to fulfill these promises with the miraculous birth of Isaac, the opportunity to buy a little plot of the Promised Land, and finally how the LORD led the servant's search for a suitable wife for Isaac.

Next, and again exceptional for the *tôlĕdôt* formula,[17] the narrator reminds Israel and us of the marriage of Isaac and Rebekah. Verse 20, "Isaac was forty years old when he married Rebekah, daughter of Bethuel the Aramean of Paddan-aram,[18] sister of Laban the Aramean." After being reminded of the LORD's providence in guiding the servant to a suitable wife for Isaac and the marriage of Isaac and Rebekah, we expect to hear next about the birth of children. But to our surprise, the narrator informs us that Rebekah is barren. Brueggemann observes, "There is an incongruity here. The father is the special child of promise (21:1-7). And the mother is of good stock (25:20). But in this best possible arrangement, there is barrenness. There are no natural guarantees for the future and no way to secure the inheritance of the family. It must trust only to the power of God."[19]

Like Sarah before her, Rebekah is barren; she waits twenty long years for a child. But in contrast to the amount of space he devotes Sarah's barrenness, the narrator does not spend much narrative time on Rebekah's barrenness. Yet with compact parallelism,[20] he manages to highlight the important point that it is the LORD who, in answer to prayer, reverses Rebekah's barrenness. Verse 21,

> Isaac prayed to the LORD for his wife,
> because she was barren;
> and the LORD granted his prayer,
> and his wife Rebekah conceived.

With his miracle-working power, the faithful covenant LORD continues the line of the seed of the woman.[21]

But instead of being overjoyed, Rebekah is deeply troubled, for the pregnancy is excruciatingly painful. Verse 22, "The children struggled together within her; and she said, 'If it is to be this way, why do I live?'" Literally it says,

17. Genesis moves from the *tôlĕdôt* of Terah (11:27–25:11), which deals with Abraham, to the *tôlĕdôt* of the older son of Abraham, Ishmael (25:12-18), and the *tôlĕdôt* of Isaac (25:19–35:29), which deals primarily with Jacob. In other words, there is no *tôlĕdôt* of Abraham, which would deal primarily with Isaac. Waltke attributes the exceptional nature of this opening verse to "the gapping of the account of Abraham's line, which would be about Isaac." *Genesis,* 357.

18. "'Paddan-Aram' . . . is the homeland of the family of Bethuel, Rebekah, and Laban, somewhere in northern Mesopotamia, probably in the vicinity of Harran (cf. 11:31)." Wenham, *Genesis 16–50,* 174.

19. Brueggemann, *Genesis,* 212.

20. For the Hebrew details, see Fokkelman, *Narrative Art in Genesis,* 88.

21. "The concentration on the barrenness of both Sarah and Rebekah, as well as Rachel (29:31) and Leah (29:35), enables the writer to reiterate the point that the promised blessing through the chosen seed of Abraham is not to be accomplished merely by human effort. The fulfillment of the promise is only possible at each crucial juncture because of a specific act of God." Sailhamer, *Genesis,* 182.

"The children smashed themselves inside her."[22] The pain is so bad that Rebekah despairs of living. This is another incongruity, that the Lord would answer earnest prayer with such an agonizing pregnancy. But it drives Rebekah "to inquire of the Lord." And the Lord responds to her, verse 23,

> "Two nations are in your womb,
> and two peoples born of you shall be divided;
> the one shall be stronger than the other,
> the elder shall serve the younger."

The Lord's words are cast into synthetic parallelism, that is, the second line develops the first as the fourth line develops the third. Two nations, yes, but divided. One stronger than the other, yes, but the elder shall serve the younger. This last line especially sounds revolutionary. "The law of primogeniture is very old. It asserts that the oldest should be first and favored (cf. Deut 21:15-17). It claims that some have 'natural rights' which cannot be questioned."[23] But here God declares that "the elder shall serve the younger." If the younger will indeed rule the elder, it can only be the result of God's sovereign grace. But it will also involve conflict. The Lord's oracle is "programmatic: it announces the God-determined career of Jacob to be one of conflict culminating in ultimate triumph."[24]

Verse 24, "When her time to give birth was at hand, there were twins in her womb. The first came out red, all his body like a hairy mantle; so they named him Esau." If we have been at all influenced by western cowboy movies, we may think of Esau as the good guy: the tanned, hairy hunter, the man of the field, the straight shooter; and we may think of Jacob as the bad guy: the foxy, deceiving, mommy's boy. But our assessments are wrong.

Esau is Edom, Israel's archenemy. When Israel came out of Egypt, Moses politely requested the king of Edom, "Thus says your *brother* Israel: . . . 'Let us pass through your land. We will not pass through field or vineyard, or drink water from any well; we will go along the King's Highway. . . .' But Edom said to him, 'You shall not pass through, or we will come out with the sword against

22. "The verb *rāṣaṣ* 'smash, crush' is most frequently used figuratively of the oppression of the poor. Literally, it is used to describe skulls being smashed (Judg 9:53; Ps 74:14) or reeds being broken (e.g., Isa 36:6)." Wenham, *Genesis 16–50*, 175.

23. Brueggemann, *Genesis*, 216. Brueggemann continues, "From that assumption of 'natural rights,' a whole theory of societal relationships is derived. In most societies, that network of rights and privileges is taken as normative and ordained of God. . . . This oracle expresses a scandalous decision on the part of God. . . . By the power of his promise, God is free to work his will in the face of every human convention and every definition of propriety."

24. Wenham, *Genesis 16–50*, 173. See ibid. for evidence of the parallel between the programmatic character of this passage for Jacob and Genesis 12:1-3 for Abraham.

you' . . ." (Num 20:14-21). After this, the fighting between Israel and Edom continued. At one point, King David "killed eighteen thousand Edomites. . . . He put garrisons in Edom . . . , and all the Edomites became David's servants" (2 Sam 8:13-14). Edom, however, regained its independence and later sided with Babylonia in driving Judah into exile. Psalm 137:7 recalls this tragedy:

> Remember, O LORD, against the Edomites the day of Jerusalem's fall, how they said, "Tear it down! Tear it down! Down to its foundations!"[25]

Given this enmity between Israel and Edom, it is not likely that the narrator would sketch Esau as a heroic figure. Already at his birth, the narrator describes Esau as "red." In those days "there was a prejudice against the ruddy or redheaded person." Further, he describes "all his body like a hairy mantle." "Hairiness or shagginess seems to have been *eo ipso* a mark of incivility."[26] Ross observes that Esau is portrayed "more like an animal of the field than an ordinary baby. . . . The first child was red-brown *('admônî)*, a description that significantly formed the basis of the sons of Esau, the Edomites. With the description of 'hairy' *(śēʿār)*, there is an allusion to Mount Seir, where Esau later dwelt (Gen 36:8)."[27]

Jacob is also described at birth; not, however, in terms of physical characteristics, but in terms of action. Verse 26, "Afterward his brother came out, with his hand gripping Esau's heel; so he was named Jacob." The original meaning of the name "Jacob" was probably, "may God protect." But the narrator here links Jacob's name to his grabbing Esau's "heel," *ʿăqēb*. This child is a "heel grabber." This name is not a compliment either.[28] In the womb Jacob already reveals himself as a ruthless fighter. "The second twin is seen trying desperately to catch up with the first. The struggle in the womb is obviously going to continue outside. The pattern for the rest of the story is set."[29]

Verse 27, "When the boys grew up, Esau was a skillful hunter, a man of the field, while Jacob was a quiet man, living in tents." The two descriptions of Esau are clear, but the description of Jacob as "a quiet man" has raised many questions for translators. Jacob is literally described as *tām*, and the basic meaning of *tām* is "blameless."[30] How can Jacob be described as "blameless" (as God

25. See also Ezek 25:12-14; Obad 10-19; and Mal 1:4.

26. Vawter, *On Genesis*, 288. See ibid., "In respect to Esau, therefore, the author's word plays go beyond mere cleverness and insinuate a bias against him from the beginning."

27. Ross, *Creation and Blessing*, 440.

28. "An audacious etymology [which] thus reveals an unusual self-irony." Von Rad, *Genesis*, 265.

29. Wenham, *Genesis 16–50*, 177.

30. *The Enhanced Brown-Driver-Briggs Hebrew and English Lexicon*, describes *tām* as "complete, sound, wholesome, morally innocent, having integrity."

pronounced Job "blameless," *tām* [Job 1:8]) in the very narrative where he swindles his brother out of his birthright?[31] The narrator may intentionally characterize Jacob as "blameless" at the beginning of the Jacob cycle in order to link him, on the one hand, to Noah who was "blameless" (*tāmîm,* Gen 6:9) and, on the other hand, to Abraham, who had to be "blameless" (*tāmîm,* 17:1). Jacob is "blameless," or at least should be "blameless" as a true seed of the woman.[32]

The second description of Jacob is that he was "living in tents." Some understand this description simply as a contrast to Esau, who was "a man of the field." But the narrator doesn't say where Esau lived. This description of Jacob "living in tents" may be an allusion to his father Isaac and his grandfather Abraham "living in tents" in the Promised Land.[33] In other words, this may be the narrator's second clue that Jacob is the seed of the woman with whom God will continue the covenant he established with Abraham and Isaac.

The distinction between the twins becomes even more apparent in verse 28, "Isaac loved Esau, because he was fond of game; but Rebekah loved Jacob." Isaac's love for Esau is motivated, strangely, by his appetite for game. Isaac's fondness of game as well as Isaac's love for Esau and Rebekah's love for Jacob will play a major role in the next narrative about Jacob and Esau striving for the blessing of the firstborn (27:1-40).

With the LORD's oracle that "the elder shall serve the younger" and these character descriptions of Esau and Jacob, the stage is set for the next episode. Verse 29, "Once when Jacob was cooking a stew, Esau came in from the field, and he was famished. Esau said to Jacob, 'Let me eat some of that red stuff, for I am famished!'" Esau's language is more coarse than the NRSV translation expresses. The verb conveys the "basic idea of gulping down food. The rabbis used it to describe the activity of cramming food down the throat of an animal."[34] A more literal translation would be, "Let me gulp down [or devour] some of that red, red." The "red, red" in Hebrew is *'ādōm, 'ādōm.* "Therefore," the narrator explains, "he was called *'ĕdôm,* Edom" (v 30).[35]

Jacob calmly responds, verse 31, "First sell me your *bĕkōrâ,* birthright." In that culture, the firstborn male *(bĕkōr)* had the rights and privileges of the

31. Fokkelman, *Narrative Art,* 91, suggests that his "singleness of purpose constitutes Jacob's 'integrity.'"

32. "*Tām* is what Jacob is *supposed* to be as the child of the promise and the one whose name will one day be synonymous with God's people. For now, he is *tām* only potentially (see Gen 35)." Frank Anthony Spina, "Genesis 25:19-34," in Van Harn (ed.), *Lectionary Commentary,* I, 50.

33. See ibid.

34. Ross, *Creation and Blessing,* 450. Cf. Alter, *Art of Biblical Narrative,* 44, "Let me cram my maw."

35. "By the choice of this word [*'ādōm*] in the telling of the story, the narrator sought to describe the Edomites as impulsive and profane as their ancestor." Ross, *Creation and Blessing,* 450.

birthright, *bĕkōrâ*. Jacob now barters for the birthright of the firstborn. "Note the omission of 'please,' the use of 'at once' [first], and the emphatic position of 'to me.' The way Jacob states his demand suggests long premeditation and a ruthless exploitation of his brother's moment of weakness."[36] Jacob lives up to his name: he is a "heel grabber."

Esau responds, "I am about to die; of what use is a birthright to me?"[37] Jacob sees his opportunity to clinch the deal. He says, verse 33, "Swear to me first." Esau can easily go back on an oral agreement, but an oath makes it a legally binding commitment. The narrator comments, "So he swore to him, and sold his birthright to Jacob" (v 33b). Jacob is now in possession of the birthright of the firstborn. At his birth he could merely grab Esau's heel. Now he has surpassed Esau and is legally considered the firstborn.

Verse 34, "Then Jacob gave Esau bread and lentil stew, and he ate and drank, and rose and went his way." It's a tragic ending for Esau: "He ate and drank, and rose and went his way." Four quick verbs. Esau satisfies his physical appetite and "rose and went his way." He simply disappears from the stage, at least for now.

But the narrator cannot forget the significance of what Esau has done in this moment of self-indulgence. He comments in verse 34c, "Thus Esau despised his birthright." "'To despise' *(bāzâ)* something means to treat it as worthless or to hold it in contempt."[38] Hebrew narrators seldom evaluate the actions of their characters, but when they do, we need to pay careful attention. Robert Alter observes, "Esau, the episode makes clear, is not spiritually fit to be the vehicle of divine election, the bearer of the birthright of Abraham's seed. He is altogether too much the slave of the moment and of the body's tyranny to become the progenitor of the people promised by divine covenant that it will have a vast historical destiny to fulfill. His selling of the birthright in the circumstances here described is in itself proof that he is not worthy to retain the birthright."[39] Esau is not worthy.[40]

36. Wenham, *Genesis 16–50*, 178. Cf. Sarna, *Genesis*, 184-87, on the importance of the birthright and the transference of the birthright. "The actual sale of the birthright by one brother to another has a remarkable parallel in one Nuzi document which provides for a certain Kurpazah to part with his future inheritance share for three sheep received immediately from his brother Tupkitilla." Ibid., 186.

37. "Esau's speech and action mark him as a primitive person. He is concerned with immediate gratification of his physical needs and cannot think about abstract things like a birthright. He does not even know what he is eating — 'that red stuff' — just that he needs to eat quickly or 'I'm going to die.' The verbs in v 34 come in a stark sequence, emphasizing the simplistic nature of the man." Berlin, *Poetics*, 39.

38. Ross, *Creation and Blessing*, 451.

39. Alter, *Art of Biblical Narrative*, 45.

40. "When in God's plan Esau lost his birthright and consequently his blessing, there was

But Jacob is not worthy either. The "heel grabber" cannot wait for God to fulfill his promise in his way. He will get the birthright by his own ingenuity. He selfishly plots to obtain the birthright without regard for his brother. He ruthlessly demands the birthright when his brother is down. Later he will deceive his father for the blessing when Isaac is old and blind. Still later he will trick his uncle Laban to line his own pockets. Jacob is a "heel-grabber," a deceiver, a self-made man. He is not worthy to be the seed of the woman. God's choice of Jacob is totally by God's grace.[41]

Although the narrator does not overtly condemn Jacob's selfish striving for the birthright and blessing, the long-range view of his life shows that God did not approve. Whereas Abraham "died in a good old age, an old man and full of years" (25:8), and Isaac died "old and full of days" (35:29), Jacob tells Pharaoh: "The years of my earthly sojourn are one hundred thirty; few and hard have been the years of my life. They do not compare with the years of my ancestors during their long sojourn" (47:9).

The LORD's oracle and these two narratives reveal that, contrary to human customs, in his grace God chooses the younger, the lesser, to be victorious: "The elder will serve the younger." Even when the younger is a selfish "heel-grabber" like Jacob! God has a history of choosing the younger over the older. He chose the younger Abel over Cain, the younger Isaac over Ishmael, here the younger Jacob over Esau, next the younger Joseph over his brothers, then the younger Ephraim over Manasseh, the younger David over his brothers, and the younger Solomon over the older Adonijah. This trail continues into the New Testament when God chooses Jesus — born in a stable, raised in despised Nazareth, poor and lowly — to be *the* Seed of the woman. And Jesus in turn chooses lowly disciples to be his representatives to the nations.

One of Jesus' central teachings is, "Many who are first will be last, and the last will be first" (Matt 19:30). Jesus illustrates this teaching with the parable of the laborers in the vineyard. "The kingdom of heaven is like a landowner who went out early in the morning to hire laborers for his vineyard." They agree to work for "a denarius," "the usual daily wage" (NRSV). The landowner hires more laborers at 9 o'clock, and again at noon, at three o'clock, and at five. These last ones work only one hour but are paid first, and, no doubt to their surprise, each receives a denarius, a full day's wage! Those who had come first are paid last and also receives a denarius, a day's wage. They grumble that they had worked the whole day and now receive the same wage as those who had worked

---

no injustice dealt him. The narrative has shown that he did not want the birthright. He despised it." Sailhamer, *Genesis,* 184.

41. Cf. Deut 7:7-8, "It was not because you were more numerous than any other people that the LORD set his heart on you and chose you — for you were the fewest of all peoples. It was because the Lord loved you and kept the oath that he swore to your ancestors."

only one hour. But the owner says to them, "I choose to give to this last the same as I give to you. Am I not allowed to do what I choose with what belongs to me? Or are you envious because I am generous?" Then Jesus drives home the point of the parable: "So the last will be first, and the first will be last" (Matt 20:1-16). When the last become first in "the kingdom of heaven" (Matt 20:1), they will know that they have not at all earned the kingdom but that it is the King's free gift. God the King is generous. Through his Son Jesus, he gives even us Gentiles the kingdom of God. The last become first only because of God's sovereign grace.[42]

As God assured his embattled people in the Old Testament of the victory, so Jesus assures his embattled New Testament church of the victory. Jesus promises his disciples, "the gates of Hades will not prevail against it [the church]" (Matt 16:18). Jesus acknowledges, "In the world you face persecution." Yet he immediately encourages his followers, "But take courage; I have *overcome* the world!" (John 16:33). The apostle John holds out the same victory for the persecuted church he addresses. He writes about "the spirit of the antichrist, of which you have heard that it is coming; and now it is already in the world. Little children, you are from God, and have *conquered* them; for the one who is in you is greater than the one who is in the world" (1 John 4:4). The one *in us* is no one less than the Spirit of Jesus Christ. He enables us to conquer. John continues, "And this is the victory that conquers the world, our faith. Who is it that conquers the world but the one who believes that Jesus is the Son of God?" (1 John 5:4-5).

In the book of Revelation we again encounter the enmity between the church and the world (e.g., Rev 12). John receives a vision of the last days when the kings of the earth and the beast make war on the Lamb. But "the Lamb will *conquer* them, for he is the Lord of lords and the King of kings, and those with him are called and chosen and faithful" (Rev 17:14). In his sovereign grace God has chosen his weak and despised people to be victorious.

42. Jesus also holds out hope for those who are first. He tells the parable of the prodigal son in which the younger son squanders his inheritance on wild living. When the younger son finally comes home, the father welcomes him with open arms. The older son complains bitterly about this unfairness. But the father says to him, "Son, you are always with me, and all that is mine is yours" (Luke 15:31). It is the parable of the father's love for his children, whether they are the younger or the older.

CHAPTER 14

Jacob's Deception of Isaac

Genesis 27:1-45

This narrative presents the preacher with several difficulties. The most obvious problem is Jacob's deception. Hermann Gunkel writes, "To deceive one's own blind, dying father appears to us simply repugnant. Especially offensive to us, however, is the role which religion plays in this story: a blessing of God is won through deception!"[1] A second problem is the apparent absence of God in this narrative. How does one preach Christ from a narrative dominated by flawed human characters and actions? A third problem is how to apply this narrative to the church today. Since Rebekah and Jacob's deception makes God's oracle come true, does the end justify the means? Or does this narrative address, as some have asserted, the issue of family conflict which only the God of Jacob can overcome?[2] A final difficulty is determining the textual unit — a question on which scholars are quite divided.

Text and Context

Many recent commentaries suggest that the narrative begins at Genesis 26:34 and does not end till 28:9.[3] One of the main arguments for this large textual unit is the structure of six scenes with two characters in each scene. J. P. Fokkelman has sketched this scenic structure as follows:

1. Hermann Gunkel as quoted in White, *Narration and Discourse in the Book of Genesis*, 204.

2. See Walton, *Genesis*, 566-67.

3. Wenham, himself in favor of this large unit, argues, "The division of the material is supported by the Jewish lectionary, which begins a new reading at 28:10, and in recent times by Dillman, Vawter, Coats, and Ross . . . , who all recognize that 26:34–28:9 constitutes a coherent unit within the present book of Genesis." Wenham, *Genesis 16–50*, 202.

A Isaac and the son of the *bĕrakâ/bĕkōrâ* (blessing/birthright), Esau (27:1-5).
  B Rebekah sends Jacob on stage (27:6-17)
    C Jacob appears before Isaac, receives blessing (27:18-29)
    C′ Esau appears before Isaac, receives anti-blessing (27:30-40)
  B′ Rebekah sends Jacob from the stage (27:41-45)
A′ Isaac and the son of the *bĕrakâ/bĕkōrâ* (now, Jacob) (27:46–28:5)[4]

To these six scenes some interpreters add a brief prologue about Esau marrying two Hittite women (Gen 26:34-35) and a brief epilogue about Esau marrying Ishmael's daughter (Gen 28:6-9).[5]

Other interpreters, however, follow Gunkel in arguing for a shorter narrative consisting of four scenes:

Scene I.	(vv 1-4)	The father prepares to bless his older son.
Scene II.	(vv 5-17)	The mother schemes for her younger son.
Scene III.	(vv 18-29)	The younger son deceives the father.
Scene IV.	(vv 30-40)	The father grieves with his older son.
	(vv 41-45)	Transitional conclusion[6]

Although arguments for the longer narrative seem compelling, the shorter text is to be preferred for preaching purposes. A shorter text, of course, is easier to handle in a twenty-minute sermon. In addition to this pragmatic argument, for narrative texts the plot line and the contents[7] trump any perceived rhetorical structure. The main issue in this narrative is, Who will receive the blessing, Esau or Jacob? This issue is resolved when Isaac gives Jacob the blessing and has only a negative[8] blessing left for Esau (Gen 27:40). Verses 41-45 show the outcome of this narrative: Esau wants to kill Jacob, and Jacob has to flee. The following verses (27:46–28:5) can be seen as the setting for the subsequent narratives: Jacob's dream at Bethel and his meeting Rachel. So we can end the literary unit at

4. Fokkelman, "Genesis," in *Literary Guide,* 46; similar to his *Narrative Art in Genesis,* 98. Cf. Fishbane, *Text and Texture,* 49. Wenham, *Genesis 16–50,* 202-3, prefers to see the two "scenes" of Genesis 27:41–28:5 as a single scene.

5. "That this material should be connected to the story can be seen from Rebekah's use of the marriages of Esau within the story and from Isaac's instructions for Jacob not to marry a Canaanite woman (27:46 and 28:1)." Ross, *Creation and Blessing,* 473.

6. Brueggemann, *Genesis,* 231. Similarly von Rad, *Genesis,* 276.

7. The plot line will be followed in the narrative sermon form, while the contents needs to be formulated in a single theme for a unified sermon. The diversity of the larger textual unit makes it practically impossible to produce a unified sermon.

8. Fokkelman, n. 4 above, speaks of "anti-blessing." I use "negative blessing" to indicate that this blessing is the opposite of the positive blessing Jacob received.

Genesis 27:45. For the beginning of the unit, we have to choose between Genesis 26:34 and 27:1. Genesis 26:34, about Esau marrying two Hittite women, is an important part of the background, but 27:1, "When Isaac was old . . ." is a natural beginning for this story. Our preaching-text, therefore, can be Genesis 27:1-45.

As to the context, an important clue for understanding this narrative is the notation that Esau marries two Hittite women (26:34). He thereby shows that he fails to appreciate Abraham's concern that they not intermarry with the Canaanites (24:2-7). By marrying outside the lineage of Terah, Esau "disinherited himself in another way than the sale of his birthright."[9] The sale of his birthright (25:29-34), of course, is another important component for understanding this narrative. In that passage we also read of the favoritism shown by Isaac and Rebekah, including the notation that his physical appetite guided Isaac's feelings: "Isaac loved Esau, because he was fond of game" (25:28). Another important part of the background is the LORD's oracle before the twins are born, "The elder shall serve the younger" (25:23). And even before that, we need to take note of God's blessing of Abraham (12:2-3), which the LORD later gave to Isaac (26:3-6, 24), and which Isaac now passes on to Jacob (27:28-29; 28:3-4).

Literary Features

In addition to the literary characteristics noted above, the most important feature for discerning the theme of this narrative is the repetition of the keyword *bārak,* bless(ing). "The root *brk* occurs no less than 22 times in this chapter, 17 times as a verb and 5 times as a noun."[10] This story is about who will receive the blessing, the older Esau or the younger Jacob. Moreover, the *contents* of the blessing are repeated several times. The first time Isaac declares to Jacob,

"May God give you of the dew of heaven,
  and of the fatness of the earth,
  and plenty of grain and wine.
Let peoples serve you,
  and nations bow down to you.
Be lord over your brothers,
  and may your mother's sons bow down to you.
Cursed be everyone who curses you,
  and blessed be everyone who blesses you!"

(27:28-29)

9. Bruce Birch et al., *A Theological Introduction to the Old Testament,* 87.
10. Hamilton, *Genesis 18–50,* 226.

The second time Isaac says to Esau, "I have already made him [Jacob] your lord, and I have given him all his brothers as servants, and with grain and wine I have sustained him." When Esau insists on a blessing, Isaac can give him only a negative blessing (the opposite of Jacob's blessing) and reassert that he will serve his brother:

> "See, away from the fatness of the earth shall your home be,
>   and away from the dew of heaven on high.
> By your sword you shall live,
>   and you shall serve your brother. . . ."
>
> (27:39-40)

We should also note the important character description at the beginning of this narrative: "Isaac was old and his eyes were dim so that he could not see" (27:1). Isaac's blindness makes the deception possible and plausible. More character description highlights the division in this family: the narrator calls Esau not "*their* son" but "*his* son" (v 5) and Jacob "*her* son" (vv 6, 17). The characters follow suit: Isaac calls *Esau* "my son" (vv 1, 21, 24, 37), while Rebekah calls *Jacob* "my son" (vv 8, 13, 43). Further character description zeroes in on the discovery of this appalling deception: "Isaac trembled violently" (v 33), while Esau "cried out with an exceedingly great and bitter cry" (v 34).[11]

The Plot Line

The distant setting of this narrative is the LORD's oracle to Rebekah, "Two nations are in your womb . . . ; the elder shall serve the younger" (25:23). Preliminary incidents consist of Esau showing himself unfit to carry on the line of the seed of the woman, first by despising his birthright (25:34), and second by marrying two Hittite women (26:34). The conflict begins when the blind Isaac still insists on passing the blessing on to Esau rather than Jacob. Rebekah's scheme to have Jacob take the place of Esau sets the tension: Will Isaac discover the deception? The tension rises as we sense the uncertainty in Isaac. Up to three times he questions, "Who are you, my son?" "Are you really my son Esau?" (vv 18, 21, 24). He wants to feel his hands (v 21) and smell his garments (v 27). Finally, convinced that Jacob is Esau, he blesses Jacob (vv 28-29) — the deception works, the tension dissipates.

11. "The verb *ḥārad* 'tremble' expressed intense fear and alarm by itself. . . . Here it is supplemented by the cognate noun 'trembling' and superlative adjective 'very great.' Hebrew can hardly express Isaac's panic more graphically. . . . [As to Esau's reaction,] once again the Hebrew is remarkable for using a strong verb, 'scream,' with a cognate noun and superlative adjective." Wenham, *Genesis 16–50*, 211.

No sooner has Jacob left Isaac's tent than Esau enters and the tension rises again. When he finds out that he has been duped, Isaac trembles violently. And Esau cries bitterly. Can Isaac perhaps take back Jacob's blessing? No, "blessed shall he be!" (v 33). Esau asks, "Have you not reserved a blessing for me?" (v 36). Not really, "I have already made him *your lord*" (v 37). But Esau insists, "Bless me also, father!" (v 38). Isaac tries, but he can utter only a negative blessing (vv 39-40). The narrrative conflict is resolved: "the elder will serve the younger." The outcome is that Esau seeks to kill Jacob, and Jacob has to flee to Haran (vv 41-45).

We can sketch the plot line of this narrative as a complex plot:

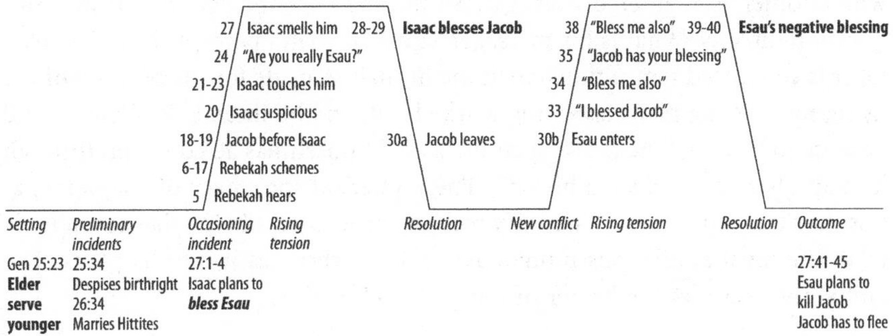

Theocentric Interpretation

Where is God in all this deception? Although God seems to be absent, the name of God is mentioned five times in this narrative. When Rebekah reports to Jacob, she quotes Isaac as saying, "Bring me game . . . that I may bless you *before the Lord* before I die" (v 7). Next, when Isaac asks Jacob, "How is it that you have found it [the game] so quickly, my son?" Jacob has to think fast and answers, "Because the Lord your God granted me success" (v 20). Finally, in blessing Jacob, Isaac speaks of "the smell of a field that the Lord has blessed," and then continues with the blessing, "May God give you . . ." (vv 27, 28).

Jacob's use of the Lord's name in deceiving his father is clearly blasphemous, but the other references are helpful in reminding us that what is at stake here is the *Lord's* blessing. The Lord had first given his blessing to Abraham and then to Isaac. Now it is Isaac's turn to pass this blessing on to the seed of the woman, his son Jacob. For the Lord had declared to Rebekah that "the elder shall serve the younger." Even if Rebekah had not shared this oracle with Isaac, he should have seen in Esau's marriages to Hittite women that Esau was not a fit agent to carry on the line of the seed of the woman. But Isaac is blind — in more ways than one. He insists on passing the blessing on to Esau. Rebekah overhears Isaac's plan and comes up with a plan of her own. It is a sinful plan — deception — but it works: Jacob receives the blessing. The prophecy of the LORD is fulfilled!

This places us before a real dilemma: Jacob the deceiver is not a fit agent either to carry on the line of the seed of the woman. Does God approve of this deception? Although the narrator does not answer this question directly, subsequent events suggest God's disapproval: the outcome of this deception is that Jacob has to flee for his life. Rebekah will never see her beloved son again, and the narrator will not even memorialize her death.[12] And Jacob will be deceived by his uncle Laban with the firstborn Leah (29:26) and later by his own sons with another "slaughtered goat" (37:31). But the narrator does not answer our question directly. What is his message? Von Rad writes perceptively, "The narrator is convinced that ultimately in the human struggle for the blessing of the dying man divine plans are being worked out, and he intends to show it. And Isaac cannot retract the blessing because God himself has acted in and through him and has accomplished his will. The mysterious prophecy of chapter 25:23 was thus truly spoken. . . . The story reckons with an act of God that sovereignly takes the most ambiguous human act and incorporates it into its plans. The guilty one becomes the bearer of the promise!"[13]

Textual Theme and Goal

In the frequent repetition of bless(ing), we have a solid clue to the theme of this narrative. Allen Ross writes, "The central theme of this story is the transference of the blessing to the (presumed) firstborn. From beginning to end, the concern for the blessing predominates. Isaac sought to bestow it, and Esau wanted it. Rebekah heard about it and ensured that Jacob got it. Isaac unwittingly gave it to Jacob, and Esau was furious over having lost it."[14] The challenge is to do justice to the narrative's various components while formulating the theme in one sentence. I suggest the following textual theme: *God can use even human deception to accomplish his plan of extending his covenant blessing to the younger Jacob.*

12. "The narrator memorializes Deborah, her nurse, not Rebekah (35:8) and makes no notice of her death (cf. 23:1-2). At the end of Genesis, however, he notes that she was given an honorable burial with the other patriarchs and matriarchs in the cave of Machpela (see 49:31)." Waltke, *Genesis*, 378-79.

13. Von Rad, *Genesis*, 280. Cf. Waltke, *Genesis*, 381, "God may use human sin to effect his purposes; compare Israel's choice of a king (1 Sam 8; 12); Assyria's boast (Isa 10); the death of Christ (1 Cor 2:8)."

14. Ross, *Creation and Blessing*, 472-73.

As to the narrator's goal, the most obvious goal is to teach Israel that not the elder Esau but their forefather Jacob was the recipient of God's covenant blessing. To arrive at a deeper, more relevant goal, we should raise the question, Why did the narrator wish to teach this fact to Israel? To answer this question, we have to recall that the descendants of Jacob and Esau, Israel and Edom, were sworn enemies. When Israel was on her way to the Promised Land and Moses requested of Edom safe passage through their land, Edom refused (Num 20:14-21). Later when Babylon attacked Jerusalem, Edom sided with Babylon, helping to slaughter Israelites and destroy the walls of Jerusalem. Given this background of recurring battles between Israel and Edom, one of the narrator's goals with this narrative probably is *to reassure Israel that their sovereign God's redemptive plan cannot be derailed.*

Ways to Preach Christ

Given the textual theme, "God can use even human deception to accomplish his plan of extending his covenant blessing to the younger Jacob," what are legitimate roads to Christ in the New Testament?

Redemptive-Historical Progression

One may wish to use the way of redemptive-historical progression to preach Christ from this narrative. We first see God using (overruling) Cain's deception and murder of Abel to select the younger Seth to continue the line of the seed of the woman. In the present narrative, God uses Rebekah and Jacob's deception to accomplish his stated plan of selecting the younger Jacob to continue the line of the seed of the woman. Later God uses David's deception and murder of Uriah, the husband of Bathsheba, to crown eventually the younger Solomon as God's chosen king. In the fullness of time, God uses the deception of Judas as well as leaders of the Jews and Romans to accomplish his redemptive plan that his Son Jesus would die for the sins of the world. Although this way of preaching Christ is possible, it will raise so many questions in the minds of the hearers that it is better to look for a more direct way.

Promise-Fulfillment

The blessing given to Jacob contains the promise, "Let peoples serve you, and nations bow down to you" (v 29). This promise received initial fulfillment when

Israel conquered the nations in Canaan, but it comes to final fulfillment only in Jacob's Son Jesus Christ, to whom has been given "all authority in heaven and on earth," and who calls for the obedience of all nations (Matt 28:18-20). When he comes again, every knee will bow and every tongue confess "that Jesus Christ is Lord, to the glory of God the Father" (Phil 2:10-11).

Typology

There is no clear type of Christ in this narrative.

Analogy

Analogy provides a more direct way of preaching Christ from this narrative: As God used human deception to further his plan of blessing Jacob as the seed of the woman, so God used human deception (that of Judas, the Jews, and the Romans) to further his plan of redeeming his creation and his people through the death of his Son Jesus. This analogy can be supported with a New Testament reference to Jesus' Last Supper with his disciples when he said, "See, the one who betrays me is with me. . . . For the Son of Man is going as it has been determined, but woe to that one by whom he is betrayed" (Matt 22:21-22; see also Acts 2:23).

Longitudinal Themes

One can also use longitudinal themes to preach Christ by tracing God's covenant blessing from Abraham to the younger Isaac, here to the younger Jacob, later to the younger David, and finally to Jesus Christ.

New Testament References

Only Hebrews 11:20 and 12:17 refer directly to this narrative, but neither text establishes a link to Christ.

Contrast

There is no contrast between this message for Israel and its application to the church today.

Sermon Theme and Goal

We formulated the textual theme as, "God can use even human deception to accomplish his plan of extending his covenant blessing to the younger Jacob." Since the New Testament does not change this message, the sermon theme can be very similar. I would make the theme a little more general so that it covers God's plan for Jacob/Israel as well as his plan for Christ and the church. We can, therefore, formulate the sermon theme as follows: *God can use even human deception to accomplish his redemptive plan.*

Our sermon goal should be in harmony with the narrator's goal. We formulated that goal as, "to reassure Israel that their sovereign God's redemptive plan cannot be derailed." In line with this goal, we can formulate our sermon goal as *to reassure God's people that our sovereign God's redemptive plan cannot be derailed.*

This particular goal shows that the message is aimed at hearers who *lack* assurance that God will accomplish his redemptive plan. The sermon could start by exploring our doubts about God accomplishing his plan of reestablishing his beautiful kingdom on this earth. Christians today are becoming disheartened. All we hear about are wars and rumors of wars. "Where is the promise of his coming?"

But there is a more engaging way to start. After the Scripture reading the hearers will undoubtedly have many questions about Jacob's deception and how that is related to God's plan. So in this case it is better not to begin with a contemporary issue but to stay *in* the story.

Sermon Exposition

Isaac and Rebekah's marriage is on the rocks! And it had looked so good in the beginning. When Abraham sent his servant back to his native land to find a wife for Isaac, the LORD led him straight to Rebekah. And when her family did not want to let her go right away, Rebekah volunteered to go. "I'll go," she said, just like Abraham before her. I'll go all the way to Canaan to marry a man I don't know. After the long journey, she saw Isaac in the distance and modestly veiled herself. Isaac took her into his mother's tent, she became his wife, and, we read, "he loved her." It was a match made in heaven.

When Rebekah did not get any children, "Isaac prayed to the LORD for his wife." And the LORD heard his prayer: Rebekah conceived. But it was a painful pregnancy, so Rebekah went "to inquire of the LORD." Notice how close they lived to the LORD. The LORD responded to her request with an oracle, a prophecy:

"Two nations are in your womb,
  and two peoples born of you shall be divided;
the one shall be stronger than the other,
  the elder shall serve the younger."

(25:23)

Strange, "the elder shall serve the younger." In that culture the firstborn had significant advantages. The firstborn would inherit "a double portion"[15] and receive a special blessing. Yet the LORD declared his plan: "The elder shall serve the younger."

Finally the twins were born. The first one came out "red, all his body like a hairy mantle." They named him Esau. The second one was right behind him, grabbing Esau's heel. They named him Jacob. When the boys grew up, Esau became a skillful hunter while Jacob became a herdsman. And this is where their parents' marriage breakdown began. The narrator tells us that "Isaac loved Esau, because he was fond of game." Can you believe it? Isaac loved his hunter son because he would bring him mouth-watering venison. Something is wrong here, loving your son because he satisfies your appetite for game. The narrator goes on to say, "but Rebekah loved Jacob" (25:28). Here is the heart of their marriage problem: favoritism. "Isaac loved Esau . . . , but Rebekah loved Jacob."

"Once when Jacob was cooking a stew, Esau came in from the field, and he was famished. Esau said to Jacob, 'Let me eat some of that red stuff, for I am famished!'" Jacob calmly responded, "First sell me your birthright." "Esau said, 'I am about to die; of what use is a birthright to me?'" (25:29-32). And Esau sold his birthright for a bowl of stew. Like his father Isaac's actions, Esau's were guided by his stomach. The narrator comments, "Thus Esau despised his birthright" (25:34). Esau despised his birthright. He was not worthy of the privilege of being the firstborn.

Later Esau shows a second time that he is not worthy of the privilege of being the firstborn. We read in chapter 26:34, "When Esau was forty years old, he married Judith daughter of Beeri the Hittite, and Basemath daughter of Elon the Hittite." Esau marries two Hittite women! You recall how adamant Abraham was that Isaac not marry a Canaanite woman. The servant had to travel over four hundred miles to Haran to find a wife for Isaac. Abraham did not wish to compromise God's call that Abraham and his family be a separate people. He did not wish to risk losing God's promise of the land by intermarrying with the Canaanites who were destined to lose the land (Gen 15:16). But Esau never considered God's special call and promise. He just acted on his physical

15. The firstborn is to receive "a double portion of all that he [the father] has; since he is the first issue of his virility, the right of the firstborn is his" (Deut 21:17).

appetites and married two Hittite women.[16] Esau was not worthy of the privilege of being the firstborn. He was not worthy of representing God's special people. But was Jacob any more worthy?

This is where our text picks up the story: chapter 27:1, "When Isaac was old and his eyes were dim so that he could not see, he called his elder son Esau and said to him, 'My son'; and he answered, 'Here I am.' He said, 'See, I am old; I do not know the day of my death. Now then, take your weapons, your quiver and your bow, and go out to the field, and hunt game for me. Then prepare for me savory food, such as I like, and bring it to me to eat,[17] so that I[18] may bless you before I die.'"

Isaac is blind in more ways than one. He should have seen that Esau's marriages to Hittite women compromised God's plan that Abraham and his seed form a separate nation. He should have noticed that Esau was not worthy of representing God's special people. But Isaac pushes blindly ahead. Isaac, like Esau, is controlled by his appetite. In this chapter, the narrator repeats the word *game* eight times and *tasty food* six times.[19] Before he dies, Isaac wishes to savor once more the delicious game and then give the blessing to Esau.

Fortunately for Jacob, Rebekah overhears Isaac's plan to cut her son Jacob out of his will.[20] Immediately she springs into action. There is no time to waste. She calls Jacob over and says to him, verse 6, "I heard your father say to your brother Esau, 'Bring me game, and prepare for me savory food to eat, that I may bless you before the LORD before I die.' Now therefore, my son, obey my word as I command you. Go to the flock, and get me two choice kids, so that I may prepare from them savory food for your father, such as he likes; and you shall take it to your father to eat, so that he may bless *you* before he dies.'"

The plan is simple: while Esau is out hunting to bring home game for his

16. "Esau's errors are threefold. He has contracted the marriage himself, thus bypassing his parents; he married exogamously rather than endogamously; he has gone against the honor of his clan group by intermarrying with the native women." Hamilton, *Genesis 18–50*, 210.

17. "If the narrator expects us to compare this deathbed scene with Abraham's (chap. 24), he implies that Isaac and Esau are both alike in putting appetite before principle, self-indulgence before justice, immediate satisfaction before long-term spiritual values." Wenham, *Genesis 16–50*, 215.

18. Literally, "my soul." "Four times the text says, '*nepeš* may bless' (vv 4, 9, 25, 31). The point is that Isaac wanted to bless Esau with all his resources — with all the blessing that he had received and with all his desire and vitality." Ross, *Creation and Blessing*, 476.

19. "The narrator's repetition of these terms in conjunction with the phrase 'tasty food I like' and its variants (27:4, 9, 14) suggests that the narrator's focus is on Isaac's sensuality, not the role the meal played in the blessing ritual." Waltke, *Genesis*, 377.

20. "It was customary for a dying man to call all his sons to his side to receive an appropriate blessing. Deliberately . . . Isaac calls only Esau to receive his blessing, and he leaves out Jacob." Wenham, *Genesis 16–50*, 215.

father, Rebekah will prepare two young goats into a delicious meal for Isaac. Then Jacob can serve his father the food and receive the blessing.

But Jacob spots a major problem in this scheme. He says to his mother, verse 11, "Look, my brother Esau is a hairy man, and I am a man of smooth skin. Perhaps my father will feel me, and I shall seem to be mocking him, and bring a curse on myself and not a blessing." This is a huge risk for Jacob, incurring a curse instead of a blessing. Israel would have known this risk, for God's law stipulates, "Cursed be anyone who misleads a blind person on the road" (Deut 27:18). But Rebekah waves the objection aside and declares, verse 13, "Let your curse be on me,[21] my son; only obey my word, and go, get them for me." The modest Rebekah has become quite domineering: "*obey* my word, and go, get them for me" (cf. 27:8 and 43).

So Jacob obeys his mother, takes two young goats, brings them to her, and watches as she carefully prepares them. But another problem looms. Even if Isaac will be fooled into thinking that the young goats are venison, how will he be fooled into thinking that the smooth Jacob is the hairy Esau? Rebekah has her plan ready. She has some of Esau's clothes in the tent and puts them on Jacob. Then she takes the skins of the young goats and puts them on Jacob's hands and the smooth part of his neck.[22] Finally she hands Jacob the food she has prepared, and Jacob is on his own. Will this deception work? Will my father recognize my voice? Will the goatskins fool him? Will he taste the difference between young goats and venison? And when is Esau coming back? Jacob must have been sweating! But he cannot back out now.

Verse 18, "So he went in to his father, and said, 'My father'; and he said, 'Here I am; who are you, my son'?" The first test, "Who are you, my son?" Jacob is ready for this one: "I am Esau your firstborn. I have done as you told me; now sit up and eat of my game, so that you may bless me" (v 19). Jacob can hardly wait to get it over with: sit up, eat, and bless me. Please hurry, for Esau is on the way!

But Isaac is in no hurry. He responds, verse 20, "How is it that you have found it so quickly, my son?" A second test. Now Jacob has to think fast. He blurts out, "Because the Lord your[23] God granted me success." He uses the name of the Lord to promote his deception. Pure blasphemy![24]

21. "The fact that she concedes the possibility of receiving a divine curse suggests that she is motivated more by her personal bias for Jacob (25:28) than by a desire to facilitate God's will decreed in 25:23." Turner, *Genesis*, 117-18.

22. "Rebekah must believe that her husband is extremely incapacitated, for he will not be able, she thinks, to distinguish between human hair and goatskins. She really thinks she can pull the wool over Isaac's eyes." Hamilton, *Genesis 18–50*, 217.

23. *Your God* is "consistent with Jacob's language elsewhere (31:5, 42; 32:9). Not until his safe return from Haran did he speak of the Lord as his own God (cf. 28:20-22; 33:18-20)." *NIV Study Bible*, Genesis 27:20, n.

24. "The low point in Jacob's conversation with his father is his statement that he is back

Isaac is not convinced. He says to Jacob, verse 21, "Come near, that I may feel you, my son, to know whether you are really my son Esau or not." A third test. Jacob approaches his father who feels his hands. Isaac wavers: "The voice is Jacob's voice, but the hands are the hands of Esau." The narrator adds, "He did not recognize him [as Jacob], because his hands were hairy like his brother Esau's hands; so he blessed him," that is, he was about to bless him.[25]

But still Isaac wavers. He asks again, "Are you really my son Esau?" The fourth test. Jacob has now been put on notice that his voice is giving him away. So he responds as briefly as he can, "I am." Then Isaac says, verse 25, "Bring it to me, that I may eat of my son's game and bless you." So Jacob brings the food and wine to him, and Isaac eats and drinks. Good, he doesn't notice that he is eating goat meat. Isaac seems to enjoy the meal. But it is all taking so long. Any time Esau can enter the door and the deceit will be discovered.

At long last Isaac says to Jacob, verse 26, "Come near and kiss me, my son." A fifth test. His heart beating in his throat, Jacob comes near and kisses his blind father. When Isaac smells the scent of Esau's clothes, he is finally convinced that this is indeed Esau. And he blesses Jacob. He exclaims, verse 27,

> "Ah, the smell of my son
> is like the smell of a field
> that the LORD has blessed."

And then follow three blessings:

The first blessing is fertility of the field:

> Verse 28, "May God give you of the dew of heaven,
> and of the fatness of the earth,
> and plenty of grain and wine."

The second blessing is political supremacy:

> Verse 29a, "Let peoples serve you,
> and nations bow down to you.
> Be lord over your brothers,
> and may your mother's sons bow down to you."

---

so quickly because God just put the game in front of him. Here is an appeal to deity to cover up duplicity." Hamilton, *Genesis 18–50*, 220. For a contrary opinion, see Turner, *Genesis*, 119 and 121.

25. The blessing is not pronounced until verse 27. See Turner, *Genesis*, 118, and Wenham, *Genesis 16–50*, 209.

This blessing echoes the birth oracle (25:23) but goes beyond it. Not only will the elder serve the younger, but peoples will "serve you, and nations[26] bow down to you."

The third blessing pertains to reciprocal curses and blessings:

Verse 29b, "Cursed be everyone who curses you,
and blessed be everyone who blesses you!"

This blessing echoes the blessing Abraham originally received (12:3). "According to this blessing, therefore, Jacob is not only blessed; he is to be a form of mediator of blessings for others."[27]

Jacob now has a threefold blessing and leaves as quickly as possible. He makes it in the nick of time. The narrator tells us, verse 30, "As soon as Isaac had finished blessing Jacob, when Jacob had *scarcely gone out* from the presence of his father Isaac, his brother Esau came in from his hunting. He also prepared savory food, and brought it to his father. He said to his father, 'Let my father sit up and eat of his son's game, so that you may bless me.'"

Isaac is understandably confused. He asks, "Who are you?" Esau answers, "I am your firstborn son, Esau." And suddenly it dawns on Isaac that he has been deceived. Wasn't the voice Jacob's voice? We read in verse 33, "Then Isaac trembled violently, and said, 'Who was it then that hunted game and brought it to me, and I ate it all before you came, and I have blessed him? — *yes, and blessed he shall be!*'" Once given, Isaac cannot take back the blessing.

Esau also understands this. Verse 34, "When Esau heard his father's words, he cried out with an exceedingly great and bitter cry, and said to his father, 'Bless me, me also, father!'" "Isaac's extreme panic is matched by his son's extreme distress."[28] But Isaac answers, "Your brother came *deceitfully,* and he has taken away your blessing" (v 35). Isaac minces no words about Jacob's heinous sin: Deceit! Jacob had deceived his blind father and walked off with the blessing Isaac wanted to give to Esau. Esau complains bitterly, verse 36, "Is he not rightly named Jacob [that is, he supplants, he deceives[29]]? For he has supplanted me

26. "The plural points to the comprehensiveness of Israel's dominion. The blessing of universal dominion ultimately falls on Christ and his church (Matt 28:18-19)." Waltke, *Genesis,* 380.

27. Brodie, *Genesis as Dialogue,* 309.

28. Wenham, *Genesis 16–50,* 211.

29. See Fokkelman, "Genesis," 46, "Sound play and reversal come together and become cogent in a chiasm forged by the duped Esau when he ascribes to the name 'Jacob' the meaning 'deceiver,' in 27:36a, which can be scanned as a two-line strophe:

Isn't he called *ya'ăqōb?*
He has deceived *(ya'qĕbēnî)* me twice:
my *bĕkōrâ* he took away,
and now he takes away my *bĕrakâ!*"

these two times. He took away my birthright; and look, now he has taken away my blessing." And grabbing at straws he asks, "Have you not reserved a blessing for me?"

Isaac responds, verse 37, "I have already made him your lord, and I have given him all his brothers as servants, and with grain and wine I have sustained him. What then can I do for you, my son?" But Esau insists, "'Have you only one blessing, father? Bless me, me also, father!' And Esau lifted up his voice and wept." His pitiful wail breaks Isaac's heart.

So Isaac decides to try to bless his son Esau as well, but the words that come out of his mouth are hardly a blessing; they are more like a negative blessing, the opposite of what he had promised Jacob. Isaac had promised Jacob fertility of the field; to Esau he announces, verse 39,

> "See, *away from*[30] the fatness of the earth shall your home be,
> and *away from* the dew of heaven on high."

Esau and his descendants will live away from the fertile fields of Canaan in the arid region of Edom. Isaac had promised Jacob political dominance; to Esau he declares, verse 40,

> "By your sword you shall live,[31]
> and *you shall serve* your brother;
> but when you break loose,
> you shall break his yoke from your neck."

"You shall serve your brother." As the LORD had announced to Rebekah in the oracle, "The elder shall serve the younger." But there is a ray of hope for Esau's descendants. At some future time, Esau, that is Edom, will also experience freedom by breaking Israel's yoke from their neck.[32]

The narrative concludes with Esau's venomous reaction. Verse 41, "Now Esau *hated* Jacob because of the blessing with which his father had blessed him, and Esau said to himself, 'The days of mourning for my father are approaching;

30. The ambiguous preposition *min* translated as "of" in verse 28 is here translated as "away from." "Most modern commentators agree that it here has a privative sense, 'away from,' because this makes best sense in the context. Esau is being condemned to a wandering existence like Cain or Ishmael, haunting the dry wilderness to the south and east of Canaan." Wenham, *Genesis 16–50,* 212. Esau is another Cain, driven "away from the soil" (4:14).

31. Esau is another Ishmael, "with his hand against everyone" (16:12).

32. "The descendants of Esau (Edomites) make a move for independence as early as the reign of Solomon (1 Kings 11:14-22), and sporadically thereafter. The total independence of Edom from Judah came as a result of a revolt against Jehoram king of Judah (2 Kings 8:20-22; 2 Chron 21:8-10)." Hamilton, *Genesis 18–50,* 228.

then *I will kill my brother* Jacob.'" "I will kill my brother" reminds us of Cain killing his younger brother Abel. Here is the third indication that Esau is not the seed of the woman. First he despised his birthright. Then he married two Canaanite women. And now he plans to murder his brother. Esau, like Cain before him, is the seed of the serpent.[33]

But Jacob receives the LORD's blessing. His descendants will inherit the fertile Promised Land. Jacob is the seed of the woman through whom God will accomplish his redemptive plan. But, you object, Jacob is a deceiver! Does God approve of deception? Certainly not: God's law forbids bearing false witness (Exod 20:16). And the narrator shows clearly that Rebekah and Jacob did not benefit from this deception. Rebekah has to send Jacob far away to her brother Laban (27:43). She will never see her beloved son again. Meanwhile his uncle Laban will deceive Jacob by giving him his firstborn daughter Leah instead of the beautiful Rachel.[34] And later Jacob's sons will deceive their father by claiming that his favorite son, Joseph, has been killed. As proof they produce Joseph's cloak covered in the blood of a goat. Jacob deceived his father with two young goats; his sons deceive him with the blood of a goat.

But the narrator's point in this narrative is not that God disapproves of deception. His message is much more profound. His point is that God can use even human deception to accomplish his plan of extending his covenant blessing to the younger Jacob. When Israel read this story, Edom was one of her archenemies. The Edomites were the descendants of Esau. With this narrative about Jacob and Esau the narrator reassures Israel that God did indeed extend his covenant blessing not to Esau but to their forefather Jacob. The descendants of Esau have to be satisfied with the parched land of Edom. According to God's covenant blessing, the fertile land of Canaan belongs to Israel. Although Jacob received that blessing by deceiving his father, Isaac had no business passing on God's blessing to Esau. "The elder shall serve the younger" (25:23). That was God's good plan for Israel and that plan cannot be derailed.

God can use even human deception to accomplish his redemptive plan. The greatest deception of all time was the trial of Jesus. At the Last Supper, Jesus said, "The Son of Man goes *as it is written of him,* but woe to that one by whom the Son of Man is betrayed" (Matt 26:24). A little later, Judas betrayed Jesus with a kiss (Matt 26:48-49). Judas would be held responsible for his betrayal, but Jesus would die as it was "written of him." God can use even human deception to accomplish his redemptive plan.

Later "the chief priests and the whole council were looking for *false* testi-

33. Cf. Waltke, *Genesis,* 381; Ross, *Creation and Blessing,* 480.

34. "With his indignant protest to Laban ['Why have you deceived me'], Jacob unwittingly condemns himself." Fishbane, *Text and Texture,* 55.

mony against Jesus so that they might put him to death." At last they found two false witnesses who agreed and the council decided: "He deserves death" (Matt 26:59, 66). God can use even human deception to accomplish his redemptive plan.

Then they took Jesus to Pilate, who represented the Roman Empire. Although Pilate knew that Jesus was innocent and even washed his hands in innocence, saying "I am innocent of this man's blood, . . . he handed him over to be crucified" (Matt 27:24, 26). God can use even human deception to accomplish his redemptive plan.

On the day of Pentecost Peter preached to the crowd, "Jesus of Nazareth . . . , *handed over to you according to the definite plan* and foreknowledge of God, you crucified and killed by the hands of those outside the law. But God raised him up, having freed him from death, because it was impossible for him to be held in its power" (Acts 2:22-24).[35] God can use even human deception to accomplish his redemptive plan! Jesus died to pay the penalty for sin once for all. And he rose again to reestablish God's good kingdom on this earth.

We do not see much of this kingdom today. We hear of wars and rumors of wars. We experience disasters and disease. Like Israel of old, we may become disheartened. Will we ever see the new heaven and the new earth "where righteousness is at home" (2 Pet 3:13)? Did God's redemptive plan fail? The message that comes to us today is that God can use even human deception to accomplish his redemptive plan. God is sovereign over all. His good plan cannot fail!

35. Cf. Acts 4:27-28, "For in this city, in fact, both Herod and Pontius Pilate, with the Gentiles and the peoples of Israel, gathered together against your holy servant Jesus, whom you anointed, to do whatever your hand and *your plan had predestined* to take place."

CHAPTER 15

Jacob's Dream at Bethel

Genesis 28:10-22

It is rather difficult to discern the plot line in this narrative. Where is the conflict and what is the resolution? One of the challenges in preaching this narrative is, therefore, to detect and communicate the tension in this story. Another challenge is to keep the application focused on the point of the narrative, for there are several elements in the story that preachers may be tempted to apply directly to people today. For example, as Jacob made a vow that the LORD would be his God, so each of the hearers should make a vow accepting the LORD as their God. Or, as Jacob made a vow to tithe, so the hearers should pledge to tithe.[1] Unlike Jacob, however, we should not set any conditions.[2] Applying mere elements of the narrative not only undermines the unity of the sermon but also short-circuits the application process in bypassing Israel. We should first ask, How did Israel hear this story? What was the application for them? Only then can we look for analogies — not between Jacob and us, but between Israel and the church today.

Text and Context

In contrast to the last narrative, the literary unit here is easy to determine. The most obvious clue is the change of location: "Jacob left Beersheba and went toward Haran" (28:10). While the preceding narratives have taken place in Beersheba, this one takes place in Bethel. Genesis 29:1 informs us of another change of location: "Then Jacob went on his journey, and came to the land of

1. For the development of the theme of tithing from the Old Testament to the New Testament, see Waltke, *Genesis,* 397-98.

2. See, e.g., Walton's application "presuming on grace," *Genesis,* 574-77.

the people of the east." The following narratives take place in Haran. The literary unit, therefore, is Genesis 28:10-22. This is "the first dream narrative in the Old Testament."[3]

The context is of critical importance to understand this narrative. The LORD meets Jacob as he is about to leave the Promised Land. Jacob has just deceived his blind father and stolen the blessing from his elder brother Esau. Now Jacob is on the run because Esau threatened to kill him. He has become a fugitive. His mother and father urged him to seek refuge with his uncle Laban, who lives in Haran, the place from which God called Abraham to the Promised Land.

When Abraham came to Canaan he built an altar to the LORD, first in Shechem and next near Bethel, the place where Jacob now finds himself. The LORD had given wonderful promises to Abraham: the LORD would be his God and would make of him a great nation, give him the land of Canaan, and through him bless all the families of the earth. Now the LORD meets Jacob at Bethel and makes himself known as "the LORD, the God of Abraham your father and the God of Isaac." Then the LORD extends all these wonderful promises to Jacob: "The land on which you lie I will give to you and to your offspring; and your offspring shall be like the dust of the earth . . . ; and all the families of the earth shall be blessed in you and in your offspring" (28:13-14). The LORD also promises to be with Jacob and bring him safely back to the Promised Land (v 15). After a twenty-year exile, Jacob will return to Canaan, where he will meet God again, first at Peniel, where he will wrestle with God and where God will change his name from Jacob to Israel (Gen 32), and later at Bethel (Gen 35).

Literary Features

The narrator again is omniscient. He travels with Jacob from Beersheba to Haran, observes his actions, knows his dream, the LORD's words, and Jacob's fear and response. The narrator shows his hand most clearly when he steps out of the narrative to tell his readers, "but the name of the city was Luz at first" (28:19).

The narrative consists of two acts:

I. Verses 10-15, "Jacob's preparations for sleep and his dream."
II. Verses 16-22, Jacob's "awakening and his reactions to the dream."[4]

3. Westermann, *Genesis,* 200.

4. Bar-Efrat, *Narrative Art in the Bible,* 103.

More detailed repetition further reveals two parallel panels in the two acts:

"place" (v 11 3×)	"place" (vv 16, 17 [19])
"stones," "headrest" (v 11)	"stone," "headrest" (v 18)
"I am really with you" (v 15)	"If God will be with me" (v 20)
"guard you wherever you go" (v 15)	"guard me on the journey I am undertaking" (v 20)
"bring you back to this land" (v 15)	"return in peace to my father's house" (v 21)
"I shall not leave you" (v 15)	"And the LORD is my God" (v 21)[5]

For determining the focus of this passage, a chiastic structure is more helpful than parallel panels. There may be a chiastic structure in this passage, centering on the LORD's promises in vv 14-15.[6]

A "He came to a certain place" (v 11)
  B "Taking one of the stones . . . , he put it under his head" (v 11)
    C "The top of it reaching to heaven" (v 12)
      D "The angels of God" (v 12)
        E "The LORD stood above it" (v 13)
          F The LORD's promises (vv 14-15)
        E′ "The LORD is in this place" (v 16)
      D′ "The house of God" (v 17)
    C′ "This is the gate of heaven" (v 17)
  B′ "He took the stone that he had put under his head" (v 18)
A′ "He called that place Bethel" (v 19)

The Plot Line

The setting of this narrative is Jacob's deception to receive the blessing, Esau's plan to kill Jacob, and Rebekah and Isaac sending Jacob to Haran (27:1–28:5). The conflict begins when Jacob is about to leave the Promised Land: "Jacob left Beersheba and went toward Haran" (28:10). After all his plotting and lying to receive God's promise of the land of Canaan, Jacob is leaving the land, and Esau remains behind in the Promised Land. Has Esau won out after all? "Jacob is a fugitive now outside all the protections of conventional meanings and social guarantees."[7]

5. Wenham, *Genesis 16–50,* 219.

6. Adapted from Fokkelman's analysis of the position of key terms in this narrative. *Narrative Art in Genesis,* 71.

7. Brueggemann, *Genesis,* 241.

The tension rises as Jacob comes to a certain place and the sun sets. Where will he spend the night? Who will protect him from the dangers that lurk in the darkness? The tension rises still further when Jacob dreams about a stairway from earth to heaven, and angels of God ascending and descending, and suddenly he sees the LORD himself. Even in his dream, Jacob must have crouched in fear. He had just deceived his blind father; he had even used the LORD's name in vain. Had the LORD come to punish him for his sins? Will the LORD curse him for his evil deeds?

The conflict begins to resolve when the LORD pronounces over him not curses but blessings — the blessings first given to Abraham. The LORD will give him the land and seed, and make him a blessing to all families of the earth. But Jacob is still moving away from the Promised Land. What will happen to him? The conflict is fully resolved when the LORD promises that he will be with him and will keep him and bring him safely back to the land.

The outcome relates Jacob's reaction to meeting the LORD. Jacob sets up his headrest for a pillar, pours oil on top of it, and calls the place Bethel, which means "the house of God." He vows that the LORD will be his God, that there he will build God's house, and that he will bring the tithe to God.

We can, therefore, sketch the plot line of this narrative as a single plot:

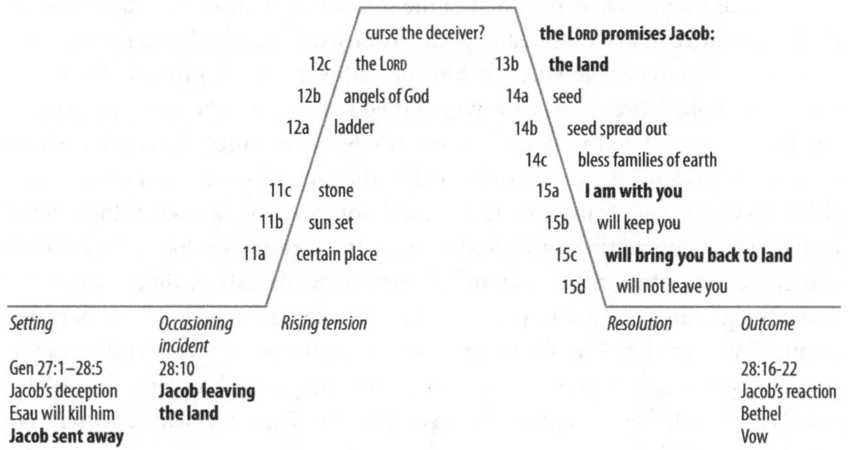

Theocentric Interpretation

God clearly takes the initiative in this narrative. Jacob is not looking for God, yet God meets him in a dream: "The LORD stood beside him and said, 'I am the LORD, the God of Abraham your father and the God of Isaac'" (v 13). Then the LORD proceeds to give him the promises he had given earlier to Abraham and Isaac. Moreover, in the light of Jacob's predicament of leaving the Promised

Land, the LORD gives him special promises: "Know that I am with you and will keep you wherever you go, and will bring you back to this land; for I will not leave you until I have done what I have promised you" (v 15).

In response to the dream and God's words, Jacob exclaims: "Surely the LORD is in this place! . . . This is none other than the house of God" (vv 16-17). Jacob calls the place Bethel, that is, "house of God." Then Jacob makes a vow to God: "If God will be with me . . . , then the LORD shall be my God, and this stone . . . shall be God's house; and of all that you give me I will surely give one tenth to you" (vv 20-22).

Textual Theme and Goal

Jacob had taken Esau's birthright by calloused bartering and the blessing by deception. As Isaac sends Jacob away from the land, he reiterates the blessing (28:3-4). In this narrative, however, the LORD himself gives Jacob the patriarchal blessing he had earlier given to Abraham (12:2-3) and to Isaac (26:3-4). We might be tempted, therefore, to formulate the theme as follows: "The LORD himself extends the patriarchal blessing to Jacob."

But this theme covers only half of the plot line and misses the specific focus of this narrative. As Jacob is leaving the Promised Land, the LORD not only extends the patriarchal blessings to him but adds a special promise for Jacob: "Know [behold][8] that I am with you and will keep you wherever you go, and will bring you back to this land; for I will not leave you until I have done what I have promised you" (v 15). As confirmed by the repetition of "I am with you . . . will keep you . . . will bring you back . . . will not leave you" as well as the symbol of the ladder connecting earth and heaven, these promises form the heart of this narrative. "Within this carefully constructed narrative, those words become the guiding motif and principle that governs the course of the narrated events."[9] We can therefore formulate the specific theme of this narrative as follows: "The LORD will be with Jacob wherever he goes." And since Jacob also stands for Israel,[10] we can make the textual theme, *The LORD will be with Jacob/Israel wherever they go.*

8. "The 'behold' of verse 15 breaks new ground — pay attention!" Brueggemann, *Genesis,* 244.

9. Sailhamer, *Genesis,* 196.

10. "Verse 14 reports that Jacob's *offspring* will be as numerous as the dust of the earth, that *Jacob* ('you' singular in Hebrew) will spread out, and that the families of the earth will be blessed through *both Jacob and his offspring;* the references to the patriarch and his descendants are grammatically intertwined in such a way that Jacob's fate is not easily distinguished from that of his descendants." Diana Lipton, *Revisions of the Night,* 71.

In seeking to discover the narrator's goal in transmitting this message to Israel, we have to put ourselves in the place of Israel. Imagine the nation of Israel after lengthy enslavement in Egypt at the border of the Promised Land. How would they hear God's message, "The LORD will be with Jacob/Israel wherever they go"? Imagine Israel hearing this story *in* the land of Canaan. Hostile enemies are invading the country: perhaps Edomites, or Moabites, or Philistines, or Assyrians. How would Israel hear this message when their existence in the land is threatened by enemies? Imagine Israel in exile in Babylon hearing this narrative. Jacob himself would go into "exile" for some twenty years, but the LORD promised to be with him and to bring him back to the land. Imagine the comfort: the LORD promises to be with Israel wherever they go. Even in Babylon, God is with us (cf. Isa 41:10; 43:2). We can therefore formulate the narrator's goal as, *To comfort Israel with the LORD's promise that he will be with them wherever they go.*

Ways to Preach Christ

Given the theme "The LORD will be with Jacob/Israel wherever they go," let us explore the ways we can move to Jesus Christ in the New Testament.

Redemptive-Historical Progression

At this stage of redemptive history, as Jacob is about to leave the Promised Land, the LORD promises Jacob that he will be with him. Later, when the LORD mandates Moses to bring Israel out of Egypt, he promises, "I will be with you" (Exod 3:12). Moses, in turn, encourages Israel to capture Canaan: "Have no fear or dread of them, because it is the LORD your God who goes with you; he will not fail you or forsake you" (Deut 31:6). The LORD also assures Joshua, "As I was with Moses, so I will be with you; I will not fail you or forsake you" (Josh 1:5). Still later, when Israel is in exile, the LORD again assures his people of his presence: "When you pass through the waters, I will be with you" (Isa 43:2; cf. 41:10). In the fullness of time, God comes to his people in his Son, Jesus. He is called "Emmanuel," which means, "God is with us" (Matt 1:23; cf. John 14:9-10; Col 2:9). After Jesus rises from the dead, he promises his disciples, "Remember, I am with you always, to the end of the age" (Matt 28:20). When Jesus ascends to heaven, he pours out the Holy Spirit to dwell in God's people (Acts 2:33). On the last day, when Jesus comes again, God will dwell with his people; "they will be his peoples, and God himself will be with them" (Rev 21:3).

Promise-Fulfillment

A more direct way to Jesus in the New Testament is the road of promise-fulfillment. The Lord promised that he would be with Jacob and return him to the land. This promise is fulfilled when Jacob returns to Canaan. But the promise takes off again and finds further fulfillment in the life of the nation of Israel when they return to the land from slavery in Egypt, and later when a remnant returns to the land from exile in Babylon. The promise that the Lord will be with his people finds its ultimate fulfillment in Jesus Christ, Emmanuel, "God is with us" (Matt 1:23), who sends the Holy Spirit to dwell in God's people (Acts 2:33) and will usher in the new creation where "God himself will be with them" (Rev 21:3).

Typology

One can also use typology to preach Christ from this narrative. The ladder Jacob sees in his dream is a symbol of the theme "God is with us." The ladder connects heaven and earth, with angels ascending and descending. God is not absent from this earth (as in deism); God is connected with his creation. The ladder is a symbol of this connection. The ladder is the "mediator" between heaven and earth. In the New Testament, Jesus suggests that the ladder prefigures Jesus as mediator. Nathanael meets Jesus and exclaims, "Rabbi, you are the Son of God! You are the King of Israel!" Jesus responds, "Very truly, I tell you, you will see heaven opened and the angels of God ascending and descending upon the Son of Man" (John 1:49, 51).[11] Jesus alludes to Jacob's ladder, but a reference to the ladder is missing. The point is that Jesus himself is the ladder. He is the link between heaven and earth, the "one mediator between God and humankind" (1 Tim 2:5). As Jesus will say later, "I am the way, and the truth, and the life. No one comes to the Father except through me" (John 14:6).

Analogy

The most direct way to preach Christ from this narrative is the road of analogy. In formulating the analogy, we can take our cue from the goal: "To comfort Israel with the Lord's promise that he will be with them wherever they go." The analogy then becomes, As God promised Israel that he would be with them wherever they go, so Jesus promises the church that he will be with them wher-

11. See further Hamilton, *Genesis 18–50*, 250.

ever they go. The New Testament supports this bridge to Christ with Jesus' promise to his church, "I am with you always, to the end of the age" (Matt 28:20).

Longitudinal Themes

The theme of God's presence with his people can be traced from Jacob (28:15; 31:3; 32:9; 46:4) to Joseph (39:2, 21, 23; 48:21) to Israel (50:24), where God's presence becomes part of the priestly blessing: "The Lord bless you and keep you" (Num 6:24). Later, when the nation of Judah is fearful of being annihilated, God gives them a sign: "Look, the young woman is with child and shall bear a son, and shall name him Immanuel" (Isa 7:14). The sign is, God is with us.

Matthew sees further fulfillment of this sign when Jesus is born: "All this took place to fulfill what had been spoken by the Lord through the prophet, 'Look, the virgin shall conceive and bear a son, and they shall name him Emmanuel,' which means 'God is with us'" (Matt 1:22-23). Jesus encourages his followers, "Abide in me as I abide in you" (John 15:4), and promises them, "I am with you always, to the end of the age" (Matt 28:20). When Jesus ascends to heaven, God's presence continues to be with the church through the Holy Spirit (Acts 2; 1 Cor 3:16; 6:19). One of the marks of the new creation is that God will dwell with his people: "they will be his peoples, and God himself will be with them" (Rev 21:3).

New Testament References

Aside from the New Testament references above, a few others could possibly be used to link this narrative to Jesus Christ in the New Testament. Matthew 18:20 quotes Jesus as saying, "Where two or three are gathered in my name, I am there among them." In Romans 8:38-39 Paul reiterates the same theme negatively: no hardships and no powers in all creation "will be able to separate us from the love of God in Christ Jesus our Lord." The author of Hebrews may allude to this narrative (more likely to Deut 31:6) when he writes, "For he has said, I will never leave you or forsake you" (13:5), but he does not link this promise to Jesus Christ.

Contrast

The New Testament confirms this message of the Old Testament that God is with his people.

Sermon Theme and Goal

The textual theme functions as the cornerstone for the sermon theme. The textual theme was, "The Lord will be with Jacob/Israel wherever they go." The New Testament expands this message to God's people everywhere (the church). Therefore we need to broaden the sermon theme to, *The Lord will be with his people wherever they go.*

The narrator's goal for Israel was, "To comfort Israel with the Lord's promise that he will be with them wherever they go." In harmony with this goal, we can make our goal in preaching this sermon, *To comfort God's people with his promise that he will be with them wherever they go.* This particular goal indicates that the need addressed is that God's people sometimes feel forsaken by God.

Sermon Exposition

The sermon introduction could set the target for this sermon by exploring the need addressed. For example, one can illustrate how people can get caught up in a particular sin and feel forsaken by God. Then one can transition either to Israel's sin and exile and then to Jacob's or directly to Jacob's sin and "exile."

Jacob is running for his life. All his planning and scheming have backfired. He wanted God's blessing so badly he could taste it. God's blessing included the promise of many offspring and possession of the land of Canaan. But Jacob was the younger twin, and his father Isaac was intent on passing the blessing on to his brother Esau. So Jacob had first swindled Esau out of his birthright. And just a few days ago he had deceived his blind father by dressing in Esau's clothes and pretending to be the hairy hunter. When father Isaac asked him how he could be back so soon with game, Jacob had even taken God's name in vain. He said to his father, "Because the Lord your God granted me success" (27:20).

Jacob would do almost anything to get the blessing: lying, deceiving, even taking God's name in vain. Jacob received the blessing, but it didn't do him much good. Esau was furious and looked for an opportunity to kill his brother (Gen 27:41). And so Jacob's planning and scheming backfired. He became a fugitive. He is running for his life, away from Esau, yes, but also away from his parental home and away from the Promised Land.

The story begins in verse 10, "Jacob left Beer-sheba [where his parental home was] and went toward Haran." Haran is the place from which the Lord had called his grandfather Abraham. The Lord had promised the land of Canaan to Abraham and his offspring. But it seems that Jacob will not inherit the land. Esau lives in the Promised Land, and Jacob is forced to flee. He has to move far away from Esau, more than 400 miles north. The journey will take about a month. And Jacob will probably have many adventures on the way. But the narrator selects just one important event that happened on Jacob's long journey.

Jacob is just a few days from his home when he comes to a certain place. The narrator underscores the significance of this place by using the word *place* three times.[12] Verse 11, "He came to a *certain place* and stayed there for the night, because the sun had set. Taking one of the stones of *the place,* he put it under his head and lay down in *that place.*" Without knowing it, Jacob has arrived at the place where his grandfather Abraham, upon reaching the Promised Land, had built an altar to the LORD (12:8). But Jacob has never met this God. He had heard his grandparents and parents talk about Yahweh, the LORD, but Jacob has personally never met him.

Jacob just "happens" upon this place. The sun has set and darkness makes further travel impossible. The fugitive is forced to sleep out in the open. This is dangerous. Who knows what animals are lurking in the darkness. Jacob quickly finds a level place and uses one of the stones as a headrest. He must have been worried about the dangers around him and the long, dangerous journey ahead: strange places and people, ferocious animals, and foreign gods. Exhausted, Jacob falls asleep.

During the night he has an awesome dream. As later Bible stories show, God sometimes revealed himself and his plans in dreams — think of Joseph's dreams of his brothers bowing down to him (37:5-11), and the dreams of the chief cupbearer, the chief baker, and of Pharaoh (40:1–41:36). So God reveals himself to Jacob in a dream. In his dream, verse 12, Jacob sees "a ladder [or stairway][13] set up on the earth, the top of it reaching to heaven; and the angels of God were ascending and descending on it." Heaven and earth are not separate worlds; the ladder links heaven and earth. And God's angels are "ascending and descending on it." "Angels (messengers) descended to embark on their errands throughout the earth and ascended when returning with reports."[14]

Verse 13 is ambiguous. The NRSV translates, "And the LORD stood beside him," with a note that "beside him" can also be translated "above it." The TNIV takes this option, "There *above it* [the ladder] stood the LORD." Although the translation can go either way, the latter is to be preferred, partly because it com-

12. "The threefold mention of *hamāqôm* 'the place' in this verse and then again in vv 16, 17, 19, culminating in the renaming of the place in v 19, hints at the significance of 'the place.'" Wenham, *Genesis 16–50*, 221.

13. As can be seen in the NRSV note, the Hebrew *sullām* can also be translated as *stairway* or *ramp.* Von Rad, *Genesis,* 284, comments, "The Hebrew word (*sullām* from *sālal,* 'heap up') points to a ramp, or, in any case, a kind of stairlike pavement."

14. Walton, *Genesis,* 571.

pletes the picture of the dream.[15] Try to visualize it. Jacob sees "a ladder set up on the earth, the top of it reaching to heaven; and the angels of God were ascending and descending on it. There above it [the ladder] stood the LORD." "The image of Yahweh at the top of the ladder forms a fitting climax to the whole and fits in with the idea that angels report back to him after patrolling the earth (1 Kgs 22:19-22; Job 1:6-8; 2:1-3; Zech 1:10)."[16]

In the New Testament, Jesus refers to this dream of Jacob.[17] When Philip brings Nathanael to Jesus, Jesus says to him, "Here is truly an Israelite in whom there is no deceit!" "Since Jacob, whose name was changed to Israel, was notable for guile as the deceiver of his father, it would seem that Jesus was comparing Nathanael favorably with his ancient ancestor."[18] Nathanael asks, "Where did you get to know me?" Jesus answers, "I saw you under the fig tree before Philip called you." Nathanael exclaims, "Rabbi, you are the Son of God! You are the King of Israel!" Jesus responds, "Very truly, I tell you, you will see heaven opened and the angels of God ascending and descending upon the Son of Man" (John 1:49, 51).

Here is Jacob's dream of heaven opened and angels of God ascending and descending. But notice that the ladder is missing. The angels are ascending and descending upon the Son of Man, that is, on Jesus. Jesus is saying that he himself is the ladder. He is the link between heaven and earth. As Jesus will later claim, "I am the way, and the truth, and the life. No one comes to the Father except through me" (John 14:6). Jesus is the way to God. Jesus is the mediator (1 Tim 2:5). No one comes to the Father except through Jesus. Jesus connects heaven and earth. Jesus is the ladder to heaven.

Jacob must have been scared to death of the vision he saw. Remember that he had just deceived his father and used the LORD's name in vain. And now the LORD meets him. Will the LORD punish him for his evil deeds? Will the LORD curse him?

15. There are several other reasons. First, the suffixes of verse 12, "the top of it" and "on it," both refer to the ladder. One would expect that the next suffix (v 13) would refer to the same ladder: "above it [the ladder] stood the LORD." Wenham, *Genesis 16–50*, 222, also points out that "the vision is described through Jacob's eyes, so 'over me' might be expected, if Jacob was the referent (cf. 40:9, 'before me')." Moreover, the context (v 12) speaks of a ladder with its top "reaching to heaven," that is, the dwelling place of God. This tilts the translation of verse 13 to, "there above it [the ladder] stood the LORD." For arguments for "beside him," see Hamilton, *Genesis 18–50*, 240-41.

16. Wenham, *Genesis 16–50*, 222.

17. One must weigh the merits of suspending the narrative at this point in order to follow the typological link to Jesus. One can justify it here because the hearers have just heard about the ladder and the angels ascending and descending. It also offers some variety from the usual pattern of completing the narrative before moving to Christ. The challenge will be to get the hearers back in the story.

18. Edmund Clowney, *Unfolding Mystery*, 66-67.

But amazingly, the LORD does not curse Jacob. Instead he blesses him with rich promises. The LORD declares, verse 13, "I am the LORD, the God of Abraham your father and the God of Isaac;[19] the *land* on which you lie I will give to you and to your offspring." The God of his fathers is speaking to Jacob and gives him the same promise he gave to Abraham, "To your offspring I will give this land" (12:7). But Abraham received this promise when he first *came* to this land; Jacob receives it when he is about to *leave* the land. So the LORD reaffirms first the promise of land.[20]

The LORD continues by extending to Jacob all the covenant promises he had given to Abraham at various times. Verse 14, "Your offspring shall be like the dust of the earth, and you shall spread abroad to the west and to the east and to the north and to the south [cf. 13:14-16];[21] and all the families of the earth shall be blessed in you and in your offspring"[22] (cf. 12:3).

This is astounding. Almighty God seeks out this fleeing scoundrel Jacob and tells him that all these rich promises given to Abraham and Isaac are now for him. He receives the blessings God bestowed on the Patriarchs. And it is completely God's initiative. Jacob has done absolutely nothing to deserve God's covenant promises. In fact, he had messed up badly. He had tried so hard to grasp God's blessings with his own cunning, and look where it got him: a fugitive running away from the Promised Land. One cannot grasp and take God's blessings. One can only receive them gratefully. God is the Giver. It is God's initiative. It is all God's grace!

But God is not finished speaking. He has a special promise for Jacob, who is setting off on a dangerous journey *away* from the Promised Land. God had promised Abraham, "I will establish my covenant between me and you, and your offspring after you throughout their generations, for an everlasting covenant, *to be God to you* and to your offspring after you" (17:7). Now God unpacks for Jacob what this promise means concretely. God says, verse 15, "Know that I

19. These titles recall "the great promises and blessings given to them and anticipates their reaffirmation and reapplication to Jacob." Wenham, *Genesis 16–50*, 222.

20. "Prominence is attached to the promise of the land, for it is mentioned before the seed promise and stressed by the word order." Ross, *Creation and Blessing*, 490.

21. "There are, of course, other passages (12:7; 15:18; 17:8; 24:7) containing the promise of land, but in no other are the terms used so close as between 28:13-14 and 13:14-16. It is noteworthy that both passages are associated with Bethel." Wenham, *Genesis 16–50*, 223.

22. "Isaac had sent Jacob on his way with two elements of the threefold Abrahamic blessing, those of nationhood and land (28:3-4). At Bethel, God himself repeats those elements but adds the third — the nations will be blessed through Jacob and his descendants." Turner, *Genesis*, 125. Hamilton comments, "God has chosen Jacob and Jacob's family as the means whereby God will mediate his blessing to the world. In spite of Jacob's behavior he is a link in the chain. Thus far in the Jacob story the emphasis has been on Jacob's 'getting' the blessing. Here the emphasis shifts to 'being' a blessing." *Genesis 18–50*, 242.

am with you and will keep you wherever you go, and will bring you back to this land; for I will not leave you until I have done what I have promised you."

The covenant promise "to be God to you" consists of three specific promises. The first is, "Know that I am with you." Even as Jacob leaves the Promised Land, he will not go alone. He will not leave God behind. God will go with him. This is a wonderful comforting thought in a culture where gods were considered local deities who give "protection only within their own territories."[23] The true God will cross borders with Jacob into other countries where other so-called gods reign.

To reinforce this thought, God says secondly, "I will keep you wherever you go." Heading for Haran, "I will *keep* you wherever you go." "The word presents the image of the shepherd who will *protect* Jacob. Israel deals with the good shepherd who cares for and protects the helpless sheep in every circumstance."[24] The import of the word *keep* is best expressed in Psalm 121:7-8,

> The Lord will keep you from all evil;
>   he will keep your life.
> The Lord will keep your going out and your coming in
>   from this time on and forevermore.

Thirdly, God promises, "I will bring you back to this land." This is the most specific promise of all. Jacob, unlike Cain (Gen 4:14), will not be a fugitive the rest of his life. He will not even be a resident alien in a foreign land. The Lord will bring him back to the land of his birth, the Promised Land.

Finally the Lord sums up his promises by assuring Jacob, "I will not leave you until I have done what I have promised you," that is to say, You can count on it that I will not leave you or forsake you, but I will be with you to do what I have promised you.

God's promises are pure grace. Jacob has messed up his life with his ambition, callousness, deceit, lying, and using the Lord's name to cover his deceit. Jacob deserves God's curse. But instead God comes to him with wonderful promises. And there are no conditions. It is pure grace.

When Jacob wakes up, he is astonished. He exclaims, verse 16, "Surely the Lord is in this place — and I did not know it! And he was afraid,[25] and said, 'How awesome is this place! This is none other than the house of God, and this is the gate of heaven.'"

23. *NIV Study Bible,* Gen 28:15, n.

24. Brueggemann, *Genesis,* 245.

25. "Perhaps the best parallel to the emotions conveyed by this verse is that found in 3:10. Adam, after his sin of disobedience, hears God walking in the garden and is afraid. Jacob, after his scenario involving his brother and father, sees God standing by him and is afraid." Hamilton, *Genesis 18–50,* 245.

Jacob is afraid, for, like Isaiah, he had received a glimpse of the sovereign God. "Woe is me! I am lost, for I am a man of unclean lips . . . ; yet my eyes have seen the King, the LORD of hosts!" (Isa 6:5). Jacob, the sinner, has seen the LORD of hosts. And he thinks of this place where God revealed himself to him as "the house of God" and the "gate of heaven." This is the place where heaven and earth are connected.[26]

At daybreak, Jacob gets up and takes the stone he had used as a headrest and places it upright as a pillar. He consecrates this pillar with oil as a shrine to the LORD.[27] And he calls the place Bethel, that is, "house of God."

Then Jacob makes a vow, saying, verse 20, "If God will be with me, and will keep me in this way that I go, and will give me bread to eat and clothing to wear, so that I come again to my father's house in peace, then the LORD shall be my God, and this stone, which I have set up for a pillar, shall be God's house; and of all that you give me I will surely give one tenth to you." "If . . . , then. . . ." Is Jacob, the calloused bargainer and deceiver, trying to strike a deal with God with a conditional, "If . . . , then . . ."? And this after God has given Jacob his unconditional promises?

Although many commentators hold that Jacob is still in a bargaining mood, it is unlikely that Jacob so soon loses the fear of the LORD. The "if . . . , then . . ." construction is the standard construction for vows: If God will do certain things, then the person who makes the vow will do certain things.[28] "Vows were not made to induce God to do something he was not willing to do. They were made to bind the worshiper to the performance of some acknowledged duty. Jacob made his vow on the basis of what God had guaranteed to do. He was thus taking God at his Word and binding himself to reciprocate with his own dedication."[29] In this case, Jacob is saying, "If God will be with me . . . and return me safely to the Promised Land [as he just promised], then the LORD shall be my God [not only the "God of Abraham" and the "God of Isaac" (v 13)

26. "'The gate of heaven' . . . , i.e., that narrow place where according to the ancient world view all intercourse between earth and the upper divine world took place." Von Rad, *Genesis*, 284.

27. "Perhaps we are to understand through these linguistic repetitions that the stone raised by Jacob is a symbol of the stairway set on the ground. This possibility is heightened by the parallel mention of the pillar's *top* (*rōʾš*, lit. 'head'), which Jacob anoints in an act of consecration, and the stairway's *top* (*rōʾš*, v 12), which reaches the sky. Both the pillar and the stairway have a 'head.'" Hamilton, *Genesis 18–50*, 246.

28. See, e.g., Judg 11:30-31 and 2 Sam 15:8. See further Hamilton, *Genesis 18–50*, 248-49.

29. Ross, *Creation and Blessing*, 493. Cf. Kidner, *Genesis*, 158, "The vow was no more a bargain than any other vow (the 'if' clause is inherent in the form); it would be fairer to say that Jacob was taking the promise of v 15 and translating the general into the particular. Further, he rightly saw his tithe (22b) not as a gift but as a giving back." Cf. Hamilton, *Genesis 18–50*, 247, "His vow underscores how utterly dependent Jacob is upon his God."

but *my* God], and this stone, which I have set up for a pillar, shall be God's house; and of all that you give me I will surely give one tenth to you."[30] Jacob's promise to return to the LORD one tenth of what the LORD gives him shows the beginning of his maturation from a "grabber" to a giver.

In Jacob's vow the central message of this narrative about God's presence and protection is repeated: "If God will be with me, and will keep me. . . ." That is God's promise. It is a promise God will later repeat to Jacob as he instructs him to return to the Promised Land: "Return to the land of your ancestors and to your kindred, and *I will be with you*" (31:3). And again, when Jacob is old and decides to bring his whole family to Egypt, God promises, "*I myself with go down with you* to Egypt, and I will also bring you up again" (46:4). The LORD promises to be with Jacob wherever he goes!

Israel later experiences the reality of these promises of God. The promise of God's presence becomes part of the priestly blessing pronounced on the Israelites: "The LORD bless you and keep you" (Num 6:24). When the nation of Judah is fearful of being annihilated by its enemies, God gives them a sign: "Look, the young woman is with child and shall bear a son, and shall name him Immanuel" (Isa 7:14). The sign is, God is with us!

Even when the LORD punishes Israel's sins with the Babylonian exile, he promises to be with them. God says to them,

> Do not fear, for *I am with you,*
> do not be afraid, for I am your God.
>
> (Isa 41:10)

> When you pass through the waters, *I will be with you.*
>
> (43:2)

The promise of God being with his people comes to its ultimate fulfillment in Jesus Christ. Matthew announces the birth of Jesus by quoting from Isaiah 7: "'Look, the virgin shall conceive and bear a son, and they shall name him Emmanuel,' which means, 'God is with us'" (Matt 1:23). As nothing else, Jesus' birth shows that God is with us. And before Jesus ascends into heaven, he promises his followers, "Remember, I am with you always, to the end of the age" (Matt 28:20). As God promised Israel that he would be with them wherever they go, so Jesus promises his church that he will be with them wherever they go.

The church today may live in this confidence that through Jesus the connection between heaven and earth, between God and humanity, has been re-

30. "In making the LORD his God and offering tithes, Jacob is imitating the actions of his grandfather Abraham (cf. 17:7; 14:20). He is also, as father of the nation, setting a pattern for all Israel to follow." Wenham, *Genesis 16–50*, 225.

stored. We are not on our own in an evil world. God is with us on our journey to the Promised Land, the new earth "where righteousness is at home" (2 Pet 3:13).

Sometimes we may indeed feel forsaken by God. Perhaps we have become ensnared in a certain sin and now feel forsaken by God. Try as we may, we cannot seem to find the way back to God. However, we can never attain God's blessings through our efforts. God's blessings are his gift to us; we can only receive them with gratitude. Jesus invites us, "Come to me, all you that are weary and are carrying heavy burdens, and I will give you rest. Take my yoke upon you, and learn from me, . . . and you will find rest for your souls" (Matt 11:28-29). "And remember," Jesus says, "I am with you always, to the end of the age" (Matt 28:20).

CHAPTER 16

Jacob's Marriage to Leah and Rachel

Genesis 29:1-35

One of the challenges in preaching this narrative is to avoid superficial, moralistic applications. Unfortunately, respected commentators sometimes guide preachers in this direction. For example, Jacob the deceiver being deceived by uncle Laban lends itself to moralizing: "The lesson is that, even though God's people may experience God's blessing on their endeavors, God will effectively discipline them by making them painfully aware of their unresolved sins."[1] Another commentator suggests, "(1) 'Out of evil came good, out of ugliness, beauty'; (2) 'he who turns to evil will, at the end, find it turned against him.' These two morals are appropriate to Jacob's life here as he learns both lessons."[2] The question, of course, is not what lessons Jacob learned but what "lesson" the narrator wants Israel and the church to learn.

A renowned preacher avoids the pitfall of moralizing but instead zeros in on Jacob's "dysfunctional family," equates it with dysfunctional families today, and concludes that "God reaches down into some of the biggest messes we can create and wrenches out of it healing and goodness."[3] Although none of the applications above are unbiblical, they are not the point of this narrative. Even if Israel knew the concept of dysfunctional families, it is not likely that they would have looked for the narrative's relevance in that direction.

A second difficulty in preaching this narrative is to delineate a proper and workable preaching unit, for the narrative that begins with Genesis 29:1 is actually not completed until 31:55.[4] Obviously, this large unit contains more infor-

1. Ross, *Creation and Blessing*, 503. Cf. Hartley, *Genesis*, 261, "Jacob finds himself married to Leah, the unwanted older daughter, powerfully portraying the theme of reaping what one sows."

2. Walton, *Genesis*, 596.

3. William Willimon, *Great Preachers*, series 1, videotape (Worcester, PA: Odyssey Productions, 1997).

4. "The extended narrative of Jacob's sojourn with Laban is a continuous, relatively self-

mation than one can handle in a single sermon, so we have to decide on the limits of a smaller narrative.

Text and Context

The beginning of this narrative is easy to detect. After Jacob's vow at Bethel, Genesis 29:1 begins, "Then Jacob went on his journey, and came to the land of the people of the east." A new location indicates a new narrative. Most commentaries end this first unit with verse 30, Jacob marrying Rachel and serving Laban for another seven years. The next narrative, Genesis 29:31–30:24, records the birth of the children in three sets of four: Leah four sons (29:31-35); Bilhah and Zilpah each two sons (30:1-13); Leah two sons and a daughter, and Rachel a son (30:14-24).

Although this division has much to commend it because the narrative conflict has been resolved at 29:30 — Jacob now being married to the woman he loves — it leaves little by way of narrative outcome or conclusion. That outcome is recorded in verses 31 to 35, "When the Lord saw that Leah was unloved, he opened her womb; but Rachel was barren. . . ." The unwanted Leah bears four children in quick succession: Reuben, Simeon, Levi, and Judah. "Then she ceased bearing" (v 35). The conflict of the next narrative begins with Rachel's demand for children (30:1), which is resolved when she finally bears Joseph (30:24). Genesis 29:31-35, then, does double duty: it functions as the outcome of the first narrative and as the setting for the next narrative.[5] As our preaching-text, therefore, we can select Genesis 29:1-35.[6]

As to the context, this wedding narrative of Jacob must be understood against the background of the wedding narrative of Isaac (Gen 24). These two narratives have much in common: There the Lord had promised Abraham and Isaac numerous offspring (22:17); here the Lord has promised Jacob numerous offspring (28:14). There the narrative conflict was that Sarah had died and her only son Isaac was still single; here the narrative conflict is that Jacob is still single — unless he finds a wife and begets children, there will not be offspring "like the dust of the earth"; in fact, there will be no Israel. There Abraham told

contained account. It is continuous in the development of its main plot. . . . It is self-contained in that it begins with Jacob's entry into Laban's sphere (29:1) and it ends with a departure (31:55)." Brueggemann, *Genesis,* 249. George Coats, "Strife without Reconciliation," 95, writes, "The story as a whole appears to me to be a novella, like the Joseph story."

5. In connection with Genesis 32, Wenham observes, "It is characteristic of Genesis to have a trailer for what follows at the close of the previous section (e.g., 4:25-26; 9:18-29; 32:2-3 [1-2])." *Genesis 16–50,* 287.

6. Fishbane, *Text and Texture,* 55-56, also identifies Genesis 29:1-35 as a unit and 30:1-24 as the next unit focusing on: "Rachel is barren and conceives."

his servant, "You will not get a wife for my son from the daughters of the Canaanites, among whom I live, but will go to my country and my kindred and get a wife for my son Isaac" (24:3-4); here Isaac told Jacob, "You shall not marry one of the Canaanite women. Go at once to Paddan-aram to the house of Bethuel, your mother's father; and take as a wife from there one of the daughters of Laban, your mother's brother" (28:1-2). There the servant came to the well at the city of Nahor (24:10) in the district of Haran; here Jacob comes to a well where he finds shepherds from Haran who know "Laban son of Nahor" (29:4-5). There the servant met Rebekah, sister of Laban; here Jacob meets Rachel, daughter of Laban. And in both narratives Laban comes running to the well to greet these strangers and invite them to his home.

But the *contrast* between Abraham's servant acquiring a wife for Isaac and Jacob acquiring a wife for himself is even more telling. Abraham's servant was entirely dependent on the LORD's guidance: Abraham said to him, "The LORD . . . will send his angel before you" (24:7); arriving at the well, the servant prayed fervently to the LORD and set up a test to make sure he would bring back the wife "appointed" by the LORD (24:12-14); when he found out that Rebekah was a relative of Abraham, he "bowed his head and worshiped the LORD and said, '. . . the LORD has led me on the way to the house of my master's kin" (24:27). The narrator's emphasis cannot be missed: in his providence, the LORD has led the servant to the future wife for Isaac. But where is the LORD in the wedding narrative of Jacob? Jacob never prays to the LORD for guidance. He never thanks the LORD for leading him to his relatives. Is Jacob, the deceiver, seeking to fulfill the LORD's promise of numerous offspring with his own ingenuity and scheming?

The narrative of Laban's deception of Jacob must also be read against the background of Genesis 27, Jacob's deception of his blind father, as well as the background of the LORD meeting Jacob at Bethel and promising him offspring "like the dust of the earth" and the LORD's presence wherever he goes (28:14-15).

Literary Features

The narrator provides some significant character description of Leah and Rachel: "Leah had weak eyes, but Rachel had a lovely figure and was beautiful" (v 17, TNIV). Although the NRSV's translation, "Leah's eyes were *lovely*," is possible, it is more likely that *rakôt* (soft) must be some negative quality since Leah is contrasted with the beautiful Rachel. "What makes eyes 'soft' . . . is unclear; most commentators think it means they had no fire or sparkle, a quality much prized in the East."[7] More character description is found in the narrator's com-

7. Wenham, *Genesis 16–50*, 235.

ments that Jacob "loved Rachel more than Leah" (29:30); that "the LORD saw that Leah was unloved" (v 31); that Leah herself felt that she was "hated" (v 33);[8] and that "Rachel was barren" (v 31).

Additional character description may be found in the dialogue, especially the first words spoken by a character.[9] Laban's first recorded words to Jacob are, "Surely you are my bone and my flesh!" (v 14). With these words the narrator probably signals more than mere kinship; he probably intimates that Laban and Jacob are cut from the same cloth (cf. 2:23): both greedy deceivers.

The narrator also uses repetition as a clue to understanding his message. Note the threefold repetition in verse 10, "Now when Jacob saw Rachel, the daughter of *his mother's brother Laban,* and the sheep of *his mother's brother Laban,* Jacob went up and rolled the stone from the well's mouth, and watered the flock of *his mother's brother Laban.*" Bar-Efrat comments, "It was Jacob's love for his mother's relatives (the very close relationship between Jacob and his mother is made clear more than once in the previous chapters) that caused him to go up and roll the stone single-handed from the mouth of the well."[10] More frequent and more important repetition is found in verses 15-30, where the narrator repeats the word *ʿbd,* "work," "serve," seven times (29:15, 18, 20, 25, 27 [2× in Hebrew], 30), "always with reference to Jacob serving Laban to wed Laban's daughters. . . . Jacob has entered a dark night of slavery. . . . Significantly, this key word is the same one used with reference to Esau serving Jacob (25:23; 27:29, 37, 40)."[11]

The narrative consists of six scenes:

1. Jacob and the shepherds (vv 1-8);
2. Jacob meets Rachel (vv 9-12);
3. Jacob meets Laban (vv 13-14);
4. Jacob serves Laban seven years (vv 15-20);
5. Laban deceives Jacob with Leah (vv 21-30);
6. Rachel barren while Leah receives four sons (vv 31-35).

The Plot Line

The setting of this narrative is Isaac's instruction to Jacob, "Go at once to Paddan-aram to the house of Bethuel, your mother's father; and take as wife

8. "Of the unloved Leah's feelings of vexation we learn a good deal through the little naming-speeches she makes after the birth of each son." Alter, *Art of Biblical Narrative,* 185.

9. See ibid., 75, on the importance of "the initial words spoken by a personage."

10. Bar-Efrat, *Narrative Art in the Bible,* 117.

11. Waltke, *Genesis,* 403. Cf. Fokkelman, *Narrative Art in Genesis,* 130.

from there one of the daughters of Laban, your mother's brother" (28:2). At the beginning of the long journey, the LORD meets Jacob at Bethel and promises him not only that the LORD will be with him and keep him but also, "your offspring shall be like the dust of the earth" (28:14).

Genesis 29:1-14 sketches the preliminary incidents. Jacob arrives at "the land of the people of the east" (v 1); at a well he meets shepherds who know Laban and point out his daughter Rachel coming with her father's sheep. When Rachel arrives at the well, Jacob rolls the heavy stone from the well's mouth, waters her flock, and identifies himself as her cousin from Canaan. Rachel runs home to tell her father Laban, and Laban in turn runs to the well to meet Jacob and invite him to his house, where he stays for a month.

The conflict is generated in verse 15 when Laban wants Jacob to serve him and asks him, "Tell me, what shall your wages be?" Before Jacob can respond, the narrator interrupts the building tension by informing us that Laban has two daughters; the older Leah, and the younger Rachel: "Leah had weak eyes, but Rachel had a lovely figure and was beautiful" (v 17, TNIV). Gordon Wenham states, "This interruption by the narrator supplies some necessary background information about Leah and Rachel that has been withheld hitherto but is necessary for understanding the story. This interruption also serves to heighten suspense. We are forced to wait a little before we hear whether Jacob will bid for Rachel and whether it will be accepted."[12]

The tension rises when Jacob offers to serve Laban seven years for his younger daughter Rachel. Can Jacob, in that culture, just skip over the older daughter? And will seven years be enough? Happily, Laban agrees, and Jacob serves him seven years (v 20). But the conflict intensifies when at the end of seven years Laban fails to act on his agreement with Jacob. Jacob has to go to Laban and admonish him, "Give me my wife" (v 21). In response Laban throws a party, and in the dark of night brings his older daughter Leah to Jacob. When will Jacob discover this deception? And when he does, will he divorce Leah and insist on marrying Rachel? Jacob wakes up in the morning light, looks at his wife, and behold, it is Leah! He storms out to confront Laban: "Why have you deceived me?" Laban calmly proposes that he complete the week of the feast with Leah and then he can marry Rachel, provided he will serve Laban for another seven years. Will Jacob accept this proposition to serve the deceiver Laban another seven years? He longs to go back to his mother. She had said his stay with uncle Laban would only be "a few days" (27:44). Now he has been gone seven years and Laban demands that he stay another seven. What will Jacob do?

The tension begins to subside when Jacob agrees to Laban's proposal: he will keep Leah, marry his beloved Rachel at the end of the week, and serve Laban an-

12. Wenham, *Genesis 16–50*, 235.

other seven years. At the end of the week Laban gives Jacob Rachel as his wife. The narrator's comment, "He loved Rachel more than Leah" (v 30), spells more trouble ahead, just as favoritism spelled trouble for Rebekah and Isaac.

The outcome of this narrative is the initial fulfillment of the LORD's promise to Jacob of a multitude of offspring. For although Jacob's beloved Rachel is barren, Leah in quick succession receives four sons: Reuben the eldest, Simeon, Levi, and Judah. "Then she ceased bearing" (vv 31-35) — end of story for now.

We can sketch this narrative, therefore, as a single plot:

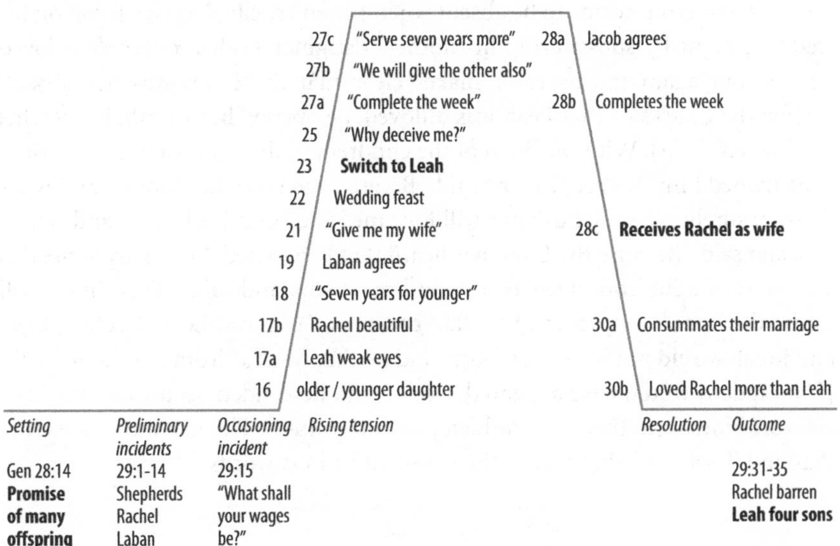

Theocentric Interpretation

In contrasting Jacob's journey to Haran with that of Abraham's servant, we asked, Where is the LORD in this narrative? Unlike the servant, Jacob never prays to the LORD for guidance and never thanks the LORD for leading him to his relatives. Is Jacob, the deceiver, still seeking to fulfill the LORD's plan with his own ingenuity and scheming?

Although Jacob may well be relying on his own ingenuity, the narrator makes sure that his readers sense God's guiding hand in Jacob's life. For this narrative follows upon the LORD meeting Jacob at Bethel and promising him, "Know that I am with you and will keep you wherever you go" (28:15). The very next narrative describes Jacob's successful month-long journey in just one verse, "Then Jacob went on his journey, and came to the land of the people of the east" (29:1). The LORD had prospered his journey. "As he looked, he saw a well" (v 2), perhaps the same well where the LORD had led Abraham's servant to

Rebekah, Laban's sister. At this well, Jacob meets Rachel, Laban's daughter. Allen Ross comments, "This passage may not explicitly refer to the Lord's leading. But the parallelism [with the journey of Abraham's servant] suggests that, just as the LORD guided the servant to Rebekah, so did he guide Jacob to Rachel. Moreover, the parallelism between the three clauses beginning with *hinneh* ['behold'] in chapter 28 and the threefold use of *hinneh* in chapter 29 also indicates how Jacob's success was to be interpreted — the vision at Bethel was the promise, and the meeting at the well was the beginning of the fulfillment."[13]

Still, the LORD seems to be absent when Laban cruelly deceives Jacob on his wedding night by substituting his homely daughter Leah for Jacob's beloved Rachel. But again the narrator makes clear that the LORD was not absent: "When the LORD saw that Leah was unloved, he opened her womb; but Rachel was barren" (v 31). With the birth of the children, Leah acknowledges the LORD: "She named him Reuben; for she said, 'Because the LORD has looked on my affliction; surely now my husband will love me.' She conceived again and bore a son, and said, 'Because the LORD has heard that I am hated, he has given me this son also'; . . . She conceived again and bore a son, and said, 'This time I will praise the LORD'" (vv 32-35). Von Rad observes, "Without Leah, Reuben, Levi, and Judah would not have been born, and neither Moses [from Levi] nor David [from Judah] would have appeared. God's work descended deeply into the lowest worldliness and there was hidden past recognition. The narrator leaves it at that and does not bring it into the open with pious words."[14]

Textual Theme and Goal

Given the narrator's efforts to reveal the LORD fulfilling his promise to Jacob even through Laban's deception, we can formulate his theme as, *By guiding Jacob to Laban's home and using even Laban's deception, the LORD begins to fulfill his promise that Jacob's descendants shall be like the dust of the earth.*

As to the narrator's goal in recording this narrative for Israel, we should recall that Laban's descendants were Israel's perennial enemies in the (north) east, the Arameans — in modern terms, the Syrians. Ross comments that "the narrative all works to develop the point that Jacob's marriages to Leah and Rachel, the two women who built the household of Israel, were the result of deception and pro-

13. Ross, *Creation and Blessing,* 500-501. Cf. Sarna, *Understanding Genesis,* 195, "The biblical narrator is careful to expose the hand of divine providence at work in the unfolding drama, fulfilling the promise of the nocturnal revelation that God would not abandon the patriarch in the land of his exile. Like Abraham's servant many years before, Jacob arrived at the well of Haran just as his own kith and kin appeared on the scene."

14. Von Rad, *Genesis,* 291-92.

longed service. But Israel could still be encouraged, for here an ancestor of the Syrians dealt underhandedly with their ancestor, but their ancestor made the best of it. After all, it was not merely a match-up between two crafty men; in spite of all that Jacob might face, God had promised to protect and bless him."[15] Against this backdrop, we can formulate the narrator's goal as, *To encourage Israel with the message that their sovereign God can fulfill his promises even through human deceit.*

Ways to Preach Christ

From the narrator's theme, "By guiding Jacob to Laban's home and using even Laban's deception, the LORD begins to fulfill his promise that Jacob's descendants shall be like the dust of the earth," what are legitimate roads to Jesus Christ in the New Testament?

Redemptive-Historical Progression

Leah, the unloved wife, gives birth to four sons: Reuben, Simeon, Levi, and Judah. With the birth of Judah, Leah exclaims, "This time I will praise the LORD." The name "Judah" means "he will be praised," or "let him be praised." "This fact permitted another play on the name in Genesis 49:8, in which Jacob prophesied that Judah's brothers would praise him . . . , meaning that the tribe of Judah would rise to prominence."[16] Judah, the youngest of the four sons, would be prominent. Jacob continues to prophesy, "The scepter shall not depart from Judah, nor the ruler's staff from between his feet" (49:10). The tribe of Judah would bring forth the royal line of kings like David and Solomon. In the fullness of time, Jesus the Messiah would be born of the house of David, of the tribe of Judah, the son of the unloved Leah.

Promise-Fulfillment

Since the theme of the narrative is about God beginning to fulfill his promise to Jacob, the road of promise-fulfillment is the most natural way to Christ in the New Testament. At Bethel, the LORD promised Jacob, "Your offspring shall be like the dust of the earth" (28:14). With the birth of four sons to Leah, the LORD begins to fulfill this promise. At the end of Genesis, when Jacob moves to Egypt,

15. Ross, *Creation and Blessing,* 503. For various meanings of "the people of the east" (29:1) see Hamilton, *Genesis 18–50,* 252.

16. Ibid., 510-11.

"the total number of people born to Jacob was seventy" (Gen 46:27). Seventy (7 × 10) is a full number of people, but it is not yet "like the dust of the earth." In Egypt, even through persecution, Israel will rapidly multiply. But still they are not "like the dust of the earth." This promise comes to final fulfillment only through Jesus Christ, who sends out his followers to "make disciples of all nations" (Matt 28:19). Through faith in Jesus, Gentiles can also be "descendants of Abraham" and inherit "the blessing of Abraham" (Gal 3:7, 14). On the last day, there will be "a great multitude that no one could count, from every nation, from all tribes and peoples and languages, standing before the throne and before the Lamb, robed in white, with palm branches in their hands" (Rev 7:9). Only through Jesus Christ will Jacob's offspring become "like the dust of the earth."

Typology

There is no clear type of Christ in this narrative.

Analogy

For the way of analogy, we can take our cue from the narrator's goal: As God encouraged Israel with the message that their sovereign God can fulfill his promises even through human deceit, so Christ encourages his church with the assurance that their sovereign God can fulfill his promises even through human deceit. This analogy can be supported, for example, by Jesus' declaration, "*Blessed* are you when people revile you and persecute you and utter all kinds of evil against you *falsely* on my account. Rejoice and be glad, for your reward is great in heaven, for in the same way they persecuted the prophets who were before you" (Matt 5:11-12).

Longitudinal Themes

One can also preach Christ from this narrative by tracing in Scripture the theme of God using human deception to fulfill his promises. In this narrative God used Laban's deception of switching Leah for Rachel — which resulted in Jacob marrying both sisters as well as their two maids — to give birth to Israel's tribal heads (Ephraim and Manasseh by way of Joseph). Later God would use the deception of Jacob's sons (selling Joseph) to save Jacob's family from famine (45:4-9). Still later, God would use David's deception and murder of Uriah to bring about his marriage to Bathsheba and the crowning of Solomon, their second son.

In the crucifixion of Jesus we can best see how God can use human deception to fulfill his promises. Judas sold Jesus for thirty pieces of silver and betrayed him with a kiss. "The chief priests and the whole council were looking for *false* testimony against Jesus so that they might put him to death." When they found two false witnesses who agreed, the council decided: "He deserves death" (Matt 26:59, 66). Pilate, the representative of the Roman Empire, knew that Jesus was innocent, yet "handed him over to be crucified" (Matt 27:26). But God used all these deceptions to fulfill his promise that Jacob's descendants would be numerous "like the dust of the earth" (Gen 28:14; see Rev 5:9-10; 7:9).

New Testament References

The appendix in the Nestle-Aland Greek New Testament lists only four New Testament references to this narrative. Acts 7:8 and Luke 1:48 are not directly linked to Jesus. The other two references are Matthew 1:2 and Luke 3:33, both referring to the genealogies of Jesus. Matthew writes: "Abraham was the father of Isaac, and Isaac the father of Jacob, and Jacob the father of Judah and his brothers, and Judah the father of Perez and Zerah by Tamar. . . . And David the father of Solomon by the wife of Uriah. . . . Joseph, the husband of Mary, of whom Jesus was born, who is called the Messiah" (Matt 1:2-16). Through this long list of names, Matthew reminds his readers of human sin and deception, particularly with names like Judah and Tamar (Gen 38), and David and "the wife of Uriah" (2 Sam 11). But through it all, God fulfills his promise of a coming Messiah, and the Savior of the world is born.

Contrast

There is no contrast between the message of this narrative and that of the New Testament.

Sermon Theme and Goal

The textual theme was, "By guiding Jacob to Laban's home and using even Laban's deception, the LORD begins to fulfill his promise that Jacob's descendants shall be like the dust of the earth." Since the New Testament does not change this message, we can keep the textual theme as sermon theme. It would be well, however, to shorten it in order to make it more memorable. This results in the following sermon theme: *The LORD can use even human deception to fulfill his promise that Jacob's descendants shall be as numerous as the dust of the earth.*

We formulated the narrator's goal as, "To encourage Israel with the message that their sovereign God can fulfill his promises even through human deceit." In harmony with the narrator's goal, we can formulate our goal in preaching the sermon as, *To encourage God's people with the message that their sovereign God can fulfill his promises even through human deceit.* The need addressed by this goal is that God's people are often discouraged by the deceit they see and experience in this sinful world.

Sermon Exposition

The introduction of the sermon could illustrate the need that we are often discouraged by the deceit we see and experience in this sinful world. Why does God allow deceit to fester? Will it frustrate God's promises?

Transition to Jacob. Jacob knew about deceit. He wanted the blessing of the firstborn so badly that he had deceived his blind father. Well, the deception worked. Jacob received the blessing from Isaac. But now Jacob is on the run, for his brother Esau wants to kill him. Jacob has to leave the home of his beloved mother and has to walk more than 400 miles to his uncle Laban's place. Jacob is a fugitive. He must have been scared. He has to travel all alone through rugged terrain, cross swift-flowing rivers, perhaps meet up with dangerous animals, hostile people, and foreign gods.

But as Jacob is about to leave the Promised Land, Yahweh, the LORD, the God of Abraham and the God of Isaac, meets him in a dream. The LORD says to Jacob, "Know that I am with you and will keep you wherever you go, and will bring you back to this land" (28:15). The LORD also promises Jacob, "The land on which you lie I will give to you and to your offspring; and your offspring shall be like the dust of the earth" (28:13-14).

With these promises ringing in his ears, Jacob continues his journey. We read in chapter 29:1, "Then Jacob went on his journey, and came to the land of the people of the east." This single verse covers a month-long dangerous journey. The LORD was indeed with him, even as he headed off into exile from the Promised Land.[17]

When Jacob is close to his destination, we read in verse 2, "As he looked, he saw a well in the field and three flocks of sheep lying there beside it; for out of that well the flocks were watered." The narrator explains, "The stone on the well's mouth

17. "In keeping with the picture of Jacob's sojourn as an exile from the Promised Land, the writer opens the account with the words, 'and he traveled toward the land of the sons of the east.'" Sailhamer, *Pentateuch*, 193.

was large, and when all the flocks were gathered there, the shepherds would roll the stone from the mouth of the well, and water the sheep, and put the stone back in its place on the mouth of the well." A well was an extremely precious resource for a community. If the stone covering the mouth of the well was left off too long, the well would eventually fill in with sand. So the shepherds would wait till all the flocks were gathered around the well. Then they would remove the stone from the well, water all the sheep, and quickly replace the stone to cover the well.

When Jacob arrives at the well, he says to the shepherds, verse 4, "My brothers, where do you come from?" They reply, "We are from Haran." Jacob asks them, "Do you know Laban son of Nahor?" They reply curtly, "We do." Jacob asks, "Is it well with him?" "Yes," they reply, "and here is his daughter Rachel, coming with the sheep."

Does the beginning of this story remind you of another wedding story in Genesis? You recall that Abraham had sent his trusted servant back to Haran to find a wife for Isaac. Abraham had told his servant, "You will not get a wife for my son from the daughters of the Canaanites, among whom I live, but will go to my country and my kindred and get a wife for my son Isaac" (24:3-4). A difficult assignment, finding a suitable wife for your master's son. But Abraham said to his servant, "The LORD . . . will send his angel before you" (24:7). And the LORD did.

The LORD led the servant straight to a well where some shepherds also watered their flocks. Arriving at the well, the servant prayed fervently, "O LORD, God of my master Abraham, please grant me success today. . . . I am standing here by the spring of water, and the daughters of the townspeople are coming out to draw water. Let the girl to whom I shall say, 'Please offer your jar that I may drink,' and who shall say, 'Drink, and I will water your camels' — let her be the one whom you have appointed for your servant Isaac. . . . *Before he had finished speaking, there was Rebekah*" (24:12-15).

The LORD has led Jacob probably to the very same well. But the narrator does not record that Jacob prays the LORD for guidance or thanks the LORD for leading him to his relatives. Instead it seems that Jacob again wishes to take matters into his own hands. As soon as the shepherds tell him that Rachel, the daughter of Laban, is coming with the sheep, he tries to send the shepherds on their way. Verse 7, "Look, it is still broad daylight; it is not time for the animals to be gathered together. Water the sheep, and go, pasture them." But they say, "We cannot[18] until all the flocks are gathered together, and the stone is rolled from the mouth of the well; then we water the sheep."[19]

18. "Some have read this statement, 'we can't,' as indicating that it required the strength of all the shepherds to remove the stone. We do not accept this. We are convinced that this was just a matter of community agreement." Aalders, *Genesis,* II, 112-13.

19. "It was the custom to remove the stone cover to the cistern, to which several parties had

Verse 9, "*While he was still speaking with them, Rachel came* with her father's sheep; for she kept them." His cousin Rachel! His mother Rebekah then, his cousin Rachel now. Is this not the LORD's leading? But Jacob does not thank the LORD for leading him to his uncle's family. He again takes matters into his own hands. Verse 10, "Now when Jacob saw Rachel, the daughter of his mother's brother Laban, and the sheep of his mother's brother Laban, Jacob went up and rolled the stone from the well's mouth, and watered the flock of his mother's brother Laban." Single-handedly he rolls away the heavy stone and, against the custom of waiting for all the flocks, Jacob waters the flock of his uncle Laban.[20] Then he kisses Rachel and explains to her that he is the son of Rebekah, her father's sister.

Like Rebekah before her, Rachel runs home to tell her father Laban about the stranger at the well: He rolled away the stone single-handedly and watered the sheep; then he said that he is your sister Rebekah's son! Laban, probably remembering the costly gifts from Abraham's servant, again runs to the well to meet Jacob. But what a disappointment: Jacob has no camels and is not loaded down with gifts. Jacob has come with only the clothes on his back. Still, Laban invites him to his home.

Once they get there, Laban naturally wants to know how it is that Jacob is all alone and dirt poor. At the end of verse 13 the narrator pointedly tells us, "Jacob told Laban all these things." What things?[21] How he had deceived his blind father Isaac for the blessing of the firstborn; how his mother heard that Esau wanted to kill him and advised him to flee to her brother Laban's house; and how his father told him to "take as wife from there one of the daughters of Laban, your mother's brother" (28:2).

Upon hearing this story, Laban exclaims, verse 14, "Surely you are my bone and my flesh!" These words remind us of Adam's exclamation when he first sees Eve, "This at last is bone of my bones and flesh of my flesh" (2:23). Laban's words, "Surely you are my bone and my flesh!" seem to imply more than simply, "Surely you are my nephew." Laban seems to be saying: You and I are cut from the same cloth; we are both greedy for more wealth; we are both willing to

---

equal rights, only when all were present, in order to avoid any mischief of individual partners." Von Rad, *Genesis,* 288.

20. "We already know him, as his name at birth *(Ya'ăqōv)* has been etymologized, as the 'heel-grabber' or wrestler, and we shall continue to see him as the contender, the man who seizes his fate, tackles his adversaries, with his own two hands." Alter, *The Art of Biblical Narrative,* 55.

21. "The text is vague, and we are left to guess, but it seems likely that Laban discovered plenty about Jacob's past and realized that Jacob had not many financial assets to offer and was very much at Laban's mercy. And this must inform our understanding of his comments." Wenham, *Genesis 16–50,* 231.

deceive to get that wealth. In any event, Laban invites Jacob to stay. He can always use a strong shepherd.

After observing Jacob for a month, Laban knows that Jacob is a hard worker. He also knows that Jacob is in love with his younger daughter Rachel. But Jacob has no money for the bride-price that was required in that culture. Craftily, Laban says to Jacob, verse 15, "Because you are my kinsman, should you therefore serve me for nothing? Tell me, what shall your wages be?" This "is an overture to a bargaining session and reveals incidentally that he has already been extracting labor from his kinsman-guest for a month."[22] Waltke notes that "Laban's smooth talk reduces Jacob to a lowly laborer under contract. Their relationship for the next twenty years is that of an oppressive lord over an indentured servant paying off a bride-price, not of an uncle helping his blood relative."[23]

Before Jacob can state his wages, the narrator raises the suspense by informing us that Laban has *two* daughters, "the name of the elder was Leah," probably meaning "cow," "and the name of the younger was Rachel," which is Hebrew for "ewe." In verse 17 he contrasts these two sisters: "Leah's eyes were soft, but Rachel was graceful and beautiful." "What makes eyes 'soft' . . . is unclear; most commentators think it means they had no fire or sparkle, a quality much prized in the East."[24] So the TNIV translates, "Leah had weak eyes." Today we would probably say that Leah was homely while Rachel was beautiful. Which one will Jacob choose to work for, the homely Leah or the beautiful Rachel?

Jacob does not put out "a fleece" as Abraham's servant did to make sure that he selected the right girl for Isaac. Jacob is attracted to Rachel's beauty.[25] The choice is easy for him. Verse 18 tells us that "Jacob loved Rachel." So he offers Laban, "I will serve you seven years for your younger daughter Rachel." We may wonder why Jacob would offer to *serve* Laban for Rachel. The reason is that Jacob is a fugitive. He has no silver or gold to pay the bride-price. So he offers to

22. Alter, *Art of Biblical Narrative,* 56. Fokkelman comments, "Wages and service — those are the two key-words which dominate the Haran phase [of Jacob], especially in regard to Laban. . . . Whenever a lord would like to take on a servant (and Laban would like to have Jacob very much) and with mealy mouth invites him to make the first proposal as to the wages . . . , there exploitation lies in wait." *Narrative Art in Genesis,* 126-27.

23. Waltke, *Genesis,* 405.

24. Wenham, *Genesis,* 235. Cf. Kidner, *Genesis,* 160, "*Tender* (AV, RV) probably means *weak* (RSV), either in vision or (as von Rad suggests) in colour." Cf. von Rad, *Genesis,* 291, "What is meant is probably their paleness and lack of luster. The Oriental likes a woman's eyes to be lively, to glow, and therefore eye make-up was used from most ancient times."

25. "There is dialogue between Jacob and Rachel (v 12), then Leah and Rachel are introduced, then attention is drawn to Rachel's pulchritude. Such a position stresses that Rachel's beauty is indeed what attracts Jacob to Rachel." Hamilton, *Genesis 18–50,* 259.

work for Rachel. But why would he offer to serve Laban *seven* years? "The Old Testament fixes the maximum marriage gift at fifty shekels (Deut 22:29), but typically the gifts were much lower."[26] If a shepherd's wage was about ten shekels a year, Jacob is offering about seventy shekels, almost twice the going rate.[27] Why does Jacob make such a high offer?

It seems that he wants to make sure that Laban cannot turn down his offer. And he is right. Laban agrees immediately. For him it is a win-win situation: he keeps the services of his daughter for seven more years, plus he gains the services of Jacob for seven years. Though Jacob pays a high bride-price for Rachel, according to verse 20, these seven years seem "but a few days[28] to him because of the love he had for her."

When Jacob has fulfilled the seven years, it seems that Laban has conveniently forgotten the agreement. For Jacob has to seek out Laban and demand bluntly, verse 21, "Give me my wife that I may go in to her, for my time is completed." In response, Laban gathers together all the people of the place, and makes a feast — "a drinking banquet!"[29] "Normally, a wedding involved processions to and from the bride's house, a reading of the marriage contract, and a large meal attended by both families and neighbors. The first day's celebration ended with the groom wrapping his cloak around the bride, who was veiled throughout the ceremony (24:65), and taking her to the nuptial chamber where the marriage was consummated. However, the feasting and celebration continued for a whole week."[30]

Verse 23, "But in the evening he [Laban] took his daughter Leah and brought her to Jacob; and he went in to her." Jacob never notices the switch: the bride is veiled, the night is dark, and the groom is probably slightly intoxicated.[31] How will Jacob react to this cruel deception? Will he divorce Leah and demand Rachel right away?

26. Wenham, *Genesis 16–50*, 235.

27. "In the texts from Nuzi the typical bride price was thirty to forty shekels. Since a shepherd's annual wage was ten shekels a year, Jacob is in effect paying a premium by working seven years." Walton, *Genesis*, 586.

28. "Rebekah had told him to stay with Laban 'for a while *(yāmîm 'ăhādîm)*' [27:44]; Jacob's love for Rachel made the seven years seem like 'a few days' *(kĕyāmîm 'ăḥādîm)*, 29:20." Turner, *Genesis*, 127.

29. "'Feast' (*mišteh*, from *šātâ*, 'to drink'), i.e., a drinking banquet." Hamilton, *Genesis 18–50*, 263.

30. Wenham, *Genesis*, 236. Cf. Judg 14:12-18.

31. "The suggestion is as old as Josephus that Jacob was 'deluded by wine and the dark' [*Ant.* 1.19.6 (par. 301)]. This is the second time in Genesis that *ṣĕʿîrâ*, 'younger,' and *bĕkîrâ*, 'firstborn,' have been used together. The same terms were used to describe Lot's two daughters. They too deceived their father, made him drunk, and then had intercourse with him." Hamilton, *Genesis 18–50*, 262-63.

The narrator keeps us in suspense at this point by inserting verse 24, "Laban gave his maid Zilpah to his daughter Leah to be her maid." In that culture, the father of the bride would give a dowry to his daughter. The dowry could be money, or clothes, or servants. Laban gives Leah his maid Zilpah. The fact that he gives only one maid may be a sign of his greedy nature.[32] In any event, with seven years of Jacob's service, he has made good money on the plain Leah. Perhaps there is more money to be gained from this source.

The narrator quickly switches back to Jacob. Verse 25, "When morning came, it was Leah!" We can imagine Jacob's shock. Jacob, who deceived his father who had "weak eyes," now discovers that his new wife has weak eyes. The deceiver has been deceived, and that by the same trick he had used on his father. Jacob had pretended to be his older brother Esau, and the deception worked because Isaac was blind and drank wine (27:25). Now Leah has pretended to be her younger sister Rachel, and the deception worked because Jacob was blind in the dark night and drank wine.

Jacob knows that Laban instigated this deception. He immediately confronts Laban, verse 25: "What is this you have done to me? Did I not serve you for Rachel? Why then have you deceived me?"[33] But Laban does not bat an eye. He simply asserts, "This is not done in our country — giving the younger before the firstborn" (v 26). You, Jacob, the younger, may have grabbed the blessing of the firstborn Esau, but in our country we don't place the younger before the firstborn.

What can Jacob say? "With his indignant protest to Laban, Jacob unwittingly condemns himself."[34] Jacob had deceived his father Isaac into giving him the blessing of the firstborn. Now Laban has deceived Jacob into marrying the firstborn, Leah.[35] Jacob has met his match in uncle Laban.

But Laban comes up with an ingenious plan by which both can get what they want. Verse 27, "Complete the week of this one, and we will give you the other also in return for serving me another seven years." Complete Leah's bridal week, then you can marry Rachel and in return serve me another seven years.

What will Jacob do? Will he agree to serve his deceiving uncle another seven years? He longs to go back to his mother. She had said his stay with uncle Laban would be only "a few days" (27:44). Now he has been gone seven years and Laban demands that he stay another seven. What will Jacob do? Jacob has

32. Note the contrast with Rebekah's gift: "Rebekah received for her part her nurse and several servants (ch. 24:59, 61)." Von Rad, *Genesis*, 292.

33. "Deceived me [*rāmâ*]. This is the same word Esau uses to describe Jacob's deceit (see 27:35-36)." Waltke, *Genesis*, 406.

34. Fishbane, *Text and Texture*, 55.

35. "The irony of such a circumstance speaks for itself. The reader was certainly expected to interpret such irony as the work of a divine plan. Jacob's past has caught up with him." Sailhamer, *Pentateuch*, 194.

little choice. He has been outmaneuvered. He can hardly begin to haggle at this point, for he agreed originally to work seven years for Rachel.

Jacob gives in to his crafty uncle. He accepts his steep offer. Verse 28, "Jacob did so, and completed her week; then Laban gave him his daughter Rachel as a wife. (Laban gave his maid Bilhah to his daughter Rachel to be her maid.) So Jacob went in to Rachel also, and he loved Rachel more than Leah. He served Laban for another seven years."

"He served Laban for another seven years." These years do not fly by like "a few days" for Jacob. They are long, difficult years. His father-in-law Laban has become his adversary, and with two wives and their maids there is constant tension in his household (see 30:8). Jacob has made a mess of his life. It seems that the LORD has forsaken him. Where is the LORD who had promised to keep him and to give him as many offspring as the dust of the earth?

It may seem like the LORD is absent, but in reality the LORD works through Laban's deception to fulfill his promise of giving Jacob a multitude of offspring. For Jacob now has two wives who each have a maid. In the following chapter we read that all four women bear children for Jacob: the sons who become the twelve tribes of Israel.

In this narrative, too, the narrator shows that the LORD was not absent during these sordid dealings. We read in verse 31, "When the LORD saw that Leah was unloved, he opened her womb; but Rachel was barren." "Jacob's intended wife . . . was barren, and it appeared to be the LORD's doing. . . . By means of such a twist in the narrative, the narrator shows again that Jacob's plans have come to naught. Jacob had planned to take Rachel as his wife, but God intended him to have Leah."[36] The irony is clear: "man proposes, but God disposes." Jacob is confronted with the fact that God blesses Leah, the firstborn, with children but does not bless the younger Rachel.

Moreover, Leah, the unloved wife, is the one who testifies to the LORD's faithfulness. Verse 32, "Leah conceived and bore a son, and she named[37] him Reuben; for she said, 'Because the LORD has looked on my affliction; surely now

36. Ibid., 194-95.

37. "The statements that are made in conjunction with the naming of each of these sons do not express an etymological description of the names as such. The names are given, rather, in connection with a certain similarity in sound between the names themselves and certain words included in these statements. Thus the name of the first-born son was Reuben — Hebrew *rĕʾûbēn*. This sounds like the combination of two of the words Leah spoke, 'seen' — Hebrew *rāʾâ*, and 'my misery' — Hebrew *bĕʿonyî*. The name of the second son was Simeon — Hebrew *šimĕʿôn*. This has a sound similar to the word translated 'heard' — Hebrew *šāmaʿ*. The third name was Levi — Hebrew *lēwî*. This relates to the word translated 'attached' — Hebrew *lāwâ*. The fourth son was Judah — Hebrew *yĕhûdâ*. This has the same sound as the word for 'praise' — Hebrew *yādâ*." Aalders, *Genesis*, II, 116.

my husband will love me.'" When Leah bears a second son, she again acknowledges the LORD, "'Because the LORD has heard that I am hated, he has given me this son also'; and she named him Simeon" (v 33). Then Leah bears a third son and says, "'Now this time my husband will be joined to me, because I have borne him three sons'; therefore he was named Levi" (v 34). "She conceived again and bore a son, and said, 'This time I will praise the LORD'; therefore she named him Judah. Then she ceased bearing" (v 35).[38]

Leah, the unwanted and unloved wife, gives birth to the forebears of four important tribes in Israel. Moses and Aaron would be born in the tribe of Levi; the LORD would choose the Levites to serve him in his temple. David would be born in the tribe of Judah; the LORD would choose the royal line of kings from the tribe of Judah. As later Israel read this story of Laban's deception and Jacob's wrong choices, they would have become aware of a deep mystery: their sovereign LORD can fulfill his promises even through human deception and scheming.

At Bethel, the LORD promised Jacob, "Your offspring shall be like the dust of the earth" (28:14). With the birth of four sons to Leah, the LORD began to fulfill this promise. At the end of Genesis, when Jacob moves to Egypt, "the total number of people born to Jacob was seventy" (Gen 46:27; Exod 1:5). Seventy (7 × 10) is a full number of people, but it is not yet "like the dust of the earth." In Egypt, even through persecution, Israel will rapidly multiply. But still they are not "like the dust of the earth." This promise comes to final fulfillment only through Jesus Christ.

Judas deceived Jesus, sold his master for thirty pieces of silver, and betrayed him with a kiss. The chief priests and the council used false testimony to condemn Jesus. Pilate, the representative of the Roman Empire, knew that Jesus was innocent, yet "handed him over to be crucified" (Matt 27:26). But God used all these deceptions to fulfill his promise that Jacob's offspring would be numerous "like the dust of the earth."

After his resurrection Jesus explained to his disciples, "*Thus it is written,* that the Messiah is to suffer and to rise from the dead on the third day, and that repentance and forgiveness of sins is to be proclaimed in his name to *all nations*" (Luke 24:46-47). Jesus sent out his followers to "make disciples of all nations" (Matt 28:19). The final result of this mission work is revealed in the book of Revelation. John heard the new song sung to the Lamb,

"You are worthy to take the scroll
    and to open its seals,

38. Hartley, *Genesis,* 265, comments, "Two explanations are possible: Leah had become infertile, or Jacob no longer slept with her." In the light of Leah's attempts to get more children by way of her maid Zilpah (30:9), it seems more likely that Leah had become infertile.

for you were slaughtered
and by your blood you ransomed for God
saints from *every tribe and language and people and nation;*
you have made them to be a kingdom and priests serving our God,
and they will reign on *earth.*"

(Rev 5:9-10)

Through Jesus Christ, Jacob's offspring will indeed become "like the dust of the earth."

Today we may have our doubts about this promise. In many countries, Christians are a struggling minority. Christians are persecuted and killed. Secularism is decimating the church in Europe. Materialism is undermining the church in North America. People follow the lies of false religions. Is God absent? Is he not aware of what is going on? What is happening to God's promise that his people will become as numerous as "the dust of the earth"?

The wedding narrative of Jacob tells us that God is never absent when human beings scheme and deceive one another. Somehow the sovereign LORD will fulfill his promise that Jacob's descendants shall be as numerous as the dust of the earth. Jesus himself predicted, "I tell you, many will come from east and west and will eat with Abraham and Isaac and Jacob in the kingdom of heaven" (Matt 8:11).

CHAPTER 17

Jacob's Wrestling with God at Peniel

Genesis 32:22-32[1]

This narrative of Jacob wrestling with God provides many challenges for contemporary preachers. First, it seems such a bizarre story: God being involved in a wrestling match with Jacob. People may wish to solve this problem by spiritualizing the match, but the fact that Jacob walks away from this encounter "limping because of his hip" (32:31) confirms that this was indeed a physical fight. Preachers may need to remind their hearers that in the world of Genesis God sometimes appeared in human form: God walked and talked with Adam and Eve in the garden of Eden; and God dined with Abraham, discussing at length his intent to destroy Sodom and Gomorrah. So God appears in this narrative as "a man."

A second problem, as the history of interpretation shows, is that this narrative is extremely difficult to interpret. Luther called this passage, "one of the most obscure in the Old Testament."[2] It raises a host of questions: Why does God attack Jacob? Why does not God prevail against Jacob? Why does he strike him on the hip socket? Why is he concerned about "the day is breaking"? What is the meaning of the name "Israel"? Why does God not tell Jacob his own name? How can Jacob say that he has "seen God face to face" when the fight took place in a canyon in the dark of night? And why is "the dietary taboo not included in the law?"[3]

A third difficulty is how to preach Christ from this narrative. From Justin Martyr[4] (ca. 150) to modern times, Christian preachers have identified Jacob's

1. Hebrew texts begin chapter 32 with the last verse of chapter 31, so that this particular narrative is numbered as 32:23-33. In this chapter I will follow the numbering of the NRSV and, where necessary, change any quotations accordingly.

2. Luther, as quoted by H. C. Leupold, *Exposition of Genesis*, II, 875.

3. Ross, *Creation and Blessing*, 547, raises many similar questions.

4. *Dialogue with Trypho* 58:10. See also my *Preaching Christ from the Old Testament*, 75.

attacker as the Angel of the LORD (see Hos 12:4), who, in turn, is identified with the preexistent Logos, that is, Christ. For example, Wilhelm Vischer writes, "We are able with Luther to say, 'without the slightest contradiction this man was not an angel, but our Lord Jesus Christ, who is the eternal God and yet was to become a man.' . . . Jesus Christ appeared as a man upon earth to wrestle with men, and to be overcome of them."[5]

Aside from the speculation involved in identifying the Angel of the LORD with the preexistent Logos, this identification is not preaching Christ as the fullness of God's revelation in Jesus of Nazareth.[6] As Hebrews 1:1-2 puts it, "Long ago God spoke to our ancestors in many and various ways by the prophets, but in these last days he has spoken to us by a Son." Preaching Christ from the Old Testament is to connect God's message "by the prophets" with his message in and by his Son Jesus Christ.

A fourth difficulty is how to apply this narrative to the church today. Preachers frequently treat this narrative as a conversion story. Von Rad quotes Luther, "And so we have this noble chapter, in which you see the marvelous expedient which God takes with his saints for our comfort and example, so that we may daily ask ourselves if he is also at work with us and be prepared for it."[7] For Charles Wesley in his "'Wrestling Jacob' it becomes a paradigm of the kind of evangelical conversion he and his brother John had undergone a few years earlier."[8] Conversely, Lawrence Toombs applies this narrative to counter "a theology in which conversion is always instantaneous, always irresistible, always complete. . . . Jacob's experience also warns against the expectation that conversion is casual or pleasant. . . . Jacob, limping from the Jabbok, testifies that it comes with pain and struggle, often with hurt. The birth of the new man involves the death of the old."[9] Before we start applying this narrative to people today, it would be well if we asked first how the narrator intended Israel to respond to this narrative. In other words, what was the narrator's goal for Israel?

5. Vischer, *The Witness of the Old Testament to Christ*, 153.

6. See "The New Testament on 'Preaching Christ,'" in my *Preaching Christ from the Old Testament*, 4-10.

7. Von Rad, *Genesis*, 321.

8. David Jasper, *The Bible and Literature: A Reader* (Oxford: Blackwell, 1999), 138.

9. Toombs, *The Old Testament in Christian Preaching*, 116. Ross, *Creation and Blessing*, 552, suggests as the first point for a sermon: "I. The Lord must on occasion 'cripple' self-sufficient believers in order to bless them." See also Roy De Brand's proposed sermon outline in my *Preaching Christ from the Old Testament*, 35-36.

Text and Context

Genesis 32:22-32 is clearly a narrative unit which relates what happened one "night" (v 22). It ends with a conclusion at verse 32, while chapter 33:1 relates what happened the next day: "Now Jacob looked up and saw Esau coming."

This narrative is a story within a story within a story. The larger narrative unit describes Jacob's experiences in Haran. It begins in Genesis 28 as Jacob is about to leave the Promised Land, and it ends in chapter 32 as Jacob is about to re-enter the Promised Land. It begins with God appearing to Jacob at Bethel, and it ends with God appearing to Jacob at Peniel. At Bethel the Lord promised Jacob, "Know that I am with you and will keep you wherever you go, and will bring you back to this land" (28:15). At Peniel God fulfills this promise by bringing Jacob back to the Promised Land.

Bethel and Peniel have much in common. "Jacob stayed in Bethel 'because the sun had set' (28:11), and when he left Penuel, 'The sun rose upon him' (32:31). At both places Jacob is granted a revelation of God at night, in both of them God blesses him and Jacob names both of them on the basis of the revelation he has experienced."[10] Moreover, "The encounter at Bethel ends with Jacob's recognition of the divine aspect of the event in 28:17; and the encounter at Peniel ends with the patriarch's recognition of the divine character of the event in 32:30. After each encounter there is a reference to a particular Israelite custom; in 28:22 it is tithing and in 32:32 it is the refrain from eating the hip sinew."[11] The structure of the Jacob narratives can be sketched geographically as follows:[12]

Canaan

Bethel (28:10-22)

Haran

Peniel (32:22-32)

Canaan

Jacob's time in Haran is marked by strife and deception. Uncle Laban deceives Jacob by giving him not the beautiful Rachel but the plain Leah as his bride. Later Laban deceives Jacob again by secretly removing from the herd the speckled goats, which he had agreed were to be Jacob's wages (30:34-36). But Jacob tricks Laban and grows "exceedingly rich, and had large flocks, and male and female slaves, and camels and donkeys" (30:43).

10. Bar-Efrat, *Narrative Art,* 135.

11. Rendsburg, *Redaction of Genesis,* 63. See ibid., pp. 62-63, for many other parallels between Gen 28:10-22 and 32:1-32.

12. Bar-Efrat, *Narrative Art,* 135.

Jacob is a self-made man, though on occasion he will grant that "the God of my father has been with me" (31:5). Jacob tells Rachel and Leah, "Your father has cheated me and changed my wages ten times, but God did not permit him to harm me" (31:7). They agree to flee from Laban when the time is right. When Laban goes away to sheer his sheep, they gather all of Jacob's possessions and flee. For good measure, Rachel steals her father's household gods (31:19). The narrator comments, "Jacob *deceived* Laban the Aramean, in that he did not tell him that he intended to flee" (31:20) — words which Laban repeats, "Why did you flee secretly and *deceive* me?" (31:27). But through all these deceptions and trickery, Jacob outsmarts Laban and becomes rich. He is ready to return to the Promised Land. But there another opponent awaits: Esau, who was waiting to kill Jacob for deceiving him and his father.

The more immediate context for the Peniel narrative is the narrative about Jacob and Esau. It consists of five scenes:

Scene 1: Messengers *(mal'ākîm)* of God meet Jacob (Mahanaim) (32:1-2)
Scene 2: Jacob sends messengers *(mal'ākîm)* to Esau in Seir (3-6)
The message: Jacob is coming and is rich (4-5)
Conflict begins: Esau is coming with four hundred men (6)
Scene 3: Terrified Jacob responds with scheming, prayer, and scheming (7-21)
He divides his possessions into two companies (7-8)
He prays to God (9-12)
He sends Esau gifts to appease him (13-21)[13]
Scene 4: Jacob at the Jabbok (22-32)
Jacob's family cross the Jabbok (22-23)
A "man" wrestles with Jacob (24-32)
Scene 5: Jacob and Esau meet and part (33:1-17)
Jacob approaches Esau (1-3)
Resolution: Esau embraces Jacob and accepts his gifts (4-11)
Jacob declines Esau's invitation to travel together (12-15)
Outcome: Jacob and Esau part (16-17)

As can be seen, the Peniel narrative is a scene within the Jacob-Esau narrative. Jacob had expected to meet Esau in the Promised Land, but before he does, *God* meets Jacob. God meets the scheming, deceiving, self-sufficient Jacob before he is allowed to enter the Promised Land. To give the congregation a sense of this context, it would be well to read Genesis 32:1-32, indicating that the preaching-text is 32:22-32.

13. "Note the . . . inclusio in 32:13 and 21 (spent the night//gift) framing this episode." Waltke, *Genesis*, 444.

Literary Features

The narrator shows his hand most clearly when he concludes the narrative: "Therefore to this day the Israelites do not eat the thigh muscle that is on the hip socket . . ." (32:32). Though the narrator is omniscient, knowing Jacob's thoughts (32:20), he describes the attack from the limited perspective of Jacob: "A man wrestled with him" (v 24). He could have written, "God wrestled with him," but he adds to the tension by making his readers wonder along with Jacob, Who is this man? Only gradually, through the increasing awareness of Jacob, do the readers discover the identity of this "man": "I have seen *God* face to face" (v 30). In retelling this narrative, it would be well to keep the same suspense.

Further, the narrator is intentionally ambiguous. "The ambiguous use of the pronouns in the Hebrew text deliberately conceals the course of the fight so that the reader feels with Jacob the deep mystery of his struggle with an ominous foe. Whose thigh was injured? Who wanted to end the fight? Who asked for the blessing?"[14]

More important is the ambiguity in the crucial name "Israel." The narrator relates that Jacob is named "Israel," "for (*kî*) you have striven (*śārîtā*) with God (*'im-'elōhîm*) . . ." (32:28). "This etymology associates 'Israel' with the root *śrh*" plus *ēl.*[15] Israel, then, means "one who strives with God." But some experts in Hebrew maintain that *Ēl* cannot be the object but must be the subject, so that Israel means "God strives."[16] This meaning, however, is still ambiguous. Is God striving *for* Jacob or *against* him? The answer appears to be, both. In this narrative God strives against Jacob when he attacks him in the dark and cripples him. God knocks the self-sufficiency out of Jacob. But, according to God's promise at Bethel, God also strives *for* Jacob, never forsaking him (28:15). God certainly strives for Jacob when he softens Esau's heart so that the brothers reconcile and when God gives the land to Jacob/Israel. In any event, the narrator explains that Jacob received the name Israel, "for (*kî*) you have striven with God."[17]

Brueggemann suggests, "Perhaps it is important that the narrative is not explicit. In its opaque portrayal of the figure, the narrative does not want us to know too much. It is part of the power of the wrestling that we do not know the name or see the face of the antagonist."[18] Of course, by the end of the story we

14. Hartley, *Genesis,* 283.

15. Zobel, *TDOT,* VI, 399.

16. "The theophorous element is not the object but the subject of the phrase name." Ibid., VI, 400. Cf. Fokkleman, *Narrative Art in Genesis,* 216, "So *Yiśrāēl* here means, 'God fights' (such a translation as Bubel's 'Fechter Gottes' is impossible.)"

17. "Popular etymologies in the Bible generally take the form of a play on a name rather than a precise historical etymology." Wenham, *Genesis 16–50,* 296.

18. Brueggemann, *Genesis,* 267.

know along with Jacob that the antagonist was God himself. Even at that, "the ending is most ambiguous: Jacob passes as a delivered man, but is lame."[19]

The repetition of keywords may aid in detecting the narrator's intended meaning.[20] The verb "to cross" or "to pass over" *(ʿābar)* is frequently used in this narrative and its context (32:10, 16, 21, 22, 23, 31). Crossing over the Jordan or the Jabbok into the Promised Land may be an important concept for the narrator. The word "face" *(pānîm)* is used five times in 32:20 and twice in verse 30 ("I have seen God face to face") (and after this narrative again twice in 33:10 where Jacob says to Esau, "Your face is like seeing the face of God"). The verb "to bless" *(brk)*, which is of crucial importance in the Jacob narratives, is here repeated in two key places in the central dialogue (32:26, 29). Note also that Jacob's cry to God for help, "Deliver me" (v 11), is the same Hebrew root *nṣl* that he uses in his exclamation, "my life is preserved" (v 30).

The narrator uses only one and a half verses to describe the fight (vv 24b-25), four verses for the dialogue (vv 26-29), one verse for naming Peniel (30), one verse for the outcome (v 31), and one verse to conclude the story (v 32). The obvious pace retardation at the dialogue in the center of the narrative would lead us to suspect that the dialogue holds the clue for the central meaning (theme) of this narrative. On the basis of repetition, Fokkelman suggests an intricate chiastic structure focusing on the dialogue, which in turn focuses on the name change from Jacob to Israel.[21] The following is a simplified version of the chiasm:[22]

A The same *night* he got up
 and *crossed (ʿābar)* the ford of the Jabbok. (22)
 B And *a man* wrestled with him until daybreak. (24)
  X a. Jacob: "I will not let you go, unless you *bless* me." (26)
   x Man: "What is your name?" Jacob: "Jacob" (27)
    Man: "You shall no longer be called Jacob, but Israel" (28)
  a′ And there he *blessed* him (29)
 B′ "I have seen *God* face to face" (30)
A′ The *sun* rose upon him
 as he *passed (ʿābar)* Penuel. (31)

19. Fokkelman, *Narrative Art in Genesis,* 222.

20. Kaiser, "Narrative," 82, notes the narrator's play on the words "Jacob" *(Yaʿăqōb)* at the "Jabbok" *(yabbōq)* and "wrestling," "the very rare Hebrew verb *(yēʾābēq)*."

21. Verse 26 is dialogue, and so are verses 27 and 29, "which mirror each other. But verse 28 is not! Verse 28 is a monologue, a solemn 'order of baptism,' spoken authoritatively. . . . A well-established nature, a long-fixed route of life must be turned back radically." Fokkelman, *Narrative Art in Genesis,* 215-16.

22. See Fokkelman, "Genesis," 51.

The Plot Line

The general background for this narrative is Jacob's deception and scheming in Haran. The more immediate setting is Jacob approaching the Promised Land and being met by "the angels of God" (32:1-2). The preliminary incidents consist of scenes 2 and 3 of the Jacob-Esau narrative: Jacob sends messengers to Esau in Seir (3-5). The messengers return with the word that Esau is coming with four hundred men (6). The terrified Jacob responds with scheming, prayer, and more scheming (7-21). The occasioning incident is that Jacob cannot sleep that night and decides to send his family, under the cover of darkness, across the Jabbok River into the Promised Land (22-23). The tension rises steadily when the narrator informs us that "Jacob was left alone; and a man wrestled with him [throughout the night] until daybreak" (24). Who is this man? Is it Esau? Or a robber? Suddenly the man touches Jacob's hip socket and his hip is pulled out of joint. Jacob is finished, yet he hangs on to the stranger for dear life. The man says, "Let me go," but Jacob responds, "I will not let you go, unless you bless me" (26). Instead of blessing him, the man asks an embarrassing question, "What is your name?" And Jacob has to admit, "I am Jacob" (27) — a deceiver from birth.

Then comes the turn in the narrative. The man declares authoritatively: "You shall no longer be called Jacob, but Israel, for you have striven with *God* and with humans, and have prevailed" (28). Jacob now knows that he has been wrestling with God. The man says it in so many words. And who but God can change a person from Jacob to Israel? Jacob asks timidly, "Please tell me your name." But God refuses to give his name. Instead he blesses Jacob (29). The conflict is completely resolved when Jacob names the place Peniel, saying, "For I have seen God face to face, and yet my life is preserved" (30). The outcome of the narrative is given in verse 31, "The sun rose upon him as he passed Penuel, limping because of his hip." The narrator adds the conclusion, "Therefore to this day the Israelites do not eat the thigh muscle that is on the hip socket, because he struck Jacob on the hip socket at the thigh muscle" (32).

We can sketch the plot line of this narrative as a single plot as shown on page 322.

Theocentric Interpretation

Angels of God meet Jacob as he approaches the Promised Land. Jacob is assured of God's presence and exclaims, "This is God's camp!" (32:1-2). Still, Jacob is terrified when he hears that Esau is coming with four hundred men, and for the

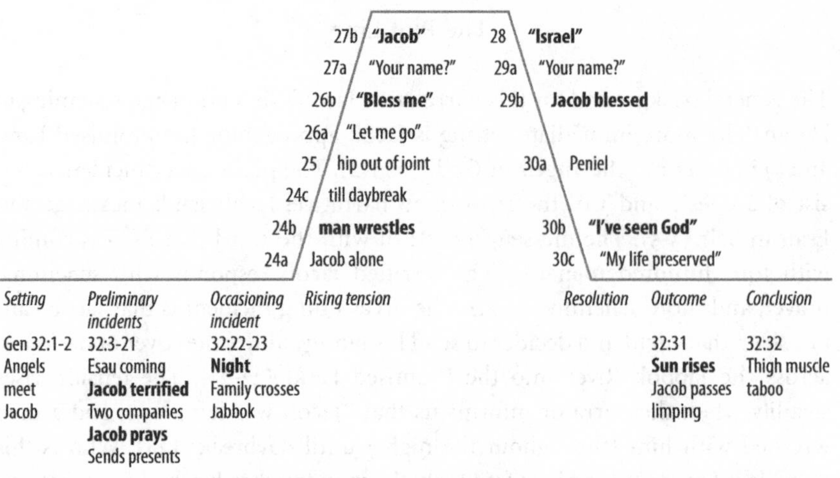

first time in his life, self-sufficient Jacob prays to God for deliverance (9-12).[23] At first Jacob thinks that it is a man wrestling with him, but gradually it dawns on him (and us) that this is no mere man. Who can immobilize Jacob with a touch?[24] Jacob recognizes a superior being and immediately asks that he bless Jacob. When the person changes Jacob's name to Israel, he thinks the person may be God, and he knows for sure when the person states, "for you have striven with God." Jacob asks God for his name, but instead of giving his name, God blesses Jacob. In response, Jacob calls the place Peniel, which means "face of God," explaining, "For I have seen God face to face."

Textual Theme and Goal

Both the chiastic structure and the plot line can guide us to the narrative's central theme. The chiastic structure focuses on the dialogue, and the dialogue, in turn, zeroes in on the monologue at its center: "You shall no longer be called Jacob, but Israel, for you have striven with God and with humans, and have prevailed" (28). The plot line also shows that verse 28 is the climax of this narrative. Taking into account also the setting of this narrative, we can formulate the textual theme as, *Before self-sufficient Jacob can enter the Promised Land, God needs to change Jacob into Israel, a person who strives with God for his blessing.*

23. Assuming that his vow at Bethel (28:20-22) was not a prayer, certainly not a prayer for deliverance.

24. To touch or strike is the same Hebrew verb, *nāgaʿ*, used for the live coal that "touched" Isaiah's lips (Isa 6:7).

In seeking to determine the narrator's goal in writing this narrative to Israel, it is important to recall that the patriarch Jacob/Israel stands also for the nation which is later called Jacob as well as Israel. Allen Ross observes, "The story of Israel the man served as an acted parable of the life of the nation, in which is here presented its relationship with God almost prophetically. The patriarch portrays the real spirit of the nation to engage in the persistent struggle with God until emerging strong in the blessing. The nation is consequently referred to as Jacob or Israel, depending on which characteristics predominate." Ross continues, "The point of the story for the nation of Israel entering the Land of Promise would be significant: Israel's victory would come not by the usual ways by which nations gain power but in the power of the divine blessing. Later in her history Israel was reminded that the restoration to the land was not by might nor by strength but by the Spirit of the Lord God, who fights for his people (Zech 4:6)."[25] Through this narrative, then, Israel would be reminded that not self-sufficient people but only those who strive with God for his blessing can live with God in the Promised Land. We can, therefore, formulate the narrator's goal for Israel as, *To warn Israel that God will not allow independent, self-sufficient people to enter the Promised Land but only those who rely on God.*

Ways to Preach Christ

Given the stated theme, "Before self-sufficient Jacob can enter the Promised Land, God needs to change Jacob into Israel, a person who strives with God for his blessing," what are legitimate roads to Jesus Christ in the New Testament?

Redemptive-Historical Progression

In Old Testament times, self-sufficient Jacob could not enter the Promised Land until God changed his name and character to Israel, a person who strives with God for his blessing, that is, a person who relies on God. When God liberated Israel from Egypt, he gave them his law at Sinai, for only a holy nation could live with God in the Promised Land. But in the wilderness, Israel often rebelled against God and went its own way. Finally, when they were about to enter the Promised Land, the spies came back with "an unfavorable report . . . saying, 'The land . . . devours its inhabitants; and all the people that we saw in it are of great size'" (Num 13:32). Hearing this report, Israel failed to trust that God would give them this land and made plans to return to Egypt. As a result, God

25. Ross, *Creation and Blessing,* 558.

decided that they could not enter the land: "None of the people who have seen my glory and the signs that I did in Egypt and in the wilderness, and yet have tested me these ten times and have not obeyed my voice, shall see the land that I swore to give to their ancestors; none of those who despised me shall see it" (Num 14:22-23). Only those who rely on God can enter the land.

Later a new generation, along with Joshua and Caleb, did indeed enter the land. The first major city they captured, Jericho, was a gift from God: "See, I have handed Jericho over to you" (Josh 6:2). It was but a token that the whole of Canaan was a gift from God to Israel, an inheritance. Israel did not have to fight for it in its own strength. But Israel would have to continue relying on God. When the Israelites in the land showed their Jacob-nature by being self-sufficient, greedy for personal gain at the cost of their neighbor, God sent them into exile in Assyria and later Babylon. Only when they were thoroughly chastened and willing to rely on God did God allow a remnant to return to the land.

In New Testament times, Jesus also warns that not everyone can enter the kingdom of God. Jesus urges, "Strive to enter through the narrow door; for many, I tell you, will try to enter and will not be able" (Luke 13:24). In fact, it is practically impossible for self-sufficient people to enter the kingdom of God: "Truly I tell you, it will be hard for a rich person to enter the kingdom of heaven. Again I tell you, it is easier for a camel to go through the eye of a needle than for someone who is rich to enter the kingdom of God" (Matt 19:23-24). Jesus makes it clear that self-sufficient people who assume they are in the kingdom will not inherit the kingdom of God: "Woe to you, scribes and Pharisees, hypocrites! For you lock people out of the kingdom of heaven. For you do not go in yourselves, and when others are going in, you stop them" (Matt 23:13). In fact, Jesus warns, "I tell you, the kingdom of God will be taken away from you and given to a people that produces the fruits of the kingdom" (Matt 21:43).

Promise-Fulfillment

There is no promise of Christ in this passage.

Typology

Perhaps we can see Jacob, the seed of the woman, who strives with God and is recreated into Israel, as a type of Jesus, the Seed of the woman, the true Israel. Jesus also strove with God and rested in him, particularly in Gethsemane when he prayed, "Father, if you are willing, remove this cup from me; yet not my will but yours be done" (Luke 22:42; cf. Heb 5:7). But the typology breaks down because Jacob was a self-sufficient sinner and Jesus is the sinless Son of God. It is advisable, therefore, not to use typology in the sermon.

Analogy

The way of analogy offers several possibilities. As God warned Israel that only those who rely on God will enter the Promised Land, so Jesus warns the church that only those who rely on God will enter the kingdom of God. Jesus states, "Truly I tell you, whoever does not receive the kingdom of God as a little child [in humble dependence] will never enter it" (Luke 18:17).

Another possibility is to draw the analogy as follows, As God came to Jacob and gave him a new name, so in Christ God has come to us and given us a new name: Christian. Paul writes in 2 Corinthians 5:17, "So if anyone is in Christ, there is a new creation; everything old has passed away; see, everything has become new." A new name is not only a privilege but also a responsibility to live up to the name. Paul writes in Ephesians 4:24, "Clothe yourselves with the new self, created according to the likeness of God in true righteousness and holiness."

Longitudinal Themes

From this narrative one can trace several longitudinal themes to Jesus Christ in the New Testament. The narrative has the subtheme of receiving a new name. God changed Abram's name to Abraham and Sarai's to Sarah. God changed Jacob's name to Israel. An angel instructed Joseph to name Mary's son "Jesus, for he will save his people from their sins" (Matt 1:21). Jesus himself changed Simon's name to Cephas, rock, "which is translated Peter" (John 1:42). In the book of Revelation, Jesus, the exalted Lord, promises those who conquer "a new name" (Rev 2:17; 3:12).

One can also trace the subtheme of the LORD's blessing from Jacob receiving God's blessing in this passage to Jesus' ninefold blessing in the Beatitudes, especially, "Blessed are the poor in spirit, for theirs is the *kingdom of heaven*. . . . Blessed are the pure in heart, for *they will see God*" (Matt 5:3, 5, 8).

New Testament References

There is only one New Testament passage that alludes to this event. For Genesis 32:30, "I have seen God face to face," the Greek New Testament lists 1 Corinthians 13:12, where Paul writes, "For now we see in a mirror, dimly, but then we will see face to face."

Contrast

There is no contrast between the message of this narrative and the New Testament. However, Edmund Clowney points out the following contrasts between Jacob and us: "The name of the LORD is too wonderful for Jacob's ears; the face of the LORD is too glorious for Jacob's eyes. Yet the LORD himself comes that Jacob may know him. His coming to Jacob anticipated his coming to us. Jacob saw the face of the LORD but dimly; we see the light of the glory of God in the face of Jesus Christ. Jacob asked for God's own name; we are baptized into the name of the triune God. Through the name of Jesus, exalted above every name, we bear the name of the Almighty God as our heavenly Father."[26]

Sermon Theme and Goal

We formulated the textual theme as follows, "Before self-sufficient Jacob can enter the Promised Land, God needs to change Jacob into Israel, a person who strives with God for his blessing." In the light of the New Testament, what is the message of this narrative for the church of Christ? The New Testament broadens the concept of the Promised Land from Canaan to the kingdom of God or the new earth. The sermon theme should reflect this broader perspective and yet stay as close as possible to the textual theme. In the New Testament, Jesus also affirms that we need to change before we can enter the kingdom of God. We can, therefore, formulate the sermon theme as follows, *Before self-sufficient people can enter the kingdom of God, God needs to change them into people who rely on God.*

We surmised that the main goal of the narrator in relating this story to Israel was, "To warn Israel that God will not allow self-sufficient people to enter the Promised Land but only those who rely on God." In line with this goal, we can make the sermon goal: *To warn the church that God will not allow independent, self-sufficient people to enter his kingdom but only those who rely on God.*

This goal exposes the need addressed in this sermon, namely, our tendency to rely on our own works to enter the kingdom of God. Preaching on this narrative, we can make our first move to Jesus in the introduction of the sermon, get people personally involved in the issue of entering the kingdom of God, and then in the body of the sermon flash back to Jacob.

26. Clowney, *Unfolding Mystery,* 75-76.

Sermon Exposition

Someone once asked Jesus, "Lord, will only a few be saved?" And Jesus responded, "Strive to enter through the narrow door; for many, I tell you, will try to enter and will not be able" (Luke 13:23-24). Can you honestly say that you have entered the kingdom of God? Or are you still wondering about it? Jesus says that it is very difficult to enter the kingdom of God, especially for rich people. Jesus declares, "Truly I tell you, it will be *hard* for a rich person to enter the kingdom of heaven. Again I tell you, it is easier for a camel to go through the eye of a needle than for someone who is rich to enter the kingdom of God" (Matt 19:23-24). "It will be *hard* for a rich person to enter the kingdom of God." Why is that? Because rich people tend to be self-sufficient. Rich people have the drive and the means to get what they want. Rich people don't have to rely on anyone else. They are independent. It will be hard for independent, self-sufficient people to enter the kingdom of God.

In the Old Testament Jacob was such a man: self-sufficient, a self-made man, grabbing opportunities as they presented themselves. Even when he was born, he was grabbing his twin brother's heel. That's why he was called Jacob, that is, "heel-grabber." Jacob wanted to be first. He wanted the blessing of the firstborn. But his brother Esau was just ahead of him at birth. So Jacob went after Esau. First he cheated Esau out of his birthright with a bowl of lentil stew. Next he deceived his blind father by pretending to be Esau and stole the blessing of the firstborn. When Esau came for the blessing, Isaac had to tell him, "Your brother came *deceitfully,* and he has taken away your blessing." Esau responded, "Is he not rightly named Jacob?" (27:35-36). Jacob is a heel-grabber, a deceiver, a self-made man.

Esau was so furious with Jacob that he planned to kill him. Jacob had to flee for his life. But before he left the Promised Land, the LORD met him in a dream at Bethel. Jacob saw a ladder with its top in the heavens and angels of God ascending and descending. And God promised him, "Know that I am with you and will keep you wherever you go, and will bring you back to this land" (28:15).

After a long journey, Jacob arrived at the home of his uncle Laban. Laban and Jacob were a good match. Laban was a greedy deceiver like Jacob. When Jacob fell in love with Laban's beautiful daughter Rachel, Laban made him work for her for seven years. Then, on the wedding night, Laban switched daughters and gave Jacob the plain Leah instead of the beautiful Rachel. Then Laban extorted another seven years of labor from Jacob for the hand of Rachel. It looked as if Jacob was no match for Laban. But that was about to change.

After working fourteen years for Rachel and Leah, Jacob agreed with Laban that he would continue working for him. His wages would be his own herd of sheep and goats. Jacob would get the speckled animals. But that very day, Laban removed the speckled animals from the herd and placed them far away in charge of his sons (30:35-36). Laban had taken the speckled breeding stock. Jacob had no chance. But through trickery Jacob still got the better of uncle Laban. Jacob complained that Laban cheated him and changed his wages ten times from speckled animals to striped ones and from striped to speckled (31:7), but Jacob still got the better of him. The Bible writer tells us that Jacob "grew exceedingly rich, and had large flocks, and male and female slaves, and camels and donkeys" (30:43). Jacob explains piously to his wives, "God has taken away the livestock of your father, and given them to me" (31:9). The independent, self-sufficient Jacob has become rich at Laban's expense.

At that point Jacob decides to flee with all his wealth. He will make his way back to the Promised Land. After a long, dangerous journey, he comes to the border of the Promised Land and is met by "the angels of God" (32:1). When he left the Promised Land, he saw "the angels of God" at Bethel (28:12), and now he is met again by "the angels of God." The Promised Land "appears to be guarded at its borders by angels"[27] — just like the garden of Eden. When Adam and Eve rebelled against God, God expelled them from Paradise, "and at the east of the garden of Eden he placed the cherubim, and a sword flaming and turning to guard the way to the tree of life" (3:24).

Now Jacob is met by "the angels of God." But Jacob does not seem to fear the angels. He fears his brother Esau, who had threatened to kill him. So Jacob sends messengers to Esau. They have to tell Esau, 32:4, "Thus says your *servant* Jacob, 'I have lived with Laban as an alien, and stayed until now; and I have oxen, donkeys, flocks, male and female slaves; and I have sent to tell my *lord,* in order that I may find favor in your sight." Jacob puts on a front of humility. He had deceived Esau for the blessing of the firstborn, but now he calls himself, "your servant Jacob," and he calls Esau, "my lord." And he tells Esau that he has become rich — so rich that he will not need any of father Isaac's estate. Surely this humble tone and generous assurance will mollify Esau.

Jacob travels further south and reaches the river Jabbok, which is the border of the Promised Land.[28] "This river in eastern Canaan flows through deep-cut canyons into the Jordan about 23 miles north of the Dead Sea."[29] Here Jacob's messengers return with alarming news, 32:6, "We came to your brother Esau, and he is coming to meet you, and four hundred men are with him." We

27. Sailhamer, *Pentateuch,* 197.

28. "The river Jabbok is mentioned several times in the Bible but always in the same context, as a boundary at the time of Israelite occupation of East Jordan. It constituted the limit of Israel's first victory against the kings of the Promised Land after it emerged from the desert wanderings." Sarna, *Understanding Genesis,* 206. See Deut 3:16.

29. Hamilton, *Genesis 18–50,* 328.

read in verse 7, "Then Jacob was greatly afraid and distressed." He is terrrified. Obviously, Esau still seeks to kill him. Why else would he come with four hundred men?

Feverishly Jacob's mind searches for a way to avert disaster. This is what he's good at. After all, he is Jacob. He is a master at turning disasters into profit. He comes up with an ingenious plan. He divides "the people that were with him, and the flocks and herds and camels, into two companies, thinking, 'If Esau comes to the one company and destroys it, then the company that is left will escape'" (32:7-8).

And then Jacob prays. For the first time in his life Jacob prays for deliverance! This is the longest prayer in the book of Genesis. Jacob is in deep distress. He prays, verse 9, "O God of my father Abraham and God of my father Isaac, O LORD who said to me, 'Return to your country and to your kindred, and I will do you good,' *I am not worthy* of the least of all the steadfast love and all the faithfulness that you have shown to your servant, for with only my staff I crossed this Jordan; and now I have become two companies." Finally Jacob the deceiver admits that he is not worthy of God's steadfast love that has kept him safe and made him rich in spite of his trickery and deceptions.

Jacob continues, verse 11, "*Deliver me,* please, from the hand of my brother, from the hand of Esau, for *I am afraid* of him; he may come and kill us all, the mothers with the children." "Deliver me." Save me! Preserve me! Finally Jacob realizes that he cannot do it alone. He needs the LORD to deliver him. And not only Jacob. Jacob is now also concerned about "the mothers with the children."

This is the beginning of a new Jacob. He is no longer self-sufficient. He prays earnestly. He confesses that he is not worthy of God's steadfast love. And he is concerned not only for himself but also for others. But Jacob remains the schemer. He is rich. Perhaps he can buy off Esau's anger with presents even a king would appreciate.[30]

That night he sets aside as a present for his brother Esau, "two hundred female goats and twenty male goats, two hundred ewes and twenty rams, thirty milch camels and their colts, forty cows and ten bulls, twenty female donkeys and ten male donkeys" (v 13). A total of five hundred and fifty animals. A gift fit for a king! "This gift is larger than towns were likely to pay in tribute to foreign kings."[31] But Jacob shrewdly decides not to give the animals all at once. He places

30. "It appears that the prayer did not change Jacob's basic approach to solving his problem. This seems to be the same approach that Jacob took to get the birthright. The only difference is that the price has gone up, and he will now have to offer more than just food." Curtis, "Structure, Style and Context," *JETS* 30/2 (June 1987), 133.

31. "For instance, in the ninth century B.C. the town of Hindanu paid to the Assyrian king Tukulti-Ninurta II some silver, bread, and beer, and 30 camels, 50 oxen, and 30 donkeys." Walton, *Genesis,* 605.

them in droves with space between each drove. And he instructs the first drivers, verse 17, "When Esau my brother meets you, and asks you, 'To whom do you belong? Where are you going? And whose are these ahead of you?' then you shall say, 'They belong to your *servant* Jacob; they are a present sent to my *lord* Esau; and moreover he is behind us.'" All the drivers of the droves are to say the same thing. Jacob is still playing the humble-servant card. With his humility and wave after wave of royal gifts he is trying to "appease" the anger of Esau. Verse 21, "So the present passed on ahead of him; and he himself spent that night in the camp."

Though Esau's presents are safely across the river Jabbok and on their way, Jacob still cannot sleep. Esau is coming to kill him and his family. How can they escape four hundred men? That's a small army. Has he done everything he can? Suppose Esau catches him just as he is fording this river with all these women, children, and herds? Esau will decimate them.

Verse 22, "The same night[32] he got up and took his two wives, his two maids, and his eleven children, and crossed the ford of the Jabbok. He took them and sent them across[33] the stream, and likewise everything that he had." He sent everything he had across the river Jabbok. This evokes a sense "of a complete letting go or a complete separation from everyone and everything."[34]

Verse 24, "Jacob was left alone." He is separated from his wives and children; he is separated from his servants; he is separated from his wealth. He is left all alone.[35] Suddenly, in the darkness, what appears to be a man[36] attacks him. Who is it? Is it Esau trying to kill him? Is it a bandit trying to rob him? Jacob fights back with all his might. This "man" wrestles[37] with him until daybreak. It is a long battle.

32. "He . . . decided to take the great risk of crossing the river during the night. Obviously he felt that this was less dangerous than a possible attack by Esau's forces during a daylight crossing of the river. . . . Since he was traveling from the north this would indicate that he crossed to the south side of the Jabbok." Aalders, *Genesis,* II, 141.

33. "The repetition in the account of the crossing suggests intensification." Brodie, *Genesis as Dialogue,* 331.

34. Ibid.

35. "Jacob's unprotected state functions as suspense. One whose life is in danger stands alone. In theological retrospect, Jacob's solitude serves an important spiritual purpose. Jacob must encounter God alone, without possessions or protection." Waltke, *Genesis,* 445.

36. "'A man [i.e., "someone"] wrestled with him,' is meant to suggest a surprise attack resembling a robbery or murder. We are not dealing with a wrestling match agreed to by both parties. Like a robber who must avoid being caught, the attacker must avoid the light of dawn; like a robber, too, he must keep his identity secret." Westermann, *Genesis: A Practical Commentary,* 229.

37. "In the ancient Near East, wrestling had very different associations from the buffoonery of TV bouts in our culture. One way in which a legal case could be settled was by the ordeal of a wrestling match — a trial by combat." Clowney, *Unfolding Mystery,* 71-72. "God wrestled *(yēʾābēq)* with Jacob *(yaʿăqōb)* by the Jabbok *(yabbōq)* — the author delighted in word play." *NIV Study Bible,* Genesis 32:24, n.

Verse 25, "When the man saw that he did not prevail[38] against Jacob, he struck him on the hip socket; and Jacob's hip was put out of joint as he wrestled with him." Just a touch on the hip socket, and Jacob's hip is out of joint. Jacob must wonder where his attacker gets this strength. Who is this person? He seems almost supernatural. Jacob is crippled; he can fight no longer; but he hangs on for dear life. Suddenly the man begins to speak. He says, verse 26, "Let me go, for the day is breaking."[39] But Jacob responds, "I will not let you go, unless you bless me." Jacob now has an inkling that the man may be God, and he wants his blessing.[40]

But the stranger is not yet ready to bless Jacob. Or rather, Jacob is not yet ready for God's blessing. The stranger asks Jacob, verse 27, "What is your name?" It's an embarrassing question because a person's name revealed his character.[41] But Jacob admits, he is "Jacob" — a heel-grabber, a deceiver. His whole life he has been a grabber and deceiver. Jacob confesses his sins in one word: "Jacob."[42]

Then follows the climax of this narrative. Verse 28, "Then the man said, 'You shall no longer be called Jacob, but Israel, for you have *striven with God* and with humans, and have prevailed.'" The man changes Jacob's name from Jacob, deceiver, to Israel. And he gives this reason for the name change, "for (*kî*) you have striven with God and with humans, and have prevailed." Jacob had striven with humans his whole life, from striving with Esau in the womb, to later getting his birthright. He had striven with his father Isaac and by deception received the blessing. He had striven with Laban and by trickery had become rich. Jacob had striven with humans and *prevailed* — unfortunately by deception and trickery. But here at the Jabbok River, Jacob has striven with God

38. "The fact that Jacob's divine opponent was not able to win this fight simply suggests that he did not make use of his divine strength but limited himself to the normal strength of the human form he had assumed for this appearance." Aalders, *Genesis,* II, 143.

39. Some commentators, often with references to 32:31 and Exod 33:20, suggest that "it is Jacob's best interests that he not see God, a sure sentence of death." Hamilton, *Genesis 18–50,* 332. Cf. Clowney, *Unfolding Mystery,* 73, and, more tentatively, Wenham, *Genesis 16–50,* 296. Aalders, *Genesis,* II, 143, counters, "This . . . suggestion fails to recognize the fact that Jacob would not have looked upon God himself, but only on a 'theophany,' which represented no real threat to a man, as is evidenced by Abraham's meeting with such a visitor (in ch. 18)."

40. "This request provides a clue that the real nature of the man is dawning on Jacob as day breaks, for the inferior would solicit a blessing from the superior." Hamilton, *Genesis 18–50,* 332.

41. "For us a name is simply a matter of *identification.* . . . For the ancient Semites, however, the name was far more important; for them it was a matter of *identity.* A man did not simply *have* his name, he *was* his name." McCurley, *Proclaiming the Promise,* 86.

42. "By divulging his name, Jacob also discloses his character. It is here a confession of guilt; as Jeremiah puts it, 'Every brother Jacobs [RSV, is a supplanter]' (Jer 9:4). In uttering his name, Jacob admits he has cheated his brother." Wenham, *Genesis 16–50,* 296.

himself and, amazingly, he has prevailed. Even with his hip out of joint, he held on to receive God's blessing. So God gives him a new name: "Israel" — "for you have striven with God." This new name reorients Jacob's character from striving deceitfully in his own strength to striving for God's blessing. God has turned Jacob around from his deceptive ways.[43] As a deceiver, Jacob is not allowed to enter the Promised Land; as Israel he may enter the land and receive it as a gift, an inheritance, from God's hand.[44]

Jacob now knows that the stranger is God, for only one in authority can give a person a new name.[45] Moreover, the stranger says, "You have striven with *God*." In order to make sure that he has been wrestling with God, Jacob asks the man, verse 29, "Please tell me your name." But the man refuses to give his name[46] and instead blesses Jacob. The new Jacob now has the blessing for which he begged earlier.

To memorialize this momentous event in his life, verse 30, "Jacob called the place Peniel, saying, 'For I have seen God face to face, and yet my life is preserved.'" "Peniel"[47] means "face of God." When Jacob says, "I have seen God face to face," he is not saying that he saw God's face, but rather that in the darkness he had had a personal encounter with God.[48] And that personal encounter, combined with God's blessing, means that his life is preserved. He can now face Esau without fear. Earlier, when Jacob heard that Esau was on the way with four hundred men, he was terrified and begged God: "*Deliver* me, please, from the hand of my brother" (v 11). Now Jacob uses the same verb, "My life is *preserved*," that is, "I am delivered." "That he has been delivered comes home to him when seeing God face to face. Jacob now understands that because he has seen God face to face he will now also see his brother Esau properly, face to face, no longer afraid, and that therefore he has been delivered."[49]

43. "The major significance of the episode derives, of course, from the change of name that resulted. This . . . portends a new destiny, effectuates a decisive break with the past and inaugurates a fresh role, all symbolized here by the substitution of Israel for Jacob." Sarna, *Understanding Genesis*, 206.

44. The name "Israel" here is a play on the Hebrew words "striving with God." But in the Hebrew the name "Israel" means, "God strives" (see p. 319 above). God strives both against and for Jacob. God strives against Jacob's self-sufficiency: God attacks him, touches his hip, and renders him helpless. An independent, self-sufficient Jacob is not welcome in the Promised Land. But God also strives for the new Jacob, Israel, mellowing the angry Esau and allowing this reoriented Jacob/Israel into the Promised Land.

45. "This renaming of Jacob is an assertion of the assailant's authority to impart a new life and new status (cf. 2 Kings 23:32; 24:17)." Ross, *Creation and Blessing*, 554.

46. "The 'man' now implicitly identified with God (cf. v 29) refuses to give his name, lest it be abused (cf. Judg 13:17-18; Exod 20:7)." Wenham, *Genesis 16–50*, 297.

47. "Elsewhere (v 31; Judg 8:8-9, 17; 1 Kgs 12:25) Peniel is called Penuel. The form Peniel may be used here [v 30] because it sounds more like 'face of God.'" Wenham, *Genesis 16–50*, 297.

48. See Hamilton, *Genesis 18–50*, 336.

49. Fokkelman, *Narrative Art in Genesis*, 220. This interpretation builds not only on the use

Verse 31, "The sun rose upon him as he passed Penuel, limping because of his hip." At Bethel "the sun had set" (28:11) when God met Jacob in the night and gave him his blessing. At Peniel God met Jacob in the night, gave him his blessing, and "the sun rose upon him." A new day is beginning for Jacob.[50] He has a new name, Israel, but also a new deformity, a limp. "The new name will forever remind Jacob of his new destiny. The new limp will forever remind him that in Elohim Jacob met for the first time one who can overpower him."[51] Jacob's limp shows that God has knocked out his self-sufficiency.

Edward Curtis sums up, "Thus the struggle at Peniel was a decisive experience in the life of Jacob in which he was taught by God that the realization of the promise must be effected by God rather than by human effort and initiative. The subsequent meeting with Esau was a test case for Jacob in that he saw clearly that God would do what he had promised as he overcame a major obstacle to Jacob's return to the land entirely apart from the schemes and devices of Jacob."[52] For when Jacob meets the dreaded Esau, Esau runs up to meet him, embraces him, falls on his neck, and kisses him; and they both weep (33:4). God has swept away Esau's anger and reconciled the brothers.

Jacob/Israel is a changed person. When he enters the Promised Land, for the first time in his life he builds an altar to God, at Shechem, just as his grandfather Abraham had done before him (12:7). And he calls the altar, significantly, "El-Elohe-Israel" (33:20), that is, "God, the God of *Israel*." The God of his fathers is now also Jacob's God. Jacob then returns to Bethel, and there builds an altar to God (35:7), just as Abraham had done before him (12:8), claiming the land for the worship of the LORD. Because God intercepted him at Peniel, Jacob is a changed person. He is now ready to receive the Promised Land as God's gift to him and his offspring. Whereas before Peniel, "his entire life had been characterized by his determination to seize the promise and the blessing for himself," now he sees that "the fulfillment of the promise must be the work of God rather than the work of Jacob. . . . God struggles with Jacob, and in the process Jacob prevails — not in the sense that he overcomes God but rather in the sense that by recognizing his dependence on God he is now able to receive the promise and the blessing of God to Abraham."[53]

---

of the same verb, "to deliver," but also on the use of the keyword "face," *pānîm,* both in 32:20, 30 and in 33:10 where Jacob tells Esau, "Truly, to see your face is like seeing the face of God — since you have received me with such favor." See Curtis, "Structure, Style and Context," *JETS* 30/2 (June 1987), 136.

50. "The rising of the sun (cf. vv 25, 27) marks the passing of the time and the dawn of a new era in Jacob's career." Wenham, *Genesis 16–50,* 297.

51. Hamilton, *Genesis 18–50,* 337.

52. Curtis, "Structure, Style and Context," *JETS* 30/2 (June 1987), 136.

53. Ibid., 135.

The narrator concludes this narrative with verse 32, "Therefore to this day the Israelites do not eat the thigh muscle that is on the hip socket, because he struck Jacob on the hip socket at the thigh muscle." Every time the Israelites butchered an animal, they were reminded of this story of God crippling their father Jacob before he could enter the Promised Land. God turned the self-sufficient Jacob into Israel before he could enter in. The nation of Israel, too, could not enter the Promised Land in their own strength. They had to rely on God alone and receive the land as a gift from God.

The same is true for us today. We receive the kingdom of God not by our hard work but only by God's grace. It is a gift. That is why Jesus warns us, "Truly I tell you, it will be hard for a rich person to enter the kingdom of heaven. Again I tell you, it is easier for a camel to go through the eye of a needle than for someone who is rich to enter the kingdom of God" (Matt 19:23-24). Self-made and self-sufficient people cannot inherit the kingdom of God. And yet Jesus urges us, "Strive to enter through the narrow door" (Luke 13:24). Do we have to work hard after all to enter the kingdom? The answer is, Yes and no. Note that Jesus says, "Strive to enter through *the narrow door*." Jesus himself is the narrow door; he is "the way, and the truth, and the life" (John 14:6; "the gate" in John 10:7). So just as Jacob strove with God for God's blessing, we are to strive for God's blessing, which is Jesus.

When the Philippian jailor asked Paul, "What must I do to be saved?" he received a simple answer, "Believe on the Lord Jesus, and you will be saved" (Acts 16:30-31). It seems so simple, and yet it is so difficult for us self-sufficient people to rely on Jesus alone. But there it is: If you wish to enter the kingdom of God, you must cling to Jesus. Jesus himself urges us to abide in him. He explains, "I am the true vine, and my Father is the vinegrower. He removes every branch in me that bears no fruit. Every branch that bears fruit, he prunes to make it bear more fruit. . . . Those who abide in me and I in them bear much fruit, because apart from me you can do nothing" (John 15:1-2, 5). Apart from Jesus we can do nothing — let alone enter the kingdom.

On another occasion, Jesus warned his disciples, "Truly I tell you, whoever does not receive the kingdom of God as a little child will never enter it" (Luke 18:17). How does a little child, a baby, receive something? Observe a baby. She can do nothing for herself but is completely dependent on her caregivers. She fully relies on her caregivers. That's the model for entering the kingdom of God: not self-sufficiency but dependence, reliance on Jesus. We must receive the kingdom as a precious gift from the Father through Jesus Christ.

CHAPTER 18

Joseph's Sale into Slavery

Genesis 37:2-36

The tenth and final *tôlĕdôt* of Genesis, about the family of Jacob, runs from Genesis 37:2 to 50:26. It is a unified narrative, often called a novella,[1] with an overarching plot. The narrative conflict begins in 37:4 with the narrator's comment that Joseph's brothers hated him so much that they "could not speak peaceably with him." Westermann states, "The peace of Jacob's household has been shattered. Here begins the narrative arc that ends with the healing of the breach by the reconciliation of the brothers in chapters 45 and 50."[2] This lengthy narrative has an overarching theme, expressed by Joseph himself, "Even though you intended to harm me, God intended it for good, in order to preserve a numerous people, as he is doing today" (50:20). One of the challenges in preaching a series of sermons on this lengthy narrative will be to select appropriate narrative units as preaching-texts. Another challenge is to understand these literary units in the context of the whole narrative and its overarching theme of God's providence, yet produce a series of sermons that each have a distinctive, textually specific, theme. For this particular narrative (37:2-36), a difficulty is to find good news as Joseph is sold into slavery. Another difficulty is how to preach Christ from a narrative that does not mention God at all.

Text and Context

In selecting this particular textual unit, the question is, Does this narrative begin at verse 1 or verse 2? Verse 1 states that Jacob settled in the land of Canaan.

1. Although von Rad argues that this is wisdom literature, "most modern writers follow Gunkel in classifying the material as a short story or novella." Ross, *Creation and Blessing,* 591. See ibid., 590-92.

2. Westermann, *Genesis: A Practical Commentary,* 263.

Although many take this to be the beginning of this narrative, it can also be read as completing the *tôlĕdôt* of Esau, who "moved to a land some distance from his brother Jacob" and "settled in the hill country of Seir; Esau is Edom" (36:6, 8). Esau's move *from* Canaan allowed Jacob to settle "in the land where his father had lived as an alien, the land of Canaan" (37:1).[3] Verse 2 reads, "This is the [*tôlĕdôt*] story of the family of Jacob." As in the nine earlier "accounts," so *tôlĕdôt* here indicates the beginning of a new narrative. The end of this first unit is easy to detect since chapter 38 deals not with Joseph but with Judah and Tamar. The narrative unit, therefore, is Genesis 37:2-36.

As to the context preceding the text, this narrative shows many similarities to the *tôlĕdôt* of Isaac. As the *tôlĕdôt* of Isaac is preceded by a brief *tôlĕdôt* of his older brother Ishmael (25:12-18), so this *tôlĕdôt* of Jacob is preceded by a brief *tôlĕdôt* of his older brother Esau (36:1–37:1). Moreover, as the *tôlĕdôt* of Isaac (25:19) is mainly about his younger son Jacob, so the *tôlĕdôt* of Jacob (37:2) is mainly about his younger son Joseph. Furthermore, as the narratives about Jacob were based on the oracle, "the elder shall serve the younger" (25:23), so the narratives about Joseph are based on his dreams that his brothers will bow down to him (37:5-11).

Other parallels between these narratives include: as "Isaac loved Esau . . . ; but Rebekah loved Jacob" (25:28), so "Israel loved Joseph more than any of his children" (37:3); as Esau sought to kill his brother Jacob (27:41), so Joseph's brothers seek to kill Joseph (37:20); as Jacob deceived his father with his brother's garments and goat's meat and skins (27:9-16), so Jacob's sons deceive their father with their brother's robe and goat's blood (37:31); and as Jacob was forced to flee to a foreign country (27:42), so Joseph is forced to go to a foreign country (37:36).

The chiastic structure of the Joseph novella suggested by Gary Rendsburg[4] provides us with a quick overview of the whole story (see p. 337). Notice that the interlude about Judah and Tamar in chapter 38 heightens the overall tension: What will happen to Joseph in Egypt? We have to wait until chapter 39 before the narrator picks up Joseph's story again. More importantly, notice that Joseph's "dream slowly works itself out in the narrative."[5] When Joseph's brothers first come to Egypt, they "bowed themselves before him with their faces to the ground" (42:6). When they come the second time, they bowed twice: they "bowed to the ground before him" and they "bowed their heads and did obei-

3. "Many commentators regard 37:1 as the start of the Joseph story, failing to realize that it is the close of the story of Esau in chapter 36 . . . , but Dillmann, Delitzsch, and Longacre . . . correctly note that 37:2 is the start of a new section in Genesis which closes at 50:26." Wenham, *Genesis 16–50*, 348-49. See also Leupold, *Genesis*, II, 952.

4. Rendsburg, *Redaction of Genesis*, 80. For a somewhat different chiastic structure, also centering in chapter 45, see Yehuda Radday, "Chiasmus in Hebrew Biblical Narrative," 102.

5. Brueggemann, *Genesis*, 290.

A Joseph and his brothers, Jacob and Joseph part	(37:1-36)
B Interlude: Joseph not present	(38:1-30)
C Reversal: Joseph guilty, Potiphar's wife innocent	(39:1-23)
D Joseph hero of Egypt	(40:1–41:57)
E Two trips to Egypt	(42:1–43:34)
F Final test	(44:1-34)
F′ Conclusion of test	(45:1-28)
E′ Two tellings of migration to Egypt	(46:1–47:12)
D′ Joseph hero of Egypt	(47:13-27)
C′ Reversal: Ephraim firstborn, Manasseh secondborn	(47:28–48:22)
B′ Interlude: Joseph nominally present	(49:1-28)
A′ Joseph and his brothers, Jacob and Joseph part	(49:29–50:26)

sance" (43:26, 28). Finally, after Jacob's death, the brothers "fell down before him, and said, 'We are here as your slaves'" (50:18).

We should also be aware of frequent doubling in the Joseph story:

> Scholars have long noted the unusual amount of doubling in the Joseph story: three sets of dreams occur in pairs — by Joseph, by his fellow prisoners, and by Pharaoh. Joseph is twice confined — in the pit and in prison. The brothers make two trips to Egypt for grain, have two audiences with Joseph on each occasion, twice find money in their grain bags, make two attempts to gain Jacob's permission to send Benjamin to Egypt, and finally receive two invitations to settle in Egypt. Both Potiphar and the prison keeper leave everything in Joseph's hands. Potiphar's wife makes two attempts to seduce Joseph and then accuses him twice. Joseph serves two prominent prisoners (and two years elapse between their dreams and those of Pharaoh). Joseph twice accuses his brothers of spying, devises two plans to force the brothers to bring Benjamin to Egypt, and on two occasions places money in their sacks. Finally, the same goods (gum, balm, and myrrh) are twice brought from Canaan to Egypt — first with Joseph and later with Benjamin.[6]

Doubling can serve several functions. Joseph himself explains to Pharaoh, "The doubling of Pharaoh's dream means that the thing is fixed by God, and God will shortly bring it about" (41:32). "Doubling can often be used for emphasis," but can also function sometimes as plot retardation, for example, in "delaying the recognition scene in which the brothers will discover the identity of the Egyptian lord."[7]

6. Ackerman, "Joseph, Judah, and Jacob," 85.

7. Ibid., 86, with credit to D. B. Redford, *A Study of the Biblical Story of Joseph (Genesis 37–50)*, vol. 20 of *Supplements to Vetus Testamentum* (Leiden: Brill), 75-76.

Literary Features

Right at the beginning the narrator describes Joseph in great detail: "Joseph, being seventeen years old, was shepherding the flock with his brothers; he was a helper to the sons of Bilhah and Zilpah, his father's wives; and Joseph brought a bad report of them to their father" (37:2). He also informs us of Jacob's favoritism: "Now Israel loved Joseph more than any other of his children, because he was the son of his old age; and he had made him a long robe with sleeves" (v 3). Joseph is further characterized by the dialogue: his insistence on telling his dreams that his brothers and even his father and mother bow down to him. The young Joseph is sketched as immature, unwise, boastful, and extremely talkative. This changes drastically when Joseph meets up with his brothers in Dothan. Here Joseph is passive and says not a single word[8] — like Abel when he was about to be killed by his older brother Cain (4:8). This change in Joseph coincides with the change in the point of view at verse 18. In the first half of the narrative Joseph is the subject — telling his dreams, searching for his brothers. Starting with verse 18, the brothers are the subject — hatching their plans, stripping Joseph of his robe, throwing him into a pit, seeing the caravan, selling Joseph, sending his blood-soaked robe back to their father.

Joseph's brothers are characterized by their ever greater hatred of Joseph (three times "they hated him [even more]" [vv 4, 5, 8]), their jealousy (v 11), their plan to kill Joseph, and their plan to deceive their old father (v 20).

Repetition of keywords may also help discern the author's emphases. We already noted the importance of Joseph's dreams for the whole Joseph story. In this chapter there are not only two dreams, but the word "dream" is repeated seven times (vv 5, 6, 8, 9 [2×], 10, 20). The word "brother(s)" is repeated twenty-one times[9] (3 × 7) to underscore the terrible nature of their crime — just as the Cain-Abel narrative (Gen 4) repeats the word "brother" seven times. The brothers' hatred of Joseph is repeated three times in ever increasing intensity (vv 4, 8, 11) and leads to "jealousy" (v 11).

Joseph's "robe" is mentioned eight times (vv 3, 23 [2×], 31 [2×], 32 [2×], 33), and that it was "long, with sleeves" is added three times (vv 3, 23, 32). The latter term (passim) is uncertain ("many-colored" comes from the Septuagint), since the word is used only here and twice in 2 Sam 13:18-19 where it describes the robe of a princess. Could it indicate a "royal robe"?[10] This would help clarify

8. This is a deliberate literary technique, for the brothers later recall, "we saw his anguish when he pleaded with us" (42:21).

9. 37:2, 4 (2×), 5, 8, 9, 10 (2×), 11, 12, 13, 14, 16, 17, 19, 23, 26 (2×), 27 (2×), 30.

10. "Many commentators suggest it has something to do with royalty." Waltke, *Genesis*, 500.

the brothers hatred, line up with Joseph's dreams of ruling over his brothers, and explain the brothers' first action on meeting Joseph: "they stripped him of his robe, the long robe with sleeves that he wore" (v 23).

In verse 28 the name "Joseph" is repeated three times (in the Hebrew): "When some Midianite traders passed by, they drew *Joseph* up, lifting him out of the pit, and sold *Joseph* to the Ishmaelites for twenty pieces of silver. And they took *Joseph* to Egypt." "The technique of 'renominalizing' (the repetition of a proper name [when pronouns could have been used]) may mark a climactic point in the text,"[11] and here it certainly does. The brothers' deception, "We shall say that a wild animal has devoured him" (v 20), is repeated verbatim by Jacob, "A wild animal has devoured him" (v 33).

The latter repetition is the basis for a possible chiastic structure in the second half of this narrative:[12]

A 18-20 conspiracy by the brothers: kill Joseph!
    "A savage beast devoured him!"
  B 21-22 speeches by Reuben: no, throw him into the pit
    C 23-24 brothers cast Joseph into the pit
      D 25 a caravan passes by
        X 26-27 proposal by Judah: sell Joseph
      D′ 28 Joseph sold to caravan
    C′ 29 Reuben finds the pit empty, rends his clothes
  B′ 30 and mourns; speech to his brothers
A′ 31-33 they deceive Jacob with the coat,
    Jacob concludes Joseph must be dead
    "A savage beast devoured him!"

Based on changes in location, the narrative can be divided into four scenes:[13]

Scene 1 (vv 5-11)
Hebron: Joseph relates his dreams;
the reaction of the brothers and father.

Scene 2 (vv 12-17)
Shechem: Joseph sent to check on the well-being of his brothers;
a man finds him wandering and directs him to Dothan.

11. Mathewson, *Art of Preaching Old Testament Narrative*, 52.

12. Fokkelman, *Reading Biblical Narrative*, 80.

13. There is no agreement among commentators on the scenic structure of this narrative, ranging from three scenes (Ross, *Creation and Blessing*, 595) to eight scenes from vv 12-35 (Wenham, *Genesis 16–50*, 349). Obviously, there is no agreement on what constitutes a scene.

Scene 3 (vv 18-31)
Dothan: The brothers plan to kill Joseph; Reuben's counterplan; Judah's plan, they sell Joseph as a slave.
Scene 4 (vv 32-35)
Hebron: Jacob recognizes Joseph's robe; he mourns for his son.
Outcome (v 36)
Egypt: Joseph sold to Potiphar, one of Pharaoh's officials.

The Plot Line

This being the first act in a long narrative, the setting is minimal: "This is the story of the family of Jacob" (37:2a). The preliminary incidents create their own tension:[14] Joseph brings a bad report of his brothers to Jacob (v 2). Jacob loves Joseph more than any of his children and makes him a long robe with sleeves (v 3). As a result the brothers "hated him, and could not speak peaceably to him" (v 4).

The hatred of the brothers increases when Joseph insists on recounting his first dream. The narrator emphasizes their increasing hatred with an inclusio of "they hated him even more" framing Joseph's retelling of the dream (vv 5, 8). But Joseph will not let up. He has a second dream and eagerly tells it to his brothers and father. The brothers' hatred now advances to jealousy (v 11) — a trait that leads to punishing action (cf. Exod 20:5; Num 25:11). The stage is set for a major confrontation.

The occasioning incident occurs when the brothers pasture Jacob's flock near Shechem (v 12), a dangerous place for them (see 34:30), and Jacob sends Joseph to check on the welfare of his brothers. Jacob says to Joseph, "Go now, see if it is well with your brothers and with the flock; and bring word back to me" (v 14). The tension heightens when Joseph cannot find his brothers near Shechem and a man finds him "wandering in the fields" (v 15). The man, however, had overheard the brothers say, "Let us go to Dothan," and so Joseph heads for Dothan, fourteen miles farther from the safety of home.

With verse 18 the perspective changes from Joseph to the brothers. This new scene places us in the brothers' camp and allows us to overhear their conversations. Joseph's brothers see him "from a distance" and begin to plan his

14. "No less than three reasons have surfaced for the anger of Joseph's brothers against him: (1) his maligning some of them (v 2); (2) the obvious favoritism lavished on him by his father (vv 3-4); (3) his insistence on sharing his seemingly pompous dreams (vv 5-11)." Hamilton, *Genesis 18–50*, 412.

murder. They say to one another, "Here comes this dreamer. Come now, let us kill him . . . and we shall see what will become of his dreams" (vv 19-20). This is the climax of the first plot. Joseph's brothers wish to kill him and with it his dreams of ruling over them. Their hatred and jealousy of Joseph is about to lead to the "shedding of blood." Will the brothers go through with fratricide?

The tension eases when the oldest brother, Reuben, urges them, "Shed no blood; throw him into this pit here in the wilderness, but lay no hand on him." Reuben wishes to rescue Joseph later and "restore him to his father" (v 22). The brothers follow his advice, but first they strip Joseph of the hated robe and then throw him into an empty cistern (vv 23-24). The brothers sit down to eat, as if nothing has happened.

Suddenly they spot a caravan in the distance. This provides brother Judah a way out of their predicament: "What profit is it if we kill our brother and conceal his blood? Come, let us sell him to the Ishmaelites, and not lay our hands on him, for he is our brother, our own flesh" (vv 26-27). His brothers agree. "When some Midianite traders passed by, they drew *Joseph* up, lifting him out of the pit, and sold *Joseph* to the Ishmaelites for twenty pieces of silver. And they took *Joseph* to Egypt" (v 28). Joseph is still alive! The initial tension is resolved.

Reuben, apparently, is elsewhere when Joseph is sold and carried off. When Reuben checks the cistern and finds Joseph gone, he tears his clothes in sorrow (v 29). "The boy is gone; and I, where can I turn?" (v 30). As the oldest son, he is responsible for the boy. What will he tell his father? This raises the second issue. The brothers decide to deceive their father. They slaughter a goat, dip Joseph's robe in the blood, and send the robe to their father with the message, "This we have found; see now whether it is your son's robe or not" (vv 31-32) — Let Jacob draw his own conclusions! The tension whether they can get away with this deception resolves when Jacob recognizes the robe and falls for the ruse: "It is my son's robe! A wild animal has devoured him; Joseph is without doubt torn to pieces" (v 33). Jacob mourns for his beloved son and refuses to be comforted (vv 34-35). The outcome of the story is that Joseph is sold in Egypt to Potiphar, "one of Pharaoh's officials" (v 36).

We can sketch this narrative as a complex plot, as shown on page 342.

Theocentric Interpretation

Where is God in this story? God is not mentioned even once. Yet God is not absent. Only God gives dreams that foretell the future: witness the dreams of the chief cupbearer and the chief baker, the two dreams of Pharaoh, and their fulfillments (40:1–41:36). Wenham writes, "Throughout the ancient world, and Genesis is no exception, dreams were viewed as revelatory, as messages from

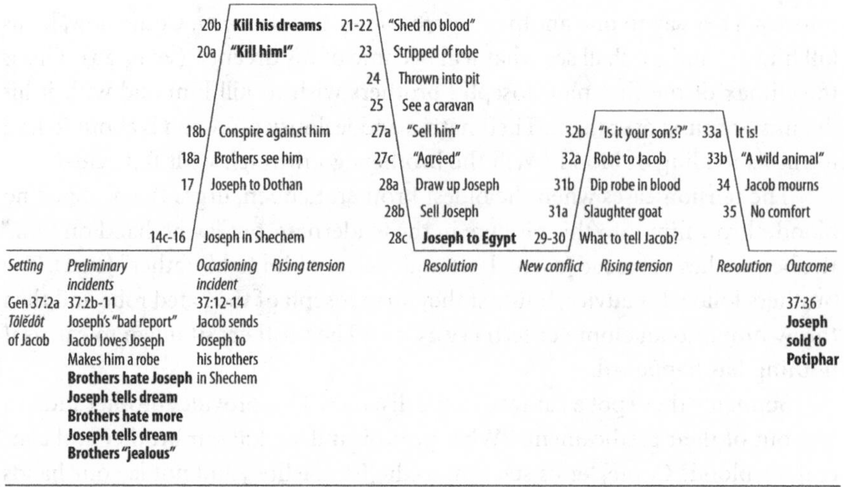

God. . . . Certainly the narrator saw these two dreams as prophetic; the sending of two dreams guarantees their fulfillment (41:32)."[15] Joseph's dreams of his brothers bowing down to him foretell God's plan for his life, as the brothers understood all too well. Their plan, "Come now, let us kill him [the dreamer] . . . and we shall see what will become of his dreams" (vv 19-20), is at bottom an attempt to kill God's plan. But God saves Joseph, first through Reuben, who "delivered him out of their hands" (v 21), then through Judah, who proposes that they sell Joseph, "and his brothers agreed" (v 27), and finally through the Midianites, who sell him "in Egypt to Potiphar, one of Pharaoh's officials" (v 36). From the beginning of Joseph's arrival in Egypt, he is near Pharaoh. Even though his suffering will increase even more when he is falsely accused and imprisoned, eventually he will rise to the highest position in Pharaoh's palace, and his brothers will come and indeed bow down to him (42:6; 43:26, 28; 50:18). Joseph's dreams will come true; God's plan is being fulfilled.

In fact, God's plan entails much more than the brothers bowing to Joseph. As ruler of Egypt, Joseph will be instrumental in saving his father Jacob and his extended family from death by famine. As Joseph later says to his brothers: "God sent me before you to preserve for you a remnant on earth, and to keep alive for you many survivors. So it was not you who sent me here, but God; he has made me a father to Pharaoh, and lord of all his house and ruler over the land of Egypt" (45:7-8). Still later, Joseph again reminds his brothers of God's providence: "Even though you intended to do harm to me, God intended it for good, in order to preserve a numerous people, as he is doing today" (50:20).

15. Wenham, *Genesis 16–50*, 359.

Textual Theme and Goal

God used the evil deeds of Joseph's brothers to set in motion his plan of making Joseph a ruler in Egypt in order to save his people Israel from famine, to have them multiply in Egypt, and eventually to return to Canaan with "great possessions" (see Gen 15:13-16). In this chapter God's plan is partially revealed in Joseph's dreams. We can, therefore, formulate the theme of this narrative as follows: *God uses the evil deeds of Joseph's brothers to begin fulfilling his plan, as revealed in Joseph's dreams, of making Joseph a ruler.*

As to the author's goal in relating this message to Israel, we should recall that Israel in its history was frequently perplexed by the evil that befell them. Often they were like father Jacob — mourning and refusing to be comforted. Where is God in such circumstances? This story about Joseph gave them comfort: no matter how dark the circumstances, our sovereign God is in control! He can overrule and even use the evil deeds of people to accomplish his plan of salvation. The author's goal, then, would be, *To comfort Israel with the knowledge that God can use even evil human deeds to fulfill his plan of salvation.*

Ways to Preach Christ

Given the theme, "God uses the evil deeds of Joseph's brothers to begin fulfilling his plan, as revealed in Joseph's dreams, of making Joseph a ruler," what are legitimate ways of moving to Jesus Christ in the New Testament?

Redemptive-Historical Progression

The road of redemptive-historical progression offers one option: God in his providence saved Joseph from the murderous intent of his brothers, who wished to kill him and his dreams. By saving Joseph from death and bringing him to Egypt, God began to fulfill his plan of making Joseph a ruler in Egypt who would be able to save Israel from death by famine. In Egypt Israel would multiply and after "four hundred years" return to the Promised Land with "great possessions" (15:13-14). Because God in his providence kept Israel alive, in the fullness of time the Messiah could be born of them.

Promise-Fulfillment

Although Joseph's dreams contain God's prediction/promise that his brothers will bow down to him (fulfilled in 42:6; 43:26, 28; 50:18), there is no messianic promise in this passage.

Typology

Typology provides an interesting bridge to Christ in the New Testament, but one must be careful to avoid typologizing (for example, some have stated that Joseph's obedience to his father in going to his brothers is a type of Jesus' obedience to his Father in going to his brothers and sisters; others have linked Joseph in the pit with Jesus in the grave). Joseph in his suffering and eventual ascension to the throne and thus saving not only Israel but "all the world" (41:57) is indeed a type of Christ as he follows the same path from humiliation to exaltation for our salvation.

Focusing on chapter 37, we can discern several parallels between Joseph and Jesus: as Joseph's brothers "conspired to kill him" (37:18), so Jesus' brothers, the chief priests and the elders, "conspired to arrest Jesus by stealth and kill him" (Matt 26:4); as Joseph's brothers sold him for twenty pieces of silver, so Jesus' disciple Judas sold Jesus for thirty pieces of silver (Matt 26:15); as Joseph's brothers handed him over to Gentiles, so Jesus' brothers handed him over to Gentiles (Matt 27:1-2),[16] as Joseph suffered in silence, so at his trial, "Jesus was silent" (Matt 26:63); and as God used the evil deeds of Joseph's brothers eventually to save his people, so God used the evil deeds of Jesus' brothers to save his people. But Jesus is more than Joseph: Jesus is the Son of God who died and rose again to save his people for all eternity. And Jesus ascended to the right hand of God the Father, from where he rules his kingdom until he comes again to establish his kingdom on earth in perfection.

Analogy

Analogy offers another way to Christ: As God taught Israel through this story that he can use even evil human deeds to fulfill his plan of salvation, so Jesus

16. See McCartney and Clayton, *Let the Reader Understand,* 158. They also caution against typologizing: "Incidental details such as the animal blood on Joseph's coat, Joseph's leaving his garment in the hand of Potiphar's wife, and his use of a cup in Benjamin's sack are probably not to be seen as having any fuller sense." Ibid., 158-59.

teaches the church that God can use evil human deeds to fulfill his plan of salvation. One can support this analogy with a New Testament passage such as Luke 21:16-18, where Jesus says, "You will be betrayed even by parents and brothers . . . ; and they will put some of you to death. You will be hated by all because of my name. But not a hair of your head will perish" — perhaps combined with Romans 8:28, "We know that all things work together for good for those who love God, who are called according to his purpose."

Longitudinal Themes

The author's deliberate portrayal of Joseph here suffering in silence (compared to 42:21) suggests the longitudinal theme of the Suffering Servant:

> He was oppressed,
>   and he was afflicted,
> yet he did not open his mouth;
> like a lamb that is led to the slaughter,
>   and like a sheep that before its shearers is silent,
>   so he did not open his mouth.
>
> (Isa 53:7)

From this Isaiah passage one can move to the New Testament and, like Philip, preach "the good news about Jesus" (Acts 8:35). Jesus "was silent and did not answer" the high priest (Mark 14:61); he "made no further reply" to Pilate (Mark 15:5); and he gave King Herod "no answer" (Luke 23:9).

One can also trace the servant theme along a broader front, as Joyce Baldwin does effectively: "Joseph was going through an experience which was to become a major theme of the Bible. The godly Servant was despised and rejected, only to become the rescuer of those who abused him (Isa 53:3-6); the Lord's shepherd was underrated (Zech 11:12-13), was struck down and his sheep scattered, but the 'sheep' found they were the Lord's people (Zech 13:7-9); the way of the cross involved for Jesus betrayal by a friend, as well as agony and death, but it was the way of life for all believers."[17]

In the New Testament, Stephen's speech in Acts 7 traces the theme of Israel rejecting its leaders. He begins this part with Joseph: "The patriarchs, jealous of Joseph, sold him into Egypt; but God was with him, and rescued him from all his afflictions, and enabled him to win favor and to show wisdom when he stood before Pharaoh, king of Egypt, who appointed him ruler over Egypt and

17. Baldwin, *Message of Genesis 12–50*, 160.

over all his household" (Acts 7:9-10). Stephen continues by recalling Israel's rejection of Moses and concludes his speech with Israel's rejection of the prophets and Christ: "Which of the prophets did your ancestors not persecute? They killed those who foretold the coming of the Righteous One, and now you have become his betrayers and murderers" (Acts 7:52).

New Testament References

The appendix of the Nestle-Aland Greek New Testament lists the following allusions to this chapter: for Genesis 37:9, Rev 12:1 ("a woman clothed with the sun"); for Genesis 37:11, both Luke 2:19 ("Mary pondered these words in her heart")[18] and Acts 7:9 (quoted above); for Genesis 37:20, Mark 12:7 (see below); and for Genesis 38:28, again Acts 7:9.

Mark 12:7 records the words of the wicked tenants in Jesus' parable: "Those tenants said to one another, 'This is the heir; come, let us kill him, and the inheritance will be ours.'" In order to use this bridge to Jesus effectively in the sermon, one would have to make the case that Jacob, by giving Joseph a royal robe, made Joseph his main heir (Joseph does indeed get Jacob's blessing of the firstborn [1 Chron 5:1-2] when Jacob adopts Joseph's sons Ephraim and Manasseh as his own [Gen 48:5]).

Victor Hamilton makes an interesting case for Matthew 1–2: "While Matthew 1–2 does not refer explicitly to the OT Joseph, Matthew appears to make the case that the NT Joseph is reliving the experiences of the OT Joseph. Both Josephs receive revelation in dreams, and go down to Egypt. Both are involved with a king (Pharaoh, Herod). Both are followed by children who are destined to be saviors and rescuers of the oppressed. Thus the parallel is:

"OT Joseph–dreams–wicked Pharaoh–infant Moses
:: NT Joseph–dreams–wicked Herod–infant Jesus."[19]

Contrast

There is no contrast between this Old Testament message and the New Testament.

18. Hamilton, *Genesis 18–50*, 411, n. 43, points out that Luke 2:51 is closer than Luke 2:19 in also using the same verb as Gen 37:11 (LXX).

19. Ibid., 714-15, with credit to R. E. Brown, *The Birth of the Messiah* (Garden City, NY: Doubleday, 1977), 111-12.

Sermon Theme and Goal

We formulated the textual theme as, "God uses the evil deeds of Joseph's brothers to begin fulfilling his plan, as revealed in Joseph's dreams, of making Joseph a ruler." The sermon theme can be similar but should be a little briefer and more focused. We can formulate the sermon theme as follows: *God uses the evil deeds of Joseph's brothers to begin fulfilling his plan of salvation.*

The author's goal was, "To comfort Israel with the knowledge that God can use even evil human deeds to fulfill his plan of salvation." We can make our goal in preaching this sermon almost the same: *To comfort the church with the knowledge that God can use even evil human deeds to fulfill his plan of salvation.* This goal addresses the church's need of being so overwhelmed by the evil in our world and society that people fear that God is absent.

Sermon Exposition

The sermon introduction can begin with a story of how God's people frequently suffer from the evil deeds of others, for example, religious persecution, genocide, murder, torture, theft. This raises the questions: Where is God? Why does he not protect us? Transition to Israel's suffering at the hands of others. How often did they not raise the questions, Where is God? Is he absent? Is he sleeping (e.g., Pss 44:23; 59:4-5)? Transition to Joseph.

Verse 2, "This is the story of the family of Jacob. Joseph, being seventeen years old, was shepherding the flock with his brothers; he was a helper to the sons of Bilhah and Zilpah, his father's wives; and Joseph brought a bad report of them to their father." The first thing the writer tells us about Joseph is that he is seventeen, an apprentice shepherd, and that he tattles on his brothers. Joseph probably exaggerates the bad things his brother did. The Hebrew indicates that he brings "an evil report," misrepresenting his brothers.[20] Joseph appears to be an unlikeable character: he is immature, tattles on his brothers, and exaggerates their flaws. In short, the narrator sketches the young Joseph as a fool: he is unwise (this will change later).

But his old father Jacob is equally unwise. We read in verse 3 that "Israel [Jacob] loved Joseph more than any of his children, because he was the son of his old age; and he had made him a long robe with sleeves." Joseph is the son of Jacob's favorite wife Rachel. After Jacob had ten sons with his other wives, Joseph was finally

20. "Although the narrator blanks the details, the word *report (dibbâ)* by itself denotes news slanted to damage the victim (see Prov 10:18)." Waltke, *Genesis,* 499. Cf. Wenham, *Genesis 16–50,* 350, "The term *dibbâ* 'tales' is always used elsewhere in a negative sense of an untrue report, and here it is qualified by the adjective 'evil' (cf. Num 13:32; 14:36-37). So it seems likely that Joseph misrepresented his brothers to his father. . . ."

born to the beautiful Rachel. So Jacob "loved Joseph more than any of his children," and he acted on his favoritism by making him "a long robe with sleeves."

The King James Version speaks here of "a coat of *many* colors."[21] But the robe was probably a special dress coat — distinguished from a normal robe by its extra length and long sleeves. This robe was probably more than a symbol of Jacob's special love for Joseph. The adjective "long with sleeves" is used in only one other place in the Old Testament, and there it is used to describe the robe of princess Tamar. For that reason "many commentators suggest it has something to do with royalty. . . . By this regal apparel (see 2 Sam 13:18-19) Jacob publicly designates Joseph as the ruler over the family."[22]

Can you imagine: With this robe Jacob publicly elevates this young brat Joseph above his older brothers! And Joseph seems to wear this symbol of his special status with pride whenever he can. Small wonder we read in verse 4 that his brothers "hated him, and could not speak peaceably to him." They refused to greet him with a friendly, "Shalom!" "Greetings were very important in this period. Even today, refusal to greet someone can mean social ostracism."[23] The brothers hated Joseph — but their hatred will grow even more furious.

Verse 5, "Once Joseph had a dream, and when he told it to his brothers, they *hated him even more.*" God sometimes revealed his plans for the future in dreams.[24] In the Joseph story, dreams always come in pairs: think of the dreams of Pharaoh's chief cupbearer and chief baker and the two dreams of Pharaoh. Joseph himself explains to Pharaoh why the dreams come in pairs: a single dream could just be an idle dream, but "the doubling of Pharaoh's dream means that the thing is fixed by God, and God will shortly bring it about" (41:32).

Joseph shows his foolish nature by insisting on telling this particular dream to his brothers. He brags, verse 6, "Listen to this dream that I dreamed. There we were, binding sheaves in the field. Suddenly my sheaf rose and stood upright; then your sheaves gathered around it, and *bowed down* to my sheaf."[25]

21. Based on an erroneous translation in the LXX and Vulgate.

22. Waltke, *Genesis,* 500. Cf. Brueggemann, *Genesis,* 304, "Jacob thereby designated his son as his special heir."

23. Westermann, *Genesis: A Practical Commentary,* 263.

24. "Throughout the biblical world, dreams were recognized as vehicles of divine communication." Sarna, *Understanding Genesis,* 212.

25. Cf. Isaac blessing Jacob (27:29):

> "Let peoples serve you,
>   and nations bow down to you.
> Be lord over your brothers,
>   and may your mother's sons bow down to you."

"We need to understand this verb *histăḥăwâ* (to bow down) in its fullest weight of meaning for that time: whoever bows down before someone else thereby acknowledges that person as an ab-

Even today, this is not the kind of dream you would want to tell your older brothers. And certainly not when you are wearing a royal robe symbolizing your father's desire that you rule the family! The brothers understand the meaning of the dream all too well. They say to Joseph, verse 8, "Are you indeed to reign over us? Are you indeed to have dominion over us?"[26] The narrator adds, "So they *hated him even more* because of his dreams and his words."

But Joseph will not let up. He has a second dream, similar to the first. He eagerly tells it to his father and brothers: verse 9, "Look, I have had another dream: the sun, the moon, and eleven stars were *bowing down* to me" (v 9). Again the meaning is clear to the hearers: the sun is father Jacob, the moon Joseph's stepmother Leah (Rachel died earlier [35:19]), and the eleven stars are the eleven brothers. All will bow down to Joseph.

This time even Jacob rebukes Joseph and says, verse 10, "What kind of dream is this that you have had? Shall we indeed come, I and your mother and your brothers, and bow to the ground before you?" Preposterous!

By talking too much, foolish Joseph is now at odds not only with his brothers but even with his father.[27] The narrator tells us in verse 11, "So his brothers were jealous of him, but his father kept the matter in mind." "His father kept the matter in mind." One never knows with these dreams. At Bethel, Jacob himself had met the Lord in a dream (28:12-17). And Jacob knew that the Lord could declare as his plan that "the elder shall serve the younger" (25:23). He had experienced this himself, and now Joseph had two dreams like this. Instead of dismissing the dreams, it is better to wait and see what happens.

But the brothers' hatred increases even more: "His brothers were *jealous* of him." Three times the narrator has mentioned the brothers' increasing hatred (vv 4, 5, 8). Now he says that they are "jealous of him." "In context, this seems to be a stronger and deeper passion than 'hatred' (vv 5, 8). Indeed, in various passages it is a feeling that is liable to spill over into violent action (e.g., Num 25:11,

---

solute authority, and he puts himself completely at the disposal of that authority." Westermann, *Joseph,* 10-11.

26. "Their anger is expressed in the two synonymous verbs in parallelism that constitute the climax of this section: the younger brother wants to reign over his older brothers! This runs counter to the familial structure of society, in which all authority derives from seniority." Westermann, *Genesis: A Practical Commentary,* 263-64. Ross, *Creation and Blessing,* 600, states that "the infinitive absolute in the question heightens the doubt." Therefore a better translation would be, "You don't mean to tell us that you will rule over us, do you? Or that you will indeed have dominion over us?"

27. "Not only was new fuel making the blaze continually hotter against Joseph in the four stages of 2, 4, 8 and 11, but the fire was also spreading. In 2b only four of the brothers seem to have been involved; in 4 it was the whole group; in 10 the father's rebuke, moderate though it was, completed the boy's isolation, leaving him apparently at odds with his entire world." Kidner, *Genesis,* 180-81.

13).... Proverbs cautions against allowing such jealousy free reign (14:30; 23:17; 24:1, 19). So the note that 'his brothers were very jealous' is ominous, suggesting that they may well seek revenge."[28] The stage is set for a major confrontation.

Once, verse 12 informs us, "his brothers went to pasture their father's flock near Shechem." Joseph is not with them. He is at home — more preferential treatment from Jacob! Shechem is about fifty miles north of the Hebron valley and a dangerous place for Jacob's sons. Here they had avenged the rape of their sister Dinah by killing "all the males" and plundering the city, thereby making Jacob "odious to the inhabitants of the land" (34:25, 27, 30). So Jacob is understandably concerned about their well-being.

Jacob says to Joseph, verse 14, "Go now, see if it is well with your brothers and with the flock; and bring word back to me." Ironically, Jacob sends Joseph to see if it is "well" *(šālôm)* with his brothers when the brothers "could not speak peaceably *(šālôm)* to him" (37:4). We wonder, What will happen to Joseph when he meets his hostile brothers so far from the safety of his father's home?

Joseph undertakes the long journey to Shechem, but, surprisingly, he cannot find his brothers. A stranger finds him "wandering in the fields" (v 15). It looks as if he is searching for lost sheep or cattle, for the stranger asks him, "What[29] are you seeking?" Joseph responds, verse 16, "I am seeking my brothers; tell me, please, where they are pasturing the flock." Providentially the stranger had overheard their plans, and replies, "They have gone away, for I heard them say, 'Let us go to Dothan'" (v 17). Dothan is another fourteen miles north.

Dothan is the place where Elisha later was surrounded by a great hostile army from Aram but said confidently to his servant, "Do not be afraid, for there are more with us than there are with them." Then the Lord opened the eyes of the servant, and he saw the mountain "full of horses and chariots of fire all around Elisha" (2 Kings 6:14-17). But Joseph does not receive a vision of a heavenly army protecting him. He lacks this assurance of God's presence.[30] All he knows is that he is facing his hostile brothers far from the protection of his father. Yet he doggedly follows the trail to Dothan. What will happen to him?

With verse 18 the perspective changes from Joseph to the brothers. This new scene places us in the brothers' camp and allows us to overhear their conversations. "They saw him from a distance, and before he came near to them, they conspired to kill him." His brothers see him "from a distance." How do they know from a distance that it is Joseph? The long robe, of course, with the

28. Wenham, *Genesis 16–50,* 352.

29. "*Mah,* 'what,' rather than *mî,* 'whom,' introduces the question, the stranger assuming that perhaps cattle had been lost." Leupold, *Genesis,* II, 962-63.

30. "God has been as watchful in his hiddenness as in any miracle. The two extremes of his methods meet in fact at Dothan, for it was here, where Joseph cried in vain (42:21), that Elisha would find himself visibly encircled by God's chariots (2 Kings 6:13-17)." Kidner, *Genesis,* 181.

long sleeves. Seeing that hated robe is enough to make their blood boil. "Here comes this dreamer,"[31] they say. "Come now, let us kill[32] him and throw him into one of the pits; then we shall say that a wild animal has devoured him, and we shall see what will become of his dreams" (vv 19-20). The dreams of Joseph still stick in their craw. By killing Joseph they think they can kill his dreams — the dreams that they, the older brothers, will bow down to this young upstart.

At this point, Jacob's oldest son, Reuben, intervenes. As the oldest, he is responsible for what happens to Joseph. Murder is out of the question. Shed blood cries out to God from the ground (4:10). God will "require a reckoning" for shed blood (9:5-6). Reuben urges, verse 22, "Shed no blood; throw him into this pit here in the wilderness,[33] but lay no hand on him." Reuben wishes to rescue Joseph later and "restore him to his father."

Fortunately for Joseph, the brothers follow his advice. Verse 23, "So when Joseph came to his brothers, they stripped him of his robe, the long robe with sleeves that he wore; and they took him and threw him into a pit." Notice that before they throw Joseph into the pit, they strip him of his royal robe.[34] Basically, the brothers "defrock" Joseph of his special status as the next ruler of the family.[35] They are still trying to kill Joseph's dreams.

The narrator again reminds us of God's providence when he emphasizes at the end of verse 24, "The pit was empty; there was no water in it." Joseph does not drown in the cistern used to collect water; he remains alive. But he is a captive to his hostile brothers and cannot escape because he is trapped in this cistern with its steep walls.[36]

31. "The expression usually translated by 'the dreamer' means much more than our English word, namely, the one empowered to prophetic dreams (*ba'al haḥălōmôt* [lord of dreams])." Von Rad, *Genesis,* 348.

32. "As long as *hārag* 'kill' is not understood judicially, we might paraphrase their comment, 'let's murder him,' for this verb is generally used of illicit taking of human life (Gen 4:8, 14; 12:12). Indeed, this is what Esau planned to do to Jacob (27:41, 42)." Wenham, *Genesis 16–50,* 353.

33. "By *wilderness* Reuben is referring to the largely unpopulated pasture lands that would ring the perimeter of Dothan. On the one hand, this locale may appeal to the brothers in that any calls for help by Joseph would go unheeded. On the other hand, perhaps Reuben can successfully retrieve Joseph from a cistern that is far enough away from the watchful eyes of his brothers." Hamilton, *Genesis 18–50,* 419.

34. "'They stripped off [a term also used for skinning animals, Lev 1:6] his tunic, the special tunic he was wearing.' This unexpected expansiveness slows down the narrative for a moment and focuses on the piece of clothing that was the mark of his father's affection and the occasion of his brothers' hatred." Wenham, *Genesis 16–50,* 354.

35. "The giving of the robe has been equivalent to enthronement (v 3). . . . Now the dream is in jeopardy as the robe serves a different function, now *de*thronement." Brueggemann, *Genesis,* 304.

36. Cisterns are "large bottle-shaped pits hewn out of rock for retaining water. They range from 6 to 20 feet in depth." Waltke, *Genesis,* 502.

Amazingly, the Joseph who earlier could not hold his tongue in check and insisted on telling his dreams, now is silent. Although the brothers later will recall that Joseph pleaded with them (42:21), the narrator here wishes to show a major change in Joseph: the loquacious Joseph suffers in silence — just as Abel suffered in silence when his brother Cain killed him.

Joseph suffering in silence reminds us of the Suffering Servant of the LORD described in Isaiah 53:7,

> He was oppressed,
>   and he was afflicted,
> yet he did not open his mouth;
> like a lamb that is led to the slaughter,
>   and like a sheep that before its shearers is silent,
>   so he opened not his mouth.

This is the passage the Ethiopian eunuch was reading and could not understand. The eunuch asked Philip, "About whom does the prophet say this?" And Philip responded by preaching to him "the good news about Jesus" (Acts 8:35). For we learn in the Gospels that Jesus suffered through his trial in silence. Jesus "was silent and did not answer" the high priest (Mark 14:61); to Pilate, he "made no further reply" (Mark 15:5); and he gave King Herod "no answer" (Luke 23:9). Joseph suffering in silence prefigures the silent suffering of Jesus.[37]

Joseph is captive in the pit. He cannot possibly escape. And his brothers sit down to eat as if nothing had happened. Verse 25, "They sat down to eat; and looking up they saw a caravan of Ishmaelites coming from Gilead, with their camels carrying gum, balm, and resin, on their way to carry it down to Egypt." The caravan route from Gilead past Dothan to Egypt "was part of the immemorial way between Damascus and the coast road to the south, and their spices were a staple trade with Egypt."[38] Seeing the caravan heading for Egypt gives brother Judah an idea. Although Judah is not the firstborn, he appears to be the leader of the brothers. He says, verse 26, "What profit is it if we kill our brother and conceal his blood? Come, let us sell him to the Ishmaelites, and not lay our hands on him, for he is our brother, our own flesh." Judah reminds his brothers that Joseph is their own brother. If they kill him, they will have to conceal his blood. But can they adequately conceal his blood? When Cain killed his brother

37. Suspending the story here to introduce the Joseph-Jesus typology is a calculated risk that one may lose one's hearers. When it is done briefly, however, it can increase the suspense in retelling Joseph's story while preparing one's hearers for the typology which will be developed later in the sermon.

38. Kidner, *Genesis*, 182.

Abel, the LORD said to Cain: "What have you done? Listen; your brother's blood is crying out to me from the ground! And now you are cursed from the ground" (4:10-11). The LORD will also see Joseph's blood and punish his brothers. "Come, let us sell him to the Ishmaelites, and not lay our hands on him."[39] Judah's plan seems like a win-win proposal: The brothers do not have to conceal Joseph's blood while he will probably die before long as a slave in Egypt. Moreover, they can make some money by selling him. The brothers agree to Judah's plan (v 27b).[40]

Verse 28, "When some Midianite traders [Midianite is another name for Ishmaelite][41] passed by, they drew Joseph up, lifting him out of the pit, and sold him to the Ishmaelites for twenty pieces of silver.[42] And they took Joseph to Egypt." The narrator repeats the name "Joseph" three times in the Hebrew: "They drew *Joseph* up, lifting him out of the pit, and sold *Joseph* to the Ishmaelites. . . . And they took *Joseph* to Egypt." "The repetition of the proper name is used to underscore that it was to *Joseph*, Jacob's favorite son, that these things were being done."[43]

It is unbelievable that this could happen to Joseph! Jacob's beloved Joseph on the way to Egypt as a slave! What will happen to Joseph? Ironically, this evil deed of Joseph's brothers begins to fulfill God's plan that Joseph will become a ruler in Egypt and that his brothers will indeed bow down to him.

Reuben, apparently, is elsewhere when Joseph is sold and carried off. After a while, Reuben goes to check on Joseph in the cistern and finds him gone. He thinks the worst has happened to Joseph. In deep sorrow he tears his clothes, runs to his brothers, and cries out, "The boy is gone; and I, where can I turn?" (v 30). As the oldest son, he is responsible for Joseph. What will he say to his father? What will *they* say to their father?

The brothers decide to deceive their old father. They will go back to plan A: "We shall say that a wild animal has devoured him" (v 20). They quickly slaughter a goat, dip Joseph's robe in the blood, and send it to their father with this

39. Judah's plan is also contrary to God's law: "If someone is caught kidnaping another Israelite, enslaving or selling the Israelite, then that kidnaper shall die" (Deut 24:7).

40. "'And his brothers agreed.' This short, very pregnant sentence is the turning point of this entire narrative. The crux of this moment is the fact that the brothers heed Judah, and in so doing, assent to his alternative plan." Westermann, *Joseph*, 16.

41. "It seems better to take Ishmaelites and Midianites as alternative designations of the same group of traders. . . . It could be that Ishmaelites is a general term meaning 'nomadic traders,' whereas 'Midianites' is a more specific ethnic designation showing which tribe they belonged to." Wenham, *Genesis 16–50*, 355. Cf. Judg 8:22, 24.

42. Twenty pieces of silver "was the average price for a male slave in Old Babylonian times (early 2nd millennium B.C.). The price gradually goes higher." Hamilton, *Genesis 18–50*, 422. Cf. Lev 27:5. Cf. Kitchen, *On the Reliability of the Old Testament*, 344-45.

43. Longacre, "Genesis as Soap Opera," 3.

message, verse 32, "This we have found; see now whether it is your son's[44] robe or not."[45]

Ironically, Jacob's sons seek to deceive their old father with their brother's robe and goat's blood, just as Jacob had earlier used his brother's garments and two little goats to deceive his blind father Isaac (27:9-27). The tension mounts again: Will the brothers get away with this deception? Can they successfully deceive the arch-deceiver Jacob?

The tension is quickly resolved when Jacob recognizes the robe as Joseph's robe. He never even considers that his sons may be deceiving him. Jacob's words are brief and filled with pain. He gasps, verse 33,

> "It is my son's robe!
> A wild animal has devoured him;
> Joseph is without doubt torn to pieces."[46]

The robe that was first used "for enthronement (v 3)," then became "an instrument of dethronement and symbolic death (v 23)," now is "used as evidence for the death of the dream."[47]

Jacob tears his garments, and puts sackcloth on his loins, and mourns for his son many days (v 34). According to verse 35, "All his sons and all his daughters sought to comfort him; but he refused to be comforted, and said, 'No, I shall go down to Sheol to my son, mourning.' Thus his father bewailed him." Father Jacob is heartbroken. His beloved son is dead.[48] He will not see him again. Jacob will mourn until the day of his death, when he will go down to Sheol, the abode of the dead.

But this is not the end of the story. The narrator ends this tragic story on a hopeful note. Verse 36, "Meanwhile the Midianites had sold him in Egypt to Potiphar, one of Pharaoh's officials, the captain of the guard." Joseph is in

44. "The language continually betrays the divisions. They speak not of their brother but of Jacob's son." Waltke, *Genesis*, 504.

45. "The bringing of the blood-dipped robe is not simply a cynical trick on the part of the brothers. Rather, it has a legal aspect, for this vestige of Joseph was considered proof of his death (cf. Exod 22:13). The father was therefore supposed to 'confirm' Joseph's death solemnly and legally; the brothers would then be released from any further liability." Von Rad, *Genesis*, 349.

46. "Jacob's three short comments . . . convey the strength of Jacob's emotions, climaxing with the mention of his favorite son's name": in the Hebrew, "He has been torn to bits, Joseph!" Wenham, *Genesis 16–50*, 356

47. Brueggemann, *Genesis*, 305.

48. "There is something singular in the Old Testament about a father and a son. So much has been entrusted to that young body. The body torn by the beast carried the future of the people. The 'added' one [Joseph] is irreplaceable. No ritual covers it. No other children can substitute." Ibid., 305.

Egypt. Though he has become a slave, he is a slave of one of Pharaoh's officials. Joseph is close to Pharaoh's palace. Even though his suffering will increase by being falsely accused and imprisoned, this way of suffering will eventually lead to his exaltation to the highest position in Pharaoh's palace. And, yes, his brothers will come and indeed bow down to him (42:6; 43:26, 28; 50:18)! Joseph's dreams will come true; God's plan for him is beginning to be fulfilled.

In fact, God's plan entails much more than the brothers bowing to Joseph. As ruler of Egypt, Joseph will be instrumental in saving his father Jacob and his extended family from death by famine. As Joseph later says to his brothers: "God sent me before you to preserve for you a remnant on earth, and to keep alive for you many survivors. So it was not you who sent me here, but God; he has made me a father to Pharaoh, and lord of all his house and ruler over the land of Egypt" (45:7-8).

In this narrative we see that God uses the evil deeds of Joseph's brothers to begin fulfilling his plan of making Joseph a ruler. The sovereign God overrules the evil intentions of Joseph's brothers to accomplish his goal: ultimately, to keep alive his people Israel — the people from whom the Messiah would be born. Later, Israel celebrated this episode of her history in Psalm 105:16-22.

When he summoned famine against the land,
  and broke every staff of bread,
he had sent a man ahead of them,
  Joseph, who was sold as a slave.
His feet were hurt with fetters,
  his neck was put in a collar of iron;
until what he had said came to pass,
  the word of the LORD kept testing him.
The king sent and released him;
  the ruler of the peoples set him free.
He made him lord of his house,
  and ruler of all his possessions,
to instruct his officials at his pleasure,
  and to teach his elders wisdom.

The Joseph story spoke to Israel of God's sovereign guidance of his people and of his covenant faithfulness. "O give thanks to the LORD, call on his name, make known his deeds among the peoples" (Ps 105:1).

In its history, Israel was frequently perplexed by the evil that befell them. Where is God? Is God sleeping? This story about Joseph gave them comfort: no matter how dark the circumstances, God is in control! He can overrule the evil deeds of people and accomplish his plan of salvation. This is profoundly good news: God uses even evil human deeds to fulfill his plan of salvation!

We see this not only in the story of Joseph but also in the story of Jesus. Joseph prefigures Jesus Christ. Through his suffering and eventual ascension to rulership Joseph saved God's people Israel. Jesus, similarly, through his suffering, death, resurrection, and ascension would save God's people. Note the parallels between Joseph and Jesus: as Joseph's brothers "conspired to kill him" (37:18), so, according to Matthew, Jesus' brothers, the chief priests and the elders, "conspired to arrest Jesus by stealth and kill him" (Matt 26:4); as Joseph's brothers sold him for twenty pieces of silver, so Jesus' disciple Judas sold Jesus for thirty pieces of silver (Matt 26:15); as Joseph's brothers handed him over to Gentiles, so Jesus' brothers "handed him over to Pilate the governor" (Matt 27:2); as Joseph suffered in silence, so Jesus suffered in silence (Matt 26:63); and as God used the evil deeds of Joseph's brothers to save his people, so God used the evil deeds of Jesus' "brothers" to save his people.

But Jesus is greater than Joseph. Jesus is God's only Son who not only became a servant and suffered humiliation and scorn; he died and *rose* again to save God's people. And whereas Joseph saved Israel from an early death through famine, Jesus saves God's people from *eternal* death caused by sin. Jesus' death accomplished our atonement. As Paul puts it, "While we were enemies, we were reconciled to God through the death of his Son" (Rom 5:10).

God uses even evil human deeds to fulfill his plan of salvation! God's people today are often perplexed by the evil that surrounds them and affects them: terrible hatred, persecution, injustice. More Christian martyrs have fallen in the last century than in the preceding nineteen centuries combined. Christians frequently ask, Where is God? How can he allow this evil to happen? Why does not God do something about this wickedness?

The story of Joseph offers us comfort in difficult times: God is not absent! He is quietly at work behind the scenes to accomplish his purposes. God can work out his plan of salvation even through the wrongdoing we experience. Even when evil seems to rule the day, God is in control! God can use sinful human deeds to accomplish his plan of salvation.

Paul writes to persecuted Christian in Rome, "I consider that the sufferings of this present time are not worth comparing with the glory about to be revealed to us. . . . We know that all things work together for good for those who love God . . ." (Rom 8:18, 28). God works all things, even evil things, together for our good!

CHAPTER 19

Judah and Tamar

Genesis 38:1-30

This is the most sexually explicit narrative in Genesis, involving sexual intercourse, coitus interruptus, and prostitution. For this reason some preachers may wish to give this chapter a wide berth in preaching a series on the Joseph narratives.[1] An additional incentive for skipping this chapter is that the Joseph story continues seamlessly from Joseph's sale to Potiphar in Genesis 37 to his experiences in Potiphar's house in Genesis 39 (see the repetition in 37:36 and 39:1).

But if the congregation is sufficiently mature, preachers may wish to include this narrative about Judah and Tamar in a series on the *tôlĕdôt of Jacob,* "the story of the family of Jacob" (37:2). After all, Judah belongs as much to the family of Jacob as does Joseph. Moreover, as we shall see, this narrative is integral to the Joseph narrative. But the challenges in preaching it are many. Aside from handling the sexual material sensitively, how does one preach Christ from a narrative that seems so secular.[2] How does it fit into the Joseph story? What is the point (theme) of this story for Israel, and why (goal) did the author record it for them?

Text and Context

The narrative unit is easy to detect. Genesis 38:1 begins the new narrative with an indication of time and a change of subject: "It happened at that time that Judah went down from his brothers." Genesis 39:1 changes the subject back to Joseph in Egypt by virtually repeating the last verse of chapter 37. The textual

1. Leupold, *Genesis,* II, 990, considers it "entirely unsuited to homiletical use, much as the devout Bible students may glean from the chapter."

2. Westermann, *Genesis 37–50,* 56, calls it "a secular narrative through and through. . . . The narrative is secular and says nothing of God's action or speech."

unit, therefore, is Genesis 38:1-30. This unit is confirmed by the inclusio of the birth of Judah's sons by his wife (38:1-5) and his sons by Tamar (38:27-30).[3]

Like many other narratives in Genesis, this narrative functions in the context of God's promises to Abraham, "I will make of you a great nation. . . . In you all the families of the earth shall be blessed" (12:2-3). Judah, the fourth son of Jacob and Leah, fails to do his part in extending the seed of the woman. He leaves his brothers, and, like Esau before him (26:34), marries a Canaanite woman. In quick succession he begets three sons. When his firstborn, Er, is of age, Judah selects Tamar as his wife. But this son is so wicked that the LORD puts him to death (38:7). The second son, for selfish reasons, refuses to impregnate the childless widow, and the LORD also puts him to death (38:10). Then Judah deceives Tamar by withholding his youngest son from her. The future of Judah's family now hangs in the balance. But through deception Tamar becomes pregnant by Judah, which results in the birth of the twins Perez and Zerah. Through deception and counterdeception, the line of the seed of the woman continues.[4]

Genesis 38 also relates ideas similar to those in earlier narratives. Previously, Jacob had deceived his father Isaac. The deceiver Jacob was in turn deceived by his sons, including Judah. And now the deceiver Judah is deceived by his daughter-in-law. "In all three episodes, goats and items of dress are used in the deception."[5] Previously, we heard of the birth of twins, Esau and Jacob, each struggling to be firstborn (25:24-26). Here Zerah seems to be the firstborn but is outmaneuvered by Perez. As Edom (red) ultimately lost out to Jacob, so Zerah (red)[6] loses out to Perez.

Beginning with Cain and Abel, we have often noted God's preference for the younger son. In this narrative God puts to death Judah's two older sons while his youngest survives. Moreover, although at birth Zerah sticks out his hand first, "making him technically the firstborn, Perez actually arrives first (vv 27-30). And it is Perez who was the ancestor of David, who was of course the youngest of Jesse's sons. This triumph-of-the-younger-son motif thus looks back to the struggle between Jacob and Esau, but more immediately to Joseph's dreams, in which he saw his brothers bowing down to him. The double rein-

3. "The final paragraph describes the birth of Perez and Zerah, which restores the number of sons to three, suggesting thereby that the full complement of heirs has been reinstated (cf. Job's reinstatement, 42:12-13)." Mathews, *Genesis 11:27–50:26*, 712.

4. "It was, of course, also the case that a line of the house of Judah was continued through the seed of Shela (Nu 26:20). What is important to note is that this line is not mentioned here, and thus the focus of the narrative is on the line of Judah that would ultimately lead to the house of David." Sailhamer, *Pentateuch as Narrative*, 209-10.

5. Wenham, *Genesis 16–50*, 364.

6. "Esau's alternate name, Edom, signified red stuff (25:30), while Zerah's name means 'scarlet' in reference to the ironic thread around his wrist." Walton, *Genesis*, 691, n. 53.

forcement of this principle in chapter 38 is an assurance that Joseph's dreams will ultimately be fulfilled."[7]

The immediate context reveals that the narrator wishes to relate "the story of the family of Jacob" (37:2). In Genesis 37 he sketches the story of Jacob, Joseph, and his brothers. Joseph unwisely brags about his dreams of ruling over his brothers. His brothers plan to kill the dreamer, but Judah convinces them to sell him as a slave to Egypt. The brothers then deceive their father Jacob with Joseph's robe dipped in goat's blood. Jacob "recognizes" the robe as Joseph's, concludes that "a wild animal has devoured him" (37:33), and mourns "for his son many days" (v 34), refusing to be comforted. Meanwhile the Midianites sell Joseph in Egypt (v 36).

"It happened *at that time* [when Joseph was sold in Egypt] that Judah went down from his brothers and settled near a certain Adullamite whose name was Hirah" (38:1). Judah was the leader of Joseph's brothers, as we have seen in the selling of Joseph and as we will see again in later narratives. In this chapter the narrator seeks to tell us more about Judah and his family. The chapter covers some twenty years in the life of Judah. This break in the Joseph narrative not only heightens its tension (What is happening to Joseph in Egypt?), it also gives readers a deeper awareness of the prolonged suffering of Joseph, his father, and his brothers. We get to experience with Joseph "the comfortless darkness of the two decades, during which hopeless and sorrowful longing was gnawing at the heart of the aged father, and the secret curse of deadly sin deceitfully concealed was weighing on the souls of his children."[8]

Literary Features

For Genesis 38 Ken Mathews suggests the following chiastic structure:[9]

A Judah's Sons and Tamar (38:1-6)
  B Tamar's Threat to Judah's Sons (38:7-11)
    C Tamar Deceives Judah (38:12-14)
      D Judah impregnates Tamar (38:15-19)
    C′ Tamar Steals Judah's Pledge (38:20-23)
  B′ Judah's Threat to Tamar (38:24-26)
A′ Judah's Sons by Tamar (38:27-30)

7. Wenham, *Genesis 16–50*, 364.

8. Franz Delitzsch, *A New Commentary on Genesis* (New York: Scribner & Welford, 1889), 266-67, quoted by Mathewson, "Exegetical Study of Genesis 38," *BSac* (Oct.-Dec. 1989) 385.

9. Mathews, *Genesis 11:27–50:26*, 713.

The narrator again is omniscient, knowing that "Er . . . was wicked in the sight of the LORD" (38:7), perceiving Onan's motive for not impregnating Tamar ("since Onan knew that the offspring would not be his," v 9), knowing that "what he [Onan] did was displeasing in the sight of the LORD" (v 10), discerning Judah's reason for withholding his third son from Tamar ("he feared that he too would die, like his brothers," v 11), knowing Tamar's reason for playing the harlot ("She saw that Shela was grown up, yet she had not been given to him in marriage," v 14), sensing Judah's thoughts ("he thought her to be a prostitute," v 15), overhearing Judah and Tamar's conversation (vv 16-18), and knowing details of the birth of Perez and Zerah (vv 27-30).[10]

After speeding through about twenty years in the first eleven verses, the narrator uses nineteen verses to cover less than a year.[11] By this pace retardation the narrator indicates that his interest lies primarily with the story that unfolds in Genesis 38:12-30.

The narrator artfully fits Genesis 38 between chapters 37 and 39 with various linguistic parallels and contrasts. Hamilton notes, "When Jacob was presented with Joseph's bloodied tunic, his sons instructed him to 'examine it' (*hakker-nā'*, 37:32); then the text says 'and he examined it' (*wayyakkîrâ*, 37:33). Holding Judah's items in her hands, Tamar says to Judah: 'identify them' (*hakker-nā'*, 38:25b); and Judah 'identified them' (*wayyakkēr*, 38:26). . . . In 37:31 we read that the brothers dipped the coat in the blood of a goat *(śĕʿîr ʿizzîm)*. In 38:17 Judah promises to give Tamar a kid from his flock *(gĕdî ʿizzim)* as payment for her services as harlot."[12] The two chapters also "contrast a Jacob who refused to be consoled (*lĕhitnaḥēm*, 37:35) over Joseph, and a Judah who was consoled (*wayyinnāḥem*, 38:12) over his wife's death."[13]

There are further parallels and contrasts between chapters 38 and 39. Alter comments, "The story begins with Judah parting from his brothers, an act conveyed with a rather odd locution, *wayyēred mē'ēt*, literally, 'he went down from' [38:1], and which undoubtedly has the purpose of connecting this separation of one brother from the rest with Joseph's, transmitted with the same verb-root . . . : 'Joseph was brought down [*hûrad*] to Egypt' [39:1]."[14] The narrator also highlights contrasts between Judah and Joseph: Judah voluntarily "went down from his brothers" and father's house, while Joseph was forcibly

10. Cf. Mathewson, *Art of Preaching Old Testament Narrative*, 75.

11. To be more exact, "while the narrated time in Genesis 38:1-11 amounts to approximately eighteen to twenty years, the narration time amounts to about 32 percent of the narrative. In Genesis 38:12-30, the narrated time amounts to approximately nine months, while the narration time amounts to about 68 percent of the narrative." Mathewson, ibid., 54-55.

12. Hamilton, *Genesis 18–50*, 431, with credit to Alter, *Art of Biblical Narrative*, 10.

13. Ibid., 432.

14. Alter, *Art of Biblical Narrative*, 6.

removed from his brothers and father's house. Richard Pratt adds the following contrasts:[15]

Judah (Genesis 38:1-30)	**Joseph (Genesis 39:1-23)**
Association with Foreign Women (38:1-3)	Separation from Foreign Women (39:6b-12)
Sexual Immorality (38:12-18)	Sexual Morality (39:6b-12)
Victimizer (38:24)	Victimized (39:13-20a)
Judgment of God (38:6-10)	Blessing of God (39:20b-23)
True Accusation of Woman (38:25)	False Accusation of Woman (39:13-20a)
Confession of Sin (38:26)	Rejection of Sin (39:10)

The narrator describes the characters primarily through their words and actions. Judah, having convinced his brothers to sell Joseph as a slave (ch. 37), now moves away from his father and brothers, befriends the Canaanite Hirah, and quickly marries the daughter of the Canaanite Shua (38:1-2) — all contrary to Abraham and Isaac's instructions that their sons not marry Canaanites (24:3; 28:1). He thus shows not only a calloused disregard for his forefathers' admonitions but also for God's covenant promises. He raises two sons who are wicked in the sight of the Lord but fails to connect their deaths to their wickedness. Instead he suspects that Tamar may be to blame (38:11), deceives her by telling her to wait until his third son grows up (v 11) and then withholding him from her (v 14). He easily turns aside to have sex with a "prostitute" but is quick to condemn Tamar when he hears that she has played the harlot. Without hearing her defense he demands the most severe punishment: death by burning. In describing Judah, a major tribal head in Israel, the narrator is brutally honest about his flawed character.

When confronted by the evidence of his own failings, however, Judah is quick to admit his guilt and declare Tamar in the right: "She is more in the right than I, since I did not give her to my son Shelah" (v 26). This is the beginning of a transformation in Judah, who will later show great concern for his father and make an impassioned speech offering himself for the freedom of Joseph's full brother, Benjamin (44:18-34).

The other main character in this narrative is Tamar. The name Tamar means palm tree, which has the positive connotations of having a beautiful figure (Song 7:7) and being fruitful. In the first half of the narrative, Tamar is passive and obedient. After the death of her husband Er, she passively accepts the sexual encounters with her brother-in-law Onan, even though he misuses her for his own gratification. When the Lord puts Onan to death, Tamar timidly obeys Judah by returning to her father's house until Shelah has come of age. But when she real-

15. Pratt, *He Gave Us Stories*, 216.

izes that she has been deceived by Judah, she swings into action to raise up seed for her dead husband — even if she has to prostitute herself to do so.

Tamar shows great boldness in posing as a prostitute, for as one betrothed she would face the death penalty for playing the harlot (cf. Deut 22:23-24). She is also highly cunning in bargaining with Judah and taking in pledge from him the very items that would publicly identify him as the father of the expected child. Tamar further reveals a great sense of loyalty and justice: she "remains true to her Israelite family in spite of its glaring failures and becomes absorbed into it. Normally Canaanite women absorb Israelite men into their debased culture (Deut 7:1, 3). In that light, her deception as a Canaanite prostitute to snare her widowed father-in-law into fathering covenant seed should be evaluated as a daring act of faith."[16]

The narrative has six scenes:[17]

vv 1-5	Judah marries a Canaanite
vv 6-11	Tamar marries Judah's sons
vv 12-19	Tamar traps Judah
vv 20-23	Judah looks for Tamar
vv 24-26	Tamar vindicated
vv 27-30	Birth of twins to Tamar and Judah

The Plot Line

The distant setting of this narrative is the LORD's promise to make of Abram "a great nation," and a blessing to "all the families of the earth" (12:2-3). The near setting is given in Genesis 38:1, At the time when Joseph arrives in Egypt, Judah "goes down from his brothers" and affiliates with Canaanites. Preliminary incidents consist of Judah marrying an unnamed Canaanite woman and in quick succession begetting three sons (vv 2-5).[18] The first narrative conflict begins when Judah takes Tamar to be the wife of his firstborn, Er, and the LORD puts Er to death for his wickedness, leaving Tamar a childless widow (vv 6-7). In that culture a widow without children was destitute and considered a failure. The custom (and later law in Israel) of levirate marriage (*levir* is Latin for "brother-in-law") provided the way for a brother-in-law to raise up seed for his deceased brother. The tension rises when Onan refuses to have a child by Tamar for his older brother.

16. Waltke, *Genesis*, 508.

17. Wenham, *Genesis 16–50*, 363.

18. "The subsequent births of three sons are 'recorded in breathless pace,' indicating the subordinate role of these events as they establish the context for what is to come." Mathewson, "Exegetical Study of Genesis 38," *BSac* (Oct.-Dec. 1989) 376.

The LORD also puts him to death (vv 8-10). Now, according to custom, it is the turn of the youngest son, Shelah, to raise up seed for his older brother. But Judah does not want to risk his last son's life on a levirate relationship with Tamar. He postpones a decision by sending Tamar home to her father's house "until my son Shelah grows up" (v 11). The tension whether all of Judah's sons will die is resolved for now, but the issue of Tamar's childlessness remains undecided.

The tension flares up again when Shelah has grown up and Judah fails to give Tamar to Shelah (v 14b). Realizing that Judah has deceived her, Tamar herself takes charge. She disguises herself as a prostitute and sets a trap for her father-in-law (v 14a). The tension rises because, if found out, she will be put to death. Fortunately for her, Judah does not recognize his daughter-in-law (vv 15-16) and for now she gets away with her scheme. Judah promises her a young goat for her favors and gives his signet, cord, and staff as a pledge (vv 17-18a). Judah "went in to her, and she conceived by him" (v 18b). Tamar quickly disappears, "and taking off her veil she put on the garments of her widowhood" (v 19). Judah sends his Canaanite friend with a young goat to fulfill his part of the agreement and to retrieve his pledge, but the "prostitute" has disappeared (vv 20-22). Rather than becoming a laughingstock among the local population, Judah decides to cut his losses and let the "prostitute" keep his signet, cord, and staff (v 23).

The conflict reaches a climax three months later when Judah is told, "Your daughter-in-law Tamar has played the whore; moreover she is pregnant as a result of whoredom" (v 24). Immediately Judah pronounces the death sentence: "Bring her out, and let her be burned" (v 24). Tamar waits till the very last minute to present her defense: "As she was being brought out, she sent word to her father-in-law, 'It was the owner of these who made me pregnant. . . . Take note, please, whose these are, the signet and the cord and the staff'" (v 25). Will Judah acknowledge them as his? Will Judah publicly acknowledge that he fathered this child?

The tension breaks when Judah not only acknowledges his fatherhood but also clears Tamar of wrongdoing: "Then Judah acknowledged them and said, 'She is more in the right than I, since I did not give her to my son Shelah" (v 26). The outcome of the narrative is the birth of the twins Perez and Zerah.

We can sketch the plot line of this narrative as a complex plot, as shown on page 364.[19]

Theocentric Interpretation

Westermann asserts, "The narrative is secular and says nothing of God's action or speech."[20] Obviously, he overlooks God's action in putting to death the first

19. See also Mathewson, *Art of Preaching Old Testament Narrative*, 46.
20. Westermann, *Genesis 37–50*, 56.

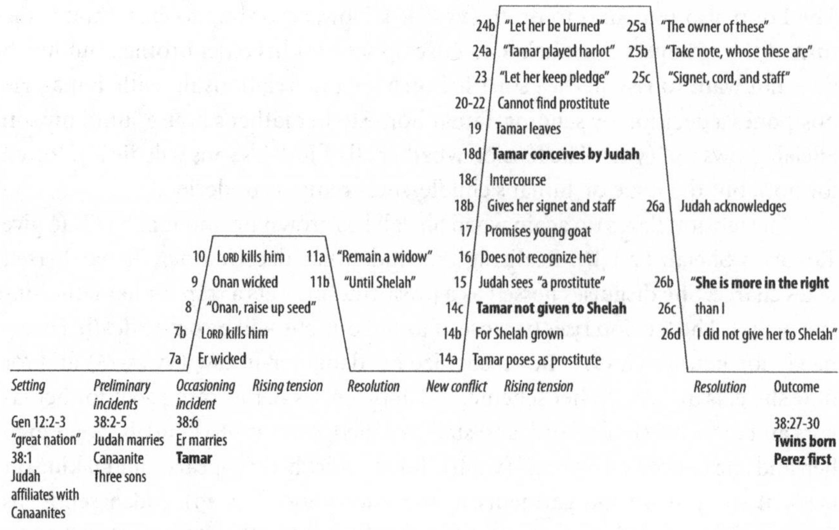

two sons of Judah (vv 7, 10). After that it does indeed look as if God goes into hiding as Judah first deceives Tamar by promising her Shelah and then withholding him. Tamar next deceives Judah by posing as a prostitute. But somehow God is still at work behind the scenes,[21] as can also be seen in the outcome: Tamar gives birth to twins — just as the barren Rebekah did in answer to Isaac's prayer (25:21-26). Only the LORD can provide new life. "Sons are indeed a heritage from the LORD, and the fruit of the womb a reward" (Ps 127:3). "Genesis 38 describes Yahweh's accomplishment of his purpose (in the continuation of the Abrahamic line) despite the unfaithfulness of Judah — the fourth link in that line. The continuation of Abraham's line . . . was accomplished by using a most unlikely person — a Canaanite woman."[22]

Textual Theme and Goal

In seeking to discover the textual theme, we should keep in mind that "the plot revolves around Tamar's right to be the mother of Judah's heir."[23] We have also seen that the narrator hurries through verses 1 to 11 but slows the pace in verses

21. "As at many points in the Joseph narrative and prominently in the theology of the Ruth account, chap. 38 implies that the hand of God is behind the events that transpire. After explicitly declaring divine involvement (vv 1-5), the passage exhibits the hiddenness of God's involvement in the lives of Israel's fathers." Mathews, *Genesis 11:27–50:26*, 704.

22. Mathewson, "Exegetical Study of Genesis 38," *BSac* (Oct.-Dec. 1989) 391.

23. Kidner, *Genesis*, 187.

12 to 26. Although the first part of the plot (vv 6-11) highlights the issue of Tamar being the childless widow of the firstborn Er, the narrator's main concern is with the second part, Judah's deception by withholding Shelah from Tamar and Tamar's counterdeception resulting in her pregnancy by her father-in-law Judah. The outcome is the birth of twins, of which the younger, Perez, becomes the firstborn and thus Judah's firstborn. We can, therefore, formulate the textual theme as follows, *God uses Tamar's deception of disobedient Judah to continue Judah's family line.*

The narrator's likely goal in communicating this message to later Israel is *to assure Israel that God can accomplish his plan of salvation even through Israel's disobedience and the deception of a Canaanite woman.* If Israel heard this message as it was about to take possession of Canaan under Joshua, this goal would be confirmed by the Canaanite woman Rahab, who deceived her king, hid the Israelite spies, and became part of Israel. On the other hand, if Israel heard this narrative in Babylonian exile where it suffered for its disobedience, this narrative would have assured Israel that God can accomplish his plan of salvation even through their disobedience and using their enemies — for example, King Evil-Merodach of Babylon freeing King Jehoiachin of Judah (2 Kings 25:27) or King Cyrus of Persia freeing Israel from Babylonian captivity (2 Chron 36:22-23). In either case, the need addressed would be the same: Israel does not fully trust God to accomplish his plan of salvation.

Ways to Preach Christ

Redemptive-Historical Progression

Redemptive-historical progression forms a solid bridge to Jesus Christ in the New Testament. In this narrative "God uses Tamar's deception of disobedient Judah to continue Judah's family line." The result is the birth of twins, of which Perez, the second, manages to become the firstborn. Perez's name appears again in a genealogy in Ruth 4:18-22 (cf. 1 Chron 2:5, 9-15) which lists ten generations[24] from Perez to the great king David. Perez and David are both younger sons, rather insignificant by human standards, but chosen by God for greatness in carrying forward the line of the seed of the woman. If Perez is a forefather of King David, then he is also a forefather of *the* Seed of the woman, Jesus Christ.

24. "The fact that ten generations separate David from Perez — symbolic of a complete and significant unit of time . . . — shows that the birth of Perez is taken to be a historical turning point." Sarna, *Genesis,* 270. Cf. the ten generations from Adam to Noah (Gen 5:1–6:8) and ten generations from Shem to Abram (Gen 11:10-26).

Indeed, Judah, Tamar, Perez, and Zerah are all mentioned in Jesus' genealogy in Matthew 1. "So this story, which at first sight seems to be so marginal to biblical history, records a vital link in saving history. Tamar, through her determination to have children, secured for Judah the honor of fathering both David and the Savior of the world."[25]

Promise-Fulfillment

There is no promise of the Messiah in this narrative.

Typology

There is no type of Christ in his narrative.

Analogy

Analogy provides a way for preaching Christ from this narrative. For example, as God assured Israel that he can accomplish his plan of salvation even through disobedience and enemies, so Christ assures his church that God can accomplish his salvation plan even through the church's disobedience and its enemies' deceptions. This analogy, of course, would require the support of one or more New Testament references to Jesus' life or teaching. One can employ, for example, God's use of Judas' betrayal of Jesus and the deception of the chief priests, the elders (Matt 26:4, 57-66), and Pilate (27:24-26) to bring about Jesus' crucifixion and atonement for all who believe in Jesus. Or, one can use Jesus' teaching about the persecution his disciples will face: "You will be dragged before governors and kings because of me, as a testimony to them and the Gentiles" (Matt 10:18), perhaps combined with John 16:33, "In the world you face persecution. But take courage; I have overcome the world!" or Romans 8:28, "We know that all things work together for good for those who love God."

Longitudinal Themes

One can also use longitudinal themes to move to Christ in the New Testament. For example, one can trace the theme of God using human deception to carry

25. Wenham, *Genesis 16–50*, 370.

forward the line of the seed of the woman. Or, one can trace from Tamar to Mary, the mother of Jesus, the unlikely unions God used to continue the line of the seed of the woman till *the* Seed of the woman is born of the virgin Mary. This longitudinal theme would overlap with Jesus' genealogy in Matthew 1.

New Testament References

The Nestle-Aland Greek New Testament lists a few New Testament citations or allusions to this narrative. For Genesis 38:8, regarding levirate marriage, it lists Matthew 22:24, Mark 12:19, and Luke 20:28, all referring to Moses' law, "If a man dies childless, his brother shall marry the widow, and raise up children for his brother" (Matt 22:24). These references show that the law of levirate marriage was still in force in Jesus' day, but they do not directly link this narrative to Jesus.

For Genesis 38:24, "she is pregnant as a result of whoredom," it lists John 8:41, "we are not illegitimate children" — again a passage that is not helpful for preaching Christ from this narrative.

Finally, for Genesis 38:29, the name Perez, it lists Luke 3:33 and Matthew 1:3 where we find his name in the genealogy of Jesus. These two New Testament references certainly expose a way for preaching Christ from Genesis 38.

John Calvin uses Philippians 2:6-7 as a link to Jesus: "Now although, at first sight, the dignity of Christ seems to be somewhat tarnished by such dishonour [the greatest disgrace of the tribe of Judah]; yet since here also is seen that 'emptying' of which St. Paul speaks, it rather redounds to his glory, than in the least degree detracts from it."[26]

Contrast

There is no contrast between the message of Genesis 38 that God can use disobedience and deception to further his cause and the message of the New Testament.

Sermon Theme and Goal

We formulated the textual theme as follows: "God uses Tamar's deception of disobedient Judah to continue Judah's family line." Since Matthew 1 clearly

26. Calvin, *Genesis,* II, 278.

shows that the line of Judah extends through Perez and David to the birth of Jesus, we can make the sermon theme, *God uses Tamar's deception of disobedient Judah to continue Judah's family line, so that, eventually, Jesus can be born of this royal line.*

We formulated the narrator's likely goal for later Israel as "to assure Israel that God can accomplish his plan of salvation even through Israel's disobedience and the deception of a Canaanite woman." The sermon goal can be similar: *To assure God's people that God can accomplish his plan of salvation even through human disobedience and deception.* This goal shows that the need addressed in this sermon is the failure of God's people to fully trust God to accomplish his plan of salvation.

Sermon Exposition

One can develop a sermon on this narrative in various ways. For example, one can begin this sermon with a Christocentric move by referring to Jesus' genealogy in Matthew 1, especially the mention of Judah, Tamar, Perez, and Zerah in verse 3. After some exploration of this genealogy, one can flash back to the Judah-Tamar narrative. But one can also begin with Genesis 38 and work one's way forward to Jesus' genealogy in Matthew 1. Here I will follow the latter approach.

Judah was a calloused, greedy character. The narrator is brutally honest in describing the flawed character of this leader in Israel. Judah was the one who said to his brothers, "What profit is it if we kill our brother [Joseph] and conceal his blood? Come, let us sell him . . ." (37:26-27). "What profit is it?" The brothers sold Joseph for "twenty pieces of silver" (37:28). Judah gave no thought to God's promises to Abram, "I will make of you a great nation. . . . In you all the families of the earth shall be blessed" (12:2-3) — promises later repeated to his father Jacob (28:14). It seems that he did not care about God's promises nor about his family: "Come, let us sell" our brother. And what about father Jacob's feelings? The brothers slaughtered a goat, dipped Joseph's robe in the blood, and sent the robe to Jacob with the message, "This we have found; see now whether it is your son's robe or not" (37:32). We read in chapter 37:33-35, Jacob "recognized it, and said, 'It is my son's robe! A wild animal has devoured him; Joseph is without doubt torn to pieces.' Then Jacob tore his garments, and put sackcloth on his loins, and mourned for his son many days. All his sons and all his daughters sought to comfort him; but he refused to be comforted, and said, 'No, I shall go down to Sheol to my son, mourning.' Thus his father bewailed him." This is what Judah's leadership among his brothers accomplished: the loss of a brother and lifelong sorrow for his father.

The present narrative begins, "It happened at that time [when Joseph arrived in Egypt] that Judah went down from his brothers and settled near a certain Adullamite [a Canaanite] whose name was Hirah" (38:1). Joseph had been forcibly removed from his father's house and his brothers, but Judah voluntarily leaves his father's house and his brothers in order to befriend the Canaanites. It is an act of disobedience. He leaves God's covenant family in order to fraternize with the enemy.

Judah's first Canaanite friend is Hirah, who lives in the town of Adullam. Soon Judah sees an attractive Canaanite woman and, like his uncle Esau who married local women, Judah marries her.[27] Again, he shows his calloused disregard for his family, particularly for his great-grandfather Abraham and his grandfather Isaac (24:3; 28:1), who had insisted that their sons not marry the accursed Canaanites (9:25), who would be dispossessed of their land (15:16). But Judah does not seem to care about God's promises or his family.

We may well wonder if God will bless with children this union of Judah and the nameless Canaanite woman. To our surprise, perhaps, in quick succession they receive three children: verse 3, "She conceived and bore a son; and he named him Er.[28] Again she conceived and bore a son whom she named Onan. Yet again she bore a son, and she named him Shelah. She was in Chezib when she bore him." Shelah was born in Chezib, which means "town of lies." With this notation, the narrator probably foreshadows Judah's lies about Shelah to Tamar.[29] In any event, "Judah's progeny looked promising with the birth of three sons, Er, Onan, and Shelah. Other notable patriarchs [also] produced three sons (Adam, Noah, Terah)."[30]

After the children have grown, verse 6, "Judah took a wife for Er his firstborn; her name was Tamar." Tamar's name means "palm tree," which would be associated with a beautiful figure (Song 7:7) and fruitfulness. Unfortunately,

27. "'Judah saw . . . took her.' Though 'take' is a perfectly proper term for marriage, the combination of 'see' and 'take' has in Genesis overtones of illicit taking (cf. 3:6; 6:2; 12:15; 34:2; cf. Judg 14:1-2), suggesting Judah's marriage may have been based on mere lust. The fact that his wife's name is not mentioned, only her father's, 'Shua' . . . , may point in the same direction." Wenham, *Genesis 16–50*, 366.

28. "Their relationship to each other is conveyed by six verbs: three for him (he meets her, marries her, and has intercourse with her, v 2), and three for her (she conceives, bears a son, and names the child, v 3). Judah and his wife relate sexually, but the text says nothing else about their relations." Hamilton, *Genesis 18–50*, 433. "The grouping of three is maintained by . . . 3 children, [and] 3 localities [Adullam (v 1), Chezib (v 5), and Timnah (v 12)]." Ibid., 434.

29. "Since 'Chezib,' or Achzib, could mean 'town of lies' or 'Lieham' (K.C., *Lugheim*), the insertion of its name as suggestive of Judah's deception in the matter of giving Shelah to Tamar is possible, yet hardly seems likely." Leupold, *Genesis*, II, 979. But this interpretation is more likely if Enaim, "opening of eyes," in v 14 is understood as foreshadowing the opening of Judah's eyes.

30. Mathews, *Genesis 11:27–50:26*, 715.

Tamar was not to be fruitful in her marriage. We read in verse 7, "But Er, Judah's firstborn, was wicked in the sight of the LORD, and the LORD put him to death." "Not since the days of Noah and Sodom and Gomorrah has God taken the life of one who displeased him, and there it was groups who were annihilated. Er is the first individual in Scripture whom Yahweh kills."[31]

Er's death leaves Tamar a childless widow. If she remains childless, she will not only be considered a failure but will probably end up destitute. Verse 8, "Then Judah said to Onan, 'Go in to your brother's wife and perform the duty of a brother-in-law[32] to her; raise up offspring for your brother.'" Judah is referring to the custom of levirate marriage (*levir* is Latin for "brother-in-law"). This common Near Eastern custom[33] would later be codified as a law for Israel: "When brothers reside together, and one of them dies and has no son, the wife of the deceased shall not be married outside the family to a stranger. Her husband's brother shall go in to her, taking her in marriage, and performing the duty of a husband's brother to her, and the firstborn whom she bears shall succeed to the name of the deceased brother, so that his name may not be blotted out of Israel" (Deut 25:5-6).

But Judah is not ordering Onan to *marry* Tamar; he is only telling him, "Go in to your brother's wife . . . ; raise up offspring for your brother." "Tamar remains Onan's sister-in-law; she does not become his wife. This point makes clear that Tamar's legitimate entitlement [as understood by Judah] extends only to a male son, not to marriage."[34] Judah seems unconcerned about the welfare of Tamar; he never even calls her by her name, Tamar. Judah is concerned only about getting offspring for his dead son.

Verse 9, "But since Onan knew that the offspring would not be his, he spilled his semen on the ground whenever he went in to his brother's wife, so that he would not give offspring to his brother." Onan, clearly, is a greedy, wicked individual. He does not wish to produce a son for his dead brother because then that son would be considered the firstborn and would get a double portion of Judah's estate. As it is, Onan himself is now the firstborn who will inherit the double portion. To prevent a pregnancy, "he practices *coitus interrup-*

31. Hamilton, *Genesis 18–50*, 434.

32. "The fact that a single Hebrew word suffices for the phrase 'perform the duty of a brother-in-law' would confirm that this was a standard practice, even if there were no record of the law in Deuteronomy 25:5ff." Kidner, *Genesis*, 188.

33. "This custom of the Levirate is found in many traditional societies and among Israel's neighbors, the Assyrians . . . and the Hittites . . . , and at Nuzi and Ugarit." Wenham, *Genesis 16–50*, 366.

34. Hamilton, *Genesis 18–50*, 435. Cf. Westermann, *Genesis 37–50*, 52, "As G. W. Coats has shown (1972), Gen 38 indicates that originally the widow had only the right to a descendant, not to marriage with the brother-in-law."

tus whenever they come together. The Hebrew emphasizes that Onan did this on every occasion of intercourse, not just once or twice."[35] Without fulfilling his obligation, he takes advantage of Tamar for his own gratification.

Verse 10 states succinctly, "What he did was displeasing in the sight of the LORD, and he put him to death also." The LORD takes Onan's life for refusing to fulfill his responsibilities to Tamar and his deceased brother. Ultimately, Onan's sin is that his greed causes him to defy the LORD's plan for Abraham's family. For God had repeatedly promised the patriarchs that he would make them fruitful. By refusing to fulfill his responsibilities, "Onan is . . . deliberately frustrating the fulfillment of those promises. The threefold reference to 'descendants' in 38:8-9 must allude to these promises, and Onan's action demonstrates his opposition to the divine agenda. For this reason, the LORD 'let him die.'"[36]

With only one son left, Judah faces a terrible predicament. Custom dictated that he now give Tamar to his third son, but Judah has become superstitious. He fails to see that the LORD put his two sons to death for their wickedness. Instead he thinks that Tamar is to blame for their deaths, and he does not wish to risk his last son on her. So Judah postpones a decision. Verse 11, "Then Judah said to his daughter-in-law[37] Tamar, 'Remain a widow in your father's house until my son Shelah grows up' — for he feared that he too would die, like his brothers." Judah has no intention of giving her to Shelah. If Shelah would also die, Judah would be childless like Tamar. Yet he does sort of promise her to his son Shelah. This leaves Tamar in limbo. She is betrothed to Shelah and thus cannot marry someone else. Yet it is very unlikely that Judah will ever give her to Shelah. Judah washes his hands of the whole thing by sending her back to her father's house.[38] But she does not belong there any more. She belongs in Judah's house. Yet Tamar quietly obeys Judah and goes "to live in her father's house" (38:11). Perhaps she still has hopes of one day being married to Shelah.

The next act in this drama begins in verse 12. "In course of time the wife of Judah, Shua's daughter, died; when Judah's time of mourning was over, he went up to Timnah to his sheepshearers, he and his friend Hirah the Adullamite." "In course of time" is literally "after many days." Shelah has grown up by now, but Judah has failed to give Tamar to Shelah. Tamar still languishes in her father's

35. Wenham, *Genesis 16–50*, 367.

36. Ibid.

37. "She is identified as 'Tamar his daughter-in-law,' an otherwise superfluous designation that reminds us of his legal obligation to provide her a husband from among his sons." Alter, *Art of Biblical Narrative*, 7.

38. "Judah's response is also wicked. Judah, with his dignity and status, is expected to care for a defenseless widow. He violates his daughter-in-law by shirking his responsibilities, denying her right to well-being and status in the community, and shifting her problem onto others." Waltke, *Genesis*, 511.

house, a childless widow, betrothed to Shelah, unable to marry someone else. She is boxed in. But Judah is also trapped in his deceit. Having promised Tamar to Shelah, Shelah can hardly marry someone else. And if he marries Tamar, Judah fears, Shelah too will die. And now Judah's wife dies, thus eliminating the possibility of Judah producing more children with his wife. It's a deadlock — with the prospect of Judah's line dying out.

When Judah's time of mourning is over,[39] he goes up to his sheepshearers. "The hard and dirty work of shearing sheep was accompanied by a festival that was noted for hilarity and much wine-drinking."[40] Verse 13, "When Tamar was told, 'Your father-in-law is going up to Timnah to shear his sheep,' she put off her widow's garments,[41] put on a veil, wrapped herself up, and sat down at the entrance to Enaim, which is on the road to Timnah. She saw that Shelah was grown up, yet she had not been given to him in marriage."[42]

When Tamar is certain that Judah has lied to her in promising her Shelah, she springs into action to secure her right to a son in Judah's family. Her plan is risky, for it could cost her her life. She puts on a veil and poses as a prostitute along the way Judah will be traveling. She will try to conceive a son by her father-in-law Judah. Although this violated later laws in Israel (Lev 18:15; 20:12), it appears that levirate customs in Tamar's days allowed a father-in-law to raise up offspring for his deceased son.[43] At any rate, at Enaim Tamar will try to deceive Judah who had deceived her.

Verse 15, "When Judah saw her, he thought her to be a prostitute, for she had covered her face.[44] He went over to her at the roadside, and said, 'Come, let

39. "Contrast Judah with Tamar, who is still dressed as a widow from the much earlier deaths of her husbands (Gen 38:14)." Waltke, ibid.

40. Mathewson, "Exegetical Study of Genesis 38," *BSac* (Oct.-Dec. 1989) 378, with references to 1 Sam 25:4, 8, 18, 36 and 2 Sam 13:23, 28.

41. Tamar "may have continued to wear such clothing beyond the usual period as a symbol of the unfulfilled levirate obligation. At any rate, the presence of the widow's garb (cf. v 19) provides a tacit contrast with Judah's completion of his period of mourning (v 12). At the same time, it forges a link with the story of Joseph, in which clothing also plays a role in deception." Sarna, *Genesis*, 267-68.

42. "Now, a clear perception of injustice done her is ascribed to Tamar (verse 14), and she suddenly races into rapid, purposeful action, expressed in a detonating series of verbs: in verse 14 she quickly takes off, covers, wraps herself, sits down at the strategic location, and after the encounter, in verse 19, there is another chain of four verbs to indicate her brisk resumption of her former role and attire." Alter, *Art of Biblical Narrative*, 8.

43. "Middle Assyrian Law number 33 and Hittite Law number 193 suggest inclusion of the father in the line of levirate responsibility. While the extant copies of these laws are dated a few hundred years later than the time of the Judah-Tamar story, they at least suggest that Tamar's action of seeking conception by Judah may have been in accord with a similar custom existing during her time." Mathewson, "Exegetical Study of Genesis 38," *BSac* (Oct.-Dec. 1989) 378, n. 32.

44. Hamilton, *Genesis 18–50*, 441-43, asserts that "there is little evidence that prostitutes in

me come in to you,' for he did not know that she was his daughter-in-law." Sarna comments, "The text is very careful to emphasize that had Judah known the identity of the woman, he would never have had relations with her: 'she had covered her face'; 'he did not know that she was his daughter-in-law' (v 16); 'he was not intimate with her again' (v 26). All this is explication by the Narrator, who is conscious of the contradiction between the moral standards of his own, later age and the fact that the offspring of Judah's venture with Tamar bore no stigma of illegitimacy."[45]

Judah and Tamar's encounter takes place at Enaim (v 14). The name *bĕpetaḥ 'ênayim* means literally "opening of [the] eyes." It is ironic that "at 'Opening of the Eyes,' even though he has sexual congress with her, Judah's eyes are closed as to the identity of his daughter-in-law, and thus he fails to recognize his partner."[46]

Tamar excels in playing the part of a prostitute. "She said to Judah, What will you give me, that you may come in to me?" "He answered," verse 17, "'I will send you a kid from the flock.'[47] And she said, 'Only if you give me a pledge, until you send it.' He said, 'What pledge shall I give you?' She replied, 'Your signet and your cord, and the staff that is in your hand.'" The signet or seal, either a stamp seal or a cylinder seal,[48] was Judah's mark of identification, much like a picture I.D. today. The staff "was a symbol of authority (cf. Num 17:2; Ps 110:2) as well as being practically useful. It had a carved top to mark ownership."[49]

Amazingly, Judah gives this unknown prostitute his personal insignia as collateral for a little goat. This is equivalent to us handing over to a stranger our driver's license and credit card. We read at the end of verse 18, "So he gave them to her, and went in to her, and she conceived by him. Then she got up and went away, and taking off her veil she put on the garments of her widowhood." Tamar is safely in her father's house again. But she conceived. She is pregnant by Judah himself.

Canaan wore veils. . . . Tamar's wearing of the veil was not to make Judah think she was a prostitute. Rather, it was intended to prevent him from recognizing her. It is not the veil but Tamar's positioning herself at Enaim (v 14) that made her appear to be a prostitute."

45. Sarna, *Genesis,* 268.

46. Hamilton, *Genesis 18–50,* 440.

47. "The fact that Judah carried nothing at that moment with which to pay for the woman's services proves that he acted on impulse in 'turning aside to her by the road' — another example of the biblical motif of God using human frailty for His own purposes." Sarna, *Genesis,* 268.

48. "Cylinder seals were usually between one and two inches in length. . . . The outer face of the seal was engraved with a design which would make an impression when it was rolled on damp clay, thus creating marks of identification. They were often attached to a cord which was strung around the owner's neck." Mathewson, "Exegetical Study of Genesis 38," *BSac* (Oct.-Dec. 1989) 379, n. 34.

49. Wenham, *Genesis 16–50,* 368.

Judah, of course, wants his personal insignia back as quickly as possible. Perhaps embarrassed to be seen with a prostitute, he sends his Canaanite friend "to recover the pledge from the woman," but "he could not find her" (v 20). Verse 21, "He asked the townspeople, 'Where is the temple prostitute[50] who was at Enaim by the wayside?' But they said, 'No prostitute has been here.' So he returned to Judah, and said, 'I have not found her; moreover the townspeople said, "'No prostitute has been here.'" Judah replied, 'Let her keep the things as her own, otherwise we will be laughed at; you see, I sent this kid, and you could not find her.'"[51]

Judah is concerned only about his own reputation. He is "like a reputable gentleman who unwittingly 'loses' his credit card in a brothel."[52] He does not want to become the laughingstock of the local population. Yet he is unconcerned about the continuing disgrace Tamar suffers as a childless widow in her father's house.

Verse 24, "About three months later Judah was told, 'Your daughter-in-law Tamar has played the whore; moreover she is pregnant as a result of whoredom.' And Judah said, 'Bring her out, and let her be burned.'" Without so much as a hearing, Judah orders that she be brought outside the town gate and be burned. In Israel the usual punishment for adultery was death by stoning (cf. Deut 22:23-24). Judah demands an even more cruel death for Tamar. He holds her responsible for the death of two of his sons. He has betrothed her to his last son but does not want to see them married lest Shelah die as well. Judah's family line is in jeopardy, and Tamar stands in the way. Here is an opportunity to get rid of Tamar. "Bring her out, and let her be burned!"

Tamar waits till the very last moment to defend herself. Verse 25, "*As she was being brought out,* she sent word to her father-in-law, 'It was the owner of these who made me pregnant.' And she said, 'Take note,[53] please, whose these

50. "While Judah was certainly out of fellowship with Yahweh, it is not necessary to suppose that he was actively practicing Canaanite religion in this situation. He was simply seeking sexual gratification. Though he certainly [?] assumed the disguised Tamar to be a temple prostitute, the less technical term *zônâ* in 38:15 emphasizes that he recognized her as a prostitute with whom he could fulfill his sexual desires." Mathewson, "Exegetical Study of Genesis 38," *BSac* (Oct.-Dec. 1989) 379, n. 33. Berlin, *Poetics,* 60, suggests that "it is not a matter of euphemism, or of putting the affair on a higher social or religious plane. It is that what Judah and the narrator (and, presumably, the reader) call *zônâ* [prostitute] was in the local idiom a *qĕdēšâ* [temple prostitute]."

51. "Fearful that he might be disgraced for not having kept his pledge, Judah attempted to clear himself . . . by making a formal pronouncement that he had sent this young goat, but Hirah could not find the woman. A play is made on the term 'pledge.' Judah sought to pay his debt to a prostitute (Tamar), even though he had failed to keep his more important pledge of arranging for his widowed daughter-in-law (Tamar) to marry Shelah." Hartley, *Genesis,* 317.

52. Waltke, *Genesis,* 513.

53. The very words the brothers used for Jacob to identify Joseph's blood-stained robe (37:32-33). See p. 360 above.

are, the signet and the cord and the staff.'" "Tamar has staked her all, chancing her honor and life, so as to get her right and prove her innocence. She takes her stand entirely on the pledge which now, at the very last moment, publicly establishes the father of the child in such a way that Judah himself has to reveal her innocence."[54]

Suddenly Judah's eyes are opened. While he did not recognize Tamar at Enaim, now he sees clearly what happened at "Opening of the Eyes." *Tamar* was the prostitute, and he, Judah, fathered this child. Verse 26, "Then Judah acknowledged them and said, 'She is more in the right than I, since I did not give her to my son Shelah.'" Judah acknowledges his insignia. Moreover, he publicly declares Tamar's innocence: "She is more in the right than I";[55] and he declares his own guilt: "since I did not give her to my son Shelah." This is the beginning of Judah's transformation. After this Judah will return to his brothers; he will show great concern for his elderly father; he will even offer himself as a slave to Joseph for Benjamin's freedom (44:18-34); and Jacob will give him the greatest blessing of all, "Judah, your brothers shall praise you. . . . The scepter shall not depart from Judah, nor the ruler's staff from between his feet . . ." (49:8-12).

In this narrative the Canaanite woman Tamar is the heroine. While Judah was doing her injustice by lying and withholding Shelah, thus placing his family line in jeopardy, Tamar was bound and determined to have a child in Judah's family. "Such determination to propagate descendants of Abraham, especially by a Canaanite woman, is remarkable, and so despite her foreign background and irregular behavior, Tamar emerges as the heroine of this story."[56]

Verse 27, "When the time of her delivery came, there were twins in her womb."[57] The twins struggled within her, just as Esau and Jacob did within Rebekah. Who would have the honor and privilege of being the firstborn? We read in verse 28, "While she was in labor, one put out a hand; and the midwife took and bound on his hand a crimson thread, saying, 'This one came out first.' But just then he drew back his hand, and out came his brother; and she said, 'What a breach[58] you have made for yourself!' Therefore he was named Perez.

54. Westermann, *Genesis 37–50*, 54.

55. "Though the root *ṣaddîq* ('righteous') often has moral connotations when applied to God's standards, its basic meaning is conformity to a standard, whether ethical or moral. The standard in this case would be the accepted social custom and duty of levirate marriage." Mathewson, "Exegetical Study of Genesis 38," *BSac* (Oct.-Dec. 1989) 380.

56. Wenham, *Genesis 16–50*, 365.

57. "It is presupposed that Tamar has been received back into her family with honor. The twins that she is expecting are legitimate, i.e., they are recognized as children of her deceased husband, fathered by a member of the family of this house." Westermann, *Genesis 37–50*, 55.

58. "Breach — Hebrew *pāreṣ*. This is a play on Perez, the only name in this chapter for

Afterward his brother came out with the crimson thread on his hand; and he was named Zerah."

The midwife is shocked: the child that should have been second somehow bypassed the first. "There is no logical or biological explanation for Perez's usurpation over Zerah, any more than there was for Jacob's over Esau. The decisions are God's. The selections are gratuitous."[59]

In this narrative God uses Tamar's deception of disobedient Judah to continue Judah's family line. God's design is amazing, for Tamar's deception of Judah results in the birth of twins: Perez and Zerah. Perez's name appears again in a genealogy in Ruth 4:18-22 (cf. 1 Chron 2:5, 9-15):

> Now these are the descendants of Perez: Perez became the father of Hezron, Hezron of Ram, Ram of Amminadab, Amminadab of Nahshon, Nahshon of Salmon, Salmon of Boaz, Boaz of Obed, Obed of Jesse, and Jesse of David.

Ten generations from Perez to David. A full number of generations from Tamar's son Perez to the great king David. Perez and David — both younger sons, rather insignificant by human standards, but chosen by God for greatness in carrying forward the line of the seed of the woman.

Perez is a forefather not only of King David but also, through David, of the King of kings, Jesus Christ. Indeed, Judah, Tamar, Perez, and Zerah are all mentioned in Jesus' genealogy in Matthew 1. Contrary to current conventions which excluded women from genealogies, Matthew lists, besides Mary, four other women in Jesus' genealogy — the first being Tamar:

> Judah the father of Perez and Zerah by *Tamar,* and Perez the father of Hezron, and Hezron the father of Aram, and Aram the father of Aminadab, and Aminadab the father of Nahshon, and Nahshon the father of Salmon, and Salmon the father of Boaz by *Rahab,* and Boaz the father of Obed by *Ruth,* and Obed the father of Jesse, and Jesse the father of King David. And David was the father of Solomon by *the wife of Uriah* . . . , and Jacob the father of Joseph the husband of Mary, of whom Jesus was born, who is called the Messiah (Matt 1:3-17).

All four women are foreigners: Tamar was probably a Canaanite; Rahab was a Canaanite; Ruth was a Moabite, and Bathsheba was probably a Hittite. But God included all four foreign women in his covenant family. Not only this, but all four received the honor of being foremothers of Israel's Messiah.

---

which an explanation is given. . . . David was descended from Perez, according to Ruth 4:18-22." Sarna, *Genesis,* 270.

59. Hamilton, *Genesis 18–50,* 453-54.

Moreover, all four women had "a highly irregular and potentially scandalous marital union."[60] Tamar had to play the harlot to conceive Perez; Rahab was a former prostitute; Ruth, also a childless widow of an Israelite, went to the threshing floor to solicit Boaz to be her kinsman-redeemer; and "the wife of Uriah" had an adulterous relationship with King David, who subsequently had her husband killed, and then married her. All these sinful acts of men and women took place in Judah's family line from which the Messiah would be born. Jesus truly "emptied himself" (Phil 2:7) by being born into the human family.[61] Yet in spite of many sins and shortcoming, "these unions were, by God's providence, links in the chain to the Messiah."[62]

The narrative of Judah and Tamar assured Israel that God can accomplish his plan of salvation even through Israel's disobedience and the deception of a Canaanite woman. They saw the family line of Perez reaching its pinnacle in the tenth generation with the great king David. From the New Testament perspective we can see that this family line of Perez continues beyond King David to an even higher summit, Jesus Christ, the King of kings. God used Tamar's deception of disobedient Judah to continue Judah's family line, so that eventually Jesus could be born of this royal line. God can accomplish his plan of salvation even through human disobedience and deception.

We are often confused about events in this world. We may sometimes wonder if there really is a God who controls this mixed-up world. This narrative shows us that God is in control even when it appears that he is absent. God punished the wicked Er and Onan who defied his plans of salvation, but he blessed the obedient Canaanite woman Tamar with children. Thus God continued Judah's family line, which would eventually result in the birth of our Savior, Jesus Christ. God is in control. We can fully trust him to accomplish his plan of salvation.

60. Hamilton, *Genesis 18–50*, 455.

61. "Now although, at first sight, the dignity of Christ seems to be somewhat tarnished by such dishonour [the greatest disgrace of the tribe of Judah]; yet since here also is seen that 'emptying' of which St. Paul speaks, it rather redounds to his glory, than in the least degree detracts from it." Calvin, *Genesis*, II, 278.

62. Hamilton, *Genesis*, 455-56.

CHAPTER 20

Joseph in Potiphar's House

Genesis 39:1-23

Preachers as good pastors will be tempted to present Joseph as a model for young people today: "Say, 'No!' Maintain your sexual purity. Flee if you have to. Just say, 'No!'" Terence Fretheim asserts, "This famous episode of Joseph and Potiphar's wife has often been interpreted as a morality tale, designed to specify the limits regarding sexuality for persons of faith."[1]

This interpretation is given some credence by von Rad's view that the "Joseph story . . . is obviously related to the older teachings of wisdom."[2] If this is wisdom literature, Joseph can indeed be depicted as the ideal Israelite whose actions ought to be imitated. Von Rad states that here "we find ourselves again in very close proximity to an important subject of wisdom literature, namely, the warning against 'strange women' (Prov 2:16; 5:3, 20; 6:24; 22:14; 23:27f.). Thus the temptation story in ch. 39 reads like a story composed *ad hoc* to illustrate these admonitions of wisdom."[3]

The Joseph story, however, is *not* wisdom literature. By beginning the Joseph narrative with, "This is the *tôlĕdôt* of Jacob" (37:2a), the author clearly indicates that he intends this narrative to be read like the foregoing narratives, that is, as redemptive history. The Joseph narrative is the tenth *tôlĕdôt,* forming the indispensable, final link in the chain from the first humans (2:4), via the patriarchs, to Israel in Egypt.

Although Allen Ross digs deeper than a superficial moralistic reading, he still approaches this text with the understanding that "Chapter 39 is essentially about the temptation of Joseph in Egypt. It actually formed another test of God's leader — if Joseph was to be a leader of God's people, he had to show himself

1. Fretheim, "Genesis," 609.
2. Von Rad, *Genesis,* 435.
3. Ibid., 436,

faithful to God. The example of Joseph makes an excellent study on how to overcome temptation."[4] This starting point leads to misconstruing the message of this chapter, as we can see in Ross's proposal: "We may reflect this lesson in an expositional idea: Dedication to the calling of God will enable the servant of God to resist temptation."[5] John Walton rightly rejects this approach: "No clear model is presented, and no exhortations or statements of approval from the narrator urge us to go and do likewise. . . . It is only when we consistently adopt the criteria of taking our lead from the overt teaching of the text that the morass of subjectivity can be avoided and the text can retain its clear vision and voice."[6]

Text and Context

Commentators are not agreed on the limits of this textual unit. It is clear after the Judah-Tamar narrative that Genesis 39:1 picks up the Joseph story again from chapter 37:36 (note the repetition). What is not so clear is where this narrative ends. Wenham and others make a strong case for ending the narrative at 39:20a. This position is based on an analysis of the scenes in the larger narrative from 39:1 to 41:57:

> Scene 1, Joseph in Potiphar's house, consists of exposition (39:1-6) followed by narration (39:7-20a);
> Scene 2, Joseph in prison, consists of exposition (39:20b-23) followed by narration (40:1-23); and
> Scene 3, Joseph in Pharaoh's court (41:1-57).

"The shift from exposition to narration is in both cases marked by the phrase 'After these things'" (39:7; 40:1).[7]

While this analysis of three distinct scenes — Potiphar's house, prison, and Pharaoh's court — is undoubtedly correct, the narrator links scenes 1 and 2 with the inclusio, "the LORD was with Joseph (with him)" (39:2 and 3) and "the LORD was with Joseph (with him)" (39:21 and 23). In other words, verses 21-23 serve a double function:[8] they conclude the first narrative of Joseph's experience in

4. Ross, *Creation and Blessing,* 621.

5. Ibid., 628. Cf. pp. 628-29, "In this passage . . . we have a paradigm for leaders (and therefore all who follow them): people cannot defiantly sin against what they know to be God's righteous will when they are on the verge of becoming what God wants them to be. . . . Equally important is the lesson that resistance to temptation does not always find immediate reward."

6. Walton, *Genesis,* 693-94. Cf. Russell, "Literary Forms," 294-97.

7. Adapted from Wenham, *Genesis 16–50,* 372, based on Gunkel's and Coats's analyses.

8. See our earlier discussion regarding Genesis 29:31-35 on p. 297 above.

Potiphar's house and form the setting for the second narrative of Joseph's experience in prison. We can, therefore, select as our text Genesis 39:1-23.

As to the context, we have already noted that this chapter continues the story of Joseph's sale to Potiphar (37:36). The Judah-Tamar narrative serves to raise the tension in the Joseph story, while Judah's sexual promiscuity serves as a foil for Joseph's conduct. The theme of the LORD's presence with Joseph reaches all the way back to God's covenant promise to Abraham to be his God (17:7-8), while the theme of the LORD blessing Joseph and through him "the Egyptian's house" (39:5) reaches all the way back to God's original promise to Abraham, "In you all the families of the earth shall be blessed" (12:3). These themes recur especially with Jacob when he leaves the Promised Land (as Joseph has done here): at Bethel the LORD promised him his special presence (28:15; cf. 31:3), and through him the LORD also blessed the house of Laban (30:27). This narrative about Joseph's rise and fall in Potiphar's house (39), will be followed by his rise in prison and being forgotten (40), and will climax with his rise to power in Egypt (41).

Literary Features

The narrator shows his hand most clearly when he *summarizes* the speech of Potiphar's wife, "When his master heard the words that his wife spoke to him, saying, 'This is the way your servant treated me,' he became enraged" (v 19). Of course, we hear the whole story through the narrator's words. Especially important is his opening statement: "The LORD was with Joseph" (v 2). "The name Yahweh occurs here at what is the most uncertain moment in the life of Joseph. His future hangs in the balance. He is alone in Egypt, separated from family, vulnerable, with a cloud over his future. Or is he alone? Only the narrator, never any of the characters, uses the name Yahweh. Thus it is the narrator who tells us, no less than five times, that in a very precarious situation, Joseph is not really alone. Yahweh is with him."[9]

The narrator provides character description for Potiphar by giving his name, titles, and nationality: "an officer of Pharaoh, the captain of the guard, an Egyptian" (v 2). He also describes him as Joseph's "master" (vv 2, 3, 19, 20) and as becoming "enraged" (19). The narrator describes Joseph as "a successful man" (v 2), finding "favor" with his master and becoming "overseer" (v 4), and being "handsome and good-looking" (v 6) — the same words used earlier to describe his mother Rachel (29:17). Potiphar's wife is nameless but is described as "his master's wife" and as "casting her eyes on Joseph."

9. Hamilton, *Genesis 18–50*, 459.

The characters are further fleshed out by dialogue. Potiphar does not say a word, but his wife speaks all the more. Her first words are only two in Hebrew, the brusque solicitation, "Lie with me" (v 7), to which Joseph responds with a long speech (vv 8-9).[10] A second time she orders, "Lie with me!" (v 12). This time Joseph flees the house. He remains silent while his master's wife frames him with clever, lengthy speeches to members of her household (vv 14-15) and then to Potiphar himself (vv 17-18). Joseph's single speech characterizes him as an upright young man, loyal to his master, and concerned to please God. Potiphar's wife's speeches, by contrast, characterize her as domineering (the command: "Lie with me!"), adulterous, devious,[11] and a liar.[12]

The narrator further enables us to discern his message by the repetition of keywords. The name *Yahweh* is used eight times in this chapter (vv 2, 3 [2×], 5 [2×], 21, 23 [2×]). This eightfold use of God's covenant name stands out here because in the entire Joseph story it is used only once more (49:18; plus three times in the Judah story [38:7 (2×), 10]). Moreover, the narrator repeats four times that "the LORD was with Joseph" (vv 2, 3, 21, 23). Three times he links this presence of the LORD with Joseph's success/prosperity (vv 2, 3, 23). Twice he mentions the LORD's blessing on "the Egyptian's house" (v 5, verb and noun). "The word 'all' *(kol)* is insisted upon five times, clearly exceeding the norm of biblical repetition and thus calling attention to itself as a thematic assertion: the scope of blessing or success this man realizes is virtually unlimited; everything prospers, everything is entrusted to him."[13]

The word "hand" *(yād)* is used eight times. The "hand" implies power. Joseph is bought from the "hand" of the Ishmaelites (v 1, literal Hebrew). The LORD prospers Joseph's hand (v 3), and Potiphar puts all that he has into his hand (vv 4, 6, 8). Unfortunately, Joseph's garment falls into the hand of his master's wife (vv 12, 13) and he ends up in prison. In prison, however, the chief jailor commits to Joseph's hand all the prisoners (v 22), and pays no heed to anything that was in Joseph's hand (v 23). Another keyword is "garment" *(beged),* which in the "hand" of the woman becomes evidence of wrongdoing. It is repeated six

10. Alter calls this "contrastive dialogue." *Art of Biblical Narrative,* 72.

11. "She starts (verse 17) with the shock of 'The Hebrew slave came to me,' which, by itself, could easily be taken to mean, in good biblical idiom, 'has had sexual intercourse with me.' Then she qualifies, 'the one you brought us, to dally with me.' This lady who before had exhibited a speech-repertoire of two carnal words here shows herself a subtle mistress of syntactic equivocation." Ibid., 110.

12. "Because she uses precisely the same series of phrases in her speech (verses 14-15) that had been used twice just before by the narrator (verses 12-13) but reverses their order, so that her calling out *precedes* Joseph's flight, the blatancy of her lie is forcefully conveyed without commentary." Ibid., 109.

13. Ibid., 107-8.

times (12 [2×], 13, 15, 16, 18). Finally, Westermann suggests that the words "see," "cast eyes" function at crucial turning points in this narrative: "One can, in fact, understand the entire episode from the perspective of three kinds of seeing that occur: the Egyptian looks at Joseph (v 3); his wife looks at Joseph (v 7); the woman sees the garment left behind [v 13]."[14]

The most important clue the narrator gives us to his intended meaning is the double inclusio of "the LORD was with Joseph":

A "The LORD was with Joseph, and he became a prosperous man." (v 2)
  B "The LORD was with him . . . , the LORD caused all that he did to prosper." (v 3)
A′ "The LORD was with Joseph and showed him steadfast love." (v 21)
  B′ "The LORD was with him; and whatever he did, the LORD made it prosper." (v 23)

The Plot Line

The setting of this narrative is given in chapter 39:1, which harks back to chapter 37:36. Preliminary incidents consist of Joseph becoming "a successful man" (v 2) because "the LORD was with him," and Joseph's rapid promotions in Potiphar's house. In contrast to the lowly field slaves, "he was in the house of his Egyptian master" (v 2); "found favor in his sight" and became his personal attendant (v 4a); became "overseer of his house" (v 4b); and finally was put "in charge of all that he had" (v 4c), "in house and field" (v 5).

The occasioning incident is his master's wife "casting her eyes" on the handsome Joseph (vv 6b-7). She follows through by bluntly ordering him: "Lie with me!" (v 7b). How will Joseph handle this temptation? The tension resolves rather quickly when Joseph refuses to obey her and justifies his refusal with a lengthy speech in which he calls her proposal "a great wickedness and sin against God" (v 9).

The tension flares up again, however, when she does not accept his refusal but instead propositions him "day after day" (v 10). The narrative reaches a climax one day when she has Joseph cornered. No one else is in the house (v 11). She sees her opportunity, grabs Joseph by his garment, and orders him, "Lie with me!" (v 12a). In response, Joseph leaves his garment in her hand and flees (v 12b). She sees his garment in her "hand" (power) (v 13) and calls the mem-

14. Westermann, *Joseph*, 28. A few other repeated words are "he left" (5×), "he fled" (4×), "to lie with (beside)" (4×). See Wilfried Warning, "Terminological Patterns and Genesis 39," *JETS* 44/3 (Sept. 2001) 409-19.

bers of her household as witnesses, accusing Joseph of attempted rape (vv 14-15). She keeps Joseph's garment with her as evidence until his master comes home (v 16). Then she repeats her trumped up story to her husband (vv 17-18), who becomes "enraged" (v 19) and throws Joseph into prison (v 20).

The outcome of the narrative follows: "The LORD was with Joseph" in prison and "gave him favor in the sight of the chief jailer" (v 21), who committed all things to Joseph's "hand" (v 22) and "paid no heed to anything . . . because the LORD was with him" (v 23).

Since this narrative has two climaxes, we could conceivably sketch it as a complex plot. But since the issue of the woman pursuing Joseph remains the same, it is better to sketch this story as a single plot, indicating at verses 8-9 an initial resolution of the tension.

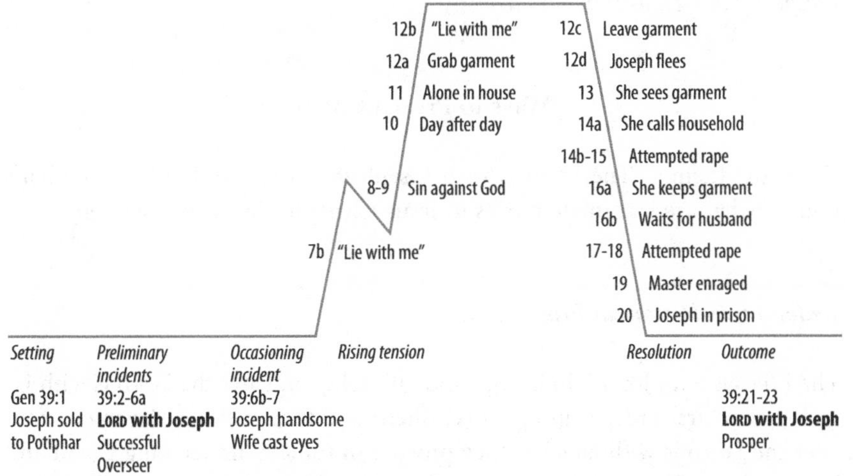

Theocentric Interpretation

The author's theocentric emphasis is evident: he uses the name "LORD" eight times in this short narrative. Although the narrative proper (from conflict to resolution, 39:6b-20) has only one reference to God (Joseph's exclamation, "sin against God, v 9), the narrative is framed by a double inclusio that "the LORD was with Joseph" (vv 2, 3, 21, 23). Moreover, because the LORD was with Joseph, he became "a successful man" in Potiphar's house (v 2); "the LORD caused all that he did to prosper" (v 3); and "the LORD [even] blessed the Egyptian's house for Joseph's sake" (v 5). When Joseph is falsely accused and thrown into prison, again "the LORD was with Joseph and showed him steadfast love" (v 21a). The LORD "gave him favor in the sight of the chief jailer" (v 21b), and "whatever he did, the LORD made it prosper" (v 23).

Textual Theme and Goal

With the double inclusio of "the LORD was with Joseph," the narrator's main point is not hard to detect. We can formulate his theme as follows: *The LORD is with Joseph in his rise and fall in Potiphar's house.*

For the author's goal in recording this story for later Israel, we should recall that Israel had also been enslaved in Egypt. Wenham writes, "Potiphar is here [v 1] called 'an Egyptian,' a designation repeated in vv 2, 5, perhaps suggesting a parallel between Joseph's slavery in Egypt and that of the Israelites some centuries later."[15] Still later, Israel would be enslaved by Assyria and Babylonia. Given Israel's suffering and enslavement to other nations, we can formulate the author's goal as follows: *To assure Israel of God's presence with them in times of prosperity as well as times of adversity.*

Ways to Preach Christ

Given the theme, "The LORD is with Joseph in his rise and fall in Potiphar's house," what are legitimate moves to Jesus Christ in the New Testament?

Redemptive-Historical Progression

The LORD is with Joseph in his rise and fall in Egypt. Later the LORD is with Israel as they first prosper in Egypt (Goshen) and then suffer enslavement. Still later the LORD is with Israel as they prosper in Canaan under King David and later as they suffer enslavement in exile in Babylonia (Isa 41:10; 43:2). In New Testament times, the Lord is with Jesus when "an angel of the Lord" warns Joseph to escape with Mary and Jesus from Herod's wrath to Egypt (Matt 2:13-15). Jesus, in turn, promises to be with his followers at all times (Matt 28:20), times of prosperity as well as times of adversity (Rom 8:35-39).

Promise-Fulfillment

There is no messianic promise in this narrative. However, the words, "The LORD blessed the Egyptian's house for Joseph's sake" (v 5), is an initial fulfillment of God's promise to Abraham, "In you all the families of the earth shall be blessed" (12:3). Through Joseph one family is blessed; through Jesus "all the

15. Wenham, *Genesis 16–50*, 373.

families of the earth shall be blessed." As Paul puts it, "Christ redeemed us from the curse of the law . . . in order that in Christ Jesus the blessing of Abraham might come to the Gentiles" (Gal 3:13-14).

Typology

The life of Joseph foreshadows the life of Jesus Christ. As Joseph moved from his high position as his father's designated heir to enslavement in Egypt to his exaltation as ruler of Egypt, so Jesus moved from his exalted position with his Father, to his humiliation on earth, to his exaltation to the Father's right hand. In this particular episode, we can also detect specific parallels between Joseph and Jesus: As God was with Joseph, so God was with Jesus (Luke 2:40; John 1:32); as Joseph was a blessing to one family, so Jesus was a blessing to all the families of the earth; as Joseph was tempted by Potiphar's wife to take a shortcut to power, so Jesus was tempted by Satan to take a shortcut to power (Matt 4:9); as Joseph was silent when falsely accused, so Jesus was silent when falsely accused (Matt 26:63), and as the innocent Joseph was punished with prison, so the innocent Jesus was punished with death.

Analogy

As God through this story assured Israel of his presence with them even in times of suffering, so Jesus assures his church of his presence with them even in times of suffering. Jesus declares, "Blessed are you when people revile you and persecute you and utter all kinds of evil against you falsely on my account. Rejoice and be glad, for your reward is great in heaven" (Matt 5:11-12). In fact, Jesus promises his church, "I am with you *always,* to the end of the age" (Matt 28:20; cf. Acts 18:10; Rom 8:35-39; 2 Tim 4:17; Heb 13:5-6).

Longitudinal Themes

The theme of God's presence with his people runs like a major thread from the patriarchs (26:3, 24; 28:13-15; 31:3) to Joseph (39:2, 3, 21, 23), to Israel (e.g., Exod 13:21; Pss 23; 46:7; Isa 41:10; 43:2), to Jesus who is Immanuel ("God with us" [Matt 1:23]), to Jesus' promise, "I am with you always" (Matt 28:20), to Jesus' pouring out his Spirit on the church at Pentecost (Acts 2), to Jesus' second coming when "God will dwell with his people" (Rev 21:3).

New Testament References

Besides the New Testament references listed above, there are few other suitable New Testament references. The appendix to the Greek New Testament lists as allusions to this narrative Acts 7:9-10 (Stephen's speech) and Matthew 24:45 (the parable of the faithful slave), neither of which forms a solid bridge from this Joseph story to Jesus in the New Testament.

Contrast

Although God was with Joseph and Israel in times of prosperity and in times of adversity (but see Isa 54:7), Jesus, at the height of his suffering, was momentarily forsaken by God (Mark 15:34). He was forsaken by God so that we might never be forsaken by him.

Sermon Theme and Goal

We formulated the textual theme as, "The LORD is with Joseph in his rise and fall in Potiphar's house." In the light of further revelation in the Old as well as the New Testament, we can broaden this specific textual theme to the sermon theme, *The Lord is with his people both in prosperity and adversity.*

The author's goal we formulated as, "To assure Israel of God's presence with them in times of prosperity as well as times of adversity." The sermon goal can be similar, *To assure God's people of his presence with them in times of prosperity as well as times of adversity.* This sermon goal addresses the need that people going through times of adversity often feel abandoned by God.

Sermon Exposition

Genesis 39 continues the Joseph story begun in chapter 37. Because of Jacob's favoritism of Joseph and Joseph's dreams of ruling over his brothers, his brothers hated him so much that they wanted to kill him. But Judah convinced his brothers to sell Joseph to a caravan headed for Egypt. Verse 1, "Now Joseph was taken down to Egypt, and Potiphar, an officer of Pharaoh, the captain of the guard, an Egyptian, bought him from the Ishmaelites who had brought him down there." Joseph is now in Egypt, far from the Promised Land. His dreams of grandeur are shattered. He has become a common slave. The narrator emphasizes Joseph's low position by contrasting it with the high position of his buyer: "Potiphar, an officer of Pharaoh, the captain of the guard, an Egyptian." Three times the narrator repeats that Joseph's master is "an Egyptian" (vv 1, 2, 5). As Israel later hears this story, they are reminded of their own enslavement to Egyptian masters. How far they have fallen: from their prosperity in the land of Goshen under the protection of friendly Pharaohs to being enslaved by Egyptian masters, who ordered their baby boys to be drowned in the Nile River.

How far Joseph has fallen: from his father's favorite and designated heir to a lowly slave in the land of Egypt, far from the Promised Land. But, amazingly, the narrator assures us in verse 2, "The LORD was with Joseph." In this narrative the narrator repeats four times that "the LORD was with Joseph" (vv 2, 3, 21, 23). Even in his descent into the lowest of human stations, "the LORD was with Joseph." Even far from the Promised Land, "the LORD was with Joseph." "Although all human supports have failed, and Joseph is far removed from the community of faith and the land of promise, God stays with him. God's presence, neither localized geographically nor dramatic or spectacular, is an unobtrusive, working-behind-the-scenes kind of presence."[16]

As a result of the LORD being with Joseph, verse 2 continues, Joseph becomes "a successful man." Three times the narrator repeats that the LORD's presence makes Joseph's work "successful"[17] or "prosperous" (vv 2, 3, 23). Right at the outset, the narrator informs us that Joseph becomes successful not because of his innate wisdom or ability but because the *LORD* is with him.

Verse 2 further relates that Joseph is "*in the house* of his Egyptian master." Instead of becoming an inferior field slave with few opportunities for advancement, Joseph works in the master's house where there are opportunities for promotion. And, indeed, Joseph, soon rises in status. Verse 3, "His master saw that the LORD was with him, and that the LORD caused all that he did to prosper in his hands. So Joseph found favor in his sight and attended him;[18] he made him overseer of his house and put him in charge of all that he had." Joseph soon becomes the personal assistant of Potiphar and then the overseer, the chief manager, of his household. He is in charge of all of Potiphar's possessions.

Verse 5, "From the time that he made him overseer in his house and over all that he had, the LORD *blessed* the Egyptian's house for Joseph's sake; the *blessing*

16. Fretheim, "Genesis," 611.

17. "The slightly complacent ring of the expression in English is no part of it: it is the word used for, e.g., the outcome of Eliezer's mission in 24:21, 40, and of the Servant's suffering in Isaiah 53:10; it speaks of achievement rather than status." Kidner, *Genesis*, 190.

18. "This 'favor' *(ḥēn)* would seem to imply a personal attachment which the Egyptian formed for him as a result of which he 'became his personal attendant.' For *yĕšāret* means 'to wait upon.' Hitherto the service had been more impersonal; now Joseph must personally attend to his master's wants." Leupold, *Genesis*, II, 994.

of the LORD was on all that he had, in house and field." The LORD had promised Abraham, "In you all the families of the earth shall be blessed" (12:3). In this narrative we see an initial fulfillment of God's promise to Abraham.[19] Here, through Joseph, the LORD's blessing flows to one family — a Gentile family at that. God's promise to Abraham will be completely fulfilled through Jesus Christ. Through him "all the families of the earth shall be blessed." Paul writes in Galatians 3:13-14, "Christ redeemed us from the curse of the law . . . in order that in Christ Jesus the blessing of Abraham might come to the Gentiles."

Verse 6, "So he left all that he had in Joseph's charge [literally, Joseph's hand]; and, with him there, he had no concern for anything but the food that he ate." Commentators are not agreed on the exception, "the food that he ate." Some take this literally, namely that Joseph was in charge of everything but the preparation of Potiphar's food, "perhaps because of a general Egyptian concern that non-Egyptians were unaware of how properly to prepare food (see 43:32), or more likely, because of ritual separation at mealtimes."[20] Others understand "food" as "an idiom for 'his private affairs.'"[21] Still others understand "food" as "a euphemism for his [Potiphar's] wife, for 'food' is here a cipher for sex."[22] If this exception refers to Potiphar's wife, it forms a natural bridge to the conflict that arises in this narrative.

At the end of verse 6, the narrator informs us that "Joseph was handsome and good-looking." Joseph is the only male person in Scripture who is described as "handsome and good-looking."[23] Unfortunately, his good looks do not bode well for him. Verse 7, "And after a time his master's wife cast her eyes on[24] Joseph and said, 'Lie with me.'" It is a brusque proposition for sex. What makes the temptation even greater for Joseph is that she is "his master's wife."[25]

19. Preachers must be careful not to turn this story into a health-and-wealth gospel. "This is not a story of the success of Joseph; rather it is a story of God's faithfulness to his promises." Sailhamer, *Genesis*, 234.

20. Hamilton, *Genesis 18–50*, 461.

21. Wenham, *Genesis 16–50*, 374.

22. Brueggemann, *Genesis*, 315. Cf. Hamilton, *Genesis 18–50*, 461, "There is an interesting rabbinic tradition (see Gen. Rabbah 86:6) to the effect that the phrase 'the food he consumed' is a euphemism, a reference to Potiphar's wife." Cf. Exod 2:20-21. This interpretation also agrees with Joseph's own words in verse 9 that his master has not "kept back anything from me except yourself, because you are his wife."

23. "Joseph's mother, Rachel, is also described as having a lovely figure and a beautiful face (29:17). They are the only two people in the OT to be awarded this double accolade." Wenham, *Genesis 16–50*, 374.

24. "Looked with desire at. The phrase is used in the same sense in Akkadian in Section 25 of the Code of Hammurabi." *NIV Study Bible*, Genesis 39:7, n.

25. "Her designation underscores Joseph's temptation not to displease such an aristocratic and powerful woman." Waltke, *Genesis*, 520.

She orders Joseph, "Lie with me!" "She presents the matter in terms of power rather than love, of command rather than seduction; she is 'his master's wife.'"[26] How can he refuse? Moreover, "sexual promiscuity was a perennial feature of all slave societies."[27] Why not obey his master's wife? Furthermore, Joseph might be able to use this opportunity "to advance his personal and selfish interests."[28] Why should he refuse?

The conflict, however, is quickly resolved with Joseph's only speech in this narrative. Verses 8-9, "But he refused and said to his master's wife, 'Look, with me here, my master has no concern about anything in the house, and he has put everything that he has in my hand. He is not greater in this house than I am, nor has he kept back anything from me *except yourself*, because you are his wife. How then could I do this great wickedness, and sin against God?'"

In refusing his master's wife, Joseph uses three arguments.[29] First, my master "has put everything that he has in my hand." Joseph cannot betray such great confidence and trust in him.[30] Second, my master has not "kept back anything from me except yourself, because you are his wife." To obey his master's wife would be to disobey his master. And third, this great wickedness against my master is to "sin against God"[31] — the God who is with him and has prospered him. Joseph wishes to be loyal to his master and loyal to his God.

But his master's wife will not let up. According to verse 10, "she spoke to Joseph day after day." Day after day she propositions Joseph. One of these days she will wear him down and he will give in to her. And Joseph cannot avoid her, for she is his master's wife. But, we read, "he would not consent to lie beside her or to be with her."

One day, however, she sees her chance to take Joseph by surprise. She is all alone in the house; there are no witnesses. Verse 11, "One day . . . when he went into the house to do his work, and while no one else was in the house, she caught hold of[32] his garment, saying, 'Lie with me!' But he left his garment in her hand,

26. Fretheim, "Genesis," 610.

27. Sarna, *Genesis*, 216.

28. Ibid.

29. See Leupold, *Genesis*, II, 997.

30. "Joseph refuses to betray the trust which his master has deposited in him. All of the talk about the 'chaste Joseph,' then, misses the real meaning of the story." Westermann, *Joseph*, 25.

31. "Adultery is a sin against God. It is not a matter of social impropriety or breach of convention. . . . It is a religious offense in which God is vitally involved. In other words, the sanction of morality is divine, not social, and for this reason morality is absolute and not relative. . . . This concept of morality as God-given, rather than utilitarian, suffuses the Torah legislation and explains a fundamental difference in its treatment of adultery from that of the ancient law codes of the Near East." Sarna, *Genesis*, 217.

32. "The verb . . . 'grab' implies violence." Wenham, *Genesis 16–50*, 376, with references to Deut 9:17; 22:28; 1 Kings 11:30.

and fled and ran outside." Fleeing is Joseph's only option. He cannot strike the woman, for she is his master's wife. All he can do is to flee away from her.

"Joseph's flight not only enrages but also compromises his mistress. He may well report her for sexual assault."[33] Shrewdly she calls together potential witnesses, twists the facts, and seeks to enlist their sympathy. Verse 13, "When she saw that he had left his garment in her hand and had fled outside, she called out to the members of her household and said to them, 'See [waving Joseph's garment], my husband has brought among us [within our household] a Hebrew [an ethnic slur] to insult us![34] He came in to me[35] to lie with me [a blatant lie], and I cried out with a loud voice [another lie];[36] and when he heard me raise my voice and cry out [another lie], he left his garment beside me [as if Joseph had "disrobed quite voluntarily as a preliminary to rape"[37]], and fled outside.'"

Verse 16, "Then she kept his garment by her until his master came home." This verse presents "a momentary still image among the hastening action. The woman remains lying down, the evidence at her side. Her husband, too, is not only to hear, but also to visualize."[38] "She kept his garment by her." Earlier Joseph's blood-smeared robe served as (false) evidence of his death; here his garment is to serve as (false) evidence of his crime.[39]

When her husband comes home, verse 17, she tells him the same story, "The Hebrew servant, whom you have brought among us, came in to me to insult me; but as soon as I raised my voice and cried out, he left his garment beside me, and fled outside." She again twists the story a little for maximum effect. Instead of calling Joseph "a Hebrew man *('îš)*," as she did to her slaves, to her husband she calls him "the Hebrew slave *('ebed)*." "To be sexually attacked by an *'îš* is bad enough. To be sexually attacked by a foreign slave makes her accusation all the more damning. In choosing this term, she is putting Joseph in as

33. Sternberg, *Poetics of Biblical Narrative*, 424.

34. "To fool with us" is a nicely ambiguous phrase used of sexual intimacy in 26:8 and of insulting behavior in 21:9." Wenham, *Genesis 16–50*, 376.

35. "She twice says that Joseph 'came in to me *(ba' 'ēlay)*' (39:14b, 17b). The same combination of verb and preposition is used in ch. 38 to mean 'had sexual intercourse with' (38:2, 8, 9, 16, 18; cf. 29:21, 23; 30:3, 4, 16). Thus the initial impression she gives is that she has been raped. Only later is this impression modified, but her opening words to the servants, and then to her husband, are weighted to arouse maximum indignation." Turner, *Genesis*, 170-71.

36. "Because she uses precisely the same series of phrases in her speech (verses 14-15) that had been used twice just before by the narrator (verses 12-13) but reverses their order, so that her calling out *precedes* Joseph's flight, the blatancy of her lie is forcefully conveyed without commentary." Alter, *Art of Biblical Narrative*, 109.

37. Ibid., 110.

38. Westermann, *Joseph*, 29.

39. In the foregoing narrative, Tamar keeps Judah's signet, cord, and staff as evidence of his crime (38:25).

despicable light as possible. It should also demand as swift redress as possible from Potiphar, the master who has been betrayed by his servant."[40]

Verse 19, "When his master[41] heard the words that his wife spoke to him, saying, 'This is the way your servant treated me,' he became enraged. And Joseph's master took him and put him into the prison, the place where the king's prisoners were confined; he remained there in prison." Joseph is fortunate that his master does not have him executed — the usual punishment for adultery in Egypt as well as Israel (cf. Lev 20:10; Deut 22:23-27). Perhaps his master really does not believe his wife's story. In any event, Joseph ends up in prison.[42] As we hear this, we are enraged at the injustice of it all: Joseph refuses Potiphar's wife's advances, he rejects evil, he follows God's law, and he is the one to end up in prison as a common criminal. This is flagrantly unjust! Where is God when his loyal servant suffers such injustice?

Surprisingly, verse 21 tells us, "But the LORD was with Joseph." The LORD was with Joseph as he prospered in Potiphar's house, and now the LORD is still with him as he is falsely accused and ends up in prison. The LORD is with Joseph not only in prosperity but also in adversity. The fact that Joseph escapes the usual death penalty can be attributed to the LORD being with him.[43] In fact, the narrator says, "But the LORD was with Joseph and *showed him steadfast love.*" Even in the depths of despair, the LORD shows Joseph his steadfast love. Joseph basks in the LORD's kindness. "He gave him favor in the sight of the chief jailer."

As a result, Joseph makes quick promotion in prison. He becomes overseer in prison as he had been earlier in Potiphar's house.[44] Verse 22, "The chief jailer committed to Joseph's care *all* the prisoners who were in the prison, and whatever was done there, he was the one who did it. The chief jailer paid no heed to anything that was in Joseph's care, because the LORD was with him; and whatever he did, the LORD made it prosper." "Whatever he did, the LORD made it prosper." It was not Joseph's wisdom or ingenuity or hard work that made him successful. "The LORD made it prosper."

The message of this narrative comes through loudly and clearly: The LORD

40. Hamilton, *Genesis 18–50*, 469.

41. "It is no accident that toward the end of the tale the narrator twice reverts to the term 'his master,' which appeared at the outset and then disappeared as the relations between Potiphar and Joseph got closer. The enraged patron again turns master and throws his seemingly ungrateful slave into prison." Sternberg, *Poetics of Biblical Narrative*, 427.

42. "'Prison,' lit. 'house of roundness,' is found only in this section of Genesis (cf. 39:21-23; 40:3-5). The term suggests it was a fortress that also served as a prison, several of which are known in Egypt. . . . It seems to have been managed by Potiphar (cf. 40:3; 41:10)." Wenham, *Genesis 16–50*, 377.

43. Herbert, *Genesis 12–50*, 130.

44. "Previously Joseph had been in charge of the house *(bayit)*, now he is in charge of the prison, literally 'the roundhouse' *(bêt hassōhar)*." Turner, *Genesis*, 172.

was with Joseph in times of prosperity as well as times of adversity. This theme is similar to the song "Footsteps in the Sand." The song writer wonders why there were two sets of footprints when he prospered (God was walking beside him) but only one set of footprints when he suffered. Had God abandoned him when he suffered? He asked God about it and God replied:

"My son, my precious child,
I love you and I would never leave you,
During your times of trial and suffering,
when you see only one set of footprints,
it was then that I carried you."[45]

The Joseph story similarly tells us that the LORD was with Joseph not only in his prosperity but also in his adversity, in his suffering. The LORD carried him at all times, no matter what his circumstances.

Through this story, the LORD assured Israel that he would always be with them. He would carry them not only up to the mountaintops but also through the dark valleys. The LORD was with them not only when they prospered in Goshen but also when a later Pharaoh enslaved them. The LORD was with them not only when they prospered under King David but also when they suffered in exile in Babylonia (see Isa 41:10; 43:2). Psalm 23 gives beautiful expression to God's constant presence with his people:

The LORD is my shepherd, I shall not want.
  He makes me lie down in green pastures;
he leads me beside still waters. . . .
  [times of prosperity; but adversity follows:]
Even though I walk through the darkest valley,
  I fear no evil;
for you are with me. . . .
  [the Psalm concludes with prosperity again:]
Surely goodness and mercy shall follow me all the days of my life,
and I shall dwell in the house of the LORD my whole life long.

In the New Testament, Jesus also assures his followers of his constant presence with them. After his resurrection, Jesus says, "Remember, I am with you *always*, to the end of the age" (Matt 28:20). Jesus is with us even in times of adversity and suffering. When it seems that God has abandoned us, he is still with us.[46] Je-

45. Author unknown.

46. "Divine presence does not mean 'preventive medicine' or a 'quick fix' of whatever may befall a person of faith." Fretheim, "Genesis," 611.

sus declares, "Blessed are you when people revile you and persecute you and utter all kinds of evil against you falsely on my account. Rejoice and be glad, for your reward is great in heaven" (Matt 5:11-12). God is with us, even in adversity. Strangely, God is with us even when he seems absent.

You know how much Paul suffered for the gospel. He writes that he was imprisoned many times, received "countless floggings, and often near death." He was "often without food, cold and naked" (2 Cor 11:23, 27). Had God abandoned him when he was suffering? Paul deals with this question in Romans 8. He asks, "Who will separate us from the love of Christ? Will hardship, or distress, or persecution, or famine, or nakedness, or peril, or sword?" And he answers confidently, "No, *in* all these things we are more than conquerors through him who loved us. For I am convinced that neither death [no matter how painful], nor life [no matter how difficult] . . . , nor anything else in all creation will be able to separate us from the love of God in Christ Jesus our Lord" (Rom 8:35-39). God is with us even in times of suffering.

CHAPTER 21

Joseph's Rise to Power in Egypt

Genesis 41:1-57

This particular narrative is rather lengthy because Pharaoh's dreams are told three times: first by the narrator (41:1-7), next by Pharaoh himself (vv 17-24), and finally by Joseph (vv 25-32). One of the challenges for expository preaching of this narrative is to keep the sermon moving and not stall it in the repeated retelling of the dreams. A related issue is to select Scripture reading that is not overly long or repetitive. I suggest reading before the sermon only Genesis 41:1-16, and then invite the congregation to keep their Bibles open so that they can read along as the rest of the story is read in the sermon.

Text and Context

The narrator has clearly marked the textual unit: he begins the narrative in verse 1 with the indication of the passage of time, "After two whole years," and he ends it with verse 57, "All the world came to Joseph in Egypt to buy grain." He begins a new narrative in chapter 42:1 with a change of location: "When Jacob [in Canaan] learned that there was grain in Egypt. . . ."

The context of this narrative relates Joseph's imprisonment in "the place where the king's prisoners were confined" (39:20), which leads to his meeting with Pharaoh's chief cupbearer and chief baker. Joseph correctly interprets their dreams: within three days the cupbearer will be restored to his office but the baker will be hanged. Joseph pleads with the cupbearer, "Remember me when it is well with you; please do me the kindness to make mention of me to Pharaoh, and so get me out of this place" (40:14). However, "the chief cupbearer did not remember Joseph, but forgot him" (40:23).

This comment leads into the present narrative: "After two whole years, Pharaoh dreamed. . . ." Pharaoh's two dreams recall the two dreams of his officers, the cupbearer and baker, and ultimately Joseph's two dreams that his brothers would bow down to him (37:1-10). But whereas Joseph's brothers immediately understood the meaning of his dreams, not even Pharaoh's wise men can interpret Pharaoh's dreams. This, in turn, causes the cupbearer to remember Joseph (41:9-13), who is quickly released from prison and brought before Pharaoh. The concluding comment of this narrative, "all the world came to Joseph in Egypt to buy grain," leads naturally into the following narrative of Jacob sending his sons to Egypt to buy grain (chapter 42) and eventually to the whole family emigrating to Egypt (chapter 46).

Literary Features

As mentioned, Pharaoh's dreams are reported three times. The narrator first relates Pharaoh's dreams rather objectively in the third person (41:1-7). Next (vv 17-24) he relates the dreams in Pharaoh's words in the first person, adding Pharaoh's perceptions: "Never had I seen such ugly ones [cows] in all the land of Egypt" (v 19). And finally he relates the dreams and their interpretation through the words of Joseph (vv 25-32).

The narrator provides character description of Joseph in the words of the cupbearer: "a young Hebrew . . . , a servant of the captain of the guard" (v 12). He describes Pharaoh as "troubled" by the dreams (v 8a) and his "wise men" as unable to interpret the dreams (v 8b). The dialogue provides further characterization. Joseph's first reply to Pharaoh reveals that Joseph is calm, unafraid of Pharaoh, and confident in God: "It is not I; God will give Pharaoh a favorable answer" (v 16). Barbara Green observes, "Interpretations come from God; dreams too. Joseph appears cool here and not particularly diplomatic, Pharaoh over-eager. Joseph's advising of Pharaoh begins before the great man has even divulged the dreams. The interpreter also commits God to a *šālôm* response for Pharaoh, perhaps to take the sting out of the rebuke to Pharaoh's inept theologizing self."[1] After Pharaoh has told Joseph his dreams, "Joseph's interpretation . . . is the first longish speech in the Joseph story [vv 25-36]. It shows him to be both clear-headed and decisive."[2]

To highlight important points, the narrator also employs pace retardation. He hurries by Pharaoh's consultation with "*all* the magicians of Egypt and *all* its wise men" in less than a verse (v 8), while drawing out the cupbearer's remembrance of Joseph over five verses (vv 9-13). He describes Joseph being "hurriedly brought out of the dungeon" in one verse: "When he had shaved

1. Green, "The Determination of Pharaoh," 158.
2. Wenham, *Genesis 16–50*, 393.

himself and changed his clothes, he came in before Pharaoh" (v 14). But he slows the pace when Pharaoh tells Joseph his dreams (vv 15-24) and Joseph responds with the interpretation (vv 25-36). Joseph, in turn, stresses especially the disastrous famine, giving only one sentence to the plenteous years (v 29) followed by five sentences on the famine (vv 30-31).[3] Joseph's rise to power in Egypt is again related in much detail (vv 37-45).

Repetition of words and phrases again provide clues to the narrator's intended meaning. The narrator sets the narrative tension by repeating twice, "but there was no one who could interpret them [the dreams] to Pharaoh"; "there was no one who could explain it to me" (vv 8, 24c). The name "Lord" is not mentioned at all, while the name "God" occurs nine times. The perfect number "seven" is repeated a total of twenty-eight (4 × 7) times: seven fat cows, seven thin cows, seven full ears of grain, seven thin ears, seven years of plenty, seven years of famine, and so on. The word "famine" is repeated twelve times,[4] the last two times with the notation that it was "severe" (vv 56-57). "The extensiveness of the famine is underscored by the repeated use of *kol* (lit., 'all') in this section [vv 53-57]. It was once used by the narrator in v 47, twice by Joseph (v 51), and eight times by the narrator in vv 54-57 (twice in each verse)."[5] Finally, the narrator provides an important clue to the meaning of this narrative with Joseph's threefold declaration to Pharaoh, "God has revealed to Pharaoh what he is about to do" (v 25); "God has shown to Pharaoh what he is about to do" (v 28); "the thing is fixed by God, and God will shortly bring it about" (v 32).

The Plot Line

The setting for this narrative is the narrator's assurance that even in Joseph's deepest descent into the pit (prison), "the Lord was with Joseph"; "the Lord was with him" (39:21, 23). The preliminary incidents consist of his experiences with Pharaoh's cupbearer and baker. They each have a dream and are "troubled" because "there is no one to interpret them." Joseph replies, "Do not interpretations belong to God? Please tell them to me" (40:8). Since Pharaoh's cupbearer will return to his office within three days, Joseph pleads with him to remember him before Pharaoh so that he can get "out of this place" (40:14). "Yet the chief cupbearer did not remember Joseph, but forgot him" (40:23). Joseph spends two more years in prison.

3. Westermann, *Genesis 37–50,* 91.

4. Gen 41:27, 30 (2×), 31, 36 (2×), 50, 54 (2×), 56 (2×), and 57.

5. Hamilton, *Genesis 18–50,* 513. See ibid., 484, n. 2, for the meaning of the sixfold repetition of the interjection *hinneh,* "behold" (vv 1, 2, 3, 5, 6, and 7), which most versions do not translate into English.

God, however, does not forget Joseph, and this becomes the occasioning incident in this narrative. God gives Pharaoh two dreams. Now Pharaoh is "troubled" (41:8) because he does not know the meaning of the dreams. Pharaoh calls together all the wise men in Egypt and tells them his dreams. But no one can interpret them. This development causes the cupbearer to remember Joseph, and he tells Pharaoh about his experience in prison (vv 9-13). The tension builds: Will Joseph be able to interpret the dreams? Pharaoh sends for Joseph: "I have heard it said of you that when you hear a dream you can interpret it" (v 15). Joseph corrects the great Pharaoh: "It is not I; God will give Pharaoh a favorable answer" (v 16). Pharaoh tells Joseph his two dreams (vv 17-24). Will God reveal their meaning to Joseph? Will Joseph succeed where all the wise men of Egypt failed?

The tension begins to dissipate when Joseph interprets the dreams: "Pharaoh's dreams are one and the same; God has revealed to Pharaoh what he is about to do. The seven good cows are seven years, and the seven good ears are seven years; the dreams are one. The seven lean and ugly cows that came up after them are seven years, as are the seven empty ears blighted by the east wind. They are seven years of famine. It is as I told Pharaoh; God has shown to Pharaoh what he is about to do" (25-28). Joseph not only tells Pharaoh what God will do but also what Pharaoh should do to ease the nation through the years of famine: "Let Pharaoh select a man who is discerning and wise, and set him over the land of Egypt" (v 33). Store one-fifth of the harvest during the seven good years to be used as a reserve for the seven years of famine (vv 34-36). The proposal pleases Pharaoh, and he sets Joseph "over all the land of Egypt" (v 41). He places his signet ring on Joseph's hand, dresses him in fine linen, and puts "a gold chain around his neck" (v 42). Pharaoh also gives Joseph an Egyptian name and an Egyptian wife (v 45).

The outcome is that Joseph gathers and stores food in storehouses in the cities during the seven good years (vv 46-49). God also blesses him with two sons (vv 50-52). When the famine hits, "all the world came to Joseph in Egypt to buy grain, because the famine became severe throughout the world" (v 57).

We can sketch the plot line as a single plot, as shown on page 398.

Theocentric Interpretation

Although this chapter says nothing about God being with Joseph, "on this occasion," writes Wenham, "God is more evidently with Joseph than ever before, for he is miraculously summoned from prison, interprets Pharaoh's dreams, and is appointed second in the kingdom to Pharaoh himself."[6] In addition to God

6. Wenham, *Genesis 16–50*, 389.

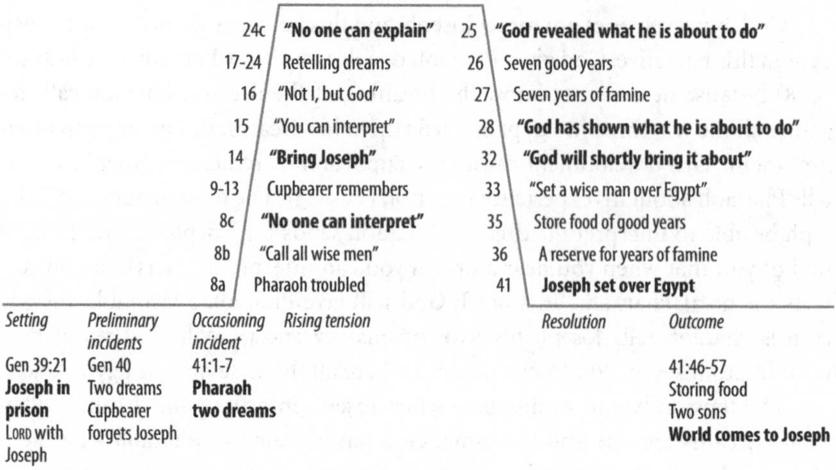

Joseph's Rise to Power in Egypt

	Rising tension		Resolution
24c	**"No one can explain"**	25	**"God revealed what he is about to do"**
17-24	Retelling dreams	26	Seven good years
16	"Not I, but God"	27	Seven years of famine
15	"You can interpret"	28	**"God has shown what he is about to do"**
14	**"Bring Joseph"**	32	**"God will shortly bring it about"**
9-13	Cupbearer remembers	33	"Set a wise man over Egypt"
8c	**"No one can interpret"**	35	Store food of good years
8b	"Call all wise men"	36	A reserve for years of famine
8a	Pharaoh troubled	41	**Joseph set over Egypt**

Setting	*Preliminary incidents*	*Occasioning incident*	*Rising tension*	*Resolution*	*Outcome*
Gen 39:21	Gen 40	41:1-7			41:46-57
Joseph in prison	Two dreams	**Pharaoh two dreams**			Storing food
LORD with Joseph	Cupbearer forgets Joseph				Two sons
					World comes to Joseph

working behind the scenes to raise Joseph from prison to ruler in Egypt, God's action is evident throughout this narrative. When the cupbearer forgets Joseph, God remembers him, for *God*[7] gives Pharaoh two dreams — dreams which no one can interpret. This, in turn, jogs the cupbearer's memory of Joseph. Joseph himself says that only God can interpret dreams: "It is not I; God will give Pharaoh a favorable answer" (v 16). In his interpretation, Joseph mentions God four times: "God has revealed to Pharaoh what he is about to do" (v 25); "God has shown to Pharaoh what he is about to do" (v 28); "the thing is fixed by God, and God will shortly bring it about" (v 32). Even Pharaoh acknowledges that "the spirit of God" is in Joseph (v 38) and declares, "Since God has shown you all this, there is no one so discerning and wise as you" (v 39). Thus when Pharaoh sets Joseph over all Egypt, it is not because of Joseph's wisdom or efforts but because Pharaoh senses the spirit of God in him. When God blesses Joseph with two sons, Joseph names the first Manasseh, "For God has made me forget all my hardship," and the second, Ephraim, "For God has made me fruitful in the land of my misfortunes" (vv 51-52).

Textual Theme and Goal

We noted above the narrator's important clue to the meaning of this narrative with Joseph's threefold declaration to Pharaoh, "God has revealed to Pharaoh what he is about to do" (v 25); "God has shown to Pharaoh what he is about to

7. "Here the double mention of God [in v 32] emphasizes the divine origin both of the dream and of its interpretation." Ibid., 399.

do" (v 28); "the thing is fixed by God, and God will shortly bring it about" (v 32). Allen Ross suggests that "the sovereignty of God is the underlying theme of this chapter, for the economy of Egypt — in fact, Egypt's whole future — was subject to the Lord God of Israel. The Bible affirms that God raises up kings and sets them down; and he controls the destinies of empires in accord with his plans for his people. In this instance, he controlled Egypt's life source, for God had determined that his wise servant would be the means to delivering Egypt."[8]

The sovereignty of God and his providence certainly are the foundation of this narrative. But these ideas are too general to capture the specific theme of this narrative. Through the dreams, the sovereign God reveals his plan to give Egypt seven bountiful years followed by seven years of famine so that the forgotten prisoner Joseph may be exalted as ruler in Egypt and save "the world" (v 57) from famine. Therefore, a more textually specific theme would be the following: *The sovereign God exalts the prisoner Joseph to ruler of Egypt in order to save the world from famine.*

As to the narrator's goal in recording this narrative for Israel, we should recall that Israel herself had been imprisoned in Egypt, being held captive for many years, and that centuries later they were imprisoned in Babylonia. How would Israel have heard this story of God liberating Joseph from prison and exalting him to rulership in Egypt? What did this narrative do for them when they were imprisoned in Babylonia? A likely goal of the narrator was, *To encourage the Israelites to entrust themselves to their sovereign God's good providence.*

Ways to Preach Christ

Given the theme "The sovereign God exalts the prisoner Joseph to ruler of Egypt in order to save the world from famine," there are several ways to move to Jesus Christ in the New Testament.

Redemptive-Historical Progression

God liberated Joseph from prison in Egypt and exalted him to ruler of Egypt in order to save the world from famine. Later God would liberate Israel from their imprisonment in Egypt and exalt them to be his holy nation in order to bless/save the world (12:3). In New Testament times, God liberated Jesus from his imprisonment in the tomb and exalted him through his resurrection and ascension to be the King of kings in order to save the world. "God so loved the world

8. Ross, *Creation and Blessing*, 637.

that he gave his only Son, so that everyone who believes in him may not perish but may have eternal life" (John 3:16).

Promise-Fulfillment

There is no messianic promise in this narrative. However, we do notice further fulfillment of God's promise to Abraham, "In you all the families of the earth shall be blessed" (12:3). Earlier, "the Lord blessed the Egyptian's [Potiphar's] house for Joseph's sake" (39:5). Here God blesses "the world" (41:57) with food through Joseph. In the fullness of time God will bless the world (John 3:16) by sending his Son Jesus. Jesus proclaims, "I am the bread of life. Whoever comes to me will never be hungry. . . . I am the living bread that came down from heaven. Whoever eats of this bread will live forever" (John 6:35, 51).

Typology

In earlier chapters we have noted that Joseph, in his humiliation and exaltation, is a type of Jesus Christ. Since this narrative focuses on Joseph's exaltation as ruler of Egypt, we should locate the typological parallel between Joseph and Jesus particularly in the area of exaltation. We can detect several related parallels between Joseph, as presented in this chapter, and Jesus, as presented in the New Testament. As the Spirit of God dwelt in Joseph (v 38), so the Spirit of God dwells in Jesus (Matt 3:16). As Joseph was God's prophet in bringing God's word to Pharaoh, so Jesus is God's prophet in bringing God's word to the people (Heb 1:1-2). But "something greater than . . . [Joseph] is here!" (Matt 12:41-42): Jesus is God's chief prophet, God's Word from eternity. As Joseph was exalted to the right hand of Pharaoh to rule as prime minister of Egypt, so Jesus was exalted to the right hand of God the Father to rule the nations as the "King of kings and Lord of lords" (1 Tim 6:15; Rev 17:14; 19:16). As all were commanded to bow before Joseph (v 43), so "at the name of Jesus every knee should bow in heaven and on earth and under the earth" (Phil 2:10). And as Joseph, with bread, saved many people from death, so Jesus, the bread of life, saves many people from eternal death — "Whoever eats of this bread will live forever" (John 6:51).

Analogy

As God with this story encouraged the Israelites to entrust themselves to their sovereign God's good providence, so Jesus encourages his people to entrust themselves to God's good providence. Jesus exhorts his followers, "Therefore do not worry, saying, 'What will we eat?' or 'What will we drink?' or 'What will we wear?' For it is the Gentiles who strive for all these things; and indeed your heavenly Father knows that you need all these things. But strive first for the kingdom of God and his righteousness, and all these things will be given to you as well" (Matt 6:31-33).

Longitudinal Themes

From Joseph to Jesus one can trace the biblical-theological theme of God exalting the oppressed and lowly: God exalted the despised slave prisoner Joseph to prime minister of Egypt; God exalted the escaped murderer Moses to be the leader of his people; God exalted the barren Hannah, making her the mother of the great prophet Samuel; God anointed the least likely of Jesse's sons, David, to be the great king of Israel; God "looked with favor on the lowliness of his servant" (Luke 1:48), Mary, and selected her to be the mother of his Son Jesus; God exalted Jesus from the grave to his right hand as "King of kings and Lord of lords" (1 Tim 6:15).

New Testament References

The appendix of the Nestle-Aland Greek New Testament lists six New Testament allusions to this narrative. Three references are to Stephen's speech, Acts 7:10-11. For Genesis 41:42 it lists the parable of the prodigal son, Luke 15:22, "But the father said to his slaves, 'Quickly, bring out a robe — the best one — and put it on him; put a ring on his finger and sandals on his feet." For 41:46 it lists Luke 3:23, "Jesus was about thirty years old when he began his work." And for 41:55 it lists the wedding at Cana, John 2:5, "His mother said to the servants, 'Do whatever he tells you.'" None of these references, however, will form a solid bridge in the sermon from Genesis 41 to Jesus in the New Testament.

Contrast

There is no contrast between the message of Genesis 41 and that of the New Testament.

Sermon Theme and Goal

We formulated the textual theme as, "The sovereign God exalts the prisoner Joseph to ruler of Egypt in order to save the world from famine." The sermon theme will have to cover the exaltation of Joseph as well as the exaltation of Jesus. We can accomplish this by broadening the textual theme as follows: *The sovereign God exalts his suffering servant to kingship in order to save the world.*

We formulated the author's goal for Israel as, "To encourage the Israelites to entrust themselves to their sovereign God's good providence." Our goal in preaching this sermon can be similar: *To encourage God's people today to entrust themselves to their sovereign God's good providence.* This goal reveals that the congregational need being addressed in this sermon is our failure to entrust ourselves fully to God's good providence.

Sermon Exposition

As a teenager, Joseph had had two dreams of someday being a ruler: all his brothers, and even his father and mother, would bow down to him. These dreams got him into deep trouble. His brothers wanted to kill the dreams by killing the dreamer. But instead of killing Joseph, they opted to sell him. Joseph ended up as a slave in Potiphar's house in Egypt. As a slave he was far removed from his dreams of rulership. He could hardly descend any lower. But then Potiphar's wife accused him falsely, and Joseph tumbled even lower than a slave. He ended up as a despised slave prisoner in Egypt.

One day the door to the prison opened and two new prisoners were brought in. They were important men, officers of Pharaoh himself, one his chief cupbearer (butler)[9] and the other his chief baker. Somehow they had offended Pharaoh, and in his anger Pharaoh ordered them locked up in prison.

One morning Joseph observes that they are "troubled" (40:6). He asks them what is bothering them and they reply, "We have had dreams, and there is no one to interpret them." Joseph responds, "Do not interpretations belong to God?[10] Please tell them to me" (40:8). And so the cupbearer tells his dream, and God enables Joseph to give the correct interpretation: "Within three days Pha-

9. The chief cupbearer "held an important office in the court of Pharaoh, and was actually a trusted advisor of the king. In a document from the time of Ramases III (12th century) we even find butlers sitting as judges." Sarna, *Understanding Genesis,* 218.

10. "In the entire Bible, only two Israelites engage in the interpretation of dreams — Joseph and Daniel — and significantly enough, each serves a pagan monarch, the one in Egypt, the other in Mesopotamia, precisely the lands in which oneiromancy flourished. Moreover, in each case, the Israelite is careful to disclaim any innate ability, attributing all to God." Sarna, ibid.

raoh will lift up your head and restore you to your office" (40:13). Joseph adds, "But remember me when it is well with you; please do me the kindness to make mention of me to Pharaoh, and so get me out of this place" (40:14).

Three days later Pharaoh does indeed restore the cupbearer to his office, but, we read in chapter 40:23, "the chief cupbearer did not remember Joseph, but forgot him." The slave Joseph languishes forgotten in an Egyptian prison — this is the depth of his humiliation. But God does not forget Joseph. After two more years of Joseph suffering in prison, at just the right time,[11] God causes the forgetful cupbearer to remember Joseph. God accomplishes this by giving Pharaoh two dreams.

In his dream Pharaoh is standing by the Nile. The river Nile is the lifeblood of Egypt. Once a year the Nile overflows its banks and inundates a narrow strip of the desert, leaving behind fertile silt. As Pharaoh stands by the Nile, he beholds "seven sleek and fat cows" coming up out of the river. The cows were probably standing in the river to counteract the heat and avoid the flies. Next Pharaoh sees another group of seven cows come out of the river, but these cows are "ugly and thin" — literally, "evil in appearance and thin of flesh."[12] These evil-looking cows eat the "seven sleek and fat cows." Pharaoh shocks awake.

But he manages to fall asleep again and has a second dream. He sees "seven ears of grain, plump and good, . . . growing on one stalk."[13] Next "seven ears, thin and blighted by the east wind,"[14] sprout, and they swallow up the seven plump and full ears. Pharaoh wakes again and realizes that it was a dream.

We read in verse 8, "In the morning his spirit was troubled." Pharaoh is troubled because he does not understand the meaning of these dreams. He probably guesses that they forecast something ominous, for they have to do with the Nile. Walter Brueggemann explains, "The Nile River is not only a geographical referent. It is also an expression of the imperial power of fertility. It is administration of the Nile which permits the king to generate and guarantee life. The failure of the Nile and its life system means that the empire does not have in itself the power of life (cf. Ezek 29:3)."[15]

Pharaoh may be troubled because he does not understand the meaning of the dreams, but in Egypt he can call on advisors to interpret the dreams for

11. "As it turns out, even the cupbearer's forgetfulness worked in Joseph's favor since, just at the opportune moment, he remembered Joseph and recounted his wisdom before the king." Sailhamer, *Introduction to Old Testament Theology,* 297.

12. Wenham, *Genesis 16–50,* 391.

13. "This is an exceptional phenomenon symbolizing abundance." Waltke, *Genesis,* 530.

14. "Resembling the Palestinian sirocco, the Egyptian *khamsin* blows in from the Sahara desert (see Hos 13:15) in late spring and early fall and often withers vegetation (see Isa 40:7; Ezek 17:10)." Waltke, ibid.

15. Brueggemann, *Genesis,* 327.

him. So he calls "for all the magicians of Egypt and all its wise men" (v 8).[16] Pharaoh tells them his dream,[17] but, amazingly, there is no one who can interpret them to Pharaoh's satisfaction. The king's court grinds to a halt. Pharaoh is troubled because he does not know the meaning of the dreams God has given him, and not one of all his wise men can help him understand God's message.

This predicament in the court finally jogs the cupbearer's memory of Joseph, who had interpreted his dream two years earlier. He tells Pharaoh his story of how Pharaoh had put him and the chief baker in prison, how they each dreamed a dream the same night, and how "a young Hebrew . . . , a servant of the captain of the guard"[18] correctly interpreted each dream for them. "Even in a modest, all-too-human event, the quiet rule of God can be perceived; the chief butler, who had completely forgotten Joseph, is reminded by the dreams of Pharaoh."[19]

We read in verse 14, "Then Pharaoh sent for Joseph, and he was hurriedly brought out of the dungeon. When he had shaved himself and changed his clothes,[20] he came in before Pharaoh." "The rush of finite verbs, 'summoned,' i.e., 'sent and called,' 'rushed,' etc., express the urgency that Pharaoh felt and the rapidity of Joseph's metamorphosis from slave to courtier. 'From the pit,' the term Joseph used to describe his prison [to the cupbearer] in 40:15, and also the place where his brothers dumped him (37:20, 22, 24, 28-29), again accentuates the sharp contrast between his humiliation and exaltation."[21]

When Joseph appears before him, Pharaoh lays out the challenge: verse 15, "I have had a dream, and *there is no one who can interpret it.* I have heard it said

16. "Every royal court in those days, and especially those in Egypt, had a complement of 'magicians' or 'wise men,' supposedly possessed with superior intelligence, who served as special advisors to the king. In Exodus 7:11, 22 and 8:7, 18, this word is used for those who performed miracles by magic and enchantments." Aalders, *Genesis,* II, 211.

17. Verse 8 reads literally, "Pharaoh told them his dream [singular], but no one could interpret them [plural]." "To Pharaoh it is one dream; to his interpreters, two. The difference helps explain why Pharaoh may be dissatisfied with the magicians' interpretations and satisfied with Joseph's." Waltke, *Genesis,* 530-31.

18. "Placed here, this comment accentuates the change in Joseph's position as dramatically as possible: one minute a forgotten imprisoned slave, the next on his way to the top of Egyptian society." Wenham, *Genesis 16–50,* 391-92.

19. Westermann, *Joseph,* 47.

20. "The clothing motif suggests that once again Joseph's status is about to change. When his brothers stripped him, it marked his descent from favoured son to slave (37:23). When Potiphar's wife disrobed him it sealed his transition from trusted slave to prisoner (39:12). He can surely descend no lower than he has now. Jacob's initial gift of the robe to Joseph elevated him among his brothers. His change of clothing in order to come before Pharaoh suggests that the clothing motif has now come full circle." Turner, *Genesis,* 175.

21. Wenham, *Genesis 16–50,* 392. Cf. Hamilton, *Genesis 18–50,* 492, n. 7, "The six imperfects with *waw* in this verse intensify the alacrity of the action."

of you that when you hear a dream you can interpret it." Can Joseph do what no one else can do? Joseph corrects the great Pharaoh, verse 16, "It is not I; *God* will give Pharaoh a favorable answer." "It is not I" is a single word in Hebrew. Joseph is quick to point out that Pharaoh is looking to the wrong person. Left to himself, Joseph can no more interpret dreams than can Pharaoh's wise men. But, he explains confidently, "God will give Pharaoh a favorable [*šālôm*] answer." Not I, but God! Gordon Wenham comments, "Joseph is as insistent as he was to the cupbearer (40:8) that not his own skill but God will interpret Pharaoh's dream. Though Joseph is thus being humble about himself, he is at the same time offering something better, divine interpretation of the dreams."[22] And because it is God who will give the answer to the troubled Pharaoh, it will give him *šālôm*, peace.[23]

Apparently Pharaoh is satisfied with Joseph's response, for he proceeds to tell him his dream. Verses 17 to 21, "In my dream I was standing on the banks of the Nile; and seven cows, fat and sleek, came up out of the Nile and fed in the reed grass. Then seven other cows came up after them, poor, very ugly, and thin. Never had I seen such ugly ones in all the land of Egypt. The thin and ugly cows ate up the first seven fat cows, but when they had eaten them no one would have known that they had done so, for they were still as ugly as before. Then I awoke." In retelling his dream Pharaoh stresses especially the negative aspect of the cows being ugly, that is, evil. They are "poor, *very ugly*, and thin." "Never had I seen such *ugly* ones in all the land of Egypt" (v 19). And when these evil cows had eaten the fat cows "no one would have known that they had done so, for they were still as *ugly* as before" (v 21). "Pharaoh is not just exaggerating; at some level he knows that his dream intimates something really terrible."[24]

Pharaoh continues telling Joseph his dream. Verses 22-24, "I fell asleep a second time and I saw in my dream[25] seven ears of grain, full and good, growing on one stalk, and seven ears, withered, thin, and blighted by the east wind, sprouting after them; and the thin ears swallowed up the seven good ears. But when I told it to the magicians, there was no one who could explain it to me." Pharaoh stresses once more the failure of his magicians to interpret the dream to his satisfaction: "there was no one who could explain it to me." Can Joseph

22. Ibid.

23. "Joseph has not yet heard the dream! *Šālôm* thus relates to Pharaoh's troubled spirit, that Pharaoh would be satisfied with Joseph's interpretation because it comes from God." Fretheim, "Genesis," 621.

24. Brodie, *Genesis as Dialogue*, 375. Cf. Sailhamer, *Pentateuch as Narrative*, 214: "In both cases [Pharaoh's additions of verses 19b and 21], the repetition seems to stress the 'evil' *(rāʿ)* appearance of the cows in contrast with the good of the first group."

25. "The Hebrew literally says 'in my dream.' Pharaoh himself knows the dream is one." Waltke, *Genesis*, 532.

do what all the magicians and wise men in Egypt cannot do? Will God reveal to him the meaning of these dreams?

Joseph says to Pharaoh, verse 25, "Pharaoh's dreams are one and the same." That's an important clue. Perhaps the magicians had tried to interpret the two dreams separately.[26] But the dreams really have a single meaning — just as Joseph's two dreams about his brothers bowing down to him had a single meaning. Joseph continues, "God has revealed to Pharaoh what he is about to do." In giving him this dream, God has disclosed what he is going to do in the near future. And now, through his servant Joseph, God will make it clear to Pharaoh: Verses 26-28, "The seven good cows are seven years, and the seven good ears are seven years; the dreams are one. The seven lean and ugly cows that came up after them are seven years, as are the seven empty ears blighted by the east wind. They are seven years of famine. It is as I told Pharaoh; God has shown to Pharaoh what he is about to do." Seven years of bountiful harvests followed by seven years of poor harvests — that's the meaning of the dream. Seven years of plenty and seven years of famine — that's what God is about to do.

But notice how Joseph stresses the years of famine. "Joseph devotes but one sentence to the years of plenty (v 29), but five sentences to the years of famine (vv 30-31)."[27] Notice verse 29, "There will come seven years of great plenty throughout all the land of Egypt." One sentence. Now notice five sentences on the years of famine, starting at verse 30, "After them there will arise seven years of famine, and all the plenty will be forgotten in the land of Egypt; the famine will consume the land. The plenty will no longer be known in the land because of the famine that will follow, for it will be very grievous." "Joseph makes his case and loudly sounds the alarm by this bounty of dramatic sentences."[28]

Seven years of famine was almost[29] unheard of in Egypt, where the Nile normally flooded the fields every year with moisture and fertile silt. But Pharaoh can count on this unusual disaster happening, as Joseph warns, verse 32, "The doubling of Pharaoh's dream means that the thing is fixed by God, and God will shortly bring it about." This plan is set by the sovereign God. God's providence calls for seven years of plenty and seven years of famine. "It is fixed by God."

But instead of resigning quietly to a sure thing, Joseph calls for action.[30] Hav-

26. See n. 17 above.

27. Hamilton, *Genesis 18–50*, 497.

28. Ibid.

29. "A late Egyptian text dealing with the reign of King Djoser (ca. twenty-eighth century B.C.E.) well illustrates the setting. It reads: 'I was in distress on the Great Throne, and those who are in the palace were in heart's affliction from a very great evil, since the Nile had not come in my time for a space of seven years. Grain was scant, fruits were dried up, and everything which they eat was short.'" Sarna, *Understanding Genesis*, 219.

30. "The emphasis in verse 32 on its certainty and imminence are calls to action, not resig-

ing explained what God will do, Joseph goes on to propose what Pharaoh can do to ease the dreadful effects of the coming famine. Verses 33-36, "Now therefore let Pharaoh select a man who is discerning and wise, and set him over the land of Egypt. Let Pharaoh proceed to appoint overseers over the land, and take one-fifth of the produce of the land of Egypt during the seven plenteous years. Let them gather all the food of these good years that are coming, and lay up grain under the authority of Pharaoh for food in the cities, and let them keep it. That food shall be a reserve for the land against the seven years of famine that are to befall the land of Egypt, so that the land may not perish through the famine."

We read in verse 37 that "the proposal pleased Pharaoh and all his servants." The news about the coming famine is not good, but Joseph's proposal sounds good to Pharaoh and his court. The troubled Pharaoh is at peace.

But Joseph is in for a surprise. Joseph would have been happy just to be set free from prison. But Pharaoh does much more than that. Pharaoh says to Joseph, verse 39, "*Since God has shown you all this,* there is no one so discerning and wise as you. You shall be over my house, and all my people shall order themselves as you command; only with regard to the throne will I be greater than you."[31] Joseph cannot believe his ears. Does Pharaoh wish to make him the prime minister of Egypt? And not because he is so smart but because God is with him and has given him wisdom? Will he become second in command only to the great Pharaoh?

Pharaoh repeats, verse 41, "See, I have set you over all the land of Egypt. Removing his signet ring from his hand, Pharaoh put it on Joseph's hand." "This gives Joseph the authority to validate documents in the king's name."[32] Next Pharaoh dresses him in robes of fine linen,[33] and puts a gold chain around his neck. Placing a gold chain around Joseph's neck "is a well-known Egyptian symbol of investiture, one of the highest distinctions the king could bestow."[34] Then, verse 43, Pharaoh "had him ride in the chariot of his second-in-

---

nation — exactly as in the preaching of the prophets." Kidner, *Genesis,* 195. Cf. von Rad, *Genesis,* 376, "What is theologically noteworthy is the way in which the strong predestinarian content of the speech is combined with a strong summons to action. The fact that God has determined the matter, that God hastens to bring it to pass, is precisely the reason for responsible leaders to take measures!"

31. This statement means "that he was to report directly to the king." Sarna, *Understanding Genesis,* 220.

32. Waltke, *Genesis,* 534.

33. "The story has returned to its starting point when Joseph was dressed by his father in lordly garb with long sleeves (37:3)." Turner, *Genesis,* 177. See n. 20 on p. 404 above.

34. Sarna, *Understanding Genesis,* 220. Cf. ibid., 219-20: "It is clear at once that Scripture exhibits an extraordinary degree of familiarity with Egyptian customs. The multiplicity of titles and functions assigned to Joseph corresponds fully to the known Egyptian penchant for the generous distribution of honors and titles to officials of the great bureaucracy." See p. 221 on the likelihood of a foreigner rising to such high office in Egypt.

command; and they cried out in front of him, 'Bow the knee!' Thus he set him over all the land of Egypt."

According to verse 45 Pharaoh also gives Joseph a new, Egyptian name, Zaphenath-paneah — probably meaning "God speaks and lives";[35] and gives him a wife of nobility, Asenath, daughter of an Egyptian priest. Joseph is transformed from an imprisoned Hebrew slave to an Egyptian nobleman; even more, he becomes prime minister of Egypt.

After this miraculous promotion from prisoner to prime minister, Joseph gathers up 20 percent of each harvest during the years of plenty and stores it in granaries in the cities. Verse 49 reports that "Joseph stored up grain in such abundance — like the sand of the sea — that he stopped measuring it; it was beyond measure." "In Egyptian fashion, at first careful records were kept of the amount of grain put into storage, but as the volume increased, keeping careful records became impossible and finally was abandoned."[36]

In addition to making the harvests fruitful, God also makes Joseph's marriage fruitful, giving him two sons. According to verse 51, Joseph names the firstborn Manasseh,[37] that is, "making to forget," for, he says, "God has made me forget all my hardship and all my father's house" — that is, the hardship associated with my father's house.[38] The second son he names Ephraim, "sounds like the Hebrew for 'twice fruitful,'"[39] for, he says, "God has made me fruitful in the land of my misfortunes."

But then the seven evil years of famine come. At first it does not seem to touch Egypt. Verse 54 states that "there was famine in every country, but throughout the land of Egypt there was bread." But soon the famine also spreads to Egypt, and Joseph gives orders to open all the storehouses and sell the grain to the hungry Egyptians. The narrative ends with verse 57, "Moreover, all the world[40] came to Joseph in Egypt to buy grain, because the famine became severe throughout the world."

John Walton observes, "On the surface, Joseph is being 'made' by Pharaoh. Everything he is given comes from Pharaoh's hand: his office, status, privilege,

35. For other suggestions, see Hamilton, *Genesis 18–50*, 507-8.

36. Aalders, *Genesis*, II, 217.

37. "Significantly, he gives his sons Hebrew, not Egyptian, names. He has not forgotten his father's household." Waltke, *Genesis*, 535.

38. "'Forget' does not mean here 'not remember' but rather to have something no longer (cf. Job 39:17; 11:16)." Von Rad, *Genesis*, 379. Cf. Hamilton, *Genesis 18–50*, 512, "With Sarna, I suggest that we understand both phrases as a hendiadys, 'my suffering in my father's home,' thus making it even clearer that the reference is to mistreatment to which Joseph had been subjected by members of his own family back in Canaan."

39. TNIV text n.

40. "The known world from the writer's perspective (the Middle East)." *NIV Study Bible*, Genesis 41:57, n.

name, wife — everything. He is 'reborn' as a servant of Pharaoh. The irony is that from the standpoint of Genesis, it is not the hand of Pharaoh that has remade Joseph but the hand of God. For all that Pharaoh did, God brought Joseph to the recognition of Pharaoh, and God gave Joseph wisdom and success. In the end, Joseph is not first and foremost Pharaoh's man, but God's man. He is not Pharaoh's instrument of economic survival; he is God's instrument of salvation."[41] According to the narrator, Joseph is God's instrument for saving "the world" (v 57).

In his providence, the sovereign God exalted the prisoner Joseph to ruler of Egypt in order to save the world from famine. God had promised Abraham, "In you all the families of the earth shall be blessed" (12:3). We see a fulfillment of this promise here when, through Joseph, God blesses "the world" with food. This promise to Abraham finds even greater fulfillment in Abraham's son, Jesus Christ. The apostle John writes, "God so loved the *world,* that he gave his only Son, so that everyone who believes in him may not perish but may have *eternal life*" (John 3:16). Jesus himself proclaims, "I am the bread of life. Whoever comes to me will never be hungry. . . . I am the living bread that came down from heaven. Whoever eats of this bread will live forever" (John 6:35, 51). The sovereign God exalts his suffering servant to kingship — Joseph then and Jesus now — in order to save the world.

Joseph reminds us of Jesus. Joseph, the servant of almighty God, prefigures Jesus, the Son of God. As the Spirit of God dwelt in Joseph (v 38), so the Spirit of God dwells in Jesus (Matt 3:16). As Joseph was God's prophet in bringing God's word to Pharaoh, so Jesus is God's prophet in bringing God's word to the people (Heb 1:1-2). But Jesus is much greater than Joseph (cf. Matt 12:41-42): Jesus is God's chief prophet, God's Word from eternity. As Joseph was exalted to the right hand of Pharaoh to rule as king of Egypt, so Jesus was exalted to the right hand of God the Father to rule the nations as the "King of kings and Lord of lords" (1 Tim 6:15; Rev 17:14; 19:16). As all were commanded to bow before Joseph (v 43), so "at the name of Jesus every knee should bow in heaven and on earth and under the earth" (Phil 2:10). And as Joseph, with bread, saved many people from death, so Jesus, the bread of life, saves many people from eternal death. Jesus proclaims, "Whoever eats of this bread will live forever" (John 6:51).

With this Joseph narrative, God encouraged the Israelites to entrust themselves to their sovereign God's good providence. Jesus did the same. Jesus encourages us, "Therefore do not worry, saying, 'What will we eat?' or 'What will we drink?' or 'What will we wear?' For it is the Gentiles who strive for all these things; and *indeed your heavenly Father knows that you need all these things.* But strive first for the kingdom of God and his righteousness, and *all these things will be given to you as well*" (Matt 6:31-33).

41. Walton, *Genesis,* 691.

CHAPTER 22

Joseph's Testing of His Brothers

Genesis 43:1–45:28

This lengthy narrative is the climax of the Joseph story. Because of its length as well as its pivotal position, the narrative challenges preachers on various fronts. First, commentators do not agree on the boundaries of this narrative. Second, the choice of three full chapters for a preaching-text makes it practically impossible to read the whole story in a worship service before preaching the sermon. And third, it is difficult to arrive at a textually specific theme for the narrative. Should one look for the theme in Joseph's prolonged testing of his brothers? Or in his emotional revelation of himself to his brothers at the climax? Or in his repeated witness, "God sent me before you to preserve life" (45:5, 7, 8)? Or all of the above?

Text and Context

The beginning of this narrative is easy to spot. After the brothers' first journey to Egypt (42:1-38), a second journey is required because "the famine was severe in the land" (43:1). The question is, Where does this narrative end? Some would end it at 43:34; others at 44:34; still others at 45:15. Building on the work of Coats and Westermann, Wenham makes a convincing case that, "despite the chapter divisions, 43:1–45:28 constitutes a single unit within the Joseph story."[1] The main argument for this position is that "the structure and contents of these chapters echo chapter 42."[2]

42:1-4	Jacob's sons sent to Egypt	43:1-14
42:5	Arrival in Egypt	43:15-25

1. Wenham, *Genesis 16–50*, 419.
2. Ibid.

42:6-10	First audience with Joseph	43:26-34
42:17	Brothers in custody	44:1-13
42:18-24	Second audience with Joseph	44:14–45:15
42:25-28	Departure from Egypt	45:16-24
42:29-38	Sons report to Jacob	45:25-28

Since chapter 42 is accepted as a narrative unit, and since chapters 43 to 45 exhibit the same structure and contents, it would follow that the narrator intended 43:1 to 45:28 also as a narrative unit. Chapter 46:1 begins a new narrative with Jacob's journey to Egypt.

In using this lengthy unit, preachers will need to be creative in fitting the Scripture reading(s) and sermon into the expected time-frame. I suggest reading only the beginning of the narrative (Gen 43:1-14) before the sermon and incorporating other key sections in the sermon itself. This approach will not only save time and avoid repetition in reading and preaching but also allow for a fresh hearing in the sermon of the buildup of narrative tension and its release.

Since this narrative is the climax of the Joseph story, many strands from the prior context come to a head here. Joseph's dreams that his brothers would bow down to him (37:5-10) come to fulfillment as all eleven bow "to the ground before him" (43:26, 28; 44:14). The brothers who sold Joseph "for twenty pieces of silver" (37:28) not only show their changed attitude when they return Joseph's money (43:21), but especially when they refuse to leave Benjamin behind when offered their own freedom (44:10, 13, 17, 33). The brothers who hated Joseph so much that they "could not speak peaceably to him" (37:4) now "talk with him" (45:15). And Jacob, who said, "I shall go down to Sheol to my son, mourning" (37:35), now cries out, "My son Joseph is still alive. I must go and see him before I die" (45:28).

This narrative also echoes earlier themes in Genesis. In a key statement, Joseph declares to his brothers, "God sent me before you to preserve for you a remnant on earth, and to keep alive for you many survivors (45:7). Gerhard von Rad comments, "The terms 'remnant' *(šĕʾērît)* and 'survivor' *(plêṭâ)* in verse 7 allude to that motif of rescue which is so thematically important for the entire narrative composition of Genesis. The story of the Flood contains it: Noah is rescued from the universal catastrophe by divine providence and made the father of a new humanity. One must also think of Abraham's departure from his family confederation, his calling and blessing, as they contrast with the gloomy background of God's judgment on the nations (chapter 11:1-9). . . . In the remnant the whole group survives to new life."[3] More specifically, the fact that God,

3. Von Rad, *Genesis*, 398-99.

through Joseph, saves the full number, 70 (46:27), of Jacob's extended family is an initial fulfillment of God's covenant promises to Abraham to make of him "a great nation" and, ultimately, through him to bless "all the families of the earth" (Gen 12:2-3).

Literary Features

As is usual in Hebrew narrative, the narrator employs minimal character description. He describes Joseph as loving his brother Benjamin (43:30) and being emotional: twice weeping secretly (42:24; 43:30), then openly before his brothers (45:2, 14-15). He pictures the brothers first as "afraid" of being enslaved (43:18), but, when Benjamin's freedom is at stake, they all, and foremost Judah, show the courage to offer themselves as Joseph's slaves (44:16, 33). The narrator describes Benjamin as "his [Joseph's] mother's son," while Joseph calls him "my son" (43:29), and Judah three times calls him "the boy" (44:33-34).

The narrator portrays the characters primarily by way of dialogue. On their first journey, Joseph put on the facade of a cold, stern Egyptian ruler, accusing the brothers of being spies, imprisoning them for three days (42:17) and Simeon (42:24) for at least a year. On their second journey, Joseph first frees Simeon and puts on a feast for them (43:16-34), but then reverts back to the role of the merciless ruler, threatening to enslave Benjamin (44:17). All along, Joseph can barely control his emotions. There can be little doubt that Joseph still loves his brothers, especially his full-brother Benjamin, as well as his father.

Of Joseph's brothers, "Judah emerges as the new leader. While he accedes to the patriarch's direction, he speaks forcefully, sensibly, and soberly"[4] to Jacob. Later he will address Joseph with the longest speech in Genesis (44:18-34), showing himself to be forthright, persuasive, and passionate. He demonstrates concern for Benjamin and especially his father when he courageously offers himself as a slave in the place of Benjamin.

The narrator again employs pace retardation to highlight important points and/or to raise the suspense. "While the long journey to Egypt is referred to in a single statement (43:15), the actual meeting with Joseph is preceded by an entire scene, which of course increases the suspense. In no fewer than ten verses the narrator describes for us the events and conversations of that morning which preceded Joseph's meal with his brothers (43:16-25)."[5] We notice pace retardation again when Joseph sees his brother Benjamin for the first time: "He looked up and saw his brother Benjamin, his mother's son, and said, 'Is this your youn-

4. Waltke, *Genesis,* 552.
5. Von Rad, *Genesis,* 388.

gest brother, of whom you spoke to me? God be gracious to you, my son!' With that, Joseph hurried out, because he was overcome with affection for his brother, and he was about to weep. So he went into a private room and wept there. Then he washed his face and came out; and controlling himself he said, 'Serve the meal'" (43:29-31). Robert Alter observes, "The specification of minute actions — wanting to weep, going into another room, weeping, washing his face, composing himself — is far beyond the Bible's laconic norm, thus focusing the event and producing an effect of dramatic retardation in the narrative tempo."[6]

The narrator also uses repetition to underscore important points. Three more times (in addition to 42:6) the brothers bow before Joseph (43:26, 28; 44:14) in fulfillment of Joseph's dreams. Three more times (in addition to 42:24) Joseph weeps (43:30-31; 45:2, 14-15) in "a beautifully regulated crescendo pattern in the story."[7] Three times Joseph makes the point: "God sent me before you to preserve life. . . . God sent me before you to preserve for you a remnant on earth, and to keep alive for you many survivors. So it was not you who sent me here, but God" (45:5, 7, 8). And in his lengthy speech persuading Joseph to set Benjamin free, Judah uses the word "father" fourteen times (2×7; 44:18-34).

The narrative is made up of seven scenes which are arranged in a chiastic pattern:[8]

Scene 1: Jacob sends sons to Egypt (43:1-14)	A
Scene 2: Arrival in Egypt: Steward and brothers (43:15-25)	B
Scene 3: Lunch with Joseph (43:26-34)	C
Scene 4: Brothers arrested (44:1-13)	D
Scene 5: Joseph discloses himself to brothers (44:14–45:15)	C′
Scene 6: Departure from Egypt: Pharaoh and brothers (45:16-24)	B′
Scene 7: Sons report to Jacob on mission (45:25-28)	A′

The Plot Line

The setting for this narrative reaches all the way back to God's promise to Abraham to make of him a great nation and a blessing to all the families of the earth (12:2-3). The intermediate setting is the beginning of the Joseph story: Joseph's brothers' hatred (they "could not speak peaceably with him" [37:4]); Joseph's dreams of his brothers bowing down to him (37:6-10); and their intent to kill

6. Alter, *Art of Biblical Narrative*, 168.
7. Ibid.
8. See Wenham, *Genesis 16–50*, 418-19.

him but settling for selling him as a slave (37:19, 27). The immediate setting is the famine which threatens to wipe out Abraham's offspring in Canaan (42:2).

The preliminary incidents consist of the brothers' first journey to Egypt and being recognized by Joseph: "But he treated them like strangers and spoke harshly to them" (42:7). He accused them of spying, and when they denied it, Joseph devised a test: "Here is how you shall be tested: as Pharaoh lives, you shall not leave this place unless your youngest brother comes here" (42:15). Joseph put them all in prison for three days and then proposed that one of them remain imprisoned until they would come back with Benjamin. The brothers "agreed to do so." Not knowing that Joseph could understand them, "they said to one another, 'Alas, we are paying the penalty for what we did to our brother. . . .' Then Reuben [the oldest son] answered them, 'Did I not tell you not to wrong the boy? But you would not listen. So now comes a reckoning for his blood. . . .' He [Joseph] turned away from them and wept. . . . And he picked out Simeon [the second oldest] and had him bound before their eyes" (42:20-24).

The other brothers return to Jacob with sacks of grain but discover to their horror that their money is in the sacks. Jacob, especially, is distraught at this trickery and gasps, "Joseph is no more, and Simeon is no more, and now you would take Benjamin. . . . My son shall not go down with you, for his brother is dead, and he alone is left. If harm should come to him on the journey that you are to make, you would bring down my gray hairs with sorrow to Sheol" (42:36, 38). No second journey to Egypt with Benjamin!

The occasioning incident is stated in chapter 43:1, "Now the famine was severe in the land." Jacob, his children, and grandchildren are about to starve to death. Although Jacob does not want Benjamin to go to Egypt, Judah convinces him: "Send the boy with me, and let us be on our way, so that we may live and not die — you and we and also our little ones. I myself will be a surety for him" (43:8-9). Jacob then instructs his sons to bring a present for the man and double the money to repay the money found in their sacks. Then, reluctantly, he allows Benjamin to go along, accompanied by the prayer, "May God Almighty grant you mercy before the man" (43:11-14).

"So the men took the present, and they took double the money with them, as well as Benjamin. Then they went on their way down to Egypt, and stood before Joseph" (43:15). What will happen to them? Will the brothers protect Benjamin at all cost? Will Jacob ever see Benjamin again?

When Joseph sees Benjamin with them (43:16), he instructs his steward to prepare a feast for his brothers. But they are suspicious of this special treatment and afraid of a setup. They seek out Joseph's steward and explain to him that they found the money in their sacks and have brought it back with them (43:21). The steward reassures them that there is no problem: he received their money. Then he brings out Simeon. Things are looking up for the brothers. When Joseph comes home, all eleven brothers bow down to the ground before him. But when Joseph sees his beloved brother Benjamin, he is "overcome with affection for his brother, and . . . about to weep" (43:30). After hurrying out and weeping in private, he returns and amazes the brothers by seating them in order of age. Then he sets them up by giving Benjamin a portion of food "five times as much as any of theirs." The brothers pass this test with flying colors: "They drank and were merry with him" (43:34).

The next test is more challenging. Joseph instructs his steward to put Joseph's silver cup in the sack of Benjamin. When the brothers leave for home, the steward chases after them. When he catches up to them, he accuses them, as instructed, of stealing Joseph's silver cup. The brothers vehemently deny this accusation and are so sure of their innocence that they declare: "Should it be found with any one of your servants, let him die; moreover the rest of us will become my lord's slaves" (44:9). The steward seems to reduce their self-prescribed punishment but actually sharpens the test: "He with whom it is found shall become my slave, but the rest of you shall go free" (44:10). The tension mounts as he searches beginning with the oldest, and finally, when he gets to the youngest, he finds the cup in Benjamin's sack (44:12). "At this they tore their clothes. Then each one loaded his donkey, and they returned to the city" (44:13). The brothers are still unified and not willing to give up Benjamin for their own freedom.

When they get to Joseph's house, Judah offers that they will all be Joseph's slaves (44:16). But, like the steward before him, Joseph cunningly narrows the punishment (and test) down to a single brother: "Only the one in whose possession the cup was found shall be my slave; but as for you, go up in peace to your father" (44:18). All the brothers can be free, if only they allow Benjamin to be enslaved. It is a virtual replay of Dothan where Judah proposed and the brothers agreed to sell Joseph as a slave. Will the brothers agree now, when the stakes are not twenty pieces of silver but their very freedom? At the height of the tension, Judah mounts an impassioned plea for the freedom of Benjamin. And he offers to be Joseph's slave in place of Benjamin.

At this offer, Joseph breaks down. He has heard enough of the brothers' changed attitude. He weeps before his brothers and reveals himself as Joseph. But they are "dismayed" at his presence (45:3). Joseph repeats, "I am your brother, Joseph, whom you sold into Egypt. And now do not be distressed, or angry with yourselves, because you sold me here; for God sent me before you to preserve life" (45:5). Since there will be five more years of famine, Joseph invites them to come to Egypt with all their possessions. When Pharaoh hears that Joseph's brothers have come, he backs up Joseph's invitation with his own generous invitation: "the best of all the land of Egypt is yours" (45:20).

The outcome of the narrative relates the brothers returning to Canaan laden with goods and the invitation to come to Egypt. Jacob is stunned at the news that Joseph is alive and is determined to travel to Egypt to see him before he dies.

We can sketch the plot line of this narrative as a single plot:

	Rising tension		Resolution
44:33b	**"Let Benjamin go back"**	45:2	**Joseph weeps loudly**
44:33a	**"I will be your slave"**	45:3a	**"I am Joseph"**
44:18-34	Judah's long speech	45:3b	Brothers dismayed
44:17b	**"You all go in peace"**	45:4	"I am your brother"
44:17a	**"No, only Benjamin"**	45:5a	"Do not be distressed"
44:16	**"We are all your slaves"**	45:5b	**"God sent me before you"**
44:14	Fall down before Joseph	45:7	**"God sent me before you"**
44:13	All tear their clothes	45:8	**"Not you sent me, but God"**
44:12b	**Cup found in Benjamin's sack**	45:9	"God made me lord of Egypt"
44:12a	Search beginning with eldest	45:10	"Settle in Goshen"
44:2	**Cup placed in Benjamin's sack**	45:14	Joseph weeps on Benjamin
43:34	**Benjamin five times as much**	45:15a	Joseph weeps on brothers
43:30	Joseph weeps	45:15b	His brothers talk with him
43:26, 28	**Brothers bow before Joseph**		
43:23	Simeon set free	45:16	Pharaoh pleased
43:16	In Joseph's house	45:18	"I give you the best land"
43:13	"Take Benjamin also"		
43:9	Judah is surety	45:22	Benjamin five garments
43:3-5	"Not without Benjamin"	45:24	"Do not quarrel on way"
43:2	"Go again, buy food"		

Setting	*Preliminary incidents*	*Occasioning incident*	*Rising tension*	*Resolution*	*Outcome*
Gen 12:2-3 Promise to Abraham 37:6-10 **Joseph's dreams** 42:2 "Buy grain in Egypt"	42:9-38 "You are spies" **Test: "Bring youngest brother"** Simeon in prison Money in sacks	43:1 Famine severe			45:25-28 Arrival at home **"Joseph is alive"** "I must go see him"

Theocentric Interpretation

Although this narrative seems to center on the human characters, especially Jacob, Benjamin, Judah, Joseph, and his steward, God is very much at work behind the scenes. Jacob sends off his sons on their dangerous mission with the prayer, "May God Almighty grant you mercy before the man" (43:14). Even Joseph's steward calms the concerned brothers, "Rest assured, do not be afraid; your God and the God of your father must have put the treasure in your sacks for you" (43:23). Joseph greets Benjamin with words of the priestly blessing, "God be gracious to you, my son" (43:23). Judah acknowledges before Joseph, "How can we clear ourselves? God has found out the guilt of your servants" (44:16).

The clearest witness to God's centrality occurs towards the end of the narrative when Joseph testifies: "God sent me before you to preserve life. . . . God sent me before you to preserve for you a remnant on earth, and to keep alive for you many survivors. So it was not you who sent me here, but God; he has made me a father to Pharaoh, and lord of all his house and ruler over all the land of Egypt. Hurry and go up to my father and say to him, 'Thus says your son Joseph, God has made me lord of all Egypt; come down to me, do not delay'" (45:5-9).

Textual Theme and Goal

With several major ideas in this lengthy narrative, it is somewhat difficult to pinpoint the narrator's overall theme. He spends much narrative time recounting how Joseph tests his brothers, and notes several times that they bow down to him, in fulfillment of Joseph's dreams. He reaches the height of emotional impact at the climax when Joseph at last reveals himself to his brothers with weeping and kissing and talking. And he makes a major point of God working behind the scenes when he has Joseph repeat three times, "God sent me before you to preserve life" ("a remnant on earth"; "many survivors").

If we consider only the plot line, we might be inclined to formulate the theme as, "Joseph tests his brothers before inviting them to settle in Egypt." This summary, however, is a description of the narrative rather than its message. The *message* of this narrative is found in Joseph's repeated testimony, "God sent me before you to preserve life" (45:5, 7, 8). One might object that the theme of God's providence is not textually specific since it is the focus of the entire Joseph story. Although it is true that God's providence underlies every narrative in the Joseph cycle, focusing on this theme particularly in this narrative is still textually specific. The narrative itself provides several reasons for this focus. First, Joseph's threefold testimony of God sending him before his family to preserve life is given in this particular narrative and in no other[9] (50:20 has a similar statement). Second, Joseph's words carry much weight in this narrative because they are spoken at the climax by the main character himself. And third, the words of Joseph's steward, "Your God and the God of your father must have put treasure in your sacks for you" (43:23) anticipate the climax of the narrative where Joseph reveals himself to his brothers and three times speaks of God's providence. We can, therefore, formulate the textual theme as follows: *In his providence God used Joseph's brothers' evil deed to send him to Egypt ahead of his family in order to preserve a remnant for Israel.*

9. "It is plain how the narrator dwells on it and underlines it, as if he wants to say to his hearers that here they can find what this story is all about." Westermann, *Joseph,* 96.

As to the author's goal in communicating this message to Israel, Joseph clearly speaks these words to comfort his brothers, who are distressed and angry with themselves for their evil deed (45:5; cf. 42:21). Later, Israel would also have many reasons to be distressed and angry with themselves because of their evil deeds — especially when God punished them by sending them into exile in Babylonia.[10] The message of this narrative of the sovereign God being able to use even evil deeds for good ends must have been a comfort to them. We can, therefore, formulate the author's goal as follows: *To comfort Israel with the message that the sovereign God is able to use even evil human deeds to fulfill his plan of preserving a remnant for Israel.*

Ways to Preach Christ

Given the theme, "In his providence God used Joseph's brothers' evil deed to send him to Egypt ahead of his family in order to preserve a remnant for Israel," what are legitimate ways to move in the sermon to Jesus Christ in the New Testament?

Redemptive-Historical Progression

God promised to make of Abraham "a great nation" (12:2). When there was a severe famine in the Promised Land, Abraham and his family moved to Egypt to survive (12:10). In Jacob's time there was a seven-year famine that would have annihilated the family. But God used the evil deed of Joseph's brothers to send him ahead of his family to Egypt, where he became a ruler, stored grain, and was able to preserve Israel from the famine. During their extended stay in Egypt, Israel would become a great multitude and later be oppressed. But God used Moses to lead them out, and Israel became a great nation. Later, when God sent Israel into exile, he promised to restore a remnant: "I myself will gather the remnant of my flock out of all the lands where I have driven them, and I will bring them back to their fold, and they shall be fruitful and multiply. I will raise up shepherds over them who will shepherd them" (Jer 23:3-4). Out of that remnant the Messiah would be born. Jesus describes himself as "the good shepherd [who] lays down his life for the sheep" (John 10:11).

10. "The otherwise slightly puzzling reference to Joseph's family being 'preserved as a remnant' (45:7) may perhaps make best sense if seen as a rewording of the story in the exilic period when this was precisely how the Jews in exile felt and when the story of Joseph was seen as offering some model for interpreting their situation." Moberly, "Genesis 12–50," 121.

Promise-Fulfillment

Although there is no messianic promise in this narrative, Joseph claims, "God sent me before you . . . to keep alive for you many survivors" (45:7). This testimony (see also 45:5) witnesses to an initial fulfillment of God's promise to Abraham to make of him "a great nation" (12:2) — a nation which would give birth, in the fullness of time, to Jesus Messiah.

Typology

Two figures in this narrative could possibly serve as a type of Christ: Joseph or Judah. Bruce Waltke writes, "Judah . . . is the first person in Scripture who willingly offers his own life for another. His self-sacrificing love for his brother for the sake of his father prefigures the vicarious atonement of Christ, who by his voluntary sufferings heals the breach between God and human beings."[11] But this is a rather incidental, weak analogy, for Judah did not "offer his life" but his freedom. As a matter of fact, he gave neither his freedom nor his life for Benjamin.

Joseph makes for a much stronger type of Jesus. Concentrating only on parallels in this particular narrative, we observe the following: As God sent Joseph to Egypt to save his family, so God sent Jesus to earth to save his people. As the brothers bowed before Joseph, so "at the name of Jesus every knee should bow" (Phil 2:10). And as Joseph invited his family to settle in Egypt, so Jesus invites his people to settle in his Father's kingdom (John 14:2-3). But "something greater than . . . [Joseph] is here" (Matt 12:41-42): Jesus saves not just from famine but from sin, and that for all eternity.

Analogy

As God teaches Israel that he is able to use evil human deeds to accomplish salvation, so Jesus teaches the church that God is able to use evil human deeds to accomplish salvation. At the Last Supper, Jesus said, "The Son of Man goes as it has been determined [by God], but woe to that one by whom he is betrayed" (Luke 22:22). On the day of Pentecost, Peter proclaimed, "Therefore let the entire house of Israel know with certainty that *God* has made him both Lord and Messiah, this Jesus whom *you* crucified" (Acts 2:36).

11. Waltke, *Genesis*, 567.

Longitudinal Themes

One can trace through Scripture from Joseph to Jesus the biblical-theological theme of God using evil deeds to accomplish his redemptive purposes. This theme runs from Joseph's brothers' hatred, to the hatred of a later Pharaoh whose daughter adopted the baby Moses, to the hatred of the Jewish leaders for Jesus, to the hatred of Saul for the early Christians, to the hatred of the Romans for the church. God used all these, and more, evil deeds to grow his church and further his redemptive plan. As Paul puts it, "We know that all things work together for good for those who love God, who are called according to his purpose" (Rom 8:28).

New Testament References

Aside from Stephen's speech in Acts 7:9-14, the appendix to the Greek New Testament lists only two New Testament allusions to this story. For 45:14, Joseph weeping, it lists Acts 20:37, "There was much weeping among them all; they embraced Paul and kissed him." And for 45:26, Jacob "could not believe them," it lists Luke 24:11, "But these words seemed to them an idle tale, and they did not believe them." None of these references support the theme of the narrative and therefore are not helpful in building a bridge to Christ in the New Testament.

Contrast

There is no contrast between this message of the Old Testament and that of the New Testament.

Sermon Theme and Goal

We formulated the textual theme as, "In his providence God used Joseph's brothers' evil deed to send him to Egypt ahead of his family in order to preserve a remnant for Israel." The sermon theme should build on this theme but extend it to God's work in Jesus as revealed in the New Testament. A succinct sermon theme would be, *In his providence God can use evil human deeds to accomplish salvation.*

We formulated the author's goal as, "To comfort Israel with the message that the sovereign God is able to use even evil human deeds to fulfill his plan of preserving a remnant for Israel." The sermon goal can be similar: *To comfort the hearers with the message that the sovereign God is able to use even evil human deeds to accomplish salvation.* This goal addresses the congregational need of people being so overwhelmed by current human evil that they have given up on God accomplishing his redemptive plan.

Sermon Exposition[12]

The narrative begins with the terrible disaster Jacob and his family face in the Promised Land: "Now the famine was severe in the land" (43:1). And "they had eaten up the grain that they had brought from Egypt" (verse 2). There is no more food. Jacob and his family are about to starve to death. That will mean the end of God's promise to Abraham that his descendants will be "exceedingly numerous" (17:2).

But Jacob knows that there is grain in Egypt. Jacob's sons had already made one trip to Egypt to buy grain. It had been a scary experience. Unknown to them, the ruler in charge of grain distribution was their brother Joseph. Twenty-two years earlier they had sold this conceited little brother into slavery. Imagine, this tattletale was the favorite son of Jacob, always getting the best. He liked to show off the beautiful coat his father had made for him. And he had dreams of grandeur — dreams of his brothers bowing down to him. When the brothers were shepherding their flocks in Dothan, they saw Joseph coming from a distance. And they conspired to kill the dreamer (37:18). But they settled for selling him as a slave to a caravan headed for Egypt. Either way, good riddance!

But under God's guidance, Joseph had been promoted quickly. The former slave and prisoner was now prime minister of Egypt. He was in charge of all grain distribution. When the brothers came to Egypt they did not recognize Joseph, but he recognized them. "He treated them like strangers and spoke harshly to them" (42:7). He accused them of spying, which they vehemently denied. Then Joseph devised a test. He said, "Here is how you shall be tested: as Pharaoh lives, you shall not leave this place *unless your youngest brother comes here!*" (42:15). Joseph wanted his full-brother Benjamin in Egypt in order to test his half-brothers. He wanted to see whether their attitude to Rachel's sons had changed over the years. So he put his half-brothers in prison for three days to show that he meant what he said. Then he set them free but had one of them, Simeon, "bound before their eyes" (42:24). Simeon would remain a prisoner in Egypt until they returned with Benjamin.

12. Considering both the length of this narrative and the time-constraints in the worship service, this exposition assumes reading only the first scene, 43:1-14, before the sermon, and reading other key sections in the sermon itself.

Joseph "gave orders to fill their bags with grain, [and] to return every man's money to his sack" (42:25). The nine remaining brothers hurried home with their bags of grain. But when they opened their bags, they discovered to their horror that all their money was in their bags. They could be accused of stealing. Jacob, especially, was distraught by this trickery and gasped, "Joseph is no more, and Simeon is no more, and now you would take Benjamin. . . . My son shall *not* go down with you, for his brother is dead, and he alone is left. If harm should come to him on the journey that you are to make, you would bring down my gray hairs with sorrow to Sheol" (42:36, 38). No second journey to Egypt with Benjamin!

But now they have finished this grain and the famine is still severe in the land. Jacob and his whole family face certain death. Jacob says to his sons, "Go again, buy us a little more food" (43:2). But he does not want Benjamin to go along on the dangerous journey. Finally Judah[13] puts his foot down. He says, 43:3, "The man solemnly warned us, saying, 'You shall not see my face unless your brother is with you.' If you will send our brother with us, we will go down and buy you food; but if you will not send him, we will *not* go down, for the man said to us, 'You shall not see my face, unless your brother is with you.'" Jacob still hesitates. He loves Benjamin as much as he had loved Joseph. He does not want to lose both sons of his favorite wife Rachel. But if his sons do not go to Egypt for more grain, they will all die! Judah speaks again, verse 8, "Send the boy[14] with me, and let us be on our way, so that we may live and not die — you and we and also our little ones." Three generations will die! Judah continues, "I myself will be a surety for him," that is, Judah will guarantee Benjamin's return.

Hardly convinced but in desperate straits, Jacob commands[15] his sons to bring a present[16] for the man to appease him, and double the money so that they will not be arrested for theft. And then, reluctantly, he allows Benjamin to

13. "Judah is the oldest son in good standing with his father (cf. 34:30; 35:22). Jacob had earlier definitively refused Reuben's weak guarantee of Benjamin's safety (42:37), and Simeon is in Egyptian custody (42:24). From this point on Judah becomes the leader of his brothers (cf. 44:14-34; 46:28)." Waltke, *Genesis,* 553.

14. Judah refers to Benjamin as a *na'ar,* a boy or a lad. However, "Benjamin is no child. Joseph is at least thirty-seven, and Benjamin can only be a few years younger than he at most. . . . This term must surely play on Jacob's emotions. Benjamin is still young, hence vulnerable (see, e.g., Isa 13:18; 40:30)." Hamilton, *Genesis 18–50,* 541-42.

15. "Jacob is clearly in charge of making arrangements for the journey to Egypt. His words to his sons are filled with imperatives, a total of seven in this unit [43:11-13]." Ibid., 545.

16. Jacob says, "Take some of the choice fruits of the land in your bags, and carry them down as a present to the man — a little balm and a little honey, gum, resin, pistachio nuts, and almonds" (43:11). "The list of the items in the present is similar to that in 37:25 with some extras. . . . It is possible that the narrator sees a parallel between this expedition to Egypt and the Ishmaelite caravan that brought Joseph there." Wenham, *Genesis 16–50,* 421.

go along. He prays, verse 14, "May God Almighty grant you mercy before the man, so that he may send back your other brother[17] and Benjamin." "*God Almighty ('ēl šadday)* was a title specially evocative of the covenant with Abraham (17:1) and therefore of God's settled purpose for this family."[18] God Almighty will remember his covenant promise to make Abraham "exceedingly numerous" (17:2). Somehow, God Almighty will save Jacob's family from the famine that threatens their lives. Somehow, God Almighty will change the ruthless Egyptian ruler and allow all the brothers to return home.

Verse 15, "So the men took the present, and they took double the money with them, as well as Benjamin. Then they went on their way down to Egypt, and stood before Joseph." In only a single verse the narrator covers the long journey to Egypt. What is important for him is not the journey but what happens to the brothers in Egypt. Will Joseph imprison them again or be merciful to them? And what will happen to Benjamin? Will his father ever see him again?

Apparently Joseph sees his brothers from a distance, for the brothers do not bow down before Joseph until later (43:26). Joseph seeing his brothers from a distance replays what happened twenty-two years earlier in Dothan. But now the roles are reversed. In Dothan the brothers saw Joseph "from a distance, and before he came near to them, they conspired to kill him" (37:18). Here Joseph sees his brothers from a distance and hatches a plan. We read in verses 16-18.

> When Joseph saw Benjamin with them, he said to the steward of his house, "Bring the men into the house, and slaughter an animal and make ready, for the men are to dine with me at noon." The man did as Joseph said, and brought the men to Joseph's house. Now the men were afraid because they were brought to Joseph's house, and they said, "It is because of the money, replaced in our sacks the first time, that we have been brought in, so that he may have an opportunity to fall upon us, to make slaves of us and take our donkeys."

The brothers think it is a ruse. They think this powerful Egyptian wants to attack them and make slaves of them, the way they had attacked Joseph at Dothan, taken his royal coat, and made him a slave.

How will the brothers overcome this threatening conspiracy? We read in verses 19-23,

> So they went up to the steward of Joseph's house and spoke with him at the entrance to the house. They said, "Oh, my lord, we came down the first time

17. "'Your other brother' in context refers to Simeon, but the narrator may have a greater answer to the prayer in view, for the other brother could be Joseph (cf. Eph 3:20)." Ibid.

18. Kidner, *Genesis*, 203-4.

> to buy food; and when we came to the lodging place we opened our sacks, and there was each one's money in the top of his sack, our money in full weight. So we have brought it back with us. Moreover we have brought down with us additional money to buy food. We do not know who put our money in our sacks." He replied, "Rest assured, do not be afraid; your *God* and the God of your father must have put treasure in your sacks for you; I received your money." Then he brought Simeon out to them.

The steward probably passes along "the answer Joseph instructed him to give":[19] "Your God and the God of your father must have put treasure in your sacks for you." As readers we know that Joseph had ordered the money put in their sacks (42:25), but the steward's words reveal that the God of Israel was working behind the scenes. God often works through human agents. In returning their money, God was working through Joseph. God working behind the scenes will become an important idea in this narrative.

Verse 26, "When Joseph came home, they brought him the present that they had carried into the house, and bowed to the ground before him." All eleven brothers bow down to him, just as Joseph had dreamt long ago about their sheaves bowing down to his sheaf and eleven stars bowing down to him (37:9). Verse 27, "He inquired about their welfare, and said, 'Is your father well, the old man of whom you spoke? Is he still alive?' They said, '*Your servant* our father is well; he is still alive.' And they bowed their heads and did obeisance." They call Jacob Joseph's "servant" and again bow before Joseph. The narrator seems to suggest that each of Joseph's two dreams is here being fulfilled — even his father is his "servant" (cf. 37:10).

Verse 29, "Then he [Joseph] looked up and saw his *brother* Benjamin, his *mother's son*." Benjamin is here called Joseph's "brother" and "his mother's son." This is Joseph's only full-brother, the second son of his mother Rachel. Joseph asks, "Is this your youngest brother, of whom you spoke to me?" And without waiting for an answer, he blesses Benjamin, "God be gracious to you,[20] my son!"

Then Joseph almost loses his composure. Verse 30, "With that, Joseph hurried out, because he was overcome with affection for his brother, and he was about to weep. So he went into a private room and wept there. Then he washed his face and came out; and controlling himself he said, 'Serve the meal.'" Joseph almost gave himself away. He almost lost the facade of severe Egyptian ruler. Happily the brothers never noticed. What they did notice, however, was astonishing. Verse 33, "When they were seated before him, the firstborn according to

19. Hamilton, *Genesis 18–50*, 550.

20. "He uses the same word which we know from the blessing in Numbers 6:25: 'the LORD make his face to shine upon you, and be gracious to you.'" Westermann, *Joseph*, 79.

his birthright and the youngest according to his youth, the men looked at one another in *amazement*." How in the world could Joseph seat them from the oldest to the youngest? How did he know their ages? How much does he know about them?

Another strange thing: when they are served, Benjamin's portion is "five times as much as any of theirs" (v 34). That is extremely unusual. If anyone would get a larger portion in that culture, it would be the oldest brother, not the youngest. What is going on? Joseph is recreating his own predicament with his ten older brothers. How jealous they had been of the favoritism Joseph received from his father. He is now testing his half-brothers to see if they are still jealous of a son of Rachel who gets special treatment. And he rubs it in by seating them from the oldest to the youngest while giving the youngest five times as much as the oldest.[21] But the brothers pass this test with flying colors. The chapter concludes "They drank and were merry with him [Joseph]."

The next test will be much more challenging.[22] In chapter 44:1-2, Joseph commands his steward, "Fill the men's sacks with food, as much as they can carry, and put each man's money in the top of his sack. Put my cup, the silver cup, in the top of the sack of the youngest, with his money for the grain." The steward does exactly as Joseph tells him: he hides Joseph's silver cup in the sack of Benjamin.

Early the next morning, the brothers are sent on their way back to Canaan. They are barely out of the city when Joseph tells his steward to chase them down. He orders, verse 4, "Go, follow after the men; and when you overtake them, say to them, 'Why have you returned evil for good? Why have you stolen my silver cup? Is it not from this that my lord drinks? Does he not indeed use it for divination? You have done wrong in doing this."

The steward soon overtakes the brothers and accuses them of stealing Joseph's silver cup. The brothers vehemently deny these accusations. They say, verses 7-9:

> "Why does my lord speak such words as these? Far be it from your servants that they should do such a thing! Look, the money that we found at the top of our sacks, we brought back to you from the land of Canaan; why then would we steal silver or gold from your lord's house? Should it be found with

21. "To exacerbate the brothers' jealousy, Joseph now shows him [Benjamin] special favor during the banquet — 'Benjamin's portion was five times as much as any of theirs' — rubbing it in through the contrast with the order of natural seniority in which he has taken care to seat them." Sternberg, *Poetics of Biblical Narrative,* 303.

22. "Joseph carefully contrives a desperate situation in which the brothers are compelled to show, once and for all, whether they have reformed since the day they so brutally sold him into slavery." Sarna, *Understanding Genesis,* 223.

any one of your servants, *let him die;* moreover *the rest of us will become my lord's slaves.*"

"Their wild offer, that if any of them is a thief, he should die and the rest of them be enslaved, shows their confidence in their innocence."[23] But the steward seems to reduce the penalty. He says, verse 10, "Even so; in accordance with your words, let it be: he with whom it is found shall become my slave, but the rest of you shall go free." Actually while the steward seems to reduce the penalty, he sharpens the test. Only the thief shall become a slave, and the rest will go free. We, the readers, know that the cup will be found in Benjamin's sack. Rachel's other son will become a slave.

The brothers are eager to prove their innocence. Verse 11, "Then each one quickly lowered his sack to the ground, and each opened his sack." The tension mounts as the steward begins searching with the eldest. No silver cup there; no silver cup in the next one; no cup in the next one. Ten brothers are innocent. The brothers are ready to give a sigh of relief when Benjamin's sack is opened — and the cup is found. At this, we read in verse 13, "They tore their clothes. Then each one loaded his donkey, and they returned to the city." "They say nothing, but their actions speak louder than words. When Joseph disappeared, it was only Jacob who tore his clothes (37:34); now all the brothers do, the first clear sign of fraternal solidarity."[24] The brothers are still unified and not willing to give up Benjamin for their own freedom.

When they arrive at Joseph's house, Judah, strangely, states that they will *all* be Joseph's slaves. He says, verse 16, "What can we say to my lord? What can we speak? How can we clear ourselves? *God has found out the guilt of your servants;* here we are then, my lord's slaves, both we and also the one in whose possession the cup has been found." "God has found out the guilt of your servants." Judah is not talking about stealing the silver cup. The brothers know that they did not steal the cup. Judah is talking about the guilt that has been gnawing at them ever since they sold Joseph into slavery. "This is God's way, says Judah, of visiting their past misdeeds upon them. They withheld mercy from Joseph (42:21). Now God will withhold mercy from them. They deserve what is happening to them even if they are not guilty of this particular crime."[25]

Judah declares that they will all be Joseph's slaves. But, like the steward before

23. Wenham, *Genesis 16–50*, 424.

24. Ibid., 425. Hamilton, *Genesis 18–50*, 564, observes, "They no more suspect they are victims of fraud [deception] than did their father suspect foul play when he was given the bloodied coat."

25. Hamilton, *Genesis 18–50*, 566. Hamilton continues, "Here is a graphic illustration of the Bible's emphasis on God's justice. The wrongs one does will be repaid, someway, somehow, somewhere."

him, Joseph cunningly narrows the punishment down to a single brother. He says, verse 17, "Far be it from me that I should do so! Only the one in whose possession the cup was found shall be my slave; but as for you, go up in peace to your father." All the brothers will go free; only Benjamin will be enslaved. It is a virtual replay of Dothan, where Judah proposed and the brothers agreed to sell Joseph as a slave. Will the brothers again agree to offer a son of Rachel when the stakes are not twenty pieces of silver but their very freedom? All ten of them can return to their father; all ten can be reunited with they families; only Benjamin will need to stay behind. Is their father not better off with ten free sons? Are their wives and children not better off with their husbands and fathers safely at home? Isn't it better to sacrifice Benjamin so that they can go free? What will the brothers do?

At the height of the tension, Judah mounts an impassioned plea for Benjamin's freedom. His concern is not for himself; not even so much for Benjamin; his concern is for father Jacob. In this speech he uses the word "father" fourteen times. This is the longest speech in the book of Genesis. It runs from verse 18 to 34:

> "O my lord, let your servant please speak a word in my lord's ears, and do not be angry with your servant; for you are like Pharaoh himself. My lord asked his servants, saying, 'Have you a father or a brother?' And we said to my lord, 'We have a father, an old man, and a young brother, the child of his old age. His brother is dead; he alone is left of his mother's children, and *his father loves him*.' Then you said to your servants, 'Bring him down to me, so that I may set my eyes on him.' We said to my lord, 'The boy cannot leave his father, for *if he should leave his father, his father would die*.' Then you said to your servants, 'Unless your youngest brother comes down with you, you shall see my face no more.' When we went back to your servant my father we told him the words of my lord. And when our father said, 'Go again, buy us a little food,' we said, 'We cannot go down. Only if our youngest brother goes with us, will we go down; for we cannot see the man's face unless our youngest brother is with us.' Then your servant my father said to us, 'You know that my wife bore me two sons [his favorite wife Rachel means so much to Jacob that he does not seem to count the other ten as his sons];[26] one left me, and I said, Surely he has been torn to pieces;[27] and I have never

26. Judah "can even bring himself to quote sympathetically (verse 27) Jacob's typically extravagant statement that his wife bore him two sons — as though Leah were not also his wife and the other ten were not also his sons." Alter, *Art of Biblical Narrative*, 175. Cf. Sternberg, *Poetics of Biblical Narrative*, 308, "That the sons of the hated wife should have come to terms with the father's attachment to Rachel ('my wife') and her children is enough to promise an end to hostilities and a fresh start."

27. "Joseph now hears for the first time what happened at home when the brothers came

seen him since. If you take this one also from me, and harm comes to him, *you will bring down my gray hairs in sorrow to Sheol* [the abode of the dead].' Now therefore, when I come to your servant my father and the boy is not with us, then, as his life is bound up in the boy's life,[28] *when he sees that the boy is not with us, he will die; and your servants will bring down the gray hairs of your servant our father with sorrow to Sheol.* For your servant became surety for the boy to my father, saying, 'If I do not bring him back to you, then I will bear the blame in the sight of my father all my life.' Now therefore, *please let your servant remain as a slave to my lord in place of the boy;* and let the boy go back with his brothers. For how can I go back to my father if the boy is not with me? I fear to see the *suffering* that would come upon my father."

Four times Judah mentions that his old father will die if he loses Benjamin: verse 22, "his father would die"; verse 29, "you will bring down my gray hairs in sorrow to Sheol"; and twice in verse 31, "he will die; and your servants will bring down the gray hairs of your servant our father with sorrow to Sheol." And he offers to become Joseph's slave in the place of Benjamin. "Judah so feels for his father that he begs to sacrifice himself for a brother more loved than himself."[29] "Twenty-two years earlier, Judah engineered the selling of Joseph into slavery; now he is prepared to offer himself as a slave so that the other son of Rachel can be set free."[30]

Joseph has heard enough to know that the brothers have changed dramatically from the day they sold him. They have passed the test. They are even willing to offer their freedom for Rachel's son Benjamin. Joseph can no longer control himself. Twice before he had wept in private. Now he can weep openly before his brothers. He no longer needs the mask of a merciless Egyptian ruler. He orders everyone but his brothers to leave the room, then breaks down sobbing, 45:3, "I am Joseph. Is my father still alive?" "Is my father well?" "Is everything OK?"[31]

---

back without him. He hears of his father's lament and grief which still persists; he hears the father's cry 'torn to pieces, torn to pieces!' which still echoes in the brothers' ears." Westermann, *Genesis 37–50,* 136.

28. "That Judah should adduce the father's favoritism as the ground for self-sacrifice is such an irresistible proof of filial devotion that it breaks down Joseph's last defenses and leads to a perfectly Aristotelian turning point." Sternberg, *Poetics of Biblical Narrative,* 308.

29. Ibid.

30. Alter, *Art of Biblical Narrative,* 175.

31. "It is likely that the Hebrew word *ḥay* (NIV 'living') asks not so much whether he is above ground or below ground, heart beating or not. It is the equivalent of our question, 'Is my father well?' or 'Is everything OK?' He wants to know on a personal level how his father is doing." Walton, *Genesis,* 682.

But, "His brothers could not answer him, so dismayed were they at his presence." They are "'dumbfounded,' a term used of a paralyzing fear sometimes felt by those involved in war."[32] Joseph repeats, verse 4, "I am your brother, Joseph, whom you sold into Egypt." Seeing their distress and anguish, he adds, "And now do not be distressed, or angry with yourselves, because you sold me here; for God sent me before you to preserve life."

Verse 5 sounds like a contradiction, "*You* sold me here; . . . *God* sent me before you to preserve life." Joseph seeks to comfort his brothers with the mystery of God's providence. The sovereign God can use even evil human deeds to accomplish his plan of salvation.[33] The brothers sold him to Egypt; they are fully responsible for this wicked deed. But God used this wicked deed for a good purpose: "God sent me before you to preserve life." The brothers can take comfort from the fact that God used their evil deed ultimately to preserve life.

We find the same teaching in the New Testament. At the Last Supper, Jesus declares, "The Son of Man is going as it has been determined, but woe to that one by whom he is betrayed" (Luke 22:22). Judas is fully responsible for his wicked deed, but God used it to accomplish his plan of salvation. Judas betrays Jesus by leading a detachment of soldiers and police to arrest Jesus in the Garden of Gethsemane. Yet Jesus accepts this betrayal as part of "the cup that *the Father has given me*" (John 18:11) — God's providence.[34]

Joseph continues by telling his brothers that "there are five more years" of famine coming (v 6). And then he makes the point of God's providence more personal for them. Verse 7, "God sent me before you to preserve *for you* a remnant[35] on earth, and to keep alive *for you* many survivors." Five more years of famine in Canaan would wipe out Jacob's family; five more years of famine would undermine God's covenant promise to Abraham of "exceedingly numerous" descendants (17:2). But God sent Joseph to Egypt ahead of his family to keep alive many survivors for Israel.

Joseph reiterates for the third time, verse 8, "So it was not you who sent me here, but God." This is a stronger statement than in verse 5. There it was, "*You* sold me here; . . . *God* sent me." Here it is, "It was *not you* who sent me, but

32. Wenham, *Genesis 16–50*, 427, with references to Exod 15:15; Judg 20:41; 1 Sam 28:21; and Ps 48:6(5).

33. "Here is the inscrutable balance between the sovereign will and the human will — they had sold him in hatred, but God sent him to Egypt to save them." Ross, *Creation and Blessing*, 670.

34. Cf. Acts 2:23, "This man, handed over to you according to the definite plan and foreknowledge of *God, you* crucified and killed by the hands of those outside the law."

35. "The translation 'remnant' is indeed appropriate, since the tribe in narrowly escaping destruction is like a remnant which is the bearer of hopes for the future existence.'" Gerhard Hasel, *The Remnant*, 154, n. 69.

God."[36] Here Joseph focuses totally on the sovereign control of God. God sent him to keep alive the seed of Abraham.

And so Joseph immediately invites Jacob and his family to settle in Egypt. He tells his brothers, verse 9, "Hurry and go up to my father and say to him, 'Thus says your son Joseph, God has made me lord of all Egypt; come down to me, do not delay. You shall settle in the land of Goshen, and you shall be near me, you and your children and your children's children, as well as your flocks, your herds, and all that you have. I will provide for you there — since there are five more years of famine to come — so that you and your household, and all that you have, will not come to poverty."

When Pharaoh hears that Joseph's brothers have come, he and his servants are pleased. He backs up Joseph's invitation with his own generous invitation and practical advice. He offers, verse 18, "Take your father and your households and come to me, so that I may give you the best of the land of Egypt, and you may enjoy the fat of the land. . . . Do this: take wagons from the land of Egypt for your little ones and for your wives, and bring your father, and come. Give no thought to your possessions, for the best of all the land of Egypt is yours."[37]

Joseph follows up by giving them wagons, provisions for the journey, garments, and special gifts for Benjamin and his father. Verse 24, "Then he sent his brothers on their way, and as they were leaving he said to them, 'Do not quarrel along the way." "Joseph's parting shot was realistic, for the ancient crime was now bound to come to light before their father, and mutual accusations were likely to proliferate (cf. 42:22)."[38]

The final scene finds the brothers back in Canaan with their father Jacob. They tell him, verse 26, "Joseph is still alive! He is even ruler over all the land of Egypt." At this news, Jacob "was stunned"; his heart seemed to stop;[39] "he could

36. "This is a remarkable passage, in which we are taught that the right course of events is never so disturbed by the depravity and wickedness of men, but that God can direct them to a good end." Calvin, *Genesis*, II, 377.

37. "Historically this is a turning-point . . . , long foretold (15:13-16): the beginning of a phase of isolation (where the family, thoroughly alien, could multiply without losing its identity), and of eventual bondage and deliverance which would produce a people that for ever after knew itself redeemed as well as called." Kidner, *Genesis*, 208.

38. Ibid. Other commentators argue that the Hebrew word *rgz* normally means to get "'worked up' or 'agitated' [see NRSV text note] in a variety of different ways, such as anger, excitement, fear, anxiety, joy, or sadness. R. Alter is probably right here that Joseph anticipates that his brothers may be fearful that he will have second thoughts and send an army after them — perhaps accusing them of plundering and thievery and slaughter them all." Walton, *Genesis*, 683, with a reference to Alter, *Genesis*, 271.

39. "'His heart went cold, for he did not believe them.' One may even say that his heart stopped: 'The Hebrew verb plainly means to stop, or more precisely, to intermit' (Alter, 271)." Brodie, *Genesis as Dialogue*, 395.

not believe them." After twenty-two years of mourning for Joseph, could he still be alive? Impossible!

Verse 27, "But when they told him all the words of Joseph that he had said to them, and when he saw the wagons that Joseph had sent to carry him, the spirit of their father Jacob revived. Israel[40] said, 'Enough! My son Joseph is still alive. I must go and see him before I die.'" Jacob is determined to travel to Egypt to see Joseph before he dies. This also means that the family will be saved from the famine.

In his providence, God used Joseph's brothers' evil deed to send him ahead of his family to Egypt in order to preserve Israel from the famine. God's promises to Abraham to make of him "a great nation" (12:2) and to make his descendants "exceedingly numerous" have not come to naught; they are still in the process of being fulfilled.

We have earlier observed that Joseph prefigures the Lord Jesus. Note the parallels in this narrative between Joseph and Jesus. As God sent Joseph to Egypt to save his family, so God sent Jesus to earth to save his people. John 3:16 makes this point: "God so loved the world that *he gave his only Son,* so that everyone who believes in him may not perish but may have eternal life." Jesus saves from more than famine. Jesus saves people from their sin so that they may receive *eternal* life.

Another parallel between Joseph and Jesus: As the brothers bowed before Joseph, so people will bow down before Jesus. Philippians 2:9-11 makes this point:

> Therefore God also highly exalted him
>   and gave him the name that is above every name,
> so that *at the name of Jesus every knee should bend,*
>   in heaven and on earth and under the earth,
> and every tongue should confess that Jesus Christ is Lord,
>   to the glory of God the Father.

A final parallel: As Joseph invited his family to settle in Egypt, so Jesus invites his people to settle in his Father's kingdom. Jesus said, "In my Father's house there are many dwelling places. . . . If I go to prepare a place for you, I will come again and take you to myself, so that where I am, there you may be also" (John 14:2-3). In this kingdom, the fear of famine will be a thing of the past. All things will be new. In the book of Revelation, John receives a vision of a great multi-

40. "It is fitting that Jacob be styled as *Israel* in the last verse. . . . Israel is Jacob's new name, a name that speaks of a new destiny and a new future. Here is Israel with a new hope and a new expectation. Joseph is alive. Israel will meet him shortly. Here is Israel in verse 28 making the decision as the head of the family to go to Egypt to see Joseph." Hamilton, *Genesis 18–50*, 587.

tude standing before God's throne and before the Lamb. One of the elders explains to him who these people are:

> "These are they who have come out of the great ordeal; they have washed their robes and made them white in the blood of the Lamb.
> For this reason they are before the throne of God,
> and worship him day and night within his temple,
> and the one who is seated on the throne will shelter them.
> They will *hunger no more*, and thirst no more;
> the sun will not strike them,
> nor any scorching heat;
> for the Lamb at the center of the throne will be their shepherd,
> and he will guide them to springs of the water of life,
> and God will wipe away every tear from their eyes."
>
> (Rev 7:14b-17)

Today we are often distressed at the evil we see all around us: stealing, drug deals, the slave trade, murders, terrorist attacks. Instead of coming closer to the peaceable kingdom of God, we seem to be slipping ever further into the kingdom of darkness. In this situation we might give up hope on the coming kingdom of God. But Joseph's story teaches us to take heart. Our God is a sovereign God. All things are under his control. He can use even evil human deeds to advance his kingdom. As the hymn writer[41] puts it,

> This is my Father's world:
> O let us not forget
> that though the wrong is great and strong,
> God is the ruler yet.

Keep praying as Jesus taught us to do:

> Your kingdom come,
> Your will be done,
> on earth as it is in heaven.
>
> (Matt 6:10)

Since our God is the sovereign God, his kingdom will surely come!

41. Mary Babcock Crawford, 1972.

CHAPTER 23

Jacob's Move to Egypt

Genesis 46:1–47:31

Preachers face several challenges in preaching this narrative. One challenge is to determine the parameters of the narrative since commentators are not at all in agreement. Moreover, the narrative includes a rather lengthy genealogical listing (46:8-27). Should the public Scripture reading include all these names? And how does one handle this section in the sermon? Moreover, since Joseph's actions in Egypt (47:13-26) are easily misunderstood as exploitation of the destitute, should one read this section without comment before the sermon?

Text and Context

As noted, the narrative unit is again a bone of contention among commentators. There is general agreement that the narrative begins at 46:1, "When Israel set out on his journey. . . ." There is also general agreement that another narrative begins at 48:1 with the narrator's signal, "After this. . . ." The question is, therefore, Where does the narrative end that begins with Jacob's move to Egypt (46:1)? Some commentators end it at 47:12 with Joseph providing food for Jacob and his family in Goshen. Others end it at 47:27 with Israel settled in the land and multiplying exceedingly. Still others end the narrative at 47:31 with Joseph swearing to Jacob that he will carry his body out of Egypt and bury him in Canaan.[1]

Although a larger narrative unit may be more difficult to preach, we are opting for the larger unit for various reasons. First, Jacob's request that he be buried not in Egypt but in Canaan (47:28-31) is a fitting conclusion to a narra-

1. For the various representatives and his arguments for the larger unit, see Wenham, *Genesis 16–50*, 437-39.

tive that focuses on Jacob moving his whole family to Egypt. Second, Jacob's request to be buried in the Promised Land "balances 46:1-4. In that unit, Jacob did not want to jeopardize the promise by leaving the land. He does not leave without the sanction given in the theophany. Now (47:27-31), he wants to embody his ultimate commitment to the land of promise even in his death."[2] Third, since the previous two journeys to Egypt concluded with Jacob speaking of his death (42:38; 45:28), it is reasonable to assume that the narrator would follow the same pattern for this third journey (see below). And fourth, if it be objected that Genesis 47:28-31 is the beginning of the next narrative about Jacob's illness and death, it should be noted, as we have seen before,[3] that a final scene can have a dual function: here it functions as the conclusion of this narrative and the setting for the next.[4]

As far as the Scripture reading is concerned, since this narrative contains a long list of foreign names and the narrative itself is plenty long, one might consider just skipping over the list of names in the Scripture reading (46:8-27a) and summarizing the list in the sermon (see Sermon Exposition below). One might also consider skipping over the section on Joseph's actions in Egypt (47:13-26), and including it in the sermon where it can be properly explained. The Scripture reading then would be Genesis 46:1-7; 46:27b-47:12; and 47:27-31.

The immediate context of this narrative is Joseph's statement to his brothers, "God sent me before you to preserve for you a remnant on earth, and to keep alive for you many survivors" (45:7), and his invitation to Jacob and his family to come to Egypt and settle in Goshen (45:10). God's providence, the famine, and Joseph's invitation all form the immediate context.

Further, this is the last of three journeys to Egypt. Gordon Wenham points out some major parallels among these three journeys: "All the journeys are prompted by Jacob's decision (42:1-2; 43:1-14; 46:1); they all climax with Joseph meeting his family (42:6-24; 43:26–45:15; 46:28–47:12); and they all conclude with Jacob mentioning his death (42:38; 45:28; 47:29-31)." But there are also new features in this third account: "First, the vision encouraging Jacob to go (46:2-4); second, the list of Jacob's descendants who moved to Egypt with him (46:8-27); and third, the devastating effects of the famine in Egypt (47:13-26)."[5]

God's instruction to "go" and his promises to Jacob recall God's instructions and promises to him at Bethel (28:13-15) and at Haran (31:11-13). They also echo God's promises to Isaac at Beer-sheba and his building an altar there (26:23-25). And finally they recall God's instruction to Abraham to "go," fol-

2. Brueggemann, *Genesis,* 355.

3. See p. 297 above at n. 5, and p. 379 at n. 8.

4. Cf. Wenham, *Genesis 16–50,* 439 and 449.

5. Ibid., 437.

lowed by God's rich promises (12:1-3). In fact, when the LORD later spoke to Abram in the night, he predicted the events that begin with Jacob's journey to Egypt: "The LORD said to Abram, 'Know this for certain, that your offspring shall be aliens in a land that is not theirs, and shall be slaves there, and they shall be oppressed for four hundred years; but I will bring judgment on the nation that they serve, and afterward they shall come out with great possessions. As for yourself, you shall go to your ancestors in peace; you shall be buried in a good old age. And they shall come back here in the fourth generation; for the iniquity of the Amorites is not yet complete'" (15:13-16).

Literary Features

The narrator's emphases can be spotted again by checking for pace retardation. As with the other journeys, he quickly passes over the journey itself (46:5-6, 28), but spends four verses (46:1-4) on the preparation for the journey at Beer-sheba (especially the theophany) and twenty-three verses (46:5-27) on the offspring that went along on the journey. Next, instead of quickly settling Jacob and his family in Goshen, the narrator in great detail relates Joseph's plan for his brothers' audience with Pharaoh, the brothers' audience and that of Jacob (46:31–47:10), revealing "the narrator's concern to base the settlement of Jacob's family and the provision made during the famine expressly on the Pharaoh's guarantee."[6] The narrator also uses a great deal of narrative time relating Joseph's actions selling the stored grain in Egypt (47:13-26), while he just notes that Jacob lives another seventeen years in Egypt (47:28).

Repetition is found primarily in the number "seven" and its multiples in the list of Jacob's descendants. "All the persons of the house of Jacob who came into Egypt were seventy [10 × 7]" (46:27), indicating the full, complete number, just like the seventy nations of Genesis 10. The children of Rachel are fourteen (2 × 7) (46:22), while her maid Bilhah has half that number, seven (46:24). The children of Leah are thirty-three (46:15), while her maid Zilpah has half that number, sixteen (46:18), for a total of forty-nine (7 × 7). The seventh son is Gad: his name is the numerical value of seven ($g = 3 + d = 4$), and Gad has seven sons (46:16).[7] And Jacob lives in Egypt seventeen years (10 + 7) (47:28), the same number of years Joseph lived in Canaan (37:2).

A few other notable repetitions should be mentioned. From the earlier journeys, the narrator repeats Jacob's concern about dying, but now, having seen Joseph, he can die in peace (46:30), and "when the time of Israel's death drew near,"

6. Westermann, *Genesis 37–50*, 167.

7. See further, Hamilton, *Genesis 18–50*, 598-99.

he makes Joseph swear to bury him in the Promised Land (47:29). Further, the narrative repeats several times that Israel is to settle in Goshen, "the best part of the land" (47:6, 11). Jacob blesses Pharaoh twice (47:7, 10), and in his short speech to Pharaoh twice calls his own life and that of his fathers a "sojourn" (47:9).

The narrative can be subdivided into seven scenes:[8]

Scene 1: God appears to Jacob (46:1-4)
Scene 2: Jacob journeys to Egypt (46:5-27)
Scene 3: Joseph meets Jacob (46:28-34)
Scene 4: Joseph's brothers meet Pharaoh (47:1-6)
Scene 5: Jacob meets Pharaoh (47:7-10)
Scene 6: Joseph cares for his family and Egypt (47:11-26)
Scene 7: Jacob prepares to die (47:27-31)

The Plot Line

The setting for this narrative is found in the previous narrative: Joseph's invitation to have Jacob and his family settle in Egypt, and Jacob's decision to "go and see" Joseph (45:9-10, 28). Preliminary incidents consist of Jacob journeying to the southern border of the Promised Land, offering sacrifices at Beer-sheba to "the God of his father Isaac," and God promising to go down to Egypt with him (46:1-4). The occasioning incident is Jacob leaving the Promised Land for Egypt (46:5). What will happen to him and his large family? Where will they settle? Will they survive another five years of famine?

The tension builds as the narrator mentions "all his offspring he brought with him into Egypt" (46:7), lists them all by name (46:8-27), and concludes, "All the persons of the house of Jacob who came into Egypt were seventy" (v 27). The full number of Jacob's offspring are going down to Egypt. Not one is left behind in the Promised Land. Will his offspring survive in Egypt?

When the family arrives in Goshen, Joseph is finally reunited with Jacob. It is an emotional meeting — Joseph "wept on his [father's] neck a good while" (46:29) — but it is not the climax of the story. The narrative tension is, Will Jacob's family survive? Joseph hatches a plan to make Pharaoh give them "the best land." He previews with his brothers what he will say to Pharaoh about them and coaches them on what they should say, so that they "may settle in the land of Goshen" (46:34). Joseph tells Pharaoh that his family with their flocks and herds are now in the land of Goshen and then presents five of his brothers

8. See Wenham, *Genesis 16–50*, 439. See there also for "a loose symmetry" between these scenes.

to Pharaoh for an audience. The brothers follow Joseph's script rather closely by telling Pharaoh that they are shepherds, but then make bold to ask to "settle in the land of Goshen" (47:5). What will Pharaoh do? Will he honor their request or send them back to Canaan?

The suspense breaks when Pharaoh responds positively: "Then Pharaoh said to Joseph, 'Your father and your brothers have come to you. The land of Egypt is before you; settle your father and your brothers in the best part of the land; let them live in the land of Goshen; and if you know that there are capable men among them, put them in charge of my livestock'" (47:5-6). The response is even better than they had hoped for. They may not only live in Goshen, but Pharaoh even offers some of them a royal office; those qualified may be in charge of his livestock. Joseph then brings Jacob before Pharaoh, and Jacob twice blesses Pharaoh (47:7, 10). Next Joseph grants his father and his brothers "a holding in the land of Egypt, in the best part of the land" (47:11) and provides food for them "according to the number of their dependents" (47:12). The tension is resolved.

The outcome of the narrative relates Joseph's actions to keep the Egyptians alive (47:13-26). The narrative concludes with a summary of Israel multiplying "exceedingly" (47:27) and Jacob's request to be buried in the Promised Land (47:28-31).

We can sketch the plot line of this narrative as a single plot:

Theocentric Interpretation

Before leaving the Promised Land, Jacob offers "sacrifices to the God of his father Isaac" (46:1). That night God calls Jacob and says, "I am God, the God of your father; do not be afraid to go down to Egypt, for I will make of you a great nation there. I myself will go down with you to Egypt, and I will also bring you up again" (46:3-4). Although God is not mentioned again in this narrative, his going down to Egypt with Jacob is evident from the results: Pharaoh assigns them "the best of the land" (47:6), Joseph grants them "a holding in the land of Egypt" (47:11), Joseph provides food for the entire family (47:12), and Israel "gained possessions" in the land, "and were fruitful and multiplied exceedingly" (47:27). God's promise to Jacob of making a great nation of him "there," in Egypt, is being fulfilled.

Textual Theme and Goal

The key to the theme of this narrative is God's promises to Jacob before he sets out for Egypt. The importance of God's promises here are underscored by the fact that this is the only time in the Joseph story that God speaks in a night vision. God promises Jacob, "I will make of you a great nation there. I myself will go down with you to Egypt, and I will also bring you up again; and Joseph's own hand shall close your eyes" (46:3-4). These promises are fulfilled in this narrative and the one that follows (48:1–50:26). In this narrative God does indeed go down with Jacob and his family: he saves them from the famine, gives them "a holding in the land of Egypt" (47:11), and makes them fruitful so that they multiply "exceedingly" (47:27) and become "a great nation." We can, therefore, formulate the theme of this narrative as follows: *In accord with his promise, God goes with his people Israel to Egypt.*

As to the author's goal in writing this message for later Israel, we should recall that Israel at that time knew "the rest of the story." Not only had God been with Jacob and his family in Egypt and made of them a great nation, he had also brought them "up again" (46:4). Whether Israel heard this story in Moab just before returning to the Promised Land, or in Canaan, or in exile in Babylonia, the probable goal of the author was, *To assure Israel that their God, unlike the local gods, goes with them wherever they go.*

Ways to Preach Christ

With the theme, "In accord with his promise, God goes with his people Israel to Egypt," how can we move legitimately to Jesus Christ in the New Testament? Since some earlier narratives (especially God's promises to Jacob at Bethel) had similar themes, we shall be traveling some of the same highways from the Old Testament to Jesus in the New Testament.

Redemptive-Historical Progression

Since Jacob is "afraid" (46:3) to leave the Promised Land without God's blessing, God promises him that he will go down to Egypt with him and will bring him up again (cf. Bethel, 28:15). In fulfillment of his promises, God saves Israel from the great famine, makes them into a great nation, and later brings Israel up out of Egypt again. God promises Moses, "I will be with you" (Exod 3:12). Moses, in turn, encourages Israel to capture Canaan: "Have no fear or dread of them, because it is the LORD your God who goes with you; he will not fail you or forsake you" (Deut 31:6). God also assures Joshua, "As I was with Moses, so I will be with you; I will not fail you or forsake you" (Josh 1:5). Still later, when Israel is in exile, the LORD again assures his people of his presence: "When you pass through the waters, I will be with you" (Isa 43:2; cf. 41:10). Thus in Old Testament times, God keeps alive the people who will give birth to the Messiah. When Jesus is born, Matthew observes fulfillment of the prophecy about Emmanuel, "which means, 'God is with us'" (Matt 1:23; cf. John 14:9-10; Col 2:9). After Jesus rises from the dead, he promises his disciples, "Remember, I am with you always, to the end of the age" (Matt 28:20). When Jesus ascends to heaven, he pours out the Holy Spirit to dwell in God's people (Acts 2:33). On the last day, when Jesus comes again, God will dwell with his people; "they will be his peoples, and God himself will be with them" (Rev 21:3).

Promise-Fulfillment

God promises Jacob that he will make a great nation of him in Egypt and that he will go down to Egypt with him and bring him up again. God fulfills these promises by giving Israel "a holding in the land of Egypt" (47:11), making them multiply "exceedingly" (47:27), and later bringing them up again through Moses (Exod 12:31-32). But God's promises find further fulfillment when, with echoes of the return from Egypt, he promises the exiles that a remnant will return: "There shall be a highway from Assyria for the remnant that is left of his people, as there was for Israel when they came up from the land of Egypt" (Isa 11:16). God's promise that he will be with his people wherever they are finds its ultimate fulfillment in Jesus Christ, God living among us, sending his disciples out to all nations with the promise, "I am with you always" (Matt 28:20), and pouring out his Holy Spirit (Acts 2:33) to be with his people forever.

Typology

Earlier we saw that Joseph in his humiliation and exaltation is a type of Christ. In this particular narrative there are also parallels between Joseph and Jesus: As Joseph granted "a holding in the land of Egypt" to God's people, so Jesus grants "a holding" in God's kingdom to God's people: "Come, you that are blessed by my Father, inherit the kingdom prepared for you from the foundation of the world" (Matt 25:34; cf. 1 Pet 1:3-5). As Joseph provided food for God's people (47:12), so Jesus provides the living bread for God's people (John 6:35). And as Joseph saved God's people from starvation, so Jesus saves God's people from sin and gives them eternal life (John 3:16).

Analogy

As God assured Israel that he would go with them wherever they go, so Jesus assures the church that he will be with them wherever they go. Jesus promises, "I am with you always, to the end of the age" (Matt 28:20).

Longitudinal Themes

The theme of God's presence with his people can be traced from God's assurance to Jacob here (46:4), to Jacob's assurance to Joseph (48:21), to Joseph's assurance to Israel (50:24), to the priestly blessing: "The LORD bless you and keep you" (Num 6:24). Later, when the nation of Judah feared being annihilated, God gives them a sign: "Look, the young woman is with child and shall bear a son, and shall name him Immanuel" (Isa 7:14). The sign is, God is with us. Matthew sees further fulfillment of this sign when Jesus is born: "All this took place to fulfill what had been spoken by the Lord through the prophet, 'Look, the virgin shall conceive and bear a son, and they shall name him Emmanuel,' which means 'God is with us'" (Matt 1:22-23). Jesus encourages his followers, "Abide in me as I abide in you" (John 15:4), and promises them, "I am with you always, to the end of the age" (Matt 28:20). When Jesus ascends to heaven, God's presence continues to be with the church through the Holy Spirit (Acts 2; 1 Cor 3:16; 6:19). One of the marks of the new creation is that God will dwell with his people: "they will be his peoples, and God himself will be with them" (Rev 21:3).

New Testament References

The appendix to the Greek New Testament again has references to Stephen's speech in Acts 7 (vv 14, 15, and 17). For Genesis 46:2, "Jacob, Jacob," it lists Acts 9:4, "Saul, Saul." For Genesis 46:30, Jacob's words, "I can die now, having seen for myself that you are still alive," it lists Luke 2:29, Simeon's words, "Master, now you are dismissing your servant in peace . . . ; for my eyes have seen your salvation." And for Genesis 47:31, "Then Israel bowed himself on the head of his bed," it lists Hebrews 11:21, Jacob "bowing in worship over the top of his staff" (based on the Septuagint). Only one of these references, Luke 2:29, is linked to Jesus. Accordingly, except for Luke 2:29, these New Testament references are not good bridges from this Old Testament narrative to Jesus.

There are, however, some other New Testament references that link the theme of God's presence with his people to Jesus. In addition to the passages mentioned earlier, one might consider Matthew 18:20, where Jesus promises, "Where two or three are gathered in my name, I am there among them." And especially Romans 8:35-39, where Paul raises the question, "Who will separate us from the love of Christ?" After enumerating many possibilities, he concludes that nothing "in all creation will be able to separate us from the love of God in Christ Jesus our Lord."

Contrast

There is no contrast since the New Testament confirms the message that God is with his people.

Sermon Theme and Goal

We formulated the textual theme as, "In accord with his promise, God goes with his people Israel to Egypt." The sermon theme can be similar but needs to extend God's promise through Jesus Christ to the church today. A succinct sermon theme would be, *In accord with his promise, God goes with his people wherever they go.*

We formulated the author's goal as, "To assure Israel that their God, unlike the local gods, goes with them wherever they go." In harmony with this goal, we can make our goal in preaching this sermon, "*To assure God's people that God goes with them wherever they go.*" This particular goal would address the congregational need of doubting God's presence with them wherever they go. This doubt may arise because their God is too small or too distant (Deism) or because of their belief that a good God cannot possibly be with them when they suffer.

Sermon Form

Most of the narratives, thus far, can best be preached in a narrative form that is developed inductively, for their theme becomes evident only toward the end of the narrative. Since this narrative reveals its theme early on, one could consider developing this sermon with inductive-deductive development, that is, begin inductively from 46:1 to 46:4, which reveals the theme, and then proceed deductively from there showing God's presence with his people in Egypt and today. The sermon outline might look something like this:

Introduction

I. God promises to go with his people Israel to Egypt
   - A. Exposition of Genesis 46:1-4.
   - B. State the textual theme: "In accord with his promise, God goes with his people Israel to Egypt."

II. We see God's presence in Egypt in:
   - A. Reuniting Jacob and his son Joseph (46:28-30).
   - B. Pharaoh giving Israel access to the best of the land of Egypt (46:31–47:6).
   - C. Jacob being able to bless Pharaoh (47:7-10).

III. We see God's presence in Egypt further in:
   - A. Joseph giving Israel "a holding" in Egypt and sufficient food (47:11-12).
   - B. Joseph saving the lives of the Egyptians (47:13-26).
   - C. God prospering Israel and multiplying them exceedingly (47:27).

IV. We see God's presence with us in Jesus (typological parallels):
   - A. As Joseph granted Israel "a holding in the land," so Jesus grants us a holding in the kingdom of God (Matt 25:34).
   - B. As Joseph provided food for Israel, so Jesus provides us with "the bread of life" (John 6:35).
   - C. As Joseph saved Israel from starvation, so Jesus saves us from sin and gives us eternal life (John 3:16).
   - D. In accord with his promise, God goes with his people wherever they go (Matt 28:20).

Conclusion

Sermon Exposition

Joseph had invited his father Jacob and his extended family to come to Egypt to survive the great famine that would plague that area for another five years. When Jacob first heard that Joseph was alive, his heart almost stopped. For twenty-two years he had thought that his favorite son was dead, and then he found out that he was alive. Jacob had cried out, "My son Joseph is still alive. I must go and see him before I die" (45:28). It was an impulsive, hasty decision. What was Jacob doing heading down to Egypt with his whole family? This was no picnic. There were at least seventy persons: men, women, and little children, as well as their flocks and herds. Would Pharaoh allow them to stay or would he send them right back to Canaan? And if he let them stay, where would that be in Egypt? Would they end up in some large city? Or in some desert area with other nomads? Or a place with good pastureland? Many questions!

Moreover, Jacob was leaving the very land God had promised to Abraham, Isaac, and Jacob himself. When his father Isaac had wanted to escape a famine by going to Egypt, God had stopped him on the way. God had said, "*Do not go down to Egypt;* settle in the land that I shall show you. Reside in this land [of the Philistines] as an alien, and I will be with you, and will bless you; for to you and to your descendants I will give all these lands, and I will fulfill the oath that I swore to your father Abraham. I will make your offspring as numerous as the stars of heaven" (26:2-4). "Do not go down to Egypt," God had said to his father. But now Jacob and his whole family are on their way to Egypt. Is he giving up on the land God had promised his grandfather Abraham and his father Isaac? Is he doing the right thing? Jacob is not sure.

The narrative begins in chapter 46:1, "When Israel set out on his journey with *all that he had* and came to Beer-sheba [on the southern border of Canaan], he offered sacrifices to the God of his father Isaac." Years ago, when Isaac was at Beer-sheba, God had appeared to him at night and said, "I am the God of your father Abraham; *do not be afraid, for I am with you* and will bless you and make your offspring *numerous* for my servant Abraham's sake" (26:24). In response, Isaac had built an altar there. Now, being uneasy about leaving the Promised Land, Jacob stops at the border and offers "sacrifices to the God of his father Isaac."

That night, God appears to Jacob. This is the only time in the Joseph story that God speaks in a night vision. This is an important message. Verses 2-4,

> God spoke to Israel in visions of the night, and said, "Jacob, Jacob." And he said, "Here I am." Then he said, "I am God, the God of your father; *do not be afraid* to go down to Egypt, for I will make of you a *great nation* there. I myself will go down with you to Egypt, and I will also bring you up again; and Joseph's own hand shall close your eyes."

"Do not be afraid to go down to Egypt." God knows his fears. When he leaves the Promised Land, what will happen to God's promises to Abraham, Isaac, and Jacob to make their offspring exceedingly numerous, to make of them a great nation (12:2; 18:18)? God says, "Do not be afraid to go down to Egypt, for I will make of you a great nation there," in Egypt.[9] Although God had promised several times that he would make the patriarchs into "a great nation," this is "the first time he announces that this formation will take place well outside the border of the Promised Land in Egypt. Egypt will become the womb of this great nation. . . . A great nation is to be formed in the relatively secluded Egyptian region of Goshen, rather than in Canaan."[10]

The readers of this narrative know, of course, that Israel will eventually be enslaved in Egypt. This "going down" to Egypt eventually becomes a "going down" into slavery. But God is working out his redemptive plan even through their suffering. Just as God "sent" (45:5) Joseph to Egypt as a slave in order to save Israel and the surrounding world from famine, so God brings Israel to Egypt, where they will be enslaved but grow into a nation. Then God will lead them out of slavery to the Promised Land. There they will eventually give birth to the Messiah who will save the world.

God also explains how he will fulfill this promise of a great nation so far from the Promised Land. God says, "I myself will go down with you[11] to Egypt."[12] This was a revolutionary idea for that culture. People at that time believed in local deities who had power only in a certain country, but beyond its borders they were powerless. Israel's God, however, is the sovereign God who controls the whole world. Earlier he went with Abraham and Sarah from Haran in Mesopotamia to Canaan. He went with Jacob from Canaan to his uncle Laban in Haran and back to Canaan again. Regional borders do not apply to Israel's God: "I myself will go down with you to Egypt."

God promises further in verse 4, "I will also bring you up again." Von Rad observes, "The promise to bring Jacob back to Canaan scarcely refers to the return of his corpse, which is reported in chapter 50:4-14, but rather to his return in his descendants. Ancient Israel considered the ancestors and the nation as connected closely with each other, in fact, it considered them both as a great liv-

9. "Joseph had told his brothers that God had engineered events so that life generally and his family in particular would be preserved. Here God tells Jacob that in Egypt he will make him into a great nation, as promised to his ancestors." Turner, *Genesis*, 193.

10. Hamilton, *Genesis 18–50*, 591.

11. This promise "reiterates another familiar theme of the patriarchal narratives, God's protecting presence that guarantees blessing (cf. 26:24; 28:15, 20; 31:3, 5, 42; 39:2-3, 21, 23)." Wenham, *Genesis 16–50*, 441.

12. "God's presence does not eliminate pain, but it does assure provision and protection in the midst of it. . . ." Waltke, *Genesis*, 574.

ing organism with a common destiny."[13] Therefore, God here promises the exodus from Egypt.[14]

God concludes his message with a personal promise for Jacob: "Joseph's own hand shall close your eyes." Jacob will see Joseph again. And though Jacob will die in Egypt, he will die in the presence of his favorite son. In Jewish culture "the eldest son or nearest relative would gently close the eyes of the deceased."[15] His beloved Joseph will perform that rite for Jacob.

Encouraged by God's promise that God will go with him to Egypt, Jacob leaves the Promised Land behind. Verses 5-7,

> Then Jacob set out from Beer-sheba; and the sons of Israel carried their father Jacob, their little ones, and their wives, in the wagons that Pharaoh had sent to carry him. They also took their livestock and the goods that they had acquired in the land of Canaan, and they came into Egypt, Jacob and all his offspring with him, his sons, and his sons' sons with him, his daughters, and his sons' daughters; *all his offspring* he brought with him into Egypt.

The emphasis here is on the fact that Jacob took along "all his offspring," literally, "all his seed." Not one remained behind in the Promised Land. He vacates the Promised Land entirely. No one is left behind "to hold the fort and preserve the family holdings."[16]

To underscore this point the narrator next lists all the names of the emigrants. As in the early chapters of Genesis, the list highlights the number "seven" and its multiples. For example, we read in verse 22, "These are the children of Rachel, who were born to Jacob — *fourteen* persons in all." Fourteen is two times seven. Rachel's maid Bilhah, on the other hand, has half that number of children. We read in verse 25, "These are the children of Bilhah, whom Laban gave to his daughter Rachel, and these she bore to Jacob — *seven* persons in all." Leah, we read in verse 15, had thirty-three children and grandchildren, while her maid Zilpah, verse 18, had sixteen. Together they had *forty-nine* children, that is, seven times seven. But the most important multiple of seven is listed at the end of verse 27, "All the persons of the house of Jacob who came into Egypt

13. Von Rad, *Genesis,* 402. Cf. Waltke, *Genesis,* 574, "The form is singular, referring both to Jacob, though in a coffin (49:29-32), and his sons in corporate solidarity with him." Cf. Herbert, *Genesis 12–50,* 144.

14. "'It is I that shall surely bring you up.' The personal pronoun 'I' and the infinitive absolute, 'surely bring up,' make this statement very emphatic. This is not merely a promise that Jacob will be buried in Canaan but, like 15:13-16, the only comparable statement in Genesis, an announcement of the exodus (cf. Exod 3:8, 17)." Wenham, *Genesis 16–50,* 441-42.

15. "Such has remained the time-honored Jewish practice to the present day." Sarna, *Genesis,* 313.

16. Walton, *Genesis,* 684.

were *seventy*." Seventy, of course, is ten times seven. Ten is the number of fullness; seven is the number of perfection. Seventy is the full, complete number of God's people.[17] "Just as the 'seventy nations' [Genesis 10] represent all the descendants of Adam, so now the 'seventy sons' represent all the descendants of Abraham, Isaac, and Jacob, the sons of Israel."[18] All God's people move down to Egypt. Not one is left behind in the Promised Land.

Verse 28, "Israel sent Judah[19] ahead to Joseph to lead the way before him into Goshen. When they came to the land of Goshen, Joseph made ready his chariot[20] and went up to meet his father Israel in Goshen. He presented himself to him,[21] fell on his neck, and wept on his neck a good while." After a twenty-two-year separation, father and son have an emotional reunion.

Jacob says to Joseph, "I can die[22] now, having seen for myself that you are still alive." "In many ways Jacob's words, upon seeing Joseph, parallel those of Simeon [when he holds the baby Jesus in his arms] in the temple: 'Lord, now let your servant depart in peace . . . for my eyes have seen your salvation' (Luke 2:29-30). Jacob can now happily accept death, knowing that he will no more go to his grave with unanswered questions about his beloved Joseph's circumstances."[23]

The question now is, Will Pharaoh still welcome such a large company of refugees? And will he still allow these nomads to settle in "the best of the land"? Joseph has a plan ready and rehearses it for the group. He says, verses 31-34,

> "I will go up and tell Pharaoh, and will say to him, 'My brothers and my father's household, who were in the land of Canaan, have come to me. The men are *shepherds*, for they have been keepers of livestock; and they have

17. "70 is understood here to be a typological rather than a literal number. It is here used, as elsewhere in the biblical literature, to express the idea of totality." Sarna, *Genesis*, 317.

18. Sailhamer, *Genesis*, 261. Sailhamer continues, "The writer has gone to great lengths to portray the new nation of Israel as a new humanity and Abraham as a second Adam. The blessing that is to come through Abraham and his offspring is a restoration of the original blessing of Adam, a blessing that was lost in the fall."

19. "It is fitting that as Judah's scheme led to the parting of father and son (37:26-27), so he should oversee their reunion." Wenham, *Genesis 16–50*, 444.

20. "He literally 'hitched his chariot.' This is not an exalted vizier waiting for his servants, but an anxious son racing to greet his father. Joseph, the second in command of Egypt, will not wait for his father to appear before him." Waltke, *Genesis*, 585.

21. Literally, "he appeared to him." "Elsewhere in the patriarchal stories this verb is always used of God appearing to man, and its use here draws attention to the overwhelming impression on Jacob of the power, grandeur, and graciousness of Joseph in his own chariot attended by numerous servants." Wenham, *Genesis 16–50*, 445.

22. "Almost all of Jacob's recorded words since 37:35 are of death, and continue to be so, but after the turning-point of 45:28 the bitterness is largely replaced by a sense of fulfillment and hope." Kidner, *Genesis*, 210.

23. Hamilton, *Genesis 18–50*, 602.

> brought their flocks, and their herds, and all that they have.' When Pharaoh calls you, and says, 'What is your occupation?' you shall say, 'Your servants have been keepers of livestock from our youth even until now, both we and our ancestors' — in order that you may settle in the land of Goshen, because all *shepherds* are abhorrent[24] to the Egyptians."

Joseph wants his family to settle in the land of Goshen, on Egypt's northeastern border. Since Goshen is on the frontier of Egypt, the family can live in relative isolation and not intermingle with the Egyptians.[25] Moreover, Goshen has ideal grazing land and is not too far from Canaan. So Joseph will emphasize to Pharaoh that they are shepherds and have brought their herds with them. Hopefully, Pharaoh will catch on that they need pastureland. But since Egyptians disdain shepherds, he will probably assign them land somewhere on the fringes of Egypt. The brothers, in turn, have to tell Pharaoh that they have been herdsmen all their lives, even to the present time. The roles having been assigned, Joseph selects five of his brothers to go with him to Pharaoh.

Joseph says to Pharaoh, chapter 47:1, "My father and my brothers, with their flocks and herds and all that they possess, have come from the land of Canaan; they are now in the land of Goshen." Then he presents his brothers to Pharaoh. Pharaoh asks, verse 3, "What is your occupation?" And they respond, "Your servants are *shepherds*, as our ancestors were. We have come to reside as aliens in the land; for there is no pasture for your servants' flocks because the famine is severe in the land of Canaan." But then the brothers go beyond their carefully rehearsed, polite little speech. They make a bold request: "Now, we ask you, let your servants settle in the land of Goshen." How will Pharaoh respond to this blunt request? Will he get angry and send them straight back to Canaan? Or will he say, "Where you settle is entirely my prerogative? I can send you to a refugee camp in the desert. Or I can place you in a city to work in the granaries."

24. This is "the perennial antipathy of the town-dweller for the nomad or the gipsy. Joseph saw the importance of emphasizing this, to ensure that Pharaoh's goodwill would be to the family's real benefit, not to their detriment by drawing them into an alien way of life at the capital." Kidner, *Genesis*, 210.

25. "Joseph emphasizes that his family are shepherds to assure the Pharaoh that they entertain no social or political ambitions and to preserve them from an alien way of life and intermarriage with the Egyptians (see 34:9)." Waltke, *Genesis*, 586. See ibid., 556, "Herein [see 43:32] lies a clue to the rationale for the Egyptian sojourn. Whereas the Canaanites are willing to integrate and absorb the sons of Israel, the Egyptians hold them in contempt. Judah's intermarriage with the Canaanites in Genesis 38 shows the danger that syncretistic Canaanites present to the embryonic family." Cf. Sarna, *Understanding Genesis*, 225, "The actual physical isolation . . . help[s] to elucidate how Israel was able to maintain its national cohesion, its language and traditions throughout the years of Egyptian bondage."

But amazingly, Pharaoh obliges their request. He even goes them one better. He says to Joseph, verse 5, "Your father and your brothers have come to you. The land of Egypt is before you; settle your father and your brothers in the best part of the land; let them live in the land of Goshen; and if you know that there are capable men among them, put them in charge of my livestock." Pharaoh not only allows them to settle in Goshen, but he offers some of them a royal position: Joseph may put qualified men in charge of the royal herd. "This office is mentioned frequently in Egyptian inscriptions since the king possessed vast herds of cattle; Rameses III is said to have employed 3,264 men, mostly foreigners, to take care of his herds. The appointment of some of Joseph's brothers to supervise the king's cattle means that they are to be officers of the crown and thus will enjoy legal protection not usually accorded aliens."[26] As the LORD had been with Joseph in Potiphar's house, in prison, and in Pharaoh's court, so clearly the LORD is now with Jacob and his family in Egypt.

Next, Joseph presents his father Jacob to Pharaoh. But instead of bowing deeply before the great Pharaoh, to everyone's surprise Jacob lifts his hands and blesses Pharaoh. Jacob blesses him for his kindness to his family. Jacob, who had cheated and lied to obtain the blessing from his father (27:18-29), here generously passes on God's blessing to Pharaoh. The importance of Jacob blessing Pharaoh "can be seen from the fact that it is mentioned twice. Lying behind such an emphasis in the narrative was God's promise to Abraham that he would bless those who blessed the offspring of Abraham. The passage shows that in Joseph and Jacob, the promise to Abraham was being fulfilled with the nations round about them."[27]

Pharaoh then asks Jacob, verse 8, "How many are the years of your life?" Jacob responds, "The years of my earthly *sojourn* are one hundred thirty; few and hard have been the years of my life. They do not compare with the years of the life of my ancestors during their long *sojourn*." Pharaoh asked a simple question: How old are you? We would expect a simple answer: a hundred and thirty. "But Jacob demurs. In his answer he does not speak of age as the Pharaoh had asked, but instead, of the years of his sojourning, thereby diverting attention from the number to the content of his years. . . . Sojourning was indeed the characteristic of the entire road of life which God had pointed out to the patriarchs. Sojourning meant renunciation of settlement and land ownership; . . . it meant a life which was oriented toward future fulfillment, namely, toward the promise of land which was often renewed to the patriarchs."[28]

Jacob characterizes his earthly sojourn as "hard." He had cheated his

26. Sarna, *Genesis*, 319.

27. Sailhamer, *Genesis*, 264.

28. Von Rad, *Genesis*, 407-8.

brother Esau and deceived his father Isaac. As a result he had to flee for his life to Mesopotamia to his uncle Laban. Laban deceived Jacob by giving him on his wedding night not the lovely Rachel but Leah. Coming back to Canaan, his daughter Dinah was raped, and his sons deceived him into thinking that his beloved son Joseph had been torn apart by wild animals. And then the famine, the imprisonment of Simeon in Egypt, his fear for Benjamin's life. His life had been hard. But he had God's promise! God would be with him even in Egypt. And eventually God would return these sojourners to the land of promise. Eventually they would dwell in the Promised Land.

In verse 11 we read that "Joseph settled his father and his brothers, and granted them a *holding* in the land of Egypt, in the best part of the land, in the land of Rameses." "Joseph exceeds the brothers' original request. They would be content to sojourn *(gûr)* in Goshen. Instead, Joseph gives them *property ('ăḥuzzâ)*. All of this confirms God's promise to Jacob that he would make of Jacob a great nation in Egypt (46:3)."[29] The sojourners now have property where they can settle down, multiply, and become a great nation. In addition to providing his family with property, verse 12 tells us that Joseph provides "his father, his brothers, and all his father's household with food, according to the number of their dependents." Everyone has enough food to eat. Not one of God's people will die of starvation, even though the famine is becoming steadily more severe.

Verse 13, "Now there was no food in all the land, for the famine was very severe. The land of Egypt *and the land of Canaan* languished because of the famine." Had Israel remained in Canaan, they would have starved to death. Even in Egypt things are becoming desperate and Joseph has to take severe measures to save the Egyptians.

We read in verses 14 to 21,

> Joseph collected all the money to be found in the land of Egypt and in the land of Canaan, in exchange for the grain that they bought; and Joseph brought the money into Pharaoh's house. When the money from the land of Egypt and from the land of Canaan was spent, all the Egyptians came to Joseph, and said, "Give us food! *Why should we die before your eyes?* For our money is gone." And Joseph answered, "Give me your livestock, and I will give you food in exchange for your livestock, if your money is gone." So they brought their livestock to Joseph; and Joseph gave them food in exchange for the horses, the flocks, the herds, and the donkeys. That year he supplied them with food in exchange for all their livestock. When that year was ended, they came to him the following year, and said to him, "We can not hide from my

29. Hamilton, *Genesis 18–50*, 613.

> lord that our money is all spent; and the herds of cattle are my lord's. There is nothing left in the sight of my lord but our bodies and our lands. *Shall we die before your eyes, both we and our land?*[30] Buy us and our land in exchange for food. We with our land will become slaves[31] to Pharaoh; just give us seed, *so that we may live and not die,* and that the land may not become desolate. So Joseph bought all the land of Egypt for Pharaoh. All the Egyptians sold their fields, because the famine was severe upon them; and the land became Pharaoh's. As for the people, he made slaves of them from one end of Egypt to the other.

We may recoil at the seeming exploitation of the destitute. But "it was axiomatic in the ancient world that one paid one's way so long as one had anything to part with — including, in the last resort, one's liberty. Israelite law accepted the principle, while modifying it with the right of redemption (Lev 25:25ff.)."[32] In essence, the Egyptians became tenant farmers on land that now belonged to the crown.

Verse 23, "Then Joseph said to the people, 'Now that I have this day bought you and your land for Pharaoh, here is seed for you; sow the land. And at the harvests you shall give one-fifth to Pharaoh, and *four-fifths shall be your own,* as seed for the field and as food for yourselves and your households, and as food for your little ones.'" "Since the people were now tenant farmers, Joseph allotted them seed for planting the fields, an indication that the famine was about to end. Under this agreement, they paid 20 percent of their crop to Pharaoh. Texts from the ancient Middle East attest that the interest rate for seed was often much higher, many times 40 percent. According to ancient standards, Joseph thus acted graciously toward the people. He stressed that the rest of the crop was theirs for *seed* and for *food.* The people gladly accepted the agreement, knowing that they had been spared from death."[33]

30. If there is no one to work the land, it will return to desert, it will become "desolate" (end of v 19).

31. "Ancient slavery at its best was like tenured employment, whereas the free man was more like someone who is self-employed. The latter may be freer, but faces more risks (cf. Exod 21:5-6; Deut 15:12-17)." Wenham, *Genesis 16–50*, 449.

32. Kidner, *Genesis*, 211. Cf. Wenham, *Genesis*, 452, "The OT law itself does not envisage the destitute simply being bailed out by the more well-to-do. Rather, if possible, members of a family should help their destitute relatives, just as Joseph did, by buying their land and employing them as slaves (cf. Lev 25:13-55). This was viewed as a great act of charity, for as the Egyptians say to Joseph, 'You have saved our lives' (45:25)."

33. Hartley, *Genesis*, 347-48. Cf. von Rad, *Genesis*, 411, "Judged by the conditions of that time, a tax of about 20 percent must be considered normal. In private business transactions the interest rates were often considerably higher. In the Babylonian economy the interest rates for the purchase of seed corn went as high as 40 percent; in the Jewish military colony of Elephantine in the fifth century B.C. they went even to 60 percent."

The Egyptians respond with gratitude.[34] They say, verse 25, "*You have saved our lives.*" Earlier Joseph had explained to his brothers God's providential leading, "You sold me here," but "God sent me before you to preserve life" (45:5). With his extreme measures, Joseph saved the lives of the Egyptians.

In the foregoing chapters we hear a lot about Joseph saving lives. Jacob tells his sons to go down to Egypt to "buy grain for us there, that we may live and not die" (42:2). Next Judah argues with his father to let them return to Egypt with Benjamin, "so that we may live and not die" (43:8). Then Joseph tells his brothers, "God sent me before you to preserve life" (45:5). In this narrative, this emphasis on Joseph saving lives continues.[35] The Egyptians come to Joseph for seed, "so that we may live and not die" (47:19).

Joseph, therefore, saves not only his family but also the Egyptians. This is clearly in fulfillment of God's promise to Abraham: "I will bless those who bless you . . . ; and in you all the families of the earth shall be blessed" (12:3). But this saving of lives is not only in fulfillment of past promises, it also extends to the future. For in keeping alive the nation of Israel, God uses Joseph to keep alive the nation that will one day give birth to the Messiah.

In fact, in his saving work, Joseph prefigures Jesus Christ. As Joseph provided food for the starving people to save their lives, so Jesus provides food for dying people. Jesus says in John 6, "I am the *bread of life.* Whoever comes to me will never be hungry, and whoever believes in me will never be thirsty. . . . This is the will of him who sent me, that I should lose nothing of all that he has given me, but raise it up on the last day. This is indeed the will of my Father, that all who see the Son and believe in him may have eternal life; and I will raise them up on the last day" (John 6:35-40).

Joseph also prefigures Jesus in granting Israel a "holding," or property, in Egypt. As Joseph granted a "holding" to God's people, so Jesus grants a "holding" in God's kingdom to God's people. Speaking of the final judgment, Jesus

34. Joseph, therefore, "is not a callous, unethical taskmaster. True, the people forfeit ownership of their land to Pharaoh, but Joseph allows them, when this measure can be put into practice, to keep 80 percent of the harvest for themselves. Only 20 percent remains Pharaoh's. (Cf. the 10 percent that is Yahweh's in OT religion.) The people are evidently grateful for this arrangement, for they say to Joseph, 'You have saved our lives' (v 25). . . . Apparently, Joseph's reforms were acceptable to later Egyptians as well, or at least to later Pharaohs. Joseph's decree was still a law in Egypt in the writer's day ('still in force today,' v 26)." Hamilton, *Genesis 18–50,* 618-19.

35. "In keeping with that emphasis, the present narrative opens with the statement of the Egyptians to Joseph as they seek to buy grain from him: 'Why should we die before you?' (47:16); then it continues with the account of their return to Joseph 'the second year' (v 18), when they again say, 'Why should we die?' and 'that we might live and not die' (47:19). Such repetitions in the surface structure of the narrative suggest a thematic strategy at work. First with his brothers and then with the Egyptians, Joseph's wisdom is seen as the source of life for everyone in the land." Sailhamer, *Pentateuch as Narrative,* 227.

says, "Come, you that are blessed by my Father, *inherit the kingdom* prepared for you from the foundation of the world" (Matt 25:34). Jesus' apostle Peter can hardly contain his excitement about this good news. He writes to "the exiles of the Dispersion": "Blessed be the God and Father of our Lord Jesus Christ! By his great mercy he has given us a new birth into a living hope through the resurrection of Jesus Christ from the dead, and into an *inheritance* that is imperishable, undefiled, and unfading, kept in heaven for you" (1 Pet 1:3-5).

The narrator sums up Israel's fruitful stay in Egypt in verse 27, "Thus Israel settled in the land of Egypt, in the region of Goshen; and they gained possessions in it, and were fruitful and *multiplied exceedingly*." God is fulfilling his promises to Abraham, Isaac, and Jacob of a multitude of descendants. At Bethel, when God changed Jacob's name to Israel, God had said to him: "I am God Almighty: be fruitful and multiply; a nation and a company of nations shall come from you, and kings shall spring from you" (35:11; cf. 28:3). In Egypt Israel is becoming a nation, because God is with them.

The narrative concludes seventeen years later with Jacob's request to be buried not in Egypt but in the Promised Land. Verse 29, "When the time of Israel's death drew near, he called his son Joseph and said to him, 'If I have found favor with you, put your hand under my thigh[36] and promise to deal loyally and truly with me. *Do not bury me in Egypt.* When I lie down with my ancestors, carry me out of Egypt and *bury me in their burial place*.'[37] He answered, 'I will do as you have said.'" But his burial in the Promised Land is so important to Jacob that he will not just take Joseph's word for it. He makes him swear an oath. Verse 31, "'Swear to me'; and he swore to him. Then Israel bowed[38] himself on the head of his bed."

Walter Brueggemann observes, "This may be simply a burial note. And yet the narrator is especially attentive to it. The paragraph balances 46:1-4. In that unit, Jacob did not want to jeopardize the promise by leaving the land. He does not leave without the sanction given in the theophany. Now (47:27-31), he wants to embody his ultimate commitment to the land of promise even in his death.

36. The ancient equivalent of swearing an oath on the Bible. Cf. 24:2, p. 238 above, n. 14.

37. "A central element of the promise to Abraham was the promise of the land. The request of the patriarchs to be buried in the land 'with their fathers' brings to the fore their trust in the faithfulness of God to his word. Henceforth a key symbol of Israel's faith in the promises of God is the bones of the faithful seed that are buried in the Promised Land." Sailhamer, *Pentateuch as Narrative,* 228.

38. "The dream has been fulfilled in its own way, with the object of the verb left ambiguously unstated. When Joseph agrees to be the agent through whom the divine promises made to Jacob in 46:4 are to be carried out, the patriarch 'bows down' — in gratitude to the son, but, more important, acknowledging and accepting the mysterious arrangements of providence." Ackerman, "Joseph, Judah, and Jacob," 108-9.

Jacob is doggedly fixed on the land. He knows he is a child of the promise. And he will not permit any imperial attractions in Goshen to turn his head from the promise. He will not be seduced into Egypt. He will be *in* Egypt, but not *of* Egypt (cf. John 17:16-17)."[39]

God had not only promised to go down to Egypt with Jacob/Israel but also to bring them up again. God is with them not only in the present but also in the future. God is present with them not only in Egypt but also, centuries later, when they return to Canaan. Jacob believes that promise. He "knows that there is to be no permanent residence in Egypt for his people. Egypt is to Jacob and his family what the ark was to Noah — a temporary shelter from the disaster on the outside. Even if represented only by his decayed remains, he wants to be a part of that redemptive act of God."[40]

This narrative, then, emphasizes the presence of God with his people wherever they go. God was present with Israel when they went down to Egypt and God is present with them when he brings them up again. In Jesus Christ, God is also present with us wherever we go. After his resurrection Jesus sent out his followers "to make disciples of *all nations*." They were to go down to Egypt where the sun god Re was still considered supreme and to Greece where Zeus was the chief of the Olympian gods. But Jesus assured his followers as they went out to the nations, "Remember, I am with you *always,* to the end of the age" (Matt 28:20). Jesus, the Son of God, the one to whom God gave "all authority in heaven and on earth" (Matt 28:18), is with us wherever we go.

However, the fact that God is with us does not mean that we will always prosper. God's presence with Jacob did not mean an end to hardship: Jacob died. God's presence with the nation of Israel did not prevent the great affliction under a Pharaoh that did not know Joseph. The Israelites were enslaved and forced to drown their baby boys in the river Nile. Somehow God was with them even in their suffering, and eventually he brought them up out of Egypt again.

The fact that Jesus promised his disciples always to be with them does not mean that they would avoid hardship and suffering. Stephen was stoned to death; James was martyred; Peter was killed; Paul suffered beatings, imprisonments, and martyrdom. God's presence with us indeed includes blessings but also suffering. Jesus asserted, "In the world you face persecution" (John 16:33; cf. 16:2 and 17:14-18). So the question arises, If God's presence with us includes both blessings and hardships, how do we benefit?

The apostle Paul, who experienced more afflictions than most of us, answers that question. First, he says in Romans 8, "We know that all things work

39. Brueggemann, *Genesis,* 355.

40. Hamilton, *Genesis 18–50,* 625.

together for good for those who love God, who are called according to his purpose. . . . Those whom he predestined he also called; and those whom he called he also justified; and those whom he justified he also glorified" (Rom 8:28, 30). Our salvation is assured! Nothing can break this chain of God's actions: predestined, called, justified, glorified. No matter how much we suffer in this life, in the end we will be "glorified." Second, Paul raises the question if our suffering in this life means that God is not present with us. "Will hardship, or distress, or persecution, or famine, or nakedness, or peril, or sword" "separate us from the love of Christ?" And he answers confidently, "No, *in all these things* [not in spite of our suffering, but *in* all these things] we are more than conquerors through him who loved us. For I am convinced that neither death, nor life . . . nor anything else in all creation, will be able to separate us from the love of God in Christ Jesus our Lord" (Rom 8:35-39). In accord with his promise, God goes with us wherever we go.

CHAPTER 24

Jacob's Death and Burial

Genesis 48:1–50:26

The final chapters of Genesis also confront preachers with several challenges. The author not only relates Jacob's final words, his death and burial, but also seeks to tie up some loose ends regarding the brothers' lingering fear of Joseph and Joseph's death. The first challenge, therefore, is to determine the narrative unit. The second challenge is to formulate a single theme for a narrative that contains so many subthemes, including Joseph's thematic summary, "Even though you intended to do harm to me, God intended it for good, in order to preserve a numerous people, as he is doing today" (50:20). A third challenge is to decide on an appropriate Scripture reading in the worship service for this lengthy narrative.

Text and Context

One could preach separate sermons on sections of this lengthy narrative: for example, Jacob blessing Joseph's sons (48:1-22), Jacob blessing his own sons (49:1-28), Jacob's death in Egypt and burial in Canaan (49:29–50:14), Joseph reassuring his brothers of his forgiveness with the reminder that God has turned their evil intentions to good results (50:15-21), and Joseph's final request that his bones be buried in Canaan and his death (50:22-26). Our challenge, however, is to preach a single sermon on the entire narrative. Gordon Wenham rightly considers Genesis 48:1 to 50:26 to be a single literary unit: "The opening of a new section in 48:1 is signaled by 'After these things,' an important structural marker throughout Genesis . . . , and the close in 50:26 is obvious."[1]

For Scripture reading in the worship service, this narrative is too long and

1. Wenham, *Genesis 16–50*, 459.

diverse. I suggest, therefore, that the Scripture reading begin with the narrative conflict: Jacob's demand that he be buried in the Promised Land (49:29-32). This opening naturally extends to his burial in Canaan (50:1-14). We can further include in the reading the fear of Joseph's brothers after Jacob's death (50:15-21), and continue to the final scene of Joseph's death (50:22-26), which echoes Jacob's desire to be buried in the Promised Land. The Scripture reading, then, would be Genesis 49:29–50:26.

As to the context, "throughout these closing chapters there are many . . . references to earlier episodes in the book."[2] The most important of these references is Abraham buying the field and cave of Machpelah as a burying place for his wife Sarah (23). Later Abraham is buried there (25:9-10) as well as Isaac (35:29), Rebekah and Leah (49:31). In the more immediate context, Jacob has moved his family to Egypt to be with Joseph and has settled in Goshen. The narrator prepares us for the final narrative in the *tôlĕdôt* of Jacob by relating:

> Jacob lived in the land of Egypt seventeen years; so the days of Jacob, the years of his life, were one hundred forty-seven years. When the time of Israel's death drew near, he called his son Joseph and said to him, "If I have found favor with you, put your hand under my thigh and promise to deal loyally and truly with me. Do not bury me in Egypt. When I lie down with my ancestors, carry me out of Egypt and bury me in their burial place." He answered, "I will do as you have said." And he said, "Swear to me"; and he swore to him. Then Israel bowed himself on the head of his bed (47:28-31).

Literary Features

The narrator passes by the seventeen years Jacob lived in Egypt in order to deal at length with Jacob's final words: blessing Joseph's sons (48:1-22) and blessing his own sons (49:1-28). He then slows the pace detailing Jacob's charge to his sons that he be buried in the Promised Land (49:29-32). He records Jacob' death in only one verse but relates the reaction to his death in great detail: Joseph weeps; physicians embalm Jacob for forty days; Egyptians weep for seventy days; Joseph addresses the household of Pharaoh, requesting Pharaoh's permission to "go up" to bury Jacob in the land of Canaan; Pharaoh responds with, "Go up, and bury your father"; Joseph "goes up" to bury his father; "With him went up. . . . a very great company" (50:7-9); near the Jordan they mourn another seven days; even the Canaanite inhabitants take notice and exclaim, "This is a grievous mourning on the part of the Egyptians,"[3] and name the place

2. Ibid., 461. See there for numerous references.

3. "For Hebrew readers the recognition of Jacob/Israel by their archenemies, the Egyptians

Abel-mizraim; the sons carry him to the land of Canaan and bury him "in the cave of the field at Machpelah, the field near Mamre, which Abraham bought as a burial site from Ephron the Hittite" (50:1-13). It is a funeral fit for a king.

The narrator deals more briefly but similarly with Joseph, passing by "the fifty-four years by which Joseph outlived his father,"[4] in order to highlight Joseph's prediction to his brothers, "God will surely come to you, and bring you up out of this land to the land that he swore to Abraham, to Isaac, and to Jacob" (50:24). Like Jacob, Joseph demands to be buried in the Promised Land. He makes the Israelites swear, "When God comes to you, you shall carry up my bones from here" (50:25). But unlike Jacob, Joseph does not receive a royal funeral: Joseph dies, is embalmed, and is "placed in a coffin in Egypt" (50:26). For Joseph there is no closure; he will wait many years for his funeral in Canaan (see Exod 13:19; Josh 24:32).

The narrator sketches Jacob's character with the extended monologues. This is "Jacob's finest hour. On his deathbed — a scene extending from 47:28 to 49:32 — Jacob has assumed total and dynamic leadership of the family. Even Joseph bows down to him."[5]

In terms of repetition, it is striking that the narrator relates in short order that both Jacob and Joseph demand to be buried in the Promised Land. Further, "that Jacob should be buried in the patriarchal tomb in Canaan [is] mentioned repeatedly (48:7, 21-22; 49:29-32; 50:5-14, cf. 25)."[6] Moreover, "the root *qbr* is a key word, repeated fourteen times (11 × 'to bury,' 49:29, 31 [3×]; 50:5 [2×]; 50:6, 7, 13, 14 [2×]; and 3 × 'grave,' 49:30; 50:5, 13). The other key term of this scene about the death of the leading patriarch and his longing for the land of his ancestors is 'father,' repeated fifteen times (49:29; 50:1, 2, 5 [2×], 6, 7, 8, 10, 14 [2×], 15, 16, 17, 22)."[7] Although the narrator repeats the word "to bury" many times, "it is the place of burial that furnishes the author's message. . . . As the family 'possession' (*'ăḥuzzâ,* 23:4, 9, 20), the burial plot represented the land as the 'everlasting possession' (*la'ăḥuzzat 'ôlām,* 17:8) promised to Abraham and his descendants. That possession was claimed by Jacob symbolically by his entombment at the 'burial place' ['burial site'] (*la'ăḥuzzat qeber,* 49:30; 50:13) of his forefathers."[8] Finally, "To 'go up' *('ālâ)* is one of the key terms in this chapter (cf. vv 6, 7, 9, 14, 24-25) and very often refers to the exodus from Egypt (e.g., Exod 1:10)."[9]

---

and Canaanites, may well have portrayed the future succession of the Israelites." Mathews, *Genesis 11:27–50:26,* 920.

4. Sarna, *Understanding Genesis,* 226.

5. Waltke, *Genesis,* 617.

6. Wenham, *Genesis 16–50,* 460.

7. Waltke, *Genesis,* 618.

8. Mathews, *Genesis 11:27–50:26,* 911.

9. Wenham, *Genesis 16–50,* 488.

The narrative can be divided into seven scenes:[10]

Scene 1: Jacob blesses Ephraim and Manasseh (48:1-22)
Scene 2: Jacob blesses his sons and dies (49:1–50:1)
Scene 3: Jacob is embalmed and mourned (50:2-3)
Scene 4: Pharaoh grants permission for Jacob's burial in Canaan (50:4-6)
Scene 5: Jacob is buried in the ancestral grave (50:7-14)
Scene 6: Joseph reassures his brothers (50:15-21)
Scene 7: Joseph's last deeds and words (50:22-26)

The Plot Line

The setting is a report Joseph receives that his father is ill (48:1). Preliminary incidents consist of Jacob blessing Joseph's sons (48:2-22) and his own sons (49:1-28). The narrative conflict begins when Jacob demands to be buried in Canaan. Will Pharaoh let the sons of Jacob go up to Canaan to bury their father? Canaan is far away; dangers lie along the way. What is wrong with burial in Egypt? The tension begins to resolve when Pharaoh responds positively, "Go up, and bury your father" (50:6), and is fully resolved when the large burial party returns to Egypt (50:14). The outcome of Jacob's death is fear among the brothers that Joseph might now take revenge on them. This fear is quickly resolved when Joseph assures them, "Do not be afraid. . . . Have no fear" (50:19-21).[11] The narrator concludes his book with a brief reference to Joseph's old age, one hundred ten years, his being blessed with great-grandchildren (50:22-23), and Joseph's prediction to his brothers, "God will surely come to you, and bring you up out of this land to the land that he swore to Abraham, to Isaac, and to Jacob" (50:24). Joseph makes them swear that they will carry his bones along for burial in the Promised Land (50:25). Joseph dies, is embalmed, and "placed in a coffin in Egypt" (50:26). The stage is set for the book of Exodus.

We can sketch the plot line of this narrative as a single plot, as shown on page 459.

Theocentric Interpretation

Jacob begins his conversation with Joseph by reminding him that "God Almighty" appeared to him in Canaan, blessed him, and promised to make him

10. See ibid., 460.

11. Although one could argue that this section (50:15-21) is a new conflict and resolution, it is better to treat it as a "complication" since it occurs after the main plot.

50:4-5	**"Let me go up to Canaan"**	50:5	**Pharaoh: "Go up"**
50:3	Egypt weeps 70 days	50:7	Joseph goes up
50:2-3	Embalm 40 days	50:7-9	With "a very great company"
50:1	Joseph weeps	50:10	7 days mourning
49:33	**Jacob dies**	50:11	Canaanites: "a grievous mourning"
49:32	**Purchased land**		
49:31	Family buried there	50:13a	**Sons carry Jacob to Canaan**
49:30	**In Canaan**	50:13b	**Bury him in cave**
49:29	**"Bury me with ancestors"**	50:14	Return to Egypt

Setting	*Preliminary incidents*	*Occasioning incident*	*Rising tension*	*Resolution*	*Outcome*	*Conclusion*
Gen 48:1 Jacob ill	48:2–49:28 Jacob blesses Joseph's sons, his own sons	49:29 **Jacob charges his sons**			50:15-21 Fear of Joseph "Have no fear"	50:22-26 Joseph 110 **"God will bring you up"** **"Carry up my bones"** Joseph dies In coffin in Egypt

fruitful and give the land of Canaan to his offspring (48:3-4). When Jacob meets the sons "God has given" (48:9) Joseph in Egypt, Jacob says to Joseph, "I did not expect to see your face; and here God has let me see your children also" (48:11). In blessing the boys, Jacob declares,

> "The God before whom my ancestors Abraham and Isaac walked,
> the God who has been my shepherd all my life to this day,
> the angel who has redeemed me from all harm,
> bless the boys."
>
> (48:15-16)

Jacob comforts Joseph, "I am about to die, but God will be with you and will bring you again to the land of your ancestors" (48:21). In the midst of blessing his sons, Jacob exclaims, "I wait for your salvation, O Lord" (49:18). In blessing Joseph, Jacob says,

> "By the hands of the Mighty One of Jacob,
> by the name of the Shepherd, the Rock of Israel,
> by the God of your father, who will help you,
> by the Almighty who will bless you with blessings of heaven above."
>
> (49:24-25)

Jacob's demand that he be buried in the Promised Land in the family burial plot speaks of his faith that the covenant God will be faithful to his promise of giving them the land of Canaan. Joseph also witnesses to this faith when he tells his brothers, "God will surely come to you, and bring you up out of this land to the land that he swore to Abraham, to Isaac, and to Jacob." Joseph makes his brothers swear, "When God comes to you, you shall carry up my bones from here" (50:24-25). Finally, Joseph sums up the theocentric thrust of the whole Joseph story in the memorable words, "Even though you intended to do harm to me, God intended it for good, in order to preserve a numerous people, as he is doing today" (50:22).

Textual Theme and Goal

Because of the various emphases in this diverse narrative, it is difficult to formulate a single theme that covers the whole. Joseph's key statement to his brothers, "Even though you intended to do harm to me, God intended it for good" (50:20), is a thematic statement of the whole Joseph story rather than of this particular narrative, though, of course, it should still be taken into account in formulating the theme of this narrative

It is clear that the narrative focuses primarily on burial in the Promised Land: in great detail the narrator sketches Jacob's demand for burial in the Promised Land, and in glowing terms he describes his actual burial there. It is a funeral fit for a king. Moreover, the narrative concludes with a similar demand by Joseph: burial in the Promised Land when God will "bring you up out of this land to the land that he swore to Abraham, to Isaac, and to Jacob" (50:24). Buried in a cave in Canaan, Jacob awaits the fulfillment of God's promise of land; lying in a coffin in Egypt, Joseph awaits the fulfillment of God's promise. Their desire to be buried in the Promised Land testifies to the fact that they die in hope that God will fulfill his covenant promise of land.

What message would Israel receive from hearing this combined testimony of Jacob and Joseph? We can formulate the textual theme of this passage somewhat as follows: *Because God is sovereign and faithful (50:20), his people can die in hope that he will fulfill his promise of land.*

If Israel first heard this message as they were on the way to Canaan, carrying along the bones of Joseph (Exod 13:19), the author's goal would probably have been to encourage Israel to trust God to fulfill his promise of land. If Israel heard this message later when they lived in the land of Canaan, the author's goal would have been to encourage Israel to trust that God will fulfill *all* his promises. If Israel heard this message in exile,[12] the author's goal would likely

12. "The use of the word 'visit' in verses 24-25 (in both cases used with an absolute infinitive for emphasis) is the same word of Jeremiah to the exiles ['Thus says the LORD: Only when Babylon's seventy years are completed will I visit you, and I will fulfill to you my promise and bring you back to this place'] (Jer 29:10). The visit of God is an *exile-ending intrusion.* That is the hope of sixth-century exiles in Babylon." Brueggemann, *Genesis,* 379.

have been *to comfort*[13] *Israel with the message that God is sovereign and faithful and can be trusted to fulfill his promise of land.*

Ways to Preach Christ

How can we carry forward to Jesus in the New Testament the theme, "Because God is sovereign and faithful, his people can die in hope that he will fulfill his promise of land"? We shall check out the seven ways to Christ:

Redemptive-Historical Progression

God gave the promise of the land of Canaan first to Abraham (12:1, 7), then to Isaac, then to Jacob, and finally to Israel. All three patriarchs were buried in their own possession (the cave) in the Promised Land and died in the hope of the complete fulfillment of God's promise. Under Joshua, Israel did indeed inherit the Promised Land (Josh 21:43-45), but it was a precarious possession. In New Testament times, Jesus expanded God's promise of land from the land of Canaan to the whole earth. Jesus proclaimed, "Blessed are the meek, for they will inherit *the earth*" (Matt 5:5). Jesus promised, "In my Father's house there are many dwelling places. . . . I go to prepare a place for you" (John 14:2). Today God's people still die in hope because God has promised them "a new earth. . . . [where] death will be no more; mourning and crying and pain will be no more" (Rev 21:1-4).

Promise-Fulfillment

God promised Abraham, Isaac, and Jacob the land of Canaan. This promise received an initial fulfillment when God enabled Abraham to buy a "burial site" in the Promised Land. The patriarchs died and were buried in their own possession in the land. They died with the hope that God would one day completely fulfill his promise of land. God fulfilled his promise when, under Joshua, he gave Israel the land. But God's promise was open to further expansion and fulfillment. Already in the Old Testament, God's promise of land begins to stretch

13. Sailhamer, *Genesis*, 283, points out the similar words used in the narrator's description of Joseph comforting his brothers and Isaiah comforting the exiles. "He comforted them [*wayĕnaḥēm 'ôtām;* NIV, 'reassured'] and spoke kindly to them [*wayĕdabbēr ʿal-libbām*]" (50:21) and Isa 40:1-2: "comfort [*naḥămû*], comfort [*naḥămû*] my people, says your God. Speak tenderly [*dabbĕrû ʿal-lēb*] to Jerusalem."

beyond the land of Canaan. Israel prayed for its king, "May he have dominion from sea to sea and from the River to the *ends of the earth*" (Ps 72:9; cf. Isa 55:5; Zech 9:10). Jesus confirms this expansion when he proclaims, "Blessed are the meek, for they will inherit *the earth*" (Matt 5:5). Accordingly, Paul writes that Abraham received the promise "that he would inherit *the world*" (Rom 4:13). And Peter encourages the early Christians, "In accordance with his [God's] promise, we wait for new heavens and a new earth, where righteousness is at home" (2 Pet 3:13). Today God's people still die and are buried in the earth. But they die with the hope that through Christ's atoning work they will inherit the new creation. God's ancient promise of land is still awaiting complete fulfillment.

Typology

In previous narratives we have seen that Joseph in his humiliation and exaltation is a type of Christ. This narrative also reveals parallels between Joseph and Christ: as Joseph forgave his brothers' crime, so Jesus, the Judge (John 5:22-29), readily forgives his brothers and sisters' sins. "There is therefore now no condemnation for those who are in Christ Jesus" (Rom 8:1). Also, as Joseph promised to provide for his brothers and their "little ones" (50:21), so Jesus, the good Shepherd, will provide for his brothers, sisters, and their little ones. But since this type is not in line with the theme, it is unlikely that we can use it in the sermon.

Analogy

As God teaches Israel to hope in the fulfillment of God's promise of land, so Jesus teaches us to hope in the fulfillment of God's promise of a new creation. Jesus proclaimed, "When the Son of Man comes in his glory, and all the angels with him, then he will sit on the throne of his glory. . . . Then the king will say to those at his right hand, 'Come, you that are blessed by my Father, inherit the kingdom prepared for you from the foundation of the world'" (Matt 25:31, 34). To his disciples Jesus said, "In my Father's house there are many dwelling places. If it were not so, would I have told you that I go to prepare a place for you?" (John 14:2). And at the Last Supper, Jesus stated, "I tell you, I will never drink of this fruit of the vine until that day when I drink it new with you in my Father's kingdom" (Matt 26:29).

Longitudinal Themes

We can trace through the Scriptures the theme of God's people's hope in God fulfilling his promise of land. The background would be Paradise lost (Gen 3) and humanity's search to recover it (Gen 11). The hope becomes concrete for Abraham when God promises him the land ("watered everywhere like the garden of the LORD," 13:10). The hope of land passes on to Isaac, to Jacob, to Joseph, to Israel in Egypt, and later to Israel in exile. In the New Testament the hope shifts from the land of Canaan to "a new heaven and a new earth" (2 Pet 3:13; Rev 21:1). Jesus promises the criminal on the cross, "Truly I tell you, today you will be with me in Paradise" (Luke 23:43). And the ascended Lord promises, "To everyone who conquers, I will give permission to eat from the tree of life that is in the paradise of God" (Rev 2:7). Paradise will be restored on earth (Rev 22:1-5), with God dwelling among his people (Rev 21:3).

New Testament References

In addition to the passages mentioned above, there are two New Testament passages that refer directly to this narrative. In his speech to the Council, Stephen recalls that the bodies of Jacob and Joseph "were brought back to Shechem[14] and laid in the tomb that Abraham had bought" (Acts 7:16). More closely related to this narrative's theme is Hebrews 11, which emphasizes the faith of Jacob and Joseph: "By faith Jacob, when dying, blessed each of the sons of Joseph, 'bowing in worship over the top of his staff.'[15] By faith Joseph, at the end of his life, made mention of the exodus of the Israelites and gave instructions about his burial" (Heb 11:21-22).

Contrast

Although the New Testament expands the land promise from the land of Canaan to "a new heaven and a new earth" (Matt 25:34; 2 Pet 3:13; Rev 21:1-4), there is no contrast between the message of our text and that of the New Testament.

Sermon Theme and Goal

We formulated the textual theme as, "Because God is sovereign and faithful, his people can die in hope that he will fulfill his promise of land." The New Testa-

14. Stephen blends Jacob's burial near Hebron and Joseph's burial in Shechem (Josh 24:32).
15. This quotation is based on the Septuagint translation of Genesis 47:31.

ment, we have seen, broadens the notion of land to the new creation, and still looks forward to the complete fulfillment of God's promise. Since the term "land" can cover both the land of Canaan and the entire earth, the sermon theme can be the same as the textual theme: *Because God is sovereign and faithful, his people can die in hope that he will fulfill his promise of land.*

The author's likely goal in sending this message to Israel was "to comfort Israel with the message that God is sovereign and faithful and can be trusted to fulfill his promise of land." Since the church today lives under the same arc of tension between God's promise of land and its fulfillment, we can maintain the same goal for the church: *to comfort God's people with the message that God is sovereign and faithful and can be trusted to fulfill his promise of land.* With this goal the congregational need for hearing this sermon would be the current lack of longing for the coming kingdom of God.

Sermon Exposition

Jacob is on his deathbed. At the end of Genesis 47 we read, "When the time of Israel's death drew near, he called his son Joseph and said to him. . . . '*Do not bury me in Egypt.* When I lie down with my ancestors, carry me out of Egypt and bury me in their burial place'" (47:29-30). Jacob is ill and about to die. With his remaining strength he lifts himself up and sits on the side of his bed. Joseph brings his two sons to Jacob, and Jacob blesses Ephraim and Manasseh. Then Jacob calls his own sons and blesses each in turn. Not the oldest son, but Judah, the younger son of Leah, receives the greatest blessing. Jacob intones, "The scepter shall not depart from Judah, nor the ruler's staff from between his feet" (49:10). From Judah's line will come the great king David and ultimately the King of kings, Jesus Christ.

After blessing all his sons, Jacob has one final request. It is more than a request; it is a demand, a command.[16] With his last bit of strength he charges them, 49:29-33,

> "I am about to be gathered to my people. Bury me with my ancestors — in the cave in the field of Ephron the Hittite, in the cave in the field at Machpelah, near Mamre, in the land of Canaan, in the field that Abraham bought from Ephron the Hittite as a burial site. There Abraham and his wife Sarah were buried; there Isaac and his wife Rebekah were buried; and there I buried Leah — the field and the cave that is in it were purchased from the Hittites."

16. "The Hebrew stem *ṣ-v-h,* 'to command' (cf. v 33) is used in the sense of laying a charge on someone in preparation for death." Sarna, *Genesis,* 346.

[The narrator adds,] When Jacob ended his charge to his sons, he drew up his feet into the bed, breathed his last, and was gathered to his people.[17]

Jacob is dead. But his final command lives on. Jacob's instructions are so detailed that his sons cannot possibly miss the burial plot: "Bury me with my ancestors — in the cave in the field of Ephron the Hittite, in the cave in the field at Machpelah, near Mamre, in the land of Canaan, in the field that Abraham bought from Ephron the Hittite as a burial site." The precision of a real estate contract emphasizes that this little piece of the Promised Land belongs legally to Jacob and his offspring.[18] Jacob's final command testifies to his faith in the covenant-keeping God. Hebrews 11: 21 says, "By *faith* Jacob, when dying, blessed each of the sons of Joseph." But also his final instructions for burial in the Promised Land testify to his faith. God had promised the land of Canaan to his grandfather Abraham, to his father Isaac, and to him and his descendants. Although God is taking his time, Jacob is convinced that God will one day fulfill his promise.[19] He wants to be part of that future fulfillment. "It is as though the dying Jacob wishes to go ahead and to be on hand in the land when it is fully given."[20] He wishes to share in the destiny of God's people.[21]

But Jacob's command creates a dilemma for his sons. Canaan is far away. The journey there will be difficult and dangerous. Why not bury Jacob in Egypt where they live? That way they won't offend the great Pharaoh, who might frown upon burial in a foreign land. In Egypt they can also visit his burial site. Why go through all the trouble of burying him in Canaan? But Jacob was adamant about being buried in the Promised Land. First he made Joseph swear to him that he would bury him not in Egypt but in Canaan. Then with his very last words he commanded all his sons, "Bury me with my ancestors — . . . in the land of Canaan." All his sons heard his instruction. All understood its signifi-

17. "The Bible appears to use different terms for three stages of the death process: one dies (here 'took his last breath'), one is gathered to one's kin, and lastly one is buried. Thus 'to be gathered to one's kin' takes place after dying but before burial, and carries with it the idea of 'being reunited with one's ancestors.'" Hamilton, *Genesis 18–50,* 689.

18. "The phraseology here, as in other passages about the patriarchal tomb, is detailed and precise, emphasizing Israel's legal title to the burial ground (cf. 23:17-20; 25:9-10; 50:13). Wenham, *Genesis 16–50,* 487.

19. "There is certitude that the promise is alive and at work. It is dependent upon and limited to no human or historical agent, because it is of God himself. Both the binding of the heirs (48) and the burial provision (49:28-33) are grounded in the promise. The heirs are to trust that promise. The burial is to anticipate it." Brueggemann, *Genesis,* 369.

20. Ibid., 367.

21. "Ancient Israel considered the ancestors and the nation as connected closely with each other, in fact, it considered them both as a great living organism with a common destiny." Von Rad, *Genesis,* 402.

cance: Not Egypt but Canaan is our home; Canaan is the land God promised to give us!

Joseph is heartbroken at his father's death. He throws himself "on his father's face," weeps over him, and kisses him (50:1). The strong bond between father and son, which survived years of separation, is now broken by Jacob's death. But soon the grieving Joseph must get to work. In the heat in Egypt a corpse would quickly decompose. And Jacob's final demand was to be buried in far-off Canaan. So Joseph commands "the physicians in his service to embalm his father" (50:2). Embalming was time-consuming; it took forty days. Meanwhile, verse 3, the Egyptians weep for Jacob "seventy days."[22] Since it was customary in Egypt to mourn the death of a Pharaoh for seventy-two days, Jacob is "mourned as a king."[23]

Despite the honor heaped on his father, Joseph faces a problem. How will he get Pharaoh's permission to bury Jacob not in Egypt but in Canaan? Egypt has been very good to Jacob and his family. Egypt welcomed the hungry nomads with plenty of food and the best of the land. Will Pharaoh not be offended by a request for burial in Canaan? Joseph handles the situation tactfully. He does not go directly to Pharaoh but asks the household of Pharaoh, that is, "other high officials at court,"[24] to intercede for him.[25] We read in verses 4 and 5, "When the days of weeping for him were past, Joseph addressed the household of Pharaoh, 'If now I have found favor with you, please speak to Pharaoh as follows: My father made me swear an oath; he said, "I am about to die. In the tomb that I hewed out for myself in the land of Canaan, there you shall bury me." Now therefore let me go up, so that I may bury my father; then I will return.'"

Notice how diplomatically Joseph puts his request. He omits Jacob's negative commands, "Do not bury me in Egypt. . . . Carry me out of Egypt" (47:29, 30). Those words might offend Pharaoh. Joseph simply quotes his father as saying, "In the tomb that I hewed out for myself in the land of Canaan, there you shall bury me."[26] And Joseph ends his request by promising to return to

22. "Jewish exegetes have by and large understood that forty days were required for embalming, followed by another thirty days of mourning. The time of mourning would be in accordance with the period of public grief observed for Aaron (Num 20:29) and Moses (Deut 34:8). Jewish law to the present time requires a thirty-day mourning period after burial . . . for close relatives, during which various restrictions are observed." Sarna, *Genesis,* 347-48.

23. Von Rad, *Genesis,* 430, referring to a report by Diodorus.

24. Westermann, *Genesis 37–50,* 199.

25. Several commentators suggest that Joseph does not approach Pharaoh directly "because of the recent contact with the corpse of his father." Hamilton, *Genesis 18–50,* 693. Cf. Herbert, *Genesis 12–50,* 159.

26. "By deleting the part of Jacob's request that has ancestral, religious aspects and replacing it with a reference to Jacob's own prepared gravesite in another country, Joseph may have been trying to make his request to Pharaoh more appealing, given the emphasis an Egyptian

Egypt: "Now therefore let me go up, so that I may bury my father; then I will return."

Notice that Joseph asks Pharaoh, "Now therefore *let me go up*." Gordon Wenham observes that "To 'go up' *(ʿālâ)* is one of the key terms in this chapter . . . and very often refers to the exodus from Egypt. . . . Jacob's insistence on being buried in Canaan is a statement of where Israel really belongs. His burial procession from Egypt to Canaan is doubtless seen as a pledge or acted prophecy of the nation's future move (cf. 50:24-25 with Exod 13:19)."[27]

Pharaoh readily approves Joseph's request. He says, "*Go up*, and bury your father, as he made you swear to do." Verses 7 to 9 describe the great funeral procession: "So Joseph *went up* to bury his father. With him *went up* all the servants of Pharaoh, the elders of his household, and all the elders of the land of Egypt, as well as all the household of Joseph, his brothers, and his father's household. Only their children, their flocks, and their herds were left in the land of Goshen. Both chariots and charioteers *went up* with him. It was a very great company." Even chariots and charioteers. It does sound like the exodus, doesn't it? Only then the chariots and charioteers will be *chasing* the Israelites.

Even Canaanites play a part in this funeral procession. We read in verses 10 and 11, "When they came to the threshing floor of Atad, which is beyond the Jordan, they held there a *very great* and sorrowful lamentation; and he observed a time of mourning for his father seven days.[28] When the Canaanite inhabitants of the land saw the mourning on the threshing floor of Atad, they said, 'This is a grievous mourning on the part of the Egyptians.' Therefore the place was named Abel-mizraim; it is beyond the Jordan."[29]

Verses 12 to 14 conclude, "Thus his sons did for him as he had instructed them. They carried him to the land of Canaan[30] and buried him in the cave of

---

would place on his own burial place, stocking it with the necessary requirements for the good life in the hereafter." Hamilton, *Genesis 18–50*, 693.

27. Wenham, *Genesis 16–50*, 488.

28. "Seven days, a full cycle of days, is the usual period of time to express great grief in Israel and in the ancient Near East (cf. 1 Sam 31:13; Job 2:13; Ezek 3:15)." Waltke, *Genesis*, 621.

29. "The site is unknown, but its position implies a detour round the Dead Sea to approach Hebron from the north-east instead of the south-west. Presumably there was political unrest at some point, which the cavalcade's arrival would have been in danger of aggravating. At the Exodus the direct route would again be impracticable (Exod 13:17). But the mention of *the Canaanites* (11) indicates that the mourning took place on the west side of the Jordan: 'near' the river, not *beyond* it. *I.e.*, the party had now crossed into Canaan; it was a suitable moment for the pause." Kidner, *Genesis*, 223. By contrast, Sarna, *Genesis*, 348, suggests that "the place most probably lies along the coastal road (the Via Maris), since this would be the shortest route for anyone traveling from Egypt to Canaan, as Exodus 13:7 notes."

30. "Apparently, the main cortege was left at Abel-Misraim, and only Jacob's sons carried his body into Canaan to bury him at the ancestral tomb at Machpela." Wenham, *Genesis 16–50*, 489.

the field at Machpelah, the field near Mamre, which Abraham bought as a burial site from Ephron the Hittite. After he had buried his father, Joseph returned to Egypt with his brothers and all who had gone up with him to bury his father." Jacob's burial in the cave "renewed the family's claim to the cave and also to the land. It was a pledge that they would one day return to occupy what had in fact been bestowed on Abraham and Sarah, Isaac and Rebekah."[31] Moreover, Jacob's burial in the Promised Land testified to Jacob's and Israel's faith that their covenant God would indeed fulfill his promise of giving them the land. Jacob died in hope and was buried in the Promised Land in hope — hope that God would fulfill his promise of a homeland for his people.

One may well ask, Why does the narrator go into so much detail describing the funeral procession of Jacob? When Abraham died, the narrator simply wrote that "his sons Isaac and Ishmael buried him in the cave of Machpelah, in the field of Ephron son of Zoar the Hittite, east of Mamre, the field that Abraham purchased from the Hittites" (25:9-10). When Isaac died, the funeral announcement was even briefer: "his sons Esau and Jacob buried him" (35:29). By contrast, the narrator exerts himself to show the immense size of Jacob's funeral procession: "*all*[32] the servants of Pharaoh, the elders of his household, and *all* the elders of the land of Egypt, as well as *all* the household of Joseph, his brothers, and his father's household. . . . Both chariots and charioteers went up with him. It was a *very great* company" (50:7-9).

This portrayal is more than a description of a royal funeral. John Sailhamer suggests that "the writer's concern focuses on God's faithfulness to his promise of the land and the hope of God's people in the eventual return to the land. In the later prophetic literature, a recurring image of the fulfillment of the promise to return to the land pictures Israel returning to the land accompanied by many from among the nations. The prophets of Israel saw the return as a time when 'all the nations [*kol haggôyim*] will stream to Jerusalem' . . . (Isa 2:2-3). . . .[33] Jacob, in his final return to the Land of Promise, was accompanied by a great congregation of the officials and elders of the land of Egypt. With him was also the mighty army of the Egyptians. Thus the story of Jacob's burial in the land foreshadows the time when God 'will bring Jacob back from captivity and will have compassion on all the people of Israel' (Ezek 39:25)."[34]

In the New Testament, Jesus takes this image one step further. When Jesus hears the Roman centurion's confession of Jesus' power, he is amazed. This Gentile centurion says to Jesus, "Lord, I am not worthy to have you come under

31. Baldwin, *The Message of Genesis 12–50*, 214.

32. "The largeness of the procession is reinforced by the threefold use of *kol* in vv 7 and 8." Hamilton, *Genesis 18–50*, 696.

33. See also Isa 66:20 and Zech 8:23. Cf. Ps 87.

34. Sailhamer, *Genesis*, 282.

my roof; but only speak the word [from a distance], and my servant will be healed." At this, Jesus exclaims, "Truly I tell you, in no one in Israel have I found such faith. I tell you, *many will come from east and west* and will eat with Abraham and Isaac and Jacob in the kingdom of heaven" (Matt 8:8-11). Jacob's large funeral procession with Egyptian officials and charioteers heading for the Promised Land foreshadows the last day when Jesus returns on the clouds of heaven. Then "many will come from east and west and will eat with Abraham and Isaac and Jacob in the kingdom of heaven." At last God will completely fill up his promise of land — a peaceful home for his people; a place where "they will hunger no more, and thirst no more" (Rev 7:16). Paradise will return to earth (Rev 22:1-5). People from all tribes and nations will eat with Abraham, Isaac, Jacob, and the children of Israel in the kingdom of God (Rev 7:4-9).

But Jacob's sons don't see the significance of his great funeral procession heading for the Promised Land. Now that Jacob is dead, they fear that Joseph may still want to get even with them. Verse 15, "Realizing that their father was dead, Joseph's brothers said, 'What if Joseph still bears a grudge against us and pays us back in full for all the wrong that we did to him?'" Perhaps they recall the story of Esau intending to wait until his father Isaac died before killing his brother Jacob. What if Joseph still bears a grudge?[35] With their father dead, Joseph can declare open season on his brothers.

Verse 16, "So they approached Joseph, saying, 'Your father gave this instruction before he died, "Say to Joseph: I beg you, forgive the crime of your brothers and the wrong they did in harming you." Now therefore please forgive the crime of the servants of the God of your father.' Joseph wept when they spoke to him."

Why does Joseph weep when his brothers beg him for forgiveness? Does he weep in frustration at their continuous mistrust of him?[36] Or does he weep because they try to deceive[37] him with the memory of their father? They say, "Your *father* gave this instruction before he died. . . ." We don't read anywhere

35. "Cf. 27:41 ["Now Esau hated (bear a grudge) Jacob . . . , and Esau said to himself, 'The days of mourning for my father are approaching; then I will kill my brother Jacob."], where the same term, 'bear a grudge,' is used." Wenham, *Genesis 16–50,* 489.

36. "He probably weeps because, after seventeen years of kindness to them that reinforced his original forgiveness of them (45:7-8), they still misunderstand his goodness and think that he will at last take his revenge." Waltke, *Genesis,* 622.

37. "This is probably a fabrication. The narrator connects their claim not to historical fact but to their fears (50:19)." Ibid., 622. Cf. Satterthwaite, "Narrative Criticism," 126, "In 50:16-17, Joseph's brothers, fearing revenge from him, attribute to Jacob words that he is never recorded as having said, but which are at points similar to the words in which they themselves express their fear in v 15 (v 15, 'all the wrongs we did to him'; v 17, 'the wrongs they committed in treating you so badly'). The narrator thereby suggests that they have invented the words they put into the dead Jacob's mouth."

that Jacob gave this instruction. Moreover, it seems very unlikely that Jacob would have said this to his sons. If Jacob had been concerned about any hostility breaking out among his sons after his death, he could have gone straight to Joseph and urged him to forgive his brothers. But the brothers are scared of Joseph. They'll do anything to appease him. According to verse 18, they fall down before him and say, "We are here as your slaves." Do they realize that they are literally fulfilling Joseph's dream that his brothers will bow down to him (37:6-7)? "Previous prostrations were done when they did not know Joseph's identity (42:6, 36; 43:28; 44:14). They now know who he is, and they know that this action fulfills to the letter the dream that predicted their subservience."[38]

Joseph answers them, verse 19, "Do not be afraid! Am I in the place of God?[39] Even though you intended to do harm to me, God intended it for good, in order to preserve a numerous people, as he is doing today. So have no fear; I myself will provide for you and your little ones." Twice Joseph urges them not to be afraid, to have no fear. He grounds this assurance in the beneficial outcome of God's providence. He says, "Even though you intended to do harm to me, God intended it for good, in order to preserve a numerous people." In his providence, God used their evil intentions to save numerous people: the Egyptians, the Israelites, and others. God is sovereign. Though he gives human beings freedom to act, God is in ultimate control of the outcome. And God's plan is good. Because God is sovereign and faithful to his plan, Israel can entrust herself to his good care.

The book of Genesis ends with a final note about Joseph. We read in verse 22 that "Joseph remained in Egypt, he and his father's household; and Joseph lived one hundred ten years."[40] God richly blesses him: Joseph even sees his grandchildren and great-grandchildren.[41] Yet for Joseph also there comes a time to die.

38. Turner, *Genesis*, 206.

39. "This is how they seem to regard him (cf. 50:17-18). The rhetorical question expects a negative answer (cf. 30:2). He is only God's instrument, not his surrogate." Waltke, *Genesis*, 623.

40. "'One hundred and ten years' was regarded as the ideal life span in Egypt." Wenham, *Genesis 16–50*, 490. Others, observing intricate numerical patterns in the ages of the patriarchs, regard the numbers as symbolic:

Abraham:	$175 = 7 \times 5^2$
Isaac:	$180 = 5 \times 6^2$
Jacob:	$147 = 3 \times 7^2$
Joseph:	$110 = 1 \times 5^2 + 6^2 + 7^2$

"That is, Joseph is the successor in the pattern 7-5-3-1, and the sum of his predecessors ($5^2 + 6^2 + 7^2$)." Hamilton, *Genesis 18–50*, 709.

41. "To live to a ripe old age and to see your grandchildren or even great-grandchildren was regarded as a mark of God's favor (Job 42:16)." Wenham, *Genesis 16–50*, 491.

When the time comes, verse 24, Joseph says to his brothers, "I am about to die; but God will surely come[42] to you, and bring you up out of this land to the land that he swore to Abraham, to Isaac, and to Jacob." This is the first time Joseph speaks of God's promise of the land. Since these are also Joseph's last words, they gain in significance. Joseph's words underscore the message of Genesis that Israel belongs not in Egypt but in Canaan. Canaan is the land of God's promise. But while Israel grows into a nation in the safety of isolation in Goshen, it will have to bide God's time. It should not lose heart if God's promise is long in coming to fulfillment. Israel should continue to trust the sovereign God, who will not fail to fulfill his promise of the land of Canaan. "God will surely come to you," Joseph says, "to bring you up out of this land to the land that he swore to Abraham, to Isaac, and to Jacob."

Joseph is so sure that God will come to them that he makes the Israelites swear an oath, verse 25, "When God comes to you, you shall carry up my bones from here." Like his father Jacob, Joseph wishes to be buried in the Promised Land. But Joseph is prepared to wait in Egypt with his brothers and sisters. Hebrews 11:22 states, "By *faith* Joseph, at the end of his life, made mention of the exodus of the Israelites and gave instructions about his burial." Joseph acts in faith. He does not see the outcome. Hebrews 11 says that "Faith is the assurance of things hoped for, the conviction of things *not* seen" (Heb 11:1). Joseph does not see the exodus from Egypt; he does not see Israel receive possession of the Promised Land; but he firmly believes that it will happen some day. And he wishes to be part of God's great deliverance of his people.[43] So he commands the Israelites, "When God comes to you, you shall carry up my bones from here."

Genesis ends with a haunting picture. Verse 26, "Joseph died, being one hundred ten years old; he was embalmed and placed in a coffin[44] in Egypt." The story of Genesis that began with God creating a beautiful Paradise on earth for his creatures ends with Joseph in a coffin in Egypt — waiting, waiting for God to bring his people back to the Promised Land.[45] Will it be Paradise? Joseph will

42. "The verb *pāqad,* 'visit,' signifies divine intervention for the sake of blessing or cursing — both, in the case of the exodus, in which Israel was delivered at the expense of the Egyptians. The word usually carries the connotation that destinies would be changed by the visitation from on high." Ross, *Creation and Blessing,* 716.

43. Joseph's "determination may indicate that he expected to participate personally in the possession of the land that had been promised." Robertson, *The Israel of God,* 23.

44. "Perhaps it is best to understand *'ārôn* as a sarcophagus here (the only time *'ārôn* has this nuance in the OT); the use of the definite article on coffin *(the coffin)* may be a way of specifying that the coffin in which Joseph was placed was similar to a sarcophagus used in Egypt for a high-ranking official." Hamilton, *Genesis 18–50,* 712.

45. "By laying it [the oath] upon his people he gave eloquent testimony to his faith in God's

have to wait a long time, but eventually God does come through for him and the people of Israel. When God finally "comes to" Israel in Egypt to lead them out, we read in the book of Exodus that "Moses took with him the bones of Joseph" (Exod 13:19). The book of Joshua records that "the bones of Joseph, which the Israelites had brought up from Egypt, were buried at Shechem, in the portion of ground that Jacob had bought from the children of Hamor" (Josh 24:32). Joseph, too, is buried in a part of the Promised Land legally owned by his ancestors. In the grave he is still waiting for God to fill completely his promise of land. For ultimately, according to the Bible, God's promise of land means the return of Paradise on earth (Gen 2; Rev 22:1-5).

When Jesus hung on the cross, one of the criminals crucified with him begged him, "Jesus, remember me when you come into your kingdom." And Jesus responded, "Truly I tell you, today you will be with me in Paradise" (Luke 23:43). Jesus died and rose again to restore us to Paradise. Jesus said to his disciples, "In my Father's house there are many dwelling places. If it were not so, would I have told you that I go to prepare a place for you?" (John 14:2). At the Last Supper, Jesus stated, "I tell you, I will never again drink of this fruit of the vine until that day when I drink it new with you in my Father's kingdom" (Matt 26:29).

Today we are much like Joseph and the Israelites — waiting, waiting for God to come to us and fulfill his promise of land — to restore Paradise on earth. Sometimes we give up hope. The world we live in seems too set on its course of violence, warfare, and disasters. It does not seem likely that God will turn things around. It is easy today to lose hope in the coming kingdom of God. Among the early Christians, too, there were people who had lost hope. They scoffed, "Where is the promise of his coming? For ever since our ancestors died, all things continue as they were from the beginning of creation." Peter encourages these Christians, "But do not ignore this one fact, beloved, that with the Lord one day is like a thousand years, and a thousand years are like one day. The Lord is not slow about his promise . . . but is patient with you, not wanting any to perish, but all to come to repentance." Peter concludes, "In accordance with his promise, we wait for new heavens and a new earth, where righteousness is at home" (2 Pet 3:4, 8-9, 13).[46]

We should not give up hope in the coming of "a new earth, where righteousness is at home," and where "death will be no more; [and] mourning and crying and pain will be no more" (Rev 21:4). "Faith is the assurance of things

---

promises, and by leaving his body in their midst he gave them a continual reminder of that gracious promise." Leupold, *Genesis,* II, 1220.

46. Like the book of Genesis, the Bible itself concludes with the note of waiting for God to act. The ascended Lord Jesus promises, "Surely I am coming soon." And his people respond with, "Amen, Come, Lord Jesus!" (Rev 22:20).

hoped for, the conviction of things *not* seen" (Heb 11:1). And God is sovereign and in control of his plan. He can use even evil human plans and turn them to fulfill his good purposes. God is faithful and will fulfill his promises. Let us not give up hope. Our ascended Lord promises, "To everyone who conquers, I will give permission to eat from the tree of life that is in the paradise of God" (Rev 2:7). Because God is sovereign and faithful, his people can die in hope that one day he will completely fulfill his promise of a homeland for his people. One day God will restore Paradise on earth. One day he will make "all things new" (Rev 21:5).

APPENDIX 1

Ten Steps from Text to Sermon

1. **Select the preaching-text.**
   Select the preaching-text with an eye to congregational needs. The text must be a literary unit and contain a vital theme.

2. **Read the text in its literary context.**
   Read and reread the text in its context and jot down initial questions.

3. **Outline the structure of the text.**
   In the Hebrew or Greek text, note the major affirmations, clausal flow, plot line, scenes, or literary structures. Mark major units with headings and verse references.

4. **Interpret the text in its own historical setting.**
   a. Literary interpretation;
   b. Historical interpretation;[1]
   c. Theocentric interpretation.
   Review your results with the help of some good commentaries.

5. **Formulate the text's theme, goal, and need addressed.**
   a. State the textual **theme** in a brief sentence that summarizes the *message* of the text for its original hearers: subject and predicate. What is the text saying?
   b. State the **goal** of the author for his original hearers. What is the text doing? Does the author aim to persuade, to motivate, to urge, to warn, to comfort? Be specific.
   c. State the **need** the author addressed — the question behind the text.

1. In order to avoid repetition, in the essays I combine historical interpretation with determining the author's goal in Step 5b.

6. **Understand the message in the contexts of canon and redemptive history.**
   a. Canonical interpretation: interpret the message in the context of the whole canon;
   b. Redemptive-historical interpretation: understand the message in the context of God's redemptive history from creation to new creation;
   c. Christocentric interpretation: explore the ways of (1) redemptive-historical progression, (2) promise-fulfillment, (3) typology, (4) analogy, (5) longitudinal themes, (6) New Testament references, and (7) contrast.

7. **Formulate the sermon theme, goal, and need addressed.**
   a. Ideally, your **sermon theme** will be the same as your textual theme (Step 5a).
   If Step 6 forces a change, stay as close as possible to the textual theme. Your theme will guide especially the development of the body of the sermon.
   b. Your **goal** must be in harmony with the author's goal (Step 5b) and match the sermon theme. Your goal will guide the style of the sermon as well as the content of its conclusion.
   c. State the **need** you are addressing. This need should be similar to the need addressed by the author. The need will inform the content of your introduction.

8. **Select a suitable sermon form.**
   Select a sermon form that respects the form of the text (didactic or narrative, deductive or inductive) and that achieves the goal of the sermon.

9. **Prepare the sermon outline.**
   If possible, follow the flow of the text (Step 3) in the body of the sermon. Main points, derived from the text, support the theme. The introduction should expose the need. The conclusion should clinch your goal.

10. **Write the sermon in oral style.**
    Say it out loud as you write it. Write in oral style, using short sentences, vivid words, strong nouns and verbs, active voice, present tense, images, and illustrations.

APPENDIX 2

An Expository Sermon Model

A. **Introduction (usually no more than 10 percent of the sermon)**
   1. Normally, begin with an illustration of the **need** addressed (Step 7c).
   2. Connect this illustration to the need of the present hearers.
   3. **Transition**: Show that this need or a similar issue was also the question behind the biblical text.
   4. State the **theme** of the text/sermon (Step 7a).

   For the sake of maintaining suspense, you may postpone disclosing the theme at the beginning (inductive development), but by statement and restatement you must make sure that the hearers catch the point of the sermon.

B. **The Sermon Body**
   1. Expose the **structure of the text.**
      The main points, affirmations, moves, scenes of the text (Step 3) normally become your main points in the sermon.
   2. The **main points** should usually support the theme and be of the same rank.
   3. Follow the **textual sequence** of the points unless there is good reason to change it, such as climactic arrangement (Step 9).
   4. Use simple, **clear transitions** that enable the hearers to sense the structure of and movement in the sermon.
      E.g., "Not only . . . but also. . . ."
      Or, "Let's first see. . . . Now we see secondly. . . ."
      Or, "Let's look at verse 8." "Now please look with me at verse 12."
   5. Use **verse references** before quoting the text so that the hearers can read along. Visual learning is nine times more effective than aural.
   6. Use some personal observations to **illustrate** difficult concepts or to

make the point. Personal illustrations are more natural and powerful than canned illustrations about Bishop Whately. Personal experiences may also be used, but be careful not to preach yourself but Christ.

C. **Conclusion**
1. Be brief.
2. Don't introduce new material. Narrow the focus; don't expand it.
3. Clinch **the goal** (Step 7b).
4. Be concrete. Can you offer some concrete suggestions of what the hearers can do in response to the Word preached?

APPENDIX 3

"The King of the Universe"

A Sermon on Genesis 1:1–2:3

I preached this sermon on September 22, 2002, in the First Christian Reformed Church of Grand Rapids, Michigan. This was one year after the infamous 9-11 attack on the World Trade Center in New York. Although the text is a narrative, the sermon uses the didactic form and deductive development. Since the pew Bibles were the NIV, I quoted the NIV in the sermon.

Text: Genesis 1:1–2:3

Theme:[2] With his powerful word, the King of the universe created the earth as his good kingdom.

Goal: To comfort God's fearful people with the knowledge that our God is the sovereign Creator who controls the world's destiny and ours.

Contemporary Need: People fear unknown, unpredictable powers.

Congregation of our Lord Jesus Christ,

A few weeks ago, an article in *The Grand Rapids Press* reported that astronomers had discovered a new asteroid. What made this item newsworthy was that this asteroid may be on a collision course with planet earth. This asteroid is a monster that is 1.2 miles wide. If it should strike the earth, its impact would cause terrible devastation around the world.

The date for a possible collision was set at February 1, 2019. But it was also

2. I always write the theme and goal at the top of the manuscript to keep me from wandering off track when I am writing the sermon.

pointed out that (quote) "the odds of the asteroid striking the Earth are about one in 250,000." A week later another article reported that astronomers had determined that the asteroid will miss the Earth in 2019. But it will come back and may strike planet earth on February 1, 2060.

I don't like the odds of one in 250,000 for the earth to be devastated in my lifetime or that of my children. I don't like to live with odds. It makes me feel powerless and at the mercy of chance happenings. And how accurate are these astronomers anyway? About two months ago "an asteroid the size of a soccer field missed the Earth by merely 75,000 miles — less than one-third of the distance to the moon." That was a near miss. And, if I'm not mistaken, astronomers discovered this "soccer field" *after* it whizzed by us. There would have been no warning at all. And even with a warning, there would have been nothing we could have done. These destructive forces are beyond our control. They make us feel helpless and fearful.

It is the way many Americans feel after September 11. We are sitting ducks for terrorists. There seems to be very little we can do to control our destiny or the safety of our families. Even Christians who believe in God's providence feel helpless and somewhat anxious and fearful.

Today we are going to listen to God's message of comfort that comes to Israel and to us in Genesis 1. Often we fail to hear this message because we focus on the conflicts between Genesis 1 and the results of modern science. I would like you to go home today with the comfort of God's message of Genesis 1. As I see it, the author of Genesis 1 is not trying to give Israel a chronological account of the origin of this world. The author was not there in the beginning, and Israel did not need a scientific account. What fearful Israel needed was a message of comfort.

For Israel was as fearful of the unknown as you and I are. Israel was as fearful of evil forces it could not control as you and I are. When God sent his message of Genesis 1 to Israel, Israel lived in fear of the power of foreign gods. While enslaved in Egypt they had experienced the fickle powers of a host of Egypt's gods, the most powerful being the sun god Re. In Canaan, the Israelites were confronted by another set of gods, especially Baal and Astarte. And when exiled to Babylon, they met up with another set of powerful gods, especially the head god Marduk, the creator of heaven and earth, but also the Sun, the Moon, and the Stars.

Place yourself in that situation of fear of the unknown, the unpredictable, the powerful foreign gods, and hear and absorb and relish this message of comfort. If I were to put this message in one sentence, it would be this: With his powerful word, the King of the universe created the earth as his good kingdom. Let me repeat this: With his powerful word, the King of the universe created the earth as his good kingdom.

Genesis 1:1, "In the beginning God created the heavens and the earth." Our

God "created the heavens and the earth." That is, he created the entire universe. He created absolutely everything. Can you taste the comfort? Our God alone is sovereign. Everything is under his control. But there is more comfort to come.

Verse 2 shifts the focus to this earth. It turns out that God's creative work was by no means complete. "Now the earth was formless and empty" — it was a wasteland, uninhabitable. Nothing could live on this earth. And "darkness was over the surface of the deep." It was pitch-black; no light at all. It was a deep, dark ocean. No plants could spring up; no creatures could thrive on this earth. It was utter chaos.

But there was a ray of hope: "the Spirit of God was hovering over the waters." The Spirit of God, you notice, was not part of the chaos; it hovered above the chaos like a mighty eagle hovering above its nest, stirring up its young. And that Spirit of God, or breath of God, is about to bring order out of chaos. God's breath is about to speak:

Verse 3, "And God *said,* 'Let there be light,' and there was light." God forced back that awful darkness with radiant light — light that would make life on earth possible. But still there was that formless watery mass. Again God spoke:

Verse 6, "And God *said,* 'Let there be an expanse between the waters to separate water from water.' So God made the expanse and separated the water under the expanse from the water above it. And it was so." Now the earth was starting to take on form: water below and the sky above. But still life as God intended was not possible.

So again God spoke: verse 9, "And God *said,* 'Let the water under the sky be gathered to one place, and let dry ground appear.' And it was so." The deep waters receded and land appeared. Now the earth had a definite form: there was not only the sky, the atmosphere, and oceans, but there was dry land. Now the earth was able to sustain life.

Ten times Genesis 1 repeats the phrase: "God said; God said; God said." Ten is the number of fullness. The Israelites would have been reminded of God's ten words on Mount Sinai, the Ten Commandments. In ten words, Exodus 20 sets forth God's law for Israel. In ten words Genesis 1 sets forth God's law word for his creation.

Psalm 33 (vv 6, 9) reflects the idea of God creating by his word:

> By the *word* of the Lord were the heavens made,
>   their starry host by the *breath* of his mouth. . . .
> For he *spoke,* and it came to be;
>   he *commanded,* and it stood firm.

Genesis 1 recounts God's ten commandments that called his creation to order. "He commanded, and it stood firm."

You see the picture? In ancient times kings were the law of the land. The king spoke and it was done. Genesis 1 portrays our God as the King of the universe. His word is powerful. He speaks and it is done; he commands and it happens; he wills it and it comes to pass. Our God is the sovereign King of the universe. Nothing on earth happens without his will. There is no such thing as odds of one in 250,000 of planet earth being destroyed. There is no such thing as chance happenings. Our King is sovereign and in control of his universe. With his powerful word he brought it into being.

When the apostle John writes his gospel of Jesus Christ, he intentionally echoes the majestic words of Genesis 1: "*In the beginning* was the *Word,* and the Word was with God, and the Word was God. He was with God in the beginning. *Through him* all things were made; without him nothing was made that has been made. In him was *life,* and that life was the light of men. The *light* shines in the darkness. . . . The Word became flesh and made his dwelling among us."

John identifies Jesus Christ as the Word of God through whom all things were made. Jesus was there in the beginning. He is one with the sovereign Creator God. In Colossians 1 (vv 15-17) Paul puts it this way: "Jesus is the image of the invisible God, the firstborn over all creation. For by him *all things* were created: things in heaven and on earth, visible and invisible, whether thrones or powers or rulers or authorities; all things were created by him and *for him.* He is *before* all things, and *in him* all things hold together."

Jesus is one with the King of the universe. By him all things were created and "in him all things hold together." Seeing the exalted nature of Jesus makes us more aware of his tremendous sacrifice in becoming a human being. Paul says in Philippians 2 that "he emptied himself and took on the nature of a servant," a slave. The King of the universe became a slave. When the world was headed for destruction, God spoke his word again through Jesus. "God so loved the world that he gave his one and only Son, that whoever believes in him shall not perish but have eternal life." The word of God created this world and the word of God redeems this world.

The first thing we have seen in Genesis 1 is that God created the earth *with his word.* Ten times the text repeats, "God said; God said; God said." Our God is the King of this universe; what he says comes to pass. Our sovereign God is in control.

Second, I would like you to notice another pattern in Genesis 1, and that is the pattern of seven: the King of the universe created everything in seven days. The author of Genesis 1 seeks to highlight the number "seven." In the Hebrew, verse 1 has exactly seven words: "In the beginning God created the heavens and the earth." Verse 2 has exactly fourteen words, 2×7. In this whole passage, the name of God is mentioned thirty-five times, 5×7.

Like the number "ten," seven is another special number. Seven is the number of perfection. Israel knew the number "seven" especially from its weekly cycle. When Israel traveled through the desert, the LORD taught them to gather manna six days a week and to trust God that the manna gathered on day six would not spoil for day seven. They were to work six days and rest the seventh, trusting the LORD's provisions.

The author of Genesis 1 uses this pattern of Israel's week to tell Israel that its God created everything. However, here the author faced a problem: a week has only six workdays and the author wished to report eight creative acts. He solved this problem by placing two acts of creation in day three and two in day six. This solution underscores the beautiful parallelism between the days. If you look on your bulletin cover, you will better be able to follow the parallelism.

We have already seen that the first three days were days of God setting limits to the forces of chaos: On day one God created light and assigned darkness to the night. On day two God created the firmament and separated the waters below from the waters above. On day three God pushed the waters back so there was space for dry land. The world that had been formless and empty and dark now had form, had light, and was about to be filled with creatures.

Notice the parallelism:

Day 1 light	Day 4 the light bearers: sun, moon, and stars
Day 2 firmament (sea and sky)	Day 5 the inhabitants of the sea and sky: fish and birds
Day 3 two creative acts: the land and vegetation	Day 6 two creative acts: land animals and human beings

Day 7 God rested

Clearly, the author is not interested in giving us a chronological report of what happened exactly. Instead of an objective chronological report, he has given us a carefully crafted literary work, a sermon to comfort Israel and us today.

Remember how Israel feared the pagan gods such as Sun, Moon, and Stars? Notice where the author places the creation of sun, moon, and stars: he places them on day four, right between the creation of vegetation and the creation of fish and birds. He is saying to Israel: These powerful pagan gods, the Sun, Moon, and Stars, are as much God's creation as is vegetation and fish and birds. Notice that in verse 16 the author deliberately avoids the names of Sun and Moon, the names of the pagan gods. "God made two great lights — the greater light to govern the day and the lesser light to govern the night." These powerful gods of the pagans are only lights made by our God to give light on the earth. Almost as an afterthought the author adds, "He also made the stars."

Do you hear what fearful Israel heard? Our God created absolutely everything in the universe. The pagan gods are mere creatures. Our destiny is not held by the stars. We need not fear odds, chance or anything in this universe. Our God made everything, and our lives are safe in his almighty hands. You think the sun is powerful; our God created it. You think our solar system, the Milky Way, is huge; our God created it. You think the millions of solar systems in the universe are mind-boggling. Our God created them. Our God is an awesome God! Whatever happens, we are safe in his almighty hands.

We have seen first that the King of the universe created everything *with his word.* Second, that the King of the universe created everything *in seven days.* As a final point, notice that the author emphasizes that the King of the universe created everything *good.* Six times we read, "and God saw that it was good."

> The light was good;
> the dry land was good;
> the vegetation was good;
> the light of sun, moon, and stars was good;
> the fish and birds were good;
> the land animals were good.
> Six times.

Finally God created human beings, and the *seventh* time, we read in v 31, "God saw all that he had made, and it was *very good.*"

God created this world very good. You can see this especially on day six and seven. On day six God created the land animals and then seems to pause. We are getting to the climax of this story. God deliberates with himself: Verse 26, "Then God said, 'Let us make man [human beings] in our image, in our likeness.'" In the ancient world, a king would place images of himself, statues, in far-off provinces. These images of the king told everyone that these provinces were part of this king's kingdom.

God made human beings in his image and placed us on this earth. In other words, the world we live in is God's domain; it is his kingdom. As images of God, we represent God in this world. As images we may manage this kingdom on God's behalf. That is God's good plan for his kingdom and for human beings.

God carefully deliberates, v 26, "'Let us make man in our image, in our likeness, and let them rule over the fish of the sea and the birds of the air, over the livestock, over all the earth, and over all the creatures that move along the ground.' So God created man in his own image, in the image of God he created him; male and female he created them."

Both male and female receive the high honor and authority of being rulers on this earth on behalf of the King of the universe. God then provides sufficient food for his creatures, and then follows verse 31: "God saw all that he had made, and it was very good." The King of the universe judges that he created everything very good. And you can see how good God was for us: the high honor of being created in his image, receiving authority and responsibility to have dominion over God's world, and God providing sufficient food for us and our offspring.

The goodness of God's creation is underscored on day seven, for God can rest and delight in his creation. We read in Genesis 2:1, "Thus the heavens and the earth were completed in all their vast array. By the seventh day God had finished the work he had been doing; so on the seventh day he rested from all his work. And God blessed the seventh day and made it holy, because on it he rested from all the work of creating that he had done."

God's creation was complete; God's kingdom on earth was well established. God blessed the seventh day and made it holy. What God created on the other days, God declared good, even very good. But this seventh day God made *holy,* that is, God set it apart from the six days of work as a very special day. God's people may rest from their labors, enjoy the fruit of their work, and focus on the worship of their great Creator God. This special day is very good for us. Jesus says, "The Sabbath was made for man, not man for the Sabbath" (Mark 2:27). The Sabbath is very good for us. We need that day of rest. Can you imagine, work, work, work, every day without letup? We would all burn out. But God provides so richly for us that we can *rest* one day in seven. We can rest from our work; we can gather for worship; we can take delight in God's creation and in our own work, we can enjoy family and friends. God created everything very good.

People of God, Genesis 1 sketches God as the King of the universe who created the earth as his good kingdom. Scientists today are discovering just how great the universe is. Especially the Hubble telescope has given us amazing pictures of the stars and the galaxies. Scientists now think that there may be a billion galaxies, each with a billion stars. And in the midst of this ever expanding universe floats a little planet called earth. For those who do not believe in the Creator God, this can be a frightening picture. We seem to be all alone in the universe. The earth is but a frail little ship floating among mighty neighbors. Who knows when the earth will be struck again by an asteroid. We seem to be at the mercy of powers that are far beyond our control.

But God's Word assures us that God is in control. "In the beginning God created the heavens and the earth." With his powerful word he created order out of chaos. This God is greater than any asteroid, greater than any star, greater than any galaxy, greater than the whole universe. And this God created everything good. In his almighty hands we are forever safe. Amen.

APPENDIX 4

"The Big Battle Begins"

A Sermon on Genesis 4:1-26

I first preached this sermon on the Cain-Abel narrative on October 6, 2002, in the First Christian Reformed Church of Grand Rapids, Michigan, under the title, "The Seed of the Woman." I preached it again on April 1, 2005, in a chapel service at Gordon-Conwell Seminary, with slight revisions and a new title. The sermon quotes the NIV, which was the Bible in the pews, and is designed in a hybrid narrative form with inductive development.

TEXT: Genesis 4:1-26

SERMON THEME: God is faithful in continuing the line of the seed of the woman till Christ gains the final victory.

SERMON GOAL: To assure the church that God is faithful in maintaining his people in human history till Christ gains the final victory.

CONTEMPORARY NEED ADDRESSED: God's people fear for the continued existence of the church under the onslaught of secularism and persecution.

Dear Friends,

I retired from preaching about five years ago. When I turned sixty-five, I realized as never before that I had only a limited number of years left to accomplish certain writing projects. So one has to set one's priorities. I let preaching go in order to focus on writing and the odd set of lectures. But I was asked to conclude the series of lectures here with a sermon. And I accepted because I believe that preaching is like swimming — once you know how to do it, you don't forget. You may get slower and more winded and less dynamic, but you don't forget. So I trust I have lowered the bar of your expectations for this morning's sermon.

You know that Gordon-Conwell is known as the "big idea school." When you get to a text you ask, What is the big idea? At noon I will be meeting with "the big idea club." So I thought I had better come up with a big title. And that was not difficult with this text. The title is "The Big Battle Begins."

But a big title is not yet the big idea, or, as I would put it, a sermon title is not yet the sermon theme. Our text this morning is a narrative, and you usually cannot discern the theme of a narrative until you have listened carefully to the whole narrative. So with me you will have to listen carefully to this narrative to discern the big idea.

But the big title you have: "The Big Battle Begins." What big battle? It is the big battle mentioned in the foregoing chapter, Genesis 3. Genesis 3 describes how Adam and Eve rebelled against God and fell for Satan's subtle temptation. But God immediately broke up the unholy alliance between Adam and Eve and Satan. In Genesis 3:15 we hear God say to the serpent: "I will put enmity between you and the woman and between your seed and her seed." Enmity. That is the big battle that began at the dawn of history and that will last till Jesus comes again. It is the battle between the kingdom of light and the kingdom of darkness, the battle between Jesus Christ and Satan, the battle between disciples of Jesus and disciples of Satan.

Our text this morning describes the beginning of this battle. Our text is addressed to Israel, which had experienced the heat of this battle firsthand. In Egypt Pharaoh had enslaved Israel. Then he had ordered all the baby boys drowned in the river Nile. But God delivered them from this evil empire. On the way to the Promised Land Israel had to fight various nations for their very existence. They must have wondered many times: Why are all these nations trying to annihilate us? And will we survive? The future looked extremely hopeless at times.

And now they are in Moab, waiting to enter the land of Canaan with its well-fortified cities, its giants, and its powerful gods. Forty years earlier their fathers stood at the edge of this land and were terrified. They felt like grasshoppers next to the Canaanites. And they refused to do battle. Now their children are again on the edge of the Promised Land. Will they do battle? Will they survive? Moses responds to their concerns by telling them about the beginning of this battle.

It all began when Satan tempted Adam and Eve to disobey God's command. In response, God *cursed* the serpent and set enmity between its seed and the seed of the woman. Genesis 3:15 also implies that ultimately the serpent will lick the dust and the seed of the woman will be victorious. The question is, Who is the seed of the woman?

Genesis 4 begins: "Adam lay with his wife Eve, and she became pregnant and gave birth to Cain. She said, 'With the help of the LORD I have brought forth a man.'" Eve must have thought that Cain was the seed of the woman. "With the help of the LORD," she says, I brought forth not just a baby, not just a boy, but *'îš*, "a man." Cain, for her, was another Adam. Surely he would conquer the devil.

And Cain had much going for him. His mother testified that he was born "with the help of the LORD." He started his life with the LORD. As the firstborn, according to the understanding of the Israelites, he would also have the rights of inheritance. Cain was the seed of the woman.

Eve also gave birth to another son, Abel. Abel may have been a twin brother, but Cain had the rights of the firstborn. Abel's name means "breath," "vanity," as in Ecclesiastes' "Vanity of vanities, all is vanity." And in this narrative Abel lives up to his name of being a mere breath. He is vulnerable; he is passive; he does not speak in this narrative; he does not defend himself.

The action begins with verse 3, "In the course of time Cain brought some of the fruits of the soil as an offering to the LORD. But Abel brought fat portions from some of the firstborn of his flock. The LORD looked with favor on Abel and his offering, but on Cain and his offering he did not look with favor."

The question has often been raised, Why did the LORD look with favor on Abel and his offering and not on Cain and his offering? The Israelites would have known the answer instinctively. We read, "Abel brought *fat* portions from some of the *firstborn* of his flock." Abel obeyed God's law, which called for an offering of the very best: the firstborn, a perfect specimen, including especially the fat portions for burning on the altar. Abel obeyed God's law; he showed total dedication to the LORD; he gave the very best.

Notice also that the LORD looks on the *person* before he looks at the gift. "The LORD looked with favor on *Abel* and his offering. The LORD looks first at the heart of a person, at the motivation, before he looks at the offering. Hebrews 11:4 says, "By faith Abel offered God a better sacrifice than Cain did." "By faith."

Cain, by contrast, just "brought some of the fruits of the soil." His offering seems rather superficial. It is something he has to do, but his heart isn't in it. Therefore, "on *Cain* and his offering God did *not* look with favor." As a result, "Cain was very angry, and his face was downcast." Cain was very angry with God for not accepting his offering. And he was jealous of his younger brother Abel. His anger even showed in his face: "His face was downcast."

But like a loving parent going after an angry child, the LORD pursues Cain. Verse 6: "Then the LORD said to Cain, 'Why are you angry? Why is your face downcast? If you do what is right, will you not be accepted?" Even after the Fall into sin, the LORD suggests that Cain can still do what is right, that is, obey God's law. He is not a helpless victim of Satan or of Adam's original sin. He can fight sin, do what is right, and be accepted.

But this is followed by the warning in verse 7, "But if you do *not* do what is right, sin is crouching at your door." Crouching sounds ominous. "If you do not do what is right, sin is crouching at your door," like an animal crouching to pounce on you. Think of a lion crouching for the kill. That is the picture Peter brings to mind in his first letter (5:8): "Your enemy the devil prowls around like a roaring lion looking for someone to devour. Resist him, standing firm in the faith. . . ."

Peter also claims that we can resist the devil. We are not helpless victims of the devil. We can do what is right: we can speak the truth, we can be faithful to our spouse, we can share our wealth with those in need — we can do what is right. No excuses! But we can also do what is not right: we can nurse our anger; we can brood over our jealousy; we can let sin build up inside us till we are open to attack. God warns Cain: "If you do not do what is right, sin is crouching at your door." If you do not do what is right, you leave yourself wide open to attack by this dangerous beast.

You could think of a lion. But in the context of Genesis another animal comes to mind. The serpent — the serpent that tempted Adam and Eve. The serpent is ready to strike again in the second generation. This time he tempts Cain, the firstborn.

God warns Cain, "Do what is right." But Cain refuses to listen to God; instead he nurses his anger at God and his jealousy of his brother Abel. Then Cain says to his brother Abel, "Let's go out to the field." For Israelites, this reference to the field had a foreboding sound. What is Cain doing, taking his brother out to the *field?* Any crime committed in the field was considered premeditated. Killing someone far away in the field does not allow the victim to get help and leaves no witnesses. Surely Cain is not planning to kill his brother? But he is: "While they were in the field, Cain attacked his brother Abel and killed him." This is not just an accident; the Hebrew word indicates that he murders his brother intentionally.

"His *brother.*" Seven times this narrative tells us that Abel is Cain's brother. He does not kill an enemy, not even a stranger. He kills his very own brother! Unbelievable! What a terrible act!! "Sin is crouching at the door of your heart if you do not do what is right." This is what Adam and Eve's sin leads to in only the second generation: fratricide — the murder of a brother.

And no witnesses — except one. God has seen Cain's awful deed. Verse 9, "Then the Lord said to Cain, 'Where is your brother Abel?'" And Cain responds: "I don't know, am I my brother's keeper?" It's a bold-faced lie. Jesus said that the devil is the father of lies. You see how Cain's lie shows that he has moved into the camp of the devil? When he was born, Eve thought he was the seed of the woman who would conquer the devil. But Cain, nursing his anger against God and his jealousy of his brother, gives an opening to the devil. He intentionally kills his brother and lies to God. It is clear that Cain is not the seed of the woman. He is the seed of the serpent out to destroy the seed of the woman.

Verse 10, "The LORD said, 'What have you done? Listen! Your brother's blood cries out to me from the ground. Now you are under a curse. . . .'" In Genesis 3 God had cursed the serpent and cursed the ground. But never Adam and Eve: they represented the seed of the woman. Now God curses Cain, confirming that Cain is the seed of the serpent. The enmity between the seed of the serpent and the seed of the woman will split the human race into two camps: some will be on the side of Satan and some will be on the side of God.

God curses Cain and drives him from the land. He "will be a restless wanderer on the earth." Cain cries out to the LORD, verse 13, "My punishment is more than I can bear. Today you are driving me from the land, and I will be hidden from your presence; I will be a restless wanderer on the earth, and whoever finds me will kill me."

In Israel when a person had been killed, a relative of the dead person would become the avenger of blood. Like a bounty hunter, he would hunt down the killer and kill him. "But the LORD said to Cain [verse 15], 'Not so; if anyone kills Cain, he will suffer vengeance seven times over' [that is, complete vengeance]. Then the LORD put a mark on Cain so that no one who found him would kill him."

People have often wondered what kind of mark the LORD put on Cain. The text doesn't tell us. That is not very important either. What is important is what the mark stood for, and that is simply amazing. Cain has switched sides in the battle between the seed of the woman and the seed of the serpent. Cain has joined forces with the devil. He has become a traitor in God's kingdom. He has murdered the seed of the woman. God rightly curses him. Now we would expect God to condemn him to hell.

But what happens? God puts a mark on him to protect his life. It is a mark of God's mercy, God's grace. God bestows his good gifts even on traitors to his cause. As Jesus says in the Sermon on the Mount, "Your Father in heaven causes his sun to rise on the evil and on the good, and sends rain on the righteous and on the unrighteous." That's common grace. Even the traitor Cain receives God's common grace.

Having received that mark of protection, verse 16, "Cain went out from the LORD's presence and lived in the land of Nod (the land of wandering), east of Eden." Sinners cannot live in the presence of God. When Adam and Eve fell into sin, they were driven out of the garden, away from the presence of God, east of Eden. Now Cain is forced to move even farther away from God's holy presence: east of Eden.

But God's common grace goes with him. God's curse on Cain does not entirely remove God's original blessing, "Be fruitful and multiply." We read in verse 17, "Cain lay with his wife, and she became pregnant and gave birth to Enoch. . . ." Verse 18, "To Enoch was born Irad, and Irad was the father of Mehujael, and Mehujael was the father of Methushael, and Methushael was the father of Lamech." Lamech is special: he represents the seventh generation from Adam in the line of Cain.

And look at the tremendous cultural developments in this line. Verse 19, "Lamech married two women, one named Adah and the other Zillah. Adah gave birth to Jabal; he was the father of those who live in tents and raise livestock [farming]. His brother's name was Jubal; he was the father of all who play the harp and flute [music]. Zillah also had a son, Tubal-Cain, who forged all kinds of tools out of bronze and iron [tools and weapons]." Again we see God's common grace in the cultural developments that enable people to cope in a harsh environment under God's curse.

But all is not well. Lamech, in the seventh generation, breaks God's creation law of a marriage of one man and one woman. He marries two women. And then he begins to brag to these two wives: Verse 23, "Adah and Zillah, listen to me; wives of Lamech, hear my words. I have killed a man for wounding me, a young man for injuring me."

Lamech is a brutal killer. He is an early Saddam Hussein. God's law for Israel demanded that punishment must fit the crime: an eye for an eye; a tooth for a tooth. Lamech moves far beyond this principle of justice: He kills a young man for injuring him. And then he brags, "If Cain is avenged seven times, then Lamech seventy-seven times." He takes God's words to Cain of complete vengeance, and goes them seventy times better. He vows unending vengeance. No one, but no one, will touch the violent Lamech. He does not need God's protection. He can fend for himself.

The story is almost finished. The author has sketched the awful development of sin in human history. Only seven generations, a complete number of generations, and sin comes to full fruition. Human beings boasting about their power to defend themselves. They don't need God; they don't need his law; they can be gods for themselves. This is the sin of Adam and Eve, only many times more defiant. With their cultural developments, they can fend for themselves. Only seven generations, and humanity has disintegrated into full-blown secularism, worldliness. And this secularism continues to the present day. With our cultural developments, with our powerful armies, with our nuclear weapons and defensive shields, we can be a law to ourselves. We can defend ourselves. We don't need God.

But instead of ending the narrative on this awful note, the author flashes back to Adam and Eve again. Verse 25, "Adam lay with his wife again, and she gave birth to a son and named him Seth, saying, 'God has granted me another child *in place of Abel,* since Cain killed him.'" Eve now knows that Cain was not the promised seed of the woman. The younger Abel was. And Cain killed him. But in his grace "God has granted me another child in place of Abel, since Cain killed him." That's the point of this passage. In the big battle between the seed of the woman and the seed of the serpent, *God is faithful in continuing the line of the seed of the woman.*

And then notice the last verse, "Seth also had a son, and he named him Enosh. At that time men began to call on the name of the LORD." This is the seventieth time Genesis uses the divine name. Thirty-five times in the creation narrative; and thirty-five times in Genesis 2–4. This seventieth time Genesis uses the name of the LORD is very special. In contrast to the seed of the serpent sketched in the line of Cain, in this line of Seth people "began to call on the name of the LORD."

In the line of Cain we see rich cultural developments but increasingly people declaring that they don't need God. In the line of the seed of the woman, people begin "to call on the name of the LORD." They recognize their dependence on the LORD, their King, and make the LORD central in their lives: they pray to God, worship him, and dedicate their lives to him.

God is faithful in continuing the line of the seed of the woman. Were God not faithful, this line of the church would have ended with the death of Abel. But God raised up Seth and his descendants to continue his church on earth. This also means, of course, that the bitter battle with the seed of the serpent continues.

Abel was the first of many martyrs. The Egyptians drowned the Israelite boys in the river Nile. Jezebel killed so many prophets of the LORD that Elijah thought he was the only one left. But God kept his church alive until the coming of Christ. Then Satan managed to kill *the* Seed of the woman, Jesus Christ. And the persecution did not stop there. Jesus had warned his disciples: "I am sending you out like sheep into the midst of wolves. . . . You will be hated by all because of my name. . . . A disciple is not above his teacher" (Matt 10:16-24). Soon these words came true.

A mob stoned the deacon Stephen; Herod Agrippa killed James; the Romans killed the apostles Peter and Paul. The early church suffered great persecution which resulted in many Christian martyrs. But the church fathers saw rightly that the blood of the martyrs was the seed of the church. Through persecution, God was faithful in continuing the line of the seed of the woman to this day.

We may think, perhaps, that we are not involved in this battle. The church in North America lives in relative peace today. But Christian martyrs are falling all around us. The twentieth century has seen more Christian martyrs than fell in all the preceding nineteen centuries. A new book, the *World Christian Ency-*

clopedia, 2001, puts the number of Christian martyrs in the twentieth century at 45 million. The author estimates that since 1990 every year an average of 160,000 Christians have been killed in countries all around us.

As Christians we are all involved in this battle. Those of you aiming for mission work will probably experience this battle more intensely than others. But as disciples of Jesus, we are all involved in this battle. Do you ever wonder, How will I handle it when my very life may be at stake in this battle? How will I handle it?

John's first letter is instructive. He writes this letter to a persecuted church. In chapter 3:12 he writes: "Do not be like Cain who was from the evil one and murdered his brother. And why did he murder him? Because his own deeds were evil and his brother's righteous. Do not be astonished, brothers and sisters, that the world hates you." John tells them about "the spirit of the antichrist, which you have heard is coming and even now is already in the world." And then he writes, "You, dear children, are from God and have overcome them, because the one who is in you is greater than the one who is in the world" (1 John 4:3-4). The seed of the woman will conquer even under the pressure of persecution today "because the one who is *in* you is greater than the one who is in the world."

One of my students had a powerful illustration of this point. I asked him for permission to use it because it shows ever so clearly how the church can survive even under great pressure. He reminded us of the nuclear submarine *Thresher*. It had heavy steel bulkheads and heavy steel armor so that it could dive deep and withstand the pressure of the ocean. Unfortunately, on a test run in 1963 the *Thresher's* nuclear engine quit and it could not get back to the surface. It sank deeper and deeper into the ocean. The pressure became immense. The heavy steel bulkheads buckled; the *Thresher* was crushed with 129 people inside.

The navy searched for the *Thresher* with a research craft that was much stronger than submarines. It was shaped like a steel ball and was lowered into the ocean on a cable. Finally they located the *Thresher* at a depth of 8400 feet, one and a half miles down. It was crushed like an egg shell. That was not a surprise, for the pressure at that depth was tremendous — 3600 pounds per square inch.

What was surprising to the searchers was that they saw fish at that great depth. And these fish did not have inches of steel to protect them. They appeared to have normal skin, a fraction of an inch thick. How can these fish survive under all that pressure? How come they are not crushed by the weight of the water? They have a secret. Their secret is that they have the same pressure inside themselves as they have on the outside. Survival under pressure.

John assures us, "The one who is in you is greater than the one who is in the world." We will be victorious in the battle against Satan because Jesus poured his Spirit into our hearts. "You, dear children, are from God and have overcome them, because the one who is *in* you is *greater* than the one who is in the world." (1 John 4:3-4). No matter how hard the battle, God is faithful in preserving his church till Christ gains the final victory. Amen.

Prayer

Father, thank you for reminding us of your faithfulness in preserving your church in the big battle. Thank you for Jesus' victory over Satan — a victory we just celebrated Easter Sunday and celebrate every Sunday again. Thank you for also promising us the victory in this battle because Jesus now lives in us. Please enable us to be faithful to you wherever you call us and to be victorious in the battle through your Spirit. Amen.

APPENDIX 5

"Building Altars to the LORD"

A Sermon on Genesis 11:27–12:9

I preached the final version of this sermon on March 25, 2001, at a combined service in the First Christian Reformed Church of London, Ontario. The sermon is designed in a hybrid narrative form with inductive development. Since the pew Bibles were in the NIV, this is the version cited in the sermon.

TEXT: Gen 11:27–12:9

SERMON THEME: The LORD calls his people to claim all nations for his kingdom.

SERMON GOAL: To motivate God's people to claim all nations for God's kingdom.

CONTEMPORARY NEED: Current materialism and consumerism sap our missionary zeal.

Congregation of our Lord Jesus Christ,

Two years ago my wife, Marie, and I visited Europe. We spent three days in Belgium and saw many beautiful cathedrals. I am always impressed by the sheer size of the cathedrals. Generation after generation worked on these monuments, sometimes for hundreds of years. It is clear what was central for these people: the worship of God. Life revolved around the Christian religion. The cathedral was the highest building in town; it was also located in the center of town. People were baptized there, worshiped there, confessed their sins there, married there, and were buried there. Worship of God in the cathedral was the focus of their lives.

But what are the highest buildings in our cities today? Not churches but the high-rises of banks and multinational corporations. And these towering high-rises also reveal what is considered important in our society. You see, a shift has taken place in modern culture. Life is no longer centered on God and his church. The center has shifted to banks and multinational corporations, the sponsors of materialism and consumerism.

Under the pressure of materialism, many churches in Europe have already collapsed. It is sad to see churches turned into warehouses, stores, sometimes even into apartments. The question arises, Could this happen to churches in Canada and the United States? Has the virus of materialism and consumerism also infected us to such an extent that we are no longer on fire for the church, for outreach, for missions? Are we perhaps more interested in seeking to live the good life than in seeking the kingdom of God?

Throughout its history the church has led a precarious existence. In the beginning God created his good kingdom on earth. God made Adam and Eve in his image to worship and obey God alone and no other creature. But Adam and Eve followed the advice of Satan and evil snuck into that harmonious world. Sin spread rapidly through the generations and totally spoiled God's good design. It got so bad that God said, "I will blot out from the earth the human beings I have created . . . , for I am sorry that I have made them" (Gen 6:7). God sent a great flood that cleaned the earth of all evildoers.

But God saved the righteous Noah and his family. Notice, now God's church is down to one family. God seeks to make a new start with Noah to spread his good kingdom across this world. And things looked promising indeed. The first thing Noah did when he came out of the ark was to build an altar to the LORD and offer burnt offerings (Gen 8:20). He dedicated this cleaned earth to God and his service.

But soon sin became rampant again. Just before our text, in Genesis 11, the author sketches a massive rebellion against God. Instead of spreading across the world, the people said, verse 4, "Come, let us build ourselves a city, with a tower that reaches to the heavens, so that we may make a name for ourselves and not be scattered over the face of the whole earth." They wanted to make a name for *themselves.* Again human sin jeopardized God's good kingdom. God put down this human rebellion by confusing their language and scattering them "over the face of the whole earth." The rebels were defeated, but there seemed to be nothing left of the kingdom of God.

To reestablish his kingdom on earth God makes a new start with a third person: First Adam, then Noah, and now Abram. Abram is an extremely unlikely candidate for this task of reestablishing God's kingdom on earth. In Genesis 11 we read Abram's family tree, but there is something very unusual about it. The writer tells us not only that Abram's father is Terah and his wife is Sarai.

He adds in verse 30, "Now Sarai was barren." And for good measure he adds, "she had no children." You see how the writer emphasizes that this is the end of the line. Abram has no future at all: "Sarai was barren; she had no children." Noah, at least, had three sons and three daughters-in-law. Abram has no children. He can contribute absolutely nothing to the new start for God's kingdom on earth. Another precarious beginning.

Abram is an unlikely candidate not only because he is childless but also because he worships idols. Of Noah we read that he was a righteous man. Of Abram we read in Joshua 24:2, "Long ago your ancestors — Terah and his sons Abraham and Nahor — lived beyond the Euphrates and served other gods." John Calvin writes, "He [Abram] was plunged in the filth of idolatry; and now God freely stretches forth his hand to bring back the wanderer" (*Genesis,* I, 343). Abram is not at all deserving. And yet, God uses him to continue his church and extend his kingdom on earth. God's call of the idolater Abram is pure grace.

In chapter 12:1 we read of God's call: "The LORD had said to Abram, 'Leave your country, your people and your father's household and go to the land I will show you.'" God wants Abram to break completely with his past and make a new start with God. "Leave your country!"

Today we can hardly imagine how difficult it must have been for Abram to leave his country. We live in a nation of immigrants. Our parents or grandparents traveled across oceans to settle in this new country. Today we also live in a highly mobile society. But in ancient times people stayed in their country: that was familiar territory; there was their livelihood; there they had a measure of security; their roots went down deeper than we'll ever know. Yet God requires that Abram leave all that behind, and more. Each of the three requests in v 1 is more difficult. "Leave your country." Very difficult. "And your people," that is, your relatives. Even more difficult. "And your father's household." Almost impossible. How could the LORD ask Abram to leave his father's house? That is his very identity. He is Abram *ben* Terah — son of Terah. His father's house is his house; his father's goods are his goods, his father's gods are his gods. Yet the LORD commands him, "Leave your country, your people, and your father's household."

In verses 2-3 God encourages Abram by promising three different blessings. God first tells Abram what great things he has in mind for him personally. "I will make you into a great nation and I will bless you: I will make your name great, and you will be a blessing." The people at Babel had said, "Let us make a name for *ourselves.*" God says to Abram, "*I* will make your name great." Abram's greatness will be totally God's work, God's grace.

Next, in verse 3, God extends the blessing from Abram personally to his contemporaries: "I will bless those who bless you, and whoever curses you I will curse." And finally God extends the blessing from Abram to all nations: "And all peoples on earth will be blessed through you." This is an amazing climax. God promises to use this one man to bless all nations of the earth. Notice, God's call of Abram has a *universal* design: "All peoples on earth." God is not giving up on his creation. He will yet spread his kingdom to all nations of the earth.

But meanwhile Abram has received God's impossible call, "Leave your country, your people, and your father's household and go to the land I will show you." "To the land I will show you" raises the conflict even further. Nothing is certain here. Abram does not even know his destination. This is no emigration to the riches of the United States or Canada. Abram is asked to walk blindly with God to an unknown land. What will he do?

Verse 4 gives us an astonishing answer: "So Abram left, as the Lord had told him." If I had been Abram, I would have wanted to think this over at least for a few nights; wouldn't you? I would have wanted to talk it over with my wife and also with relatives and friends. But Abram apparently leaves his entire past without raising any questions or objections and, as far as we can tell, without so much as checking with Sarai. "So Abram left, as the Lord had told him." He shows unquestioning trust in the Lord and obeys him immediately.

How can Abram leave his country, his people, and his father's house just like this? Later the author of Hebrews 11 will use this as an illustration of what true faith is like: "By faith Abraham obeyed when he was called to set out for a place that he was to receive as an inheritance; and he set out, not knowing where he was going." Abram the idol worshiper now has true faith, complete trust in the Lord, the only true God.

So Abram gathers all his worldly possessions and sets out for the land God will show him. The writer spends very little time on the long, arduous journey — over 400 miles with flocks and herds. All he records at the end of verse 5 is that "they set out for the land of Canaan, and they arrived there." That part of the journey isn't all that important. What is important is what happens once Abram arrives in the land of Canaan. Here the writer slows the pace of the story and records the details.

If you check a map you will see that Abram passes through the land of Canaan from north to south. Verse 6 tells us that "Abram traveled through the land as far as the site of the great tree of Moreh at Shechem." Shechem was considered the very center of the land of Canaan. Here was a famous Canaanite shrine, "the great tree of Moreh," probably a soothsayers' tree where the Canaanites sought to hear oracles from their gods (Gen 35:4; Judg 9:37).

The writer adds ominously, "At that time the *Canaanites* were in the land." The Canaanites were the descendants of Canaan, the grandson whom Noah had cursed (Gen 9:25). What a tremendous letdown for Abram. Here he has come all this way, blindly trusting the Lord, and now he finds a land already occupied. And not only is the land occupied, it is occupied by the accursed Canaanites. Will he begin to doubt now? Will he turn around and go back to his homeland?

But precisely at that spot in the midst of the land of the Canaanites, the LORD appears to Abram and says, verse 7, "To your offspring I will give this land" — this land of the Canaanites.

Abram's response to God's promise of this land is profound. As soon as he hears that this is the land God will give his offspring, "he built an altar there to the LORD [Yahweh, the Hebrew name], who had appeared to him." In the very center of the land of Canaan, within view of the Canaanite shrine, Abram erects the first altar to the LORD, Yahweh. Then he moves further south to Bethel. And again, verse 8b, "he built an altar to the LORD and called on the name of the LORD [Yahweh]." Then he continues traveling south to the Negev. And if you check the last verse of chapter 13, you will see that in Hebron, too, near the great trees of Mamre (another Canaanite shrine), Abram built an altar to the LORD.

Building altars to the LORD! Why does the author emphasize that Abram built altars to the LORD? A Jewish commentator made me aware of the fact that Abram is never portrayed as building altars outside the Promised Land; he always builds altars in the Promised Land. What is the significance of Abram building altars to the LORD only in the Promised Land? And that at strategic locations such as Shechem, Bethel, Hebron?

You remember from Genesis 8 Noah's first act when he stepped from the ark? He built an altar to the LORD. With it, he dedicated this cleansed earth to the worship of the LORD. But human sin led again to the worship of human might (the tower of Babel) and the worship of other false gods.

Now Abram is in the land God promised to his offspring, Israel. Abram sees the Canaanites worshiping their false gods at the sacred shrines. And within sight of these shrines he builds altars to the only true God, the LORD. In other words, Abram *claims this land for the LORD*. At key locations, we might say, he raises the LORD's flag of ownership: This is the LORD's country! This is where the LORD is King!

By building altars to the LORD, Abram dedicates this land to the worship and service of the LORD; in this land the LORD will be worshiped and obeyed. John Calvin writes perceptively, Abram "endeavoured, as much as in him lay, to dedicate to God, every part of the land to which he had access, and perfumed it with the odour of his faith" (*Genesis,* I, 357).

As Israel later heard this story about father Abram, the message must have been obvious to them. They were about to try to conquer the land of Canaan under Joshua. But like their fathers before them, they still feared the mighty Canaanites and their powerful gods. Their fathers had refused to enter the land.

Now, forty years later, the next generation is at the edge of the Promised Land waiting for orders to attack the Canaanites. In that setting this story about father Abram told them clearly: *The LORD calls us to claim the Promised Land for the LORD, for his kingdom.*

But in calling Israel to claim the land of Canaan for God's kingdom, God has a universal design. Remember verse 3, "All peoples on earth will be blessed through you." God has the whole earth in mind. The land of Canaan is only a small start. It's like the liberation of Europe in 1945. The allied forces tried to free Europe from the occupation of an evil power. But liberation did not come to all of Europe at once. It started on D-day with a beach in Normandy. And from that beach freedom spread throughout Europe.

Just so, Canaan would be the beachhead from which the kingdom of God would spread throughout the world. Abram was the first to build altars to the LORD in this land. Later God commanded King Solomon to build a temple to the LORD in the capital city of Jerusalem. Just outside the temple was a huge altar where Israel was to bring its sacrifices. The Promised Land is God's country. At the temple God's law would be proclaimed. Israel was to worship the LORD in this land, praise his name, obey his commands. Israel was to reveal in its national life the justice and peace of the kingdom of God. It was to show the reality of God's kingdom in Canaan — not for its own sake but for the sake of the whole world.

Unfortunately, Israel failed to manifest the justice and peace of God's kingdom. So the LORD banished the people into exile — back to Babylon where Abram had come from. It looked as if the kingdom of God collapsed once again. But God made a new start with Abram's son, God's own Son, Jesus Christ.

In the New Testament we read that Jesus came preaching, "The time is fulfilled, and the *kingdom of God* has come near . . ." (Mark 1:15). Jesus showed the reality of God's kingdom by feeding the hungry, healing the sick, raising the dead, casting out demons. When some people accused Jesus of casting out demons by Beelzebul, the ruler of the demons, Jesus said, "If it is by the finger of God that I cast out the demons, then the kingdom of God has come to you" (Luke 11:20). Jesus' mission was again to establish a beachhead on earth for the kingdom of God. From that beachhead the justice and peace of God's kingdom was to spread into all the earth.

After his death and resurrection, Jesus mandated his disciples to "Go and make disciples of all nations" (Matt 28:19). Did you notice the parallel with God's command to Abram? God had said to Abram, "Go to a *land* I will show you." Jesus says to his disciples, "Go and make disciples of *all nations*" — go to the ends of the earth! God's design to save all nations is being fulfilled.

There is a further parallel: as God gave Abram the difficult assignment,

"Leave your country, your people and your father's house," so Jesus tells his disciples, "Anyone who loves his father or mother more than me is not worthy of me; anyone who loves his son or daughter more than me is not worthy of me; and anyone who does not take his cross and follow me is not worthy of me. Whoever finds his life will lose it, and whoever loses his life for my sake will find it" (Matt 10:37-39).

You see, our King, Jesus Christ, is inviting us to be part of his mission. And it's a difficult mission: we have to lose our own life with its self-interests and instead focus our life totally on the worship of God; we have to dedicate our life totally to the service of God and his kingdom; building altars to the LORD around the world; raising the flag of God's kingdom in strategic places: planting churches, Christian schools, and other Christian organizations — reclaiming this world, its people and institutions, for God. It's a difficult mission, and the opposition of secularism and materialism is fierce.

If we tried to build God's kingdom on earth in our own strength, we would fail miserably. But remember, God enabled Abram to fulfill his calling by pronouncing on him a threefold blessing. Jesus does even more: In his Sermon on the Mount, he pronounces a ninefold blessing on his people: "Blessed are the poor in spirit, for theirs is the *kingdom of heaven.* Blessed are those who mourn, for they will be comforted. Blessed are the meek, for they will inherit *the earth.* Blessed are those who hunger and thirst for *righteousness*, for they will be filled . . ." (Matt 5:3-6). Nine times, "Blessed are those." We work not in our own strength but under God's call and blessing.

Still, you may wonder, Why should I get involved in this tough mission? Why should I not live for a good time? Why should I not join our society of pleasure seekers? Why not serve the gods of this age: materialism and consumerism?

The reason why not is simple: the gods of this age lead to death. Whereas service of the true God leads to life — a wonderful, satisfying, and meaningful life. For it puts our lives in the service of something far greater than our personal desires, far greater even than company profits or the national interest; it puts our lives in the service of the kingdom of God which is breaking into this world. We can be co-workers with Christ.

Moreover, joining this mission will place us on the winning side. For this mission, difficult though it is, will succeed. In the book of Revelation, John records a glimpse of this final triumph when he heard the new song being sung in heaven after Jesus' ascension:

> "You are worthy to take the scroll and to open its seals,
> because you were slain, and with your blood you purchased men for God
> *from every tribe and language and people and nation.*

> You have made them to be *a kingdom and priests to serve our God,*
> and they will reign on the *earth.*"
>
> (Rev 5:9-10)

That is where the story of God's call of Abram will end: people from every tribe, language and nation serving the Lord as priests and reigning on the earth.

And we may be part of this unfolding drama. Jesus himself invites us to be part of this history God is making in the world. Jesus tells us not to get distracted by false gods such as money: "You cannot serve God and Mammon" (Matt 6:24). Instead, Jesus invites us to take up our cross and to serve God alone; to serve God in everything we do; to build altars to the Lord in our community and around the world; to raise the flag of God's kingdom everywhere; to get involved in spreading on earth the justice and peace of God's kingdom. That is God's calling for Christians. Accepting that calling will give our lives a single focus and fill them with meaning, both now and for eternity. Amen.

Select Bibliography

Aalders, G. C. *Genesis: Bible Student's Commentary.* Vols. 1 and 2. Trans. William Heynen. Grand Rapids: Zondervan, 1981.

Achtemeier, Elizabeth. *The Old Testament and the Proclamation of the Gospel.* Philadelphia: Westminster, 1973.

———. *Preaching from the Old Testament.* Louisville: Westminster/John Knox, 1989.

———. "Genesis 12:1-9." In *The Lectionary Commentary: Theological Exegesis for Sunday's Texts.* The First Readings: *The Old Testament and Acts.* Ed. Roger E. Van Harn. Grand Rapids, Eerdmans, 2001. Pp. 23-26.

Ackerman, James. "Joseph, Judah, and Jacob." In *Literary Interpretations of Biblical Narratives.* Vol. 2. Ed. Kenneth R. R. Gros Louis. Nashville: Abingdon, 1982. Pp. 85-113.

Alexander, T. Desmond. "From Adam to Judah: The Significance of the Family Tree in Genesis," *EvQ* 61 (1989) 7-18.

———. "Genealogies, Seed and the Compositional Unity of Genesis." *TynBul* 44/2 (1993) 255-70.

———. "Messianic Ideology in the Book of Genesis." In *The Lord's Anointed.* Eds. Philip E. Satterthwaite et al. Grand Rapids: Baker, 1995. Pp. 19-39.

———. *From Paradise to the Promised Land: An Introduction to the Main Themes of the Pentateuch.* Grand Rapids: Baker, 1998.

Allen, Ronald J., and John C. Holbert. *Holy Root, Holy Branches: Christian Preaching from the Old Testament.* Nashville: Abingdon, 1995.

Alter, Robert. *The Art of Biblical Narrative.* New York: Basic Books, 1981.

———. *Genesis: Translation and Commentary.* New York: Norton, 1996.

Amit, Yairah. *Reading Biblical Narratives: Literary Criticism and the Hebrew Bible.* Minneapolis: Fortress, 2001.

Anderson, Bernhard W. "From Analysis to Synthesis: The Interpretation of Genesis 1–11." *JBL* 97 (1978) 23-39. Reprinted in *I Studied Inscriptions from before the Flood: Ancient Near Eastern, Literary, and Linguistic Approaches to Genesis 1–11.* Eds. Richard S. Hess and David Toshio Tsumura. Winona Lake, IN: Eisenbrauns, 1994. Pp. 416-35.

———. *Understanding the Old Testament.* Englewood Cliffs, NJ: Prentice-Hall, 1986.

———. *From Creation to New Creation: Old Testament Perspectives.* Minneapolis: Fortress, 1994.

———. *Contours of Old Testament Theology.* Minneapolis: Fortress, 1999.

Baldwin, Joyce G. *The Message of Genesis 12–50.* Downers Grove, IL: InterVarsity Press, 1986.

Bar-Efrat, S. "Some Observations on the Analysis of Structure in Biblical Narrative." *VT* 30 (1980) 154-73.

———. *Narrative Art in the Bible.* Sheffield: Almond, 1989.

Bartholomew, Craig G., and Michael W. Goheen. *The Drama of Scripture: Finding Our Place in the Biblical Story.* Grand Rapids: Baker, 2004.

Baylis, Albert H. *From Creation to the Cross: Understanding the First Half of the Bible.* Grand Rapids: Zondervan, 1996.

Berlin, Adele. *Poetics and Interpretation of Biblical Narrative.* Sheffield: Almond, 1983.

———. *The Dynamics of Biblical Parallelism.* Bloomington: Indiana University, 1985.

Birch, Bruce C., Walter Brueggemann, Terence E. Fretheim, and David L. Peterson. *A Theological Introduction to the Old Testament.* Nashville: Abingdon, 1999.

Brodie, Thomas L. *Genesis as Dialogue: A Literary, Historical, and Theological Commentary.* Oxford: Oxford University Press, 2001.

Brueggemann, Walter. *Genesis: A Bible Commentary for Teaching and Preaching.* Atlanta: John Knox, 1982.

———. *Theology of the Old Testament: Testimony, Dispute, Advocacy.* Minneapolis: Fortress, 1997.

Calvin, John. *Commentaries on the Book of Genesis.* Vols. 1 and 2. Trans. John King. Grand Rapids: Eerdmans, 1963.

Cassuto, Umberto. *Commentary on the Book of Genesis: Part 1, From Adam to Noah, Genesis 1–6:8.* Trans. Israel Abrahams. Jerusalem: Hebrew University, Magnes Press, 1961.

Chapell, Bryan. *Christ-Centered Preaching: Redeeming the Expository Sermon.* 2nd rev. ed. Grand Rapids: Baker, 2005.

Childs, Brevard S. *Old Testament Theology in a Canonical Context.* Philadelphia: Fortress, 1985.

Clines, David J. A. "The Theology of the Flood Narrative." *Faith and Thought* 100 (1972-73) 128-42.

———. "Theme in Genesis 1–11." *CBQ* 38 (1976) 483-507.

———. *The Theme of the Pentateuch.* Sheffield: JSOT Press, 1978.

Clowney, Edmund P. *Preaching and Biblical Theology.* Grand Rapids: Eerdmans, 1961.

———. "Preaching Christ from All the Scriptures." In *The Preacher and Preaching.* Ed. S. Logan, Jr. Phillipsburg, NY: Presbyterian and Reformed, 1986. Pp. 163-91.

———. *The Unfolding Mystery: Discovering Christ in the Old Testament.* Colorado Springs: Nav Press, 1988.

Coats, George W. "Strife without Reconciliation: A Narrative Theme in the Jacob Traditions." In *Werden und Wirken des alten Testaments: Festschrift für Claus Westermann zum 70 Geburtstag.* Eds. Rainer Albertz et al. Göttingen: Vandenhoeck & Ruprecht, 1980. Pp. 82-106.

———. *Genesis: With an Introduction to Narrative Literature.* Grand Rapids: Eerdmans, 1983.

Curtis, "Structure, Style and Context as a Key to Interpreting Jacob's Encounter at Peniel." *JETS* 30/2 (June 1987) 129-37.

Davidson, JoAnn. "Eschatology and Genesis 22." *Journal of the Adventist Theological Society* 11/1-2 (2000) 232-47.

De Graaf, S. G. *Promise and Deliverance.* Vol. 1. Trans. H. Evan and Elisabeth Runner. St. Catharines, ON: Paideia, 1977.

Dillard, Raymond B., and Tremper Longman, III. *An Introduction to the Old Testament.* Grand Rapids: Zondervan, 1994.

Duguid, Iain M. *Living in the Gap between Promise and Reality: The Gospel according to Abraham.* Phillipsburg, NJ: Presbyterian and Reformed, 1999.

Dumbrell, William J. *Covenant and Creation: A Theology of Old Testament Covenants.* Nashville: Thomas Nelson, 1984.

Dunn, James D. G. *Christology in the Making: A New Testament Inquiry into the Origins of the Doctrine of the Incarnation.* London: SCM, 1980.

Fishbane, Michael. *Text and Texture: A Literary Reading of Selected Texts.* Oxford: Oneworld, 1998.

Fokkelman, Jan P. *Narrative Art in Genesis: Specimens of Stylistic and Structural Analysis.* Assen/Amsterdam: Van Gorcum, 1975.

———. "Genesis." In *The Literary Guide to the Bible.* Eds. Robert Alter and Fred Kermode. Cambridge, MA: Harvard University Press, 1987. Pp. 36-55.

———. *Reading Biblical Narrative: An Introductory Guide.* Trans. Ineke Smit. Louisville: Westminster/John Knox, 1999.

Francisco, Clyde T. "Preaching from the Primeval Narratives of Genesis." In *Biblical Preaching: An Expositor's Treasury.* Ed. James W. Cox. Philadelphia: Westminster, 1983. Pp. 17-35.

Fretheim, Terence E. "Genesis." In *The New Interpreter's Bible.* Vol. 1. Nashville: Abingdon, 1994. Pp. 319-674.

Gilgamesh. In *The Context of Scripture.* Vol. 1. Ed. William W. Hallo. New York: Brill, 1996. Pp. 458-60.

Goldingay, John. "The Patriarchs in Scripture and History." In *Essays on the Patriarchal Narratives.* Eds. A. R. Millard and D. J. Wiseman. Leicester: InterVarsity Press, 1980. Pp. 11-42.

Goldsworthy, Graeme. *Preaching the Whole Bible as Christian Scripture: The Application of Biblical Theology to Expository Preaching.* Grand Rapids: Eerdmans, 2000.

Gowan, Donald E., *Reclaiming the Old Testament for the Christian Pulpit.* Atlanta: John Knox, 1980.

———. *From Eden to Babel: A Commentary on the Book of Genesis 1–11.* Grand Rapids: Eerdmans, 1988.

Green, Barbara. "Determination of Pharaoh: His Characterization in the Joseph Story (Genesis 37–50)." In *The World of Genesis: Persons, Places, Perspectives.* Eds. Philip R. Davies and David Clines. *JSOT Supplement* 257. Sheffield: Sheffield Academic Press, 1998. Pp. 150-71.

Greidanus, Sidney. *The Modern Preacher and the Ancient Text: Interpreting and Preaching Biblical Literature.* Grand Rapids: Eerdmans, 1988.

———. "The Value of a Literary Approach for Preaching." In *A Complete Literary Guide to the Bible.* Eds. Leland Ryken and Tremper Longman, III. Grand Rapids: Zondervan, 1993. Pp. 509-19.

———. "Application in Preaching Old Testament Texts." In *Reading and Hearing the Word: From Text to Sermon.* Essays in Honor of John H. Stek. Ed. Arie C. Leder. Grand Rapids: Calvin Theological Seminary and CRC Publications, 1998. Pp. 233-44.

———. *Preaching Christ from the Old Testament: A Contemporary Hermeneutical Method.* Grand Rapids: Eerdmans, 1999.

Hallo, William W., ed. *The Context of Scripture.* Vol. 1. New York: Brill, 1996.

Hamilton, Victor P. *The Book of Genesis: Chapters 1–17.* NICOT. Grand Rapids: Eerdmans, 1995.

———. *The Book of Genesis: Chapters 18–50.* NICOT. Grand Rapids: Eerdmans, 1995.

———. "Genesis." In his *Handbook on the Pentateuch: Genesis, Exodus, Leviticus, Numbers, Deuteronomy.* Grand Rapids: Baker, 1982. Pp. 17-138.

———. "Genesis: Theology of." In *NIDOTTE,* 4. Ed. Willem A. VanGemeren. Grand Rapids: Zondervan, 1997. Pp. 663-75.

Harrison, R. K. *Biblical Criticism: Historical, Literary and Textual.* Grand Rapids: Zondervan, 1978.

Hartley, John E. *Genesis.* NIBC. Peabody, MA: Hendrickson, 2000.

Hasel, Gerhard F. *The Remnant: The History and Theology of the Remnant Idea from Genesis to Isaiah.* Berrien Springs, MI: Andrews University Press, 1972.

Hauser, Alan J. "Linguistic and Thematic Links between Genesis 4:1-16 and Genesis 2–3." *JETS* 23/4 (Dec. 1980) 297-305.

Herbert, A. S. *Genesis 12–50: Abraham and His Heirs.* London: SCM, 1962.

Holbert, John C. *Preaching Old Testament: Proclamation and Narrative in the Hebrew Bible.* Nashville: Abingdon, 1991.

Holmgren, Fredrick C. "Abraham and Isaac on Mount Moriah: Genesis 22:1-19." *CovQ* 39/3-40/1 (Aug. 1981-Feb. 1982) 75-85.

Holwerda, David E. *Jesus and Israel: One Covenant or Two?* Grand Rapids: Eerdmans, 1995.

Hughes, R. Kent. *Genesis: Beginning and Blessing.* Wheaton, IL: Crossway, 2004.

Kaiser, Jr., Walter C. *Toward an Old Testament Theology.* Grand Rapids: Zondervan, 1978.

———. "Narrative." In *Cracking Old Testament Codes: A Guide to Interpreting the Literary Genres of the Old Testament.* Eds. D. Brent Sandy and Ronald L. Giese, Jr. Nashville: Broadman and Holman, 1995. Pp. 69-88.

———. *The Messiah in the Old Testament.* Grand Rapids: Zondervan, 1995.

———. *Preaching and Teaching from the Old Testament: A Guide for the Church.* Grand Rapids: Baker, 2003.

Kidner, Derek. *Genesis: An Introduction and Commentary.* Chicago: InterVarsity Press, 1967.

Kitchen, Kenneth A. "Genesis 12–50 in the Near Eastern World." In *He Swore an Oath: Biblical Themes from Genesis 12–50.* Eds. Richard A. Hess, P. E. Satterthwaite, and G. J. Wenham. Grand Rapids: Baker, 1994. Pp. 67-92.

———. "The Patriarchal Age: Myth or History?" *BAR* (Mar./Apr. 1995) 48-57.

———. *On the Reliability of the Old Testament.* Grand Rapids: Eerdmans, 2003.

Kline, Meredith G. *By Oath Consigned: A Reinterpretation of the Covenant Signs of Circumcision and Baptism.* Grand Rapids: Eerdmans, 1968.

Lambe, Anthony J. "Genesis 38: Structure and Literary Design." In *The World of Genesis.*

Eds. Philip R. Davies and David Clines. Sheffield: Sheffield Academic Press, 1998. Pp. 102-20.

LaSor, William S., David A. Hubbard, and Frederic W. Bush. *Old Testament Survey: The Message, Form, and Background of the Old Testament.* Grand Rapids: Eerdmans, 1982.

Leupold, H. C. *Exposition of Genesis.* Vols. 1 and 2. Grand Rapids: Baker, 1960.

Lipton, Diana. *Revisions of the Night: Politics and Promises of the Patriarchal Dreams of Genesis. JSOT Supplement* 288. Sheffield: Sheffield Academic Press, 1999.

Long, Philips. "Reading the Old Testament as Literature." In *Interpreting the Old Testament: A Guide for Exegesis.* Ed. Craig C. Broyles. Grand Rapids: Baker, 2001. Pp. 85-123.

Longacre, R. E. "Genesis as Soap Opera: Some Observations about Storytelling in the Hebrew Bible." *Journal of Text and Translation* 7/1 (1995) 1-8.

Longman, III, Tremper. "The Literary Approach to the Study of the Old Testament: Promises and Pitfalls." *JETS* 28/4 (1985) 385-98.

McCartney, Dan, and Charles Clayton. *Let the Reader Understand: A Guide to Interpreting and Applying the Bible.* Wheaton, IL: Victor, 1994.

McCurley, Foster R. *Proclaiming the Promise: Christian Preaching from the Old Testament.* Philadelphia: Fortress, 1974.

———. *Genesis, Exodus, Leviticus, Numbers.* Proclamation Commentaries. Philadelphia: Fortress, 1979.

McEvenue, Sean E. *The Narrative Style of the Priestly Writer.* Rome: Biblical Institute Press, 1971.

Mathews, Kenneth A. "Preaching Old Testament Genealogies." *Preaching* 5 (Nov.-Dec. 1988) 7-12.

———. "Preaching in the Pentateuch." In *Handbook of Contemporary Preaching.* Ed. Michael Duduit. Nashville: Broadman, 1992. Pp. 257-79.

———. "Preaching Historical Narrative." In *Reclaiming the Prophetic Mantle: Preaching the Old Testament Faithfully.* Ed. George L. Klein. Nashville: Broadman, 1992. Pp. 19-50.

———. *Genesis 1–11:26.* Nashville: Broadman and Holman, 1996.

———. "Genesis." In *New Dictionary of Biblical Theology.* Ed. T. Desmond Alexander. Downers Grove, IL: InterVarsity Press, 2000. Pp. 140-46.

———. *Genesis 11:27–50:26.* Nashville: Broadman and Holman, 2005.

Mathewson, Steven D. "Exegetical Study of Genesis 38." *BSac* (Oct.-Dec. 1989) 373-92.

———. *The Art of Preaching Old Testament Narrative.* Grand Rapids: Baker, 2002.

Merrill, Eugene H. "A Theology of the Pentateuch." In *A Biblical Theology of the Old Testament.* Ed. Roy B. Zuck. Chicago: Moody, 1991. Pp. 7-87.

———. "Old Testament History: A Theological Perspective." In *A Guide to Old Testament Theology and Exegesis.* Ed. Willem A. VanGemeren. Grand Rapids: Zondervan, 1997. Pp. 65-82.

Moberly, R. Walter L. "Christ as the Key to Scripture: Genesis 22 Reconsidered." In *He Swore an Oath: Biblical Themes from Genesis 12–50.* Eds. Richard A. Hess, P. E. Satterthwaite, and G. J. Wenham. Cambridge: Tyndale House, 1993.

———. "Genesis 12–50." In *Genesis and Exodus.* Eds. John W. Rogerson, R. W. L. Moberly, and William Johnstone. Sheffield: Sheffield Academic Press, 2001. Pp. 100-179.

Nestle, Erwin, and Kurt Aland. *Novum Testamentum Graece.* 27th ed. Stuttgart: Deutsche Bibelgesellschaft, 1993.

NIV Study Bible: New International Version. Grand Rapids: Zondervan, 1985.

Osborne, Grant R. *The Hermeneutical Spiral: A Comprehensive Introduction to Biblical Interpretation.* Downers Grove: InterVarsity Press, 1991.

———. "Historical Narrative and Truth in the Bible." *JETS* 48/4 (Dec. 2005) 673-88.

Pratt, Jr., Richard L. *He Gave Us Stories: The Bible Student's Guide to Interpreting Old Testament Narratives.* Phillipsburg, NJ: Presbyterian and Reformed, 1990.

Provan, Iain, V. Philips Long, and Tremper Longman, III. *A Biblical History of Israel.* Louisville: Westminster/John Knox, 2003.

Rad, Gerhard von. *Old Testament Theology.* Vol. 1: *The Theology of Israel's Historical Traditions.* Trans. D. M. G. Stalker. Edinburgh: Oliver and Boyd, 1962.

———. *Genesis: A Commentary.* Trans. John H. Marks. Rev. ed. Philadelphia: Westminster, 1972.

———. *Biblical Interpretations in Preaching.* Trans. John E. Steely. Nashville: Abingdon, 1977.

Radday, Yehuda T. "Chiasmus in Hebrew Biblical Narrative." In *Chiasmus in Antiquity.* Ed. John W. Welch. Hildesheim: Gerstenberg, 1981. Pp. 50-117.

Rendsburg, Gary A. *Redaction of Genesis.* Winona Lake, IN: Eisenbrauns, 1986.

Rendtorff, Rolf. "'Covenant' as a Structuring Concept in Genesis and Exodus." *JBL* 108/3 (1989) 385-93.

Robertson, O. Palmer. *The Israel of God: Yesterday, Today, and Tomorrow.* Phillipsburg, NJ: Presbyterian and Reformed, 2000.

Ross, Allen P. *Creation and Blessing: A Guide to the Study and Exposition of the Book of Genesis.* Grand Rapids: Baker, 1990.

Russell, III, Walter B. "Literary Forms in the Hands of Preachers and Teachers." In *Cracking Old Testament Codes: A Guide to Interpreting the Literary Genres of the Old Testament.* Eds. D. Brent Sandy and Ronald L. Giese, Jr. Nashville: Broadman and Holman, 1995. Pp. 281-98.

Ryken, Leland. *How to Read the Bible as Literature.* Grand Rapids: Zondervan, 1984.

Ryken, Leland, and Tremper Longman, III, eds. *A Complete Literary Guide to the Bible.* Grand Rapids: Zondervan, 1993.

Sailhamer, John H. "Genesis." In *Genesis–Numbers: The Expositor's Bible Commentary.* Vol. 2. Gen. ed. Frank E. Gaebelein. Grand Rapids: Zondervan, 1990.

———. *The Pentateuch as Narrative.* Grand Rapids: Zondervan, 1992.

———. *Introduction to Old Testament Theology: A Canonical Approach.* Grand Rapids: Zondervan, 1995.

Sarna, Nahum M. *Understanding Genesis.* New York: Schocken, 1970.

———. *The JPS Torah Commentary: Genesis.* Philadelphia: Jewish Publication Society, 1989.

———. "Genesis Chapter 23: The Cave of Machpelah." *Hebrew Studies* 23 (1982) 17-21.

Satterthwaite, Philip E. "Narrative Criticism: The Theological Implications of Narrative Techniques." In *A Guide to Old Testament Theology and Exegesis.* Ed. Willem A. VanGemeren. Grand Rapids: Zondervan, 1999. Pp. 122-30.

Speiser, E. A. *Genesis.* Anchor Bible Commentary. Garden City, NY: Doubleday, 1964.

Spina, Frank Anthony. "Genesis 12:1-4a," and "Genesis 25:19-34." In *The Lectionary Commentary: Theological Exegesis for Sunday's Texts.* The First Readings: *The Old Testament and Acts.* Ed. Roger Van Harn. Grand Rapids: Eerdmans, 2001. Pp. 20-23 and 48-51.

Stek, John. "What Says the Scripture?" in *Portraits of Creation: Biblical and Scientific Explanations on the World's Formation.* Ed. Howard J. Van Till. Grand Rapids: Eerdmans, 1990. Pp. 232-40.

Sternberg, Meir. *The Poetics of Biblical Narrative: Ideological Literature and the Drama of Reading.* Bloomington, IN: Indiana University Press, 1985.

Stordalen, T. *Echoes of Eden: Genesis 2–3 and Symbolism of the Eden Garden in Biblical Hebrew Literature.* Leuven, Belg.: Peeters, 2000.

Stratton, Beverly J. *Out of Eden: Reading, Rhetoric, and Ideology in Genesis 2–3. JSOT Supplement* 208. Sheffield: Sheffield Academic Press, 1995.

Throntveit, Mark A. "Preaching from the Book of Genesis." *WW* 14 (Spring 1994) 208-13.

Toombs, Lawrence E. *The Old Testament in Christian Preaching.* Philadelphia: Westminster, 1961.

Townsend, P. Wayne. "Eve's Answer to the Serpent: An Alternative Paradigm for Sin and Some Implications for Theology." *CTJ* 33 (1998) 399-420.

Turner, Laurence A. *Announcements of Plot in Genesis.* Sheffield: JSOT Press, 1990.

———. *Genesis.* Sheffield: Sheffield Academic Press, 2000.

VanGemeren, Willem A. *The Progress of Redemption: The Story of Salvation from Creation to the New Jerusalem.* Grand Rapids: Zondervan, 1988.

Van Groningen, Gerard. *Messianic Revelation in the Old Testament.* Grand Rapids: Baker, 1990.

Van Harn, Roger, ed. *The Lectionary Commentary: Theological Exegesis for Sunday's Texts.* The First Readings: *The Old Testament and Acts.* Grand Rapids: Eerdmans, 2001.

Van Wolde, Ellen. *Words Become Worlds: Semantic Studies of Genesis 1–11.* Leiden: Brill, 1994.

Vawter, Bruce. *On Genesis: A New Reading.* Garden City, NY: Doubleday, 1977.

Vischer, Wilhelm. *The Witness of the Old Testament to Christ.* Vol. 1. Trans. A. B. Crabtree. Trans. of *Das Christuszeugnis des Alten Testaments,* 1935. London: Lutterworth, 1949.

Walsh, Jerome T. "Genesis 2:4b–3:24: A Synchronic Approach." *JBL* 96/2 (1977) 161-77.

Walters, Stanley. "Wood, Sand and Stars: Structure and Theology in Gn 22:1-19." *Toronto Journal of Theology* 3 (1987) 301-30.

Waltke, Bruce K. *Genesis: A Commentary.* Grand Rapids: Zondervan, 2001.

Walton, John H. *Genesis.* The NIV Application Commentary. Grand Rapids: Zondervan, 2001.

Walton, John H., and Victor Matthews. *The IVP Bible Background Commentary: Genesis-Deuteronomy.* Downers Grove, IL: InterVarsity Press, 1997.

Warning, Wilfried. "Terminological Patterns and Genesis 39." *JETS* 44/3 (Sept. 2001) 409-19.

Wenham, Gordon J. "The Coherence of the Flood Narrative." *VT* 28 (1978) 336-48. Reprinted in *I Studied Inscriptions from before the Flood: Ancient Near Eastern, Literary, and Linguistic Approaches to Genesis 1–11.* Eds. Richard S. Hess and David Toshio Tsumura. Winona Lake, IN: Eisenbrauns, 1994. Pp. 436-47.

———. "Sanctuary Symbolism in the Garden of Eden Story." In *Proceedings of the Ninth World Congress of Jewish Studies, Division A: The Period of the Bible.* Jerusalem: World Union of Jewish Studies, 1986. Reprinted in *I Studied Inscriptions from before the Flood: Ancient Near Eastern, Literary, and Linguistic Approaches to Genesis 1–11.* Eds.

Select Scripture Index